CW00691029

ISBN 978-0-266-18488-1
PIBN 11010304

A COLLECTION

OF

STATUTES RELATING TO INDIA.

IN TWO VOLUMES.

Agents for the sale of Books published by the Superintendent of Government Printing, India, Calcutta.

IN LONDON.

E. A. Arnold, Esq., 37, Bedford Street, Strand, W. C.

Messrs. Constable & Co., 2, Whitehall Gardens, S. W.

Messrs. Sampson Low, Marston & Co., St. Dunstan's House, Fetter Lane, E. C.

Messrs. P. S. King & Son, 9, Bridge Street, Westminster, S. W.

Messrs. Luzac & Co., 46, Great Russell Street, W. C.

Messrs. Kegan Paul, Trench, Trübner & Co., Charing Cross Road, W. C.

B. Alfred Quaritch, Esq , 15, Piccadilly, W.

Messrs. William and Norgate, Oxford.

" Deighton Bell & Co., Cambridge.

ON THE CONTINENT.

Messrs. Friedländer & Sohn, 11, Carlstrasse, Berlin, N. W.

Otto Harrassowitz, Esq., Leipzig.

Karl W. Hiersemann, Esq., Leipzig.

Ernest Leroux, Esq., 28, Rue Bonaparte, Paris.

Martinus Nijhoff, Esq , The Hague.

IN INDIA.

Messrs. Thacker, Spink & Co., Calcutta and Simla.

Messrs. Newman & Co., Calcutta.

Messrs. Thacker & Co., Ld., Bombay.

E. Seymour Hale, Esq., Fort, Bombay.

Messrs. Higginbotham & Co , Madras.

Superintendent, American Baptist Mission Press, Rangoon.

Rai Sahib M. Gulab Singh & Sons, Mufid-I Am Press, Lahore.

Manager, Educational Book Depôts, Nagpur and Jubbulpore.

A COLLECTION

OF

STATUTES RELATING TO INDIA.

IN TWO VOLUMES.

VOL. II.

FROM 1871 UP TO 1899.

CALCUTTA:

OFFICE OF THE SUPERINTENDENT OF GOVERNMENT PRINTING, INDIA.

1901.

Price Eight Rupees. *English Price Twelve Shillings.*

PREFACE.

THE first volume of this Collection, which has but recently been issued, contains the *Statutes relating to India* up to the end of the year 1870. This volume brings the Collection up to date and has been prepared on the same lines as its predecessor.

The two Appendices to the first volume (giving a list of Statutes affected by legislation in India, and a table of the various Statute Law Revision Acts which have been passed by Parliament) would have been reserved for inclusion in this volume had its early issue been anticipated.

A fresh index for both volumes has been added at the end of this.

The Coinage Act, 1870 (33 & 34 Vict, c. 10), would have been included in the first volume, had it been issued after the decision to apply that Statute to India and provide for the coinage of gold in this country. It has now been reproduced as an Appendix to this volume, the amending Act of 1891 (54 & 55 Vict., c. 72), being printed in its proper place therein.

SIMLA;
The 15th October, 1899.

H. W. C. CARNDUFF,
Deputy Secy. to the Govt. of India,
Legislative Department.

CONTENTS.

CHRONOLOGICAL TABLE OF THE STATUTES RELATING TO INDIA.

VOLUME II—(FROM 1871 UP TO THE END OF 1899).

Year.	Regnal No. and Chapter.	Short title or subject.	How repealed or otherwise affected.	Remarks.
1871	34 & 35 Vict., c. 29.	The India Stock Dividends Act, 1871.	...... S. 1 rep. in pt. (U. K.) 46 & 47 Vict., c. 39 (S. L. R.).	See p. 521.
"	34 & 35 Vict., c. 34.	The Indian Councils Act, 1871.	......	See p. 521.
"	34 & 35 Vict., c. 62.	The Indian Bishops Act, 1871.	...... S. 1 rep. in pt. 46 & 47 Vict., c. 39 (S. L. R.).	See p. 522.
"	34 & 35 Vict., c. 91.	Judicial Committee of Privy Council.	Rep. (U. K.) 56 & 57 Vict., c. 54 (S. L. R.).	Omitted as being inapplicable to India.
1872	35 & 36 Vict., c. 39.	The Naturalization Act, 1872.	......	See p. 523.
"	35 & 36 Vict., c. 76.	Lady Mayo's Annuity.	......	See p. 525. The title only is reproduced.
1873	36 & 37 Vict., c. 17.	The East India Stock Dividend Redemption Act, 1873.	...... Ss. 3—9 rep. (U. K.) 46 & 47 Vict., c. 39.	See p. 525. Omitted as being spent.
			S. 10 rep. in pt. (U. K.) 46 & 47 Vict., c. 39.	Part omitted as being obsolete and inapplicable to India.
			Ss. 11—15, 19—23, 26, 35, 36 rep. (U. K.) 46 & 47 Vict., c. 39 (S. L. R.).	Omitted as being spent.
"	36 & 37 Vict., c. 32.	The East India Loan Act, 1873.	...... S. 1 rep. in pt. (U. K.) 46 & 47 Vict., c. 39 (S. L. R.).	See p. 529.

Year.	Regnal No. and Chapter.	Short title or subject.	How repealed or otherwise affected.	Remarks.
1873	36 & 37 Vict., c. 32—*contd.*	......	S. 14 rep. 37 & 38 Vict., c. 3, s. 15.	Omitted as being spent.
"	36 & 37 Vict., c. 43.	The Indian Railway Companies Act, 1873.	......	See p. 533.
"	36 & 37 Vict., c. 59.	The Slave Trade (East African Courts Act, 1873).	...... S. 1 rep. in pt. 42 & 43 Vict., c. 38, s. 2.	See p. 535.
			S. 8 and schedule rep. (U. K.) 46 & 47 Vict., c. 39 (S. L. R.).	Omitted as being spent.
"	36 & 37 Vict., c. 60.	The Extradition Act, 1873.	...... Ext. IX of 1895, s. 2.	See p. 537.
"	36 & 37 Vict., c. 88.	The Slave Trade Act, 1873.	...... S. 20, as far as relates to the taxation of any costs, charges and expenses which can be taxed in pursuance of 53 & 54 Vict., c. 27, rep. by s. 18 of that Act, and as respects any courts out of Her Majesty's dominions, as from the date of any order applying that Act. S. 23 rep. in pt. 53 & 54 Vict., c. 27, as respects any British Possession as from the commencement of that Act in that possession, and as respects any courts out of Her Majesty's dominions, as from the date of any order applying that Act.	See p. 540.
			S. 30 and second schedule rep. (U. K.) 46 & 47 Vict., c. 39 (S. L. R.).	Omitted as being spent.
1874	37 & 38 Vict., c. 3.	The East India Loan Act, 1874.	...... S. 14 rep. (U. K.) 46 & 47 Vict., c. 39 (S. L. R.).	See p. 551. Omitted as being obsolete.

Chronological Table.

STATUTES RELATING TO INDIA—*contd.*

Year.	Regnal No. and Chapter.	Short title or subject.	How repealed or otherwise affected.	Remarks.
1874	37 & 38 Vict., c. 3—*contd.*	......	S. 15 rep in pt. (U. K.) 46 & 47 Vict., c. 39 (S. L. R.). S. 18 rep. (U. K.) 46 & 47 Vict., c. 39 (S. L. R.).	Omitted as being spent.
"	37 & 38 Vict., c. 12.	The East India Annuity Funds Act, 1874.	...... S 1 rep. (U. K.) 56 & 57 Vict., c. 14 (S. L. R.) No. 2.	See p. 555. Omitted as being obsolete.
"	37 & 38 Vict., c. 27.	The Courts (Colonial) Jurisdiction Act, 1874.	......	See p. 556.
"	37 & 38 Vict., c. 41.	The Colonial Attorney's Relief Act, 1874.	......	See p. 557.
"	37 & 38 Vict., c. 61.	The Royal (late Indian) Ordnance Corps Act, 1874.	...... S. 3—5 rep. (U. K) 46 & 47 Vict., c. 39 (S. L. R.).	See p. 558. Omitted as being obsolete.
"	37 & 38 Vict., c. 77.	The Colonial Clergy Act, 1874.	...... Ss 2 & 10 rep. (U. K.) 46 & 47 Vict., c. 39 (S. L R.) Schedules A & B rep. (U. K.) 46 & 47 Vict., c. 39 (S. L. R).	See p. 559. Omitted as being spent. Omitted as being spent.
"	37 & 38 Vict., c. 91.	The Indian Councils Act, 1874.		See p. 562.
1875	38 & 39 Vict., c. 12.	The International Copyright Act, 1875.	......	See p. 563.
1876	39 & 40 Vict., c. 7.	The Council of India Act, 1876.	......	See p. 563.
"	39 & 40 Vict., c. 10.	The Royal Titles Act, 1876.	......	See p. 564.
"	39 & 40 Vict., c. 20.	The Statute Law Revision (Substituted Enactments) Act, 1876.	......	See p. 565.

Chronological Table.

STATUTES RELATING TO INDIA—*contd.*

Year.	Regnal No. and Chapter.	Short title or subject.	How repealed or otherwise affected.	Remarks.
1876	39 & 40 Vict., c. 36.	The Customs Consolidation Act, 1876.	......	See p. 565.
"	39 & 40 Vict., c. 46.	The Slave Trade Act, 1876.	...... Ss. 4 & 6 rep. 53 & 54 Vict., c. 37, s. 18.	See p. 567.
1877	40 & 41 Vict., c. 51.	The East India Loan Act, 1877.	...... S. 16 rep. (U. K.) 57 & 58 Vict., c. 56 (S. L. R.).	See p. 570. Omitted as being obsolete.
			S. 19 rep. (U. K.) 46 & 47 Vict., c. 39(S. L. R.).	Omitted as being spent.
1878	41 & 42 Vict., c. 33.	The Dentists Act, 1878.	...... Am. 49 & 50 Vict., c. 48, ss. 23, 26. S. 4 rep. in pt. 49 & 50 Vict., c. 48, s. 26.	See p. 573.
"	41 & 42 Vict., c. 47.	The Elders' Widows' Fund (India) Act, 1878.	...... S. 1 rep. (U. K.) 46 & 47 Vict., c. 39 (S. L. R.).	See p. 587. Omitted as being spent.
"	41 & 42 Vict., c. 73.	The Territorial Waters Jurisdiction Act, 1878.	......	See p. 589.
1879	42 & 43 Vict., c. 8.	The Registration of Births, Deaths and Marriages (Army) Act, 1879.	...... S. 5 rep. (U. K.) 57 & 58 Vict., c. 56 (S. L. R.).	See p. 592. Omitted as being spent.
"	42 & 43 Vict., c. 38.	The Slave Trade (East African Courts) Act, 1879.	...... S. 2 rep. in pt. (U. K.) 57 & 58 Vict., c. 56 (S. L. R.).	See p. 593.
"	42 & 43 Vict., c. 41.	The Indian Guaranteed Railways Act, 1879.	......	See p. 594.
"	42 & 43 Vict., c. 43.	The East Indian Railway (Redemption of Annuities) Act, 1879.	...... S. 1 rep. (U. K.) 57 & 58 Vict., c. 56 (S. L. R.).	See p. 597. Omitted as being spent.
"	42 & 43 Vict., c. 60.	The East India Loan Act, 1879.	...... S. 16 rep. (U. K.) 57 & 58 Vict., c. 56 (S. L. R.).	See p. 599. Omitted as being spent.
			S. 19 rep. (U. K.) 61 & 62 Vict, c. 22 (S. L. R.).	Omitted as being spent.

STATUTES RELATING TO INDIA—*contd.*

Year.	Regnal No. and Chapter.	Short title or subject.	How repealed or otherwise affected.	REMARKS.
1880	43 Vict., c. 3.	The Indian Salaries and Allowances Act, 1880.	...... S. 5 rep. (U. K.) 57 & 58 Vict., c. 56 (S. L. R.). The second schedule rep. (U. K.) 57 & 58 Vict., c. 56 (S. L. R.).	See p. 603.
"	" c. 10.	The East India Loan (East Indian Railway Debentures) Act, 1880.	......	See p. 604.
"	" c. 11.	The India Stock (Powers of Attorney) Act, 1880.	......	See p. 607.
1881	44 & 45 Vict., c. 3.	The Judicial Committee Act, 1881.	......	See p. 607.
"	44 & 45 Vict., c. 7.	The India Office (Sale of Superfluous Land) Act, 1881.	......	See p. 608.
"	44 & 45 Vict., c. 53.	The East India Railway (Redemption of Annuities) Act, 1881.	...... S. 2 am. 48 & 49 Vict., c. 25, s. 25 (2).	See p. 610.
"	44 & 45 Vict., c. 57.	The Regulation of the Forces Act, 1881.	......	See p 613.
"	44 & 45 Vict., c. 58.	The Army Act .	......	See p. 614. Printed in accordance with the Army (Annual) Act, 1885 (48 & 49 Vict, c. 8), s. 8. (2), with amendments made by successive Army (Annual) Acts down to the end of 1899. Of these Army (Annual) Acts only the last—that passed in 1899—has been reproduced in this Collection. As to s. 156, see Act XIII of 1889, s. 21 (1) (a).

Chronological Table.

STATUTES RELATING TO INDIA—*contd.*

Year.	Regnal No. and Chapter.	Short title or subject.	How repealed or otherwise affected.	Remarks.
1881	44 & 45 Vict., c. 63.	The India Office Auditor Act, 1881.	......	See p. 733.
"	44 & 45 Vict., c. 69.	The Fugitive Offenders Act, 1881	...... Ss. 40, 41 & schedule rep. (U. K.) 57 & 58 Vict., c. 56 (S. L. R.).	See p. 734. Omitted as being spent.
1882	45 & 46 Vict., c. 9.	The Documentary Evidence Act 1882.	...... Am. 58 & 59 Vict., c. 9.	See p. 748.
"	45 & 46 Vict., c. 45.	The Bombay Civil Fund Act, 1882.	......	See p. 749.
"	45 & 46 Vict., c. 48.	The Reserve Forces Act, 1882.	......	See p. 752.
"	45 & 46 Vict., c. 79.	The India (Home Charges Arrears) Act, 1882.	......	See p. 766.
"	46 & 47 Vict., c. 30.	The Companies (Colonial Registers) Act, 1883.	...... S. 3 (7) am. 52 & 53 Vict., c. 42, s. 18.	See p. 767.
1883	46 & 47 Vict., c. 52.	The Bankruptcy Act, 1883.	......	See p. 770.
1884	47 & 48 Vict., c. 24.	The Colonial Attorneys Relief Act Amendment Act, 1884.	......	See p. 770.
"	47 & 48 Vict., c. 31.	The Colonial Prisoners Removal Act, 1884.	......	See p. 771.
"	47 & 48 Vict., c. 38.	The Indian Marine Service Act, 1884.	......	See p. 778.
"	47 & 48 Vict, c. 39.	The Naval Discipline Act, 1884.	......	See p. 780.
"	47 & 48 Vict., c. 64.	The Criminal Lunatics Act, 1884.	......	See p. 785.
1885	48 & 49 Vict., c. 25.	The East India Unclaimed Stock Act, 1885.	......	See p. 786.
"	48 & 49 Vict., c. 49.	The Submarine Telegraph Act, 1885.	...... S. 4 rep. 50 Vict., c. 3, s. 8.	See p. 800.

Chronological Table.

STATUTES RELATING TO INDIA—*contd.*

Year.	Regnal No. and Chapter.	Short title or subject.	How repealed or otherwise affected.	Remarks.
1885	48 & 49 Vict., c. 67.	The Indian Army Pension Deficiency Act, 1885.	......	See p. 808.
"	48 & 49 Vict., c. 74.	The Evidence by Commission Act, 1885.	......	See p. 812.
1886	49 & 50 Vict., c. 33.	The International Copyright Act, 1886.	......	See p. 813.
"	49 & 50 Vict., c. 48.	The Medical Act, 1886.	......	See p. 822.
"	50 Vict., c. 3.	The Submarine Telegraph Act, 1886.	......	See p. 836.
1887	50 & 51 Vict., c. 11.	The Conversion of India Stock Act, 1887.	......	See p. 837.
"	50 & 51 Vict., c. 54.	The British Settlements Act, 1887.	......	See p. 840.
"	50 & 51 Vict., c. 67.	The Superannuation Act, 1887.	......	See p. 842.
"	50 & 51 Vict., c. 70.	The Appellate Jurisdiction Act, 1887.	......	See p. 847.
1888	51 & 52 Vict., c. 5.	The Oudh and Rohilkhand Railway Purchase Act, 1888.	......	See p. 849.
1889	52 & 53 Vict., c. 10.	The Commissioners for Oaths Act, 1889.	...... Expld. & am. 53 & 54 Vict., c. 7, & 54 & 55 Vict., c. 50. S. 6 am. 54 & 55 Vict., c. 50, s. 2.	See p. 853.
"	52 & 53 Vict., c. 52.	The Official Secrets Act, 1889.	......	See p. 858.
"	52 & 53 Vict., c. 63.	The Interpretation Act, 1889.	......	See p. 862.
"	52 & 53 Vict., c. 65.	The Council of India Reduction Act, 1889.	.....	See p. 876.

STATUTES RELATING TO INDIA—*contd.*

Year.	Regnal No. and Chapter.	Short title or subject.	How repealed or otherwise affected.	REMARKS.
1890	53 & 54 Vict., c. 6.	The South Indian Railway Purchase Act, 1890.	......	See p. 876.
"	53 & 54 Vict., c. 7.	The Commissioners for Oaths Act, 1891.	......	See p. 879.
"	53 & 54 Vict., c. 27.	The Colonial Courts of Admiralty Act, 1890.	......	See p. 880.
"	53 & 54 Vict., c. 37.	The Foreign Jurisdiction Act, 1890.	......	See p. 891.
1891	54 & 55 Vict., c. 31.	The Mail Ships Act, 1891.	......	See p. 898.
"	54 & 55 Vict., c. 50.	The Commissioners for Oaths Act, 1891.	......	See p. 906.
"	54 & 55 Vict., c. 72.[1]	The Coinage Act, 1891.	......	See p. 906.
1892	55 & 56 Vict., c. 6.	The Colonial Probates Act, 1892.	......	See p. 908.
"	55 & 56 Vict., c. 14.	The Indian Councils Act, 1892.	......	See p. 911.
"	55 & 56 Vict., c. 23.	The Foreign Marriage Act, 1892.	......	See p. 914.
"	55 & 56 Vict., c. 40.	The Superannuation Act, 1892.	......	See p. 924.
1893	56 & 57 Vict., c. 5.	The Regimental Debts Act, 1893.	......	See p. 926.
"	56 & 57 Vict., c. 53.	The Trustee Act, 1893.	Am. 57 & 58 Vict., c. 10. S. 30 rep. in pt. 57 & 58 Vict., c. 10, s. 1. S. 41 ext. 57 & 58 Vict., c. 10, s. 2. S. 44 am. 57 & 58 Vict., c. 10, s. 3.	See p. 936.
"	56 & 57 Vict., c. 62.	The Madras and Bombay Armies Act, 1893.	S. 1 expld., 59 & 60 Vict., c. 2, s. 4.	See p. 959.
"	56 & 57 Vict., c. 70.	The East India Loan Act, 1893.	......	See p. 962.

[1] The Coinage Act, 1870 (33 Vict., c. 10), which is amended by this Act, is printed as an appendix to this Volume, p. 1263.

Chronological Table.

STATUTES RELATING TO INDIA—*contd.*

Year	Regnal No. and Chapter.	Short title or subject.	How repealed or otherwise affected.	Remarks.
1894	57 & 58 Vict., c. 10.	The Trustee Act, 1893, Amendment Act, 1894.	......	See p. 965.
"	57 & 58 Vict., c. 12.	The Indian Railways Act, 1894.	......	See p. 965.
"	57 & 58 Vict., c. 30.	The Finance Act, 1894.	......	See p. 967. S. 20 alone is reproduced, the rest being inapplicable to India.
"	57 & 58 Vict., c. 39.	The Prize Courts Act, 1894.	......	See p. 969.
"	57 & 58 Vict., c. 45.	The Uniforms Act, 1894.	......	See p. 970.
"	57 & 58 Vict., c. 60.	The Merchant Shipping Act, 1894.	......	See p. 971. Pts. IV & X, ss. 634—669 in pt. XI, ss. 702—710 in pt. XIII, and Sch. XXI omitted as being inapplicable to India.
1895	58 & 59 Vict., c. 43.	The Naturalization Act, 1895.	......	See p. 1253.
"	58 & 59 Vict., c. 44.	The Judicial Committee Amendment Act, 1895.	......	See p. 1254.
1896	59 & 60 Vict., c. 12.	The Derelict Vessels (Report) Act, 1896.	......	See p. 1255.
"	59 & 60 Vict., c. 14.	The Short Titles Act, 1896.	......	See p. 1255. As the short titles conferred by this Act on the Statutes printed in this Collection have been given *in loco.*, the schedules of short titles have not been reproduced.

STATUTES RELATING TO INDIA—*concld.*

Year.	Regnal No. and Chapter.	Short title or subject.	How repealed or otherwise affected.	Remarks.
1898	61 & 62 Vict., c. 13.	The East India Loan Act, 1898.	......	See p. 1256.
1899	62 & 63 Vict., c. 3.	The Army (Annual) Act, 1899.	......	See p. 1257. This is the only one of the successive Army (Annual) Acts which is printed in this Collection—see the note to 44 & 45 Vict., c. 58, *ante* p. v.
"	62 & 63 Vict., c. 40.	The Reserve Forces Act, 1899.	......	See p. 1260.

A COLLECTION

OF

STATUTES RELATING TO INDIA.

VOLUME II.

THE INDIA STOCK DIVIDENDS ACT, 1871.[1]

(34 & 35 Vict., c. 29.)

An Act to facilitate the payment of Dividends on India Stocks.

[29th June, 1871.]

[*Preamble recites 33 & 34 Vict., c. 71, s. 20 (as to payment of dividends on India Stock by Banks of England and Ireland).*]

[2]1. THE power given to the said Banks, as above recited, to make arrangements for payment of dividends on stock by sending warrants through the post shall, as regards the payment of dividends on India five per cent. stock and India capital four per cent. stock, and on any stock which may be in future created under the powers in that behalf vested in the Secretary of State for India in Council by Acts of Parliament now in force, be exercised with the sanction of the Secretary of State for India in Council instead of the Treasury; and, where a holder of any such stock desires to have his dividend warrants sent him by post, he shall make his request as in the said Act provided, but in a form approved by the Bank and the Secretary of State for India in Council; and the provisions of sections 20 and 21 of the said Act, shall, with this variation, apply to payment of dividends on the aforesaid India stocks, and to warrants for the same sent by post. Sending dividend warrants by post.

THE INDIAN COUNCILS ACT, 1871.[3]

(34 & 35 Vict., c. 34.)

An Act to extend in certain respects the power of Local Legislatures in India as regards European British subjects.

[29th June, 1871.]

[*Preamble recites 24 & 25 Vict., c. 67, s. 42.*]

1. No law or regulation heretofore made or hereafter to be made by any Governor or Lieutenant-Governor in Council in India in manner prescribed by Power to Local Legislatures to

[1] This Act may be cited, with eighteen others, as the East India Loans Acts, 1859 to 1893—*see* the Short Titles Act, 1896 (59 & 60 Vict., c. 14), *post*, p. 1255.

[2] This section is repealed as to the U. K. so far as it applies 33 & 34 Vict., c. 71, s. 20, last para., by 46 & 47 Vict. c. 39 (S. L. R.).

[3] For digest, *see* Ilbert's *Government of India*, p. 323.

confer jurisdiction over European British subjects to magistrates in certain cases.

the aforesaid Act shall be invalid only by reason that it confers on magistrates, being justices of the peace, the same jurisdiction over European British subjects as such Governor or Lieutenant-Governor in Council, by regulations made as aforesaid, could have lawfully conferred or could lawfully confer on magistrates in the exercise of authority over natives in the like cases.

Committal of defendant (being an European British subject) to the High Court (Indian Act No. XXV of 1861, s. 226).

2. When evidence has been given in any proceeding under this Act before a magistrate, being a justice of the peace, which appears to be sufficient for the conviction of the accused person, being an European British subject, of an offence for which, if a native, he would under existing law be triable exclusively before the Court of Session, or which, in the opinion of the Magistrate, is one which ought to be tried by the High Court, the accused person, if such European British subject, shall be sent for trial by the Magistrate before the High Court.

Power to Local Legislatures to amend and repeal certain laws.

3. And whereas by an Act passed by the Governor General of India in Council, Indian Act No. XXII of 1870, it is provided that certain Acts heretofore passed by the Governors of Madras and Bombay respectively in Council, and by the Lieutenant-Governor of Bengal in Council, shall, so far as regards the liability of European British subjects to be convicted and punished thereunder, be and be deemed to be as valid as if they had been passed by the Governor General of India in Council at a meeting for the purpose of making laws and regulations: Be it further enacted, that the said Governors and Lieutenant-Governor in Council respectively shall have power to repeal and amend any of the said Acts so declared valid, by Acts to be passed under the provisions of the Indian Councils Act.

The Indian Bishops Act, 1871.[1]

(34 & 35 Vict., c. 62.)

An Act to enable Her Majesty to make regulations relative to the leave of absence of Indian Bishops on furlough and medical certificates.

[*31st July, 1871.*]

[*Preamble recites 5 & 6 Vict., c. 119.*]

Rules for leave of absence for bishops.

1. It shall be lawful for Her Majesty to make such rules as to the leave of absence of Indian bishops on furlough or medical certificate as may seem to be expedient.

Provided that no further expenditure of the revenues of India be incurred thereby than is already authorized under existing Acts of Parliament.

* * * * * * * * * * * *[2]

[1] For digest, see Ilbert's *Government of India*, p. 323. See, too, *Phillimore*, p. 1800.
[2] The remainder of the section has been repealed by 46 & 47 Vict., c. 39 (S. L. R.) and is omitted.

The Naturalization Act, 1872.[1]

(35 & 36 Vict., c. 39.)

An Act for amending the Law in certain cases in relation to Naturalization.

[*25th July, 1872.*]

[*Preamble recites Supplementary Convention which is set out in the Schedule.*]

1. This Act may be cited for all purposes as the Naturalization Act, 1872, and this Act and "The Naturalization Act, 1870", may be cited together as "The Naturalization Acts, 1870 and 1872". Short title.

2. Any renunciation of naturalization or of nationality made in manner provided by the said supplementary convention by the persons and under the circumstances in the said convention in that behalf mentioned shall be valid to all intents, and shall be deemed to be authorized by the said Naturalization Act, 1870. This section shall be deemed to take effect from the date at which the said supplementary convention took effect. Confirmation of renunciation of nationality under the convention.

3. Nothing contained in "The Naturalization Act, 1870", shall deprive any married woman of any estate or interest in real or personal property to which she may have become entitled previously to the passing of that Act, or affect such estate or interest to her prejudice. Saving clause as to property of married women.

SCHEDULE.

Convention between Her Majesty and the United States of America, supplementary to the Convention of May 13th, 1870, respecting naturalization.

Signed at Washington, 23rd February, 1871.

[*Ratifications exchanged at Washington, May 4, 1871.*]

Whereas by the second article of the convention between Her Majesty the Queen of the United Kingdom of Great Britain and Ireland and the United States of America for regulating the citizenship of subjects and citizens of the contracting parties who have emigrated or may emigrate from the dominions of the one to those of the other party, signed at London, on the 13th of May, 1870, it was stipulated that the manner in which the renunciation by such subjects and citizens of their naturalization, and the resumption of their native allegiance, may be made and publicly declared, should be agreed upon by the governments of the respective countries; Her Majesty the Queen of the United Kingdom of Great Britain and Ireland and the President of the United States of America, for the purpose of effecting such

[1] *See Chitty's Statutes*, Tit. Alien, p. 16.

agreement, have resolved to conclude a supplemental convention, and have named as their plenipotentiaries, that is to say, Her Majesty the Queen of the United Kingdom of Great Britain and Ireland, Sir Edward Thornton, Knight Commander of the Most Honourable Order of the Bath, and Her Envoy Extraordinary and Minister Plenipotentiary to the United States of America; and the President of the United States of America, Hamilton Fish, Secretary of State; who have agreed as follows:

ARTICLE I.

Any person being originally a citizen of the United States who had, previously to May 12, 1870, been naturalized as a British subject, may at any time before August 10, 1872, and any British subject who, at the date first aforesaid, had been naturalized as a citizen within the United States, may at any time before May 12, 1872, publicly declare his renunciation of such naturalization by subscribing an instrument in writing, substantially in the form hereunto appended, and designated as annex A.

Such renunciation by an original citizen of the United States, of British nationality shall, within the territories and jurisdiction of the United States, be made in duplicate, in the presence of any court authorized by law for the time being to admit aliens to naturalization, or before the clerk or prothonotary of any such court: if the declarant be beyond the territories of the United States, it shall be made in duplicate, before any diplomatic or consular officer of the United States. One of such duplicates shall remain on record in the custody of the court or officer in whose presence it was made; the other shall be, without delay, transmitted to the department of State.

Such renunciation, if declared by an original British subject, of his acquired nationality as a citizen of the United States, shall, if the declarant be in the United Kingdom of Great Britain and Ireland, be made in duplicate, in the presence of a justice of the peace; if elsewhere in Her Britannic Majesty's dominions, in triplicate, in the presence of any judge of civil or criminal jurisdiction, or any justice of the peace, or of any other officer for the time being authorized by law, in the place in which the declarant is, to administer an oath for any judicial or other legal purpose; if out of Her Majesty's dominions, in triplicate, in the presence of any officer in the diplomatic or consular service of Her Majesty.

ARTICLE II.

The contracting parties hereby engage to communicate each to the other, from time to time, lists of the persons who, within their respective dominions and territories, or before their diplomatic and consular officers, have declared their renunciation of naturalization, with the dates and places of making such declarations, and such information as to the abode of the declarants, and the times and places of their naturalization, as they may have furnished.

ARTICLE III.

The present convention shall be ratified by Her Britannic Majesty, and by the President of the United States by and with the advice and consent of the Senate thereof, and the ratifications shall be exchanged at Washington as soon as may be convenient.

In witness whereof, the respective plenipotentiaries have signed the same, and have affixed thereto their respective seals.

Done at Washington, the twenty-third day of February, in the year of our Lord one thousand eight hundred and seventy-one.

(L. S.) EDWD. THORNTON.
(L. S.) HAMILTON FISH.

(Annex A.)

I, *A. B.* of (*insert abode*), being originally a citizen of the United States of America (*or a British subject*), and having become naturalized within the dominions of Her Britannic Majesty as a British subject (*or as a citizen within the United States of America*), do hereby renounce my naturalization as a British subject (*or citizen of the United States*); and declare that it is my desire to resume my nationality as a citizen of the United States (*or British subject*).

(Signed) *A. B.*

Made and subscribed before me in (*insert country or other subdivision, and state, province, colony, legation, or consulate*), this day of , 187 .

(Signed) *E. F.*,
Justice of the Peace (or other title).

(L. S.) Edwd. Thornton.
(L. S.) Hamilton Fish.

(35 & 36 Vict., c. 76.)

An Act to settle an annuity on the Honourable Blanche Julia, Countess of Mayo, in consideration of the eminent services of the late Earl of Mayo as Viceroy and Governor General of India.[1]

[6th August, 1872.]

The East India Stock Dividend Redemption Act, 1873.[2]

(36 & 37 Vict., c. 17.)

An Act to provide for the Redemption or Commutation of the Dividend on the Capital Stock of the East India Company, and for the transfer of the Security Fund of the India Company to the Secretary of State in Council of India, and for the Dissolution of the East India Company.

[15th May, 1873.]

[Preamble.]

1. This Act may be cited as "The East India Stock Dividend Redemption Act, 1873". Short title.

[1] It has been thought sufficient only to print the title of this Statute.

[2] This Act may be cited, with eighteen others, as the East India Loans Acts, 1859 to 1893—see the Short Titles Act, 1896 (59 & 60 Vict., c. 14), *post*, p. 1255.

Interpretation of terms.

2. In this Act—

"East India stock" means the capital stock of the East India Company:

The expression "proprietors of East India stock" means and includes all persons, bodies politic or corporate, and the executors or administrators of all persons in whose names any portion or share of East India stock may be standing in the books kept for or on behalf of the East India Company by the governor and company of the Bank of England.

3 to 9. [*Rep. as to U. K. 46 & 47 Vict., c. 39 (S. L. R.). Omitted as being spent.*]

Payment of dividends on stock, etc., accepted in lieu of East India stock.

10. * * * *[1] The dividends to accrue on such stocks, funds, or securities as may be accepted in lieu of East India stock, under this provision, shall continue to be paid and dealt with in like manner as the dividends on such East India stock would have been paid and dealt with in case this Act had not been passed until the Court of Chancery shall make further order therein; and the said paymaster-general and accountant-general respectively shall be fully indemnified against all actions, suits, or proceedings for or in respect of any act, matter, or thing done by them respectively in pursuance of this Act.

11 to 15. [*Rep. as to U. K. 46 & 47 Vict., c. 39 (S. L. R.). Omitted as being spent.*]

Power to Secretary of State in Council to grant letter of attorney for sale, etc., of stock on account of security fund.

16. The Secretary of State in Council, by letter of attorney executed by two members of the Council, and countersigned by the Secretary of State or one of his under-secretaries, or his assistant under-secretary, may authorize all or any of the cashiers of the Bank of England to sell and transfer all or any part of the stock or stocks standing, or that may thereafter stand, in the books of the said bank to the accounts intituled "the stock account of the Secretary of State in Council of India in respect of the security fund of the India Company", and to purchase and accept stock on the said accounts, and to receive the dividends due and to become due on the several stocks standing, or that may thereafter stand, on the said accounts, and by any writing signed by two members of the Council and countersigned as aforesaid, may direct the application of the moneys to be received in respect of such sales and dividends; but no stock shall be purchased or sold and transferred by any of the said cashiers, under the authority of such general letter of attorney, except upon an order directed to the chief cashier and chief accountant of the Bank of England from time to time, and duly signed and countersigned as aforesaid.

Account how to be drawn upon.

17. The account to be intituled "the account of the Secretary of State in Council of India in respect of the security fund of the India Company", to be

[1] The words omitted have been repealed as to the U. K. by 46 & 47 Vict, c. 39 (S. L. R.), and are omitted as being obsolete and inapplicable to India.

opened at the Bank of England pursuant to this Act, shall be drawn upon by such person or persons, and in such manner as may from time to time be directed by the Secretary of State in Council, and the said account shall be deemed a public account.

18. No part of the stocks to be transferred to the accounts to be intituled "the stock account of the Secretary of State in Council of India in respect of the security fund of the India Company", or of the dividends to accrue due on such stocks, or of the moneys to be paid to the account to be intituled "the account of the Secretary of State in Council of India in respect of the security fund of the India Company", or of the cash to arise from the temporary investment of moneys standing to such last-mentioned account, shall be applied to any purposes other than the redemption or commutation of the dividend on East India stock or the accumulation of a fund for the redemption of such dividend, unless and until the total amount payable for the use of proprietors of East India stock who shall not signify their assents to commute their respective shares of the dividend on the said stock shall have been actually paid to such account as shall be raised at the Bank of England in pursuance of the directions in that behalf hereinbefore contained.

No part of transferred stocks to be applied otherwise than to redemption of dividends until certain claims satisfied.

19 to 23. [*Rep. as to U. K. 46 & 47 Vict., c. 39 (S. L. R.). Omitted as being spent.*]

24. All principal sums of money payable to any proprietors of East India stock, the dividend whereon is redeemed in pursuance of this Act, which shall not be claimed for ten years after the thirtieth day of April one thousand eight hundred and seventy-four, or for such period after the thirtieth day of April one thousand eight hundred and seventy-four, as with the period immediately preceding the said thirtieth day of April, during which the dividends on such stock shall not have been claimed, shall make up ten years, shall be transferred to the account of the Secretary of State in Council at the Bank of England.

Transfer of unclaimed redemption money to Secretary of State in Council.

25. Immediately after every such transfer as last aforesaid the name or names in which the stock stood on the thirtieth day of April one thousand eight hundred and seventy-four, the residence and description of the parties, the amount transferred, and the date of transfer, shall be entered on a list to be kept for the purpose by the Secretary of State in Council, which list shall be open for inspection at such place and at such times as the Secretary of State in Council shall appoint.

List of names in which the stock stood in respect whereof redemption money unclaimed.

26. [*Rep. as to U. K. 46 & 47 Vict., c. 39 (S. L. R.). Omitted as being spent.*]

27. All other dividends on any portions or shares of East India stock remaining unclaimed on the said thirtieth day of May one thousand eight

Other unclaimed dividends to be

transferred to East India stock dividend account.

hundred and seventy-four, shall be paid by the East India Company to an account to be opened at the Bank of England and to be intituled "East India Stock dividend account"; and such dividends, when claimed within the period of ten years from the date of the same having accrued due, shall be paid by the Bank of England out of such account. Any dividend on that account, if and when unclaimed for the period of ten years from the date of such dividend having accrued due, and all dividends subsequently accrued due in respect of the same portion or share of stock and unclaimed, shall be transferred to the account of the Secretary of State in Council at the Bank of England.

Dividends on that account unclaimed for ten years to be transferred to Secretary of State in Council.

Redemption money and dividends transferred to Secretary of State in Council to be applied as part of revenues of India.

28. All principal sums of money and dividends transferred or paid to the account of the Secretary of State in Council in pursuance of the directions hereinbefore contained, shall be held by the Secretary of State in Council and applied as part of the revenues of India, subject to the claims of the parties entitled thereto.

Repayment to person showing title.

29. The Secretary of State in Council shall pay any principal sums of money and dividends so transferred or paid to the account of the Secretary of State in Council to any person showing his right thereto to the satisfaction of the Secretary of State in Council.

But in case the Secretary of State in Council is not satisfied of the right of any person claiming to be entitled to any such principal moneys or dividends, the claimant may apply by petition in respect thereof in a summary way to the Court of Chancery.

The petitions shall be served upon the solicitor to the India Office, and the court shall make such order thereon (for payment of the principal moneys and dividends to which the petition relates, or otherwise), and in respect of the costs of the application, as to the court seems just.

Three months notice before payment.

30. Principal sums exceeding the sum of twenty pounds shall not be paid, nor shall dividends exceeding twenty pounds in the whole be paid to a claimant under the preceding section of this Act until three months after application made for the same, nor until public notice has been given thereof as hereinafter provided.

Advertisements before payment.

31. The Secretary of State in Council shall require the applicant to give such public notice as the Secretary of State in Council shall think fit by advertisements in one or more newspapers circulating in London and elsewhere.

Every such notice shall state the name or names, residence, and description of the person or persons in whose name or names the stock stood on the thirtieth day of April one thousand eight hundred and seventy-four, the amount of the stock, the name of the claimant, and the time at which payment of the principal money due in respect thereof, and of the dividends, if any, will be made, if no other claimant sooner appears and makes out his claim.

Where any such payment is ordered by the Court of Chancery the notice shall also state the purport of the order.

32. At any time before payment to a claimant any person may apply to the Court of Chancery by motion or petition to rescind or vary any order made for such payment.

Application to court to rescind order.

33. Where any principal moneys or dividends having been paid as aforesaid to a claimant by the Secretary of State in Council are afterwards claimed by another person, the Secretary of State in Council shall not be responsible for the same to such other claimant, but such other claimant may have recourse against the person to whom payment was made.

Secretary of State in Council not responsible to second claimant.

34. Provided that if in any case a new claimant establishes his title to any principal moneys or dividends paid to a former claimant, and is unable to obtain payment thereof from the former claimant, the Court of Chancery shall, on application by petition by the new claimant, verified as the Court requires, order the Secretary of State in Council to pay to the new claimant such sum of money, or make such other order on the application, as the court thinks just.

Order in favour of second claimant, showing title.

35 and 36. [*Rep. as to U. K. 46 & 47 Vict., c. 39 (S. L. R.). Omitted as being spent.*]

37. This Act shall be and is hereby declared to be a full and complete indemnity and discharge to the East India Company, and the directors thereof and the commissioners for the reduction of the national debt, and the governor and company of the Bank of England, their officers and servants, and every of them, for all things done or permitted to be done pursuant thereto, and the same shall not be questioned or impeached in any court of law or equity whatever to their prejudice or detriment.

Indemnity to East India Company, commissioners for reduction of national debt, and Bank of England.

The East India Loan Act, 1873.[1]

(36 & 37 Vict., c. 32.)

An Act to enable the Secretary of State in Council of India to raise Money in the United Kingdom for the Service of the Government of India.

[*16th June, 1873.*]

[*Preamble recites that the Security Fund of the India Company is insufficient to redeem or commute the capital stock of the East India Company.*]

1. It shall be lawful for the Secretary of State in Council of India, at any time or times, to raise in the United Kingdom for the service of the Govern-

Power to the Secretary of State in Council of India

[1] This Act may be cited, with eighteen others, as the East India Loans Acts, 1859 to 1893—see the Short Titles Act, 1896 (59 & 60 Vict., c. 14), *post*, p. 1256.

to raise any sums not exceeding 8,000,000*l.*

ment of India, such sum or sums of money not exceeding in the whole six millions of pounds sterling, as may be requisite to effect such redemption or commutation, such sum or sums to be raised by the creation and issue of bonds or debentures, or capital stock bearing interest, or annuities, or partly by one of such modes and partly by another or others, and also to raise any further sum or sums of money not exceeding two millions of pounds sterling due at any one time, such last-mentioned sum or sums to be raised by the creation and issue of bonds and debentures, but not of capital stock bearing interest, or of annuities.

* * * * * * * *[1]

Bonds may be issued under the hands of two members of the Council countersigned by Secretary of State.

2. ALL bonds issued under the authority of this Act may be issued under the hands of two members of the Council of India, and countersigned by the Secretary of State for India, or one of his under-secretaries, or his assistant under-secretary, and shall be for such respective amounts, payable after such notice, and at such rate or rates of interest as the said Secretary of State in Council may think fit.

Debentures may be issued.

3. ALL debentures issued under the authority of this Act may be issued under the hands of two members of the Council, and countersigned as aforesaid, for such respective amounts, and at such rate or rates of interest, as the Secretary of State in Council may think fit, and shall be issued at or for such prices and on such terms as may be determined by the Secretary of State in Council.

As to payment of principal and interest on debentures.

4. ALL debentures issued under the authority of this Act shall be paid off at par at a time or times to be mentioned in such debentures respectively; and the interest on all such debentures shall be paid half-yearly on such days as shall be mentioned therein; and the principal moneys and interest secured by such debentures, or by any debentures issued by the Secretary of State in Council of India under the authority of former Acts, shall be payable either at the treasury of the Secretary of State in Council in London or at the Bank of England.

Debentures transferable by delivery.

5. ALL or any number of the debentures issued under the authority of this Act, and all right to and in respect of the principal and interest moneys secured thereby, shall be transferable by the delivery of such debentures; and the coupons for interest annexed to any debenture issued under the authority of this Act shall also pass by delivery.

Coupons by delivery.

Capital stock and annuities may be created and issued.

6. ANY capital stock created under the authority of this Act shall bear such a rate of interest, and any annuities to be created under the authority of this Act, shall be at such rate per centum per annum, as the Secretary of

[1] The proviso to this section has been repealed as to the U. K. by 46 & 47 Vict., c. 39 (S. L. R.), and is omitted as being obsolete.

State in Council may think fit; and such capital stock and such annuities may be issued on such terms as may be determined by the Secretary of State in Council; and any such capital stock may bear interest during such period, and be paid off at par at such time, as the Secretary of State in Council may prescribe previously to the issue of such capital stock; and such annuities may be terminable at such period as the Secretary of State in Council may prescribe previously to the issue of such annuities.

Transfer books of such capital stock and annuities to be kept.

7. In case of the creation and issue of any such capital stock or of any such annuities, there shall be kept, either at the office of the Secretary of State in Council in London or at the Bank of England, books wherein entries shall be made of the said capital stock and annuities respectively, and wherein all assignments or transfers of the same respectively, or any part thereof respectively, shall be entered and registered, and shall be signed by the parties making such assignments or transfers, or, if such parties be absent, by his, her, or their attorney or attorneys thereunto lawfully authorized by writing under his, her, or their hands and seals, to be attested by two or more credible witnesses; and the person or persons to whom such transfer or transfers shall be made may respectively underwrite his, her, or their acceptance thereof; and no other mode of assigning or transferring the said capital stock or the said annuities, or any part thereof respectively, or any interest therein respectively, shall be good and available in law, and no stamp duties whatsoever shall be charged on the said transfers or any of them.

Annuities deemed personal estate.

8. All annuities created and issued under the authority of this Act shall be deemed and taken to be personal and not real estate, and shall go to the executors or administrators of the person or persons dying possessed thereof, interested therein, or entitled thereto, and not to the heir-at-law, nor be liable to any foreign attachment by the custom of London, or otherwise.

The whole amount charged on revenue of India not to exceed 8,000,000*l*.

9. The whole amount of the principal moneys to be charged on the revenues of India under this Act shall not exceed eight millions, nor shall it be lawful to increase under this Act the permanent debt in England, secured on the revenues of India, beyond six millions, or such lesser sum as may be required to redeem or commute the said capital stock.

Power to raise money for payment of principal money.

10. Upon or for the repayment of any principal money secured under the authority of this Act, the Secretary of State in Council may at any time borrow or raise, by all or any of the modes aforesaid, all or any part of the amount of principal money repaid or to be repaid, and so from time to time as all or any part of any principal money under this Act may require to be repaid, but the amount to be charged upon the revenues of India shall not in any case exceed the principal money required to be repaid.

Securities, etc., to be charged on revenues of India.

11. All bonds and debentures to be issued under this Act, and the principal moneys and interest thereby secured, and all capital stock to be issued under this Act, and the interest thereon, and all annuities to be issued under this Act, shall be charged on and payable out of the revenues of India, in like manner as other liabilities incurred on account of the government of the said territories.

Provisions as to compositions for stamp duties on India bonds extended to bonds, etc., under this Act.

12. The provisions contained in section four of the Act of the session holden in the fifth and sixth years of King William the Fourth, chapter sixty-four, with respect to the composition and agreement for the payment by the East India Company of an annual sum in lieu of stamp duties on their bonds, and the exemption of their bonds for stamp duties, shall be applicable with respect to the bonds and debentures to be issued under the authority of this Act as if such provisions were here repeated and re-enacted with reference thereto.

Forgery of debentures to be punishable as forgery of East India bonds.

13. All provisions now in force in anywise relating to the offence of forging or altering, or offering, uttering, disposing of, or putting off, knowing the same to be forged or altered, any East India bond, with intent to defraud, shall extend and be applicable to and in respect of any debenture issued under the authority of this Act, as well as to and in respect of any bond issued under the same authority.

14. [*Rep. 37 & 38 Vict., c. 3, s. 15. Omitted as being spent.*]

Saving powers of the Secretary of State in Council.

15. This Act shall not prejudice or affect any power of raising or borrowing money vested in the said Secretary of State in Council at the time of passing thereof.

Stock created hereunder to be deemed East India stock.

16. Any capital stock created under this Act shall be deemed to be East India stock, within the Act twenty-second and twenty-third Victoria, chapter thirty-five, section thirty-two, unless and until Parliament shall otherwise provide; and any capital stock created under this Act or under Act of the thirty-second and thirty-third Victoria, chapter one hundred and six, shall be deemed to be and shall mean India stock within the Act of the twenty-sixth and twenty-seventh Victoria, chapter seventy-three, anything in the said last-mentioned Act to the contrary notwithstanding.

THE INDIAN RAILWAY COMPANIES ACT, 1873.

(36 & 37 Vict., c. 43.)

An Act to enable Indian Railway Companies to issue and register Shares and Securities in India.

[*21st July, 1873.*]

[*Preamble.*]

Every Indian railway company may establish offices in India for the issue and registration of shares.

1. EVERY company now formed, or which shall hereafter be formed, whether by amalgamation or otherwise, for constructing, maintaining, and working railways in India, may establish at such places in India as they think fit an office for the issue, registration, and transfer of shares, stock, bonds, and securities of the company, and the registration of transfers of shares, stock, bonds, and securities, and the registration of shareholders, and may from time to time remove or alter the place of any such office, and may make such regulations, consistent with the provisions of this Act, as they think fit, for enabling and facilitating the issue, registration, and transfer of shares, stock, bonds, and securities, and the registration of transfers of shares, stock, bonds, and securities, and the registration of shareholders at such office, and all and every the powers and provisions in relation to the issue, transfer, and registration of shares, stock, bonds, and securities, and the registration of shareholders in Great Britain, contained in any deed of settlement or Act of Parliament under or by which the company shall be constituted or governed, shall apply and be in force as to the shares, stock, bonds, and securities, and the registration of transfers thereof, and the registration of shareholders, to be issued, transferred, registered and made at such office in India, except so far as the same are inconsistent with the provisions of this Act.

Registers to be kept in India.

2. EVERY such company may keep at their office in India books to be called respectively "the India register of shareholders", "the India register of holders of consolidated stock", "the India shareholders address book", "the India register of transfers", and also books for the registration of bonds, debentures, mortgages, and the debenture stock, and the transfers thereof respectively, and the books so kept shall be of the like validity and effect as the books kept for the like purposes by the company in England, and accounts of all entries and alterations made in the books of the company in India shall be transmitted to the principal office of the same company in England.

Registers at several offices.

3. PROVIDED always, that if and when the company have offices in India at more places than one, then the company shall substitute for or add to the

In India to be distinguished

word "India" in the titles of the register kept at every such office, the name of the place at which the particular office is established.

Where transfers to be registered.

Shares, etc., to be registered at one office only.

4. All transfers of any such shares, stock, bonds, and securities as aforesaid shall be made at the office at which the same respectively shall for the time being be registered, and no share, stock, bond, or security shall be on the registry of more than one office at one time and the same time: Provided always, that the company may keep in England duplicates of any of its books of register kept in India, but no such duplicate book shall be deemed a register.

Shares, etc., may be transferred from one register to another at the option of the holder.

5. Subject to the regulations from time to time made by such companies respectively, with respect to the issue, registration, and transfer of shares, stock, bonds, and securities respectively, and the registration of transfers of shares, stock, bonds, and securities respectively, every such company may and shall, on notice in writing by the holder of any share, stock, bond, or security to the person for the time being acting as secretary, managing director, or principal clerk at the office in England or in India where such share, stock, bond, or security shall then be registered, transfer the share, stock, bond, or security from the register thereof at that office to the corresponding register at any other office of the company where for the time being a register shall be kept to be appointed and named in such notice, and as soon as conveniently may be after the receipt of any such notice such secretary, managing director, or principal clerk shall transmit advice thereof to the office to which the transfer is directed to be made.

Locality of shares, etc.

6. For the purpose of determining any question as to the place or jurisdiction within which any share, stock, bond, or security shall be deemed to be or to have been situate at any given time, the locality, whether in India or in Great Britain, of the register in which such share, stock, bond, or security shall be or have been actually registered for the time being, shall be deemed to be or have been at such time the locality of such share, stock, bond, or security, and so soon as notice shall have been given as aforesaid for the transfer of any share, stock, bond, or security from one register to another, the share, stock, bond, or security shall for the purpose of this section be deemed to be actually registered in the register to which it is so directed to be transferred.

Saving of rights.

7. Nothing in this Act shall interfere with or affect any powers which are now vested in any Indian railway company by any Acts of Parliament by which the company is governed.

THE SLAVE TRADE (EAST AFRICAN COURTS) ACT, 1873.

(36 & 37 Vict., c. 59.)

An Act for regulating and extending the Jurisdiction in matters connected with the Slave Trade of the Vice-Admiralty Court at Aden and of Her Majesty's Consuls under Treaties with the Sovereigns of Zanzibar, Muscat, and Madagascar, and under future Treaties.[1]

[*5th August, 1873.*]

[*Preamble recites 6 & 7 Vict., c. 94; 32 & 33 Vict., c. 75.*]

1. THIS Act may be cited as the Slave Trade (East African Courts) Act, 1873. Short title.

2. IN this Act— Definition of terms.

The term "vessel" means any vessel used in navigation:

The term "treaty" includes any convention, agreement, engagement, or arrangement:

The term "foreign state" includes any foreign nation, people, tribe, sovereign, prince, chief, or headman:

The term "existing East African slave trade treaty" means a treaty made by or on behalf of Her Majesty with any foreign state in Arabia or on the east coast of Africa, or the shores of the Persian Gulf, or in any island lying off Arabia, or off such coast or shores, including the islands of Zanzibar and Madagascar and the Comoro islands, for the more effectual suppression of the slave trade, and in force at the passing of this Act:

* * * * * * *[2]

3. ALL jurisdiction which is by any Act conferred on the Vice-Admiralty Courts in Her Majesty's possessions abroad, in regard to British vessels seized by the commander or officer of any of Her Majesty's ships on suspicion of being engaged in or fitted out for the slave trade, and in regard to the persons, slaves, goods, and effects on board thereof, is hereby conferred on the East African courts, in regard to vessels seized by the commander or officer of any of Her Majesty's ships on suspicion of being engaged in or fitted out for the slave trade, and to the persons, slaves, goods, and effects on board thereof, in the following cases; namely, Jurisdiction of courts in regard to slave vessels, slaves, goods, and effects.

(1) where the vessel seized is a British vessel;

---

[1] Amended and repealed in part, by 42 & 43 Vict., c. 38, printed *post*, p. 593.

[2] The remainder of this section has been repealed by 42 & 43 Vict., c. 38, s. 2, and is omitted.

(2) where the vessel seized has been seized in pursuance of any existing East African slave trade treaty; and

(3) where the vessel seized is not shown to the court to be entitled to claim the protection of the flag of any foreign state.

Each of the East African courts shall have the same jurisdiction in regard to any person who has been seized either at sea or land, on the ground that he has or is suspected to have been detained as a slave, for the purpose of the slave trade, as the court would have under this section if he had been so detained on board a vessel that was seized and brought in for adjudication.

All jurisdiction exercised under this section shall for the purposes of any such Act as above mentioned be deemed to be exercised in pursuance of that Act.

Appeal to Her Majesty in Council.

4. The provisions of the Vice-Admiralty Courts Act, 1863, with respect to appeals to Her Majesty in Council from any decree or order of a Vice-Admiralty Court shall apply, *mutatis mutandis*, to appeals from any decree or order of the East African courts made or purporting to be made in the exercise of their jurisdiction under this Act.

Making of rules and tables of fees under 26 & 27 Vict., c. 24, ss. 14 to 18.

5. The provisions of the Vice-Admiralty Courts Act, 1863, with respect to rules touching the practice to be observed in the Vice-Admiralty Courts, and table of fees to be taken by the officers and practitioners thereof, shall apply in like manner as if they were herein enacted, with the substitution of the East African Courts for the Vice-Admiralty Courts, and of the place in which any such court is held for the British possession in which the Vice-Admiralty Court is established.

Application of Act to cases already adjudicated.

6. This Act shall apply to all cases of vessels, slaves, goods, and effects seized by the commander or officer of any of Her Majesty's ships, and adjudicated upon by any of the East African courts, whether before or after the passing of this Act.

Extension of Act to future treaties.

7. Where any treaty in relation to the slave trade is made after the passing of this Act, by or on behalf of Her Majesty, with any foreign state in Arabia, or on the east coast of Africa, or on the shores of the Persian Gulf, or in any island lying off Arabia or off such coast or shores, including the islands of Zanzibar and Madagascar and the Comoro islands, Her Majesty may by Order in Council direct that as from such date, not being earlier than the date of the treaty, as may be specified in the order, such treaty shall be deemed, and thereupon (as from the said date, or if no date is specified, as from the date of such order) such treaty shall be deemed to be an existing East African slave trade treaty within the meaning of this Act, and the provisions of this Act shall apply and be construed accordingly

Her Majesty may by such order, or any subsequent order referring to the same treaty, render the application of this Act subject to such conditions, exceptions, and qualifications as may be deemed expedient, and limit or exclude the jurisdiction of any of the East African courts.

Her Majesty may by such order, or any subsequent order referring to the same treaty, direct that any court, consul, or person authorized by or in pursuance of an Order in Council to exercise within the dominions of the foreign state with whom the treaty is made jurisdiction in matters relating to the slave trade, shall, subject to the conditions, exceptions, and limitations, if any, contained in the order, exercise all the jurisdiction conferred by this Act on the East African courts; and such court, consul or person when exercising such jurisdiction shall be deemed to be one of the East African courts within the meaning of this Act.

Every such order shall recite or embody the terms of the treaty, so far as they relate to the slave trade, and shall be laid before both Houses of Parliament within six weeks after it is made, or, if Parliament be not then sitting, within six weeks after the then next meeting of Parliament, and shall also be published in the *London Gazette*.

A treaty, whether made before or after the passing of this Act, which ceases to be in force, shall cease to be an existing East African slave trade treaty within the meaning of this Act.

8 & Sch. [*Rep. as to U. K. 46 & 47 Vict., c. 39 (S. L. R.). Omitted as being spent.*]

THE EXTRADITION ACT, 1873.[1]

(36 & 37 Vict., c. 60.)

An Act to amend the Extradition Act, 1870.[2]

[*5th August, 1873.*]

[*Preamble.*]

1. THIS Act shall be construed as one with the Extradition Act, 1870, (in this Act referred to as the principal Act) and the principal Act and this Act may be cited together as the Extradition Acts, 1870 and 1873, and this Act may be cited alone as the Extradition Act, 1873. **Construction of Act and short title. 33 & 34 Vict., c. 52.**

2. WHEREAS by section six of the principal Act it is enacted as follows: **Explanation of sect. 6 of 33 & 34 Vict., c. 52.**

" Where this Act applies in the case of any foreign state, every fugitive
" criminal of that state who is in or suspected of being in any part of Her

[1] *See Chitty's Statutes*, Tit. Extradition, p. 14.

[2] Extended by the Extradition (India) Act, 1895 IX of 1895), s. 2, printed, General Acts, Vol. VI, Ed. 1898.

" Majesty's dominions, or that part which is specified in the order applying " this Act (as the case may be), shall be liable to be apprehended and surrendered " in manner provided by this Act, whether the crime in respect of which the " surrender is sought was committed before or after the date of the order, and " whether there is or is not any concurrent jurisdiction in any court of Her " Majesty's dominions over that crime."

And whereas doubts have arisen as to the application of the said section to crimes committed before the passing of the principal Act, and it is expedient to remove such doubts, it is therefore hereby declared that—

a crime committed before the date of the order includes in the said section a cri e committed before the passing of the principal Act, and the principal Act and this Act shall be construed accordingly.

3. [*Recital.*]

Every person who is accused or convicted of having counselled, procured, commanded, aided, or abetted the commission of any extradition crime, or of being accessory before or after the fact to any extradition crime, shall be deemed for the purposes of the principal Act and this Act to be accused or convicted of having committed such crime, and shall be liable to be apprehended and surrendered accordingly.

Explanation of sect. 14 of 33 & 34 Vict., c. 52, as to statements on oath including affirmations.

4. * * * * The provisions of the principal Act relating to depositions and statements on oath taken in a foreign state, and copies of such original depositions and statements do and shall extend to affirmations taken in a foreign state, and copies of such affirmations.

Power of taking evidence in United Kingdom for foreign criminal matters.

5. A SECRETARY OF STATE may, by order under his hand and seal, require a police Magistrate or a justice of the peace to take evidence for the purposes of any criminal matter pending in any court or tribunal in any foreign state; and the police magistrate or justice of the peace, upon the receipt of such order, shall take the evidence of every witness appearing before him for the purpose in like manner as if such witness appeared on a charge against some defendant for an indictable offence, and shall certify at the foot of the depositions so taken that such evidence was taken before him, and shall transmit the same to the Secretary of State; such evidence may be taken in the presence or absence of the person charged, if any, and the fact of such presence or absence shall be stated in such deposition.

Any person may, after payment or tender to him of a reasonable sum for his costs and expenses in this behalf, be compelled, for the purposes of this section, to attend and give evidence and answer questions and produce documents, in like manner and subject to the like conditions as he may in the case of a charge preferred for an indictable offence.

Every person who wilfully gives false evidence before a police magistrate or justice of the peace under this section shall be guilty of perjury.

Provided that nothing in this section shall apply in the case of any criminal matter of a political character.

6. The jurisdiction conferred by section sixteen of the principal Act on a stipendiary magistrate, and a sheriff or sheriff substitute, shall be deemed to be in addition to, and not in derogation or exclusion of, the jurisdiction of the police magistrate. Explanation of sect. 16 of 33 & 34 Vict., c. 52.

7. For the purposes of the principal Act and this Act a diplomatic representative of a foreign state shall be deemed to include any person recognized by the Secretary of State as a consul general of that state, and a consul or vice-consul shall be deemed to include any person recognized by the governor of a British possession as a consular officer of a foreign state. Explanation of diplomatic representative and consul.

8. The principal Act shall be construed as if there were included in the first schedule to that Act the list of crimes contained in the schedule to this Act. Addition to list of crimes in schedule.

SCHEDULE.

List of Crimes.

The following list of crimes is to be construed according to the law existing in England or in a British possession (as the case may be) at the date of the alleged crime, whether by common law or by statute made before or after the passing of this Act:

Kidnapping and false imprisonment.

Perjury, and subornation of perjury, whether under common or statute law.

Any indictable offence under the Larceny Act, 1861, or any Act amending or substituted for the same, which is not included in the first schedule to the principal Act. 24 & 25 Vict., c. 96, etc.

Any indictable offence under the Malicious Damage Act, 1861, or any Act amending or substituted for the same, which is not included in the first schedule to the principal Act.

Any indictable offence under the Forgery Act, 1861, or any Act amending or substituted for the same, which is not included in the first schedule to the principal Act.

Any indictable offence under the Coinage Offences Act, 1861, or any Act amending or substituted for the same, which is not included in the first schedule to the principal Act.

Any indictable offence under the Offences against the Person Act, 1861, or any Act amending or substituted for the same, which is not included in the first schedule to the principal Act.

Any indictable offence under the laws for the time being in force in relation to bankruptcy which is not included in the first schedule to the principal Act.

The Slave Trade Act, 1873.[1]

(36 & 37 Vict., c. 88.)

An Act for consolidating with amendments the Acts for carrying into effect Treaties for the more effectual Suppression of the Slave Trade, and for other purposes connected with the Slave Trade.

[*5th August, 1873.*]

[*Preamble.*]

Preliminary.

Short title. 1. This Act may be cited as the Slave Trade Act, 1873.

Interpretation. 2. In this Act—

* * * * * *

the term "vessel" means any vessel used in navigation:

the term "British possession" means any plantation, territory, settlement, or place situate within Her Majesty's dominions, and not forming part of the United Kingdom:

the term "governor" includes the officer for the time being administering the government of any colony; and where there is a local governor or lieutenant-governor under a governor general, means the local governor or lieutenant-governor:

* * * * * *

the term "foreign state" includes any foreign nation, people, tribe, sovereign, prince, chief, or headman:

the term "vessel of a foreign state" means a vessel which is justly entitled to claim the protection of the flag of a foreign state, or which would be so entitled if she did not lose such protection by being engaged in the slave trade:

the term "treaty" includes any convention, agreement, engagement, or arrangement:

the term "slave trade" when used in relation to any particular treaty does not include anything declared by such treaty not to be comprised in the term or in such treaty:

---

[1] *See Chitty's Statutes*, Tit. Admiralty, 4.

the term "Vice-Admiralty Court" does not include any Vice-Admiralty Court which for the time being has under its commission a limited jurisdiction only in matters relating to the slave trade:

the term "British slave court" means the High Court of Admiralty of England, every Vice-Admiralty Court in Her Majesty's dominions out of the United Kingdom, and every East African Court for the time being within the meaning of the Slave Trade (East African Courts) Act, 1873:

the term "slave court" means every British slave court, every mixed commission or court established under any existing slave trade treaty, and the court of any foreign state having jurisdiction to try and condemn a vessel engaged in the slave trade:

the term "existing slave trade treaty" means a treaty made by or on behalf of Her Majesty or Her Royal predecessors with any foreign state for the more effectual suppression of the slave trade and in force at the passing of this Act.

Seizure of Slave Ships.

Visitation and seizure by cruisers, etc., of suspected slave ships.

3. Where a vessel is, on reasonable grounds, suspected of being engaged in or fitted out for the slave trade, it shall (subject, in the case either of the vessel of a foreign state, or of the commander or officer of a cruiser of a foreign state, to the limitations, restrictions, and regulation, if any, applicable thereto contained in any existing slave trade treaty made with such state) be lawful—

(*a*) if the vessel is a British vessel, or is engaged in the slave trade within British jurisdiction, or is not a vessel of a foreign state, for any commander or officer of any of Her Majesty's ships, for any officer bearing Her Majesty's commission in the army or navy, for any officer of Her Majesty's customs in the United Kingdom, Channel Islands, or Isle of Man, for the governor of a British possession, or any person authorized by any such governor, and for any commander or officer of any cruiser of a foreign state authorized in pursuance of any existing slave trade treaty; and

(*b*) if the vessel is the vessel of a foreign state, for any commander or officer of any of Her Majesty's ships, when duly authorized in that behalf, in pursuance of any treaty with that state, and for any commander or officer of any cruiser of that foreign state,

to visit and seize and detain such vessel, and to seize and detain any person found detained or reasonably suspected of having been detained as a slave, for the purpose of the slave trade, on board any such vessel,[1] and to carry away such vessel and person, together with the master and all persons, goods, and effects on board any such vessel, for the purpose of bringing in such vessel, persons, goods, and effects for adjudication.

All vessels, slaves, persons, goods, and effects which may be forfeited under the enactments with which this Act is to be construed as one, as hereinafter mentioned, may be visited, seized, and detained by any commander, officer, governor, or person authorized by this section to seize a British vessel.

Vessels equipped for traffic in slaves to be deemed engaged in the slave trade.

4. Where any of the particulars mentioned in the first schedule to this Act are found in the equipment or on board of any vessel visited, seized or detained in pursuance of this Act, such vessel shall, unless the contrary be proved, be deemed to be fitted out for the purposes of and engaged in the slave trade, and in such case, even though the vessel is restored, no damages shall be awarded against the seizor under this Act in respect of such visitation, seizure, or detention, or otherwise upon such restoration.

Provided that this section shall not extend to the vessel of any foreign state except so far as may be consistent with the treaty made with such state.

Courts.

Jurisdiction of courts in regard to slave vessels, slaves, goods, and effects.

5. The High Court of Admiralty of England and Vice-Admiralty Court in Her Majesty's dominions out of the United Kingdom shall have jurisdiction to try and condemn or restore any vessel, slave, goods, and effects alleged to be seized, detained, or forfeited, in pursuance of this Act, and on restoring the same to award such damages in respect of the visitation, seizure, and detention of such vessel, goods, and effects, and of any person on board such vessel, and in respect of any act or thing done in relation to such visitation, seizure, or detention, or in respect of any of such matters, and in any case to make such order as to costs as, subject to the provisions of this Act and of any existing slave trade treaty, the court may think just.

Provided that nothing in this section shall give to any court any jurisdiction inconsistent with any existing slave trade treaty over a vessel which is shown to such court to be the vessel of any foreign state and which has not been engaged within British jurisdiction in the slave trade, but where any vessel of a foreign state is liable to be condemned by a British slave court, such court shall have the same jurisdiction as if she were a British vessel.

---

[1] This does not justify a British officer in seizing slaves on board a British vessel within the waters of a foreign state, without the consent, by treaty or otherwise, of such state, even in cases where the vessel is engaged in, or fitted out for, the slave trade.—*Opinion of law-officers of the Crown and Dr. Deane, 15th January 1881.*

Each of the said courts shall have the same jurisdiction in regard to any person who has been seized, either at sea or on land, on the ground that he has or is suspected to have been detained as a slave, for the purpose of the slave trade, as the court would have under this section if he had been so detained on board a vessel that was seized and brought in for adjudication.

6. Where any vessel or slave seized by the commander or officer of the cruiser of any foreign state is brought in for adjudication in a British slave court, all proceedings for the condemnation of such vessel and slave, and the goods and effects on board such vessel, shall be taken in the name of Her Majesty by some person duly authorized in that behalf. Proceedings upon seizure by a foreigner.

Mixed Courts.

7. Where any existing slave trade treaty contains provisions for the time being in force for the appointment of any mixed court or commission for deciding cases under such treaty, it shall be lawful for Her Majesty from time to time to appoint such commissioners, judges, arbitrators, secretary, registrar, and other officers as are mentioned in such provisions. Appointment of judges, arbitrators, secretary, etc., to mixed courts and commissions.

There shall be paid to every commissioner, judge, arbitrator, secretary, registrar, and other officer so appointed, such salary as the Treasury may from time to time direct.

In case of the death, or sickness, or absence either on leave or from any other lawful impediment, of any such commissioner, judge, arbitrator, secretary, registrar, or other officer, whether British or not, the vacancy shall be temporarily filled in manner provided by the treaty

8. The regulations contained in any existing slave trade treaty for the time being in force, with respect to any mixed court or commission, shall have effect as if they were enacted in this Act, and such court or commission shall have all necessary jurisdiction for the purpose of carrying into effect any treaty referring to them, and in particular shall have jurisdiction to try, condemn, and restore British vessels seized in pursuance of such treaty on suspicion of being engaged in the slave trade, and shall, for the purpose of their jurisdiction, have the same power as any Vice-Admiralty Court in Her Majesty's dominions has, and may accordingly take evidence, administer oaths, summon and enforce the attendance of witnesses, and require and enforce the production of documents in like manner as any such court. Regulations as to powers of mixed courts.

Disposal of Vessels and Slaves.

9. A vessel seized in pursuance of this Act, when condemned by a slave court, may be taken into Her Majesty's service upon payment of such sum as the Admiralty deem to be a proper price for the same (which sum is in this Disposal of condemned vessels.

Act called the appraised value of such vessel) or, if not so taken, shall be broken up, and the materials thereof shall be publicly sold in separate parts.

Provided that nothing herein shall prejudice the right of the government of any foreign state, under any treaty, to require such vessel to be broken up, or to take such vessel into its service upon payment of a sum fixed in accordance with such treaty, and any sum paid by the government of a foreign state for a vessel taken into its service after condemnation by a slave court shall be deemed for the purposes of this Act to be the appraised value of the vessel.

Disposal of slaves.

10. Where any slaves are seized in pursuance of this Act, they shall, for the purpose only of seizure, prosecution, and condemnation, be deemed to be property, and shall be condemned as forfeited to the sole use of Her Majesty for the purpose only of divesting all other right or interest therein, and shall not be treated as slaves, but shall be provided for, pending the proceedings for their condemnations, in such manner, and shall on condemnation be disposed of in such manner, or delivered over to such persons, as the court having cognizance of the case may adjudge, subject to the regulations (if any) which are from time to time made by the Treasury; and the Treasury may from time to time make, alter, and revoke regulations for this purpose so that they be consistent with any provisions in this behalf contained in any existing slave trade treaty.

Bounties.

Bounty and other payments to seizors when British cruisers.

11. Where a vessel (whether British or not) or slave, goods, or effects seized in pursuance of this Act by any commander or officer of any of Her Majesty's ships have been condemned by a slave court, there shall be paid to the commander, officers, and crew of such ship the following sums:

(1) A slave bounty of five pounds for every slave so condemned who is delivered over, or, if the commander of the ship so elect, a tonnage bounty of four pounds for every ton of the tonnage of the vessel condemned:

(2) That part to which Her Majesty is entitled of the appraised value of the vessel condemned, or, if such vessel was broken up and the materials thereof publicly sold in separate parts, of the net proceeds of such sale after deducting the charges of prosecution:

(3) Where the condemned vessel

(*a*) was brought into port and was broken up in pursuance of the order of the slave court, and the materials thereof publicly sold in separate parts; or

(*b*) was abandoned or destroyed prior to condemnation, and the slave court by the decree of condemnation declared that, after full consideration by the court of the circumstances of the case, the seizors had satisfied the court that such abandonment or destruction was inevitable, or otherwise under the circumstances proper and justifiable,

a further tonnage bounty at the rate of thirty shillings for every ton of the tonnage of the vessel; and

(4) The net proceeds to which Her Majesty is entitled (after deducting the charges of prosecution) of any such goods and effects which the slave court ordered to be sold.

Where any slave so condemned is not delivered over in consequence of death, sickness, or other inevitable circumstances, the Treasury may, if they think fit, pay to the seizors of such slave one moiety of the slave bounty which would have been due in respect of such slave if he had been delivered over.

Bounty and other payments where vessel, slave, or goods not seized by cruisers.

12. Where any vessel, slave, goods, or effects seized in pursuance of this Act otherwise than by the commander or officer of one of Her Majesty's ships, or of the cruiser of a foreign state, have been condemned by a slave court, there shall be paid the following sums :

(1) Two-thirds of the appraised value of the vessel or (if the vessel was broken up and the materials thereof publicly sold in separate parts) of the net proceeds of such sale, and two-thirds of the net proceeds of such goods and effects (after deducting from such appraised value or net proceeds the charges of prosecution) for the use of Her Majesty, to such persons as the Treasury may from time to time appoint, to be carried to the Consolidated Fund :

(2) The remaining third part of the said appraised value or net proceeds of the vessel and of the net proceeds of such goods and effects to the person who lawfully seized and prosecuted the ship, goods, and effects respectively to condemnation :

(3) For every slave so condemned who is delivered over, a slave bounty of five pounds to the person who prosecuted the same to condemnation.

Where any slave so condemned is not delivered over in consequence of death, sickness, or other inevitable circumstances, the Treasury may, if they think fit, pay in respect of such slave one moiety of the slave bounty which would have been due in respect of such slave if he had been delivered over.

Payment of proceeds of vessels, etc., when seized by a foreign cruiser.

13. Where any vessel, goods, or effects have been seized in pursuance of this Act by the commander or officer of a cruiser of any foreign state, and been condemned by a British slave court, such portion of the appraised value of the vessel, or (if the vessel was broken up and the materials thereof publicly sold in separate parts) of the net proceeds of such sale, and of the net proceeds of the goods and effects, as is, under any treaty with such state, payable to the seizors, shall be paid to such person as the Treasury may direct, to be disposed of in accordance with such treaty.

Regulations as to payment of bounty.

14. In order to obtain payment of the bounty, there shall be produced to the Treasury the following evidence, or such other evidence as the Treasury may deem sufficient; namely,

(a) a copy, duly certified, of the decree of condemnation of the vessel or slave :

(b) if any tonnage bounty is claimed, a certificate from some person authorized for the time being to act as a registrar of British ships of the dimensions and tonnage of the vessel :

(c) if a slave bounty is claimed, a certificate from the person appointed to receive the slaves of the number of slaves condemned and delivered over.

For the purpose of bounty the tonnage of a vessel shall be calculated and ascertained in the like manner in which, for the time being, the tonnage of a vessel is calculated and ascertained for the purpose of registering the same as a British vessel, or, if the same cannot be satisfactorily ascertained in that manner, shall be ascertained in such manner as the Treasury may consider satisfactory.

Payment by Treasury of costs, damages, and expenses.

15. Where any visitation, seizure, detention, or prosecution purports to have been made or instituted in pursuance of this Act, the Treasury when required under any treaty shall, and in any other case may, if they think fit, pay the whole or any part of any costs, expenses, compensation, and damages which may have been awarded against the person making or instituting such visitation, seizure, detention, or prosecution, or any costs and expenses which may have been incurred in respect of the same, or on account of any person on board any vessel so visited, seized, or detained; but nothing in this section shall exempt the commander or officer of the ship or other person by whom the visitation, seizure, detention, or prosecution was made or instituted from his liability to make good any sum so paid when required by the Treasury so to do, and when any such commander or officer, or other person serving under the Admiralty, or any person serving under any other department of the Government, is so required to make good any sum, that sum shall, if the Treasury so direct, be deducted by the Admiralty or other department of the Government under whom such person is serving, from any payment to which such commander, officer, or person is entitled on account of salary, pay, prize, or bounty.

16. The bounties and all other sums payable by the Treasury in pursuance of this Act shall be paid out of moneys provided by Parliament for the purpose. Payment and distribution of bounties and other sums.

27 & 28 Vict., c. 24. The provisions of "The Naval Agency and Distribution Act, 1864", shall apply to all money payable to the commanders, officers, and crews of Her Majesty's ships in pursuance of this Act.

Miscellaneous.

17. All persons authorized to make seizures under this Act shall, in making and prosecuting any such seizure, have the benefit of all the protection granted to persons authorized to make seizures under any Act for the time being in force relating to Her Majesty's customs in the United Kingdom, in like manner as if the enactments granting such protection were herein enacted and in terms made applicable thereto. Protection of persons authorized to seize.

18. In either of the following cases, namely,

(a) where any proceeding has been instituted in any slave court for the condemnation or restitution of any vessel, slave, goods, or effects purporting to have been seized in pursuance of this Act and is still pending; or Pendency of suit or decree a bar to proceeding for recovery of vessel, damages, etc.

(b) where any vessel, slave, goods, or effects purporting to have been seized in pursuance of this Act, have been condemned or restored, or any other final judgment has been pronounced thereon by any slave court,

the pendency of such proceeding, or the condemnation or restitution, or other final judgment thereon, as the case may be, shall be a complete bar to every legal proceeding whatever for the recovery of such vessel, slave, goods, or effects, or of damages for any costs, expenses, loss, or injury sustained by any person by or in consequence of the visitation, seizure, or detention of such vessel, slave, goods, or effects, or of any person on board such vessel, or by or in consequence of any act or thing done in relation to such visitation, seizure, or detention, or in pursuance of this Act or any existing slave trade treaty, and may be pleaded in bar, or given in evidence under the general issue.

19. The High Court of Admiralty of England shall have jurisdiction to hear and determine any question arising with respect to the right of any person to any payment in pursuance of this Act in respect of any condemned vessel, slave, goods, or effects, and any question of joint capture or seizure which may arise in respect of any vessel, slave, goods, or effects seized in pursuance of this Act, and also as well to review as to enforce any decree, declaration, or order of any British slave court made in pursuance of this Act. Power of High Court of Admiralty of England as to bounties, reviewing and enforcing decrees, etc.

Review of taxation by registrar of Court of Admiralty.

[1] **20.** The registrar of the High Court of Admiralty of England may, on the application of any person aggrieved, or of the Treasury, tax or review the taxation of any costs, charges, or expenses incurred or alleged to be incurred in any proceeding taken in any British slave court, or in any mixed commission or court in Her Majesty's dominions, and shall for this purpose have the same jurisdiction and powers as he has in the taxation of any costs, charges or expenses incurred in any proceeding in the High Court of Admiralty.

Appeal by Treasury.

21. The Treasury may appeal from any decree, order, or declaration which is made by any British slave court in pursuance of this Act and involves the payment by the Treasury of any bounty, costs, expenses, compensation, damages, or other moneys in like manner as if they were parties to the proceeding in which such decree, order, or declaration was made.

Prosecution for false evidence.

22. Any person who wilfully gives false evidence in any proceeding taken in pursuance of this Act in any slave court shall be guilty of an offence against this Act and shall be liable to the like penalty as if he had been guilty of perjury, or in a British possession, of the offence, by whatever name called, which if committed in England would be perjury.

Returns by registrars.

23. The registrar of every British slave court, and if appointed by Her Majesty, of every other slave court, shall from time to time make returns of the cases adjudged in such court in pursuance of this Act, at such times and in such form and containing such particulars as may be from time to time directed by any rule established with respect to such court [2] * * * or if there is no such rule by Order in Council.

Slave Trade Act, 1824.

Incorporation with unrepealed portions of 5 Geo. 4, c. 113.

24. This Act shall be construed as one with the enactments of the Slave Trade Act, 1824, and any enactments amending the same, so far as they are in force at the time of the passing of this Act, and are not repealed by this Act; and the expression "this Act", when used in this Act, shall include those enactments.

Recovery of forfeitures under 5 Geo. 4, c. 113.

25. All pecuniary forfeitures and penalties imposed by the said enactments, with which this Act is to be construed as one, may be sued for, prosecuted, and recovered in any Court of Record or of Vice-Admiralty in any part of Her Majesty's dominions wherein the offence was committed, or where the offender may be, in like manner as any penalty or forfeiture incurred in the

---

[1] Section 20, as far as relates to the taxation of any costs, charges, and expenses which can be taxed in pursuance of 53 & 54 Vict., c. 27, is repealed by s. 18 of that Act, and as respects any courts out of Her Majesty's dominions as from the date of any order applying that Act. For 53 & 54 Vict., c. 27, *see post*, p. 880.

[2] The words "under the Vice-Admiralty Courts Act, 1863", are repealed by 53 & 54 Vict., c. 27, which came into force in India on the 1st July, 1891, *see post*, p. 880.

United Kingdom under any Act for the time being in force relating to Her Majesty's Customs, or (in the case of the High Court of Admiralty or of a Court of Vice-Admiralty) in like manner as any vessel seized in pursuance of this Act.

Such pecuniary penalties and forfeitures shall, subject to the express provisions of the said enactments, be paid and applied in like manner as the net proceeds of a vessel seized otherwise than by the commander or officer of one of Her Majesty's ships, or of the cruiser of a foreign state.

26. ANY offence against this Act or the said enactments with which this Act is to be construed as one, or otherwise in connexion with the slave trade, shall for all purposes of and incidental to the trial and punishment of a person guilty of such offence, and all proceedings and matters preliminary and incidental to and consequential on such trial and punishment, and for all purposes of and incidental to the jurisdiction of any court, constable, and officer with reference to such offence, be deemed to have been committed either in the place in which the offence was committed, or in the county of Middlesex, or in any place in which the person guilty of the offence may for the time being be, either in Her Majesty's dominions, or in any foreign port or place in which Her Majesty has jurisdiction; and the offence may be described in any indictment or other document relating thereto as having been committed at the place where it was wholly or partly committed, or as having been committed on the high seas or out of Her Majesty's dominions, and the venue or local description in the margin may be that of the place in which the trial is held.

Jurisdiction of Court over offences under 5 Geo. 4, c. 113.

Where any such offence is commenced at one place and completed at another, the place at which such offence is to be deemed to have been committed shall be either the place where the offence was commenced or the place where the offence was completed.

Where a person being in one place is accessory to or aids or abets in any such offence committed in another place, the place at which such offence is to be deemed to have been committed shall be either the place in which the offence was actually committed or the place where the offender was at the time of his being so accessory, aiding, or abetting.

Where it appears to any court or the judge of any court having jurisdiction to try any such offence that the removal of an offender charged with such offence to some other place in Her Majesty's dominions for trial would be conducive to the interests of justice, such court or judge may by warrant, or instrument in the nature of a warrant, direct such removal, and such offender may be removed and tried accordingly; and section two hundred and sixty-eight of the Merchant Shipping Act, 1854, shall apply to the removal of an offender under this section in the same manner as if the term "consular officer" in that section included the court or judge making such warrant or instrument. 17 & 18 Vict., c. 104.

Extension of 33 & 34 Vict., c. 52, to slave trade offences. 27. OFFENCES committed against this Act or the enactments with which this Act is to be construed as one or otherwise in connexion with the slave trade, whether committed on the high seas or on land, or partly on the high seas or partly on land, shall be deemed to be inserted in the first schedule to the Extradition Act, 1870, and that Act, and any Act amending the same, shall be construed accordingly.

Application of Act.

Application of Act to cases already adjudicated. 28. THIS Act shall apply to all cases of vessels, slaves, goods, and effects seized and adjudicated upon by any slave court, whether before or after the passing of this Act.

Extension of Act to future treaties. 29. WHERE any treaty in relation to the slave trade is made after the passing of this Act, by or on behalf of Her Majesty, with any foreign state, Her Majesty may by Order in Council direct that as from such date, not being earlier than the date of the treaty, as may be specified in the order, such treaty shall be deemed, and thereupon (as from the said date, or if no date is specified as from the date of such order) such treaty shall be deemed to be an existing slave trade treaty within the meaning of this Act, and all the provisions of this Act shall apply and be construed accordingly.

Her Majesty may, by the same or any subsequent order referring to the same treaty, render the application of this Act subject to such conditions, exceptions, and qualifications as may be deemed expedient.

Every such order shall recite or embody the terms of the treaty so far as they relate to the slave trade, and shall be laid before both Houses of Parliament within six weeks after it is made, or, if Parliament be not then sitting, within six weeks after the then next meeting of Parliament, and shall also be published in the *London Gazette*.

A treaty, whether made before or after the passing of this Act, which ceases to be in force shall cease to be an existing slave trade treaty within the meaning of this Act.

Repeal.

30 & Second Sch. [*Rep. as to U. K. 46 & 47 Vict., c. 39 (S. L. R.). Omitted as being spent.*]

FIRST SCHEDULE.

EQUIPMENTS WHICH ARE *PRIMÂ FACIE* EVIDENCE OF A VESSEL BEING ENGAGED IN THE SLAVE TRADE.

First.—Hatches with open gratings, instead of the close hatches which are usual in merchant vessels.

Secondly.—Divisions or bulkheads in the hold or on deck more numerous than are necessary for vessels engaged in lawful trade.

Thirdly.—Spare plank fitted for being laid down as a second or slave deck.

Fourthly.—Shackles, bolts, or handcuffs.

Fifthly.—A larger quantity of water in casks or in tanks than is requisite for the consumption of the crew of the vessel as a merchant vessel.

Sixthly.—An extraordinary number of water casks or of other vessels for holding liquid unless the master shall produce a certificate from the custom-house at the place from which he declared outwards, stating that a sufficient security had been given by the owners of such vessel that such extra quantity of casks or of other vessels should only be used for the reception of palm oil, or for other purposes of lawful commerce.

Seventhly.—A greater quantity of mess tubs or kids than are requisite for the use of the crew of the vessel as a merchant vessel.

Eighthly.—A boiler or other cooking apparatus of an unusual size, and larger or fitted for being or capable of being made larger than requisite for the use of the crew of the vessel as a merchant vessel, or more than one boiler or other cooking apparatus of the ordinary size.

Ninthly.—An extraordinary quantity either of rice or of the flour of Brazil, manioc, or cassada, commonly called farina, of maize or of Indian corn, or of any other article of food whatever, beyond what might probably be requisite for the use of the crew, such rice, flour, maize, Indian corn, or other article of food not being entered on the manifest as part of the cargo for trade.

Tenthly.—A quantity of mats or matting larger than is necessary for the use of the crew of the vessel as a merchant vessel.

Eleventhly.—Any other equipment, article, or thing, which is declared by any existing slave trade treaty to be *primâ facie* evidence of a vessel being engaged in the slave trade.

THE EAST INDIA LOAN ACT, 1874.[1]

(37 & 38 Vict., c. 3.)

An Act to enable the Secretary of State in Council of India to raise Money in the United Kingdom for the Service of the Government of India.

[*30th March, 1874.*]

[*Preamble.*]

1. IT shall be lawful for the Secretary of State in Council of India, at any time or times before the thirtieth day of April one thousand eight hundred and Power to the Secretary of

[1] This Act may be cited, with eighteen others, as the East India Loans Acts, 1859 to 1893—*see* the Short Titles Act, 1896 (59 & 60 Vict., c. 14), *post*, p 1266.

State in Council of India to raise any sum not exceeding 10,000,000*l.*

seventy-nine, or, if Parliament be then sitting, before the end of the then Session of Parliament, to raise in the United Kingdom, for the service of the Government of India, any sum or sums of money not exceeding in the whole ten millions of pounds sterling, and such sum or sums may be raised by the creation and issue of bonds or debentures, or capital stock bearing interest, or annuities, or partly by one of such modes and partly by another or others.

Bonds may be issued under the hands of two members of the Council, and countersigned by the Secretary of State.

2. All bonds issued under the authority of this Act may be issued under the hands of two members of the Council of India, and countersigned by the Secretary of State for India, or one of his under-secretaries, or his assistant under-secretary, and shall be for such respective amounts, payable after such notice, and at such rate or rates of interest as the said Secretary of State in Council may think fit.

Debentures may be issued.

3. All debentures issued under the authority of this Act may be issued under the hands of two members of the Council, and countersigned as aforesaid, for such respective amounts, and at such rate or rates of interest, as the Secretary of State in Council may think fit, and shall be issued at or for such prices and on such terms as may be determined by the Secretary of State in Council.

As to payment of principal and interest on debentures.

4. All debentures issued under the authority of this Act shall be paid off at par at a time or times to be mentioned in such debentures respectively; and the interest on all such debentures shall be paid half-yearly on such days as shall be mentioned therein; and the principal moneys and interest secured by such debentures shall be payable either at the treasury of the Secretary of State in Council in London or at the Bank of England.

Debentures transferable by delivery.

Coupons by delivery.

5. All or any number of the debentures issued under the authority of this Act, and all right to and in respect of the principal and interest moneys secured thereby, shall be transferable by the delivery of such debentures; and the coupons for interest annexed to any debenture issued under the authority of this Act shall also pass by delivery.

Capital stock and annuities may be created and issued.

6. Any capital stock created under the authority of this Act shall bear such a rate of interest, and any annuities to be created under the authority of this Act shall be at such rate per centum per annum, as the Secretary of State in Council may think fit; and such capital stock and such annuities may be issued on such terms as may be determined by the Secretary of State in Council; and any such capital stock may bear interest during such period, and be paid off at par at such time, as the Secretary of State in Council may prescribe previously to the issue of such capital stock; and such annuities may be terminable at such period as the Secretary of State in Council may prescribe previously to the issue of such annuities.

(*Secs. 7-11.*)

Transfer books of such capital stocks and annuities to be kept.

7. In case of the creation and issue of any such capital stock or of any such annuities, there shall be kept, either at the office of the Secretary of State in Council in London or at the Bank of England, books wherein entries shall be made of the said capital stock and annuities respectively, and wherein all assignments or transfers of the same respectively, or any part thereof respectively, shall be entered and registered, and shall be signed by the parties making such assignments or transfers, or, if such parties be absent, by his, her, or their attorney or attorneys thereunto lawfully authorized by writing under his, her, or their hands and seals, to be attested by two or more credible witnesses; and the person or persons to whom such transfer or transfers shall be made may respectively underwrite his, her, or their acceptance thereof, and no other mode of assigning or transferring the said capital stock or the said annuities, or any part thereof respectively, or any interest therein respectively, shall be good and available in law, and no stamp duties whatsoever shall be charged on the said transfers or any of them.

Annuities deemed personal estate.

8. All annuities created and issued under the authority of this Act shall be deemed and taken to be personal and not real estate, and shall go to the executors or administrators of the person or persons dying possessed thereof, interested therein, or entitled thereto, and not to the heir-at-law, nor be liable to any foreign attachment by the custom of London or otherwise.

The whole amount charged on revenues of India not to exceed 10,000,000*l.*

9. The whole amount of the principal moneys to be charged on the revenues of India under this Act shall not exceed ten millions; and no money shall be raised or secured under the authority of this Act after the said thirtieth day of April one thousand eight hundred and seventy-nine, or, if Parliament be then sitting, after the end of the then session of Parliament, save for or upon the repayment of principal moneys previously secured under this Act as hereinafter provided.

Power to raise money for payment of principal money.

10. Upon or for the repayment of any principal money secured under the authority of this Act, the Secretary of State in Council may at any time borrow or raise, by all or any of the modes aforesaid, all or any part of the amount of principal money repaid or to be repaid, and so from time to time as all or any part of any principal money under this Act may require to be repaid, but the amount to be charged upon the revenues of India shall not in any case exceed the principal money required to be repaid.

Securities, etc., to be charged on revenues of India.

11. All bonds and debentures to be issued under this Act, and the principal moneys and interest thereby secured, and all capital stock to be issued under this Act, and the interest thereon, and all annuities to be issued under this Act, shall be charged on and payable out of the revenues of India, in like manner as other liabilities incurred on account of the government of the said territories.

Provisions as to composition for stamp duties on India bonds extended to bonds and debentures under this Act.

12. THE provisions contained in section four of the Act of the session holden in the fifth and sixth years of King William the Fourth, chapter sixty-four, with respect to the composition and agreement for the payment by the East India Company of an annual sum in lieu of stamp duties on their bonds, and the exemption of their bonds from stamp duties, shall be applicable with respect to the bonds and debentures to be issued under the authority of this Act, as if such provisions were here repeated and re-enacted with reference thereto.

Forgery of debentures to be punishable as forgery of East India bonds.

13. ALL provisions now in force in anywise relating to the offence of forging or altering, or offering, uttering, disposing of, or putting off, knowing the same to be forged or altered, any East India bond, with intent to defraud, shall extend and be applicable to and in respect of any debenture issued under the authority of this Act, as well as to and in respect of any bond issued under the same authority.

14. [*Rep. as to U. K., 46 & 47 Vict., c. 39 (S. L. R.). Omitted as being obsolete.*]

Accounts of all loans and liabilities to be included in account annually laid before Parliament.

15. THE Secretary of State in Council shall include in the account to be laid before both Houses of Parliament, pursuant to the fifty-third section of the Act of the twenty-first and twenty-second Victoria, chapter one hundred and six, within the first fourteen days during which Parliament may be sitting next after the first day of May in every year, accounts of all stocks, loans, debts, and liabilities chargeable on the revenues of India, at home and abroad, at the commencement and close of the year to which such account shall relate, the loans, debts, and liabilities raised or incurred within that year and the amounts paid off or discharged during that year; * * *[1]

Saving powers of the Secretary of State in Council.

16. THIS Act shall not prejudice or affect any power of raising or borrowing money vested in the said Secretary of State in Council at the time of passing thereof.

Stock created hereunder to be deemed East India stock.

17. ANY capital stock created under this Act shall be deemed to be East India stock, within the Act twenty-second and twenty-third Victoria, chapter thirty-five, section thirty-two, unless and until Parliament shall otherwise provide; and any capital stock created under this Act shall be deemed to be and shall mean India stock within the Act of the twenty-sixth and twenty-seventh Victoria, chapter seventy-three, anything in the said last-mentioned Act to the contrary notwithstanding.

18. [*Rep. as to U. K. by 46 & 47 Vict., c. 39 (S. L. R.). Omitted as being spent.*]

---

[1] The remainder of this section has been repealed as to U. K. by 46 & 47 Vict., c. 39 (S. L. R.), and is omitted as being spent.

The East India Annuity Funds Act, 1874.

(37 & 38 Vict., c. 12.)

An Act to make provision for the transfer of the Assets and Liabilities of the Bengal and Madras Civil Service Annuity Funds, and the Annuity Branch of the Bombay Civil Fund, to the Secretary of State for India in Council.

[*8th June, 1874.*]

[*Preamble.*]

1. [*Rep. as to U. K., 56 & 57 Vict., c. 14 (S. L. R.), No. 2. Omitted as being obsolete.*]

2. * * * * * All existing liabilities of the said funds shall be deemed to be liabilities of the revenues of India, and all such liabilities may be enforced against the Secretary of State for India in Council in like manner as they might have been enforced against the trustees of the said Funds if this Act had not been passed, and every civil servant who shall at the date of such notification be an incumbent of an annuity from any of the said Civil Annuity Funds, or from any earlier fund the assets and liabilities of which shall have been transferred as aforesaid, shall be entitled to receive from time to time the amount of such annuity from the revenues of India; and every covenanted civil servant who shall be a subscriber to any of the said Civil Annuity Funds at or after the date of such notification shall be entitled on retirement to the benefits granted by the despatch of the Secretary of State in Council to the Government of India, dated the tenth of February, one thousand eight hundred and seventy-one; namely, Annuities charged on said funds to be payable from revenues of India.

If he shall have completed twenty-five years' service and twenty-one years' residence in India a full annuity of one thousand pounds payable in England, or Company's rupees ten thousand six hundred and sixty-six ten annas and eight pies payable in Bengal, or Company's rupees ten thousand six hundred and fifty payable in Madras or Bombay:

And if he shall be compelled to resign the service on account of ill health, clearly proved by medical certificate,

if under five years' service, a grant of five hundred pounds;

if of five years' service and under six, an invalid annuity of one hundred and fifty pounds;

if of six years' service and under seven, an invalid annuity of one hundred and seventy pounds;

and so on, an increase of twenty pounds being made to the annuity for each year's service, the highest invalid annuity being four hundred and fifty pounds for a service of twenty years.

Nothing to prejudice subscribers' claims.

3. PROVIDED, that nothing in this Act contained shall prejudice any claim which may be made by any subscriber to the said Civil Service Annuity Funds or by the representatives of any such subscriber, upon the funds so transferred; and in case any question shall arise between any such subscriber or the representatives of any deceased subscriber on the one hand, and the Secretary of State for India in Council on the other, as to any liability or alleged liability of the said funds, such question shall be determined by the Court of Appeal appointed by the Judicature Act, 1873, in such manner as may be provided by any general orders, or as the said Court may, on special application, think fit to prescribe, anything in the Statute of Limitations to the contrary notwithstanding.

THE COURTS (COLONIAL) JURISDICTION ACT, 1874.[1]

(37 & 38 Vict., c. 27.)

An Act to regulate the Sentences imposed by Colonial Courts where jurisdiction to try is conferred by Imperial Acts.

[*30th June, 1874.*]

[*Preamble.*]

Short title.

1. THIS Act may be cited for all purposes as The Courts (Colonial) Jurisdiction Act, 1874.

Definition of term "colony".

2. FOR the purposes of this Act,—

the term "colony" shall not include any places within the United Kingdom, the Isle of Man, or the Channel Islands, but shall include such territories as may for the time being be vested in Her Majesty by virtue of an Act of Parliament for the government of India, and any plantation, territory, or settlement situate elsewhere within Her Majesty's dominions, and subject to the same local government; and for the purposes of this Act all plantations, territories, and settlements under a central legislature shall be deemed to be one colony under the same local government.

At trials in any colonial courts by virtue of Im-

3. WHEN, by virtue of any Act of Parliament now or hereafter to be passed, a person is tried in a court of any colony for any crime or offence committed upon the high seas or elsewhere out of the territorial limits of such

---

[1] *See Chitty's Statutes*, Tit. Colonies, p. 6.

colony and of the local jurisdiction of such court, or if committed within such local jurisdiction made punishable by that Act, such person shall, upon conviction, be liable to such punishment as might have been inflicted upon him if the crime or offence had been committed within the limits of such colony and of the local jurisdiction of the court, and to no other, anything in any Act to the contrary notwithstanding: Provided always, that if the crime or offence is a crime or offence not punishable by the law of the colony in which the trial takes place, the person shall, on conviction, be liable to such punishment (other than capital punishment) as shall seem to the court most nearly to correspond to the punishment to which such person would have been liable in case such crime or offence had been tried in England. perial Acts, courts empowered to pass sentences as if crimes had been committed in the colony.

The Colonial Attorneys' Relief Act, 1874.[1]

(37 & 38 Vict., c. 41.)

An Act to amend "The Colonial Attornies Relief Act".

[*30th July, 1874.*]

[*Preamble recites 20 & 21 Vict., c. 39.*]

1. So much of the Colonial Attornies Relief Act as enacts that no person shall be deemed qualified to be admitted as attorney or solicitor under the provisions of the said Act unless he shall pass an examination to test his fitness and capacity, and shall further make affidavit that he has ceased for the space of twelve calendar months at the least to practise as attorney or solicitor in any colonial court of law, and also so much of the said Act and of any orders and regulations made thereunder as relate to such examination, shall not apply to, nor shall compliance therewith respectively be required of, any person seeking to be admitted as attorney or solicitor under the provisions of the said Act who shall have been in actual practice for the period of seven years at the least as attorney and solicitor in any colony or dependency as to which an Order in Council has been or may be made as mentioned in the said Act, and who shall have served under articles and passed an examination previously to his admission as attorney and solicitor in any such colony or dependency. Examination and ceasing to practise dispensed with where colonial attorney and solicitor has actually practised for seven years, and passed examination previous to admission.

2. The expression "The Colonial Attornies Relief Act" shall henceforth be deemed to include this Act. Short title.

---

[1] *See Chitty's Statutes*, Tit. Solicitors, p. 42.

THE ROYAL (LATE INDIAN) ORDNANCE CORPS ACT, 1874.

(37 & 38 Vict., c. 61.)

An Act for granting Compensation to Officers of the Royal (late Indian) Ordnance Corps.

[*7th August, 1874.*]

[*Preamble.*]

Short title.

1. THIS Act may be cited for all purposes as "The Royal (late Indian) Ordnance Corps Act, 1874".

Compensation to officers of the Royal (late Indian) Ordnance Corps.

2. SUBJECT as hereinafter mentioned, the army purchase commissioners, acting under the Regulation of the Forces Act, 1871, in this Act referred to as the commissioners, shall have power to consider the claims on retirement of any officers, who on the first day of November, one thousand eight hundred and seventy-one, were serving in any one of the corps following, that is to say,

The Royal (late Bengal) Artillery,
The Royal (late Bengal) Engineers,
The Royal (late Madras) Artillery,
The Royal (late Madras) Engineers,
The Royal (late Bombay) Artillery, or
The Royal (late Bombay) Engineers;

and to grant to any of the said officers who have retired since the said first day of November, or who may hereafter be permitted to retire, a compensation equal to the sums they would have received according to the custom, if any, of their corps, as or in the nature of a bonus for such retirement had they retired from their regiment on the said day, after deducting such sums (if any) as they may have received from the Indian revenues in respect or on account of such bonus.

3 to 5. [*Rep. as to U. K., 46 & 47 Vict., c. 39 (S. L. R.). Omitted as being obsolete.*]

Powers of commissioners applicable for purposes of this Act.

6. ALL powers vested in the commissioners by the said Regulation of the Forces Act, 1871, for or in relation to their proceedings under that Act, shall apply to their proceedings under this Act, and may be exercised by them for ascertaining any matter or fact, or doing any act required to be ascertained or done by them for the purposes of this Act, in the same manner in all respects as if their proceedings under this Act were proceedings under the said Regulation of the Forces Act, 1871.

Provision for expenses of compensating officers.

7. ALL expenses incurred by the commissioners in carrying into effect his Act shall be defrayed out of moneys provided by Parliament.

The Colonial Clergy Act, 1874.[1]

(37 & 38 Vict., c. 77.)

An Act respecting Colonial and certain other Clergy.

[*7th August, 1874.*]

[*Preamble.*]

1. This Act may be cited as The Colonial Clergy Act, 1874. Short title.

2. [*Rep. as to U. K., 46 & 47 Vict., c. 39 (S. L. R.). Omitted as being spent.*]

3. Except as hereinafter mentioned, no person who has been or shall be ordained priest or deacon, as the case may be, by any bishop other than a bishop of a diocese, in one of the churches aforesaid shall, unless he shall hold or have previously held preferment or a curacy in England, officiate as such priest or deacon in any church or chapel in England, without written permission from the archbishop of the province in which he proposes to officiate, and without also making and subscribing so much of the declaration contained in "The Clerical Subscription Act, 1865", as follows, that is to say, Colonial and certain other clergy not to officiate without permission from the archbishop;

"I assent to the thirty-nine articles of religion, and to the Book of Common Prayer, and of the ordering of bishops, priests, and deacons. I believe the doctrine of the Church of England as therein set forth to be agreeable to the Word of God; and in public prayer and administration of the sacraments, I, whilst ministering in England, will use the form in the said book prescribed, and none other, except so far as shall be ordered by lawful authority."

4. Except as hereinafter mentioned, no person who has been or shall be ordained priest or deacon, as the case may be, by any bishop other than a bishop of a diocese in one of the churches aforesaid, shall be entitled as such priest or deacon to be admitted or instituted to any benefice or other ecclesiastical preferment in England, or to act as curate therein, without the previous consent in writing of the bishop of the diocese in which such preferment or curacy may be situate. nor to hold preferment nor act as curates without consent of bishop.

5. Any person holding ecclesiastical preferment, or acting as curate in any diocese in England under the provisions of this Act, may, with the written consent of the bishop of such diocese, request the archbishop of the province to give him a license in writing under his hand and seal in the following form, that is to say, As to license.

"To the Rev. *A. B.*,

"We, *C.*, by Divine Providence archbishop of *D.*, do hereby give you the said *A. B.* authority to exercise your office of priest (*or* deacon) according to

[1] For digest, see Ilbert's *Government of India*, p. 323. See, too, *Chitty's Statutes*, Tit. Church and Clergy, p. 226. See, too, *Phillimore*, pp. 117, 1762, 1795, 1798, 1808, 1811, 1812, 1813.

the provisions of an Act of the thirty-seventh and thirty-eighth years of Her present Majesty, intituled 'An Act respecting Colonial and certain other Clergy.'

"Given under our hand and seal on the day of

"*C.* (L. S.) *D.*"

And if the archbishop shall think fit to issue such license, the same shall be registered in the registry of the province, and the person receiving the license shall thenceforth possess all such rights and advantages, and be subject to all such duties and liabilities as he would have possessed and been subject to if he had been ordained by the bishop of a diocese in England: Provided that no such license shall be issued to any person who has not held ecclesiastical preferment or acted as curate for a period or periods exceeding in the aggregate two years.

Appointments, etc., contrary to Act void.

6. All appointments, admissions, institutions, or inductions to ecclesiastical preferment in England, and all appointments to act as curate therein, which shall hereafter be made contrary to the provisions of this Act, shall be null and void.

Penalty for officiating contrary to Act.

7. If any person shall officiate as priest or deacon in any church or chapel in England contrary to the provisions of this Act, or if any bishop not being bishop of a diocese in England shall perform episcopal functions in any such church or chapel without the consent in writing of the bishop of the diocese in which such church or chapel is situate, he shall for every such offence forfeit and pay the sum of ten pounds to the Governors of Queen Anne's Bounty, to be recovered by action brought within six months after the commission of such offence by the treasurer of the said Bounty in one of Her Majesty's Superior Courts of Common Law; and the incumbent or curate of any church or chapel who shall knowingly allow such offence to be committed therein shall be subject to a like penalty, to be recovered in the same manner.

Persons ordained under 15 & 16 Vict., c. 52, exempt.

8. Any person ordained a priest or deacon in pursuance of such request and commission as are mentioned in an Act of the fifteenth and sixteenth years of Her present Majesty, chapter fifty-two, shall, for the purposes of this Act, be deemed to have been so ordained by the bishop of a diocese in England, and it shall not be necessary that the bishop to whom such commission shall have been given should have exercised his office within Her Majesty's dominions, or by virtue of Her Majesty's Royal Letters Patent, provided that such bishop be a bishop in communion with the Church of England; and such commission shall not become void by the death of the grantor until after seven days: Provided always, that any such act of ordination by any such bishop as aforesaid shall be subject to the same laws and provisions as to the titles and as to the oaths and subscriptions of the persons to be ordained, and as to the registration

of such act, as if it had been performed by the bishop of the diocese; and that the letters of orders of any persons so ordained by any such bishop shall be issued in the name of, and be subscribed with the signature of such bishop as commissary of the bishop of the diocese, and shall be sealed with the seal of the bishop of such diocese.

9. Any person ordained a deacon or priest under the provisions of an Act of the second session of the twenty-fourth year of King George the Third, chapter thirty-five, or under the first section of an Act of the fifty-ninth year of King George the Third, chapter sixty, shall be subject to the provisions contained in this Act.

Persons ordained under 24 Geo. 3, sess. 2, c. 35, or 59 Geo. 3, c. 60, s. 1, subject to Act.

10. [*Rep. as to U. K., 46 & 47 Vict., c. 39 (S. L. R.). Omitted as being spent.*]

11. Nothing in this Act contained shall alter or affect any of the provisions of an Act of the twenty-seventh and twenty-eighth years of Her present Majesty, chapter ninety-four, intituled "An Act to remove disabilities affecting the bishops and clergy of the Protestant Episcopal Church in Scotland".

Saving of 27 & 28 Vict., c. 94.

12. It shall be lawful for the archbishop of Canterbury or the archbishop of York for the time being, in consecrating any person to the office of bishop for the purpose of exercising episcopal functions elsewhere than in England, to dispense, if he think fit, with the oath of due obedience to the archbishop.

Archbishops may dispense with oath of due obedience.

13. Nothing contained in an Act of the fifty-third year of King George the Third, chapter one hundred and fifty-five, or in an Act of the third and fourth years of King William the Fourth, chapter eighty-five, or in any letters patent issued as mentioned in the said Acts, or either of them, shall prevent any person who shall be or shall have been bishop of any diocese in India from performing episcopal functions, not extending to the exercise of jurisdiction, in any diocese or reputed diocese at the request of the bishop thereof.

Indian bishops.

14. In this Act the word "bishop" shall, when not inconsistent with the context, include archbishop; the words "bishop" and "archbishop", in the matters of "permission" and "consent", and of "consent and license", shall include the lawful commissary of a bishop or an archbishop; the word "England" shall include the Isle of Man and the Channel Islands; and the term "church or chapel" shall mean church or chapel subject to the ecclesiastical law of the Church of England.

Interpretation of terms.

SCHEDULES.

[*Rep. as to U. K., 46 & 47 Vict., c. 39 (S. L. R.). Omitted as being spent.*]

The Indian Councils Act, 1874.[1]

(37 & 38 Vict., c. 91.)

An Act to amend the law relating to the Council of the Governor General of India.

[*7th August, 1874.*]

[*Preamble.*]

Number of ordinary members of Governor General's Council may be increased. 24 & 25 Vict., c. 67. 32 & 33 Vict., c. 97.

1. It shall be lawful for Her Majesty, if she shall see fit, to increase the number of the ordinary members of the Council of the Governor General of India to six, by appointing any person, from time to time, by warrant under Her Royal Sign Manual, to be an ordinary member of the said Council in addition to the ordinary members thereof appointed under section three of "The Indian Councils Act, 1861," and under section eight of the Act of the thirty-second and thirty-third years of Her present Majesty, chapter ninety-seven. The law for the time being in force with reference to ordinary members of the Council of the Governor General of India shall apply to the person so appointed by Her Majesty under this Act, who shall be called the member of Council for public works purposes.

Number of members of Council may be subsequently diminished.

2. Whenever a member of Council for public works purposes shall have been appointed under the first section of this Act, it shall be lawful for Her Majesty, if she shall see fit, to diminish, from time to time, the number of the ordinary members of the Council of the Governor General of India to five, by abstaining so long as she shall deem proper from filling up any vacancy or vacancies occurring in the offices of the ordinary members of the said Council appointed under section three of "The Indian Councils Act, 1861," and under section eight of the Act of the thirty-second and thirty-third years of Her present Majesty, chapter ninety-seven, not being a vacancy in the office of the ordinary member of Council required by law to be a barrister or a member of the Faculty of Advocates in Scotland; and whenever the Secretary of State for India shall have informed the Governor General of India that it is not the intention of Her Majesty to fill up any vacancy, no temporary appointment shall be made to such vacancy under section twenty-seven of "The Indian Councils Act, 1861." and if any such temporary appointment shall have been made previously to the receipt of such information, the tenure of office of the person temporarily appointed shall cease and determine from the time of the receipt of such information by the Governor General.

Not to affect power of

3. Nothing in this Act contained shall affect the provisions of section eight of "The Indian Councils Act, 1861," or the provisions of section five

[1] For digest, see Ilbert's *Government of India*, p. 324.

of the Act of the thirty-third year of Her Majesty, chapter three, or any power or authority vested by law in the Governor General of India in respect of his Council or of the members thereof. Governor General in respect of his Council.

THE INTERNATIONAL COPYRIGHT ACT, 1875.[1]

(38 & 39 Vict., c. 12.)

An Act to amend the Law relating to International Copyright.

[*13th May, 1875.*]

[*Preamble recites 15 & 16 Vict., c. 12, ss. 4, 5.*]

1. IN any case in which, by virtue of the enactments hereinbefore recited, any Order in Council has been or may hereafter be made for the purpose of extending protection to the translations of dramatic pieces first publicly represented in any foreign country, it shall be lawful for Her Majesty by Order in Council to direct that the sixth section of the said Act shall not apply to the dramatic pieces to which protection is so extended; and thereupon the said recited Act shall take effect with respect to such dramatic pieces and to the translations thereof as if the said sixth section of the said Act was hereby repealed. Section 6 of 15 & 16 Vict., c. 12, not to apply to dramatic pieces in certain cases.

THE COUNCIL OF INDIA ACT, 1876.[2]

(39 & 40 Vict., c. 7.)

An Act to amend the Law relating to certain Appointments to the Council of India. [*7th April, 1876.*]

[*Preamble recites 32 & 33 Vict., c. 97.*]

1. NOTWITHSTANDING anything in the Act of 1869, the Secretary of State for India may, if he thinks fit, subject to the condition as to the number of appointments hereinafter laid down, appoint any person having professional or other peculiar qualifications to be a member of the said Council under this Act; and every person so appointed shall hold his office in the same manner, and shall be entitled to the same salary, pension, and other rights and privileges, and be subject to the same disabilities, as if he had been elected or appointed before the passing of the Act of 1869. Appointment of persons with professional or other qualifications.

Where any person appointed under this Act is at his appointment a member of the Council, his period of service for the purposes of this Act shall be reckoned from the time of his first appointment or election to the Council.

---

[1] This Act may be cited, with four others, as the International Copyright Acts—*see* the Short Titles Act, 1896 (59 & 60 Vict., c. 14), *post*, p. 1255, and *see*, too, *Chitty's Statutes*, Tit. Copyright, p. 47; also *Scrutton*, p. 242.

[2] For digest, *see* Ilbert's *Government of India*, p. 324.

The special reasons for every appointment under this Act shall be stated in a minute of the Secretary of State for India, and shall be laid before both Houses of Parliament. Not more than three persons appointed under this Act shall be members of the Council at the same time; nor shall the provisions of sections seven and ten of the Act of 1858, with reference to the number of the Council and the qualification of the major part of the members, be affected by this Act.

The Royal Titles Act, 1876.

(39 & 40 Vict., c. 10.)

An Act to enable Her most Gracious Majesty to make an addition to the Royal Style and Titles appertaining to the Imperial Crown of the United Kingdom and its Dependencies.

[*27th April, 1876.*]

Whereas by the Union with Ireland Act, 1800, it was provided that after such union as aforesaid the royal style and titles appertaining to the imperial Crown of the United Kingdom and its Dependencies should be such as His Majesty by His Royal proclamation under the Great Seal of the United Kingdom should be pleased to appoint: 39 & 40 Geo. 3, c. 67, A. D. 1800.

And whereas by virtue of the said Act and of a Royal proclamation under the Great Seal, dated the first day of January, one thousand eight hundred and one, the present style and titles of Her Majesty are "Victoria by the Grace of God of the United Kingdom of Great Britain and Ireland, Queen, Defender of the Faith":

And whereas by the Government of India Act, 1858,[1] it was enacted that the government of India, theretofore vested in the East India Company in trust for Her Majesty, should become vested in Her Majesty, and that India should thenceforth be governed by and in the name of Her Majesty, and it is expedient that there should be a recognition of the transfer of Government so made by means of an addition to be made to the style and titles of Her Majesty: 21 & 22 Vict., c. 106.

Addition to style and titles of Crown.

1. It shall be lawful for Her most gracious Majesty with a view to such recognition as aforesaid of the transfer of the government of India, by Her Royal proclamation under the Great Seal of the United Kingdom, to make such addition to the style and titles at present appertaining to the imperial Crown of the United Kingdom and its Dependencies as to Her Majesty may seem meet.

---

[1] Printed, Vol. I, 1899, p. 300.

The Statute Law Revision (Substituted Enactments) Act, 1876.

(39 & 40 Vict., c. 20.)

An Act to facilitate the Revision of the Statute Law by substituting in certain Acts, incorporating enactments which have been otherwise repealed, a reference to recent Enactments still in force.

[*27th June, 1876.*]

* * * * * * * * * *

2. * * * The penalty under section two of the Portuguese Deserters Act, 1849, shall be recovered, paid, and applied in the same manner as a penalty for harbouring or secreting any seaman deserting from a British ship is for the time being recoverable, payable, and applicable. **Substitution for repealed enactments mentioned in 12 & 13 Vict., c. 25.**

* * * * * * * * * *

The Customs Consolidation Act, 1876.

(39 & 40 Vict., c. 36.)

[*24th July, 1876.*]

[*Preamble.*]

* * * * * * * * * *

As to the Channel Islands and other possessions.

149. The powers and authorities vested in the Commissioners of Customs with regard to any act or thing relating to the Customs, or to trade or navigation in any of the British possessions abroad, shall continue to be vested in the governor, lieutenant-governor, or other person administering the government in any such possession; and every act required by any law to be done by or with any particular officer or at any particular place, if done by or with any such officer or at any place appointed or nominated by such governor, lieutenant-governor or other person so administering such government, shall be deemed to have been done by or with such particular officer or at such particular place, as the case may be, and as required by law; and all commissions, deputations and appointments granted to any officers of Customs in force at the commencement of this Act shall have the same force and effect to all intents and purposes as if the same had been granted or made in the first instance by such governor, lieutenant-governor or person so administering the government of any such possession; and all bonds or other securities which shall have been given by or for any such officers and their **Powers of Commissioners as to colonies extended to governors, etc.**

respective sureties for good conduct or otherwise shall remain in force and shall and may be enforced and put in suit at the instance of or by directions of any such governor, lieutenant-governor or person administering the government of any such possession.

* * * * * *

Customs Acts to extend to British possessions abroad, except where otherwise provided for.

151. The Customs Acts shall extend to and be of full force and effect in the several British possessions abroad, except where otherwise expressly provided for by the said Acts, or limited by express reference to the United Kingdom or the Channel Islands, and except also as to any such possession as shall by local Act or ordinance have provided, or may hereafter, with the sanction and approbation of Her Majesty, make entire provision for the management and regulation of the Customs of any such possession, or make in like manner express provisions in lieu or variation of any of the clauses of the said Act for the purposes of such possession.

Foreign reprints of books under copyright prohibited.

[1] **152.** Any books wherein the copyright shall be subsisting first composed or written or printed in the United Kingdom, and printed or reprinted in any other country, shall be and are hereby absolutely prohibited to be imported into the British possessions abroad: Provided always, that no such books shall be prohibited to be imported as aforesaid unless the proprietor of such copyright, or his agent, shall have given notice in writing to the Commissioners of Customs that such copyright subsists, and in such notice shall have stated when the copyright will expire; and the said Commissioners shall cause to be made and transmitted to the several ports in the British possessions abroad, from time to time to be publicly exposed there, lists of books respecting which such notice shall have been duly given, and all books imported contrary thereto shall be forfeited; but nothing herein contained shall be taken to prevent Her Majesty from exercising the powers vested in her by the Colonial Copyright Act, 1847, to suspend in certain cases such prohibitions. 10 & 11 Vict., c. 95.

Foreign manufactures with British marks.[1]

153. If any articles of foreign manufacture, and any packages of such articles, bearing any names, brands, or marks being or purporting to be the names, brands, or marks of manufacturers resident in the United Kingdom, shall be imported into any of the British possessions abroad, the same shall be forfeited.

* * * * * *

Colonial laws repugnant to Acts of Parliament void.

161. All laws, bye-laws, usages or customs at this time, or which hereafter shall be in practice, or endeavoured or pretended to be in force or practice, in any of the British possessions, which are in anywise contrary to the Customs Acts, are and shall be null and void.

* * * * * *

[1] *See Chitty's Statutes*, Tit. Customs, p. 3.

As to collusive seizures.

217. If any officer of Customs or other person duly employed for the prevention of smuggling shall make any collusive seizure, or deliver up, or make any agreement to deliver up or not to seize any vessel or boat or any goods liable to forfeiture, or shall take any bribe, gratuity, recompense, or reward for the neglect or non-performance of his duty, or conspire or connive with any person to import or bring into the United Kingdom or the Channel Islands or any of the British possessions abroad, or be in any way concerned in the importation or bringing into the United Kingdom or the said Islands or possessions, of any goods prohibited to be imported or liable to duties of Customs, for the purpose of seizing any ship, boat or goods, and obtaining any reward for such seizure or otherwise, every such officer or other person shall forfeit for every such offence the sum of five hundred pounds, and be rendered incapable of serving Her Majesty in any office, either civil, naval, or military; and every person who shall give or offer, or promise to give or procure to be given, any bribe, recompense or reward to, or shall make any collusive agreement with, any such officer or person as aforesaid to induce him in any way to neglect his duty, or to do, conceal or connive at any act whereby any of the provisions or any Act or Parliament relating to the Customs may be evaded, shall forfeit the sum of two hundred pounds.

Penalty on officers and persons making collusive seizures, or taking bribes, and on persons offering them.

THE SLAVE TRADE ACT, 1876.

(39 & 40 Vict., c. 46.)

An Act for more effectually punishing Offences against the Laws relating to the Slave Trade.

[*11th August, 1876.*]

[*The first two paragraphs of the preamble recite 32 & 33 Vict., c. 98; 28 & 29 Vict., c. 17.*]

AND whereas the several princes and states in India in alliance with Her Majesty have no connexions, engagements, or communications with foreign powers, and the subjects of such princes and states are, when residing or being in the place hereinafter referred to, entitled to the protection of the British

Government, and receive such protection equally with the subjects of Her Majesty:

Certain offenders on high seas punished as though offence committed in India.

1. If any person, being a subject of Her Majesty or of any prince or state in India in alliance with Her Majesty, shall, upon the high seas or in any part of Asia or Africa which Her Majesty may from time to time think fit to specify by any Order in Council in this behalf, commit any of the offences defined in sections 367, 370, and 371 (in the schedule to this Act respectively recited) of Act XLV of 1860, passed by the Governor General of India in Council and called "The Indian Penal Code", or abet within the meaning of the fifth chapter of the said Penal Code the commission of any such offence, such person shall be dealt with, in respect of such offence or abetment, as if the same had been committed in any place within British India in which he may be or may be found.

Sect. 1 may be made to apply to future amendments of this Act.

2. If the Governor General of India in Council shall, at a meeting for making laws and regulations, amend the provisions of the said sections 367, 370, and 371 of the said Penal Code, or any of them, or the said fifth chapter thereof so far as relates to the abetment of any of the offences forbidden by such sections, or make any further provision for preventing or suppressing the making, buying, or selling of slaves or any of the offences comprised in the said three sections, the Secretary of State for India shall, unless Her Majesty has disallowed such amendment or further provision, lay a copy of the amending Act before each House of Parliament, and after the same shall have lain on the table of both Houses of Parliament for the space of forty days, it shall be lawful for Her Majesty, unless either House of Parliament shall present an address to Her Majesty to the contrary, to direct by Order in Council that the provisions of the first section of this Act shall apply to the law so amended or enlarged, and the same shall be applicable accordingly.

Powers of High Court for purpose of obtaining evidence.

3. For the purpose of obtaining evidence of the commission of the offences made punishable by this Act or any Act of Parliament relating to slavery or the slave trade, every High Court in India shall have, as respects the persons in the first section of this Act referred to, and as respects any British colony, settlement, plantation, or territory, wherein any witness may be, the same powers as are conferred on the Court of Queen's Bench by the fourth section of an Act made and passed in the session of Parliament holden in the sixth and seventh years of Her Majesty's reign, chapter ninety-eight, with respect to such British colonies, settlements, plantations, and territories as are therein referred to.

And every High Court may, if it thinks fit, issue such commission as is mentioned in section 330 of Act X of 1872,[1] passed by the Governor General of India in Council, and called "The Code of Criminal Procedure", to any consular officer of Her Majesty in the parts of Asia or Africa specified in any Order of Her Majesty in Council under section 1 of this Act, or to any political officer or agent of the Governor General of India in Council or of any Indian Government in the said parts or in the dominions of any prince or state in India in alliance with Her Majesty, or to any magistrate in Her Majesty's Indian dominions.

And the depositions taken by virture of the said powers or under such commission shall be deemed by every court of original or appellate jurisdiction in India in any trial or proceeding under this Act or any Act of Parliament relating to slavery or the slave trade to be as good and competent evidence as if the witnesses deposing had been present and examined *vivâ voce*, had made oath or affirmation as required by law.

4. [*Rep. 53 & 54 Vict., c. 37, s. 18.*]

5. NOTHING in this Act shall be deemed to restrict the legislative power which the Governor General of India in Council possesses at meetings for the purposes of making laws and regulations. Saving powers of Governor General.

6. [*Rep. 53 & 54 Vict., c. 37, s. 18.*]

SCHEDULE.

S. 367 of the Indian Penal Code.—Whoever kidnaps or abducts any person, in order that such person may be subjected or may be so disposed of as to be put in danger of being subjected to grievous hurt, or slavery, or to the unnatural lust of any person, or knowing it to be likely that such person will be so subjected or disposed of, shall be punished with imprisonment of either description for a term which may extend to ten years, and shall also be liable to a fine.

S. 370.—Whoever imports, exports, removes, buys, sells, or disposes of, any person as a slave, or accepts, receives, or detains against his will any person as a slave, shall be punished with imprisonment of either description for a term which may extend to seven years, and shall also be liable to a fine.

S. 371.—Whoever habitually imports, exports, removes, buys, sells, traffics, or deals in slaves, shall be punished with transportation for life, or with imprisonment of either description for a term not exceeding ten years, and shall also be liable to a fine.

---

[1] See now the Code of Criminal Procedure, 1898 (Act V of 1898), General Acts, Vol. VI, Ed. 1898.

The East India Loan Act, 1877.[1]

(40 & 41 Vict., c. 51.)

An Act to enable the Secretary of State in Council of India to raise Money in the United Kingdom for the Service of the Government of India.

[*14th August, 1877.*]

[*Preamble.*]

Power to the Secretary of State in Council of India to raise any sum not exceeding 5,000,000*l*.

1. It shall be lawful for the Secretary of State in Council of India, at any time or times after the passing of this Act, to raise in the United Kingdom, for the service of the Government of India, any sum or sums of money not exceeding in the whole five millions of pounds sterling, of which two millions five hundred thousand pounds sterling may be raised by the creation and issue of capital stock bearing interest, or annuities, bonds, debentures, or bills, or partly by one of such modes and partly by another or others, and the whole or any portion of the remaining two millions five hundred thousand pounds sterling may be raised by the creation and issue of bonds, debentures, or bills, but not by the creation and issue of capital stock bearing interest, or of annuities.

Bonds may be issued under the hands of two members of the Council and countersigned by Secretary of State.

2. All bonds issued under the authority of this Act may be issued under the hands of two members of the Council of India, and countersigned by the Secretary of State for India, or one of his under-secretaries, or his assistant under-secretary, and shall be for such respective amounts, payable after such notice, and at such rate or rates of interest as the said Secretary of State in Council may think fit.

Debentures may be issued.

3. All debentures issued under the authority of this Act may be issued under the hands of two members of the Council, and countersigned as aforesaid, for such respective amounts, and at such rate or rates of interest, as the Secretary of State in Council may think fit, and shall be issued at or for such prices and on such terms as may be determined by the Secretary of State in Council.

As to payment of principal and interest on debentures.

4. All debentures issued under the authority of this Act shall be paid off at par at a time or times to be mentioned in such debentures respectively; and the interest on all such debentures shall be paid half-yearly on such days as shall be mentioned therein; and the principal moneys and interest secured by such debentures shall be payable either at the treasury of the Secretary of State in Council in London or at the Bank of England.

Debentures transferable by delivery.

5. All or any number of the debentures issued under the authority of this Act, and all right to and in respect of the principal and interest moneys secured thereby, shall be transferable by the delivery of such debentures; and the

[1] This Act may be cited, with eighteen others, as the East India Loans Acts, 1859 to 1893—*see* the Short Titles Act, 1896 (59 & 60 Vict., c. 14), *post*, p. 1255.

coupons for interest annexed to any debenture issued under the authority of this Act shall also pass by delivery. Coupons by delivery.

6. All bills issued under the authority of this Act may be issued under the hands of two members of the Council, and countersigned as aforesaid, for such respective amounts as the Secretary of State in Council may think fit, and shall be issued at or for such prices and on such terms as may be determined by the Secretary of State in Council. Bills may be issued.

7. A bill issued under the authority of this Act shall be a bill for the payment of the principal sum named therein at the date therein mentioned, so that the date be not more than twelve months from the date of the bill; and the principal sum secured by such bill shall be payable either at the treasury of the Secretary of State in Council in London or at the Bank of England. Interest shall be payable in respect of such bill at such rate and in such manner as the Secretary of State in Council may determine. Description, currency of, and interest on bills.

8. Any capital stock created under the authority of this Act shall bear such a rate of interest, and any annuities to be created under the authority of this Act shall be at such rate per centum per annum, as the Secretary of State in Council may think fit; and such capital stock and such annuities may be issued on such terms as may be determined by the Secretary of State in Council; and any such capital stock may bear interest during such period, and be paid off at par at such time, as the Secretary of State in Council may prescribe previously to the issue of such capital stock; and such annuities may be determinable at such period as the Secretary of State in Council may prescribe previously to the issue of such annuities. Capital stock and annuities may be created and issued.

9. In case of the creation and issue of any such capital stock or of any such annuities, there shall be kept, either at the office of the Secretary of State in Council in London or at the Bank of England, books wherein entries shall be made of the said capital stock and annuities repectively, and wherein all assignments or transfers of the same respectively, or any part thereof respectively, shall be entered and registered, and shall be signed by the parties making such assignments or transfers, or, if such parties be absent, by his, her, or their attorney or attorneys thereunto lawfully authorized by writing under his, her, or their hands and seals, to be attested by two or more credible witnesses; and the person or persons to whom such transfer or transfers shall be made may respectively underwrite his, her, or their acceptance thereof; and no other mode of assigning or transferring the said capital stock or the said annuities, or any part thereof respectively, or any interest therein respectively, shall be good and available in law, and no stamp duties whatsoever shall be charged on the said transfers or any of them. Transfer books of such capital stock and annuities to be kept.

Annuities deemed personal estate.

10. All annuities created and issued under the authority of this Act shall be deemed and taken to be personal and not real estate, and shall go to the executors or administrators of the person or persons dying possessed thereof, interested therein, or entitled thereto, and not to the heir-at-law, nor be liable to any foreign attachment by the custom of London, or otherwise.

The whole amount charged not to exceed 5,000,000*l.*

11. The whole amount of the principal moneys to be charged on the revenues of India under this Act shall not exceed five millions.

Power to raise money for payment of principal money.

12. Upon or for the repayment of any principal money secured under the authority of this Act, the Secretary of State in Council may at any time borrow or raise, by all or any of the modes aforesaid, all or any part of the amount of principal money repaid or to be repaid, and so from time to time as all or any part of any principal money under this Act may require to be repaid, but the amount to be charged upon the revenues of India shall not in any case exceed the principal money required to be repaid, and the total amount raised under this section by the creation and issue of capital stock bearing interest or of annuities shall not at any one time exceed two millions five hundred thousand pounds sterling.

Securities, etc., to be charged on revenues of India.

13. All bonds, debentures, and bills, to be issued under this Act, and the principal moneys and interest thereby secured, and all capital stock to be issued under this Act, and the interest thereon, and all annuities to be issued under this Act, shall be charged on and payable out of the revenues of India, in like manner as other liabilities incurred on account of the government of the said territories.

Provisions as to composition for stamp duties on India bonds extended to bonds and debentures under this Act.

14. The provisions contained in section four of the Act of the session holden in the fifth and sixth years of King William the Fourth, chapter sixty four, with respect to the composition and agreement for the payment by the East India Company of an annual sum in lieu of stamp duties on their bonds, and the exemption of their bonds from stamp duties, shall be applicable with respect to the bonds and debentures to be issued under the authority of this Act, as if such provisions were here repeated and re-enacted with reference thereto.

Forgery of debentures and bills to be punishable as forgery of East India bonds.

15. All provisions now in force in anywise relating to the offence of forging, or altering, or offering, uttering, disposing of, or putting off, knowing the same to be forged or altered, any East India bond, with intent to defraud, shall extend and be applicable to and in respect of any debenture or bill issued

under the authority of this Act, as well as to and in respect of any bond issued under the same authority.

16. [*Rep. as to U. K., 57 & 58 Vict., c. 56 (S. L. R.). Omitted as being obsolete.*]

17. This Act shall not prejudice or affect any power of raising or borrowing money vested in the said Secretary of State in Council at the time of passing thereof. Saving powers of the Secretary of State in Council.

18. Any capital stock created under this Act shall be deemed to be East India stock, within the Act twenty-second and twenty-third Victoria, chapter thirty-five, section thirty-two, unless and until Parliament shall otherwise provide; and any capital stock created under this Act shall be deemed to be and shall mean India stock within the Act of the twenty-sixth and twenty-seventh Victoria, chapter seventy-three, anything in the said last-mentioned Act to the contrary notwithstanding. Stock created hereunder to be deemed East India stock.

19. [*Rep. as to U. K., 46 & 47 Vict., c. 39 (S. L. R.). Omitted as being spent.*]

The Dentists Act, 1878.[1]

(41 & 42 Vict., c. 33.)

An Act to amend the Law relating to Dental Practitioners.

[*22nd July, 1878.*]

Whereas it is expedient that provision be made for the registration of persons specially qualified to practise as dentists in the United Kingdom, and that the law relating to persons practising as dentists be otherwise amended.

* * * * * * *

1. This Act may for all purposes be cited as the Dentists Act, 1878. Short title.

2. In this Act "General Council" means the General Council of Medical Education and Registration of the United Kingdom, established under the Interpretation.

---

[1] Amended by 49 & 50 Vict., c. 48, ss. 23 and 26, *post*, p. 823.

Medical Act, 1858; and "Branch Council" means a branch of the said council as constituted by the same Act: 21 & 22 Vict., c. 90.

"General registrar" means the person appointed to be the registrar by the General Council, and "local registrar" means the registrar appointed by a branch council under the Medical Act, 1858:

"British possession" means any part of Her Majesty's dominions exclusive of the United Kingdom:

"Medical authorities" means the bodies and universities who choose members of the General Council.

Registration.

Penalty on unregistered persons using title of "dentist", etc.

3. From and after the first day of August, one thousand eight hundred and seventy-nine, a person shall not be entitled to take or use the name or title of "dentist" (either alone or in combination with any other word or words), or of "dental practitioner", or any name, title, addition, or description implying that he is registered under this Act or that he is a person specially qualified to practise dentistry, unless he is registered under this Act.

Any person who, after the first day of August, one thousand eight hundred and seventy-nine, not being registered under this Act, takes or uses any such name, title, addition, or description as aforesaid, shall be liable, on summary conviction, to a fine not exceeding twenty pounds; provided that nothing in this section shall apply to legally qualified medical practitioners.

Provision as to offence of unregistered person taking name, etc., and as to offence of person taking title he does not possess.

4. With respect to the offence of a person not registered under this Act taking or using any name, title, addition, or description as above in this Act mentioned, the following provisions shall have effect:

(1) He shall not be guilty of an offence under this Act—

(*a*) If he shows that he is not ordinarily resident in the United Kingdom and that he holds a qualification which entitles him to practise dentistry or dental surgery in a British possession or foreign country, and that he did not represent himself to be registered under this Act; or,

(*b*) If he shows that he has been registered and continues to be entitled to be registered under this Act, but that his name has been erased on the ground only that he has ceased to practise.

* * * * * * *[1]

If a person takes or uses the designation of any qualification or certificate in relation to dentistry or dental surgery which he does not possess, he shall

---

[1] Clause (2) of the first para is repealed by 49 & 50 Vict, c. 48, s. 26.

be liable, on summary conviction on such prosecution as hereinafter mentioned, to a fine not exceeding twenty pounds.

* * * * * * * [1]

Privileges of registered persons.

5. A PERSON registered under this Act shall be entitled to practise dentistry and dental surgery in any part of Her Majesty's dominions, and from and after the first day of August, one thousand eight hundred and seventy-nine, a person shall not be entitled to recover any fee or charge, in any court, for the performance of any dental operation or for any dental attendance or advice, unless he is registered under this Act or is a legally qualified medical practitioner.

Qualification necessary for registration.

6. ANY person who—

(*a*) is a licentiate in dental surgery or dentistry of any of the medical authorities; or,

(*b*) is entitled as hereinafter mentioned to be registered as a foreign or colonial dentist; or,

(*c*) is at the passing of this Act *bonâ fide* engaged in the practice of dentistry or dental surgery, either separately or in conjunction with the practice of medicine, surgery or pharmacy,

shall be entitled to be registered under this Act.

Registration of persons in dentists' register.

7. WHERE a person entitled to be registered under this Act produces or sends to the general registrar the document conferring or evidencing his licence or qualification, with a statement of his name and address and the other particulars, if any, required for registration, and pays the registration fee, he shall be registered in the dentists' register.

Provided that a person shall not be registered under this Act as having been at the passing thereof engaged in the practice of dentistry unless he produces or transmits to the registrar, before the first day of August, one thousand eight hundred and seventy-nine, information of his name and address, and a declaration signed by him in the form in the schedule to this Act or to the like effect; and the registrar may, if he sees fit, require the truth of such declaration to be affirmed in manner provided by the Act of the session held in the fifth and sixth years of the reign of King William the Fourth, chapter sixty-two, intituled "An Act to repeal an Act of the present session of Parliament, intituled 'An Act for the more effectual abolition of oaths and affirmations taken and made in various departments of the State, and to substitute declarations in lieu thereof, and for the more entire suppression of voluntary and extra-judicial oaths and affidavits'; and to make other provisions for the abolition of unnecessary oaths".

5 & 6 W. 4, c. 62.

---

[1] The third para is repealed by 49 & 50 Vict., c. 48, s. 26

A person resident in the United Kingdom shall not be disqualified for being registered under this Act by reason that he is not a British subject; and a British subject shall not be disqualified for being registered under this Act by reason of his being resident or engaged in practice beyond the limits of the United Kingdom.

Registration of colonial dentist with recognised certificate.

8. WHERE a person who either is not domiciled in the United Kingdom, or has practised for more than ten years elsewhere than in the United Kingdom, or in the case of persons practising in the United Kingdom at the time of the passing of this Act for not less than ten years either in the United Kingdom or elsewhere, shows that he holds some recognized certificate (as hereinafter defined) granted in a British possession, and that he is of good character, such person shall upon payment of the registration fee be entitled, without examination in the United Kingdom, to be registered as a colonial dentist in the dentists' register.

Registration of foreign dentist with recognized certificate.

9. WHERE a person who is not a British subject, or who has practised for more than ten years elsewhere than in the United Kingdom, or in the case of persons practising in the United Kingdom at the time of the passing of this Act for not less than ten years either in the United Kingdom or elsewhere, shows that he obtained some recognized certificate (as hereinafter defined) granted in a foreign country, and that he is of good character, and either continues to hold such certificate, or has not been deprived thereof for any cause which disqualifies him for being registered under this Act, such person shall upon payment of the registration fee be entitled, without examination in the United Kingdom, to be registered as a foreign dentist in the dentists' register.

Recognized certificates of colonial and foreign dentist.

10. THE certificate granted in a British possession or in a foreign country, which is to be deemed such a recognized certificate as is required for the purposes of this Act, shall be such certificate, diploma, membership, degree, licence, letters, testimonial or other title, status or document as may be recognized for the time being by the General Council as entitling the holder thereof to practise dentistry or dental surgery in such possession or country, and as furnishing sufficient guarantees of the possession of the requisite knowledge and skill for the efficient practice of dentistry or dental surgery.

If a person is refused registration as a colonial dentist or as a foreign dentist, the general registrar shall, if required by him, state in writing the reason for such refusal, and if such reason be that the certificate held or obtained by him is not such a recognized certificate as above defined, such person may appeal to the Privy Council, and the Privy Council, after hearing the General Council, may dismiss the appeal or may order the General Council to recognize such certificate, and such order shall be duly obeyed.

(*Sec. 11.*)

Contents and form of dentists' register, and other provisions as to register.

11. (1) A REGISTER shall be kept by the general registrar to be styled the dentists' register; and that register shall—

(*a*) contain in one alphabetical list all United Kingdom dentists, that is to say, all persons who are registered under this Act as having been at the passing thereof engaged in the practice of dentistry or dental surgery, and all persons who are registered as licentiates in dentistry or dental surgery of any of the medical authorities of the United Kingdom; and,

(*b*) contain in a separate alphabetical list all such colonial dentists as are registered in pursuance of this Act; and,

(*c*) contain in a separate alphabetical list all such foreign dentists as are registered in pursuance of this Act.

(2) The dentists' register shall contain the said lists made out alphabetically according to the surnames, and shall state the full names and addresses of the registered persons, the description and date of the qualifications in respect of which they are registered, and, subject to the provisions of this Act, shall contain such particulars and be in such form as the General Council from time to time direct.

(3) The General Council shall cause a correct copy of the dentists' register to be from time to time and at least once a year printed under their direction, and published and sold, which copy shall be admissible in evidence.

(4) The dentists' register shall be deemed to be in proper custody when in the custody of the general registrar, and shall be of such a public nature as to be admissible as evidence of all matters therein on its mere production from that custody.

(5) Every local registrar shall keep such register and perform such duties in relation to registration under this Act as the General Council from time to time direct, and receive such remuneration out of the registration fees as the General Council assign him.

Every registrar shall in all respects in the execution of his discretion and duty in relation to any register under this Act, conform to any orders made by the General Council under this Act, and to any special directions given by the General Council.

(6) The General Council may, if they think fit, from time to time make, and when made, revoke and vary, orders for the registration in (on payment of the fee fixed by the orders) and the removal from the dentists' register of any additional diplomas, memberships, degrees, licences or letters held by a person registered therein, which appear to the Council to be granted after examination

Correction of dentists' register.

by any of the medical authorities in respect of a higher degree of knowledge than is required to obtain a certificate of fitness under this Act.

12. (1) The general registrar shall from time to time insert in the dentists' register any alteration which may come to his knowledge in the name or address of any person registered.

(2) The general registrar shall erase from the dentists' register the name of every deceased person.

(3) The general registrar may erase from the dentists' register the name of a person who has ceased to practise (but not save as hereinafter provided) without the consent of that person; and the general registrar may send by post to a person registered in the dentists' register a notice inquiring whether or not he has ceased to practise, or has changed his residence; and if the general registrar does not, within three months after sending the notice, receive any answer thereto from the said person, he may, within fourteen days after the expiration of the three months, send him by post in a registered letter another notice, referring to the first notice, and stating that no answer thereto has been received by the registrar, and if the general registrar either before the second notice is sent receives the first notice back from the dead letter office of the Postmaster General, or receives the second notice back from that office, or does not within three months after sending the second notice receive any answer thereto from the said person, that person shall, for the purpose of the present section, be deemed to have ceased to practise, and his name may be erased accordingly.

(4) In the execution of his duties the general registrar shall act on such evidence as in each case appears sufficient.

Erasing from dentists' register name of practitioner convicted of crime or guilty of disgraceful conduct.

13. The General Council shall cause to be erased from the dentists' register any entry which has been incorrectly or fraudulently made.

Where a person registered in the dentists' register has, either before or after the passing of this Act, and either before or after he is so registered, been convicted either in Her Majesty's dominions or elsewhere of an offence which, if committed in England, would be a felony or misdemeanor, or been guilty of any infamous or disgraceful conduct in a professional respect, that person shall be liable to have his name erased from the register.

The General Council may, and upon the application of any of the medical authorities shall, cause inquiry to be made into the case of a person alleged to be liable to have his name erased under this section, and, on proof of such conviction or of such infamous or disgraceful conduct, shall cause the name of such person to be erased from the register:

Provided that the name of a person shall not be erased under this section on account of his adopting or refraining from adopting the practice of any particular theory of dentistry or dental surgery, nor on account of a conviction for a political offence out of Her Majesty's dominions, nor on account of a conviction for an offence which, though within the provisions of this section, does not, either from the trivial nature of the offence or from the circumstances under which it was committed, disqualify a person for practising dentistry. Any name erased from the register in pursuance of this section shall also be erased from the list of licentiates in dental surgery or dentistry of the medical authority of which such person is a licentiate.

Restoration of name to dentists' register.

14. Where the General Council direct the erasure from the dentists' register of the name of any person, or of any other entry, the name of that person, or that entry, shall not be again entered in the register, except by direction of the General Council, or by order of a court of competent jurisdiction.

If the General Council think fit in any case, they may direct the general registrar to restore to the dentists' register any name or entry erased therefrom, either without fee or on payment of such fee, not exceeding the registration fee, as the General Council from time to time fix, and the registrar shall restore the same accordingly.

The name of any person erased from the dentists' register at the request of such person or with his consent shall, unless it might, if not so erased, have been erased by order of the General Council, be restored to the register on his application, on payment of such fee not exceeding the registration fee as the General Council from time to time fix.

Where the name of a person restored to the register in pursuance of this section has been erased from the list of licentiates in dental surgery or dentistry of any medical authority, that name shall be restored to such list of licentiates.

Committee of General Council for purpose of erasure from and restoration to the register.

15. The General Council shall, for the purpose of exercising in any case the powers of erasing from and of restoring to the dentists' register the name of a person or an entry, ascertain the facts of such case by a committee of their own body, not exceeding five in number, of whom the quorum shall be not less than three, and a report of the Committee shall be conclusive as to the facts for the purpose of the exercise of the said powers by the General Council.

The General Council shall from time to time appoint and shall always maintain a committee for the purposes of this section, and subject to the provisions of this section may from time to time determine the constitution, and the number and tenure of office of the members, of the committee.

The committee from time to time shall meet for the despatch of business, and subject to the provisions of this section, and of any regulations from time to time made by the General Council, may regulate the summoning, notice, place, management, and adjournment of such meetings, the appointment of a chairman, the mode of deciding questions, and generally the transaction and management of business, including the quorum, and if there is a quorum the committee may act notwithstanding any vacancy in their body. In the case of any vacancy the committee may appoint a member of the General Council to fill the vacancy until the next meeting of that Council.

A committee under this section may, for the purpose of the execution of their duties under this Act, employ at the expense of the Council such legal or other assessor or assistants as the committee think necessary or proper.

Fees.

16. There shall be payable in respect of the registration of any person who, before the first day of January, one thousand eight hundred and seventy-nine, applies to be registered under this Act, a fee not exceeding two pounds; and in respect of the registration of any person who after that day applies to be registered, a fee not exceeding five pounds.

Orders of General Council.

17. Subject to the provisions of this Act, the General Council may from time to time make, alter, and revoke such orders and regulations as they see fit for regulating the general register and the local registers, and the practice of registration under this Act, and the fees to be paid in respect thereof.

Examinations.

Examinations in dental surgery.

18. Notwithstanding anything in any Act of Parliament, charter, or other document, it shall be lawful for any of the medical authorities (hereinafter referred to as colleges or bodies) who have power for the time being to grant surgical degrees, from time to time to hold examinations for the purpose of testing the fitness of persons to practise dentistry or dental surgery who may be desirous of being so examined, and to grant certificates of such fitness; and any person who obtains such a certificate from any of those colleges or bodies shall be a licentiate in dental surgery or dentistry of such college or body, and his name shall be entered on a list of such licentiates to be kept by such college or body.

Each of the said colleges or bodies shall admit to the examinations held by them respectively under this section any person desirous of being examined who has attained the age of twenty-one years, and has complied with the regulations in force (if any) as to education of such college or body.

Board of examiners.

19. Subject to the provisions hereinafter contained with reference to a medical board, the council or other the governing body of the Royal College of

Surgeons of Edinburgh, and of the Faculty of Physicians and Surgeons of Glasgow, and of the Royal College of Surgeons in Ireland, and of any university in the United Kingdom respectively, may from time to time appoint a board of examiners for the purpose of conducting the examinations and granting the certificates hereinbefore mentioned.

Each of such board shall be called the Board of Examiners in Dental Surgery or Dentistry, and shall consist of not less than six members, one-half of whom at least shall be persons registered under this Act, and such registration shall (notwithstanding anything in any Act of Parliament, charter, or other document) be deemed the only qualification necessary for the membership of such board.

The persons appointed by each such council or other governing body shall continue in office for such period, and shall conduct the examinations in such manner, and shall grant certificates in such form, as such council or other governing body may from time to time, by byelaws or regulations, respectively direct.

A casual vacancy in any such board of examiners may be filled by the council or other governing body which appointed such board, but the person so appointed shall be qualified as the person in whose stead he is appointed was qualified, and shall hold office for such time only as the person in whose stead he is appointed would have held office.

Fees for examination.

20. Such reasonable fees shall be paid for the certificates to be granted under this Act by the board of examiners of the Royal College of Surgeons of Edinburgh, the Faculty of Physicians and Surgeons of Glasgow, and of the Royal College of Surgeons in Ireland, and of any such university as aforesaid respectively, as the council or other the governing body of each of those colleges or bodies may from time to time, by byelaws or regulations, respectively direct.

Continuance of examination in dental surgery by Royal College of Surgeons of England.

21. The Royal College of Surgeons of England shall continue to hold examinations and to appoint a board of examiners in dentistry or dental surgery for the purpose of testing the fitness of persons to practise dentistry or dental surgery who may be desirous of being so examined, and to grant certificates of such fitness, subject and according to the provisions of their charter dated the eighth day of September, one thousand eight hundred and fifty-nine, and the byelaws made, or to be made, in pursuance thereof; and any person who obtains such a certificate shall be a licentiate in dental surgery of the said college, and his name shall be entered on a list of such licentiates to be kept by the said college.

General Council may require information as to examinations.

22. Every medical authority shall from time to time, when required by the General Council, furnish such Council with such information as such Council may require as to the course of study and examinations to be gone through in order to obtain such certificates as are in this Act mentioned, and generally as to the requisites for obtaining such certificates; and any member or members of the General Council, or any person or persons deputed for this purpose by such Council, or by any branch council, may attend and be present at any such examinations.

Representation to Privy Council of defects in examination.

23. Where it appears to the General Council that the course of study and examinations to be gone through in order to obtain such certificate as is in this Act mentioned from any of the said colleges or bodies are not such as to secure the possession by persons obtaining such certificate of the requisite knowledge and skill for the efficient practice of dentistry or dental surgery, the General Council may represent the same to Her Majesty's Privy Council.

Powers of Privy Council, on representation, to make order.

24. The Privy Council, on any representation made as aforesaid, may, if they see fit, order that a certificate granted by any such college or body after such time as may be mentioned in the order shall not confer any right to be registered under this Act.

Any such order may be revoked by the Privy Council on its being made to appear to them, by further representation from the General Council or otherwise, that such college or body has made effectual provision, to the satisfaction of the General Council, for the improvement of such course of study or examination.

Consequences of order.

25. After the time mentioned in this behalf in any such Order in Council, no person shall be entitled to be registered under this Act in respect of a certificate granted by the college or body to which such order relates after the time therein mentioned, and the revocation of any such order shall not entitle any person to be registered in respect of a certificate granted before such revocation.

Privy Council may prohibit attempts to impose restrictions as to any theory of dentistry by bodies entitled to grant certificates.

26. If it appears to the General Council that an attempt has been made by any medical authority to impose on any candidate offering himself for examination an obligation to adopt or refrain from adopting the practice of any particular theory of dentistry or dental surgery as a test or condition of admitting him to examination, or granting a certificate of fitness under this Act, the General Council may represent the same to the Privy Council, and the Privy Council may thereupon issue an injunction to the authority so acting directing them to desist from such practice, and in the event of their not complying therewith, then to order that such authority shall cease to have power to confer any right to be registered under this Act so long as they continue such practice.

27. A CERTIFICATE under this Act shall not confer any right or title to be registered under the Medical Act, 1858, in respect of such certificate, nor to assume any name, title, or designation implying that the person mentioned in the certificate is by law recognized as a licentiate or practitioner in medicine or general surgery.

Saving as to registration under 21 & 22 Vict., c. 90.

28. In the event of a board being at any time after the passing of this Act established, whether under the name of a medical board or otherwise, for nominating on behalf of any two or more of the medical authorities examiners of persons desirous of practising medicine and surgery, whether such board (in this Act referred to as a medical board) is established under the Medical Act, 1858, or otherwise, a person shall not receive a certificate of fitness to practise as a dentist from any medical authority represented on such board, or, if such board is established for the whole of England, Scotland, or Ireland, shall not be entitled to be registered in respect of any certificate obtained in England, Scotland, or Ireland, as the case may be, unless he has obtained from such board a certificate that he has shown by examination that he is qualified to practise dentistry or dental surgery: Provided that one-half at least of the examiners at any such examination shall be persons registered under this Act.

Provision for conduct of examinition by medical boards, if established.

21 & 22 Vict., c. 90.

The medical board shall, in such manner as may be from time to time directed by the General Council, certify to the general registrar and to the medical authorities the persons who have shown by examination that they are qualified to practise dentistry or dental surgery, and every person so certified shall on application receive from the Royal College of Surgeons of England or the Royal College of Surgeons of Edinburgh or the Faculty of Physicians and Surgeons of Glasgow, or the Royal College of Surgeons of Ireland, a certificate of fitness constituting such person a licentiate in dental surgery or dentistry of such college or faculty.

If a medical authority certify to the general registrar the names and addresses of the persons who, having been so certified by a medical board, have received certificates from that authority, together with the other particulars required for the registration of such persons, the general registrar may, upon payment of the registration fee, register every such person in the dentists' register without application from that person.

The General Council shall have the same power of making rules respecting the examination of persons desiring to obtain certificates of being qualified to practise dentistry or dental surgery as they have for the time being in respect of the examination of persons desiring to obtain a qualification to practise medicine and surgery, and there shall be the same right of appeal to the Privy Council against such rules.

The General Council and the Privy Council shall have the same control over the medical board, so far as regards the examination of persons desiring to practise dentistry or dental surgery, as they have as regards the examination of persons desiring to practise medicine and surgery, and shall have the same power of dismissing the members of such board.

The General Council may cause to be framed, and may approve, and when approved, submit to the Privy Council, a scheme to carry into effect the provisions of this Act with respect to a medical board, and rules respecting examinations and for extending, with or without any exception or modification, to the examination of persons desirous of practising dentistry or dental surgery, the provisions of any Act for the time being in force with respect to the examination of persons desiring to practise medicine or surgery, and any such scheme when confirmed by the Privy Council shall have full effect.

Any such scheme may provide for the fees to be paid on admission to the examinations, and for the application of such fees for public purposes and generally for such matters as appear to be necessary or proper for carrying into effect the scheme and regulating the examinations.

Supplemental.

Evidence of registration.

29. A COPY of the register of dentists for the time being, purporting to be printed and published in pursuance of this Act, shall be evidence in all cases (until the contrary be made to appear) that the persons therein specified are registered according to the provisions of this Act; and the absence of the name of any person from such copy shall be evidence (until the contrary be made to appear) that such person is not registered according to the provisions of this Act: Provided that, in the case of any person whose name does not appear in such copy, a certified copy under the hand of the registrar of the General Council of the entry of the name of such person in the dentists' register shall be evidence that such person is registered according to the provisions of this Act.

Exemptions of registered persons.

30. EVERY person registered under this Act shall be exempt, if he so desires, from serving on all juries and inquests whatsoever, and from serving all corporate, parochial, ward, hundred, and town-ship offices and from serving in the militia; and the name of any registered person shall not be returned in any list of persons liable to serve in the militia or in any such office as aforesaid.

Exercise of powers by Privy Council.

31. THE powers by this Act vested in the Privy Council may be exercised by any two or more o the Lords and others of Her Majesty's most honourable Privy Council.

Any order made by the Privy Council, on any appeal to them under this Act, may be made conditionally, or unconditionally, and may contain such terms and directions as to the Privy Council seem just.

32. All moneys arising from fees paid on registration or from the sale of copies of the registers, or otherwise received by the General Council under this Act, shall be applied, in accordance with such regulations as may be from time to time made by the General Council, in defraying the expenses of registration and the other expenses of the execution of this Act, and subject thereto, towards the support of museums, libraries or lectureships, or for public purposes connected with the profession of dentistry or dental surgery, or towards the promotion of learning and education in connexion with dentistry or dental surgery. Application of fees.

33. The treasurers of the General and Branch Councils shall enter in books to be kept for that purpose a true account of all sums of money by them, received and paid under this Act; and such accounts shall be submitted by them to the General Council and Branch Councils respectively at such times as the councils may respectively require. Such accounts shall be published annually, and shall be laid before both Houses of Parliament in the month of March in every year, if Parliament be then sitting, or if Parliament be not sitting, then within one month after the commencement of the next sitting of Parliament. Account to be published.

34. Any registrar who wilfully makes or causes to be made any falsification in any matter relating to any register under this Act shall be deemed guilty of a misdemeanor in England or Ireland, and in Scotland of a crime or offence punishable by fine or imprisonment, and shall, on conviction thereof, be liable to be imprisoned for any term not exceeding twelve months. Penalty on wilful falsification of registers.

35. Any person who wilfully procures or attempts to procure himself to be registered under this Act, by making or producing, or causing to be made or produced, any false or fraudulent representation, or declaration, either verbally or in writing, and any person aiding and assisting him therein, shall be deemed guilty of a misdemeanor in England and Ireland, and in Scotland of a crime or offence punishable by fine or imprisonment, and shall, on conviction thereof, be liable to be imprisoned for any term not exceeding twelve months. Penalty for obtaining registration by false representation.

36. Every registrar of deaths in the United Kingdom, on receiving notice of the death of any person registered under this Act, shall forthwith transmit by post, to the registrar of the General Council and to the registrar of the Branch Council for that part of the United Kingdom in which the death occurs, a certificate under his own hand of such death, with the particulars of time and place of death, and may charge the cost of such certificate and transmission as an expense of his office. Notice of death of practitioner

Provision for certain students.

37. ANY person who has been articled as a pupil and has paid a premium to a dental practitioner entitled to be registered under this Act in consideration of receiving from such practitioner a complete dental education shall, if his articles expire before the first day of January, one thousand eight hundred and eighty, be entitled to be registered under this Act as though he had been in *bonâ fide* practice before the passing of this Act. Moreover, it shall be lawful for the General Council by special order to dispense with such of the certificates, examinations, or other conditions for registration in the dentists' register required under the provisions of this Act, or under any byelaws, orders, or regulations made by its authority, as to them may seem fit, in favour of any dental students or apprentices who have commenced their professional education or apprenticeship before the passing of this Act.

Byelaws.

38. ALL byelaws, orders, and regulations made by the General Council, or by any medical authority under the authority of this Act, shall be made and may be from time to time altered or revoked in such manner, and subject to such approval or confirmation if any, as in the case of other byelaws, orders, or regulations made by such medical authority.

Services of notices by post.

39. SUBJECT to the other provisions of this Act, all notices and documents required by or for the purposes of this Act to be sent may be sent by post, and shall be deemed to have been received at the time when the letter containing the same would be delivered in the ordinary course of post, and in proving such sending it shall be sufficient to prove that the letter containing the notice or document was prepaid, and properly addressed, and put into the post.

Such notices and documents may be in writing or in print, or partly in writing and partly in print, and when sent to the General Council, or a medical board, or a medical authority, shall be deemed to be properly addressed if addressed to the General Council, medical board, or medical authority, or to some officer of such Council, board, or authority, at the principal office or place of business of such Council, board, or authority; and when sent to a person registered in the medical register, shall be deemed to be properly addressed if addressed to him according to his address registered in that register.

Recovery of penalties.

40. ALL fees under this Act may be recovered as ordinary debts due to the General Council, and all penalties under this Act may be recovered and enforced as follows, that is to say:—In England, before two or more justices of the peace, in manner directed by the Act of the session of the eleventh and twelfth years of the reign of Her present Majesty, chapter forty-three, intituled "An Act to facilitate the performance of the duties of justices of the peace out of sessions within England and Wales with respect to summary convic-

tions and orders", and any Act amending the same; and in Scotland, before the sheriff or sheriff substitute, or two justices, in manner provided by
27 & 28 Vict., c. 53. the Summary Procedure Act, 1864, and any Act amending the same; and in Ireland, within the police district of Dublin metropolis, in manner directed by the Acts regulating the powers and duties of justices of the peace for such district or of the police of such district, and elsewhere in Ireland, before two or more justices of the peace, in manner directed by the Petty Ses-
14 & 15 Vict., c. 93. sions (Ireland) Act, 1851, and any Act amending the same.

SCHEDULE.

DECLARATION required to be made by a person who claims to be registered under the Dentists Act, 1878, on the ground that he was bonâ fide engaged in the practice of dentistry at the date of the passing of the Dentists Act, 1878.

I, , residing at
, hereby declare that I was bonâ fide engaged in the practice of dentistry at
, at the date of the passing of the Dentists Act, 1878.

(Signed)

(Witness)

Dated this day of 18

NOTE.—Any person who wilfully procures or attempts to procure himself to be registered under this Act, by making or producing, or causing to be made or produced, any false or fraudulent representation or declaration, either verbally or in writing, and any person aiding and assisting him therein is liable under the Dentists Act, 1878, to imprisonment for twelve months.

THE ELDERS' WIDOWS' FUND (INDIA) ACT, 1878.

(41 & 42 Vict., c. 47.)

An Act to enable the Trustees of the Elders' Widows' Fund to apply the capital of the said Fund in aid of Income; and for other purposes in relation thereto.

[*8th August, 1878.*]

[Preamble recites that in 1820 a fund, commonly known as "The Elders' Widows' Fund", was established for the relief of the widows and orphans of persons employed in the Extra Department of the Home Service of the East India Company: that in 1834, at the request of the trustees of the said fund it was resolved by the Court of Directors of the East India Company, with the sanction of the Commissioners for the affairs of India, that the deficiency should be made good by the East India Company as compensation under 3 & 4 Will. 4, c. 85, s. 7, on condition that, if the capital of the said fund and the income thereof from interest and subscriptions should be more than sufficient to provide for the permanent charge for pensions, the excess should be appropriated, so far as it would go, to repay to the East India Company the advance which they might make under that arrangement, together with interest: that on the 17th May, 1860, the said fund was closed, and since that date no fresh subscribers had been admitted: that in 1877 a fund, entitled the India Office Provident Fund, was established for the relief of the widows and orphans of persons on the permanent home establishment of the Secretary of State for India in Council, and it was provided by the rules of the said fund that the subscribers to the Elders' Widows' Fund who were in the service at the date of the establishment of the Provident Fund should be entitled to become subscribers to the Provident Fund in case an Act of Parliament should be passed enabling the trustees of the Elders' Widows' Fund to transfer to the account of the Provident Fund such a portion of the invested capital of the Elders' Widows' Fund as should, in the opinion of an actuary to be named by the Secretary of State for India in Council, represent the claims on the Elders' Widows' Fund, as upon the 26th March, 1877, of the subscribers to that fund who might have elected to become subscribers to the Provident Fund, and that upon such transfer being made, the latter fund should alone be liable for the payment of pensions to the widows and orphans of the subscribers to the Elders' Widows' Fund who should have elected to become subscribers to the Provident Fund: that thirty-six subscribers to the Elders' Widows' Fund had elected to become subscribers to the Provident Fund, and a valuation had accordingly been made of their claims upon the Elders' Widows' Fund as upon the 26th March, 1877, and such valuation amounted to the sum of £3,317-3-6.]

1. [*Rep. as to U. K. 46 & 47 Vict., c. 39 (S. L. R.). Omitted as being spent.*]

Liability of Provident Fund.

2. The India Office Provident Fund shall alone be liable to the claims of those subscribers to the Elders' Widows' Fund who have elected to subscribe to the India Office Provident Fund.

Annual contribution of Secretary of State.

3. The annual contribution in aid of the Elders' Widows' Fund payable by the Secretary of State for India in Council shall be reduced to five hundred pounds a year.

4. The trustees of the Elders' Widows' Fund shall from time to time, until the liabilities of the said fund are satisfied or the invested capital thereof is exhausted, raise, by sale of sufficient portions of such invested capital, such an amount as may be from time to time required, in addition to the income of the fund, to meet the current liabilities thereof. Trustees empowered to raise, by sale of invested capital, sufficient amount to meet liabilities.

5. Any ultimate surplus which may remain in the hands of the trustees of the Elders Widows' Fund, after satisfying all the liabilities thereof, shall be transferred and paid to the Secretary of State for India in Council as part of the revenues of India. Ultimate surplus to be transferred to Secretary of State.

6. In case the invested capital of the Elders' Widows' Fund shall be exhausted before all the liabilities thereof are satisfied, the Secretary of State for India in Council shall from time to time, out of the revenues of India, pay to the trustees of the said fund such sums or sum as may be required to make good the deficiency in accordance with the said resolution of one thousand eight hundred and thirty-four, and to enable the said trustees from time to time to meet the current liabilities of the said fund. In case capital should be exhausted, Secretary of State to meet liabilities.

The Territorial Waters Jurisdiction Act, 1878.[1]

(41 & 42 Vict., c. 73.)

An Act to regulate the Law relating to the Trial of Offences committed on the Sea within a certain distance of the Coasts of Her Majesty's Dominions.

[*16th August, 1878.*]

Whereas the rightful jurisdiction of Her Majesty, her heirs and successors, extends and has always extended over the open seas adjacent to the coasts of the United Kingdom and of all other parts of Her Majesty's dominions to such a distance as is necessary for the defence and security of such dominions:

And whereas it is expedient that all offences committed on the open sea within a certain distance of the coasts of the United Kingdom and of all other parts of Her Majesty's dominions, by whomsoever committed, should be dealt with according to law:

Be it therefore enacted by the Queen's most excellent Majesty, by and with the advice and consent of the lords spiritual and temporal, and commons, in this present Parliament assembled, and by the authority of the same, as follows:

1. This Act may be cited as The Territorial Waters Jurisdiction Act, 1878. Short title.

---

[1] See *Chitt's Statutes*, Tit. Criminal Law, p. 148.

Amendment of the law as to the jurisdiction of the Admiral.

2. An offence committed by a person, whether he is or is not a subject of Her Majesty, on the open sea within the territorial waters of Her Majesty's dominions, is an offence within the jurisdiction of the Admiral, although it may have been committed on board or by means of a foreign ship, and the person who committed such offence may be arrested, tried, and punished accordingly.

Restriction on institution of proceedings for punishment of offence.

3. Proceedings for the trial and punishment of a person who is not a subject of Her Majesty, and who is charged with any such offence as is declared by this Act to be within the jurisdiction of the Admiral, shall not be instituted in any court of the United Kingdom, except with the consent of one of Her Majesty's Principal Secretaries of State, and on his certificate that the institution of such proceedings is in his opinion expedient, and shall not be instituted in any of the dominions of Her Majesty out of the United Kingdom, except with the leave of the Governor of the part of the dominions in which such proceedings are proposed to be instituted, and on his certificate that it is expedient that such proceedings should be instituted.

Provisions as to procedure.

4. On the trial of any person who is not a subject of Her Majesty for an offence declared by this Act to be within the jurisdiction of the Admiral, it shall not be necessary to aver in any indictment or information on such trial that such consent or certificate of the Secretary of State or Governor as is required by this Act has been given, and the fact of the same having been given shall be presumed unless disputed by the defendant at the trial; and the production of a document purporting to be signed by one of Her Majesty's Principal Secretaries of State as respects the United Kingdom, and by the Governor as respects any other part of Her Majesty's dominions, and containing such consent and certificate, shall be sufficient evidence for all the purposes of this Act of the consent and certificate required by this Act.

Proceedings before a justice of the peace or other magistrate previous to the committal of an offender for trial or to the determination of the justice or magistrate that the offender is to be put upon his trial shall not be deemed proceedings for the trial of the offence committed by such offender for the purposes of the said consent and certificate under this Act.

Saving as to jurisdiction.

5. Nothing in this Act contained shall be construed to be in derogation of any rightful jurisdiction of Her Majesty, her heirs or successors, under the law of nations, or to affect or prejudice any jurisdiction conferred by Act of Parliament or now by law existing in relation to foreign ships or in relation to persons on board such ships.

Saving as to piracy.

6. This Act shall not prejudice or affect the trial in manner heretofore in use of any act of piracy as defined by the law of nations, or affect or

prejudice any law relating thereto; and where any act of piracy as defined by the law of nations is also any such offence as is declared by this Act to be within the jurisdiction of the Admiral, such offence may be tried in pursuance of this Act, or pursuance of any other Act of Parliament, law, or custom relating thereto.

7. In this Act, unless there is something inconsistent in the context, the following expressions shall respectively have the meanings hereinafter assigned to them; that is to say, Definitions.

"The jurisdiction of the Admiral", as used in this Act, includes the jurisdiction of the Admiralty of England and Ireland, or either of such jurisdictions as used in any Act of Parliament; and for the purpose of arresting any person charged with an offence declared by this Act to be within the jurisdiction of the Admiral, the territorial waters adjacent to the United Kingdom or any other part of Her Majesty's dominions, shall be deemed to be within the jurisdiction of any judge, magistrate, or officer having power within such United Kingdom, or other part of Her Majesty's dominions, to issue warrants for arresting or to arrest persons charged with offences committed within the jurisdiction of such judge, magistrate, or officer: "Jurisdiction of the Admiral";

"United Kingdom" includes the Isle of Man, the Channel Islands, and other adjacent islands: "United Kingdom";

"The territorial waters of Her Majesty's dominions," in reference to the sea, means such parts of the sea adjacent to the coast of the United Kingdom, or the coast of some other part of Her Majesty's dominions, as is deemed by international law to be within the territorial sovereignty of Her Majesty; and for the purpose of any offence declared by this Act to be within the jurisdiction of the Admiral, any part of the open sea within one marine league of the coast measured from low-water mark shall be deemed to be open sea within the territorial waters of Her Majesty's dominions: "Territorial waters of Her Majesty's dominions";

"Governor", as respects India, means the Governor General or the Governor of any presidency; and where a British possession consists of several constituent colonies, means the Governor General of the whole possession or the Governor of any of the constituent colonies; and as respects any other British possession, means the officer for the time being administering the government of such possession; also any person acting for or in the capacity of Governor shall be included under the term "Governor": "Governor";

"Offence" as used in this Act means an act, neglect, or default of such a description as would, if committed within the body of a country in "Offence";

England, be punishable on indictment according to the law of England for the time being in force:

"Ship": "Ship" includes every description of ship, boat, or other floating craft:

"Foreign ship". "Foreign ship" means any ship which is not a British ship.

THE REGISTRATION OF BIRTHS, DEATHS AND MARRIAGES (ARMY) ACT, 1879.

(42 & 43 Vict., c. 8.)

An Act to make further provision for the Registration of Deaths, Marriages, and Births occurring out of the United Kingdom among officers and soldiers of Her Majesty's Forces, and their families.

[*23rd May, 1879.*]

[*Preamble.*]

Short title. 1. THIS Act may be cited as the Registration of Births, Deaths, and Marriages (Army) Act, 1879.

Transmission to registrar of registers of births, deaths, and marriages of army kept in pursuance of Her Majesty's regulations. 2. IF Her Majesty is pleased from time to time to make regulations respecting the registration of deaths and births occurring and marriages solemnized out of the United Kingdom among officers and soldiers of Her Majesty's land forces and their families or any of them, the registers kept from time to time in pursuance of the said regulations shall, in manner provided by the regulations for the time being in force, be authenticated and transmitted to the registrar general of births and deaths in England.

Where it appears from any such register that an officer or soldier whose death or marriage is entered therein, or to whose family a person whose death, marriage, or birth is entered therein belonged, was a Scotch or Irish subject of Her Majesty, the registrar general of births and deaths in England shall, as soon as may be after receiving the register, send a certified copy of so much thereof as relates to such death, marriage, or birth to the registrar general of births and deaths in Scotland or Ireland, as the case may require.

Every registrar general of births and deaths to whom a register or certified copy of a register is sent, in pursuance of this section, shall cause the same to be filed and preserved in or copied in a book to be kept by him for the purpose, and to be called the army register book, and such book shall be deemed to be a certified copy of the register book within the meaning of the Acts relating to the registration of births and deaths in England, Scotland, and Ireland respectively.

Provision as to existing 3. WHEREAS under the directions of Her Majesty, or of one of Her Majesty's Principal Secretaries of State, or the Commander-in-Chief or other lawful authority, various documents, such as registers, muster-rolls, and pay-lists have been kept, showing the deaths and births which have occurred and the marriages which have been solemnized among officers and soldiers of Her Majesty's land forces and their families:

documents evidencing deaths, marriages, and births among officers and soldiers of the army, and their families.

And whereas it is expedient to make further provision respecting the said documents: Be it therefore enacted as follows:

Where any of such documents, or any certified extracts thereof made under the direction of one of Her Majesty's Principal Secretaries of State, have either before or after the passing of this Act been transmitted to the registrar general of births and deaths in England, such documents or extracts shall be deemed to be in the legal custody of the said registrar general, and shall be admissible in evidence; and a copy of any such document or extract of, or any part thereof, if purporting to be certified to be a true copy under the seal of the register office of the registrar general, shall be admissible in evidence of such document, extract, or part.

Saving as to births, deaths, and marriages in the United Kingdom.

4. NOTHING in this Act shall apply to any deaths, marriages, or births which occur in the United Kingdom, except where the same occurred before the commencement of this Act.

5. [*Rep. as to U. K. 57 & 58 Vict., c. 56 (S. L. R.). Omitted as being spent.*]

THE SLAVE TRADE (EAST AFRICAN COURTS) ACT, 1879.

(42 & 43 Vict., c. 38.)

An Act to amend the Slave Trade (East African Courts) Act, 1873.

[*11th August, 1879.*]

[*Preamble.*]

Short title and construction.

1. THIS Act may be cited as the Slave Trade (East African Courts) Act, 1879.

36 & 37 Vict., c. 59.

This Act shall be construed as one with the Slave Trade (East African Courts) Act, 1873, and that Act and this Act may be cited together as the Slave Trade (East African Courts) Acts, 1873 and 1879.

Definition of "East African Courts" in 36 & 37 Vict., c. 59.

2. * * * * * * * *.[1]

36 & 37 Vict., c. 59.

In the Slave Trade (East African Courts) Act, 1873, the term "East African Courts" shall mean the Vice-Admiralty Court at Aden, and any of

---

[1] The first and last paragraphs of this section have been repealed as to the U. K. by 57 & 58 Vict., c. 56 (S. L. R.).

Her Majesty's consular officers within the dominions of the sovereigns of Zanzibar, Muscat, and Madagascar on whom jurisdiction in relation to vessels captured on suspicion of being engaged in the slave trade, or otherwise in relation to the slave trade, has been conferred by an Order in Council, made whether before or after the passing of this Act.

* * * * * * * *[1].

Definition of treaty in 36 & 37 Vict., c. 59, s. 7.

3. * * * * * * * *

A treaty in relation to the slave trade made either before or after the passing of this Act by or on behalf of Her Majesty with the Government of Egypt shall be deemed to be a treaty in relation to the slave trade to which section seven of the Slave Trade (East African Courts) Act, 1873, applies, and Orders in Council in relation to such treaty may be made accordingly in pursuance of the said section. 36 & 37 Vict, c. 59.

Amendment of 36 & 37 Vict., c. 59, s. 3, as to jurisdiction over British vessels.

4. Each of the East African court shall have the same jurisdiction in regard to a British vessel seized on suspicion of being engaged in or fitted out for the slave trade, and to the persons, slaves, goods, and effects on board thereof, when the vessel, in pursuance of any existing East African Slave Trade treaty, is seized and brought for trial by the commander or officer of any ship belonging to the foreign state with whom such treaty is made, as such court would have if the vessel had been seized by the commander or officer of any of Her Majesty's ships.

The Indian Guaranteed Railways Act, 1879.

(42 & 43 Vict., c. 41.)

An Act to enable guaranteed Railway Companies in India and the Secretary of State for India in Council to enter into Agreements with respect to the working of Railways, and with respect to Telegraphs, and to confer upon those Companies additional powers with respect to their undertakings.

[*11th August, 1879.*]

[*Preamble.*]

Interpretation.

1. In and for the purposes of this Act,—

the term "guaranteed company" means any of the companies specified in the schedule to this Act, and any railway company which for the time being

---

[1] *See* footnote on preceding page.

constructs, maintains, or works a railway under any guarantee from or arrangement with the Secretary of State for India in Council:

the term "railway company" includes any person or body of persons being the owner or lessee of or working a railway, except the East Indian Railway Company, and except any railway company of which the undertaking is after the passing of this Act purchased by the Secretary of State for India in Council:

the term "railway" means a railway constructed before or after the passing of this Act, and belonging to the Secretary of State for India in Council, or situate in Her Majesty's territories in India, or in any territory in the East Indies belonging to any native prince or state in alliance with Her Majesty or to any European power, and includes any tramway so belonging or situate and worked by steam power, and any ferry so belonging or situate and worked or used in connection with a railway.

Power for guaranteed company to enter into working agreements.

2. A GUARANTEED company may from time to time make with the Secretary of State for India in Council, and carry into effect, or, with the sanction of the Secretary of State for India in Council, make with any railway company, and carry into effect, any agreement with respect to any of the following purposes; namely,

(*a*) the working, use, management, and maintenance of any railway or part of a railway:

(*b*) the supply of rolling stock and machinery necessary for any of the purposes hereinbefore mentioned, and of officers and servants for the conduct of the traffic of any such railway or part:

(*c*) the payments to be made and the conditions to be performed with respect to such working, use, management, and maintenance:

(*d*) the interchange, accommodation, and conveyance of traffic on, coming from, or destined for the respective railways of the contracting parties, and the fixing, collecting, apportionment, and appropriation of the revenues arising from that traffic:

(*e*) generally the giving effect to any such provisions or stipulations with respect to any of the purposes hereinbefore mentioned as the contracting parties may think fit and mutually agree on.

Power for guaranteed company to make agreements with the Secretary of State as to telegraphs.

3. A GUARANTEED company may from time to time make with the Secretary of State for India in Council, and carry into effect, any agreement with respect to any of the following purposes; namely,

(*a*) the surrendering, selling, or letting by the company to the Secretary of State of all or any part of the telegraphs belonging to the company:

(*b*) the doing of anything connected with the working, use, management, or maintenance of or otherwise relating to any telegraphs in India which belong to the Secretary of State in Council or a guaranteed company, or in which the Secretary of State in Council or any such company is for the time being interested, including the application of the revenue to arise from any such telegraphs:

(*c*) generally the giving effect to any such provisions or stipulations with respect to any such telegraphs as the Secretary of State in Council and any such company may think fit and mutually agree on.

Additional powers of guaranteed company.

4. A GUARANTEED company may from time to time, with the sanction of the Secretary of State for India in Council, exercise all or any of the following powers:

(*a*) they may use, maintain, farm, or work and take tolls in respect of any bridge or ferry used in connection with their railway:

(*b*) they may construct, use, maintain, and take tolls in respect of any road in connection with a railway bridge:

(*c*) they may provide any means of transport which may be required for the reasonable convenience of persons or goods carried or to be carried on their railway, but not between any places between which any company shall for the time being be carrying on the business of carriers by water:

provided always, that the capital outlay on the works mentioned in the three preceding sub-sections shall not in the case of any guaranteed company exceed in all ten lacs of rupees:

(*d*) they may make and carry into effect agreements with the Secretary of State for India in Council for the construction of rolling stock, plant, or machinery used on or in connection with railways, or for leasing or taking on lease any rolling stock, plant, machinery, or equipments required for use on a railway.

A guaranteed company shall have, for the purpose of recovering any tolls which they are authorized to take under this section, such powers as may be conferred upon them by laws and regulations made by the Governor General of India in Council.

Secretary of State may delegate to Governor General right of sanction under this Act.

5. THE Secretary of State for India in Council may from time to time, with respect to any case or class of cases, delegate to the Governor General of India in Council the power to give any sanction required under this Act.

6. The powers conferred by this Act shall be in addition to and not in derogation of any powers existing independently of this Act. **Powers of Act cumulative.**

7. Any agreement made before the passing of this Act by a guaranteed company for any of the purposes specified in this Act shall be as valid as if it had been made after the passing of this Act. **Validation of past agreements.**

8. This Act may be cited as the Indian Guaranteed Railways Act, 1879. **Short title.**

SCHEDULE.

The Great Indian Peninsular Railway Company.
The Madras Railway Company.
The Bombay, Baroda, and Central India Railway Company.
The Scinde, Punjab, and Delhi Railway Company.
The Eastern Bengal Railway Company.
The South Indian Railway Company.
The Oudh and Rohilcund Railway Company (Limited).

The East Indian Railway (Redemption of Annuities) Act, 1879.

(42 & 43 Vict., c. 43.)

An Act to enable the Secretary of State in Council of India to create and issue Capital Stock in the United Kingdom in exchange for so much of the Annuity created under the East Indian Railway Company Purchase Act, 1879, and thereby made chargeable on the Revenues of India as may be purchased by the Secretary of State under that Act.

[*11th August, 1879.*]

[*Preamble recites 42 & 43 Vict., c. 206.*]

1. [*Rep. as to U. K. 57 & 58 Vict., c. 56 (S. L. R.). Omitted as being spent.*]

2. The Secretary of State may create and issue so much capital stock, bearing interest at the rate of four per centum per annum, as may be required for the purpose of completing any purchase or purchases authorized by the East Indian Railway Company Purchase Act, 1879, of any portion or portions of the said annuity of one million four hundred and seventy-three thousand seven hundred and fifty pounds, created under the authority of that Act. **Power to the Secretary of State in Council of India to create and issue so much capital stock as may be required for the purposes of 42 & 43 Vict., c. 206.**

As to terms of issue and date of payment off.

3. Any capital stock created under this Act may be issued on such terms as may be determined by the Secretary of State, and may bear interest during such period and be paid off at par at such time as the Secretary of State may prescribe.

Transfer books of such capital stock to be kept.

4. * * * * * * * * *
There shall be kept, either at the office of the Secretary of State in London or at the Bank of England, books wherein entries shall be made of the said capital stock, and wherein all assignments or transfers of the same, or any part thereof, shall be entered and registered and shall be signed by the party or parties making such assignments or transfers, or if such party or parties be absent, by his, her, or their attorney or attorneys thereunto lawfully authorized by writing under his, her, or their hands and seals to be attested by two or more credible witnesses; and the person or persons to whom such transfer or transfers shall be made may respectively underwrite his, her, or their acceptance thereof, and no other mode of assigning or transferring the said capital stock, or any part thereof, or any interest therein, shall be good and available in law; and no stamp duties whatsoever shall be charged on the said transfers, or any of them.

Power to raise money for payment of principal money.

5. Upon or for the payment off or repayment ofa ny principal money secured under this Act, the Secretary of State may at any time borrow or raise by the creation and issue of capital stock, bearing interest at such rate per centum per annum as the Secretary of State may think fit, all or any part of the amount of principal money required to be paid off or repaid, and so from time to time as all or any part of the principal money secured under this Act may require to be repaid, but the amount to be charged upon the revenues of India shall not in any case exceed the principal money required to be paid off or repaid: Provided that nothing in this Act contained shall authorize the Secretary of State to re-issue any capital stock or securities which may, by the operation of the said sinking fund, be cancelled or redeemed in reduction of the public debt of India created under the authority of Parliament.

Capital stock and interest to be charged on revenues of India.

6. All capital stock to be issued under this Act, and the interest thereon, shall be charged on and payable out of the revenues of India in like manner as other liabilities incurred on account of the Government of India.

Half-yearly returns of loans to include sinking fund under 42 & 43 Vict., c. 206.

7. The half-yearly returns to Parliament of loans raised in England chargeable upon the revenues of India shall include the amount of the sinking fund created by the Secretary of State under the East Indian Railway Company Purchase Act, 1879, and the application thereof.

Saving of borrowing powers.

8. This Act should not prejudice or affect any power of raising or borrowing money vested in the Secretary of State at the time of passing thereof.

9. Any capital stock created under this Act shall be deemed to be East India stock within the Act twenty-second and twenty-third Victoria, chapter thirty-five, section thirty-two, unless and until Parliament shall otherwise provide; and any capital stock created under this Act shall be deemed to be and shall mean India stock within the Act of the twenty-sixth and twenty-seventh Victoria, chapter seventy-three, anything in the said last-mentioned Act to the contrary notwithstanding. Stock created hereunder to be deemed East India stock.

10. The provisions contained in the third section of the Married Women's Property Act, 1870, and all other enactments in the said Act relating to or affecting such provisions shall be extended and be applicable to any capital stock created under this Act. 33 & 34 Vict., c. 93, s. 3, etc. extended to capital stock created under this Act.

The East India Loan Act, 1879.[1]

(42 & 43 Vict., c. 60.)

An Act to enable the Secretary of State in Council of India to raise Money in the United Kingdom for the Service of the Government of India.

[*15th August, 1879.*]

[*Preamble.*]

[2]1. It shall be lawful for the Secretary of State in Council of India, at any time or times after the passing of this Act, to raise in the United Kingdom, for the service of the Government of India, any sum or sums of money not exceeding in the whole five millions of pounds sterling, of which two millions five hundred thousand pounds sterling may be raised by the creation and issue of capital stock bearing interest; and the whole or any portion of the remaining two millions five hundred thousand pounds sterling may be raised by the creation and issue of bonds, debentures, or bills, but not by the creation and issue of capital stock bearing interest, and so that the total sum raised by bills current at any time shall not exceed one million pounds sterling. Power to the Secretary of State in Council of India to raise any sum not exceeding 5,000,000*l.*

2. All bonds issued under the authority of this Act may be issued under the hands of two members of the Council of India, and countersigned by the Secretary of State for India, or one of his under secretaries, or his assistant under secretary, and shall be for such respective amounts, payable after such notice, and at such rate or rates of interest, as the said Secretary of State in Council may think fit. As to issue of bonds.

---

[1] This Act may be cited, with eighteen others, as the East India Loans Acts, 1859 to 1893—*See* the Short Titles Act, 1896 (59 & 60 Vict., c. 14), *post*, p. 1255.

[2] By 56 & 57 Vict., c. 70, s. 20 [printed *post*, p. 962], the whole or any part of the money, which by this Act the Secretary of State is authorized to borrow, may be raised by the creation of capital stock.

As to issue of debentures.

3. All debentures issued under the authority of this Act may be issued * * * * *, for such respective amounts, and at such rate or rates of interest, as the Secretary of State in Council may think fit, and shall be issued at or for such prices and on such terms as may be determined by the Secretary of State in Council.

As to payment of principal and interest on debentures.

4. All debentures issued under the authority of this Act shall be paid off at par at a time or times to be mentioned in such debentures respectively, and the interest on all such debentures shall be paid half-yearly on such days as shall be mentioned therein, and the principal moneys and interest secured by such debentures shall be payable either at the treasury of the Secretary of State in Council in London or at the Bank of England.

Debentures and coupons for interest transferable by delivery.

5. All or any number of the debentures issued under the authority of this Act, and all right to and in respect of the principal and interest moneys secured thereby, shall be transferable by the delivery of such debentures; and the coupons for interest annexed to any debenture issued under the authority of this Act shall also pass by delivery.

As to issue of bills.

6. All bills issued under the authority of this Act may be issued under the hands of two members of the Council, and countersigned as aforesaid, for such respective amounts as the Secretary of State in Council may think fit, and shall be issued at or for such prices and on such terms as may be determined by the Secretary of State in Council.

Description, currency of, and interest on bills.

7. A bill issued under the authority of this Act shall be a bill for the payment of the principal sum named therein at the date therein mentioned, so that the date be not more than twelve months from the date of the bill; and the principal sum secured by such bill shall be payable either at the treasury of the Secretary of State in Council in London or at the Bank of England. Interest shall be payable in respect of such bill at such rate and in such manner as the Secretary of State in Council may determine.

Capital stock may be created and issued.

8. Any capital stock created under the authority of this Act shall bear such a rate of interest as the Secretary of State in Council may think fit, and such capital stock may be issued on such terms as may be determined by the Secretary of State in Council; and any such capital stock may bear interest during such period, and be paid off at par at such time, as the Secretary of State in Council may prescribe previously to the issue of such capital stock.

Transfer books of such capital stock to be kept.

9. * * * * There shall be kept, either at the office of the Secretary of State in Council in London or at the Bank of England, books wherein entries shall be made of the said capital stock, and wherein all assignments or transfers of the same, or any part thereof, shall be entered and registered, and shall be signed by the parties making such assignments or transfers, or, if such parties

be absent, by his, her, or their attorney or attorneys thereunto lawfully authorized by writing under his, her, or their hands and seals, to be attested by two or more credible witnesses; and the person or persons to whom such transfer or transfers shall be made may respectively underwrite his, her, or their acceptance thereof, and no other mode of assigning or transferring the said capital stock or any part thereof, or any interest therein, shall be good and available in law, and no stamp duties whatsoever shall be charged on the said transfers or any of them.

10. THE whole amount of the principal moneys to be charged on the revenues of India under this Act shall not exceed five millions. Amount charged on revenues of India not to exceed 5,000,000*l*.

11. UPON or for the repayment of any principal money secured under the authority of this Act, the Secretary of State in Council may at any time borrow or raise, by all or any of the modes aforesaid, all or any part of the amount of principal money repaid or to be repaid, and so from time to time as all or any part of any principal money under this Act may require to be repaid, but the amount to be charged upon the revenues of India shall not in any case exceed the principal money required to be repaid; and the total amount raised under this section by the creation and issue of capital stock bearing interest shall not, at any one time, exceed two millions five hundred thousand pounds sterling. Power to raise money for payment of principal money.

12. ALL bonds, debentures, and bills to be issued under this Act, and the principal moneys and interest thereby secured, and all capital stock to be issued under this Act, and the interest thereon, shall be charged on and payable out of the revenues of India, in like manner as other liabilities incurred on account of the government of the said territories. Securities, etc., to be charged on revenues of India.

13. THE provisions contained in section four of the Act of the session holden in the fifth and sixth years of King William the Fourth, chapter sixty-four, with respect to the composition and agreement for the payment by the East India Company of an annual sum in lieu of stamp duties, on their bonds, and the exemption of their bonds from stamp duties, shall be applicable with respect to the bonds and debentures to be issued under the authority of this Act, as if such provisions were here repeated and re-enacted with reference thereto. Provisions as to composition for stamp duties on India bonds extended to bonds and debentures issued under this Act.

14. ALL provisions now in force in anywise relating to the offence of forging or altering, or offering, uttering, disposing of, or putting off, knowing the same to be forged or altered, any East India bond, with intent to defraud, shall extend and be applicable to and in respect of any debenture or bill issued under the authority of this Act, as well as to and in respect of any bond issued under the same authority. Forgery of debentures and bills to be punishable as forgery of East India bonds.

Half-yearly returns of moneys raised on loan, etc., to be presented to Parliament.

15. PROVIDED always, that, at the end of each of the half years ending on the thirty-first day of March and the thirtieth day of September in every year, the Secretary of State in Council shall prepare or cause to be prepared a return of all loans raised in England under the provisions of this Act or of any other Acts, chargeable on the revenues of India, outstanding at the commencement of each half year, with the rates of interest and total amount payable thereon, and the date of the termination of each loan, the debt incurred during the half year, the moneys raised thereby during the half year, the loans paid off or discharged during the half year, and the loans outstanding at the close of the half year, stating, so far as the public convenience will allow, the purpose or service for which moneys have been raised during the half year; and that a similar return shall also be prepared of all loans raised in India; that such returns shall be presented to both houses of Parliament within fifteen days after the expiration of the said half-yearly periods as regards the loans raised in England, and within three months as regards the loans raised in India, if Parliament be then sitting, or if not sitting, then within one week after Parliament shall be next assembled; and the various conditions in respect to terms, prices, dates of payment, and rates of interest on which bills have been issued during the half year under the authority of sections six and seven of this Act, shall be shown in the return in a form admitting of a comparison with previous years.

16. [*Rep. as to U. K. 57 & 58 Vict., c. 56 (S. L. R.). Omitted as being spent.*]

Saving of borrowing powers of Secretary of State in Council.

17. THIS Act shall not prejudice or affect any power of raising or borrowing money vested in the said Secretary of State in Council at the time of passing thereof.

Stock created under this Act to be India stock.

18. ANY capital stock created under this Act shall be deemed to be East India stock, within the Act twenty-second and twenty-third Victoria, chapter thirty-five, section thirty-two, unless and until Parliament shall otherwise provide; and any capital stock created under this Act shall be deemed to be and shall mean India stock within the Act of the twenty-sixth and twenty-seventh Victoria, chapter seventy-three, anything in the said last-mentioned Act to the contrary notwithstanding.

19. [*Rep. as to U. K. 61 & 62 Vict., c. 22 (S. L. R.). Omitted as being spent.*]

THE INDIAN SALARIES AND ALLOWANCES ACT, 1880.[1]

(43 Vict., c. 3.)

An Act to amend the Law relating to the Salaries and Allowances of certain Officers in India; and for other purposes relating thereto.

[*15th March, 1880.*]

[*Preamble.*]

1. THIS Act may be cited as the Indian Salaries and Allowances Act, 1880. Short title.

2. IT shall be lawful for the Secretary of State in Council of India from time to time to fix, alter, or abolish the allowances for equipment and voyage of the several officers specified in the first schedule to this Act, or any of them. Power to regulate certain allowances for equipment, etc.

3. IT shall be lawful for the Secretary of State in Council of India from time to time to fix and alter the salaries, and to fix, alter, or abolish the allowances of the bishops and archdeacons of Calcutta, Madras, and Bombay, or any of them: Power to regulate certain ecclesiastical salaries.

Provided that nothing in this section shall affect the salary or allowance, of any person who is such bishop or archdeacon at the passing of this Act.

4. NOTHING in this Act shall authorize the imposition of any additional charge on the revenues of India. Charges on Indian revenues not to be increased.

5. [*Rep. as to U. K. 57 & 58 Vict., c. 56 (S. L. R.).*]

SCHEDULES.

FIRST SCHEDULE.

The Governor General of India and the Members of his Council.
The Governors of Madras and Bombay and the Members of their Councils.
The Commander-in-Chief of the Forces in India.

* * * * * * * * * * * *

The Bishops and Archdeacons of Calcutta, Madras, and Bombay.

Second Schedule. [*Rep. as to U. K. 57 & 58 Vict., c. 56 (S. L. R.).*]

[1] For digest, *see* Ilbert's *Government of India*, p. 324.

THE EAST INDIA LOAN (EAST INDIAN RAILWAY DEBENTURES) ACT, 1880.

(43 Vict., c. 10.)

An Act to enable the Secretary of State in Council of India to raise money in the United Kingdom for the purpose of paying off or redeeming Debentures of the East India Railway Company.

[*19th March, 1880.*]

[*Preamble recites 42 & 43 Vict., c. 206.*]

Power to Secretary of State to raise any sum not exceeding 2,950,000*l.*

1. IT shall be lawful for the Secretary of State at any time or times to raise in the United Kingdom for the service of the Government of India such sum or sums of money, not exceeding in the whole two millions nine hundred and fifty thousand pounds, as may be required for the purpose of paying off or redeeming the principal moneys, secured by the debentures specified in the schedule hereto, such sum or sums to be raised by the creation and issue of bonds, debentures, or capital stock bearing interest, or partly by one of such modes and partly by another or others.

As to issue of bonds.

2. ALL bonds issued under the authority of this Act may be issued under the hands of two members of the Council of India, and countersigned by the Secretary of State, or one of his under secretaries, or his assistant under secretary, and shall be for such respective amounts, payable after such notice, and at such rate or rates of interest, as the Secretary of State may think fit.

As to issue of debentures.

3. ALL debentures issued under the authority of this Act may be issued * * * * for such respective amounts, and at such rate or rates of interest, as the Secretary of State may think fit, and shall be issued at or for such prices and on such terms as may be determined by the Secretary of State.

As to payment of principal and interest on debentures.

4. ALL debentures issued under the authority of this Act shall be paid off at par at a time or times to be mentioned in such debentures respectively; and the interest on all such debentures shall be paid half-yearly on such days as shall be mentioned therein; and the principal moneys and interest secured by such debentures shall be payable either at the treasury of the Secretary of State in London or at the Bank of England.

Debentures and coupons for interest transferable by delivery.

5. ALL or any number of the debentures issued under the authority of this Act and all right to and in respect of the principal and interest moneys secured thereby, shall be transferable by the delivery of such debentures; and the coupons for interest annexed to any debenture issued under the authority of this Act shall also pass by delivery.

Interest, etc., of capital stock.

6. ANY capital stock created under the authority of this Act shall bear such a rate of interest as the Secretary of State may think fit; and such capital stock may be issued on such terms as may be determined by the

Secretary of State; and any such capital stock may bear interest during such period, and be paid off at par at such time, as the Secretary of State may prescribe previously to the issue of such capital stock.

Transfer books of such capital stock to be kept.

7. In case of the creation and issue of any such capital stock there shall be kept, either at the office of the Secretary of State in London or at the Bank of England, books wherein entries shall be made of the said capital stock, and wherein all assignments or transfers of the same, or any part thereof, shall be entered and registered, and shall be signed by the parties making such assignments or transfers, or, if such parties be absent, by his, her, or their attorney or attorneys thereunto lawfully authorized by writing under his, her, or their hands and seals, to be attested by two or more credible witnesses; and the person or persons to whom such transfer or transfers shall be made may respectively underwrite his, her, or their acceptance thereof; and no other mode of assigning or transfering the said capital stock or any part thereof or any interest therein, shall be good and available in law, and no stamp duties whatsoever shall be charged on the said transfers or any of them.

Amount to be charged on revenues of India.

8. The whole amount of the principal moneys to be charged on the revenues of India under this Act shall not exceed two millions nine hundred and fifty thousand pounds.

Power to raise money for payment of principal money.

9. Upon or for the repayment of any principal money secured under the authority of this Act, the Secretary of State may at any time borrow or raise by all or any of the modes aforesaid, all or any part of the amount of principal money repaid or to be repaid, and so from time to time as all or any part of any principal money under this Act may require to be repaid, but the amount to be charged upon the revenues of India shall not in any case exceed the principal money required to be repaid.

Securities, etc., to be charged on revenues of India.

10. All bonds and debentures to be issued under this Act, and the principal moneys and interest thereby secured, and all capital stock to be issued under this Act, and the interest thereon, shall be charged on and payable out of the revenues of India, in like manner as other liabilities incurred on account of the Government of India.

Provisions as to composition for stamp duties on India bonds extended to bonds and debentures issued under this Act.

11. The provisions contained in section four of the Act of the session holden in the fifth and sixth years of King William the Fourth, chapter sixty-four, with respect to the composition and agreement for the payment by the East India Company of an annual sum in lieu of stamp duties on their bonds, and the exemption of their bonds from stamp duties, shall be applicable with respect to the bonds and debentures to be issued under the authority of this Act as if such provisions were here repeated and re-enacted with reference thereto.

Forgery of debentures and bills to

12. All provisions now in force in anywise relating to the offence of forging or altering, or offering, uttering, disposing of, or putting off, knowing the

be punishable as forgery of East India bonds.

same to be forged or altered, any East India bond, with intent to defraud, shall extend and be applicable to and in respect of any debenture or bond issued under the authority of this Act.

Saving of borrowing powers of Secretary of State

13. THIS Act shall not prejudice or affect any power of raising or borrowing money vested in the Secretary of State at the time of passing thereof.

Stock created under this Act to be deemed East India stock.

14. ANY capital stock created under this Act shall be deemed to be East India stock, within the Law of Property Amendment Act, 1859,[1] section thirty-two, unless and until Parliament shall otherwise provide; and any capital stock created under this Act shall be deemed to be and shall mean India stock within the Act of the twenty-sixth and twenty-seventh Victoria, chapter seventy-three, anything in the said last-mentioned Act to the contrary notwithstanding. 22 & 23 c. 35.

Sect. 3, etc., of 33 & 34 Vict., c. 93, extended to capital stock created under this Act.

15. THE provisions contained in the third section of the Married Women's Property Act, 1870,[1] and all other enactments in the said Act relating to or affecting such provisions, shall be extended and be applicable to any capital stock created under this Act.

34 & 35 Vict., c. 29, extended to all capital stock issued by the Secretary of State under the authority of Parliament.

16. THE provisions contained in the Act of the thirty-fourth and thirty-fifth Victoria, chapter twenty-nine, shall be extended and be applicable to all capital stock issued or to be issued by the Secretary of State under the authority of Parliament.

Short title.

17. THIS Act may be cited as the East Indian Loan (East Indian Railway Debentures) Act, 1880.

SCHEDULE.

REDEEMABLE DEBENTURES OF EAST INDIAN RAILWAY COMPANY.

Principal moneys secured.	When payable.	Rate of interest per annum.
£		
1,000,000	1 January 1881	4½ per cent.
1,279,850	12 July 1882	4 per cent.
230,150	1 December 1882	4 per cent.
440,000	19 March 1883	4 per cent.
2,950,000		

[1] Cf. 42 & 43 Vict., c. 43, ss. 9, 10, ante, p. 597.

THE INDIA STOCK (POWERS OF ATTORNEY) ACT, 1880.[1]

(43 Vict., c. 11.)

An Act to make Powers of Attorney and Requests for Transmission of Dividend Warrants by Post relating to India Five per centum Stock applicable to India Four per centum Stock.

[*19th March, 1880.*]

[*Preamble.*]

1. THIS Act may be cited as India Stock (Powers of Attorney) Act, 1880. Short title.

2. EVERY power of attorney in force at the time of the passing of this Act for the sale and transfer of any India five per cent. stock shall, unless it be legally revoked or become void, remain in force for the purpose of enabling the attorney or attorneys therein named or referred to to receive and give receipt for any principal sum of such India five per cent. stock, and to sell and transfer any India four per cent. stock that may be accepted in exchange for such five per cent. stock, and to receive the consideration money and give receipts for the same. Powers of attorney for sale and transfer of India five per cent. stock to apply to India four per cent. stock.

EVERY power of attorney in force at the time of the passing of this Act for the receipt of dividends on any India five per cent. stock, shall, unless it be legally revoked or become void, remain in force for the purpose of enabling the attorney or attorneys therein named or referred to to receive the dividends to accrue on India four per cent. stock, * * * * Powers of attorney for receipt of dividends on India five per cent. stock to apply to India four per cent. stock.

* * * * * *

4. EVERY request for the transmission of dividend warrants by post relating to India five per cent. stock in force at the time of the passing of this Act, or which may hereafter be made, in pursuance of the Act of the India Stock Dividends Act, 1871, shall, unless it be legally revoked or become void, extend and apply to India four per cent. stock as if the stock mentioned in such request were therein described as India four per cent. stock. Requests for post dividend warrants in respect of India five per cent. stock to apply to India four per cent. stock.

THE JUDICIAL COMMITTEE ACT, 1881.[2]

(44 & 45 Vict., c. 3.)

An Act to further improve the Administration of Justice in the Judicial Committee of the Privy Council.

[*17th February, 1881.*]

WHEREAS it is expedient that further provision should be made for the administration of justice in the Judicial Committee of the Privy Council:

---

[1] This Act may be cited, with eighteen others, as the East India Loans Acts, 1879 to 1893—*see* the Short Titles Act, 1896 (59 & 60 Vict., c 14), *post*, p. 1255.

[2] See *Chitty's Statutes*, Tit. Privy Council, p. 19.

Be it therefore enacted by the Queen's most excellent Majesty, by and with the advice and consent of the lords spiritual and temporal, and commons, in this present Parliament assembled, and by the authority of the same, as follows:

Lords Justices of Appeal to be members of Judicial Committee. 1. Every person holding or who has held in England the office of a Lord Justice of Appeal shall, if a member of Her Majesty's Privy Council in England, be a member of the Judicial Committee of the Privy Council.

Short title. 2. This Act may be cited as the Judicial Committee Act, 1881.

The India Office (Sale of Superfluous Land) Act, 1881.

(44 & 45 Vict., c. 7.)

An Act to authorise the Secretary of State for India in Council to sell a piece of land in Charles Street, Westminster, to the Commissioners of Her Majesty's Works and Public Buildings for the Public Service.

[*29th March, 1881.*]

Whereas in pursuance of the India Office Site and Approaches Act, 1865, 28 & 29 Vict., c. 32. the Secretary of State in Council of India purchased certain land, and such land is now vested in Her Majesty, her heirs and successors, for the service of the Government of India, according to the provisions of the Act of the session of the twenty-first and twenty-second years of the reign of Her present Majesty, 21 & 22 Vict., c. 106. chapter one hundred and six, intituled "An Act for the better government of India," in this Act referred to as the India Act, 1858:

And whereas that portion of the land so purchased and vested in Her Majesty as aforesaid which is described in the schedule to this Act, and delineated on the plan deposited as in the schedule mentioned, is not required for the service of the Government of India:

And whereas the Secretary of State in Council of India has agreed to sell to the Commissioners of Her Majesty's Works and Public Buildings (in this Act referred to as the Commissioners of Works), and the Commissioners of Works have agreed to buy the said portion of land described in the schedule to this Act for the sum of sixty-eight thousand six hundred pounds, to be paid out of moneys provided by Parliament:

And whereas it is expedient to provide as hereinafter appearing for carrying into effect the said sale:

* * * * * *

Short title. 1. This Act may be cited as the India Office (Sale of Superfluous Land) Act, 1881.

Transfer of site in Charles Street from Indian Secretary to Commissioners of Works.

2. As soon as the Commissioners of Works have paid into the Bank of England to the account of the Secretary of State in Council of India the sum of sixty-eight thousand six hundred pounds, the piece of land described in the schedule to this Act, and delineated on the plan deposited as in that schedule mentioned, shall be vested in the Commissioners of Works, and their successors and assigns, for all the estate and interest of Her Majesty therein, and all powers in relation to the said piece of land which, by the India Office Site and Approaches Act, 1865, are vested in Her Majesty, her heirs and successors, shall vest in the Commissioners of Works, their successors and assigns.

28 & 29 Vict., c. 32.

The Commissioners of Works shall hold the said piece of land for the public service in like manner as if it had been duly purchased by them under the Act of the fifteenth and sixteenth years of the reign of Her present Majesty, chapter twenty-eight, intituled "An Act to amend an Act of the fourteenth and fifteenth years of Her present Majesty for the direction of Public Works and Buildings, and to vest the buildings appropriated for the accommodation of the Supreme Court of Justice in Edinburgh in the Commissioners of Her Majesty's Works and Public Buildings."

Provided that in the event of the sale, exchange, or lease of the said piece of land, or any part thereof, it shall not be necessary for the person who purchases or takes the same in exchange or lease to ascertain that the direction of the Commissioners of Her Majesty's Treasury has been given to such purchase, exchange, or lease.

The receipt of one of Her Majesty's Principal Secretaries of State or the above-mentioned sum shall be recorded at the Queen's Remembrancer's office among the records of the High Court of Justice, and shall be conclusive evidence to any purchaser that the above sum was duly paid, and that the land became under this Act vested in the Commissioners of Works.

Land to continue subject to land tax.

3. Such portion of the piece of land described in the schedule to this Act as, at the time of the passing of this Act, is subject to land tax, shall continue liable thereto until duly discharged, but shall not be assessed to the land tax at a higher value than that at which such land was assessed at the time at which it was purchased in pursuance of the India Office Site and Approaches Act, 1865.

Exemption from operation of 18 & 19 Vict., c. 122.

4. All buildings erected on the land mentioned in the schedule to this Act by or under the direction of the Commissioners of Works shall be exempt from the operation of the Metropolitan Buildings Act, 1855, and any Act amending the same, whether passed before or after the passing of this Act, except so far as any future Act expressly negatives this section.

Disposition of moneys received for purchase.

5. All moneys received by the Secretary of State in Council of India in pursuance of this Act shall be applied as other moneys received from the sale of land vested in Her Majesty for the service of the Government of India under the India Act, 1858, are by law applicable. 21 & 22 Vict., c. 106.

SCHEDULE.

All the piece of land, containing twenty-seven thousand four hundred and forty square feet, or thereabouts, situate in the parish of St. Margaret, in the city of Westminster, and abutting on the north on Charles Street, on the west on Delahay Street, on the south on Gardener's Lane, and on the east on land belonging to the Commissioners of Works, as the same land is delineated on a plan signed by the Right Honourable George John Shaw Lefevre, First Commissioner of Her Majesty's Works and Public Buildings, and by the Right Honourable Spencer Compton Cavendish, commonly called the Marquis of Hartington, one of Her Majesty's Principal Secretaries of State, and deposited at the Queen's Remembrancer's office among the records of Her Majesty's High Court of Justice, and coloured red on the said plan.

The East Indian Railway (Redemption of Annuities) Act, 1881.

(44 & 45 Vict., c. 53.)

An Act for making further provision with respect to the Redemption of the Annuity created under the East Indian Railway Company Purchase Act, 1879; and for other purposes.

[*22nd August, 1881.*]

Whereas by the East Indian Railway Company Purchase Act, 1879, (hereinafter called the Purchase Act), provision was made for transferring to and vesting in the Secretary of State in Council of India, hereinafter called the Secretary of State, the undertaking of the East Indian Railway, hereinafter called the Company, and all other the property of the Company, save and except as therein mentioned, and for the creation of an annuity of one million four hundred and seventy-three thousand seven hundred and fifty pounds, terminating on the fourteenth of February, one thousand nine hundred and fifty-three, to be charged on the revenues of India, and to be paid to the 42 & 43 Vict. c. 206.

Company as therein mentioned for the purpose of being distributed among the proprietors of stock of the Company :

And whereas by section forty-six of the Purchase Act it was enacted that the Secretary of State might purchase by agreement from any proprietor of stock of the Company the amount of annuity to which such proprietor was entitled, or any portion thereof, paying in exchange for the same as thereby provided, to any such proprietor on the register in London India four per centum stock, and to any such proprietor on the register at Calcutta India four per centum rupee debt in India, at the respective rates therein specified, subject to the proviso that no such purchase should be made by means of India four per centum stock unless the Secretary of State should be authorized by Parliament to create and issue such stock for the purpose:

And whereas by the same Act (section forty-eight) provision was made for the registration in the name of the Secretary of State of the annuities so to be purchased, and (section forty-nine) for the retention by the Secretary of State of the amount therein mentioned in respect of the annuity registered in his name, and (section fifty) for the rights and liabilities of the Secretary of State in respect of the annuity so registered:

And whereas by section fifty-one of the same Act the Secretary of State was required to invest one equal ninth part of the amount retained by him in respect of the annuity registered in his name, in order to provide a sinking fund to be applied in the reduction of the public debt of India created under the authority of Parliament:

42 & 43 Vict., c. 43. And whereas by an Act of the same session, chapter forty-three, "to enable the Secretary of State in Council of India to create and issue capital stock in the United Kingdom in exchange for so much of the annuity created under the East Indian Railway Company Purchase Act, 1879, and thereby made chargeable on the revenues of India, as may be purchased by the Secretary of State under that Act" (hereinafter called the Redemption Act), the Secretary of State was authorized to create and issue India four per centum stock for the purposes of the Purchase Act, and such stock has accordingly been created and issued, and paid in exchange for a portion of the annuity created under the Purchase Act:

And whereas by reason of the conversion of the stock of the Company into the annuities created under the Purchase Act there are no longer any proprietors of that stock, and it is expedient that the powers of the Secretary of State be extended to authorize the purchase of the said annuities from the holders thereof:

And whereas it is expedient that the Secretary of State be authorized to create and issue such capital stock, bearing interest at a lower rate than four per centum per annum, as may be required either for the purpose of this purchase, or for the purpose of reducing the liabilities charged on the revenues of India by the redemption of any part of those liabilities which may for the time being bear interest at a rate not lower than the stock so created:

* * * * * * * * *

Power to purchase annuities from annuitants by means of India stock.

1. (*1*) The Secretary of State may purchase by agreement from any holder of the annuity created under the Purchase Act the whole or any part of the annuity held by him, paying in exchange for the same India stock created under this Act at such a rate of exchange that the annual interest on the stock given in exchange for any annuity shall not exceed eight-ninths of the annuity.

(*2*) The annuities purchased under this section shall be registered in the books of the Company in the name of the Secretary of State by his official style, and sections forty-nine and fifty of the Purchase Act shall apply to them as if they were so registered in pursuance of that Act.

Power to create India stock for the purpose of reducing the public debt or liabilities of India.

2. (*1*) The Secretary of State may from time to time create and issue so much capital stock, bearing interest at the rate of three and a half per centum per annum, or at any other rate not higher than four per centum per annum, as may be required either for the purpose of redeeming the annuities created under the Purchase Act by the purchase thereof under this Act, or for the purpose of redeeming any other liability now charged [or contingently chargeable][1] on the revenues of India and bearing interest or involving an annual payment at a rate not lower than the interest of the stock so created; subject, nevertheless, to the following provisoes:—

(*a*) the difference between the interest or annual payment in respect of the liability redeemed and the interest on the stock created for redemption thereof shall be set aside and invested in manner directed by section fifty-one of the Purchase Act with respect to the amount of annuity retained by the Secretary of State under that Act, so as to provide a sinking fund to be applied in reduction of the public debt of India created under the authority of Parliament:

(*b*) any stock or securities that may be cancelled or redeemed for the purposes of such reduction shall not be re-issued without the authority of Parliament:

(*c*) the amount so set aside shall be sufficient to repay the principal of the stock created at the expiration of the period during which the Secretary of State was liable to pay the interest or annual

---

[1] The words in square brackets were inserted by 48 & 49 Vict., c. 25, s. 25 (2), *post*, p. 266.

payment redeemed by means of the creation of the stock, if that period does not exceed ninety-nine years, but if it does exceed ninety-nine years then at the expiration of ninety-nine years from the date of the creation of the stock:

(*d*) when and so soon as the public debt of India created under the authority of Parliament shall by the operation of the said sinking fund be reduced by an amount equivalent to the amount of the public debt of India, attributable to the redemption effected under this section, any obligation imposed on the Secretary of State under or by virtue of this section shall cease and determine.

(*2*) All the provisions of the Redemption Act with respect to the capital stock created or issued under that Act shall apply to the capital stock created or issued under this Act.

3. This Act may be cited as the East Indian Railway (Redemption of Annuities) Act, 1881. Short title.

THE REGULATION OF THE FORCES ACT, 1881.

(44 & 45 Vict., c. 57.)

An Act to amend the Law respecting the Regulation of Her Majesty's Forces, and to amend the Army Discipline and Regulation Act, 1879.

[*27th August, 1881.*]

Be it enacted by the Queen's most excellent Majesty, by and with the advice and consent of the lords spiritual and temporal, and commons, in this present Parliament assembled, and by the authority of the same, as follows:—

* * * * * * * * *

[1]55. Whereas under the Act of the session of the twenty-fourth and twenty-fifth years of the reign of Her present Majesty, chapter seventy-four, intituled "An Act to render lawful the enlistment of persons transferred from the Indian to the general forces of Her Majesty, and to provide in certain respects for the rights of such persons," it was provided that where a soldier was transferred from Her Majesty's Indian forces to Her Majesty's general forces it should be lawful for the Commissioners of Chelsea Hospital to calculate the pension of Pensions of soldiers formerly in Indian forces.

---

[1] This is the only extant section applicable to India.

such person in accordance with the regulations either of Her Majesty's Indian or of Her Majesty's general forces, according as such soldier might choose.

And whereas doubts have arisen as to whether certain additions to pensions granted by Royal Warrant to the above-mentioned soldiers in respect of service over and above the term of twenty-one years can, having regard to the above-recited Act, be lawfully granted by the said Commissioners to the said soldiers, and it is expedient to remove such doubts: Be it therefore enacted as follows:

Nothing in the Act above in this section recited shall prevent the Commissioners of Chelsea Hospital from granting to a soldier such pension as is for the time being authorized by Royal Warrant.

ARMY ACT.[1]

(44 & 45 Vict., c. 58.)

An Act to consolidate the Army Discipline and Regulation Act, 1879, and the subsequent Acts amending the same.

[*Printed in accordance with the Army (Annual) Act, 1885 (48 & 49 Vict., c. 8, s. 8 (2)); with the Amendments made down to the end of 1900.*]

Preliminary.

Preliminary. **Short title of Act.** 1. THIS Act may be cited for all purposes as the Army Act.

Mode of bringing Act into force. 2. THIS Act shall continue in force only for such time and subject to such provisions as may be specified in an annual Act of Parliament bringing into force or continuing the same.[2]

Division of Act. 3. THIS Act is divided into five parts, relating to the following subject-matters; that is to say,

Part I., Discipline:

Part II., Enlistment:

Part III., Billeting and impressment of carriages:

Part IV., General provisions:

Part V., Application of military law, saving provisions, and definitions.

---

[1] See *Chitty's Statutes*, Tit. Army, p. 8.

[2] The Army Act is continued yearly by the passing of an Army (Annual) Act. The last of these Army (Annual) Acts, *viz.*, the Army (Annual) Act, 1899 (62 & 63 Vict., c. 3), alone is reproduced in this Collection, see *post*, p. 1257.

PART I.

DISCIPLINE.

Crimes and Punishments.

Offences in respect of Military Service.

Offences in respect of Military Service.

Offences in relation to the enemy punishable with death.

4. Every person subject to military law who commits any of the following offences; that is to say,

(1) Shamefully abandons or delivers up any garrison, place, post, or guard, or uses any means to compel or induce any governor, commanding officer, or other person shamefully to abandon or deliver up any garrison, place, post, or guard, which it was the duty of such governor, officer, or person to defend; or

(2) Shamefully casts away his arms, ammunition, or tools in the presence of the enemy; or

(3) Treacherously holds correspondence with or gives intelligence to the enemy, or treacherously or through cowardice sends a flag of truce to the enemy; or

(4) Assists the enemy with arms, ammunition, or supplies, or knowingly harbours or protects an enemy not being a prisoner; or

(5) Having been made a prisoner of war, voluntarily serves with or voluntarily aids the enemy; or

(6) Knowingly does when on active service any act calculated to imperil the success of Her Majesty's forces or any part thereof; or

(7) Misbehaves or induces others to misbehave before the enemy in such manner as to show cowardice,

shall, on conviction by court-martial, be liable to suffer death, or such less punishment as in this Act mentioned.

Offences in relation to the enemy not punishable with death.

5. Every person subject to military law who on active service commits any of the following offences; that is to say,

(1) Without orders from his superior officer leaves the ranks, in order to secure prisoners or horses, or on pretence of taking wounded men to the rear; or

(2) Without orders from his superior officer wilfully destroys or damages any property; or

Offences in respect of Military Service.

(3) Is taken prisoner, by want of due precaution or through disobedience of orders, or wilful neglect of duty, or having been taken prisoner fails to rejoin Her Majesty's service when able to rejoin the same; or

(4) Without due authority either holds correspondence with, or gives intelligence to, or sends a flag of truce to the enemy; or

(5) By word of mouth or in writing or by signals or otherwise spreads reports calculated to create unnecessary alarm or despondency; or

(6) In action, or previously to going into action, uses words calculated to create alarm or despondency,

shall, on conviction by court-martial, be liable to suffer penal servitude, or such less punishment as is in this Act mentioned.

Offences punishable more severly on active service than at other times.

6. (*1*) Every person subject to military law who commits any of the following offences; that is to say,

(*a*) Leaves his commanding officer to go in search of plunder; or

(*b*) Without orders from his superior officer, leaves his guard, picquet, patrol, or post; or

(*c*) Forces a safeguard; or

(*d*) Forces or strikes a soldier when acting as sentinel; or

(*e*) Impedes the provost marshal or any assistant provost marshal or any officer or non-commissioned officer or other person legally exercising authority under or on behalf of the provost marshal, or, when called on, refuses to assist in the execution of his duty the provost marshal, assistant provost marshal, or any such officer, non-commissioned officer, or other person; or

(*f*) Does violence to any person bringing provisions or supplies to the forces; or commits any offence against the property or person of any inhabitant of or resident in the country in which he is serving; or

(*g*) Breaks into any house or other place in search of plunder; or

(*h*) By discharging firearms, drawing swords, beating drums, making signals, using words, or by any means whatever, intentionally occasions false alarms in action, on the march, in the field, or elsewhere; or

(*i*) Treacherously makes known the parole, watchword, or countersign to any person not entitled to receive it; or treacherously gives a parole, watchword, or countersign different from what he received; or (*j*) Irregularly detains or appropriates to his own corps, battalion or detachment any provisions or supplies proceeding to the forces, contrary to any orders issued in that respect; or *Offences in respect of Military Service.*

(*k*) Being a soldier acting as sentinel, commits any of the following offences; that is to say, Misbehaviour of sentinel.

(i) sleeps or is drunk on his post; or

(ii) leaves his post before he is regularly relieved,

shall, on conviction by court-martial,

if he commits any such offence on active service, be liable to suffer death, or such less punishment as is in this Act mentioned; and if he commits any such offence not on active service, be liable, if an officer, to be cashiered, or to suffer such less punishment as is in this Act mentioned, and if a soldier, to suffer imprisonment or such less punishment as is in this Act mentioned.

(2) Every person subject to military law who commits any of the following offences; that is to to say,

(*a*) By discharging firearms, drawing swords, beating drums, making signals, using words, or by any means whatever, negligently occasions false alarms in action, on the march, in the field, or elsewhere; or

(*b*) Makes known the parole, watchword, or countersign to any person not entitled to receive it; or, without good and sufficient cause, gives a parole, watchword, or countersign different from what he received,

shall, on conviction by court-martial, be liable, if an officer, to be cashiered, or to suffer such less punishment as is in this Act mentioned, and if a soldier, to suffer imprisonment, or such less punishment as is in this Act mentioned.

Mutiny and Insubordination.

Mutiny and Insubordination.

7. Every person subject to military law who commits any of the following offences; that is to say, Mutiny and sedition.

(1) Causes or conspires with any other persons to cause any mutiny or sedition in any forces belonging to Her Majesty's regular, reserve, or auxiliary forces or Navy; or

(2) Endeavours to seduce any person in Her Majesty's regular, reserve, or auxiliary forces, or Navy, from allegiance to Her Majesty, or to persuade any person in Her Majesty's regular, reserve, or auxiliary forces, or Navy, to join in any mutiny or sedition; or

Mutiny and Insubordination.

(3) Joins in, or being present does not use his utmost endeavours to suppress, any mutiny or sedition in any forces belonging to Her Majesty's regular, reserve, or auxiliary forces, or Navy ; or

(4) Coming to the knowledge of any actual or intended mutiny or sedition in any forces belonging to Her Majesty's regular, reserve, or auxiliary forces, or Navy, does not without delay inform his commanding officer of the same,

shall, on conviction by court-martial, be liable to suffer death, or such less punishment as is in this Act mentioned.

Striking or threatening superior officer.

8. (*1*) Every person subject to military law who commits any of the following offences ; that is to say,

Strikes or uses or offers any violence to his superior officer, being in the execution of his office,

shall, on conviction by court-martial, be liable to suffer death, or such less punishment as is in this Act mentioned ; and

(*2*) Every person subject to military law who commits any of the following offences ; that is to say,

Strikes or uses or offers any violence to his superior officer, or uses threatening or insubordinate language to his superior officer,

shall, on conviction by court-martial, if he commits such offence on active service, be liable to suffer penal servitude, or such less punishment as is in this Act mentioned ; and

if he commits such offence not on active service, be liable, if an officer, to be cashiered, or to suffer such less punishment as is in this Act mentioned, and if a soldier, to suffer imprisonment, or such less punishment as is in this Act mentioned.

Disobedience to superior officer.

9. (*1*) Every person subject to military law who commits the following offence ; that is to say,

Disobeys in such manner as to show a wilful defiance of authority any lawful command given personally by his superior officer in the execution of his office, whether the same is given orally, or in writing, or by signal, or otherwise,

shall, on conviction by court-martial, be liable to suffer death, or such less punishment as is in this Act mentioned ; and

(*2*) Every person subject to military law who commits the following offence ; that is to say,

Disobeys any lawful command given by his superior officer,

shall, on conviction by court-martial, if he commits such offence on active service, be liable to suffer penal servitude, or such less punishment as is in this Act mentioned; and *Mutiny and Insubordination.*

if he commits such offence not on active service, be liable, if an officer, to be cashiered, or to suffer such less punishment as is in this Act mentioned, and if a soldier, to suffer imprisonment, or such less punishment as is in this Act mentioned.

10. Every person subject to military law who commits any of the following offences; that is to say, Insubordination.

(1) Being concerned in any quarrel, fray, or disorder, refuses to obey any officer (though of inferior rank) who orders him into arrest, or strikes or uses or offers violence to any such officer; or

(2) Strikes or uses or offers violence to any person, whether subject to military law or not, in whose custody he is placed, and whether he is or is not his superior officer; or

(3) Resists an escort whose duty it is to apprehend him or to have him in charge; or

(4) Being a soldier breaks out of barracks, camp, or quarters,

shall, on conviction by court-martial, be liable, if an officer, to be cashiered, or to suffer such less punishment as is in this Act mentioned, and if a soldier, to suffer imprisonment, or such less punishment as is in this Act mentioned.

11. Every person subject to military law who commits the following offence; that is to say, Neglect to obey garrison or other orders

neglects to obey any general or garrison or other orders,

shall, on conviction by court-martial, be liable, if an officer, to be cashiered, or to suffer such less punishment as is in this Act mentioned, and if a soldier, to suffer imprisonment, or such less punishment as is in this Act mentioned.

Provided that the expression "general orders" in this section shall not include Her Majesty's regulations and orders for the army or any similar order in the nature of a regulation published for the general information and guidance of the army.

Desertion, Fraudulent Enlistment, and Absence without Leave. *Desertion, Fraudulent Enlistment, and Absence without Leave.*

12. (*1*) Every person subject to military law who commits any of the following offences; that is to say, Desertion.

(*a*) Deserts or attempts to desert Her Majesty's service; or

Desertion, Fraudulent Enlistment, and Absence without Leave.

(*b*) Persuades, endeavours to persuade, procures or attempts to procure, any person subject to military law to desert from Her Majesty's service,

shall, on conviction by court-martial—

if he committed such offence when on active service or under orders for active service, be liable to suffer death, or such less punishment as is in this Act mentioned; and

if he committed such offence under any other circumstances, be liable for the first offence to suffer imprisonment, or such less punishment as is in this Act mentioned; and for the second or any subsequent offence to suffer penal servitude, or such less punishment as is in this Act mentioned.

(*2*) Where an offender has fraudulently enlisted once or oftener, he may, for the purposes of trial for the offence of deserting or attempting to desert Her Majesty's service, be deemed to belong to any one or more of the corps to which he has been appointed or transferred as well as to the corps to which he properly belongs; and it shall be lawful to charge an offender with any number of offences against this section at the same time, and to give evidence of such offences against him, and if he be convicted thereof to punish him accordingly; and further it shall be lawful on conviction of a person for two or more such offences to award him the higher punishment allowed by this section for a second offence as if he had been convicted by a previous court-martial of one of such offences.

(*3*) For the purposes of the liability under this section to the higher punishment for second offence, a previous offence of fraudulent enlistment may be reckoned as a previous offence under this section.

Fraudulent enlistment.

13. (*1*) Every person subject to military law who commits any of the following offences; that is to say,

(*a*) When belonging to either the regular forces or the militia when embodied, without having first obtained a regular discharge therefrom, or otherwise fulfilled the conditions enabling him to enlist, enlists in Her Majesty's regular forces, or

(*b*) When belonging to the regular forces without having fulfilled the conditions enabling him to enlist, enrol, or enter, enrol himself, or enlists in the militia or in any of the reserve forces, not subject to military law, or enters the Royal Navy, shall be deemed to have been guilty of fraudulent enlistment, and shall, on conviction by court-martial, be liable— *Desertion, Fraudulent Enlistment, and Absence without Leave.*

(i) for the first offence to suffer imprisonment, or such less punishment as is in this Act mentioned; and

(ii) for the second or any subsequent offence to suffer penal servitude, or such less punishment as is in this Act mentioned.

(*2*) Where an offender has fraudulently enlisted on several occasions he may, for the purposes of this section, be deemed to belong to any one or more of the corps to which he has been appointed or transferred, as well as to the corps to which he properly belongs; and it shall be lawful to charge an offender with any number of offences against this section at the same time, and to give evidence of such offences against him, and if he be convicted thereof to punish him accordingly; and further it shall be lawful on conviction of a person for two or more such offences to award him the higher punishment allowed by this section for a second offence as if he had been convicted by a previous court-martial of one of such offences.

(*3*) Where an offender is convicted of the offence of fraudulent enlistment then for the purposes of his liability under this section to the higher punishment for a second offence, the offence of deserting or attempting to desert Her Majesty's service may be reckoned as a previous offence of fraudulent enlistment under this section, with this exception, that the absence of the offender next before any fraudulent enlistment shall not upon his conviction for that fraudulent enlistment be reckoned as a previous offence of deserting or attempting to desert.

Persuasion of or connivance at desertion.

14. Every person subject to military law who commits any of the following offences; that is to say,

(*1*) Assists any person subject to military law to desert Her Majesty's service; or

(*2*) Being cognisant of any desertion or intended desertion of a person subject to military law, does not forthwith give notice to his commanding officer, or take any steps in his power to cause the deserter or intending deserter to be apprehended,

shall, on conviction by court-martial, be liable to suffer imprisonment, or such less punishment as is in this Act mentioned.

Absence from duty without leave.

15. Every person subject to military law who commits any of the following offences; that is to say,

(1) Absents himself without leave; or

Desertion, Fraudulent Enlistment, and Absence without Leave.

(2) Fails to appear at the place of parade or rendezvous appointed by his commanding officer, or goes from thence without leave before he is relieved, or without urgent necessity quits the ranks; or

(3) Being a soldier, when in camp or garrison or elsewhere, is found beyond any limits fixed or in any place prohibited by any general garrison or other order, without a pass or written leave from his commanding officer; or

(4) Being a soldier without leave from his commanding officer, or without due cause, absents himself from any school when duly ordered to attend there,

shall, on conviction by court-martial, be liable, if an officer, to be cashiered, or to suffer such less punishment as is in this Act mentioned, and if a soldier, to suffer imprisonment, or such less punishment as is in this Act mentioned.

Disgraceful Conduct.

Disgraceful Conduct.

Scandalous conduct of officer.

16. Every officer who, being subject to military law, commits the following offence; that is to say,

Behaves in a scandalous manner, unbecoming the character of an officer and a gentleman,

shall, on conviction by court-martial, be cashiered.

Fraud by persons in charge of moneys or goods.

17. Every person subject to military law who commits any of the following offences; that is to say,

Being charged with or concerned in the care or distribution of any public or regimental money or goods, steals, fraudulently misapplies, or embezzles the same, or is concerned in or connives at the stealing, fraudulent misapplication or embezzlement thereof, or wilfully damages any such goods,

shall, on conviction by court-martial; be liable to suffer penal servitude, or such less punishment as is in this Act mentioned.

Disgraceful conduct of soldier.

18. Every soldier who commits any of the following offences; that is to say,

(1) Malingers, or feigns or produces disease or infirmity; or

(2) Wilfully maims or injures himself or any other soldier, whether at the instance of such other soldier or not, with intent thereby to render himself or such other soldier unfit for service, or causes himself to be maimed or injured by any person, with intent thereby to render himself unfit for service; or

(3) Is wilfully guilty of any misconduct, or wilfully disobeys, whether in hospital or otherwise, any orders, by means of which miscon-

duct or disobedience he produces or aggravates disease or infirmity or delays its cure; or *Disgraceful Conduct.*

(4) Steals or embezzles or receives knowing them to be stolen or embezzled any money or goods the property of a comrade or of an officer, or any money or goods belonging to any regimental mess or band, or to any regimental institution, or any public money or goods; or,

(5) Is guilty of any other offence of a fraudulent nature not before in this Act particularly specified, or of any other disgraceful conduct of a cruel, indecent, or unnatural kind,

shall, on conviction by court-martial, be liable to suffer imprisonment, or such less punishment as is in this Act mentioned.

Drunkenness.

Drunkenness.

19. Every person subject to military law who commits the following offence; that is to say, Drunkenness.

The offence of drunkenness, whether on duty or not on duty,

shall, on conviction by court-martial, be liable, if an officer, to be cashiered, or to suffer such less punishment as is in this Act mentioned, and if a soldier, to suffer imprisonment, or such less punishment as is in this Act mentioned, and, either in addition to or in substitution for any other punishment, to pay a fine not exceeding one pound.

Offences in relation to Prisoners.

Offences in relation to Prisoners.

20. Every person subject to military law who commits any of the following offences; that is to say, Permitting escape of prisoner.

(1) When in command of a guard, picket, patrol, or post, releases without proper authority, whether wilfully or otherwise, any prisoner committed to his charge; or

(2) Wilfully or without reasonable excuse allows to escape any prisoner who is committed to his charge, or whom it is his duty to keep or guard,

shall, on conviction by court-martial, be liable, if he has acted wilfully to suffer penal servitude, or such less punishment as is in this Act mentioned, and in any case to suffer imprisonment, or such less punishment as is in this Act mentioned.

Offences in relation to Prisoners.

Irregular imprisonment.

21. Every person subject to military law who commits any of the following offences; that is to say,

(1) Unnecessarily detains a prisoner in arrest or confinement without bringing him to trial, or fails to bring his case before the proper authority for investigation; or

(2) Having committed a person to the custody of any officer, non-commissioned officer, provost marshal, or assistant provost marshal, fails without reasonable cause to deliver at the time of such committal, or as soon as practicable, and in any case within twenty-four hours thereafter, to the officer, non-commissioned officer, provost marshal, or assistant provost marshal, into whose custody the person is committed, an account in writing signed by himself of the offence with which the person so committed is charged;

(3) Being in command of a guard, does not as soon as he is relieved from his guard or duty, or if he is not sooner relieved, within twenty-four hours after a prisoner is committed to his charge, give in writing to the officer to whom he may be ordered to report the prisoner's name and offence so far as known to him; and the name and rank of the officer or other person by whom he was charged, accompanied, if he has received the account above in this section mentioned, by that account,

shall, on conviction by court-martial, be liable, if an officer, to be cashiered, or to suffer such less punishment as is in this Act mentioned, and if a soldier, to suffer imprisonment, or such less punishment as is in this Act mentioned.

Escape from confinement.

22. Every person subject to military law who commits the following offence; that is to say,

Being in arrest or confinement, or in prison or otherwise in lawful custody, escapes, or attempts to escape,

shall, on conviction by court-martial, be liable, if an officer, to be cashiered, or to suffer such less punishment as is in this Act mentioned, and if a soldier, to suffer imprisonment, or such less punishment as is in this Act mentioned.

Offences in relation to Property.

Corrupt dealings in respect of supplies to forces.

Offences in relation to Property.

23. Every person subject to military law who commits any of the following offences; that is to say,

(1) Connives at the exaction of any exorbitant price for a house or stall let to a sutler; or

(2) Lays any duty upon, or takes any fee or advantage in respect of, or is in any way interested in, the sale of provisions or merchandise brought into any garrison, camp, station, barrack, or place, in which he has any command or authority, or the sale or purchase of any provisions or stores for the use of any of Her Majesty's forces, *Offences in relation to Property.*

shall, on conviction by court-martial, be liable to suffer imprisonment, or such less punishment as is in this Act mentioned.

Deficiency in and injury to equipment.

24. Every soldier who commits any of the following offences; that is to say,

(1) Makes away with, or is concerned in making away with (whether by pawning, selling, destruction, or otherwise howsoever) his arms, ammunition, equipments, instruments, clothing, regimental necessaries, or any horse of which he has charge; or

(2) Loses by neglect anything before in this section mentioned; or

(3) Makes away with (whether by pawning, selling, destruction, or otherwise however) any military decoration granted to him; or

(4) Wilfully injures anything before in this section mentioned or any property belonging to a comrade, or to an officer, or to any regimental mess or band, or to any regimental institution, or any public property; or

(5) Ill-treats any horse used in the public service,

shall, on conviction by court-martial, be liable to suffer imprisonment, or such less punishment as is in this Act mentioned.

For the purposes of this section, the expression "equipments" includes any article issued to a soldier for his use, or entrusted to his care for military purposes.

Offences in relation to False Documents and Statements.

Offences in relation to False Documents and Statements.

Falsifying official documents and false declarations.

25. Every person subject to military law who commits any of the following offences; that is to say,

(1) In any report, return, muster roll, pay list, certificate, book, route, or other document made or signed by him, or of the contents of which it is his duty to ascertain the accuracy—

(*a*) Knowingly makes or is privy to the making of any false or fraudulent statement; or

(*b*) Knowingly makes or is privy to the making of any omission with intent to defraud; or

Offences in relation to False Documents and Statements.

(2) Knowingly and with intent to injure any person, or knowingly and with intent to defraud, suppresses, defaces, alters, or makes away with any document which it is his duty to preserve or produce; or

(3) Where it is his official duty to make a declaration respecting any matter, knowingly makes a false declaration,

shall, on conviction by court-martial, be liable to suffer imprisonment, or such less punishment as is in this Act mentioned.

Neglect to report, and signing in blank.

26. Every person subject to military law who commits any of the following offences; that is to say,

(1) When signing any document relating to pay, arms, ammunition, equipments, clothing, regimental necessaries, provisions, furniture, bedding, blankets, sheets, utensils, forage, or stores, leaves in blank any material part for which his signature is a voucher; or

(2) Refuses or by culpable neglect omits to make or send a report or return which it is his duty to make or send,

shall, on conviction by court-martial, be liable, if an officer, to be cashiered, or to suffer such less punishment as is in this Act mentioned, and if a soldier, to suffer imprisonment, or such less punishment as is in this Act mentioned.

False accusation or false statement by soldier.

27. Every person subject to military law who commits any of the following offences; that is to say,

(1) Being an officer or soldier, makes a false accusation against any other officer or soldier, knowing such accusation to be false; or

(2) Being an officer or soldier, in making a complaint where he thinks himself wronged, knowingly makes any false statement affecting the character of an officer or soldier, or knowingly and wilfully suppresses any material facts; or

(3) Being a soldier, falsely states to his commanding officer that he has been guilty of desertion or of fraudulent enlistment, or of desertion from the Navy, or has served in and been discharged from any portion of the regular forces, reserve forces or auxiliary forces, or the Navy; or

(4) Being a soldier, makes a wilfully false statement to any military officer or justice in respect of the prolongation of furlough,

shall, on conviction by court-martial, be liable to suffer imprisonment, or such less punishment as is in this Act mentioned.

Offences in relation to Courts-martial.

Offences in relation to Courts-martial.

Offences in relation to courts-martial.

28. Every person subject to military law who commits any of the following offences; that is to say,

(1) Being duly summoned or ordered to attend as a witness before a court-martial, makes defau t in attending; or

(2) Refuses to take an oath or make a solemn declaration legally required by a court-martial to be taken or made; or

(3) Refuses to produce any document in his power or control legally required by a court-martial to be produced by him; or

(4) Refuses when a witness to answer any question to which a court-martial may legally require an answer; or

(5) Is guilty of contempt of a court-martial by using insulting or threatening language, or by causing any interruption or disturbance in the proceedings of such court,

shall, on conviction by a court-martial, other than the court in relation to or before whom the offence was committed, be liable, if an officer, to be cashiered, or to suffer such less punishment as is in this Act mentioned, and if a soldier, to suffer imprisonment, or such less punishment as is in this Act mentioned:

Provided that where a person subject to military law is guilty of contempt of a court-martial by using insulting or threatening language, or by causing any interruption or disturbance in the proceedings of such court, that court, if they think it expedient, instead of the offender being tried by another court-martial, may, by order under the hand of the president, commit such offender to prison, there to be imprisoned, with or without hard labour, for a period not exceeding twenty-one days.

False evidence.

29. Every person subject to military law who commits the following offence; that is to say,

When examined on oath or solemn declaration before a court-martial or any court or officer authorized by this Act to administer an oath, wilfully gives false evidence,

shall be liable, on conviction by court-martial, to suffer imprisonment, or such less punishment as is in this Act mentioned.

Offences in relation to Billeting.

Offences in relation to Billeting.

Offences in relation to billeting.

30. Every person subject to military law who commits any of the following offences (in this Act referred to as offences in relation to billeting); that is to say,

(1) Is guilty of any ill-treatment, by violence, extortion, or making disturbances in billets, of the occupier of a house in which any person or horse is billeted; or

Offences in relation to Billeting.

(2) Being an officer, refuses or neglects, on complaint and proof of such ill-treatment by any officer or soldier under his command, to cause compensation to be made for the same; or

(3) Fails to comply with the provisions of this Act with respect to the payment of the just demands of the person on whom he or any officer or soldier under his command, or his or their horses, have been billeted, or to the making up and transmitting of an account of the money due to such person; or

(4) Wilfully demands billets which are not actually required for some person or horse entitled to be billeted; or

(5) Takes or knowingly suffers to be taken from any person any money or reward for excusing or relieving any person from his liability in respect of the billeting or quartering of officers, soldiers, or horses, or any part of such liability; or

(6) Uses or offers any menace to or compulsion on a constable or other civil officer to make him give billets contrary to this Act, or tending to deter or discourage him from performing any part of his duty under the provisions of this Act relating to billeting, or tending to induce him to do anything contrary to his said duty; or

(7) Uses or offers any menace to or compulsion on any person tending to oblige him to receive, without his consent, any person or horse not duly billeted upon him in pursuance of the provisions of this Act relating to billeting, or to furnish any accommodation which he is not thereby required to furnish,

shall, on conviction by court-martial, be liable, if an officer, to be cashiered, or to suffer such less punishment as is in this Act mentioned, and if a soldier, to suffer imprisonment, or such less punishment as is in this Act mentioned.

Offences in relation to Impressment of Carriages.

Offences in relation to Impressment of Carriages.

Offences in relation to the impressment of carriages, and their attendants.

31. Every person subject to military law who commits any of the following offences (in this Act referred to as offences in relation to the impressment of carriages); that is to say,

(1) Wilfully demands any carriages, animals, or vessels which are not actually required for the purposes authorized by this Act; or

(2) Fails to comply with the provisions of this Act relating to the impressment of carriages as regards the payment of sums due for carriages or as regards the weighing of the load; or

(3) Constrains any carriage, animal, or vessel furnished in pursuance of the provisions of this Act relating to the impressment of carriages to travel against the will of the person in charge thereof beyond the proper distance, or to carry against the will of such person any greater weight than he is required by the said provisions to carry; or

Offences in relation to Impressment of Carriages.

(4) Does not discharge as speedily as practicable any carriage, animal, or vessel furnished in pursuance of the provisions of this Act relating to the impressment of carriages; or

(5) Compels the person in charge of any such carriage, animal, or vessel, or permits him to be compelled, to take thereon any baggage or stores not entitled to be carried, or, except where the carriage or animal is furnished upon a requisition of emergency, to take thereon any soldier or servant (except such as are sick), or any woman or person; or

(6) Ill-treats or permits such person in charge to be ill-treated; or

(7) Uses or offers any menace to or compulsion on a constable to make him provide any carriage, animal, or vessel, which he is not bound in pursuance of the provisions of this Act relating to the impressment of carriages to provide, or tending to deter or discourage him from performing any part of his duty in relation to the providing of carriages, animals, or vessels, or tending to induce him to do anything contrary to his said duty; or

(8) Forces any carriage, animal, or vessel from the owner thereof,

shall, on conviction by court-martial, be liable, if an officer, to be cashiered, or to suffer such less punishment as is in this Act mentioned, and if a soldier, to suffer imprisonment, or such less punishment as is in this Act mentioned.

Offences in relation to Enlistment.

Offences in relation to Enlistment.

Enlistment of soldier or sailor discharged with ignominy or disgrace.

32. (*1*) Every person having become subject to military law, who is discovered to have committed the following offence; (that is to say),

Having been discharged with disgrace from any part of Her Majesty's forces, or having been dismissed with disgrace from the Navy, has afterwards enlisted in the regular forces without declaring the circumstances of his discharge, or dismissal,

shall, on conviction by court-martial, be liable to suffer imprisonment, or such less punishment as is in this Act mentioned.

(*2*) For the purpose of this section, the expression "discharged with disgrace from any part of Her Majesty's forces" means discharged with

Offences in relation to Enlistment.

ignominy, discharged as incorrigible and worthless, discharged for misconduct, or discharged on account of conviction for felony or of a sentence of penal servitude.

False answers or declarations on enlistment.

33. Every person having become subject to military law who is discovered to have committed the following offence; that is to say,

To have made a wilfully false answer to any question set forth in the attestation paper which has been put to him by or by direction of the justice before whom he appears for the purpose of being attested,

shall, on conviction by court-martial, be liable to suffer imprisonment or such less punishment as is in this Act mentioned.

General offences in relation to enlistment.

34. Every person subject to military law who commits any of the following offences; that is to say,

(1) Is concerned in the enlistment for service in the regular forces of any man, when he knows or has reasonable cause to believe such man to be so circumstanced that by enlisting he commits an offence against this Act; or

(2) Wilfully contravenes any enactments or the regulations of the service in any matter relating to the enlistment or attestation of soldiers of the regular forces,

shall, on conviction by court-martial, be liable to suffer imprisonment, or such less punishment as is in this Act mentioned.'

Miscellaneous Military Offences.

Miscellaneous Military Offences.

Traitorous words.

35. Every person subject to military law who commits the following offence; that is to say,

Uses traitorous or disloyal words regarding the Sovereign,

shall, on conviction by court-martial, be liable, if an officer, to be cashiered, or to suffer such less punishment as is in this Act mentioned, and if a soldier, to suffer imprisonment, or such less punishment as is in this Act mentioned.

Injurious disclosures.

36. Every person subject to military law who commits the following offence; that is to say,

Whether serving with any of Her Majesty's forces or not, without due authority, either verbally or in writing or by signal or otherwise, discloses the numbers or position of any forces, or any magazines or stores thereof, or any preparations for, or orders relating to, operations or movements of any forces, at such time and in such manner as in the opinion of the court to have produced effects injurious to Her Majesty's service, shall, on conviction by court-martial, be liable, if an officer, to be cashiered, or to suffer such less punishment as is in this Act mentioned, and if a soldier, to suffer imprisonment, or such less punishment as is in this Act mentioned. *Miscellaneous Military Offences.*

Ill-treating soldier.

37. Every officer or non-commissioned officer who commits any of the following offences; that is to say,

(1) Strikes or otherwise ill-treats any soldier; or

(2) Having received the pay of any officer or soldier, unlawfully detains or unlawfully refuses to pay the same when due,

shall, on conviction by court-martial, be liable, if an officer, to be cashiered or to suffer such less punishment as is in this Act mentioned, and if a non-commissioned officer, to suffer imprisonment or such less punishment as is in this Act mentioned.

Duelling and attempting to commit suicide.

38. Every person subject to military law who commits any of the following offences; that is to say,

(1) Fights, or promotes or is concerned in or connives at fighting a duel; or

(2) Attempts to commit suicide,

shall, on conviction by court-martial, be liable, if an officer, to be cashiered, or to suffer such less punishment as is in this Act mentioned, and if a soldier, to suffer imprisonment, or such less punishment as is in this Act mentioned.

Refusal to deliver to civil power officers and soldiers accused of civil offences.

39. Every person subject to military law who commits any of the following offences; that is to say,

On application being made to him, neglects or refuses to deliver over to the civil magistrate, or to assist in the lawful apprehension of, any officer or soldier accused of an offence punishable by a civil court,

shall, on conviction by court-martial, be liable, if an officer, to be cashiered, or to suffer such less punishment as is in this Act mentioned, and if a soldier, to suffer imprisonment, or such less punishment as is in this Act mentioned.

Conduct to prejudice of military discipline.

40. Every person subject to military law who commits any of the following offences; that is to say,

Is guilty of any act, conduct, disorder, or neglect, to the prejudice of good order and military discipline,

shall, on conviction by court-martial, be liable, if an officer, to be cashiered, or to suffer such less punishment as is in this Act mentioned, and if a soldier, to suffer imprisonment, or such less punishment as is in this Act mentioned: Provided that no person shall be charged under this section in respect of any offence for which special provision is made in any other part of this Act, and which is not a civil offence; nevertheless the conviction of a person so charged shall not be invalid by reason only of the charge being in contravention of this proviso, unless it appears that injustice has been done to the person charged by reason of such contravention; but the responsibility of any officer for that contravention shall not be removed by the validity of the conviction.

Offences punishable by ordinary Law.

Offences punishable by ordinary Law.

Offences punishable by ordinary law of England.

41. SUBJECT to such regulations for the purpose of preventing interference with the jurisdiction of the civil courts as are in this Act after mentioned, every person who, whilst he is subject to military law, shall commit any of the offences in this section mentioned shall be deemed to be guilty of an offence against military law, and if charged under this section with any such offence (in this Act referred to as a civil offence) shall be liable to be tried by court-martial, and on conviction to be punished as follows; that is to say,

(1) If he is convicted of treason, be liable to suffer death, or such less punishment as is in this Act mentioned; and

(2) If he is convicted of murder, be liable to suffer death; and

(3) If he is convicted of manslaughter or treason-felony, be liable to suffer penal servitude, or such less punishment as is in this Act mentioned; and

(4) If he is convicted of rape, be liable to suffer penal servitude, or such less punishment as is in this Act mentioned; and

(5) If he is convicted of any offence not before in this section particularly specified which when committed in England is punishable by the law of England, be liable, whether the offence is committed in England or elsewhere, either to suffer such punishment as might be awarded to him in pursuance of this Act in respect of an act to the prejudice of good order and military discipline, or to suffer any punishment assigned for such offence by the law of England.

Provided as follows:—

(a) A person subject to military law shall not be tried by court-martial for treason, murder, manslaughter, treason-felony, or rape committed in the United Kingdom, and shall not be tried by court-martial for treason, murder, manslaughter, treason-felony, or rape committed in any place within Her Majesty's dominions, other than the United Kingdom and Gibraltar, unless such person at the time he committed the offence was on active service, or such place is more than one hundred miles as measured in a straight line from any city or town in which the offender can be tried for such offence by a competent civil court.

(*b*) A person subject to military law when in Her Majesty's dominions may be tried by any competent civil court for any offence for which he would be triable if he were not subject to military law.

Offences punishable by ordinary Law.

Redress of Wrongs.

Redress of Wrongs.

42. If an officer thinks himself wronged by his commanding officer, and on due application made to him does not receive the redress to which he may consider himself entitled, he may complain to the Commander-in-Chief in order to obtain justice, who is hereby required to examine into such complaint, and through a Secretary of State make his report to Her Majesty in order to receive the directions of Her Majesty thereon.

Mode of complaint by officer.

43. If any soldier thinks himself wronged in any matter by any officer other than his captain, or by any soldier, he may complain thereof to his captain, and if he thinks himself wronged by his captain, either in respect of his complaint not being redressed or in respect of any other matter, he may complain thereof to his commanding officer, and if he thinks himself wronged by his commanding officer, either in respect of his complaint not being redressed or in respect of any other matter, he may complain thereof to the general or other officer commanding the district or station where the soldier is serving; and every officer to whom a complaint is made in pursuance of this section shall cause such complaint to be inquired into, and shall, if on inquiry he is satisfied of the justice of the complaint so made, take such steps as may be necessary for giving full redress to the complainant in respect of the matter complained of.

Mode of complaint by soldier.

Punishments.

Punishments.

44. Punishments may be inflicted in respect of offences committed by persons subject to military law and convicted by courts-martial,—

Scale of punishments by courts-martial.

In the case of officers, according to the scale following:

a. Death.

b. Penal servitude for a term not less than three years.

c. Imprisonment, with or without hard labour, for a term not exceeding two years.

d. Cashiering.

e. Dismissal from Her Majesty's service.

f. Forfeiture in the prescribed manner of seniority of rank, either in the army or in the corps to which the offender belongs, or in both.

g. Reprimand, or severe reprimand.

Punishments. In the case of soldiers, according to the scale following:

h. Death.

j. Penal servitude for a term not less than three years.

k. Imprisonment, with or without hard labour, for a term not exceeding two years.

l. Discharge with ignominy from Her Majesty's service.

m. Reduction in the case of a non-commissioned officer to a lower grade, or to the ranks.

n. Forfeitures, fines and stoppages.

Provided that—

(1) Where in respect of any offence under this Act there is specified a particular punishment, or such less punishment as is in this Act mentioned, there may be awarded in respect of that offence, instead of such particular punishment (but subject to the other regulations of this Act as to punishments, and regard being had to the nature and degree of the offence) any one punishment lower in the above scales than the particular punishment.

(2) An officer shall be sentenced to be cashiered before he is sentenced to penal servitude or imprisonment.

(3) An officer when sentenced to forfeiture of seniority of rank may also be sentenced to reprimand or severe reprimand.

(4) A soldier when sentenced to penal servitude or imprisonment may, in addition thereto, be sentenced to be discharged with ignominy from Her Majesty's service.

(5) Where a soldier on active service is guilty of an aggravated offence of drunkenness, or of an offence of disgraceful conduct, or of any offence punishable with death or penal servitude, it shall be lawful for a court-martial to award for that offence such summary punishment other than flogging as may be directed by rules to be made from time to time by a Secretary of State; and such summary punishment shall be of the character of personal restraint or of hard labour, but shall not be of a nature to cause injury to life or limb, and shall not be inflicted where the confirming officer is of opinion that imprisonment can with due regard to the public service be carried into execution.

(6) The said summary punishment shall not be inflicted upon a non-commissioned officer, or upon a reduced non-commissioned officer, for any offence committed while holding the rank of non-commissioned officer.

(*Sec. 45.*)

Punishments.

(7) "An aggravated offence of drunkenness" for the purposes of this section means drunkenness committed on the march or otherwise on duty, or after the offender was warned for duty, or when by reason of the drunkenness the offender was found unfit for duty; and notwithstanding anything in this Act it shall not be incumbent on the commanding officer to deal summarily with such aggravated offence of drunkenness.

(8) "An offence of disgraceful conduct" for the purposes of this section means any offence specified in section eighteen of this Act.

(9) All rules with respect to summary punishment made in pursuance of this section shall be laid before Parliament as soon as practicable after they are made, if Parliament be then sitting, and if Parliament be not then sitting, as soon as practicable after the beginning of the then next session of Parliament.

(10) For the purpose of commutation of punishment the summary punishment above mentioned shall be deemed to stand in the scale of punishments next below imprisonment.

(11) In addition to or without any other punishment in respect of any offence, an offender convicted by court-martial may be subject to forfeiture of any deferred pay, service towards pension, military decoration or military reward, in such manner as may for the time being be provided by Royal Warrant, but shall not, save as may be provided by Royal Warrant, be liable to any forfeiture under the Regimental Debts Act, 1893, or under any Act relating to the military savings banks, or any regulations made in pursuance of either of the above-mentioned Acts.

26 & 27 Vict., c. 57, now 56 & 57 Vict., c. 5. [See 52 & 53 Vict., c. 63, s. 38 (1).]

(12) In addition to or without any other punishment in respect of any offence, an offender may be sentenced by court-martial to any deduction authorised by this Act to be made from his ordinary pay.

(13) No officer or non-commissioned officer shall, under or by virtue of any power or authority derived from any foreign potentate or ruler, inflict or cause to be inflicted on any person subject to military law under this Act, for or in respect of any offence against such law, any punishment not authorised by this Act.

ARREST AND TRIAL.

Arrest.

Arrest. Custody of persons charged with offences.

45. THE following regulations shall be enacted with respect to persons subject to military law when charged with offences punishable under this Act:

(1) Every person subject to military law when so charged may be taken into military custody: Provided, that in every case where any

Arrest.

officer or soldier not on active service remains in such military custody for a longer period than eight days without a court-martial for his trial being ordered to assemble, a special report of the necessity for further delay shall be made by his commanding officer in manner prescribed; and a similar report shall be forwarded every eight days until a court-martial is assembled or the officer or soldier is released from custody:

(2) Military custody means, according to the usages of the service, the putting the offender under arrest or the putting him in confinement:

(3) An officer may order into military custody an officer of inferior rank or any soldier, and any non-commissioned officer may order into military custody any soldier, and an officer may order into military custody any officer (though he be of higher rank) engaged in a quarrel, fray, or disorder; and any such order shall be obeyed, notwithstanding the person giving the order and the person in respect of whom the order is given do not belong to the same corps, arm, or branch of the service:

(4) An officer or non-commissioned officer commanding a guard, or a provost-marshal, or assistant provost-marshal, shall not refuse to receive or keep any person who is committed to his custody by any officer or non-commissioned officer, but it shall be the duty of the officer or non-commissioned officer who commits any person into custody to deliver at the time of such committal or as soon as practicable, and in every case within twenty-four hours thereafter to the officer, non-commissioned officer, provost-marshal, or assistant provost-marshal into whose custody the person is committed, an account in writing, signed by himself, of the offence with which the person so committed is charged:

(5) The charge made against every person taken into military custody shall without unnecessary delay be investigated by the proper military authority, and, as soon as may be, either proceedings shall be taken for punishing the offence, or such persons shall be discharged from custody.

Power of Commanding Officers.

Power of Commanding Officer.

Power of Commanding Officers.

46. (*1*) The commanding officer shall, upon an investigation being had of a charge made against a person subject to military law under his command of having committed an offence under this Act, dismiss the charge, if he in his discretion thinks that it ought not to be proceeded with, but where he thinks the charge ought to be proceeded with, he may take steps for bringing the offender to a court-martial, or in the case of a soldier may deal with the case summarily. *Power of Commanding Officer.*

(2) Where he deals with a case summarily, he may,—

(*a*) Award to the offender imprisonment, with or without hard labour, for any period not exceeding fourteen days; and

(*b*) In the case of the offence of drunkenness, may order the offender to pay a fine not exceeding ten shillings either in addition to or without imprisonment with or without hard labour; and

(*c*) In addition to or without any other punishment, may order the offender to suffer any deduction from his ordinary pay authorised by this Act to be made by the commanding officer.

(3) Where the charge is against a soldier for drunkenness not on duty, and it is not an aggravated offence of drunkenness within the meaning of section forty-four of this Act, the commanding officer shall deal with the case summarily unless the soldier has been guilty of drunkenness on not less than four occasions in the preceding twelve months; but nothing in this sub-section shall affect the jurisdiction of any court-martial or the right of the soldier to be tried by a district court-martial.

(4) In the case of absence without leave, the commanding officer may award imprisonment, with or without hard labour, for any period not exceeding twenty-one days.

(5) Provided that, where imprisonment is awarded for absence without leave, the commanding officer shall have regard to the number of days during which the offender has been absent, and in no case shall the term of imprisonment awarded, if exceeding seven days, exceed the term of absence.

(6) Provided that, in every case where the power of summary award by a commanding officer exceeds a sentence of seven days' imprisonment, the accused person may demand that the evidence against him should be taken on oath, and the same oath or solemn declaration as that required to be taken by witnesses before a court-martial shall be administered to each witness in such case.

(7) An offender shall not be liable to be tried by court-martial for any offence which has been dealt with summarily by his commanding officer, and shall not be liable to be punished by his commanding officer for any

Power of Commanding Officer. offence of which he has been acquitted or convicted by a competent civil court or by a court-martial.

(*8*) Where a commanding officer has power to deal with a case summarily under this section, and, after hearing the evidence, considers that he may so deal with the case, he shall, unless he awards one of the minor punishments referred to in this section, ask the soldier charged whether he desires to be dealt with summarily or to be tried by a district court-martial, and if the soldier elects to be tried by a district court-martial the commanding officer shall take steps for bringing him to trial by a district court-martial, but otherwise shall proceed to deal with the case summarily.

(*9*) Nothing in this section shall prejudice the power of a commanding officer to award such minor punishments as he is for the time being authorised to award, so, however, that a minor punishment shall not be awarded for any offence for which imprisonment exceeding seven days is awarded.

Courts-martial.

Courts-martial.

Regimental courts-martial.

47. (*1*) ANY officer authorised by or in pursuance of this Act to convene general and district courts-martial or either of them, also any commanding officer of a rank not below the rank of captain, also any officer of a rank not below the rank of captain when in command of two or more corps or portions of two or more corps, also on board a ship, a commanding officer of any rank may, without warrant and by virtue of this Act, convene a regimental court-martial for the trial of offences committed by soldiers under his command.

(*2*) Such court-martial shall consist of not less than three officers, each of whom must have held a commission during not less than one whole year.

(*3*) The convening officer shall appoint the president.

(*4*) The president of a regimental court-martial shall not be under the rank of captain, unless where the court-martial is held on the line of march, or on board any ship, or unless, in the opinion of the convening officer, such opinion to be expressed in the order convening the court and to be conclusive, a captain is not, with due regard to the public service, available, in any of which cases an officer of any rank may be president.

(*5*) A regimental court-martial shall not try an officer, nor award the punishment of death or penal servitude, or of imprisonment in excess of forty-two days, or of discharge with ignominy; but, subject as aforesaid, and save as in this Act specially mentioned, any offence under this Act committed by a person subject to military law, and triable by court-martial, may be tried and punished by a regimental court-martial.

General and district courts-martial.

48. THE following rules are enacted with respect to general courts-martial and district courts-martial:

(1) A general court-martial shall be convened by Her Majesty, or some officer deriving authority to convene a general court-martial immediately or mediately from Her Majesty: *Courts-martial.*

(2) A district court-martial shall be convened by an officer authorised to convene general courts-martial, or some officer deriving authority to convene a district court-martial from an officer authorised to convene general courts-martial:

(3) A general court-martial shall consist in the United Kingdom, India, Malta, and Gibraltar of not less than nine and elsewhere of not less than five officers, each of whom must have held a commission during not less than three whole years, and of whom not less than five must be of a rank not below that of captain:

(4) A district court-martial shall consist of not less than three officers, each of whom must have held a commission during not less than two whole years:

(5) The minimum number mentioned in this section for a general or a district court-martial shall be the legal minimum for that court-martial:

(6) A district court-martial shall not try a person subject to military law as an officer, nor award the punishment of death or penal servitude; but, subject as aforesaid, any offence under this Act committed by a person subject to military law, and triable by court-martial, may be tried and punished by either a general or district court-martial:

(7) An officer under the rank of captain shall not be a member of a court-martial for the trial of a field officer:

(8) Sentence of death shall not be passed on any prisoner without the concurrence of two-thirds at the least of the officers serving on the court-martial by which he is tried:

(9) The president of a court-martial, whether general or district, shall be appointed by order of the authority convening the court, but he shall not be under the rank of field officer, unless the officer convening the court is under that rank, or unless in the opinion of the officer who convenes the court, such opinion to be expressed in the order convening the court, and to be conclusive, a field officer is not, with due regard to the public service, available, in either of which cases an officer not below the rank of captain may be the president of such court-martial, and he shall not be under the rank of captain, except in the case of a district court-martial,

Courts-martial.

where in the opinion of the officer who convenes the court, such opinion to be expressed in the order convening the court, and to be conclusive, a captain is not, having due regard to the public service, available.

Field general courts-martial.

49. (*1*) WHERE a complaint is made to any officer in command of any detachment or portion of troops in any country beyond the seas, or to the commanding officer of any corps or portion of a corps on active service, or to any officer in immediate command of a body of forces on active service, that an offence has been committed by any person subject to military law,

then, if in the opinion of such officer it is not practicable that such offence should be tried by an ordinary general court-martial, it shall be lawful for him, although not authorised to convene general courts-martial to convene a court-martial, in this Act referred to as a field general court-martial, for the trial of the person charged with such offence, provided as follows:

(*a*) An officer in command of a detachment or portion of troops not on active service shall not convene a field general court-martial for the trial of any person, unless that person is under his command, nor unless the offence with which the person is charged is an offence against the property or person of an inhabitant of, or resident in, the country in which the offence is alleged to have been committed;

(*b*) A field general court-martial shall consist of not less than three officers, unless the officer convening the same is of opinion that three officers are not available, having due regard to the public service, in which case the court-martial may consist of two officers;

(*c*) The convening officer may preside, but he shall, whenever he deems it practicable, appoint another officer as president, who may be of any rank, but shall, if practicable in the opinion of the convening officer, be not below the rank of captain;

(*d*) Where a field general court-martial consists of less than three officers, the sentence shall not exceed such summary punishment as is allowed by this Act, or imprisonment.

(*2*) Section forty-eight of this Act shall not apply to a field general court-martial, but sentence of death shall not be passed on any prisoner by a field general court-martial without the concurrence of all the members.

(*3*) A field general court-martial may, notwithstanding the restrictions enacted by this Act in respect of the trial by court-martial of civil offences within the meaning of this Act, try any person subject to military law who is under the command of the convening officer, and is charged with any such offence as is mentioned in this section, and may award for such offence any sentence which a general court-martial is competent to award for such offence; *Courts-martial.*

Provided always, that no sentence of any such court-martial shall be executed until confirmed as provided by this Act.

50. (*1*) THE officers sitting on a court-martial may belong to the same or different corps, or may be unattached to any corps, and may try persons belonging or attached to any corps. **Courts-martial in general.**

(*2*) The officer who convened a court-martial shall not, save as is otherwise expressly provided by this Act, sit on that court-martial.

(*3*) Any of the following persons, that is to say, a prosecutor or witness for the prosecution of any prisoner, or the commanding officer of the prisoner within the meaning of the provisions of this Act which relate to dealing with a case summarily, or the officer who investigated the charges on which a prisoner is arraigned, shall not, save in the case of a field general court-martial, sit on the court-martial for the trial of such prisoner, nor shall he act as judge advocate at such court-martial.

51. (*1*) A PRISONER about to be tried by any court-martial may object, for any reasonable cause, to any member of the court, including the president, whether appointed to serve thereon originally or to fill a vacancy caused by the retirement of an officer objected to, so that the court may be constituted of officers to whom the prisoner makes no reasonable objection. **Challenges by prisoner.**

(*2*) Every objection made by a prisoner to any officer shall be submitted to the other officers appointed to form the court.

(*3*) If the objection is to the president, such objection, if allowed by one-third or more of the other officers appointed to form the court, shall be allowed, and the court shall adjourn for the purpose of the appointment of another president.

(*4*) If an objection to the president is allowed, the authority convening the court shall appoint another president, subject to the same right of the prisoner to object.

(*5*) If the objection is to a member other than the president, and is allowed by one-half or more of the votes of the officers entitled to vote, the objection shall be allowed, and the member objected to shall retire, and his vacancy may be filled in the prescribed manner by another officer, subject to the same right of the prisoner to object.

(*6*) In order to enable a prisoner to avail himself of his privilege of objecting to any officer, the names of the officers appointed to form the court shall be read over in the hearing of the prisoner on their first assembling, and before they are sworn, and he shall be asked whether he objects to any of such

Courts-martial

officers, and a like question shall be repeated in respect of any officer appointed to serve in lieu of a retiring officer.

Administration of oaths.

52. (*1*) An oath shall be administered by the prescribed person to every member of every court-martial before the commencement of the trial in the following form; that is to say,

'You do swear, that you will well and 'truly try the prisoner [*or* prisoners] before the court according to the evidence 'and that you will duly administer justice according to the Army Act now in 'force, without partiality, favour or affection, and you do further swear that you 'will not divulge the sentence of the court until it is duly confirmed, and you 'do further swear that you will not on any account at any time whatsoever dis-'close or discover the vote or opinion of any particular member of this court-'martial unless thereunto required in due course of law. So help you GOD.'

(*2*) An oath in the prescribed form or forms shall be administered by the prescribed person to the judge advocate or person officiating as judge advocate (if any) and also to every officer in attendance on a court-martial for the purpose of instruction (if any) and also to every short-hand writer (if any) in attendance on the court-martial.

(*3*) Every witness before a court-martial shall be examined on oath which the president or other prescribed person shall administer in the prescribed form.

(*4*) If a person by this Act required either as a member of, or person in attendance on, or witness before a court-martial or otherwise in respect of a court-martial, to take an oath, objects to take an oath or is objected to as incompetent to take an oath, the court if satisfied of the sincerity of the objection, or, where the competence of the person to take an oath is objected to, of the oath having no binding effect on the conscience of such person, shall permit such person instead of being sworn to make a solemn declaration in the prescribed form, and for the purposes of this Act such solemn declaration shall be deemed to be an oath.

Procedure.

53. (*1*) If a court-martial after the commencement of the trial is by death or otherwise reduced below the legal minimum, it shall be dissolved.

(*2*) If after the commencement of the trial the president dies or is otherwise unable to attend, and the court is not reduced below the legal minimum, the convening authority may appoint the senior member of the court, if of sufficient rank, to be president, and the trial shall proceed accordingly; but if he is not of sufficient rank the court shall be dissolved.

(*3*) If, on account of the illness of the prisoner before the finding, it is impossible to continue the trial, a court-martial shall be dissolved.

(*4*) Where a court-martial is dissolved under the foregoing provisions of this section the prisoner may be tried again. *Courts-martial.*

(*5*) The president of any court-martial may, on any deliberation amongst the members, cause the court to be cleared of all other persons.

(*6*) The court may adjourn from time to time.

(*7*) The court may also, where necessary, view any place.

(*8*) In the case of an equality of notes on the finding the prisoner shall be deemed to be acquitted. In the case of an equality of votes on the sentence, or any question arising after the commencement of the trial except the finding, the president shall have a second or casting vote.

(*9*) When a court-martial recommend a prisoner to mercy, such recommendation shall be attached to and form part of the proceedings of the court, and shall be promulgated and communicated to the prisoner, together with the finding and sentence.

Confirmation, revision, and approval of sentences.

54. (*1*) The following authorities shall have power to confirm the findings and sentences of courts-martial; that is to say,

(*a*) In the case of a regimental court-martial the convening officer or officer having authority to convene such a court-martial at the date of the submission of the finding and sentence thereof:

(*b*) In the case of a general court-martial, Her Majesty, or some officer deriving authority to confirm the findings and sentences of general courts-martial immediately or mediately from Her Majesty:

(*c*) In the case of a district court-martial an officer authorised to convene general courts-martial or some officer deriving authority to confirm the findings and sentences of district courts-martial from an officer authorised to convene general courts-martial:

(*d*) In the case of a field general court-martial, an officer authorised to confirm the findings and sentences of general courts-martial for the trial of offences in the force of which the detachment or portion of troops under the command of the convening officer forms part, or, where the offence was committed on active service, any such officer as may under the rules made in pursuance of this Act be authorised to confirm the findings and sentences of the field general court-martial awarding the sentence: Provided that a sentence of death or penal servitude awarded by a field general court-martial shall not be carried into effect unless or until it has been confirmed by the general or field officer commanding the force with which the prisoner is present at the date of his sentence.

Courts-martial.

(*2*) The authority having power to confirm the finding and sentence of a court-martial may send back such finding and sentence or either of them for revision once, but not more than once, and it shall not be lawful for the court on any revision to receive any additional evidence; and where the finding only is sent back for revision, the court shall have power without any direction to revise the sentence also. In no case shall the authority recommend the increase of a sentence nor shall the court-martial on revisal of the sentence, either in obedience to the recommendation of an authority, or for any other reason, have the power to increase the sentence awarded.

(*3*) The finding of acquittal whether on all or some of the offences with which the prisoner is charged shall not require confirmation or be subject to be revised and if it relates to the whole of the offences shall be pronounced at once in open court and the prisoner shall be discharged.

(*4*) A member of a court-martial shall not have authority to confirm the finding or sentence of that court-martial, and where a member of a court-martial becomes confirming officer he shall refer the finding and sentence of the court-martial to a superior authority competent to confirm the findings and sentences of the like description of courts-martial, and that authority shall, for the purposes of this Act, be deemed to be in that instance the confirming authority; and where a court-martial is held in a colony, and there is no such superior authority in that colony, the governor of that colony shall have power to confirm the finding and sentence of such court-martial in like manner in all respects as if he were such superior authority as above mentioned : Provided that where a member of a field general court-martial trying a prisoner would but for his being a member of the court have power to confirm the finding and sentence of the court, and is of opinion that it is not practicable, having due regard to the public service, to delay the case for the purpose of referring it to any other officer, he may confirm the finding and sentence.

(*5*) An officer having authority to confirm the finding and sentence of a court-martial may withhold his confirmation wholly or partly, and refer such finding and sentence or the part not confirmed to any superior authority competent to confirm the findings and sentences of the like description of courts-martial, and that authority shall for the purposes of this Act be deemed to be in that instance and to the extent of such reference the confirming authority.

(*6*) Subject to the provisions of this Act with respect to the finding of acquittal, the finding and sentence of a court-martial shall not be valid except in so far as the same may be confirmed by an authority authorised to confirm the same.

(7) Sentence of death when passed in a colony shall not unless passed in respect of an offence committed on active service be carried into effect, unless, in addition to the confirmation otherwise required by this Act, it is approved by the governor of the colony. *Courts-martial.*

(8) Sentence of death when passed in India in respect of the offence of treason or murder shall not (except where the offence was committed on active service) be carried into effect, unless in addition to the confirmation otherwise required by this Act it is approved by the Governor General.

(9) When a person subject to military law is convicted of manslaughter or rape or any other civil offence under the section of this Act relating to the trial by court-martial of civil offences, and is sentenced to penal servitude, such sentence shall not be carried into execution unless, in addition to the confirmation otherwise required by this Act, it is approved, if the offender has been tried in India, by the Governor General, or, if he has been tried in a colony, by the governor of the colony.

55. [*Rep.* 56 & 57 *Vict., c.* 4., *s.* 9 (8).]

Conviction of less offence permissible on charge of greater.

56. (1) A PRISONER charged before a court-martial with stealing may be found guilty of embezzlement or of fraudulently misapplying money or property.

(2) A prisoner charged before a court-martial with embezzlement may be found guilty of stealing or fraudulently misapplying money or property.

(3) A prisoner charged before a court-martial with desertion may be found guilty of attempting to desert or of being absent without leave.

(4) A prisoner charged before a court-martial with attempting to desert may be found guilty of desertion or of being absent without leave.

(5) A prisoner charged before a court-martial with any other offence under this Act may, on failure of proof of an offence being committed under circumstances involving a higher degree of punishment, be found guilty of the same offence as being committed under circumstances involving a less degree of punishment.

Execution of Sentence.

Execution of Sentence. Commutation and remission of sentences.

57. (1) THE confirming authority may, when confirming the sentence of any court-martial, mitigate or remit the punishment thereby awarded, or commute such punishment for any less punishment or punishments to which the offender might have been sentenced by the said court-martial, or if such punishment is death, awarded for the offence of murder, then for penal servitude or such less punishment as is in this Act mentioned. The confirming authority may also suspend for such time as seems expedient the execution of a sentence.

Execution of Sentence.

(2) When a sentence passed by a court-martial has been confirmed, the following authorities shall have power to mitigate or remit the punishment thereby awarded, or to commute such punishment for any less punishment or punishments to which the offender might have been sentenced by the said court-martial, or, if such punishment is death, awarded for the offence of murder, then for penal servitude or such less punishment as is in this Act mentioned; that is to say,

(*a*) As respects persons undergoing sentence in any place whatever, Her Majesty or the Commander-in-Chief or the officer commanding the district or station where the prisoner subject to such punishment may for the time being be, or any prescribed officer; and

(*b*) As respects persons undergoing sentences in India, the Commander-in-Chief of the forces in India, or such officer as the Commander-in-Chief of the forces in India, with the approval of the Governor-General of India in Council may appoint; and

(*c*) As respects persons undergoing sentences in any colony, the officer commanding the forces in that colony; and

(*d*) As respects persons undergoing sentences in any place not in the United Kingdom, India, or a colony, the officer commanding the forces in such place.

(3) Provided that the power given by this section shall not be exercised by an officer holding a command inferior to that of the authority confirming the sentence, unless such officer is authorised by such confirming authority or other superior military authority to exercise such power.

(4) An authority having power under this section to mitigate, remit, or commute any punishment may, if it seem fit, do all or any of those things in respect of a person subject to such punishment.

(5) The provisions of this Act with respect to an original sentence of penal servitude or imprisonment shall apply to a sentence of penal servitude or imprisonment imposed by way of commutation.

Effect of sentence of penal servitude.

58. When a person subject to military law is convicted by a court-martial, whether in the United Kingdom or elsewhere, either within or without Her Majesty's dominions, and is sentenced to penal servitude, such conviction and sentence shall be of the same effect as if such person (in this Act referred to as a military convict) had been convicted in the United Kingdom of an offence punishable by penal servitude and sentenced to penal servitude by a competent civil court, and all enactments relating to a person sentenced to penal servitude by a competent civil court shall, so far as circumstances admit, apply accordingly.

(*Secs. 59-60.*)

Execution of Sentence.

Execution of sentences of penal servitude passed in the United Kingdom.

59. (*1*) WHERE a sentence of penal servitude is passed by a court-martial in the United Kingdom, the military convict on whom such sentence has been passed shall, as soon as practicable, be transferred to a penal servitude prison to undergo his sentence according to law, and until so transferred shall be kept in military custody.

(*2*) The order of the committing authority (hereafter in this section mentioned) shall be a sufficient warrant for his transfer to a penal servitude prison.

(*3*) At any time before his arrival at a penal servitude prison the discharging authority (hereafter in this section mentioned) may by order discharge the military convict.

(*4*) Any one or more of the following officers shall be the committing authority for the purposes of this section, namely,—

(*a*) The Commander-in-Chief,

(*b*) The Adjutant General,

(*c*) The commanding officer of the military convict, and

(*d*) Any other prescribed officer.

(*5*) Any one of the following officers shall be the discharging authority for the purposes of this section, namely,—

(*a*) The Commander-in-Chief,

(*b*) The Adjutant General, and

(*c*) Any other prescribed officer.

Execution of sentences of penal servitude passed in India or a colony.

60. (*1*) WHERE a sentence of penal servitude is passed by a court-martial in India or any colony, the military convict on whom such sentence has been passed shall, as soon as practicable, be transferred to a penal servitude prison to undergo his sentence according to law.

(*2*) The order of the committing authority (hereafter in this section mentioned) shall be a sufficient warrant for his transfer to a penal servitude prison.

(*3*) The military convict during the period which intervenes between the passing of his sentence and his arrival at the penal servitude prison (in this section referred to as the term of his intermediate custody) shall be deemed to be in legal custody.

(*4*) The military convict during his term of intermediate custody may be kept in military custody or in civil custody, or partly in one description of custody and partly in the other, and may from time to time be transferred from military custody to civil custody and from civil custody to military custody as occasion may require, and may, during his conveyance from place to place, or when on board ship or otherwise, be subjected to such restraint as is necessary for his detention and removal.

Execution of Sentence.

(*5*) "Civil custody" for the purposes of this section, means custody in any authorised prison; nevertheless, where it is not practicable to place the military convict in an authorised prison, he may, by way of civil custody, be confined temporarily in any other prison with the assent of the authority having jurisdiction over that prison.

(*6*) The military convict whilst in any prison in which he may legally be placed may be dealt with, in respect of hard labour and otherwise, according to the rules of that prison.

(*7*) An order of the removing authority (hereafter in this section mentioned) shall be a sufficient authority for the transfer of the military convict from military custody to civil custody and from civil custody to military custody, and his removal from place to place, and for his detention in civil custody, and generally for dealing with such convict in such manner as may be thought expedient during the term of his intermediate custody.

(*8*) The removing authority during the term of the intermediate custody of the military convict may from time to time by order provide for his being brought before a court-martial, or any civil court, either as a witness or for trial or otherwise, and an order of such authority shall be a sufficient warrant for the delivering him into military custody, and detaining him in custody until he can be returned, and for returning him to the place from whence he is brought, or to such other place as may be determined by the removing authority.

(*9*) Any directions of the removing authority relating to the mode in which the military convict is to be dealt with during the term of his intermediate custody may be contained in the same order or in several orders; and if the orders are more than one, they may be by different officers and at different times.

(*10*) At any time before the military convict arrives at a penal servitude prison the discharging authority (hereafter in this section mentioned) may by order discharge the military convict.

(*11*) Any one or more of the following officers shall be the committing authority for the purposes of this section; that is to say,

(*a*) In India—

(i) The Commander-in-Chief of the forces in India;

* * * * *

(iii) The Adjutant General in India; and

* * * * *

(*b*) In a colony, the officer commanding the forces in that colony; and

(*c*) In any case, whether in India or in a colony, the prescribed officer.

(*12*) Any one or more of the following officers shall be the removing authority for the purposes of this section; that is to say, *Execution of Sentence.*

(*a*) Any officer in this section named as the committing authority; also

(*b*) The officer commanding the military district or station where the military convict may for the time being be; also

(*c*) Any other prescribed officer.

(*13*) Any of the following officers shall be the discharging authority for the purposes of this section; that is to say,

(*a*) The officer who confirmed the sentence; also

(*b*) Any officer in this section named as the committing authority; also

(*c*) Any other prescribed officer.

61. (*1*) Where a sentence of penal servitude is passed by a court-martial in any foreign country, the military convict on whom such sentence has been passed shall, as soon as practicable, be transferred to a penal servitude prison for the purpose of undergoing his sentence according to law, and, until so transferred, may be kept in military custody. Execution of sentences of penal servitude passed in a foreign country.

(*2*) The order of the committing authority (hereafter in this section mentioned) shall be a sufficient warrant for the transfer of the military convict to a penal servitude prison.

(*3*) If at any time before his arrival in the United Kingdom the military convict is brought into India or any colony, he may be dealt with by the competent military authority in India or such colony in the same manner in all respects as if he had been there sentenced by court-martial to penal servitude.

(*4*) The military convict may, at any time before he arrives at any place in the United Kingdom, India, or any colony, be discharged by the discharging authority (hereafter in this section mentioned) having jurisdiction in any place where the military convict may for the time being be.

(*5*) Any one or more of the following officers shall be the committing authority for the purposes of this section; that is to say,

(*a*) The officer commanding the army or force with which the military convict was serving at the time of his being sentenced;

(*b*) The officer who confirmed the sentence of the court;

(*c*) Any other prescribed officer.

(*6*) Any committing authority under this section shall also be the discharging authority for the purposes of this section.

Execution of Sentence.

General provisions applicable to penal servitude.

62. (*1*) A PENAL servitude prison for the purposes of the provisions of this Act relating to penal servitude means any prison or place in which a prisoner sentenced to penal servitude by a civil court in the United Kingdom can for the time being be confined, either permanently or temporarily.

(*2*) "An authorised prison" for the purposes of the provisions of this Act relating to penal servitude means any prison in India or any colony which the Governor General of India or the governor of such colony may, with the concurrence of a Secretary of State, have appointed as a prison in which military convicts may, during the period of their intermediate custody, be confined.

(*3*) After a military convict has arrived at the penal servitude prison to undergo his sentence, he shall be dealt with in the like manner as an ordinary civil prisoner under sentence of penal servitude.

Execution of sentences of imprisonment.

63. (*1*) WHERE a sentence of imprisonment is passed by court-martial or a commanding officer, the person on whom such sentence has been passed (in the provisions of this Act relating to imprisonment referred to as a military prisoner) shall undergo the term of his imprisonment either in military custody or in a public prison or partly in one way and partly in the other.

(*2*) The order of the committing authority hereafter mentioned shall be a sufficient warrant for the transfer of a military prisoner to a public prison.

(*3*) A military prisoner while in a public prison shall be confined, kept to hard labour, and otherwise dealt with in the like manner as an ordinary prisoner under a like sentence of imprisonment; and where the hospital or place for the reception of sick prisoners in such prison is detached from the prison may be detained in such hospital or place and conveyed to and from the same as circumstances require.

(*4*) A military prisoner during his conveyance from place to place, or when on board ship or otherwise, may be subjected to such restraint as is necessary for his detention and removal.

(*5*) The discharging authority hereafter mentioned may, at any time during the period of a military prisoner undergoing his imprisonment, by order discharge the prisoner.

(*6*) The committing authority or any other prescribed authority may at any time by order remove a military prisoner from one public prison to another, so that he be not removed from a prison in the United Kingdom to a prison elsewhere.

(*7*) The removing authority hereafter mentioned may, at any time during the period of the military prisoner undergoing his sentence in a public prison, from time to time, by order provide for his being brought before a court-martial, or any civil court, either as a witness, or for trial or otherwise, and an order of such authority shall be a sufficient warrant for delivering him into military custody and detaining him in custody until he can be returned and for returning him to the place from whence he is brought, or to such other place as may be determined by the removing authority.

Execution of Sentence.

Supplemental provisions as to sentences of imprisonment passed or being undergone in the United Kingdom

64. Where a sentence of imprisonment is passed or is being undergone in the United Kingdom, then for the purposes of the provisions of this Act relating to imprisonment—

(1) The expression "public prison" means any prison in the United Kingdom in which offenders sentenced by a civil court to imprisonment can for the time being be confined:

(2) Any one or more of the following officers shall be the committing authority:

(*a*) The Commander-in-Chief;
(*b*) The Adjutant General;
(*c*) The officer who confirmed the sentence;
(*d*) The commanding officer of the military prisoner; and
(*e*) Any other prescribed officer:

(3) Any one of the following officers shall be the discharging authority:

(*a*) The Commander-in-Chief;
(*b*) The Adjutant General;
(*c*) The officer commanding the military district in which the prisoner may be;
(*d*) The officer who confirmed the sentence;
(*e*) Any other prescribed officer; also
(*f*) Where the sentence was passed by the commanding officer, the commanding officer.

(4) Any one or more of the following officers shall be the removing authority:

(*a*) The Commander-in-Chief;
(*b*) The Adjutant General;
(*c*) The officer commanding the military district in which the prisoner may be;
(*d*) Any other prescribed officer; also
(*e*) Where the sentence was passed by the commanding officer, the commanding officer.

Execution of Sentence.

Supplemental provision as to sentences of imprisonment passed or being undergone in India or a colony.

65. WHERE a sentence of imprisonment is passed or being undergone in India or any colony, then for the purposes of the provisions of this Act relating to imprisonment—

(1) The expression "public prison" means any of the following prisons; that is to say—

(*a*) where the sentence was passed in India, any authorised prison in India;

(*b*) where the sentence was passed in a colony, any authorised prison in that colony;

(*c*) any such authorised prison in any part of Her Majesty's dominions other than that in which the sentence was passed as may be prescribed; and

(*d*) any public prison in the United Kingdom as above defined for the purpose of the provisions of this Act relating to imprisonment in the United Kingdom:

(2) "Authorised prison" means any prison in India or any colony which the Governor General of India or the governor of such colony, with the concurrence of the Secretary of State, may have appointed as a prison in which military prisoners may be confined.

(3) A military prisoner may temporarily be confined in a prison not a public prison, with the assent of the authority having jurisdiction over such prison And a military prisoner, who is to undergo his sentence in the United Kingdom until he reaches a prison in the United Kingdom, in which he is to undergo his sentence, may be kept in military custody or in civil custody, and partly in one description of custody and partly in the other, and may from time to time be transferred from military custody to civil custody, and from civil custody to military custody, as occasion may require;

(4) Any one or more of the following officers shall be the committing authority; that is to say,

(*a*) In India—

(i) The Commander-in-Chief of the forces in India;

* * * * *

(iii) The Adjutant General in India; and

* * * * *

(*b*) In a colony, the officer commanding the forces in that colony; and

(*c*) In any case, whether in India or in a colony—

(i) The officer who confirmed the sentence ;

(ii) The commanding officer of the military prisoner; and

(iii) Any other prescribed officer.

(5) Any of the following officers shall be the discharging authority: *Execution of Sentence.*

(*a*) The officer commanding the military district or station in which the prisoner may be;

(*b*) Any officer in this section named as a committing authority, with this exception, that the commanding officer shall only be a discharging authority where the sentence was passed by a commanding officer; and

(*c*) Any other prescribed officer.

(6) Any one or more of the following officers shall be the removing authority:

(*a*) Any officer in this section named as a committing authority;

(*b*) The officer commanding the military district or station where the prisoner may be; and

(*c*) Any other prescribed officer.

66. Where a sentence of imprisonment is passed by a court-martial or commanding officer in any foreign country, then if and as soon as the military prisoner on whom such sentence has been passed is brought into the United Kingdom or India, or any colony, the provisions of this Act shall apply in the same manner in all respects as if the sentence of imprisonment had been passed in the United Kingdom, India, or any colony, as the case may be, with this addition, that the officer commanding the army or force to which the military prisoner belonged at the time of his being sentenced shall also be deemed to be a committing authority. **Supplemental provision as to sentences of imprisonment passed in a foreign country.**

67. (*1*) The competent military authority (hereafter in this section mentioned) may give directions for the delivery into military custody of any military prisoner for the time being undergoing his sentence of imprisonment, and the removal of such prisoner, whether with his corps or separately, to any place beyond the seas where the corps, or any part thereof, to which for the time being he belongs, is serving or under orders to serve. **Removal of prisoner to place where corps is serving.**

(*2*) The directions of such competent military authority, or an order of the removing authority issued in pursuance of such directions, shall be sufficient authority for the removal of such prisoner from the prison in which he is confined, and for his conveyance in military custody to any place designated, and for his intermediate custody during such removal and conveyance.

(*3*) The competent military authority may further give directions for the discharge of the prisoner either conditionally or unconditionally at any time while he is in military custody under this section.

Execution of Sentence.

(4) For the purposes of this section any one or more of the following officers shall be the competent military authority:

(*a*) In the United Kingdom—

(i) The Commander-in-Chief;

(ii) The Adjutant General; and

(iii) Any other prescribed officer:

(*b*) In India—

(i) The Commander-in-Chief of the forces in India;

* * * *

(iii) The Adujtant General in India; and

* * * * *

(*c*) In a colony, the officer commanding the forces in that colony; and

(*d*) In any case, whether in India or in a colony, the prescribed officers.

Commencement of term of penal servitude or imprisonment.

68. (*1*) The term of penal servitude or imprisonment to which a person is sentenced by a court-martial, whether the sentence has been revised or not, and whether the prisoner is already undergoing sentence or not, shall be reckoned to commence on the day on which the original sentence and proceedings were signed by the president of the court-martial.

(*2*) An offender under this Act shall not be subject to imprisonment for more than two consecutive years, whether under one or more sentences.

Articles of War and Rules of Procedure.

MISCELLANEOUS.

Articles of War and Rules of Procedure.

Power of Her Majesty to make Articles of War.

69. It shall be lawful for Her Majesty to make Articles of War for the better government of officers and soldiers, and such Articles shall be judicially taken notice of by all judges and in all courts whatsoever: Provided that no person shall, by such Articles of War, be subject to suffer any punishment extending to life or limb, or to be kept in penal servitude, except for crimes which are by this Act expressly made liable to such punishment as aforesaid, or be subject, with reference to any crimes made punishable by this Act, to be punished in any manner which does not accord with the provisions of this Act.

Power of Her Majesty to make rules of procedure.

70. (*1*) Subject to the provisions of this Act Her Majesty may, by rule to be signified under the hand of a Secretary of State, from time to time make, and when made repeal, alter, or add to, provisions in respect of the following matters or any of them; that is to say,

(*a*) The assembly and procedure of courts of inquiry;

(*b*) The convening and constitution of courts-martial;

(*c*) The adjournment, dissolution, and sittings of courts-martial;

(*d*) The procedure to be observed in trials by court-martial;

(*e*) The confirmation and revision of the findings and sentences of courts-martial, and enabling the authority having power under section fifty-seven of this Act to commute sentences to substitute a valid sentence for an invalid sentence of a court-martial; *Articles of War and Rules of Procedure.*

(*f*) The carrying into effect sentences of courts-martial;

(*g*) The forms of orders to be made under the provisions of this Act relating to courts-martial, penal servitude, or imprisonment;

(*h*) Any matter in this Act directed to be prescribed;

(*i*) Any other matter or thing expedient or necessary for the purpose of carrying this Act into execution so far as relates to the investigation, trial, and punishment of offences triable or punishable by military law.

(*2*) Provided always, that no such rules shall contain anything contrary to or inconsistent with the provisions of this Act.

(*3*) All rules made in pursuance of this section shall be judicially noticed.

(*4*) All rules made in pursuance of this section shall be laid before Parliament as soon as practicable after they are made, if Parliament be then sitting, and if Parliament be not then sitting, as soon as practicable after the beginning of the then next session of Parliament.

Command.

Command.

71. (*1*) For the purpose of removing doubts as to the powers of command vested or to be vested in officers and others belonging to Her Majesty's forces, it is hereby declared that Her Majesty may, in such manner as to Her Majesty may from time to time seem meet, make regulations as to the persons to be invested as officers, or otherwise, with command over Her Majesty's forces, or any part thereof, or any person belonging thereto and as to the mode in which such command is to be exercised; provided that command shall not be given to any person over a person superior in rank to himself. Removal of doubts as to military command.

(*2*) Nothing in this section shall be deemed to be in derogation of any power otherwise vested in Her Majesty.

Inquiry as to and Confession of Desertion.

Inquiry as to and Confession of Desertion.

72. (*1*) When any soldier has been absent without leave from his duty for a period of twenty-one days, a court of inquiry may as soon as practicable be assembled, and inquire in the prescribed manner on oath or solemn declaration (which such court is hereby authorised to administer) respecting the fact of such absence, and the deficiency (if any) in the arms, ammunition, equipments, instruments, regimental necessaries, or clothing of the soldier, and if satisfied of the fact of such soldier having absented himself without leave or Inquiry by court on absence of soldier.

Inquiry as to and Confession of Desertion.

other sufficient cause, the court shall declare such absence and the period thereof, and the said deficiency, if any, and the commanding officer of the absent soldier shall enter in the regimental books a record of the declaration of such court.

(*2*) If the absent soldier does not afterwards surrender or is not apprehended, such record shall have the legal effect of a conviction by court-martial for desertion.

Confession by soldier of desertion or fraudulent enlistment.

73. (*1*) WHERE a soldier signs a confession that he has been guilty of desertion or of fraudulent enlistment, a competent military authority may, by the order dispensing with his trial by a court-martial, or by any subsequent order, award the same forfeitures and the same deductions from pay (if any) as a court-martial could award for the said offence, or as are consequential upon conviction by a court-martial for the said offence, except such of them as may be mentioned in the order.

(*2*) If upon any such confession, evidence of the truth or falsehood of such confession cannot then be conveniently obtained, the record of such confession, countersigned by the commanding officer of the soldier, shall be entered in the regimental books, and such soldier shall continue to do duty in the corps in which he may then be serving, or in any other corps to which he may be transferred, until he is discharged or transferred to the reserve, or until legal proof can be obtained of the truth or falsehood of such confession.

(*3*) The competent military authority for the purposes of this section means the Commander-in-Chief or Adjutant General, or any general or other officer commanding a military district, or, in the case of India, the Commander-in-Chief of the forces in India, or such officer as the Commander-in-Chief of the forces in India, with the approval of the Governor General of India in Council, may appoint, and in the case of a colony and elsewhere the general or other officer commanding the forces, subject in the case of India, or a colony, or elsewhere, to any directions given by the Commander-in-Chief.

Provost Marshal.

Provost Marshal.

Provost Marshal.

74. (*1*) FOR the prompt repression of all offences which may be committed abroad, provost marshals with assistants may from time to time be appointed by the general order of the general officer commanding a body of forces.

(*2*) A provost marshal or his assistants may at any time arrest and detain for trial persons subject to military law committing offences, and may also carry into execution any punishments to be inflicted in pursuance of a court-martial, but shall not inflict any punishment of his or their own authority.

Restitution of Stolen Property.

Restitution of Stolen Property.

Power as to restitution of stolen property.

75. (*1*) WHERE a person has been convicted by court-martial of having stolen, embezzled, received, knowing it to be stolen, or otherwise unlawfully obtained, any property, and the property or any part thereof is found in the possession of the offender, the authority confirming the finding and sentence of such court-martial, or the Commander-in-Chief, may order the property so found to be restored to the person appearing to be the lawful owner thereof.

(*2*) A like order may be made with respect to any property found in the possession of such offender, which appears to the confirming authority or Commander-in-Chief to have been obtained by the conversion or exchange of any of the property stolen, embezzled, received, or unlawfully obtained.

(*3*) Moreover where it appears to the confirming authority or Commander-in-Chief from the evidence given before the court-martial, that any part of the property stolen, embezzled, received, or unlawfully obtained was sold to or pawned with any person without any guilty knowledge on the part of the person purchasing or taking in pawn the property, the authority or Commander-in-Chief may, on the application of that person, and on the restitution of the said property to the owner thereof, order that out of the money (if any) found in the possession of the offender, a sum not exceeding the amount of the proceeds of the said sale or pawning shall be paid to the said person purchasing or taking in pawn.

(*4*) An order under this section shall not bar the right of any person, other than the offender, or any one claiming through him, to recover any property or money delivered or paid in pursuance of an order under this section from the person to whom the same is so delivered or paid.

PART II.

ENLISTMENT.

Period of Service.

Period of Service.

Limit of original enlistment.

76. A PERSON may be enlisted to serve Her Majesty as a soldier of the regular forces for a period of twelve years, or for such less period as may be from time to time fixed by Her Majesty, but not for any longer period, and the period for which a person enlists is in this Act referred to as the term of his original enlistment.

Terms of original enlistment.

77. THE original enlistment of a person under this Act shall be as follows, either—

(1) For the whole of the term of his original enlistment in army service; or

Period of Service.

(2) For such portion of the term of his original enlistment as may be from time to time fixed by a Secretary of State, and specified in the attestation paper, in army service, and for the residue of the said term in the reserve.

Change of conditions of service.

78. (*1*) A SECRETARY of State may from time to time, by general or special regulations, vary the conditions of service, so as to permit a soldier of the regular forces in army service, with his assent, either—

(*a*) To enter the reserve at once for the residue unexpired of the term of his original enlistment; or

(*b*) To extend his army service for all or any part of the residue unexpired of such term; or

(*c*) To extend the term of his original enlistment up to the period of twelve years.

(*2*) A Secretary of State may from time to time, by general or special regulations, vary the conditions of service so as to permit a man in the reserve, with his assent, to re-enter upon army service for all or any part of the residue unexpired of the term of his original enlistment, or for any period of time not exceeding twelve years in the whole from the date of his original enlistment.

Reckoning and forfeiture of service.

79. IN reckoning the service of a soldier of the regular forces for the purpose of discharge or of transfer to the reserve—

(1) The service shall begin to reckon from the date of his attestation; but

(2) Where a soldier of the regular forces has been guilty of any of the following offences:

(*a*) Desertion from Her Majesty's service, or

(*b*) Fraudulent enlistment,

then either upon his conviction by court-martial of the offence, or (if, having confessed the offence, he is liable to be tried) upon his trial being dispensed with by order of the competent military authority, the whole of his prior service shall be forfeited, and he shall be liable to serve as a soldier of the regular forces for the term of his original enlistment, reckoned from the date of such conviction or such order dispensing with trial, in like manner as if he had been originally attested at that date:

Provided that a Secretary of State may restore all or any part of the service forfeited under this section to any soldier who may perform good and faithful service, or may otherwise be deemed by such Secretary of State to merit such restoration of service, or may be recommended for such restoration of service by a court-martial. *Period of Service.*

Proceedings for Enlistment.

Proceedings for Enlistment.

80. (*1*) Every person authorised to enlist recruits in the regular forces (in this Act referred to as the "recruiter") shall give to every person offering to enlist a notice in the form for the time being authorised by a Secretary of State, stating the general requirements of attestation and the general conditions of the contract to be entered into by the recruit, and directing such person to appear before a justice of the peace either forthwith or at the time and place therein mentioned. Mode of enlistment and attestation.

(*2*) Upon the appearance before a justice of the peace of a person offering to enlist, the justice shall ask him whether he has been served with and understands the notice and whether he assents to be enlisted, and shall not proceed with the enlistment if he considers the recruit under the influence of liquor.

(*3*) If he does not appear before a justice, or on appearing does not assent to be enlisted, no further proceedings shall be taken.

(*4*) If he assents to be enlisted—

(*a*) The justice, after cautioning such person that if he makes any false answer to the questions read to him he will be liable to be punished as provided by this Act, shall read or cause to be read to him the questions set forth in the attestation paper for the time being authorised by a Secretary of State, and shall take care that such person understands each question so read, and after ascertaining that the answer of such person to each question has been duly recorded opposite the same in the attestation paper, shall require him to make and sign the declaration as to the truth of those answers set forth in the said paper, and shall then administer to him the oath of allegiance contained in the said paper:

(*b*) Upon signing the declaration and taking the oath, such person shall be deemed to be enlisted as a soldier of Her Majesty's regular forces:

(*c*) The justice shall attest by his signature, in manner required by the said paper, the fulfilment of the requirements as to attesting a recruit, and shall deliver the attestation paper, duly dated, to the recruiter:

Proceedings for Enlistment.

(*d*) The fee for the attestation of a recruit, and for all acts and things incidental thereto, shall be one shilling and no more, and shall be paid to the clerk of the justice:

(*e*) The officer who finally approves of a recruit for service shall, at his request, furnish him with a certified copy of his attestation paper.

(*5*) The date at which the recruit signs the declaration and takes the oath in this section in that behalf mentioned shall be deemed to be the date of the attestation of such recruit.

(*6*) The competent military authority, if satisfied that there is any error in the attestation paper of a recruit, may cause the recruit to attend before some justice of the peace, and that justice, if satisfied that such error exists, and is not so material as to render it just that the recruit should be discharged, may amend the error in the attestation paper, and the paper as amended shall thereupon be deemed as valid as if the matter of the amendment had formed part of the original matter of such paper.

(*7*) Where the regulations of a Secretary of State under this part of this Act require duplicate attestation papers to be signed and attested, this section shall apply to both such duplicates, and in the event of any amendment of an attestation paper the amendment shall be made in both of the duplicate attestation papers.

Power of recruit to purchase discharge.

81. If a recruit within three months after the date of his attestation pays for the use of Her Majesty a sum not exceeding ten pounds, he shall be discharged with all convenient speed, unless he claims such discharge during a period when soldiers in army service who otherwise would be transferred to the reserve are required by a proclamation of Her Majesty in pursuance of this Act to continue in army service, in which case he may be retained in Her Majesty's service during that period, and at the termination thereof shall, if he so require it, on the payment then of the said sum be discharged.

Appointment to Corps and Transfers.

Appointment to Corps and Transfers.

Enlistment for general service and appointment to corps.

82. (*1*) Recruits may, in pursuance of any general or special regulation from time to time made by a Secretary of State, be enlisted for service in particular corps of the regular forces, but save as is provided by such regulations, if any, recruits shall be enlisted for general service.

(*2*) The competent military authority shall as soon as practicable appoint a recruit, if enlisted for service in a particular corps, to that corps, and if enlisted for general service, to some corps of the regular forces.

Appointment to Corps and Transfers.

Effect of appointment to a corps and provision for transfer.

83. A SOLDIER of the regular forces, whether enlisted for general service or not, when once appointed to a corps, shall serve in that corps for the period of his army service, whether during the term of his original enlistment or during the period of such re-engagement as is in this Act mentioned, unless transferred under the following provisions:

(1) A soldier of the regular forces enlisted for general service may within three months after the date of his attestation be transferred to any corps of the regular forces of the same arm or branch of the service by order of the competent military authority.

(2) A soldier of the regular forces may at any time with his own consent be transferred by order of the competent military authority to any corps of the regular forces.

(3) Where a soldier of the regular forces is in pursuance of any of the foregoing provisions transferred to a corps in an arm or branch different from that in which he was previously serving, the competent military authority may by order vary the conditions of his service so as to correspond with the general conditions of service in the arm or branch to which he is transferred.

(4) A soldier of the regular forces in any branch of the service may be transferred by order of the competent military authority to any corps of the same branch which is serving in the United Kingdom in either of the following cases:

(*a*) When he has been invalided from service beyond the seas; or

(*b*) When, in the case of his corps or the part thereof in which he is serving being ordered on service beyond the seas, he is either unfit for such service by reason of his health, or is within two years from the end either of the period of his army service in the term of his original enlistment, or of such re-engagement as is in this Act mentioned.

(5) Where a soldier of the regular forces in any branch of the service, who was enlisted to serve part of the term of his original enlistment in the reserve, and has not extended his army service for the whole of that time, is on service beyond the seas, and at the time of his corps or the part thereof in which he is serving being ordered to another station or to return home has more than two years of his army service in the term of his original enlistment unexpired, he may be transferred by order of the competent military authority to any corps of the same branch which or a part of which is on service beyond the seas.

(6) Where a soldier of the regular forces has been transferred to serve, either as a warrant officer not holding an honorary commission, or on the staff,

Appointment to Corps and Transfers.

or in any corps not being a corps of infantry, cavalry, artillery, or engineers, he may by order of the competent military authority, either during the term of his original enlistment or during the period of his re-engagement, be removed from such service and transferred to any corps of the regular forces serving in the United Kingdom, or to any corps of the regular forces serving on the station beyond the seas on which he is serving at the time of his removal, or to the corps of the regular forces in which he was serving prior to such first-mentioned transfer, either in the rank he holds at the time of his removal or any lower rank.

(7) Where a soldier of the regular forces—

(*a*) Has been guilty of the offence of desertion from Her Majesty's service or of fraudulent enlistment, and has either been convicted of the same by a court-martial, or, having confessed the offence, is liable to be tried, but his trial has been dispensed with by order of the competent military authority; or

(*b*) Has been sentenced by a court-martial for any offence to a punishment not less than imprisonment for a term of six months,

such soldier shall be liable, in commutation wholly or partly of other punishment, to general service, and may from time to time be transferred to such corps of the regular forces as the competent military authority may from time to time order.

(8) A soldier of the regular forces delivered into military custody or committed by a court of summary jurisdiction in any part of Her Majesty's dominions as a deserter shall be liable to be transferred by order of the competent military authority to any corps of the regular forces near to the place where he is delivered or committed, or to any other corps to which the competent military authority think it desirable to transfer him, and to serve in the corps to which he is so transferred without prejudice to his subsequent trial and punishment.

Re-engagement and Prolongation of Service.

Re-engagement and Prolongation of Service.

Re-engagement of soldiers.

84. (*1*) Subject to any general or special regulations from time to time made by a Secretary of State, a soldier of the regular forces, if in army service, and after the expiration of nine years from the date of his original term of enlistment, may on the recommendation of his commanding officer, and with the approval of the competent military authority, be re-engaged for such further period of army service as will make up a total continuous period of twenty-one years of army service, reckoned from the date of his attestation, and inclusive of any period previously served in the reserve.

(*2*) A soldier of the regular forces during his period of re-engagement shall be liable to forfeit his previous serivce during such period of re-engagement in like manner as he is liable under this part of this Act during the term of his original enlistment. *Re-engagement and Prolongation of Service.*

(*3*) A soldier of the regular forces who so re-engages shall make before his commanding officer a declaration in accordance with the said regulations.

85. A SOLDIER of the regular forces who has completed, or will within one year complete, a total period of twenty-one years' service, inclusive of any period served in the reserve, may give notice to his commanding officer of his desire to continue in Her Majesty's service in the regular forces; and if the competent military authority approve he may be continued as a soldier of the regular forces in the same manner in all respects as if his term of service were still unexpired, except that he may claim his discharge at the expiration of any period of three months after he has given notice to his commanding officer of his wish to be discharged. Continuance in service after twenty-one years' service.

86. THE regulations from time to time made in pursuance of this part of this Act may, if it seems expedient, provide that a non-commissioned officer of the regular forces who extends his army service for the residue unexpired of his original term of enlistment shall have the right at his option to re-engage, under section eighty-four, and to continue his service under section eighty-five of this Act, or to do either of such things, subject, nevertheless, to the veto of the Secretary of State or other authority mentioned in the regulations, and to such other conditions as are specified in the regulations. Re-engagement and continuance of service of non-commissioned officers.

87. (*1*) WHERE the time at which a soldier of the regular forces would otherwise be entitled to be discharged occurs while a state of war exists between Her Majesty and any foreign power, or while such soldier is on service beyond the seas, or while soldiers in the reserve are required by a proclamation, in pursuance of the enactments relating to the calling out of the reserve on permanent service, to continue in or re-enter upon army service, the soldier may be detained, and his service may be prolonged for such further period, not exceeding twelve months, as the competent military authority may order; but at the expiration of that period, or any earlier period at which the competent military authority considers his services can be dispensed with, the soldier shall, as provided by this Act, be discharged with all convenient speed. Prolongation of service in certain cases.

(*2*) Where the time at which a soldier of the regular forces would otherwise be entitled to be transferred to the reserve occurs while a state of war exists between Her Majesty and any foreign power, the soldier may be detained in army service for such further period, not exceeding twelve months, as the competent military authority may order, but at the expiration of that period,

Re-engagement and Prolongation of Service.

or any earlier period at which the competent military authority considers his services can be dispensed with, the soldier shall with all convenient speed be sent to the United Kingdom for the purpose of being transferred to the reserve.

(*3*) If a soldier required under this section to be discharged or sent to the United Kingdom desires, while a state of war exists between Her Majesty and any foreign power, to continue in Her Majesty's service, and the competent military authority approve, he may agree to continue as a soldier of the regular forces in the same manner in all respects as if his term of service were still unexpired, except that he may claim his discharge at the end of such state of war, or, if it is so provided by such agreement, at the expiration of any period of three months after he has given notice to his commanding officer of his wish to be discharged.

(*4*) A soldier who so agrees to continue shall make before his commanding officer a declaration in accordance with any general or special regulations from time to time made by a Secretary of State.

In imminent national danger, Her Majesty may continue soldiers in army service or call out reserve for permanent service.

88. (*1*) It shall be lawful for Her Majesty in Council in case of imminent national danger or of great emergency, by proclamation, the occasion being first communicated to Parliament if Parliament be then sitting or if Parliament be not then sitting declared by the proclamation, to order that the soldiers who would otherwise be entitled in pursuance of the terms of their enlistment to be transferred to the reserve shall continue in army service.

(*2*) It shall be lawful for Her Majesty by any such proclamation to order a Secretary of State from time to time to give, and when given to revoke or vary, such directions as may seem necessary or proper for causing all or any of the soldiers mentioned in the proclamation to continue in army service.

(*3*) Every soldier for the time being required by or in pursuance of such directions to continue in army service shall continue to serve in army service for the same period for which he might be required to serve, if he had been transferred to the reserve and called out for permanent service by a proclamation of Her Majesty under the enactments relating to the reserve.

(*4*) Any man who has entered the reserve in pursuance of the terms of his enlistment may be called out for permanent service by a proclamation of Her Majesty under the enactments relating to the calling out of the reserve on permanent service.

Discharge and Transfer to Reserve Force.

Discharge and Transfer to Reserve Force.

Transfer of soldier to reserve when corps ordered abroad.

89. In the following cases; that is to say,

(1) Where a soldier of the regular forces has been invalided from service beyond the seas; or

(*Sec. 90.*)

(2) Where a corps to which a soldier of the regular forces belongs, or the part thereof in which he is serving is ordered on service beyond the seas, and the soldier is either unfit for such service by reason of his health, or is within two years of the end of the period of his army service in the term of his original enlistment, *Discharge and Transfer to Reserve Force.*

the competent military authority may by order transfer him to the reserve in like manner as if the period of his actual service were specified in his attestation paper as the portion of the term of his original enlistment which was to be spent in army service.

90. (*1*) Save as otherwise provided by this Act or the Acts relating to the reserve forces, every soldier of the regular forces upon the completion of the term of his original enlistment, or of the period of his re-engagement, shall be discharged with all convenient speed, but until so discharged shall be subject to this Act as a soldier of the regular forces. Discharged or transferred to reserve.

(*2*) Where a soldier of the regular forces enlisted in the United Kingdom is, when entitled to be discharged, serving beyond the seas, he shall, if he so requires, be sent to the United Kingdom, and in such case shall, with all convenient speed, be sent there free of expense, and on his arrival be discharged. If such soldier is permitted, at his request, to stay at the place where he is serving, he shall not afterwards have any claim to be sent at the public expense to the United Kingdom or elsewhere.

(*3*) Every soldier of the regular forces upon the completion of the period of his army service, if shorter than the term of his original enlistment, shall be transferred to the reserve, but until so transferred shall be subject to this Act as a soldier of the regular forces.

(*4*) Where a soldier of the regular forces, when entitled to be transferred to the reserve, is serving beyond the seas, he shall be sent to the United Kingdom free of expense with all convenient speed, and on his arrival shall be transferred to the reserve.

(*5*) A soldier of the regular forces who is discharged on the completion of the term of his original enlistment or his re-engagement, as mentioned in the second sub-section of this section, or is transferred to the reserve, shall be entitled to be conveyed free of cost from the place in the United Kingdom where he is discharged or transferred to the place in which he appears from his attestation paper to have been attested, or to any place at which he may at the time of his discharge or transfer decide to take up his residence, and to which he can be conveyed without greater cost. Provided that in the case of transfer to the reserve he shall not be entitled to be so conveyed to any place out of the United Kingdom.

(*Sec. 91.*)

Delivery of lunatic soldier on discharge with his wife or child at workhouse or of dangerous lunatic at asylum.

91. (*1*) A SECRETARY of State or any officer deputed by him for the purpose may, if he think proper, on account of a soldier's lunacy, cause any soldier of the regular forces on his discharge, and his wife and child, or any of them, to be sent to the parish or union to which under the Statutes for the time being in force, he appears, from the statements made in his attestation paper and other available information, to be chargeable; and such soldier, wife, or child, if delivered after reasonable notice, in England or Ireland at the workhouse in which persons settled in such parish or union are received, and in Scotland to the inspector of poor of such parish, shall be received, by the master or other proper officer of such workhouse or such inspector of poor, as the case may be.

(*2*) Provided that a Secretary of State or any officer deputed by him for the purpose, where it appears to him that any such soldier is a dangerous lunatic, and is in such a state of health as not to be liable to suffer bodily or mental injury by his removal, may, by order signified under his hand, send such lunatic direct to an asylum, registered hospital, licensed house, or other place in which pauper lunatics can legally be confined, and for the purpose of the said order the above-mentioned parish or union shall be deemed to be the parish or union from which such lunatic is sent.

(*3*) In England the lunatic shall be sent to the asylum, hospital, house, or place to which a person in the workhouse aforesaid, on becoming a dangerous lunatic, can by law be removed, and an order of the Secretary of State or officer under this section shall be of the same effect as a summary reception order within the meaning of the Lunacy Act, 1890, and the like proceedings shall be taken thereon as on an order under that Act. 53 & 54 Vict., c. 5

(*4*) The Secretary of State, or officer before making the said order in respect of a lunatic who is liable to be delivered to the inspector of poor of a parish in Scotland, may require the inspector of poor of that parish to specify the aslyum to which such lunatic if in the parish would be sent, and it shall be the duty of such inspector forthwith to specify such asylum, and thereupon the Secretary of State or officer may make the said order for sending the lunatic to that asylum, and such order shall be of the same effect as an order by the sheriff within the meaning of section fifteen of the Lunacy (Scotland) Act, 1862, and the like proceedings shall be taken thereon as on an order under that section. 25 & 26 Vict., c. 54

(*5*) In the case of any such lunatic, who is liable to be delivered at a workhouse in Ireland, at which persons settled in the said union are received, a Secretary of State or any officer deputed by him for the purpose may, by order under his hand, send such lunatic to the asylum of the district in which such union is situate, and such order shall be of the same effect as a warrant under the hands and seals of two justices given under the provisions of the tenth section of the Act of the session of the thirtieth and thirty-first years of the reign of Her present Majesty, chapter one hundred and eighteen, intituled "An Act to provide for the appointment of the officers and servants of district lunatic asylums in Ireland, and to alter and amend the law relating to "the custody of dangerous lunatics and dangerous idiots in Ireland." *Discharge and Transfer to Reserve Force.*

92. (*1*) A SOLDIER of the regular forces shall not be discharged from those forces, unless by sentence of court-martial with ignominy, or by order of the competent military authority, or by authority direct from Her Majesty and until duly discharged in manner provided by this Act and by regulations of the Secretary of State under this Act shall be subject to this Act. **Regulations as to discharge of soldiers.**

(*2*) To every soldier of the regular forces who is discharged, for whatever reason he is discharged, there shall be given a certificate of discharge, stating such particulars as may be from time to time required by regulations of a Secretary of State under this Act.

Authorities to enlist and attest Recruits.

Authorities to enlist and attest Recruits.

93. A SECRETARY of State may from time to time make and when made revoke and alter a general or special order making such regulations, giving such directions, and issuing such forms as he may think necessary or expedient respecting the persons authorised to enlist recruits for Her Majesty's regular forces, and for the purpose of such enlistment, and generally for carrying this part of this Act into effect; and any such order shall be of the same effect as if enacted in this Act. **Regulations as to persons to enlist and enlistment of soldiers.**

94. FOR the purposes of the attestation of soldiers in pursuance of this part of this Act— **Justices of the peace for the purposes of enlistment.**

An officer in the United Kingdom or elsewhere, if authorised in that behalf under the regulations of a Secretary of State, also every person exercising the office of a magistrate in India or a colony, and also each of the following persons, shall have the authority of a justice of the peace, and be deemed to be included in the expression "justice of the peace" wherever used in this part of this Act in relation to the attestation of soldiers; that is to say,

In India, any person duly authorised in that behalf by the Governor General; and in the territories of any native state in India the person performing the duties of the office of British resident or political agent therein, or any other person authorised in that behalf by the Governor General of India; and

In a colony, any person duly authorised in that behalf by the governor of the colony; and

Authorities to enlist and attest Recruits.

Beyond the limits of the United Kingdom, India, and a colony, any British consul general, or vice-consul, consul, or person duly exercising the authority of a British consul.

Special Provisions as to Persons to be enlisted.

Special Provisions as to Persons to be enlisted.

Enlistment of aliens, negroes, etc.

95. (*1*) ANY person who is for the time being an alien may, if Her Majesty think fit to signify her consent through a Secretary of State, be enlisted in Her Majesty's regular forces, so however that the number of aliens serving together at any one time in any corps of the regular forces shall not exceed the proportion of one alien to every fifty British subjects, and that an alien so enlisted shall not be capable of holding any higher rank in Her Majesty's regular forces than that of a warrant officer or non-commissioned officer:

(*2*) Provided that notwithstanding the above provisions of this section any negro or person of colour, although an alien, may voluntarily enlist in pursuance of this part of this Act, and when so enlisted shall, while serving in Her Majesty's regular forces, be deemed to be entitled to all the privileges of a natural-born British subject.

Claims of masters to apprentices.

96. THE master of an apprentice in the United Kingdom who has been attested as a soldier of the regular forces may claim him while under the age of twenty-one years as follows, and not otherwise:

(1) The master, within one month after the apprentice left his service, must take before a justice of the peace the oath in that behalf specified in the First Schedule to this Act, and obtain from the justice a certificate of having taken such oath, which certificate the justice shall give in the form in the said schedule, or to the like effect :

(2) A court of summary jurisdiction within whose jurisdiction the apprentice may be, if satisfied on complaint by the master that he is entitled to have the apprentice delivered up to him, may order the officer under whose command the apprentice is to deliver him to the master, but if satisfied that the apprentice stated on his attestation that he was not an apprentice may, and if required by or on behalf of the said commanding officer shall try the apprentice for the offence of making such false statement, and if need be may adjourn the case for the purpose:

(3) Except in pursuance of an order of a court of summary jurisdiction, an apprentice shall not be taken from Her Majesty's service:

(4) An apprentice shall not be claimed in pursuance of this section unless he was bound for at least four years by a regular indenture, and was under the age of sixteen years when so bound: *Special Provisions as to Persons to be enlisted.*

(5) A master who gives up the indenture of his apprentice within one month after the attestation of such apprentice shall be entitled to receive to his own use so much of the bounty (if any) payable to such apprentice on enlistment as has not been paid to the apprentice before notice was given of his being an apprentice.

Application of apprentice provisions to indentured labourers.

97. The provisions of this part of this Act with respect to apprentices shall apply to a person who at the time of his attestation is an indentured labourer in a colony, with these qualifications, that such indentured labourer, if imported at the expense of the employer or of the colony in consideration of the indenture under which he is serving, may be claimed, although above the age of twenty-one years, and though bound for a less period or at an older age than is above specified.

Offences as to Enlistment.

Offences as to Enlistment.

Penalty on unlawful recruiting.

98. If a person without due authority—

(1) Publishes or causes to be published notices or advertisements for the purpose of procuring recruits for Her Majesty's regular forces, or in relation to recruits for such forces; or

(2) Opens or keeps any house, place of rendezvous, or office as connected with the recruiting of such forces; or

(3) Receives any person under any such advertisement as aforesaid; or

(4) Directly or indirectly interferes with the recruiting service of such forces,

he shall be liable on summary conviction to a fine not exceeding twenty pounds.

Recruits punishable for false answers.

99. (*1*) If a person knowingly makes a false answer to any question contained in the attestation paper, which has been put to him by or by direction of the justice before whom he appears for the purpose of being attested, he shall be liable on summary conviction to be imprisoned with or without hard labour for any period not exceeding three months.

(*2*) If a person guilty of an offence under this section has been attested as a soldier of the regular forces, he shall be liable, at the discretion of the competent military authority, to be proceeded against before a court of summary jurisdiction, or to be tried by court-martial for the offence.

Miscellaneous as to Enlistment.

Miscellaneous as to Enlistment.

Validity of attestation and enlistment or re-engagement.

100. (*1*) Where a person after his attestation on his enlistment or the making of his declaration on re-engagement, has received pay as a soldier of the regular forces during three months, he shall be deemed to have been duly attested and enlisted or duly re-engaged, as the case may be, and shall not be entitled to claim his discharge on the ground of any error or illegality in his enlistment, attestation, or re-engagement, or on any other ground whatsoever, save as authorised by this Act, and, if within the said three months such person claims his discharge, any such error or illegality or other ground shall not until such person is discharged in pursuance of his claim affect his position as a soldier in Her Majesty's service, or invalidate any proceedings, act, or thing taken or done prior to such discharge.

(*2*) Where a person is in pay as a soldier in any corps of Her Majesty's regular forces, such person shall be deemed for all the purposes of this Act to be a soldier of the regular forces, with this qualification, that he may at any time claim his discharge, but until he so claims and is discharged in pursuance of that claim, he shall be subject to this Act as a soldier of the regular forces legally enlisted and duly attested under this Act.

(*3*) Where a person claims his discharge on the ground that he has not been attested or re-engaged, or not duly attested or re-engaged, his commanding officer shall forthwith forward such claim to the competent military authority, who shall as soon as practicable submit it to a Secretary of State, and if the claim appears well grounded, the claimant shall be discharged with all convenient speed.

Definition for purposes of Part Two of competent military authority and reserve.

101. (*1*) Any act authorised or required by this part of this Act to be done by, to, or before the competent military authority may be done by, to, or before the commander-in chief or the adjutant general, or any officer prescribed in that behalf.

(*2*) For the purposes of this part of this Act the expression "reserve" means the first class of the army reserve force.

PART III.

Billeting and Impressment of Carriages.

Billeting of Officers and Soldiers.

Billeting of Officers and Soldiers.

Suspension of 3 Chas. 1, c. 1; 31 Chas. 2, c. 1; 6 Anne (I), c. 4, as to billeting.

102. During the continuance in force of this Act, so much of any law as prohibits, restricts, or regulates the quartering or billeting of officers and soldiers on any inhabitant of this realm without his consent is hereby suspended, so far as such quartering or billeting is authorised by this Act.

Billeting of Officers and Soldiers.

Obligation of constable to provide billets or officers, soldiers, and horses.

103. (*1*) EVERY constable for the time being in charge at any place in the United Kingdom mentioned in the route issued to the commanding officer of any portion of Her Majesty's regular forces shall, on the demand of such commanding officer, or of an officer or soldier authorised by him, and on production of such route, billet on the occupiers of victualling houses and other premises specified in this Act as victualling houses in that place such number of officers, soldiers, and horses entitled under this Act to be billeted as are mentioned in the route and stated to require quarters.

(*2*) A route for the purposes of this part of this Act shall be issued under the authority of Her Majesty, signified through a Secretary of State, and shall state the forces to be moved in pursuance of the route, and that statement shall be signed by such officer as the commander-in-chief may from time to time order in that behalf.

(*3*) A route purporting to be issued and signed as required by this section shall be evidence until the contrary is proved of its having been duly issued and signed in pursuance of this Act, and if delivered to an officer or soldier by his commanding officer shall be a sufficient authority to such officer or soldier to demand billets, and when produced by an officer or soldier to a constable shall be conclusive evidence to such constable of the authority of the officer or soldier producing the same to demand billets in accordance with such route.

Liability to provide billets.

104. (*1*) THE provisions of this part of this Act with respect to victualling houses shall extend to all inns, hotels, livery stables, or alehouses, also to the houses of sellers of wine by retail, whether British or foreign, to be drunk in their own houses or places thereunto belonging, and to all houses of persons selling brandy, spirits, strong waters, cider, or metheglin by retail; and the occupier of a victualling house, inn, livery stable, alehouse, or any such house as aforesaid shall be subject to billets under this Act, and is in this Act included under the expression "keeper of a victualling house," and the inn, hotel, house, stables, and premises of such occupier are in this Act included under the expression "victualling house."

(*2*) Provided that an officer or soldier shall not be billeted—

(*a*) In any private house; nor

(*b*) In any canteen held or occupied under the authority of a Secretary of State; nor

(*c*) On persons who keep taverns only, being vintners of the City of London admitted to their freedom of the said company in right of patrimony or apprenticeship, notwithstanding the persons who keep such taverns have taken out licenses for the sale of any intoxicating liquor; nor

Billeting of Officers and Soldiers.

(*d*) In the house of any distiller kept for distilling brandy and strong waters, so as such distiller does not permit tippling in such house; nor

(*e*) In the house of any shopkeeper whose principal dealing is more in other goods and merchandise than in brandy and strong waters, so as such shopkeeper does not perm tippling in such house; nor

(*f*) In a house of a person licensed only t sell beer or cider not to be consumed on the premises; nor

(*g*) In the house of residence of any oreign consul duly accredited as such.

Officers, soldiers, and horses entitled to be billeted.

105. (*1*) ALL officers and soldiers of Her Majesty's regular forces; and

(*2*) All horses belonging to Her Majesty's regular forces; and

(*3*) All horses belonging to the officers of such forces for which forage is for the time being allowed by Her Majesty's regulations,

shall be entitled to be billeted.

Accommodation and payment on billet.

106. (*1*) THE keeper of a victualling house upon whom any officer, soldier, or horse is billeted shall receive such officer, soldier, or horse in his victualling house, and furnish there the accommodation following; that is to say lodging and attendance for the officer; and lodging, attendance, and food for the soldier; and stable room and forage for the horse, in accordance with the provisions of the Second Schedule to this Act.

(*2*) Where the keeper of a victualling house on whom any officer, soldier, or horse is billeted desires, by reason of his want of accommodation of his victualling house being full or otherwise, to be relieved from the liability to receive such officer, soldier, or horse in his victualling house, and provides for such officer, soldier, or horse in the immediate neighbourhood such good and sufficient accommodation as he is required by this Act to provide, and as is approved by the constable issuing the billets, he shall be relieved from providing the same in his victualling house.

(*3*) There shall be paid to the keeper of a victualling house for the accommodation furnished by him in pursuance of this Act the prices for the time being authorised in this behalf by Parliament.

(*4*) An officer or soldier demanding billets in pursuance of this Act shall, before he departs, and if he remains longer than four days, at least once in every four days, pay the just demands of every keeper of a victualling house on whom he and any officers and soldiers under his command, and his or their horses (if any) have been billeted.

Billeting of Officers and Soldiers.

(5) If by reason of a sudden order to march, or otherwise, an officer or soldier is not able to make such payment to any keeper of a victualling house as is above required, he shall before he departs make up with such keeper of a victualling house an account of the amount due to him, and sign the same, and forthwith transmit the account so signed to a Secretary of State, who shall forthwith cause the amount named in such account as due to be paid.

Annual list of keepers of victualling house liable to billets.

107. (1) The police authority for any place may cause annually a list to be made out of all keepers of victualling houses within the meaning of this Act in such place, or any particular part thereof, liable to billets under this Act, specifying the situation and character of each victualling house, and the number of soldiers and horses who may be billeted on the keeper thereof.

(2) The police authority shall cause such list to be kept at some convenient place open for inspection at all reasonable times by persons interested, and any person who feels aggrieved either by being entered in such list, or by being entered to receive an undue proportion of officers, soldiers, or horses, may complain to a court of summary jurisdiction, and the court, after such notice as the court think necessary to persons interested, may order the list to be amended in such manner as the court may think just.

Regulations as to grant of billets.

108. The following regulations shall be observed with respect to billeting in pursuance of this Act; that is to say,

(1) No more billets shall at any time be ordered than there are effective officers, soldiers, and horses present to be billeted:

(2) All billets, when made out by the constable, shall be delivered into the hands of the commanding officer or non-commissioned officer who demanded the billets, or of some officer authorised by such commanding officer:

(3) If a keeper of a victualling house feels aggrieved by having an undue proportion of officers, soldiers, or horses billeted on him, he may apply to a justice of the peace, or if the billets have been made out by a justice may complain to a court of summary jurisdiction, and the justice or court may order such of the officers, soldiers, or horses to be removed and to be billeted elsewhere as may seem just:

(4) A constable having authority in a place mentioned in the route may act for the purposes of billeting in any locality within one mile from such place, unless some constable ordinarily having authority in such locality is present and undertakes to billet therein the due proportion of officers, soldiers, and horses:

Billeting of officers and soldiers.

(5) The regulations with respect to billets contained in the Second Schedule to this Act shall be duly observed by the constable:

(6) A justice of the peace on the request of an officer or non-commissioned officer authorised to demand billets, may vary a route by adding any place or omitting any place, and also may direct billets to be given above one mile from a place mentioned in the route:

(7) A justice of the peace may require a constable to give an account in writing of the number of officers, soldiers, and horses billeted by such constable, together with the names of the keepers of victualling houses on whom such officers, soldiers, and horses are billeted, and the locality of such victualling houses.

Offences in relation to billeting.

Offences in relation to Billeting.

Offences by constables.

109. If a constable commits any of the offences following; that is to say,

(1) Billets any officer, soldier, or horse, on any person not liable to billets without the consent of such person; or

(2) Receives, demands, or agrees for any money or reward whatsoever to excuse or relieve a person from being entered in a list as liable or from his liability to billets, or from any part of such liability; or

(3) Billets or quarters on any person or premises, without the consent of such person or the occupier of such premises, any person or horse not entitled to be billeted; or

(4) Neglects or refuses after sufficient notice is given to give billet demanded for any officer, soldier, or horse entitled to be billeted;

he shall, on summary conviction, be liable to a fine of not less than forty shillings and not exceeding ten pounds.

Offences by keepers of victualling houses.

110. If a keeper of a victualling house commits any of the offences following; that is to say,

(1) Refuses or neglects to receive any officer, soldier, or horse billeted upon him in pursuance of this Act, or to furnish such accommodation as is required by this Act; or

(2) Gives or agrees to give any money or reward to a constable to excuse or relieve him from being entered in a list as liable, or from his liability to billets, or any part of such liability; or

(3) Gives or agrees to give to any officer or soldier billeted upon him in pursuance of this Act any money or reward in lieu of receiving an officer, soldier, or horse, or furnishing the said accommodation ;

Offences in relation to Billeting.

he shall, on summary conviction, be liable to a fine of not less than forty shillings and not exceeding five pounds.

Offences by officers or soldiers.

111. (*1*) If any officer quarters or causes to be billeted any officer, soldier, or horse, otherwise than is allowed by this Act upon any person, he shall be guilty of a misdemeanor.

(*2*) If any officer or soldier commits any offence in relation to billeting for which he is liable to be punished under Part One of this Act, other than an offence in respect of which any other remedy is given by this part of this Act to the person aggrieved, he shall, upon summary conviction, be liable to a fine not exceeding fifty pounds.

(*3*) A certificate of a conviction for an offence under this section shall be transmitted by the court making such conviction to a Secretary of State.

Impressment of Carriages.

Impressment of Carriages.

Supply of carriages, etc., for regimental baggage and stores on the march.

112. (*1*) Every justice of the peace in the United Kingdom having jurisdiction in any place mentioned in a route issued to the commanding officer of any portion of Her Majesty's regular forces shall, on the demand of such commanding officer, or of an officer or non-commissioned officer authorised by him, and on production of such route, issue his warrant requiring some constable or constables having authority in such place to provide, within a reasonable time to be named in the warrant, such carriages, animals, and drivers as are stated to be required for the purpose of moving the regimental baggage and regimental stores of the forces mentioned in the route in accordance with the route; and the constable or constables shall execute such warrant, and persons having carriages and animals suitable for the said purpose shall, when ordered by a constable in pursuance of such warrant, furnish the same in a state fit for use for the aforesaid purpose.

(*2*) The route for the purpose of this section shall be such route as is mentioned in the foregoing provisions of this part of this Act with respect to billeting.

(*3*) A route purporting to be issued and signed as required by those provisions, if delivered to an officer or non-commissioned officer by his commanding officer, shall be a sufficient authority to such officer or non-commissioned officer to demand carriages and animals in pursuance of this Act, and when produced by an officer or non-commissioned officer shall be conclusive evidence to a justice and constable of the authority of the officer or non-commissioned officer producing the same to demand carriages and animals in accordance with such route.

Impressment of Carriages.

(*4*) The warrant ordering carriages, animals and drivers to be provided shall specify the number and description of the carriages, and also the places from and to which the same are to travel, and the distances between such places.

(*5*) When sufficient carriages or animals cannot be procured within the jurisdiction of the said justice, any justice having jurisdiction in the next adjoining place shall, by a like course of proceeding, supply the deficiency.

(*6*) A fee of one shilling and no more shall be paid for the warrant by the officer or non-commissioned officer applying for the same, and shall be paid to the clerk of the justice.

Payment for and regulations as to carriages, animals, etc.

113. (*1*) THERE shall be paid in respect of the carriages and animals furnished in pursuance of this part of this Act, the rates specified in the Third Schedule to this Act, and the regulations contained in that schedule with respect to the carriages and animals furnished shall be duly observed.

(*2*) The following authorities; that is to say,

(*a*) In England the court of general or quarter sessions of a county or of a borough subject to the Municipal Corporations Act, 1882; and 45 & 46 Vict., c. 50.

(*b*) In Scotland, the commissioners of supply of a county, or the magistrates of a Royal or Parliamentary burgh; and

(*c*) In Ireland, the grand jury for a county, a county of a city, a county of a town and city, or a city or town and county, also any council of any such county, town or city having by law the fiscal powers of a grand jury,

may from time to time, as respects places within their jurisdiction, by order increase the rates authorised in the said schedule by such amount in respect of each rate, not exceeding one-third, as may seem reasonable, and the amount of such increase shall be notified in writing by the justice granting a warrant in pursuance of this Act to the person demanding the warrant.

(*3*) The order shall specify the average price of hay and oats at the nearest market town at the time of fixing such increased rates, and the order shall not be in force for more than ten days beyond the next meeting of such authority, but may be renewed from time to time by a fresh order or orders, and while in force shall have effect as part of the said schedule.

(*4*) A copy of every such order, duly authenticated, shall be transmitted to a Secretary of State within three days after the making thereof.

(*5*) The officer or non-commissioned officer who demands carriages or animals in pursuance of this part of this Act shall pay the sums due in respect of the same to the owners or drivers of the carriages or animals, and one-third part of such payment shall in each case, if required, be made before the carriage is loaded; and such payments shall be made, if required, in the presence of a justice or constable. *Impressment of Carriages.*

(*6*) If an officer or non-commissioned officer is from any cause unable to pay the amount due to the owner or driver of any carriage or animal, he shall make up with such owner or driver and sign an account of the amount due to him, and forthwith transmit the account so signed to a Secretary of State, who shall forthwith cause the amount named therein to be paid to such owner or driver.

Annual list of persons liable to supply carriages.

114. (*1*) The police authority for any place may cause annually a list to be made out of all persons in such place, or any particular part thereof, liable to furnish carriages and animals under this Act, and of the number and description of the carriages and animals of such persons; and where a list is so made, any justice may by warrant require any constable or constables having authority within such place to give from time to time, on demand by an officer or non-commissioned officer under this Act, orders to furnish carriages and animals, and such warrant shall be executed as if it were a special warrant issued in pursuance of this Act on such demand, and the orders shall specify the like particulars as such special warrant.

(*2*) The police authority shall cause such list to be kept at some convenient place open for inspection at all reasonable times by persons interested, and any person who feels aggrieved either by being entered in such list, or by being entered to furnish any number or description of carriages or animals which he is not liable to furnish, may complain to a court of summary jurisdiction, and the court, after such notice as the court think necessary to persons interested, may order the list to be amended in such manner as the court may think just.

(*3*) All orders given by constables for furnishing carriages and animals shall, as far as possible, be made from such list in regular rotation.

Supply of carriages and vessels in case of emergency.

115. (*1*) Her Majesty by order distinctly stating that a case of emergency exists and signified by a Secretary of State, and also in Ireland the Lord Lieutenant by a like order, signified by the Chief Secretary or Under Secretary, may authorise any general or field officer commanding Her Majesty's regular forces in any military district or place in the United Kingdom to issue a requisition under this section (herein-after referred to as a requisition of emergency).

(*2*) The officer so authorised may issue a requisition of emergency under his hand, reciting the said order, and requiring justices of the peace to issue their warrants for the provision, for the purpose mentioned in the requisition,

Impressment of Carriages. of such carriages and animals as may be provided under the foregoing provisions, and also of carriages of every description, and of horses of every description, whether kept for saddle or draught, and also of vessels (whether boats, barges, or other) sued for the transport of any commodities whatsoever upon any canal or navigable river.

(3) A justice of the peace, on demand by an officer of the portion of Her Majesty's forces mentioned in a requisition of emergency, or by an officer of a Secretary of State authorised in this behalf, and on production of the requisition, shall issue his warrant for the provision of such carriages, animals, and vessels as are stated by the officer producing the requisition of emergency to be required for the purpose mentioned in the requisition; the warrant shall be executed in the like manner, and all the provisions of this Act as to the provision or furnishing of carriages and animals, including those respecting fines on officers, non-commissioned officers, justices, constables, or owners of carriages or animals, shall apply in like manner as in the case where a justice issues, in pursuance of the foregoing provisions of this Act, a warrant for the provision of carriages and animals, and shall apply to vessels as if the expression carriages included vessels.

(4) A Secretary of State shall cause due payment to be made for carriages, animals, and vessels furnished in pursuance of this section, and any difference respecting the amount of payment for any carriage, animal, or vessel shall be determined by a county court judge having jurisdiction in any place in which such carriage, animal, or vessel was furnished or through which it travelled in pursuance of the requisition.

(5) Canal, river, or lock tolls are hereby declared not to be demandable for vessels while employed in any service in pursuance of this section or returning therefrom. And any toll collector who demands or receives toll in contravention of this exemption shall, on summary conviction, be liable to a fine not exceeding five pounds nor less than ten shillings.

(6) A requisition of emergency, purporting to be issued in pursuance of this section and to be signed by an officer therein stated to be authorised in accordance with this section, shall be evidence, until the contrary is proved of its being duly issued and signed in pursuance of this Act, and if delivered to an officer of Her Majesty's forces or of a Secretary of State shall be a sufficient authority to such officer to demand carriages, animals, and vessels in pursuance of this section, and when produced by such officer shall be conclusive evidence to a justice and constable of the authority of such officer to demand carriages, animals, and vessels in accordance with such requisition; and it shall be lawful to convey on such carriages, animals, and vessels, not only the baggage, provisions, and military stores of the troops mentioned in

the requisition of emergency, but also the officer, soldiers, servants, women, children, and other persons of and belonging to the same. *Impressment of Carriages.*

(7) Whenever an order for the embodiment of the militia is in force, the order of Her Majesty authorising an officer to issue a requisition of emergency may authorise him to extend such requisition to the provision of carriages, animals, and vessels for the purpose of being purchased, as well as of being hired, on behalf of the Crown.

(8) Where a justice, on demand by an officer and on production of a requisition of emergency, has issued his warrant for the provision of any carriages, animals, or vessels and any person ordered in pursuance of such warrant to furnish a carriage, animal or vessel refuses or neglects to furnish the same according to the order, then, if an order for the embodiment of the militia is in force, the said officer may seize (and if need be by force) the said carriage, animal, or vessel, and may use the same in like manner as if it had been furnished in pursuance of the order, but the said person shall be entitled to payment for the same in like manner as if he had duly furnished the same according to the order.

Offences in relation to the Impressment of Carriages.

Offences in relation to the Impressment of Carriages.

Offences by constables.

116. Any constable who—

(1) Neglects or refuses to execute any warrant of a justice requiring him to provide carriages, animals, or vessels; or

(2) Receives, demands, or agrees for any money or reward whatsoever to excuse or relieve any person from being entered in a list as liable to furnish, or from being required to furnish, or from furnishing any carriage, animal, or vessel; or

(3) Orders any carriage, animal, or vessel to be furnished for any person or purpose or on any occasion for and on which it is not required by this Act to be furnished,

shall, on summary conviction, be liable to a fine of not less than twenty shillings nor more than twenty pounds.

Offences by persons ordered to furnish carriages, animals, or vessels.

117. A person ordered by any constable in pursuance of this Act to furnish a carriage, animal, or vessel who—

(1) Refuses or neglects to furnish the same according to the orders of such constable and this Act; or

(2) Gives or agrees to give to a constable or to any officer or noncommissioned officer any money or reward whatsoever to be excused from being entered in a list as liable to furnish, or from being required to furnish, or from furnishing, or in lieu of furnishing, any carriage, animal, or vessel in pursuance of this Act; or

Offences in relation to the Impressment of Carriages.

(3) Does any act or thing by which the execution of any warrant or order for providing or furnishing carriages, animals, or vessels is hindered,

shall, on summary conviction, be liable to pay a fine of not less than forty shillings nor more than ten pounds.

Offences by officers or soldiers.

118. (*1*) Any officer or soldier who commits any offence in relation to the impressment of carriages for which he is liable to be punished under Part One of this Act, other than an offence in respect of which any other remedy is given by this part of this Act to the person aggrieved, shall, on summary conviction, be liable to a fine not exceeding fifty pounds nor less than forty shillings.

(2) A certificate of a conviction for an offence under this section shall be transmitted by the court making such conviction to a Secretary of State.

Supplemental Provisions as to Billeting and Impressment of Carriages.

Supplemental Provisions as to Billeting and Impressment of Carriages.

Application to court of summary jurisdiction respecting sums due to keepers of victualling houses or owners of carriages, etc.

119. (*1*) The following persons; that is to say,

(*a*) If any officer or soldier fails to comply with the provisions of this part of this Act with respect to the payment of a sum due to a keeper of a victualling house or in respect of carriages or animals, or to the making up of an account of the sum due, the person to whom the sum is due; or

(*b*) If a keeper of a victualling house suffers any ill-treatment by violence, extortion, or making disturbance in billets from any officer or soldier billeted upon him, or if the owner or driver of any carriage, animal or vessel furnished in pursuance of this part of this Act suffers any ill-treatment from any officer or soldier, the person suffering such ill-treatment, but, when there is an officer commanding such officer or soldier present at the place only after first making due complaint, if practicable to such commanding officer,

may apply to a court of summary jurisdiction, and such court, if satisfied on oath of such failure or such ill-treatment, and of the amount fairly due to the applicant, including the costs of his application to the court of summary jurisdiction, shall certify the same to a Secretary of State, who shall forthwith cause the amount due to be paid.

(2) Provided that the Secretary of State, if it appear to him that the amount named in such certificate is not justly due, or is in excess of the amount justly due, may direct a complaint to be made to a court of summary jurisdiction for the county, borough, or place for which the court giving the certificate acted and the court after hearing the case may by order confirm the said certificate, or vary it in such manner as to the court seems just.

Supplemental Provisions as to Billeting and Impressment of Carriages

Provisions as to constables, police authorities, and justices.

120. (*1*) A CONSTABLE shall observe the directions given to him for the due execution of this part of this Act, by the police authority; and the police authority, or any member thereof, and every justice of the peace may, if it seem necessary, and in the absence of a constable shall, themselves or himself exercise the powers and perform the duties by this part of this Act vested in or imposed on a constable, and in such case every such person is in this part of this Act included in the expression "constable."

(*2*) A person having or executing any military office or commission in any part of the United Kingdom shall not, directly or indirectly, be concerned, as a justice or constable, in the billeting of or appointing quarters for any officer or soldier or horse of the corps or part of a corps under his immediate command, and all warrants, acts, and things made, done, and appointed by such person for or concerning the same shall be void.

Fraudulent claim for carriages, animals, etc.

121. IF any person—

(1) Forges or counterfeits any route or requisition of emergency, or knowingly produces to a justice or constable any route or requisition of emergency so forged or counterfeited; or

(2) Personates or represents himself to be an officer or soldier authorised to demand any billet, or any carriage, animal, or vessel, or to be entitled to be billeted, or to have his horse billeted; or

(3) Produces to a justice or constable a route or requisition which he is not authorised to produce, or a document falsely purporting to be a route or requisition,

he shall be liable, on summary conviction, to imprisonment for a period not exceeding three months, with or without hard labour, or to a fine not less than twenty shillings and not more than five pounds.

PART IV.

GENERAL PROVISIONS.

Supplemental Provisions as to Courts-martial.

Supplemental Provisions as to Courts-martial.

Royal warrant required for convening and confirming general courts-martial.

122. (*1*) HER Majesty may, subject to the provisions of this Act, by any warrant or warrants under Her Sign Manual, in such form as Her Majesty may from time to time direct, from time to time—

(*a*) Convene or authorise any qualified officer to convene a general court-martial for the trial under this Act of any person subject to military law; and

(*b*) Give a general authority to any qualified officer to convene general courts-martial for the trial, under this Act, of such persons

Supplemental Provisions as to Courts-martial.

subject to military law as may for the time being be under or within the territorial limits of his command; and

(*c*) Empower any qualified officer to delegate to any officer under his command, not below the degree of field officer, a general authority to convene general courts-martial for the trial, under this Act, of such persons subject to military law, as are for the time being under or within the territorial limits of his command; and

(*d*) Reserve for confirmation by Her Majesty, or empower any qualified officer to confirm, the findings and sentences of general courts-martial; and

(*e*) Empower any officer for the time being authorised to confirm the findings and sentences of general courts-martial to reserve for confirmation findings or sentences of general courts-martial, or to delegate a power of confirming such findings or sentences to any officer under his command not below the degree of field officer; and

(*f*) Revoke any warrant for the time being in force, or any part of any warrant, leaving the remainder in full force:

Provided that where it appears to Her Majesty that, in any place out of the United Kingdom, where no field officer is for the time being in command, hardship would be inflicted on persons accused of offences by reason of there being no means of speedily trying such persons for offences, a warrant under this section may empower an officer to delegate to an officer not below the degree of captain any authority and power authorised under this section to be delegated to a field officer.

(*2*) The same officer may or may not be appointed convening and confirming officer.

(*3*) The power of convening general courts-martial, and of confirming the findings and sentences of general courts-martial, or either of such powers, may be granted subject to such restrictions, reservations, exceptions, and conditions as to Her Majesty may seem meet, and when delegated by any officer empowered in that behalf may, subject to the provisions of any warrant granting him such power, be delegated subject to such restrictions, reservations, exceptions, and conditions as to such officer may seem fit.

(*4*) Warrants under this section may be addressed to officers by name or by designation of their offices, or partly in one way and partly in the other, and any warrant may or may not, according to the terms of such warrant and the mode in which the same is addressed, be limited to an officer named, or be extended to a person for the time being performing the duties of the office named, or be extended to the successors in command of an officer.

Supplementa Provisions as to Courts-martial.

(5) Any warrant of Her Majesty issued in pursuance of this section shall be of the same force as if the provisions thereof were enacted by this Act.

(6) "Qualified officer" for the purposes of this Act, in so far as it relates to convening or confirming the findings and sentences of general courts-martial, means the Commander-in-Chief and any officer not below the rank of a field officer commanding for the time being any body of the regular forces either within or without Her Majesty's dominions; it also includes the Lord Lieutenant of Ireland, the Governor General of India, and a Governor of any colony on whom the command of any body of regular forces may be conferred by Her Majesty.

Authority of officer empowered to convene general courts-martial required for convening and confirming district courts-martial.

123. (*1*) Any officer or person authorised to convene general courts-martial may—

(*a*) Convene a district court-martial for the trial under this Act of any person under his command who is subject to military law; and

(*b*) Empower any person under his command not below the rank of captain to convene a district court-martial for the trial under this Act of any person under the command of such last-mentioned officer who is subject to military law; and

(*c*) Confirm the finding and sentence of any district court-martial, or empower any officer whom he has power to authorise to convene district courts-martial to confirm the finding and sentence of any district court-martial.

(*2*) The same officer may or may not be appointed convening and confirming officer under this section.

(*3*) The power of convening, and of confirming the findings and sentences of, district courts-martial, or either of such powers, may be granted under this section, subject to such restrictions, reservations, exceptions, and conditions as to the officer granting such power may seem meet.

(*4*) Any authority under this section for convening district courts-martial may be addressed to an officer by name or by designation of his office, or partly in one way and partly in the other, and may or may not, according to the terms thereof and the mode in which the same is addressed, be limited to an officer named, or be extended to a person holding for the time being or performing the duties of the office, or be extended to the successors in command of such officer.

Right of person tried to copy of

124. Any person tried by a court-martial shall be entitled on demand, at any time in the case of a general court-martial within seven years, and in

proceedings of court-martial.

the case of any other court-martial within three years, after the confirmation of the finding and sentence of the court, to obtain from the officer or person having the custody of proceedings of such court a copy thereof, including the proceedings with respect to revision and confirmation thereof, upon payment for the same at the prescribed rate, not exceeding two pence for every folio of seventy-two words, and for the purposes of this section the proceedings of courts-martial shall be preserved in the prescribed manner.

Summoning and privilege of witnesses at courts-martial.

125. (*1*) Every person required to give evidence before a court-martial may be summoned or ordered to attend in the prescribed manner.

(*2*) Every person attending in pursuance of such summons or order as a witness before any court-martial shall, during his necessary attendance in or on such court, and in going to and returning from the same, have the same privilege from arrest as he would have if he were a witness before a superior court of civil jurisdiction.

Misconduct of civilian at court-martial.

126. (*1*) Where any person who is not subject to military law commits any of the following offences; that is to say,

(*a*) On being duly summoned as a witness before a court-martial, and after payment or tender of the reasonable expenses of his attendance, makes default in attending; or

(*b*) Being in attendance as a witness—

(i) Refuses to take an oath legally required by a court-martial to be taken; or

(ii) Refuses to produce any document in his power or control legally required by a court-martial to be produced by him; or

(iii) Refuses to answer any question to which a court-martial may legally require an answer, the president of the court-martial may certify the offence of such person under his hand to any court of law in the part of Her Majesty's dominions where the offence is committed which has power to punish witnesses if guilty of like offences in that court, and that court may thereupon inquire into such alleged offence, and after examination of any witnesses that may be produced against or for the person so accused, and after hearing any statement that may be offered in defence, if it seem just, punish such witness in like manner as if he had committed such offence in a proceeding in that court.

(*2*) Where a person not subject to military law when examined on oath or solemn declaration before a court-martial wilfully gives false evidence, he shall be liable on indictment or information to be convicted of and punished for the offence of perjury, or the offence by whatever name called in the part of

Her Majesty's dominions in which the offence is tried which, if committed in England, would be perjury.

Supplemental Provisions as to Courts-martial.

(3) Where a person not subject to military law is guilty of any contempt towards a court-martial, by using insulting or threatening language, or by causing any interruption or disturbance in its proceedings, or by printing observations or using words calculated to influence the members of or witnesses before such court, or to bring such court into disrepute, the president of the court-martial may certify the offence of such person, under his hand, to any court of law in the part of Her Majesty's dominions where the offence is committed which has power to commit for contempt, and that court may thereupon inquire into such alleged offence, and after hearing any witnesses that may be produced against or on behalf of the person so accused, and after hearing any statement that may be offered in defence, punish or take steps for the punishment of such person in like manner as if he had been guilty of contempt of that court.

Court-martial governed by English law only.

127. A COURT-MARTIAL under this Act shall not, as respects the conduct of its proceedings, or the reception or rejection of evidence, or as respects any other matter or thing whatsoever, be subject to the provisions of the Indian Evidence Act, 1872,[1] or to any Act, law, or ordinance of any legislature whatsoever other than the Parliament of the United Kingdom.

Rules of evidence to be the same as in civil courts.

128. THE rules of evidence to be adopted in proceedings before courts-martial shall be the same as those which are followed in civil courts, in England, and no person shall be required to answer any question or to produce any document which he could not be required to answer or produce in similar proceedings before a civil court.

Position of counsel at courts-martial.

129. WHEREAS it is expedient to make provision respecting the conduct of counsel when appearing on behalf of the prosecution or defence at courts-martial in pursuance of rules under this Act, be it therefore enacted as follows:

(1) Any conduct of a counsel which would be liable to censure, or a contempt of court, if it took place before Her Majesty's High Court of Justice in England, shall likewise be deemed liable to censure, or a contempt of court, in the case of a court-martial; and the rules laid down for the practice of courts-martial and the guidance of counsel shall be binding on counsel appearing before such courts-martial, and any wilful disobedience of such rules shall be professional misconduct, and, if persevered in, be deemed a contempt of court.

(2) Where a counsel is guilty of conduct liable to censure, or a contempt of court, such offence shall be deemed to be an offence within the meaning of section one hundred and twenty-six of this Act, and the president of the court-martial may certify the same to a court of law accordingly; and the court of

[1] Printed, Genl. Acts, Vol. II, Ed. 1898.

Supplemental Provisions as to Courts-martial.

law to which the same is certified shall deal with such offence in the same manner as if it had been committed in a proceeding before that court.

(3) A court-martial may, by order under the hand of the president, cause a counsel to be removed from the court who is guilty of such an offence as may, in the opinion of the court-martial, require his removal from court, but in every such case the president shall certify the offence committed to a court of law in manner provided by the above-mentioned section.

Provision in case of insane persons.

130. (*1*) WHERE it appears on the trial by court-martial of a person charged with an offence that such person is by reason of insanity unfit to take his trial, the court shall find specially that fact; and such person shall be kept in custody in the prescribed manner until the directions of Her Majesty thereon are known, or until any earlier time at which such person is fit to take his trial.

(*2*) Where on the trial by court-martial of a person charged with an offence it appears that such person committed the offence, but that he was insane at the time of the commission thereof, the court shall find specially the fact of his insanity, and such person shall be kept in custody in the prescribed manner until the directions of Her Majesty thereon are known.

(*3*) In either of the above cases Her Majesty may give orders for the safe custody of such person during Her pleasure, in such place and in such manner as Her Majesty thinks fit.

(*4*) A finding under this section shall be subject to confirmation in like manner as any other finding.

[1](*5*) If a person imprisoned by virtue of this Act becomes insane, then, without prejudice to any other provision for dealing with such insane prisoner, a Secretary of State in any case, and in the case of a prisoner confined in India, the Governor General of India, or the Governor of any presidency in which the person is confined, and in the case of a prisoner confined in a colony, the Governor of that colony, may, upon a certificate of such insanity by two qualified medical practitioners, order the removal of such prisoner to an asylum or other proper place for the reception of insane persons in the United Kingdom, India, or the colony, according as the prisoner is confined in the United Kingdom, India, or the colony, there to remain for the unexpired term of his imprisonment, and, upon such person being certified in the like manner to be again of sound mind, may order his removal to any prison in which he might have been confined if he had not become insane, there to undergo the remainder of such punishment.

---

[1] NOTE.—So much of sub-section (*5*) as relates to a person imprisoned in England is repealed by the Criminal Lunatics Act, 1884 (47 & 48 Vict., c. 64), s. 17. Printed post, p. 785.

General Provisions as to Prisons.

General Provisions as to Prisons.

Arrangements with Indian and colonial government as to prisons.

131. (*1*) A Secretary of State may from time to time make arrangements with the Governor General of India or the Governor of a colony for the reception in any prison in India or in such colony of prisoners under this Act, and of deserters or absentees without leave from Her Majesty's service, on payment of such sums as are provided by the arrangement, and the governor of any prison to which any such arrangement relates shall be under the same obligation as the governor of a prison in the United Kingdom to receive and detain such prisoners, deserters and absentees without leave.

(*2*) Provided that where a prisoner has been sentenced in India or in a colony to a term of imprisonment exceeding twelve months or to a term of penal servitude, he shall be transferred as soon as practicable to a prison or convict establishment within the United Kingdom, unless in the case of imprisonment the court shall for special reasons otherwise order, there to undergo his sentence; or unless he belongs to a class with respect to which a Secretary of State has declared that, by reason of the climate or place of his birth or the place of his enlistment, or otherwise, it is not beneficial to the prisoner to transfer him to the United Kingdom; every such declaration shall be laid before both Houses of Parliament.

(*3*) Any order which can be made under this section by the court may be made by the confirming authority in confirming the finding and sentence, and in the case of any commutation or remission of sentence may be made by the authority commuting or remitting the sentence.

Duty of governor of prison to receive prisoners, deserters, and absentees without leave.

132. (*1*) The governor of every prison in the United Kingdom, and the governor of every prison in India or a colony who is under the same obligation as the governor of a prison in the United Kingdom, shall receive and confine, until discharged or delivered over in due course of law, all prisoners sent to such prison in pursuance of this Act, and every person delivered into his custody as a deserter or absentee without leave by any person conveying him under legal authority, on production of the warrant of a court of summary jurisdiction on which such deserter or absentee without leave has been taken or committed, or of some order from a Secretary of State, or from the Governor General of India, or the Governor of a colony, which order shall continue in force until the deserter or absentee without leave has arrived at his destination.

(*2*) Every such governor shall also receive into his custody for a period not exceeding seven days any soldier in military custody upon delivery to him of a written order purporting to be signed by the commanding officer of such soldier.

(*3*) The provisions of this section with respect to the governor of a prison in the United Kingdom shall apply to a person having charge of any police station or other place in which prisoners may legally be confined.

(Sec. 133.)

Militar Prisons.

Military Prisons.

Establishment and regulation of military prisons.

133. (1) It shall be lawful for a Secretary of State, and in India for the Governor General, to set apart any building or part of a building under the control of the Secretary of State or Governor General as a military prison, or as a public prison for the imprisonment of military prisoners, and to declare that any such building or part of a building shall be a military prison, or a public prison, as the case may be, and every military prison so declared shall be deemed to be a public prison within the meaning of the provisions of this Act relating to imprisonment, and if such prison is in India shall be deemed to be an authorised prison.

(2) It shall be lawful for a Secretary of State, and in India for the Governor General, from time to time to make, alter, and repeal rules for the government, management, and regulation of military prisons, and for the appointment and removal and powers of inspectors, visitors, governors, and officers thereof, and for the labour of military prisoners therein, and for the safe custody of such prisoners, and for the maintenance of discipline among them, and for the punishment by personal correction, not exceeding twenty-five lashes in the case of corporal punishment, restraint, or otherwise of offences committed by such prisoners, so, however, that such rules shall not authorise corporal punishment to be inflicted for any offence in addition to the offences for which such punishment can be inflicted in pursuance of the Prison Act, 1865, and the Prison Act, 1877, nor render the imprisonment more severe than it is under the law in force for the time being in any public prison in England subject to the Prison Act, 1877, and provided that all the regulations in the Prison Act, 1865, and in the Prison Act, 1877, as to the duties of gaolers, medical officers, and coroners, shall be contained in such rules, so far as the same can be made applicable.

28 & 29 Vict. c. 126. 40 & 41 Vict. c. 21.

(3) On all occasions of death by violence or attended with suspicious circumstances in any military prison in India, an inquest is to be held, to make inquiry into the cause of death. The commanding officer shall cause notice to be given to the nearest magistrate, duly authorised to hold inquests, and such magistrate shall hold an inquest into the cause of any such death, in the manner and with the powers provided in the case of similar inquiries held under the law for the time being in force in India for regulating criminal procedure.

(4) Where from any cause there is no competent civil authority available the commanding officer shall convene a court of inquest. Such court shall be convened and shall hold the inquest in such manner as may be prescribed.

(5) Such rules may apply to such prisons any enactments of the Prison Act, 1865, imposing punishments on any persons not prisoners.

28 & 29 Vict. c. 126.

(6) All rules made by a Secretary of State in pursuance of this section shall be laid before Parliament as soon as practicable after they are made, if Parliament be then sitting, and if not, as soon as practicable, after the commencement of the then next session of Parliament. *Military Prisons.*

134. No soldiers shall be confined, longer than is absolutely necessary, in prisons other than military prisons in India and the colonies where the rules for the government and management of such prisons differ from those made by the Governor General of India and a Secretary of State in the case of India and the colonies respectively. *Restrictions on confinement in prisons in India or colonies, not being military prisons.*

135. Whereas it is expedient that a clear difference should be made between the treatment of prisoners convicted of breaches of discipline and the treatment of prisoners convicted of offences of an immoral, dishonest, shameful, or criminal character, or sentenced to be discharged from the service with ignominy, a Secretary of State shall from time to time make rules for the classification and treatment of such prisoners. *Classification of prisoners.*

Pay.

Pay.

136. The pay of an officer or soldier of Her Majesty's regular forces shall be paid without any deduction other than the deductions authorised by this or any other Act or by any Royal Warrant for the time being or by any law passed by the Governor General of India in Council. *Authorised deductions only to be made from pay.*

137. The following penal deductions may be made from the ordinary pay due to an officer of the regular forces: *Penal stoppages from ordinary pay of officers.*

(1) All ordinary pay due to an officer who absents himself without leave or overstays the period for which leave of absence has been granted him, unless a satisfactory explanation has been given through the commanding officer of such officer, and has been notified as satisfactory by the Commander-in-Chief to a Secretary of State:

(2) The sum required to make good such compensation for any expenses, loss, damage, or destruction occasioned by the commission of any offences may be awarded by the court-martial by whom he is convicted of such offence:

(3) The sum required to make good the pay of any officer or soldier which he has unlawfully retained or unlawfully refused to pay.

138. The following penal deductions may be made from the ordinary pay to a soldier of the regular forces: *Penal stoppages from ordinary pay of soldiers.*

(1) All ordinary pay for every day of absence either on desertion or without leave, or as prisoner of war, and for every day of imprisonment either under sentence for an offence awarded by a civil

court or court-martial, or by his commanding officer, or if he is on board one of Her Majesty's ships by the commanding officer of that ship, or under detention on the charge for an offence of which he is afterwards convicted by a civil court or court-martial, or under detention on the charge for absence without leave for which he is afterwards awarded imprisonment by his commanding officer;

(2) All ordinary pay for every day on which he is in hospital on account of sickness certified by the proper medical officer attending on him at the hospital to have been caused by an offence under this Act committed by him;

(3) The sum required to make good such compensation for any expenses, loss, damage, or destruction occasioned by the commission of any offence as may be awarded by the court-martial by whom he is convicted of such offence, or if he is on board of one of Her Majesty's ships by the commanding officer of that ship, or where he has confessed the offence and his trial is dispensed with by order under section seventy-three of this Act, as may be awarded by that order or by any other order of a competent military authority under that section;

(4) The sum required to make good such compensation for any expenses caused by him, or for any loss of or damage or destruction done by him to any arms, ammunition, equipment, clothing, instruments, or regimental necessaries or military decoration, or to any buildings or property, as may be awarded by his commanding officer, or, in case he requires to be tried by a court-martial, by that court-martial, or if he is on board one of Her Majesty's ships, by the commanding officer of that ship;

(5) Where a soldier at the time of his enlistment belonged to any part of the auxiliary forces, the sum required to make good any compensation for which at the time of his enlistment he was under stoppage of pay as a member of the auxiliary forces and any sum which he is liable to pay by reason of his quitting the said part of the auxiliary forces upon his enlistment;

(6) Where a soldier's liquor ration is stopped by his commanding officer on board any ship, whether commissioned by Her Majesty or not, the sum equivalent to such ration, whether previously drawn by the soldier or not, not exceeding one penny a day for twenty-eight days;

(7) The sum required to pay a fine awarded by a court-martial, his commanding officer, or a civil court; and *Pay.*

(8) The sum required to pay any sum ordered by a Secretary of State or any officer deputed by him for the purpose to be paid as mentioned in this Act for the maintenance of his wife or child, or of any bastard child, or towards the cost of any relief given by way of loan to his wife or child:

Provided that—

(*a*) the total amount of deductions from the ordinary pay due to a soldier in respect of the sums required to pay any compensation, fine, or sum awarded or ordered to be paid as aforesaid shall not exceed such sum as will leave to the soldier, after paying for his messing and washing, less than one penny a day; and

(*b*) a person shall not be subjected in respect of any compensation, fine, or sum awarded or ordered to be paid as aforesaid to any deductions greater than is sufficient to make good the expenses, loss, damage, or destruction for which such compensation is awarded, or to pay the said sum.

139. Any deduction of pay authorised by this Act may be remitted in such manner and by such authority as may be from time to time provided by Royal Warrant, and subject to the provisions of any such warrant may be remitted by the Secretary of State.

How deduction of pay may be remitted.

140. (*1*) Any sum authorised by this Act to be deducted from the ordinary pay of an officer or soldier may, without prejudice to any other mode of recovering the same, be deducted from the ordinary pay or from any sums due to such officer or soldier, in such manner, and when deducted or recovered may be appropriated in such manner, as may be from time to time directed by any regulation or order of the Secretary of State.

Supplemental as to deductions from ordinary pay.

(*2*) And any such regulation or order may from time to time declare what shall be deemed for the purposes of the provisions of this Act relating to deductions from pay to constitute a day of absence or a day of imprisonment, so, however, that no time shall be so reckoned as a day unless the absence or imprisonment has lasted for six hours or upwards, whether wholly in one day or partly in one day and partly in another, or unless such absence prevented the absentee from fulfilling any military duty which was thereby thrown upon some other person.

(*3*) In cases of doubt as to the proper issue of pay or the proper deduction from pay due to any officer or soldier, the pay may be withheld until Her Majesty's order respecting it has been signified through a Secretary of State, which order shall be final.

Pay.

Prohibition of assignment of military pay, pensions, etc.

141. Every assignment of, and every charge on, and every agreement to assign or charge, any deferred pay, or military reward payable to any officer or soldier of any of Her Majesty's forces, or any pension, allowance, or relief payable to any such officer or soldier, or his widow, child, or other relative, or to any person in respect of any military service, shall, except so far as the same is made in pursuance of a Royal Warrant for the benefit of the family of the person entitled thereto, or as may be authorised by any Act for the time being in force, be void.

Punishment of false oath and personation.

142. (*1*) Where any regulations made by the Secretary of State or the Commissioners of Her Majesty's Treasury, with respect to the payment of any military reward, pension, or allowance, or any sum payable in respect of military service, or with respect to the payment of money or delivery of property in the possession of the military authorities, provide for proving, whether on oath or by statutory declaration, the identity of the recipient or any other matter in connexion with such payment, such oath may be administered and declaration taken by the persons specified in the regulations, and any person who in such oath or declaration wilfully makes any false statement shall be liable to the punishment of perjury.

(*2*) Any person who falsely represents himself to any military, naval, or civil authority to belong to, or to be a particular man in, the regular reserve or auxiliary forces shall be deemed to be guilty of personation.

(*3*) Any person who is guilty of an offence under the False Personation Act, 1874, in relation to any military pay, reward, pension, or allowance, or to any sum payable in respect of military service, or to any money or property in the possession of the military authorities, or is guilty of personation under this section, shall be liable, on summary conviction, to imprisonment, with or without hard labour, for a term not exceeding three months, or to a fine not exceeding twenty-five pounds.

37 & 38 Vict., c. 36.

(*4*) Provided that nothing in this section shall prevent any person from being proceeded against and punished under any other enactment or at common law in respect of any offence, so that he be not punished twice for the same offence.

Exemptions of Officers and Soldiers.

Exemptions of Officers and Soldiers.

Exemptions of officers and soldiers from tolls.

143. (*1*) All officers and soldiers of Her Majesty's regular forces on duty or on the march; and

Their horses and baggage; and

All prisoners under military escort; and

All carriages and horses belonging to Her Majesty or employed in her military service, when conveying any such persons as above in this section mentioned, or baggage or stores, or returning from conveying the same, shall be exempted from payment of any duties or tolls on embarking or disembarking from or upon any pier, wharf, quay, or landing place, or in passing along or over any turnpike or other road or bridge, otherwise demandable by virtue of any Act of Parliament already passed or hereafter to be passed, or by virtue of any Act, Ordinance, order, or direction of the legislature or other authority in India or any colony: *Exemptions of Officers and Soldiers.*

Provided that nothing in this section shall exempt any boats, barges, or other vessels employed in conveying the said persons, horses, baggage, or stores along any canal from payment of tolls in like manner as other boats, barges, and vessels.

(*2*) When any soldiers have occasion in their march by route to pass regular ferries in Scotland, the officer commanding may, at his option, pass over with his soldiers as passengers, and shall pay for himself and each soldier one-half only of the ordinary rate payable by single persons, or may hire the ferry boat for himself and his party, debarring others for that time, and shall in all such cases pay only half the ordinary rate for such boat.

(*3*) Any person who demands and receives any duty, toll, or rate in contravention of this section shall, on summary conviction, be liable to a fine not exceeding five pounds nor less than ten shillings.

144. (*1*) A SOLDIER of Her Majesty's regular forces shall not be liable to be taken out of Her Majesty's service by any process, execution, or order of any court of law or otherwise, or to be compelled to appear in person before any court of law, except in respect of the following matters, or one of them; that is to say, Exemption of soldiers in respect of civil process.

(*a*) On account of a charge of or conviction for crime; or

(*b*) On account of any debt, damages, or sum of money, when the amount exceeds thirty pounds over and above all costs of suit.

(*2*) For the purposes of this section a crime shall mean a felony, misdemeanor, or other crime or offence punishable, according to the law in force in that part of Her Majesty's dominions in which such soldier is, with fine or imprisonment or some greater punishment, and shall not include the offence of a person absenting himself from his service, or neglecting to fulfil his contract, or otherwise misconducting himself respecting his contract.

(*3*) For the purposes of this section a court of law shall be deemed to include a court of summary jurisdiction and any magistrate.

(*4*) The amount of the debt, damages, or sum shall be proved for the purpose of any process issued before the court has adjudicated on the case by an affidavit of the person seeking to recover the same or of some one on his behalf, and such affidavit shall be sworn, without payment of any fee, in the

Exemptions of Officers and Soldiers.

manner in which affidavits are sworn in the court in which proceedings are taken for the recovery of the sum, and a memorandum of such affidavit shall, without fee, be indorsed upon any process or order issued against a soldier.

(*5*) All proceedings and documents in or incidental to a process, execution, or order in contravention of this section shall be void; and where complaint is made by a soldier or his commanding officer that such soldier is dealt with in contravention of this section by any process, execution, or order issued out of any court, and is made to that court or to any court superior to it, the court or some judge thereof shall examine into the complaint, and shall, if necessary, discharge such soldier without fee, and may award reasonable costs to the complainant, which may be recovered as if costs had been awarded in his favour in any action or other proceeding in such court.

Provided that—

(1) Any person having cause of action or suit against a soldier of the regular forces may, notwithstanding anything in this section, after due notice in writing given to the soldier, or left at his last quarters, proceed in such action or suit to judgment, and have execution other than against the person, pay, arms, ammunition, equipments, regimental necessaries, or clothing of such soldier; and

(2) This section shall not prevent such proceeding with respect to apprentices and indentured labourers as is authorised by this Act.

Liability of soldier to maintain wife and children.

145. (*1*) A SOLDIER of the regular forces shall be liable to contribute to the maintenance of his wife and of his children, and also to the maintenance of any bastard child of which he may be proved to be the father, to the same extent as if he were not a soldier; but execution in respect of any such liability or of any order or decree in respect of such maintenance shall not issue against his person, pay, arms, ammunition, equipments, instruments, regimental necessaries, or clothing; nor shall he be liable to be punished for the offence of deserting or neglecting to maintain his wife or family, or any member thereof, or of leaving her or them chargeable to any union, parish, or place.

(*2*) When any order or decree is made under any Act or at common law for payment by a man who is or subsequently becomes a soldier of the regular forces either of the cost of the maintenance of his wife or child, or of any bastard child of whom he is the putative father, or of the cost of any relief given to his wife or child by way of loan, a copy of such order or decree shall be sent to a Secretary of State or any officer deputed by him for the purpose, and in the case—

(*a*) Of such order or decree being so sent; or

(*b*) Of it appearing to the satisfaction of a Secretary of State or any officer deputed by him for the purpose that a soldier of the regular forces has deserted or left in destitute circumstances, without reasonable cause, his wife or any of his legitimate children under fourteen years of age, *Exemptions of Officers and Soldiers.*

the Secretary of State or officer shall order a portion not exceeding sixpence of the daily pay of a non-commissioned officer who is not below the rank of sergeant, and not exceeding threepence of the daily pay of any other soldier, to be deducted from such daily pay, and to be appropriated, in the first case, in liquidation of the sum adjudged to be paid by such order or decree, and in the second case, towards the maintenance of such wife or children, in such manner as the Secretary of State or officer thinks fit.

(3) Where a proceeding is instituted against a soldier of the regular forces under any Act, or at common law, for the purpose of enforcing against him any such liability as above in this section mentioned, and such soldier is quartered out of the jurisdiction of the court, or, if the proceeding is before a court of summary jurisdiction, out of the petty sessional division in which the proceeding is instituted, the process shall be served on the commanding officer of such soldier, and such service shall not be valid unless there be left therewith, in the hands of the commanding officer, a sum of money (to be adjudged as costs incurred in obtaining the order or decree, if made against the soldier) sufficient to enable him to attend the hearing of the case and return to his quarters, and such sum may be expended by the commanding officer for that purpose; and no process whatever under any Act or at common law in any proceeding in this section mentioned shall be valid against a soldier of the regular forces if served after such soldier is under orders for service beyond the seas.

146. An officer of the regular forces on the active list within the meaning of any Royal Warrant for regulating the pay and promotion of the regular forces shall not be capable of being nominated or elected to be sheriff of any county, borough, or other place, or to be mayor or alderman of, or to hold any office in, any municipal corporation in any city, borough, or place in the United Kingdom: Provided that nothing in this section shall disqualify any officer for being elected to or being a member of a county council. Officers not to be sheriffs or mayors.

147. Every soldier in Her Majesty's regular forces shall be exempt from serving on any jury. Exemption from jury.

148—150. [*Rep. by the Army (Annual) Act, 1888 (51 & 52 Vict., c. 4), s. 6.*]

151. [*Rep. by the Army (Annual) Act, 1895 (58 & 59 Vict., c. 7), s. 5.*]

Legal Penalties in Matters respecting Forces.

(*Secs. 152-154.*)

Legal Penalties in Matters respecting Forces.

Punishment for pretending to be a deserter.

152. Any person who falsely represents himself to any military, naval, or civil authority to be a deserter from Her Majesty's regular forces shall, on summary conviction, be sentenced to be imprisoned, with or without hard labour, for any period not exceeding three months.

Punishment for inducing soldiers to desert.

153. Any person who in the United Kingdom or elsewhere by any means whatsoever—

(1) Procures or persuades any soldier to desert, or attempts to procure or persuade any soldier to desert; or

(2) Knowing that a soldier is about to desert, aids or assists him in deserting; or

(3) Knowing any soldier to be a deserter, conceals such soldier, or aids or assists him in concealing himself, or aids or assists in his rescue,

shall be liable on summary conviction to be imprisoned, with or without hard labour, for a term not exceeding six months.

Apprehension of deserters.

154. With respect to deserters the following provisions shall have effect:—

(1) Upon reasonable suspicion that a person is a deserter, it shall be lawful for any constable, or if no constable can be immediately met with, then for any officer or soldier or other person, to apprehend such suspected person, and forthwith to bring him before a court of summary jurisdiction:

(2) A justice of the peace, magistrate, or other person having authority to issue a warrant for the apprehension of a person charged with crime may, if satisfied by evidence on oath that a deserter is or is reasonably suspected to be within his jurisdiction, issue a warrant authorising such deserter to be apprehended and brought forthwith before a court of summary jurisdiction:

(3) Where a person is brought before a court of summary jurisdiction charged with being a deserter under this Act, such court may deal with the case in like manner as if such person were brought before the court charged with an indictable offence, or in Scotland an offence:

(4) The court if satisfied either by evidence on oath or by the confession of such person that he is a deserter, shall forthwith, as it may seem to the court most expedient with regard to his safe custody, cause him either to be delivered into military custody in such manner as the court may deem most expedient, or, until he can be so delivered, to be committed to some prison,

police station, or other place legally provided for the confinement of persons in custody, for such reasonable time as appears to the court reasonably necessary for the purpose of delivering him into military custody: *Legal Penalties in Matters respecting Forces.*

(5) Where the person confessed himself to be a deserter, and evidence of the truth or falsehood of such confession is not then forthcoming, the court shall remand such person for the purpose of obtaining information as to the truth or falsehood of the said confession, and for that purpose the court shall transmit, if sitting in the United Kingdom to a Secretary of State, or as he may direct, and if in India to the general or other officer commanding the forces in the military district or station where the court sits, and if in a colony to the general or other officer commanding the forces in that colony, a return (in this Act referred to as a descriptive return) containing such particulars and being in such form as is specified in the Fourth Schedule to this Act, or as may be from time to time directed by a Secretary of State:

(6) The court may from time to time remand the said person for a period not exceeding eight days in each instance and not exceeding in the whole such period as appears to the court reasonably necessary for the purpose of obtaining the said information:

(7) Where the court cause a person either to be delivered into military custody or to be committed as a deserter, the court shall send, if in the United Kingdom to a Secretary of State or as he may direct, and if in India or a colony to the general or other officer commanding as aforesaid, a descriptive return in relation to such deserter, for which the clerk of the court shall be entitled to a fee of two shillings:

(8) A Secretary of State shall direct payment of the said fee.

155. Every person (except the Army Purchase Commissioners and persons acting under their authority by virtue of the Regulation of the Forces Act, 1871, who negotiates, acts as agent for, or otherwise aids or connives at— Penalty on trafficking in commissions.

5 Vict.,

(1) The sale or purchase of any commission in Her Majesty's regular forces; or

(2) The giving or receiving of any valuable consideration in respect of any promotion in or retirement from such forces, or any employment therein; or

Legal Penalties in Matters respecting Forces.

(3) Any exchange which is made in manner not authorised by regulations made in pursuance of the Regimental Exchanges Act, 1875, and in respect of which any sum of money or other consideration is given or received, 38 & 39 Vict. c. 16.

shall be liable on conviction on indictment or information to a fine of one hundred pounds, or to imprisonment for any period not exceeding six months, and if an officer, on conviction by court-martial, to be dismissed the service.

Penalty on purchasing from soldiers regimental necessaries, equipments, stores, etc.

156.[1] (*1*) Every person who—

(*a*) Buys, exchanges, takes in pawn, detains, or receives from a soldier or any person acting on his behalf, on any pretence whatsoever; or

(*b*) Solicits or entices any soldier to sell, exchange, pawn, or give away; or

(*c*) Assists or acts for a soldier in selling, exchanging, pawning, or making away with,

any of the property following, namely, any arms, ammunition, equipments, instruments, regimental necessaries, or clothing, or any military decorations of an officer or soldier, or any furniture, bedding, blankets, sheets, utensils, and stores in regimental charge, or any provisions or forage issued for the use of an officer or soldier, or his horse, or of any horse employed in Her Majesty's service, shall, unless he proves either that he acted in ignorance of the same being such property as aforesaid, or of the person with whom he dealt being or acting for a soldier, or that the same was sold by order of a Secretary of State or some competent military authority, be liable on summary conviction, in the case of the first offence, to a fine not exceeding twenty pounds, together with treble the value of any property of which such offender has become possessed by means of his offence; and in the case of a second offence, to a fine not less than five pounds, and not exceeding twenty pounds, together with treble the value of any property of which such offender has become possessed by means of his offence, or to imprisonment, with or without hard labour, for a term not exceeding six months.

(*2*) Where any such property as above in this section mentioned is found in the possession or keeping of any person, such person may be taken or summoned before a court of summary jurisdiction, and if such court have reasonable ground to believe that the property so found was stolen, or was bought, exchanged, taken in pawn, obtained or received in contravention of this section, then if such person does not satisfy the court that he came by the

[1] As to fines recovered under this section in British Indian cantonments, *see* s 21 (*1*) (*a*) of the Cantonments Act, 1889 (XIII of 1889), printed, General Acts, Vol. V, Ed. 1898.

property so found lawfully and without any contravention of this Act, he shall be liable on summary conviction to a penalty not exceeding five pounds. *Legal Penalties in Matters respecting Forces.*

(*3*) A person charged with an offence against this section, and the wife or husband of such person, may, if he or she think fit, be sworn and examined as an ordinary witness in the case.

(*4*) A person found committing an offence against this section may be apprehended without warrant, and taken, together with the property which is the subject of the offence, before a court of summary jurisdiction; and any person to whom any such property as above mentioned is offered to be sold, pawned, or delivered, who has reasonable cause to suppose that the same is offered in contravention of this section, may, and if he has the power shall, apprehend the person offering such property, and forthwith take him, together with such property, before a court of summary jurisdiction.

(*5*) A court of summary jurisdiction, if satisfied on oath that there is reasonable cause to suspect that any person has in his possession, or on his premises, any property on or with respect to which any offence in this section mentioned has been committed, may grant a warrant to search for such property, as in the case of stolen goods; and any property found, on such search shall be seized by the officer charged with the execution of such warrant, who shall bring the person in whose possession the same is found before some court of summary jurisdiction, to be dealt with according to law.

(*6*) For the purposes of this section property shall be deemed to be in the possession or keeping of a person if he knowingly has it in the actual possession or keeping of any other person, or in any house, building, lodging, apartment, field, or place, open or inclosed, whether occupied by himself or not, and whether the same is so had for his own use or benefit, or for the use or benefit of another.

(*7*) Articles which are public stores within the meaning of the Public 39 Vict., Stores Act, 1875, and are not included in the foregoing description, shall not be deemed to be stores issued as regimental necessaries or otherwise within the meaning of section thirteen of that Act.

(*8*) It shall be lawful for the Governor General of India or for the legislature of any colony, on the recommendation of the governor thereof, but not otherwise, by any law or ordinance to reduce a minimum fine under this section to such amount as may to such Governor General or legislature appear to be better adapted to the pecuniary means of the inhabitants.

(*9*) Every person who receives, detains, or has in his possession the identity certificate or life certificate of a person entitled to a military pension or to reserve pay as a pledge or security for a debt, or with a view to obtain

Legal Penalties in Matters respecting Forces.

payment from the pensioner or person entitled to the pay of a debt, due either to himself or to any other person, shall be liable on summary conviction to the like penalty as for an offence under sub-section one of this section, and the certificate shall be deemed to be property within the meaning of this section.

Jurisdiction.

Jurisdiction.

Person not to be tried twice.

157. Where a person subject to military law has been acquitted or convicted of an offence by a court-martial, he shall not be liable to be tried again by a court-martial in respect of that offence.

Liability to military law in respect of status.

158. (*1*) Where an offence under this Act has been committed by any person while subject to military law, such person may be taken into and kept in military custody, and tried and punished for such offence, although he, or the corps or battalion to which he belongs, has ceased to be subject to military law, in like manner as he might have been taken into and kept in military custody, tried or punished, if he or such corps or battalion had continued so subject.

Provided that where a person has since the commission of an offence ceased to be subject to military law, he shall not be tried for such offence, except in the case of the offence of mutiny, desertion, or fraudulent enlistment, unless his trial commences within three months after he has ceased to be subject to military law; but this section shall not affect the jurisdiction of a civil court in the case of any offence triable by such court as well as by court-martial.

(2) Where a person subject to military law is sentenced by court-martial to penal servitude or imprisonment, this Act shall apply to him during the term of his sentence, notwithstanding that he is discharged or dismissed from Her Majesty's service, or has otherwise ceased to be subject to military law, and he may be kept, removed, imprisoned, and punished accordingly as if he continued to be subject to military law.

Liability to military law in respect of place of commission of offence.

159. Any person subject to military law who within or without Her Majesty's dominions commits any offence for which he is liable to be tried by court-martial may be tried and punished for such offence at any place (either within or without Her Majesty's dominions) which is within the jurisdiction of an officer authorised to convene general courts-martial, and in which the offender may for the time being be, in the same manner as if the offence had been committed where the trial by court-martial takes place, and the offender were under the command of the officer convening such court-martial.

Punishment not increased by trial elsewhere than offences committed.

160. No person shall be subject to any punishment or penalties under the provisions of this Act other than those which could have been inflicted if he had been tried in the place where the offence was committed.

Jurisdiction. Liability to military law in respect of time for trial of offences.

161. A PERSON shall not in pursuance of this Act be tried or punished for any offence triable by court-martial committed more than three years before the date at which his trial begins, except in the case of the offence of mutiny, desertion, or fraudulent enlistment; but this section shall not affect the jurisdiction of a civil court in the case of any offence triable by such court, as well as by court-martial; and where a soldier has served continuously in an exemplary manner for not less than three years in any corps of Her Majesty's regular forces he shall not be tried for any such offence of desertion (other than desertion on active service), or of fraudulent enlistment, as was committed before the commencement of such three years, but where such offence was fraudulent enlistment all service prior to such enlistment shall be forfeited.

Adjustment of military and civil law

162. (*1*) IF a person sentenced by a court-martial in pursuance of this Act to punishment for an offence is afterwards tried by a civil court for the same offence, that court shall, in awarding punishment, have regard to the military punishment he may have already undergone.

(*2*) Save as aforesaid, nothing in this Act shall exempt an officer or soldier from being proceeded against by the ordinary course of law, when accused or convicted of any offence, except such an offence as is declared not to be a crime for the purpose of the provisions of this Act relating to taking a soldier out of Her Majesty's service.

(*3*) If an officer—

(*a*) Neglects or refuses on application to deliver over to the civil magistrate any officer or soldier under his command, who is so accused or convicted as aforesaid; or

(*b*) Wilfully obstructs or neglects or refuses to assist constables or other ministers of justice in apprehending any such officer or soldier;

such commanding officer shall, on conviction in any of Her Majesty's superior courts in the United Kingdom, or in a supreme court in India, be guilty of a misdemeanor.

(*4*) A certificate of a conviction of an officer under this section, with the judgment of the court thereon in such form as may be directed by a Secretary of State, shall be transmitted to such Secretary of State.

(*5*) Any offence committed by any such commanding officer out of the United Kingdom shall for the purpose of the apprehension, trial and punishment of the offender be deemed to have been committed within the jurisdiction of Her Majesty's High Court of Justice in England; and such court shall have jurisdiction as if the place where the offence was committed or the offender may for the time being be were in England.

Jurisdiction.

(*6*) Where a person subject to military law has been acquitted or convicted of an offence by a competent civil court, he shall not be liable to be tried in respect of that offence under this Act.

Evidence.

Evidence.

Regulations as to evidence.

163. (*1*) THE following enactments shall be made with respect to evidence in proceedings under this Act, whether before a civil court or a court-martial; that is to say,

(*a*) The attestation paper purporting to be signed by a person on his being attested as a soldier, or the declaration purporting to be made by any person upon his re-engagement in any of Her Majesty's regular forces, or upon any enrolment in any branch of Her Majesty's service, shall be evidence of such person having given the answers to questions which he is therein represented as having given:

The enlistment of a person in Her Majesty's service may be proved by the production of a copy of his attestation paper purporting to be certified to be a true copy by the officer having the custody of the attestation paper without proof of the handwriting of such officer, or of his having the custody of the paper:

(*b*) A letter, return, or other document respecting the service of any person in or the discharge of any person from any portion of Her Majesty's forces, or respecting a person not having service in or belonged to any portion of Her Majesty's forces, if purporting to be signed by or on behalf of a Secretary of State, or of the Commissioners of the Admiralty, or by the commanding officer of any portion of Her Majesty's forces, or of any of Her Majesty's ships, to which such person appears to have belonged, or alleges that he belongs or had belonged, shall be evidence of the facts stated in such letter, return, or other document:

(*c*) Copies purporting to be printed by a Government printer of Queen's regulations or regulations referred to in section 142 of this Act, of royal warrants, of army circulars, or orders, and of rules made by Her Majesty, or a Secretary of State, in pursuance of this Act, shall be evidence of such regulations, royal warrants, army circulars or orders, and rules:

(*d*) An army list or gazette purporting to be published by authority and either to be printed by a Government printer or to be issued, if in the United Kindgom, by Her Majesty's Stationery Office, and if in India by some office under the Governor General of India or the Governor of any presidency in India, shall be evidence of the status and rank of the officers therein mentioned, and of any appointment held by such officers, and of the corps or battalion or arm or branch of the service to which such officers belong: *Evidence.*

(*e*) Any warrants or orders made in pursuance of his Act by any military authority shall be deemed to be evidence of the matters and things therein directed to be stated by or in pursuance of this Act, and any copies of such warrants or orders purporting to be certified to be true copies by the officer therein alleged to be authorised by a Secretary of State or Commander-in-Chief to certify the same shall be admissible in evidence:

* * * * * *

(*g*) Where a record is made in one of the regimental books in pursuance of any Act or of the Queen's regulations, or otherwise in pursuance of military duty, and purports to be signed by the commanding officer or by the officer whose duty it is to make such record, such record shall be evidence of the facts thereby stated:

(*h*) A copy of any record in one of the said regimental books purporting to be certified to be a true copy by the officer having the custody of such book shall be evidence of such record:

(*i*) A descriptive return within the meaning of this Act, purporting to be signed by a justice of the peace, shall be evidence of the matters therein stated.

(2) For the purpose of this Act the expression "Government printer" means any printer to Her Majesty, and in India any Government press.

164. WHENEVER any person subject to military law has been tried by any civil court, the clerk of such court, or his deputy, or other officer having the custody of the records of such court, shall, if required by the commanding officer of such person, or by any other officer, transmit to him a certificate setting forth the offence for which the person was tried, together with the judgment of the court thereon if he was convicted, and the acquittal if he was acquitted, and shall be allowed for such certificate a fee of three shillings. Any such certificate shall be sufficient evidence of the conviction and sentence or of the acquittal of the prisoner, as the case may be. *Evidence of civil conviction or acquittal.*

165. THE original proceedings of a court-martial, purporting to be signed by the president thereof and being in the custody of the Judge Advocate General, or of the officer having the lawful custody thereof, shall be deemed to be of such a public nature as to be admissible in evidence on their mere *Evidence of conviction by Court-martial.*

Evidence. production from such custody; and any copy purporting to be certified by such Judge Advocate General or his deputy authorised in that behalf, or by the officer having such custody as aforesaid, to be a true copy of such proceedings or of any part thereof, shall be admissible in evidence without proof of the signature of such Judge Advocate General, deputy, or officer; and a Secretary of State, upon production of any such proceedings or certified copy, may, by warrant under his hand, authorise the offender appearing therefrom to have been convicted and sentenced to any punishment, to be imprisoned and otherwise dealt with in accordance with the sentence in the proceedings or certified copy mentioned.

Summary and other Legal Proceedings.

Summary and other Legal Proceedings. Prosecution of offences, and recovery and application of fines.

166. (*1*) A COURT of summary jurisdiction having jurisdiction in the place where the offence was committed or in the place where the offender may for the time being be shall have jurisdiction over all offences triable in a civil court under this Act, except any such offence as is declared by this Act to be a misdemeanor or to be punishable on indictment; and any offence within the jurisdiction of a court of summary jurisdiction may be prosecuted, and the fine and forfeiture in respect thereof may be recovered on summary conviction, in manner provided by the Summary Jurisdiction Acts.

(*2*) Any proceedings taken before a court of summary jurisdiction in pursuance of this Act shall be taken in accordance with the Summary Jurisdiction Acts so far as applicable.

(*3*) A court of summary jurisdiction imposing a fine in pursuance of this Act may, if it seem fit, order a portion of such fine not exceeding one half to be paid to the informer.

(*4*) Where the maximum fine or imprisonment which a court of summary jurisdiction in England, when sitting in an occasional court-house is authorised by law to impose is less than the minimum fine or imprisonment fixed by this Act, the court may impose the maximum fine or imprisonment which such court is authorised by law to impose, but if required by either party, shall adjourn the case to the next practicable petty sessional court.

(*5*) The court of summary jurisdiction in Ireland, when hearing and determining a case arising under this Act, shall be constituted either of two or more justices of the peace sitting at some court or public place at which justices are for the time being accustomed to assemble for the purpose of holding petty sessions, or of some magistrate or officer sitting alone or with others at some court or other place appointed for the public administration of justice and for the time being empowered by law to do alone any act authorised to be done by more than one justice of the peace.

(6) Subject to the provisions of this Act with regard to the payment to the informer, fines and other sums recovered before a court of summary jurisdiction in pursuance of this Act shall, notwithstanding anything contained in any other Act, if recovered in England, be paid into the Exchequer, and if recovered in Ireland, shall be applied in manner directed by the Fines Act (Ireland), 1851, and any Acts amending the same. *Summary and other Legal Proceedings.*

14 & 15 Vict., c. 90.

167. (1) In Scotland, offences and fines which may be prosecuted and recovered on summary conviction may be prosecuted and recovered and proceedings under this Act may be taken at the instance of the procurator fiscal of the court, or of any person in that behalf authorised by a Secretary of State or the Commander-in-Chief, or of any person authorised by this Act to complain. Summary proceedings in Scotland.

(2) All fines under this Act in default of payment, and all orders made under this Act failing compliance, may be enforced by imprisonment for a term to be specified in the order or conviction, but not exceeding three months, and the conviction and warrant may be in the form number three of Schedule K. of the Summary Procedure Act, 1864.

27 & 28 Vict., c. 53.

(3) All fines and other sums recovered under this Act before a court of summary jurisdiction, subject to any payment made to the informer, shall be paid to the Queen's and Lord Treasurers' Remembrancer on behalf of Her Majesty.

(4) It shall be no objection to the competency of a person to give evidence as a witness in any prosecution for offences under this Act, that such prosecution is brought at the instance of such person.

(5) Every person convicted of an offence under this Act shall be liable in the reasonable costs and charges of such conviction.

(6) All jurisdictions, powers, and authorities necessary for the purposes of this Act are conferred on the sheriffs and their substitutes and on justices of the peace.

(7) The court may make, and may also from time to time alter or vary, summary orders under this Act on petition by the procurator fiscal of the court, or such person as aforesaid, presented in common form.

168. All offences under this Act which may be prosecuted, and all fines under this Act which may be recovered on summary conviction, and all proceedings under this Act which may be taken before a court of summary jurisdiction, may be prosecuted and recovered and taken in the Isle of Man, Channel Islands, India, and any colony in such courts and in such manner as may be from tme to time provided therein by law, or if no express provision is made, then in and before the courts and in the manner in which the like offences and Summary proceedings in Isle of Man, Channel Islands, India, and the colonies.

Summary and other Legal Proceedings.

fines may be prosecuted and recovered and proceedings taken therein by law, or as near thereto as circumstances admit.

Power of Governor General of India and legislature of colony as to fines.

169. It shall be lawful for the Governor General of India, and for the legislature of any colony, to provide by law for reducing any fine directed by this Act to be recovered on summary conviction to such amount as may appear to the Governor General or legislature to be better adapted to the pecuniary means of the inhabitants and also to declare the amount of the local currency which is to be deemed for the purposes of this Act to be equivalent to any sum of British currency mentioned in this Act.

Protection of persons acting under Act.

170. (*1*) Any action, prosecution, or proceeding against any person for any act done in pursuance or execution or intended execution of this Act, or in respect of any alleged neglect or default in the execution of this Act, shall not lie or be instituted unless it is commenced within six months next after the act, neglect, or default complained of, or, in case of a continuance of injury or damage, within six months next after the ceasing thereof.

(*2*) In any such action tender of amends before the action was commenced may, in lieu of or in addition to any other plea, be pleaded. If the action was commenced after such tender, or is proceeded with after payment into court of any money in satisfaction of the plaintiff's claim, and the plaintiff does not recover more than the sum tendered or paid, he shall not recover any costs incurred after such tender or payment, and the defendants shall be entitled to costs, to be taxed as between solicitor and client, as from the time of such tender or payment; but this provision shall not affect costs on any injunction in the action.

(*3*) Every such action, and also every action against a member or minister of a court-martial in respect of a sentence of such court, or of anything done by virtue or in pursuance of such sentence, shall be brought in one of Her Majesty's superior courts in the United Kingdom (which courts shall have jurisdiction to try the same wherever the matter complained of occurred) or in a supreme court in India, or in any Colonial court of superior jurisdiction, provided the matter complained of occurred within the jurisdiction of such Indian or Colonial court respectively, and in no other court whatsoever.

Miscellaneous.

Miscellaneous.

Exercise of powers vested in holder of military office.

171. Any power or jurisdiction given to, and any act or thing to be done by, to, or before any person holding any military office may be exercised by, or done by, to, or before any other person for the time being authorised in that behalf according to the custom of the service, or according to rules made under section seventy of this Act.

Miscellaneous. Provisions as to warrants and orders of military authorities.

172. (*1*) WHERE any order is authorised by this Act to be made by the Commander-in-Chief or the Adjutant-General, or by the Commander-in-Chief or Adjutant-General of the forces in India, or by any general or other officer commanding, such order may be signified by an order, instruction, or letter under the hand of any officer authorised to issue orders on behalf of such Commander-in-Chief, Adjutant-General, or General or other officer commanding, and an order, instruction, or letter purporting to be signed by any officer appearing therein to be so authorised shall be evidence of his being so authorised.

(*2*) The foregoing enactment of this section shall extend to any order or directions issued in pursuance of this Act in relation to a military convict or military prisoner, and any such order or directions shall not be held void by reason of the death or removal from office of the officer signing or ordering the issue of the same, or by reason of any defect in such order or directions, if it be alleged in such order or directions that the convict or prisoner has been convicted, and there is a good and valid conviction to sustain the order or directions.

(*3*) An order in any case if issued in the prescribed form shall be valid, but an order deviating from the prescribed form if otherwise valid shall not be rendered invalid by reason only of such deviation.

(*4*) Where any military convict or military prisoner is for the time being in custody, whether military or civil, in any place or manner in which he might legally be kept in pursuance of this Act, the custody of such convict or prisoner shall not be deemed to be illegal only by reason of any informality or error in or as respects the order, warrant or other document, or the authority by or in pursuance whereof such convict or prisoner was brought into or is detained in such custody, and any such order, warrant, or document may be amended accordingly.

(*5*) Where a military convict, or a military prisoner, or a person who is subject to military law and charged with an offence, is a prisoner in military custody, and for the purpose of conveyance by sea is delivered on board a ship to the person in command of the ship or to any other person, on board the ship acting under the authority of the commander, the order of the military authority which authorises the prisoner to be conveyed by sea shall be a sufficient authority to such person, and to the person for the time being in command of the ship, to keep the said prisoner in custody and convey him in accordance with the order, and the prisoner while so kept shall be deemed to be kept in military custody.

Furlough in case of sickness.

173. IF any soldier on furlough is detained by sickness or other casualty rendering necessary any extension of such furlough in any place, and there is

Miscellaneous.

not any officer in the performance of military duty of the rank of captain, or of higher rank, within convenient distance of the place, any justice of the peace who is satisfied of such necessity may grant an extension of furlough for a period not exceeding one month; and the said justice shall by letter immediately certify such extension and the cause thereof to the commanding officer of such soldier, if known, and if not, then to a Secretary of State. The soldier may be recalled to duty by his commanding officer or other competent military authority, and the furlough shall not be deemed to be extended after such recall; but, save as aforesaid, the soldier shall not in respect of the period of such extension of furlough, be liable to be treated as a deserter, or as absent without leave.

Licenses of canteens.

174. (*1*) When a person holds a canteen under the authority of a Secretary of State or the Admiralty, it shall be lawful for any two justices within their respective jurisdictions to grant, transfer, or renew any license for the time being required to enable such person to obtain or hold any excise license for the sale of any intoxicating liquor, without regard to the time of year, and without regard to the requirements as to notices, certificates, or otherwise, of any Acts for the time being in force affecting such licenses; and excise licenses may be granted to such persons accordingly.

(*2*) For the purposes of this section the expression license includes any license or certificate for the time being required by law to be granted, renewed, or transferred by any justices of the peace, in order to enable any person to obtain or hold any excise license for the sale of any intoxicating liquor.

Use of recreation room without license.

174A. Notwithstanding anything in the Disorderly Houses Act, 1751, or in the Theatres Act, 1843, where a recreation room is managed or conducted under the authority of a Secretary of State or the Admiralty, it may be used for public dancing, music, or other public entertainment of the like kind or for the public performance of stage plays, without any license in pursuance of those Acts, or either of them.

25 Geo. 2, c. 36. 6 & 7 Vict., c. 68.

PART V.

Application of military law, saving provisions, and definitions.

Persons subject to Military Law.

Persons subject to Military Law. Persons subject to military law as officers.

175. The persons in this section mentioned are persons subject to military law as officers, and this Act shall apply accordingly to all the persons so specified; that is to say,

(1) Officers of the regular forces on the active list, within the meaning of any Royal Warrant for regulating the pay and promotion of the

regular forces, and officers not on such active list who are employed on military service under the orders of an officer of the regular forces, who is subject to military law: *Persons subject to Military Law.*

(2) Officers who are members of the permanent staffs of any of the auxiliary forces, and are not otherwise subject to military law:

(3) Officers of the militia other than members of the permanent staff:

(4) All such persons not otherwise subject to military law as may be serving in the position of officers of any troops or portion of troop raised by order of Her Majesty beyond the limits of the United Kingdom and of India, and serving under the command of an officer of the regular forces:

Provided that nothing in this Act shall affect the application to such persons of any Act passed by the legislature of a colony:

(5) Officers of the yeomanry, and officers of the volunteers, whenever in actual command of men who are in pursuance of this Act subject to military law, or when their corps is on actual military service:

(6) Any officer of the yeomanry or volunteers, whether in receipt of pay or otherwise, during and in respect of the time when with his own consent he is attached to or doing duty with any body of troops for the time being subject to military law, whether of the regular or auxiliary forces, or, with his own consent, is ordered on duty by the military authorities:

(7) Every person not otherwise subject to military law who under the general or special orders of a Secretary of State or of the Governor General of India accompanies in an official capacity equivalent to that of officer any of Her Majesty's troops on active service in any place beyond the seas, subject to this qualification, that where such person is a native of India he shall be subject to Indian Military law as an officer:

(8) Any person, not otherwise subject to military law, accompanying a force on active service, who shall hold from the commanding officer of such force a pass, revocable at the pleasure of such commanding officer entitling such person to be treated on the footing of an officer:

(9) The persons holding commissions as officers in the Indian army reserve when such officers are called out in any military capacity.

176. The persons in this section mentioned are persons subject to military law as soldiers, and this Act shall apply accordingly to all the persons so specified; that is to say, *Persons subject to military law as soldiers.*

(1) All soldiers of the regular forces:

Persons subject to Military Law.

(2) All non-commissioned officers and men of the permanent staff of any of the auxiliary forces who are not otherwise subject to military law:

(3) All non-commissioned officers and men serving in a force raised by order of Her Majesty beyond the limits of the United Kingdom and of India, and serving under the command of an officer of the regular forces:

Provided that nothing in this Act shall affect the application to such non-commissioned officers and men of any Act passed by the legislature of a colony:

(4) All pensioners not otherwise subject to military law who are employed in military service under the orders of an officer of the regular forces:

(5) All non-commissioned officers and men belonging to the army reserve force or the militia reserve force,—

(*a*) When called out for training and exercise; and
(*b*) When called out for duty in aid of the civil power; and
(*c*) When called out on permanent service under Her Majesty's proclamation:

(6) All non-commissioned officers and men in the militia of the United Kingdom,—

(*a*) During their preliminary training; and
(*b*) When they or the body of militia to which they belong are being trained or exercised either alone or with any portion of the regular forces or otherwise; and
(*c*) When attached to or otherwise acting as part of or with any regular forces; and
(*d*) When embodied:

(7) All non-commissioned officers and men belonging to the yeomanry force of the United Kingdom,—

(*a*) When they or their corps are being trained or exercised, either alone or with any portion of regular forces, or with any portion of the militia when subject to military law; and
(*b*) When they are attached to or otherwise acting as part of or with any regular forces; and
(*c*) When their corps is on actual military service; and
(*d*) When serving in aid of the civil power:

(8) All non-commissioned officers and men belonging to the volunteer forces of the United Kingdom,— *Persons subject to Military Law.*

(*a*) When they are being trained or exercised with any portion of the regular forces or with any portion of the militia when subject to military law; and

(*b*) When they are attached to or otherwise acting as part of or with any regular forces; and

(*c*) When their corps is on actual military service:

Provided that it shall be the duty of the commanding officer of any part of the volunteer force not in actual military service, when he knows that any non-commissioned officers or men belonging to that force are about to enter upon any service which will render them subject to military law, to provide for their being informed that they will become so subject, and for their having an opportunity of abstaining from entering on that service.

(9) All persons who are employed by or are in the service of any of Her Majesty's troops when employed on active service beyond the seas, and who are not under the former provisions of this Act subject to military law:

(10) All persons not otherwise subject to military law who are followers of or accompany Her Majesty's troops, or any portion thereof, when employed on active service beyond the seas; subject to this qualification that, where any such persons are employed by or are followers of, or accompany any portion of, Her Majesty's forces, consisting partly of Her Majesty's Indian forces subject to Indian military law, and such persons are natives of India, they shall be subject to Indian military law.

177. Where any force of volunteers, or of militia, or any other force, is raised in India or in a colony, any law of India or the colony may extend to the officers, non-commissioned officers and men belonging to such force, whether within or without the limits of India or the colony; and where any such force is serving with part of Her Majesty's regular forces, then so far as the law of India or the colony has not provided for the government and discipline of such force, this Act and any other Act for the time being amending the same shall, subject to such exceptions and modifications as may be specified in the general orders of the general officer commanding Her Majesty's forces with which such force is serving, apply to the officers, non-commissioned officers, and men of such force, in like manner as they apply to the officers, non-commissioned officers, and men respectively mentioned in the two preceding sections of this Act. *Persons belonging to colonial forces, and subject to military law as officers or soldiers.*

Persons subject to Military Law. Mutual relations of regular forces and auxiliary forces.

178. When officers, non-commissioned officers, and men belonging to the auxiliary forces, or any pensioners, are subject to military law in pursuance of this Act, such officers, non-commissioned officers, men and pensioners shall be subject to this Act in all respects as if they were part of the regular forces, and the provisions of this Act shall be construed as if such officers, non-commissioned officers, men and pensioners were included in the expression "regular forces" : Provided that nothing in this section contained shall affect the conditions of service of any officer, non-commissioned officer, or man belonging to such auxiliary forces, or of any pensioner.

Modification of Act with respect to Royal Marines.

179. In the application of this Act to Her Majesty's Royal Marines the following modifications shall be made:

(1) Nothing in this Act shall prejudice any power of the Admiralty to make Articles of War for the Royal Marines or otherwise prejudice the authority of the Admiralty over the Royal Marines or confer on any officers who are not officers of the Royal marines any greater authority to command the Royal Marines than they have heretofore used; and a general court-martial for the trial of an officer or man in the Royal Marines shall not be convened except by an officer authorised by a warrant from the Admiralty in pursuance of this section, and except that, where such officer or man while subject to this Act is serving beyond the seas with any other portion of the regular forces, and in the opinion of the general or other officer commanding those forces (such opinion to be stated in the order convening the court and to be conclusive), there is not present any officer authorised by warrant from the Admiralty to convene a general court-martial, a general court-martial convened by such general or other officer, if authorised to convene general courts-martial, may try such officer or man:

(2) A district court-martial for the trial of a man in the Royal Marines may be convened by any officer having authority to convene a district court-martial for the trial of any soldier of any other portion of the regular forces:

(3) Any power in relation to the convening of courts-martial, or of authorising an officer to convene courts-martial, or to delegate the powers of convening courts-martial, or of confirming the findings and sentences of courts-martial, or otherwise in relation to courts-martial, which under this Act Her Majesty may exercise by any warrant or warrants, may be exercised in Her Majesty's name by a warrant or warrants from the Admiralty;

and any such warrant may be addressed to any officer to whom any warrant of Her Majesty can be addressed:

Persons subject to Military Law.

(4) Any power vested by this Act in Her Majesty in relation to the confirmation of the findings and sentences of courts-martial, or otherwise in relation to courts-martial, may be exercised by the Admiralty:

(5) Without prejudice to any power of confirmation, the findings and sentences of any general or district court-martial on an officer or man of the Royal Marines may be confirmed by an officer authorised under this section to convene the same, or by any officer otherwise authorised under this Act to confirm the findings and sentences of general or district courts-martial, as the case may be, for the trial of any soldier of any other portion of the regular forces:

(6) Any power vested in Her Majesty by this Act in relation to the making of rules, or to any order with respect to pay, or to any complaint in respect of an officer who thinks himself wronged, shall be vested in and exercised by the Admiralty, and the provisions of this Act respectively relating to such rules, orders and complaints shall be construed, so far as respects the Royal Marines, as if "the Admiralty" were substituted for Her Majesty, as well as for the Secretary of State:

(7) Anything required or authorised by this Act to be done by, to, or before a Secretary of State, the Commander-in-Chief, Adjutant-General, or Judge Advocate-General, may, as regards the Royal Marines, be done by, to, or before the Admiralty; the provisions of this Act shall be construed, so far as respects the Royal Marines, as if "the Admiralty" were substituted for "Secretary of State," "Commander-in-Chief," "Adjutant-General," and "Judge Advocate-General," wherever those words occur:

(8) Anything required or authorised by this Act to be done by, to, or before the Commander-in-Chief of the forces in India, or the general or other officer commanding the forces in any colony or elsewhere, may, as regards the Royal Marines, be done by, to, or before such officer as the Admiralty may by warrant from time to time appoint in that behalf, and, if no such appointment is made, by such Commander-in-Chief or general or other officer:

ons ... to ...tary

(9) Anything authorised by this Act to be done by Royal Warrant may be done, as regards the Royal Marines, by Warrant of the Admiralty, and the provisions of this Act with respect to Royal Warrants printed by the Government printer shall apply to any warrants of the Admiralty under this Act:

(10) Anything authorised to be done by the deputy of the Judge Advocate-General may be done by any one of the Commissioners for executing the office of Lord High Admiral, or by a secretary of the Admiralty:

(11) In the provisions of this Act with respect to evidence, the expression "Queen's regulations" shall be deemed to include Admiralty Regulations:

(12) Nothing in the provisions of this Act relating to the term of enlistment, to the conditions of service, to appointment or transfer, to transfer to the reserve, to the re-engagement or prolongation of service, or to forfeiture of service of a soldier of the regular forces, or to the rules for reckoning service for discharge or transfer to the reserve, shall apply to the Royal Marines:

Save that if regulations made by a Secretary of State and the Admiralty provide for the transfer of men of the Royal Marines to any other part of Her Majesty's regular forces, a man of the Royal Marines may, with his consent, be so transferred in accordance with the said regulations, and subject to those regulations shall become a soldier of the said part of Her Majesty's regular forces in like manner, so nearly as circumstances admit, as if he had been enlisted in pursuance of this Act:

And save that if any regulations so made provide for the transfer to the Royal Marines of men belonging to any other part of Her Majesty's regular forces, a man belonging to such part may, with his consent, be so transferred in accordance with the said regulations, and subject to those regulations, shall become a man of the Royal Marines in like manner, so nearly as circumstances admit, as if he had been enlisted in pursuance of the Acts relating to the Royal Marines:

(13) A marine on his re-engagement shall make a declaration, either before a justice of the peace or person having under this Act the same authority as a justice of the peace, for the purposes of enlistment, or before a naval officer commanding any ship commissioned by Her Majesty, or before the commanding officer of any battalion or detachment of Royal Marines in the form from time to time directed by the Admiralty:

(*Sec. 179.*)

(14) A man in the Royal Marines shall, for absence without leave, on conviction of that offence by court-martial, and for fraudulent enlistment, forfeit his service in like manner as he forfeits it for desertion under the Acts relating to the Royal Marines: *Persons subject to Military Law.*

(15) Officers and men of the Royal Marines, during the time that they are borne on the books of any ship commissioned by Her Majesty (otherwise than for service on shore), shall be subject to the Naval Discipline Act, and to the laws for the government of officers and seamen in the Royal Navy, and to the rules for the discipline of the Royal Navy for the time being, and shall be tried and punished for any offence in the same manner as officers and seamen in the Royal Navy:

9 & 30 Vict., 109, as amended by 7 & 48 Vict., 39.

Provided that—

(*a*) The last-mentioned provision shall not prevent the application of this Act to any person dealing with or having any relations with any such officer or man of the Royal Marines or to any such officer or man if found on shore as a deserter or absentee without leave; and

(*b*) If any such officers or men of the Royal Marines are employed on land, the senior naval officer present may, if it seems to him expedient, order that they shall, during such employment, be subject to military law under this Act, and while such order is in force they shall be subject to military law under this Act accordingly:

(16) If any officer or man of the Royal Marines who is borne on the books of any ship commissioned by Her Majesty commits an offence for which he is not amenable to a naval court-martial, but for which he can be punished under this Act, he may be tried and punished for such offence under this Act:

(17) The Admiralty may direct that an officer or man of the Royal Marines may be tried under this Act for any offence committed by him on shore, whether he be or be not amenable to a naval court-martial for such offence, or be or be not borne on the books of any ship commissioned by Her Majesty:

(18) Where any officer or man of the Royal Marines is on board any ship commissioned by Her Majesty, but is borne on the books thereof for service on shore, he shall be subject to the Naval Discipline Act to such extent and under such regulations as Her Majesty by Order in Council from time to time directs, and, so

9 & 30 Vict., 109, as amended by 7 & 48 Vict., 39.

Persons subject to Military Law.

far as she does not so direct, as is for the time being directed by Order in Council with respect to the other regular forces:

(19) Any naval prison within the meaning of the Naval Discipline Act shall be deemed to be included in the definition of a public prison for the purposes of this Act, and the Admiralty shall not have any authority to establish any military prison under this Act:

(20) In this section the expression "Admiralty" means the Lord High Admiral or the Commissioners for executing the office of the Lord High Admiral for the time being, or any two of them:

(21) The expression "man of the Royal Marines" includes a non-commissioned officer of the Royal Marines:

Modification of Act with respect to Her Majesty's Indian forces.

180. (*1*) In the application of this Act to Her Majesty's forces when serving in India the following modification shall be made:

A court-martial may take the same proceedings for the punishment of a person not subject to military law who, in any part of India, commits any offence as a witness before a court-martial, or is guilty of a contempt of a court-martial, as might be taken by any civil court in that part of India in the case of the like offence in that court, and any court in which such proceedings are taken shall have jurisdiction to punish such person accordingly.

(2) In the application of this Act to Her Majestys' Indian forces the following modifications shall be made:

(*a*) Nothing in this Act shall prejudice or affect the Indian military law respecting officers or soldiers or followers in Her Majesty's Indian forces being natives of India; and on the trial of all offences committed by any such native officer, soldier, or follower, reference shall be had to the Indian military law for such native officers, soldiers, or followers, and to the established usages of the service, but courts-martial for such trials may be convened in pursuance of this Act:

(*b*) For the purposes of this Act the expression "Indian military law" means the Articles of War or other matters made, enacted, or in force, or which may hereafter be made, enacted, or in force under the authority of the Government of India; and such articles or other matters shall extend to such native officers, soldiers, and followers, wherever they are serving:

(*c*) The Governor General of India may suspend the proceedings of any court-martial held in India on an officer or soldier belonging to Her Majesty's Indian forces:

(*d*) An officer belonging to Her Majestys' Indian forces who thinks himself wronged by his commanding officer, and on due appleiation made to him does not receive the redress to which he may consider himself entitled, may complain to the officer appointed in that behalf by the Commander-in-Chief of the forces in India with the approval of the Governor General, and that officer shall cause his complaint to be inquired into, and thereupon report to the Governor General in order to receive the further directions of the Governor General: *Persons subject to Military Law.*

(*e*) A court-martial may sentence an officer of the Indian staff corps to forfeit all or any part of his army or staff service, or all or any part of both:

(*f*) The Governor General of India may reduce any warrant officer not holding an honorary commission to a lower grade of warrant rank, or may remand any such warrant officer to regimental duty in the regimental rank held by him immediately previous to his appointment to be a warrant officer:

(*g*) The provisions of this Act relating to warrant officers not holding honorary commissions shall apply to hospital apprentices in India although not appointed by warrant:

(*h*) Part Two of this Act shall not apply to Her Majesty's Indian forces, but persons may be enlisted and attested in India for medical service or for other special service in Her Majesty's Indian forces for such periods, by such persons, and in such manner, as may be from time to time authorised by the Governor General of India.

(*3*) In this Act, so far as regards India, any reference to an indictable offence, or an offence punishable on indictment, shall be deemed to refer to an offence punishable with rigorous imprisonment.

181. (*1*) The provisions of this Act with respect to enlistment shall not apply to a person enlisted or enrolled in any of Her Majesty's auxiliary forces, except so far as such person enlists or attempts to enlist in the regular forces, and except so far as the said provisions may be applied by any other Act: Modification of Act with respect to auxiliary forces.

(*2*) The provisions of this Act shall apply to the permanent staff of the auxiliary forces who are not otherwise part of the regular forces, in like manner as if such permanent staff were part of the regular forces.

(*3*) The provisions of this Act with respect to billeting and impressment of carriages shall apply to Her Majesty's auxiliary forces when subject to military law, in like manner as if they were part of the regular forces, subject to the following modification.

Persons subject to Military Law.

(4) An order issued and signed as a route or an order signed by the officer commanding the battalion of militia, or the battalion or corps of yeomanry, or volunteers, shall be substituted for a route,—

(*a*) In the case of any militiaman attending for his preliminary training; and

(*b*) In the case of any militia officer, non-commissioned officer, or man, assembled for training and exercise at the place in the United Kingdom apppointed by Her Majesty in that behalf; and

(*c*) In the case of any militia officer, non-commissioned officer, or man, embodied under an order of Her Majesty, who has joined his corps at the place appointed for his assembling; and

(*d*) In the case of any officer, non-commissioned officer, or man of the yeomanry, or volunteers attending at the place at which his corps is required to assemble;

and an order to billet such officer, non-commissioned officer, or man, purporting to be signed in manner required by this Act in the case of a route or by the officer commanding a battalion of militia, or a battalion or corps of yeomanry, or volunteers, as the case may be, shall be evidence, until the contrary is proved, of the order being issued in accordance with this Act, and when delivered to an officer, non-commissioned officer, or man, of the militia, yeomanry, or volunteers, shall be a sufficient authority to such officer, non-commissioned officer, or man, to demand billets, and when produced by an officer, non-commissioned officer, or man, to a constable shall be conclusive evidence to such constable of the authority of the officer, non-commissioned officer, or man, producing the same to demand billets in accordance with the order.

(5) The competence or liability of an officer of the auxiliary forces to be nominated or elected to, or to hold, the office of sheriff, mayor, or alderman, or an office in a municipal corporation, shall not be affected by reason of the battalion or corps to which he belongs being assembled for annual training at the time of such nomination or election, or during the time of his tenure of office.

(6) When a member of the volunteers, being a non-commissioned officer or private, is subject to military law, dismissal may be awarded to him as a punishment, in the event of his committing any offence triable by court-martial or punishable by a commanding officer under this Act.

Special provisions as to warrant officers.

182. The provisions of this Act shall apply to a warrant officer not holding an honorary commission in like manner as if he were a non-commissioned

officer, subject nevertheless (in addition to the modifications for a non-commissioned officer) to the following modifications: *Persons subject to Military Law.*

(1) He shall not be punished by his commanding officer, nor tried by regimental court-martial, nor sentenced by a district court-martial to any punishment not in this section mentioned; and

(2) He may be sentenced—

(*a*) by a district court-martial to such forfeitures, fines, and stoppages as are allowed by this Act, and, either in addition to or in substitution for any such punishment, to be dismissed from the service, or to be suspended from rank and pay and allowances, for any period stated by the court-martial, or to be reduced to the bottom or any other place in the list of the rank which he holds, or to be reduced to an inferior class of warrant officer (if any), or, if he was originally enlisted as a soldier but not otherwise, to be reduced to a lower grade, or to the ranks; or

(*b*) by any court-martial having power to try him, other than a district court-martial, to any punishment which under this section a district court-martial has power to award, either in addition to or in substitution for any other punishment;

(3) A warrant officer reduced to the ranks or remanded to regimental duty in the rank of private shall not be required to serve in the ranks as a soldier;

(4) The president of a court-martial for the trial of a warrant officer shall in no case be under the rank of captain.

183. In the application of this Act to a non-commissioned officer the following modifications shall apply: Special provisions as to non-commissioned officer.

(1) The obligation on a commanding officer to deal summarily with a soldier charged with drunkenness shall not apply to a non-commissioned officer charged with drunkenness:

(2) The Commander-in-Chief, and in India the Commander-in-Chief of the forces in India or such officers as the Commander-in-Chief of the forces in India, with the approval of the Governor General of India in Council, may appoint, may reduce any non-commissioned officer to any lower grade or to the ranks:

(3) A non-commissioned officer may be reduced by the sentence of a court-martial to any lower grade or to the ranks, either in addition to or without any other punishment, in respect of an offence:

(4) A non-commissioned officer sentenced by court-martial to penal servitude or imprisonment shall be deemed to be reduced to the ranks.

Persons subject to Military Law.

Provided that—

(*a*) An army schoolmaster shall not be liable to be reduced to the ranks (unless he has been transferred from the ranks in which case he may be reduced to the rank which he held at the date of transfer), but may nevertheless be sentenced by a court-martial to penal servitude or imprisonment, or to a lower grade of pay, or to be dismissed, and if sentenced to penal servitude or imprisonment shall be deemed to be dismissed; but

(*b*) The Commander-in-Chief, and in India the Commander-in-Chief of the forces in India, or such officer as the Commander-in-Chief of the forces in India, with the approval of the Governor General of India in Council, may appoint, may dismiss an army schoolmaster;

(*c*) A soldier being an acting non-commissioned officer by virtue of his employment either in a superior rank or in an appointment may be ordered by his commanding officer either for an offence or otherwise to revert to his permanent grade as a non-commissioned officer, or, if he has no permanent grade above the ranks, to the ranks.

Special provisions as to application of Act to persons not belonging to Her Majesty's forces.

184. In the application of this Act to persons who do not belong to Her Majesty's forces, the following modifications shall be made:

(1) Where an offence has been committed by any person subject to military law who does not belong to Her Majesty's forces, such person may be tried by any description of court-martial other than a regimental court-martial, convened by an officer authorised to convene such description of court-martial, within the limits of whose command the offender may for the time being be, and may be tried and on conviction dealt with and punished accordingly:

(2) Any person subject to military law who does not belong to Her Majesty's forces shall, for the purposes of this Act relating to offences, be deemed to be under the command of the commanding officer of the corps or portion of a corps (if any) to which he is attached, and if he is not attached to any corps or a portion of a corps under the command of any officer who may for the time being be named as his commanding officer by the general or other officer commanding the force with which such person may for the time being be, or of any other prescribed officer, or, if no such officer is named or prescribed, under the command of the said general or other officer commanding, but such person shall not be liable

to be punished by a commanding officer or by a regimental court-martial:

Provided that a general or other officer commanding shall not place a person under the command of an officer of rank inferior to the official rank of such person if there is present, at the place where such person is, any officer of higher rank under whose command he can be placed.

Saving Provisions. *Saving Provisions.*

185. All jurisdiction and powers of a Secretary of State under this Act with respect to military convicts or military prisoners, or to prisons other than military prisons, shall in Ireland be vested in the General Prisons Board, and shall be exercised by that board in the manner and subject to the regulations in and under which the jurisdiction and powers of that board are exercised under the General Prisons (Ireland) Act, 1877, and the provisions of this Act with respect to the orders and regulations of the Secretary of State shall apply to the orders and regulations of such board. Special provision as to prisoners and prisons in Ireland. [margin: 40 & 41 Vict., c. 49.]

186. Nothing in this Act shall affect the application of the Naval Discipline Act, or any Order in Council made thereunder, to any of Her Majesty's forces when embarked on board any ship commissioned by Her Majesty, and the auxiliary forces shall be deemed to be part of Her Majesty's forces within the meaning of that Act. Saving of Naval Discipline Act as to forces when on board Her Majestys' ships. [margin: 29 & 30 Vict., c. 109.]

Definitions. *Definitions.*

187. This Act shall apply to the Channel Islands and the Isle of Man in like manner as if they were part of the United Kingdom, subject to the following modifications: Application of Act to Channel Islands and Isle of Man.

(1) The provisions of this Act relating to billeting and the impressment of carriages shall not extend to the Channel Islands and the Isle of Man:

(2) For the purposes of the provisions of this Act relating to the execution of sentences of penal servitude or imprisonment, and to prisons, the Channel Islands and the Isle of Man shall be deemed to be colonies, and any sentence of penal servitude or imprisonment passed in any of those islands shall be deemed to have been passed in a colony:

(3) For the purposes of the provisions of this Act relating to the auxiliary forces the Channel Islands shall be deemed to be colonies:

(4) For the purposes of the provisions of this Act relating to the militia the Isle of Man shall be deemed to be a colony.

188. Where a person subject to military law is on board a ship, this Act shall apply until he arrives at the port of disembarkation in like manner as if he and the officers in command of him were on land at the place at which he Application of Act to ships.

Definitions.

embarked on board the said ship, subject to this proviso, that, if he is tried and sentenced while so on board ship, any finding and sentence, so far as not confirmed and executed on board ship, may be confirmed and executed in like manner as if such person had been tried at the port of disembarkation.

Interpretation of term "on active service."

189. (*1*) In this Act, if not inconsistent with the context, the expression "on active service" as applied to a person subject to military law means whenever he is attached to or forms part of a force which is engaged in operations against the enemy or is engaged in military operations in a country or place wholly or partly occupied by an enemy or is in military occupation of any foreign country.

(*2*) Where the governor of a colony in which any of Her Majesty's forces are serving, or if the forces are serving out of Her Majesty's dominions, the general officer commanding such forces declares at any time or times that, by reason of the imminence of active service or of the recent existence of active service, it is necessary for the public service that the forces in the colony or under his command, as the case may be, should be temporarily subject to this Act, as if they were on active service, then, on the publication in general orders of any such declaration, the forces to which the declaration applies shall be deemed to be on active service for the period mentioned in the declaration, so that the period mentioned in any one declaration do not exceed three months from the date thereof.

(*3*) If at any time during the said period the governor or general officer for the time being is of opinion that the necessity continues he may from time to time renew such declaration for another period not exceeding three months, and such renewal shall be published and have effect as the original declaration, and if he is of opinion that the said necessity has ceased, he shall state such opinion, and on the publication in general orders of such statement, the forces to which the declaration applies shall cease to be deemed to be on active service.

(*4*) Every such declaration, renewal of declaration, and statement by the governor of a colony shall be made by proclamation published in the official gazette of the colony, and it shall be the duty of every governor or general officer making a declaration or renewal of a declaration under this section, if he has the means of direct telegraphic communication with the Secretary of State, to obtain the previous consent of the Secretary of State to such declaration or renewal, and in any other case to report the same with the utmost practicable speed to the Secretary of State.

(*5*) The Secretary of State may, if he thinks fit, annul a declaration or renewal purporting to be made in pursuance of this section without prejudice to anything done by virtue thereof before the date at which the annulment takes effect, and until that date any such declaration or renewal shall be deemed to have been duly made in accordance with this section, and shall have full effect. *Definitions.*

190. In this Act, if not inconsistent with the context, the following expressions have the meanings hereinafter respectively assigned to them; that is to say, Interpretation of terms.

(1) The expression "Secretary of State" means one of Her Majesty's Principal Secretaries of State:

(2) The expression "Lord Lieutenant of Ireland" includes the lords justices or other chief governor or governors of Ireland:

(3) The expression "Commander-in-Chief" means the field-marshal or other officer commanding in chief Her Majesty's forces for the time being:

(4) The expression "officer" means an officer commissioned or in pay as an officer in Her Majesty's forces or any arm, branch or part thereof, it also includes a person who, by virtue of his commission, is appointed to any department or corps of Her Majesty's forces, or of any arm, branch, or part thereof; it also includes a person, whether retired or not, who, by virtue of his commission or otherwise, is legally entitled to the style and rank of an officer of Her Majesty's said forces, or of any arm, branch or part thereof:

Warrant and other officers holding honorary commissions are officers within the meaning of this Act, subject to the exceptions in this Act mentioned:

(5) The expression "non-commissioned officer" includes an acting non-commissioned officer, and includes an army schoolmaster when not a warrant officer, but save as is in this Act mentioned does not include a warrant officer not holding an honorary commission:

(6) The expression "soldier" does not include an officer as defined by this Act, but, with the modifications in this Act contained in relation to warrant officers, and non-commissioned officers, does include a warrant officer not having an honorary commission and a non-commissioned officer, and every person subject to military law during the time that he is so subject:

(7) The expression "superior officer" when used in relation to a soldier, includes a warrant officer not holding an honorary commission, and also includes non-commissioned officer as above defined:

Definitions.

(8) The expressions "regular forces" and "Her Majesty's regular forces" mean officers and soldiers who by their commission, terms of enlistment, or otherwise, are liable to render continuously for a term military service to Her Majesty in any part of the world, including, subject to the modifications in this Act mentioned, the Royal Marines and Her Majesty's Indian forces, and the Royal Malta Artillery, and subject to this qualification that when the reserve forces are subject to military law such forces become during the period of their being so subject part of the regular forces:

(9) The expression "reserve forces" means the army reserve force and the militia reserve force:

* * * * * *

(12) The expression "auxiliary forces" means the militia, the yeomanry, and the volunteers:

(13) The expression "militia" includes the general and the local militia:

(14) The expression "volunteers and volunteer forces" includes the Honourable Artillery Company of London:

(15) The expression "corps"—

(A) In the case of Her Majesty's regular forces—

(i) Means any such military body whether known as a territorial regiment or by any different name, as may be from time to time declared by Royal Warrant to be a corps for the purpose of this Act, and is a body formed by Her Majesty, and either consisting of associated battalions of the regular and auxiliary forces, or consisting wholly of a battalion or battalions of the regular forces, and in either case with or without the whole or any part of the permanent staff of any of the auxiliary forces not included in such military body; and

(ii) Means the Royal Marine forces in this Act referred to as the Royal Marines; and also

(iii) Means any portion of Her Majesty's regular forces, by whatever name called, which is declared by Royal Warrant to be a corps for the purposes of this Act; and also

(iv) Means any other portion of Her Majesty's regular forces employed on any service and not attached to any corps as above defined;

(v) And any reference in Part II of this Act to a corps of the regular forces shall be deemed to refer to any such military body as is hereinbefore defined to form a corps; and

(B) In the case of Her Majesty's auxiliary forces— *Definitions.*

(i) Means any such military body, whether known as a territorial regiment or by any different name as may be from time to time declared by Royal Warrant to be a corps for the purposes of this Act, and is a body formed by Her Majesty, and either consisting of associated battalions of the regular and auxiliary forces, or consisting wholly of a battalion or battalions of the auxiliary forces, and either inclusive or exclusive of the whole or any part of the permanent staff of any part of the auxiliary forces; and

(ii) Means any other portion of Her Majesty's auxiliary forces employed in any service, and not attached to any corps as above defined:

(16) The expression "battalion" in the application of this Act to cavalry, artillery, or engineers shall be construed to mean regiment, brigade, or other body into which Her Majesty may have been pleased to divide such cavalry, artillery, or engineers:

(17) The expression "regimental" means connected with a corps, or with any battalion or other sub-division of a corps:

(18) The expression "military decoration" means any medal, clasp, good conduct badge, or decoration:

(19) The expression "military reward" means any gratuity or annuity for long service or good conduct; it also includes any good-conduct pay or pension and any other military pecuniary reward:

(20) The expression "enemy" includes all armed mutineers, armed rebels, armed rioters and pirates:

(21) The expression "India" means British India, together with any territories of any native prince or chief under the suzerainty of Her Majesty exercised through the Governor General of India, or through any governor or other officer subordinate to the Governor General of India; and the expression "British India" means all territories and places within Her Majesty's dominions which are for the time being governed by Her Majesty through the Governor General of India, or through any governor or other officer subordinate to the Governor General of India:

(22) The expression "native of India" means a person triable and punishable under Indian military law as defined by this Act:

(23) The expression "colony" means any part of Her Majesty's dominions exclusive of the British Islands and of British India, and includes Cyprus, and where parts of such dominions are

itions.

under both a central and a local legislature, all parts under the central legislature shall, for the purposes of this definition, be deemed to be one colony:

(24) The expression "foreign country" means any place which is not situate in the United Kingdom, a colony, or India, as above defined, and is not on the high seas:

(25) The expression "beyond the seas" means out of the United Kingdom, the Channel Islands, and Isle of Man; and the expression "station beyond the seas" includes any place where any of Her Majesty's forces are serving out of the United Kingdom, the Channel Islands, and Isle of Man:

(26) The expression "governor general" in its application to India means the Governor General of India in Council:

(27) The expression "governor" as respects the presidency of Bengal means the Governor General of India in Council, and as respects the presidencies of Madras and Bombay means the Governor in Council of the presidency, and in its application to a colony includes the lieutenant-governor or other officer administering the government of the colony:

(28) The expressions "oath" and "swear," and other expressions relating thereto, include affirmation or declaration, affirm or declare, and expressions relating thereto, in cases where an affirmation or declaration is by law allowed instead of an oath:

(29) The expression "superior court," in the United Kingdom, means Her Majesty's High Court of Justice in England, the Court of Session in Scotland, and Her Majesty's High Court of Justice at Dublin:

(30) The expression "supreme court" means, as regards India, any high court or any chief court; and the expression "court of superior jurisdiction," as regards a colony, means a court exercising in that colony the like authority as the High Court of Justice in England:

(31) The expression "civil court" means, with respect to any crime or offence, a court of ordinary criminal jurisdiction, and includes a court of summary jurisdiction:

(32) The expression "prescribed" means prescribed by any rules of procedure made in pursuance of this Act:

(33) The expression "misdemeanor," as far as regards Scotland, means a crime or offence, and so far as regards India, means a crime punishable by fine and rigorous or simple imprisonment at the discretion of the court:

8 & 42 Vict., c. 49. (34) The expression "Summary Jurisdiction Acts"— *Definitions.* "Summary Jurisdiction Acts."

(*a*) As regards England, has the same meaning as in the Summary Jurisdiction Act, 1879;

27 & 28 Vict., c. 53. (*b*) As regards Scotland, means the Summary Procedure Act, 1864, and any Acts amending the same; and

14 & 15 Vict., c. 93. (*c*) As regards Ireland, means within the police district of Dublin metropolis, the Acts regulating the powers and duties of justices of the peace for such district, or of the police of such district; and elsewhere in Ireland, the Petty Sessions (Ireland) Act, 1851, and any Act amending the same:

(35) The expression "court of summary jurisdiction"— "Court of summary jurisdiction."

(*a*) As regards England has the same meaning as in the Summary Jurisdiction Act, 1879; and

(*b*) As regards Ireland, means any justice or justices of the peace, police magistrate, stipendiary or other magistrate, or officer, by whatever name called, to whom jurisdiction is given by the Summary Jurisdiction Acts or any Acts therein referred to; and

27 & 28 Vict., c. 53. (*c*) As regards Scotland, means the sheriff or sheriff substitute, or any two justices of the peace sitting in open court; or any magistrate or magistrates to whom jurisdiction is given by the Summary Procedure (Scotland) Act, 1864; and

(*d*) As regards India, a colony, the Channel Islands and Isle of Man, means the court, justices, or magistrates who exercise jurisdiction in the like cases to those in which the summary Jurisdiction Acts are applicable:

(36) The expression "court of law" includes a court of summary jurisdiction:

(37) The expression "county court judge" includes—

(*a*) In the case of Scotland, the sheriff or sheriff substitute; and

(*b*) In the case of Ireland, the judge of the Civil Bill Court;

(38) The expression "constable" includes a high constable and a commissioner, inspector, or other officer of police:

(39) The expression "police authority" means the commissioner, commissioners, justices, watch committee, or other authority having the control of a police force:

(40) The expression "horse" includes a mule, and the provisions of this Act shall apply to any beast of whatever description, used for burden or draught or for carrying persons in like manner as if such beast were included in the expression "horse."

PART VI.

191 to 193. [*Rep. as to U. K., 56 & 57 Vict., c. 54. Omitted as being spent.*]

Section 96.

FIRST SCHEDULE.

Form of Oath to be taken by a Master whose apprentice has absconded, and of Justice's Certificate annexed.

I, *A. B.*, of , do make oath, that I am by trade a , and that was bound to serve as an apprentice to me in the said trade, by indenture dated the day of for the term of years; and that the said did on or about the day of abscond and quit my service without my consent; and that to the best of my knowledge and belief the said is aged about years. Witness my hand at the day of one thousand eight hundred and .

(Signed) *A. B.*

I hereby certify that the foregoing affidavit was sworn before me at this day of one thousand nine hundred and .

Signed *C. D.*
Justice of the Peace for .

Form of Oath to be taken by a Master whose indentured Labourer in India or a Colony has absconded, and of Justice's Certificate annexed.

of do make oath, that was bound to me to serve as an indentured labourer by indenture dated the day of for the term of years, and that the said did on or about the day of abscond and quit my service without my consent. Witness my hand at the day of one thousand nine hundred and .

(Signed) *A. B.*

hereby certify, etc. [*as for apprentice.*]

s. 166.

SECOND SCHEDULE.

Billeting.

PART I.

Accommodation to be furnished by Keeper of Victualling House.

A keeper of a victualling house on whom any officer, soldier, or horse is billeted—

(1) Shall furnish the officer and soldier with lodging and attendance; and

(2) Shall, if required by the soldier, furnish him for every day of the march and for not more than two days, if the soldier is halted at an intermediate place on the march for more than two days, and on the day of arrival at the place of final destination, with one hot meal on each day, the meal to consist of such quantities of diet and small beer as may be from time to time fixed by Her Majesty's regulations, not exceeding one pound and a quarter of meat previous to being dressed, one pound of bread, one pound of potatoes or other vegetables, and two pints of small beer, and vinegar, salt, and pepper, and with a breakfast consisting of half a pound of bread and a cup of tea; and

(3) When the soldier is not so entitled to be furnished with a hot meal shall furnish the soldier with candles, vinegar, and salt, and allow him the use of fire, and the necessary utensils for dressing and eating his meat; and

(4) Shall furnish stable room and ten pounds of oats, twelve pounds of hay, and eight pounds of straw on every day for each horse.

PART II.

Regulations as to Billets.

(1) When the troops are on the march the billets given shall, except in case of necessity or of an order of a justice of the peace, be upon victualling houses in or within one mile from the place mentioned in the route.

(2) Care shall always be taken that the billets be made out to the less distant victualling houses in which suitable accommodation can be found before billets are made out for the more distant victualling houses:

(3) Except in case of necessity, where horses are billeted, each man and his horse shall be billeted on the same victualling house:

(4) Except in case of necessity, one soldier at least shall be billeted where there are one or two horses, and two soldiers at least where there are four horses, and so in proportion for a greater number:

(5) Except in case of necessity, a soldier and his horse shall not be billeted at a greater distance from each other than one hundred yards:

(6) When any soldiers with their horses are billeted upon the keeper of a victualling house who has no stables, on the written requisition of the commanding officer present the constable shall billet the soldiers and their horses, or the horses only, on the keeper of some other victualling house who has stables, and a court of summary jurisdiction upon complaint by the keeper of the last-mentioned victualling house may order a proper allowance to be paid to him by the keeper of the victualling house relieved:

(7) An officer demanding billets may allot the billets among the soldiers under his command and their horses as he thinks most expedient for the public service, and may from time to time vary such allotment:

(8) The commanding officer may, where it is practicable, require that not less than two men shall be billeted in one house.

THIRD SCHEDULE.

Sec. 112.

Impressment of Carriages.

Table of Rates of Payment for Carriages and Animals.

Carriages and Animals.	Rate per Mile.
In Great Britain.	
A wagon with four or more horses, or wain with six oxen, or four oxen, and two horses.	One shilling.
A wagon with narrow wheels, or a cart with four horses, carrying not less than fifteen hundredweight.	Ninepence.
Any other cart or carriage, with less than four horses, and not carrying fifteen hundredweight.	Sixpence.
In Ireland.	
For every hundredweight loaded on any wheeled vehicle.	One halfpenny.

The mileage when reckoned for the purposes of payment shall include the distance from home to the place of starting, and the distance home from the place of discharge.

Regulations as to Carriages and Animals.

(1) Where the whole distance for which a carriage is furnished is under one mile the payment shall be for a full mile.

(2) In Ireland, the minimum sum payable for a car shall be threepence, and for a dray, sixpence per mile.

(3) In Great Britain, when the day's march exceeds fifteen miles, the justice granting his warrant may fix a further reasonable compensation for every mile travelled not exceeding, in respect of each mile, the rate of hire authorised to be charged by this Act; when any such additional compensation is granted, the justice shall insert in his own hand in the warrant the amount thereof.

(4) In Ireland the payment shall be at the same rate for each hundredweight in excess of the amount which the carriage is liable under this schedule to carry.

(5) A carriage shall not be required to travel more than twenty-five miles.

(6) A carriage shall not, except in case of pressing emergency, be required to travel more than one day's march prescribed in the route.

(7) In Great Britain a carriage shall not be required to carry more than twenty hundredweight.

(8) In Ireland a carriage shall not be required to carry, if a car, more than six hundredweight, and if a dray more than twelve hundredweight.

(9) The load for each carriage shall, if required, at the expense of the owner of the carriage, and if the same can be done within a reasonable time without hindrance to Her Majesty's service, be weighed before it is placed in the carriage.

FOURTH SCHEDULE.

Sec. 154.

Form of Descriptive Return.

Descriptive Return of who* at on the day of , and was committed to confinement at on the day of as a deserter [*or* absentee without leave] from the Bn. of the Regiment of .

* After the word "who" to be inserted either the words "was apprehended," or "surrendered himself," as the case may be.

Age	
Height	*Feet.* Inches.
Complexion	
Hair	
Eyes	
Marks	
In uniform or plain clothes	
Probable date and place of attestation . . .	
Probable date of desertion or beginning of absence, and from what place.	
Name, occupation, and address of the person by whom or through whose means the deserter [*or* absentee without leave] was apprehended and secured.†	
Particulars in the evidence on which the prisoner is committed, and showing whether he surrendered or was apprehended, and in what manner and upon what grounds. The fullest possible details to be given.	

† It is important for the public service, and for the interest of the deserter or absentee without leave, that his part of the return should be accurately filled up, and the details should be inserted by the justice in his own handwriting, or, under his direction, by his clerk.

I do hereby certify, that the prisoner has been duly examined before me as to the circumstances herein stated, and has declared in my presence that he * the before-mentioned Corps, and I recommend † for a reward of s.	———— *Signature* } *of committing magistrate.* ———— *Residence* ———— *Post Town* ———— *Signature of prisoner.* ———— *Signature of informant.*

Or where the prisoner confessed, and evidence of the truth or falsehood of such confession is not then forthcoming:

I hereby certify that the abovenamed prisoner confessed to the circumstances above stated, but that evidence of the truth or falsehood of such confession is not forthcoming, and that the case was adjourned until the day of for the purpose of obtaining such evidence from a Secretary of State.	———— *Signature.* ———— *Residence.* ———— *Post Town.*

* Insert *is* or *is not a deserter or absentee without leave*, from or belongs or does not belong to, as the case may be.

† The justice will insert the name of the person to whom the reward is due, and the amount [5*s.*, 10*s.*, 15*s.*, or 20*s.*,] which, in his opinion, should be granted in this particular case.

FIFTH SCHEDULE.

[*Rep. as to U. K. 56 & 57 Vict., c. 54. Omitted as being spent.*]

THE INDIA OFFICE AUDITOR ACT, 1881.[1]

(44 & 45 Vict., c. 63.)

An Act for providing a Superannuation Allowance for the Auditor of the accounts of the Secretary of State for India in Council and his Assistants.

[*27th August, 1881.*]

WHEREAS by section fifty-two of an Act of the session held in the twenty-first and twenty-second years of Her Majesty, chapter one hundred and six, "for the better government of India," (hereinafter referred to as the Act of 1858,) provision is made for the appointment, and for the payment out of the revenues of India, of an auditor of the accounts of the Secretary of State for India in Council and his assistants;

[1] For digest, *see* Ilbert's *Government of India*, p. 325.

And whereas by section eighteen of the same Act provision is made for granting superannuation allowances to Secretaries, officers, and servants on the establishment of the Secretary of State for India in Council, but the auditor and his assistants are not persons on that establishment, and no provision is made by the Act of 1858 or any other Act for granting superannuation allowances to them, and it is expedient that the law be in this respect amended:

And whereas the existing auditor was appointed to his present office on his resigning a situation in the permanent Civil Service entitling him to superannuation allowance under the Superannuation Act, 1859, and doubts have been entertained whether under these circumstances he has been transferred from his previous employment to his present office within the meaning of the Act twenty-three and twenty-four Victoria, chapter eighty-nine, and it is expedient that such doubts be removed: 22 Vict., c.

And whereas some of the assistants of the existing auditor have been appointed without having obtained the requisite certificates from the Civil Service Commissioners such certificates not having been required by law as a condition of their appointment, and their right to a superannuation allowance ought not to be prejudiced by this circumstance:

* * * * * * * * *

Pension rights of India Office auditor.

1. The auditor of the accounts of the Secretary of State for India in Council and his assistants, including the persons who hold those offices at the time of the passing of this Act, notwithstanding that some of such last mentioned persons have not obtained certificates from the Civil Service Commissioners, shall, for the purposes of superannuation allowance, be in the same position as if they were secretaries, officers, or servants appointed on the establishment of the Secretary of State for India in Council under section sixteen of the Act of 1858; and for the above purposes the existing auditor shall be deemed to have been transferred to his present office from the employment previously held by him.

Short title.

2. This Act may be cited as the India Office Auditor Act, 1881.

The Fugitive Offenders Act, 1881.[1]
(44 & 45 Vict., c. 69.)

An Act to amend the law with respect to Fugitive Offenders in Her Majesty's Dominions, and for other Purposes connected with the Trial of Offenders.

[27th August, 1891.]

Be it enacted by the Queen's most excellent Majesty, by and with the advice and consent of the lords spiritual and temporal, and commons, in this

---

1 *See Chitty's Statutes,* Tit. Criminal Law, p. 157.

present Parliament assembled, and by the authority of the same, as follows; (that is to say,)

Short title.

1. This Act may be cited as the Fugitive Offenders Act, 1881.

PART I.

Return of Fugitives.

Liability of fugitive to be apprehended and returned.

2. Where a person accused of having committed an offence to (which this part of this Act applies) in one part of Her Majesty's dominions has left that part, such person (in this Act referred to as a fugitive from that part) if found in another part of Her Majesty's dominions, shall be liable to be apprehended and returned in manner provided by this Act to the part from which he is a fugitive.

A fugitive may be so apprehended under an endorsed warrant or a provisional warrant.

Endorsing of warrant for apprehension of fugitive.

3. Where a warrant has been issued in one part of Her Majesty's dominions for the apprehension of a fugitive from that part, any of the following authorities in another part of Her Majesty's dominions in or on the way to which the fugitive is or is suspected to be; (that is to say,)

(1) a judge of a superior court in such part; and

(2) in the United Kingdom a Secretary of State and one of the magistrates of the metropolitan police court in Bow Street; and

(3) in a British possession the governor of that possession,

if satisfied that the warrant was issued by some person having lawful authority to issue the same, may endorse such warrant in manner provided by this Act, and the warrant so endorsed shall be a sufficient authority to apprehend the fugitive in the part of Her Majesty's dominions in which it is endorsed, and bring him before a magistrate.

Provisional warrant for apprehension of fugitives.

4. A magistrate of any part of Her Majesty's dominions may issue a provisional warrant for the apprehension of a fugitive who is or is suspected of being in or on his way to that part on such information, and under such circumstances, as would in his opinion justify the issue of a warrant if the offence of which the fugitive is accused had been committed within his jurisdiction, and such warrant may be backed and executed accordingly.

A magistrate issuing a provisional warrant shall forthwith send a report of the issue, together with the information or a certified copy thereof, if he is in the United Kingdom, to a Secretary of State, and if he is in a British possession, to the governor of that possession, and the Secretary of State or governor may, if he think fit, discharge the person apprehended under such warrant.

Dealing with fugitive when apprehended.

5. A FUGITIVE when apprehended shall be brought before a magistrate, who (subject to the provisions of this Act) shall hear the case in the same manner and have the same jurisdiction and powers, as near as may be (including the power to remand and admit to bail), as if the fugitive were charged with an offence committed within his jurisdiction.

If the endorsed warrant for the apprehension of the fugitive is duly authenticated, and such evidence is produced as (subject to the provisions of this Act) according to the law ordinarily administered by the magistrate, raises a strong or probable presumption that the fugitive committed the offence mentioned in the warrant, and that the offence is one to which this part of this Act applies, the magistrate shall commit the fugitive to prison to await his return, and shall forthwith send a certificate of the committal and such report of the case as he may think fit, if in the United Kingdom to a Secretary of State, and if in a British possession to the governor of that possession.

Where the magistrate commits the fugitive to prison he shall inform the fugitive that he will not be surrendered until after the expiration of fifteen days, and that he has a right to apply for a writ of *habeas corpus*, or other like process.

A fugitive apprehended on a provisional warrant may be from time to time remanded for such reasonable time not exceeding seven days at any one time, as under the circumstances seems requisite for the production of an endorsed warrant.

Return of fugitive by warrant.

6. UPON the expiration of fifteen days after a fugitive has been committed to prison to await his return, or if a writ of *habeas corpus* or other like process is issued with reference to such fugitive by a superior court, after the final decision of the court in the case,

(1) if the fugitive is so committed in the United Kingdom, a Secretary of State; and

(2) if the fugitive is so committed in a British possession, the governor of that possession,

may, if he thinks it just, by warrant under his hand order that fugitive to be returned to the part of Her Majesty's dominions from which he is a fugitive, and for that purpose to be delivered into the custody of the persons to whom the warrant is addressed, or some one or more of them, and to be held in custody, and conveyed by sea or otherwise to the said part of Her Majesty's dominions, to be dealt with there in due course of law as if he had been there apprehended, and such warrant shall be forthwith executed according to the tenor thereof.

The governor or other chief officer of any prison, on request of any person having the custody of a fugitive under any such warrant, and on payment or tender of a reasonable amount for expenses, shall receive such fugitive and detain him for such reasonable time as may be requested by the said person for the purpose of the proper execution of the warrant.

Discharge of person apprehended if not returned within one month.

7. If a fugitive who, in pursuance of this part of this Act, has been committed to prison in any part of Her Majesty's dominions to await his return, is not conveyed out of that part within one month after such committal, a superior court, upon application by or on behalf of the fugitive, and upon proof that reasonable notice of the intention to make such application has been given, if the said part is the United Kingdom to a Secretary of State, and if the said part is a British possession to the governor of the possession, may, unless sufficient cause is shown to the contrary, order the fugitive to be discharged out of custody.

Sending back of persons apprehended if not prosecuted within six months or acquitted.

8. Where a person accused of an offence and returned in pursuance of this part of this Act to any part of Her Majesty's dominions, either is not prosecuted for the said offence within six months after his arrival in that part, or is acquitted of the said offence, then if that part is the United Kingdom a Secretary of State, and if that part is a British possession the governor of that possession, may, if he think fit, on the request of such person, cause him to be sent back free of cost and with as little delay as possible to the part of Her Majesty's dominions in or on his way to which he was apprehended.

Offences to which this part of this Act applies.

9. This part of this Act shall apply to the following offences, namely, to treason and piracy, and to every offence, whether called felony, misdemeanor, crime, or by any other name, which is for the time being punishable in the part of Her Majesty's dominions in which it was committed, either on indictment or information, by imprisonment with hard labour for a term of twelve months or more, or by any greater punishment; and for the purposes of this section, rigorous imprisonment, and any confinement in a prison combined with labour, by whatever name it is called, shall be deemed to be imprisonment with hard labour.

This part of this Act shall apply to an offence notwithstanding that by the law of the part of Her Majesty's dominions in or on his way to which the fugitive is or is suspected of being it is not an offence, or not an offence to which this part of this Act applies; and all the provisions of this part of this Act, including those relating to a provisional warrant and to a committal to prison, shall be construed as if the offence were in such last-mentioned part of Her Majesty's dominions an offence to which this part of this Act applies.

Powers of superior court to discharge

10. Where it is made to appear to a superior court that by reason of the trivial nature of the case, or by reason of the application for the return of a

Fugitive when case frivolous or return unjust.

fugitive not being made in good faith in the interests of justice or otherwise, it would, having regard to the distance, to the facilities for communication and to all the circumstances of the case, be unjust or oppressive or too severe a punishment to return the fugitive either at all or until the expiration of a certain period, such court may discharge the fugitive, either absolutely or on bail, or order that he shall not be returned until after the expiration of the period named in the order, or may make such other order in the premises as to the court seems just.

Power of Lord Lieutenant in Ireland.

11. In Ireland the Lord Lieutenant or Lords Justices or other chief governor or governors of Ireland, also the chief secretary of such Lord Lieutenant may, as well as a Secretary of State, execute any portion of the powers by this part of this Act vested in a Secretary of State.

PART II.

Inter-Colonial Backing of Warrants, and Offences.

Application of Part of Act.

Application of part of Act to group of British possessions.

12. This part of this Act shall apply only to those groups of British possessions to which, by reason of their contiguity or otherwise, it may seem expedient to Her Majesty to apply the same.

It shall be lawful for Her Majesty from time to time by Order in Council to direct that this part of this Act shall apply to the group of British possessions mentioned in the Order, and by the same or any subsequent Order to except certain offences from the application of this part of this Act, and to limit the application of this part of this Act by such conditions, exceptions, and qualifications as may be deemed expedient.

Backing of Warrants.

Backing in one British possession of warrant issued in another of same group.

13. Where in a British possession of a group to which this part of this Act applies a warrant has been issued for the apprehension of a person accused of an offence punishable by law in that possession, and such person is or is suspected of being in or on the way to another British possession of the same group, a magistrate in the last-mentioned possession, if satisfied that the warrant was issued by a person having lawful authority to issue the same, may endorse such warrant in manner provided by this Act, and the warrant so endorsed shall be a sufficient authority to apprehend, within the jurisdiction of the endorsing magistrate, the person named in the warrant, and bring him

before the endorsing magistrate or some other magistrate in the same British possession.

Return of prisoner apprehended under backed warrant.

14. THE magistrate before whom a person so apprehended is brought, if he is satisfied that the warrant is duly authenticated as directed by this Act and was issued by a person having lawful authority to issue the same, and is satisfied on oath that the prisoner is the person named or otherwise described in the warrant, may order such prisoner to be returned to the British possession in which the warrant was issued, and for that purpose to be delivered into the custody of the persons to whom the warrant is addressed, or any one or more of them, and to be held in custody and conveyed by sea or otherwise into the British possession in which the warrant was issued, there to be dealt with according to law as if he had been there apprehended. Such order for return may be made by warrant under the hand of the magistrate making it, and may be executed according to the tenor thereof.

A magistrate shall, so far as is requisite for the exercise of the powers of this section, have the same power, including the power to remand and admit to bail a prisoner, as he has in the case of a person apprehended under a warrant issued by him.

Backing in one British possession of summons, etc., of witness issued in another possession of same group.

15. WHERE a person required to give evidence on behalf of the prosecutor or defendant on a charge for an offence punishable by law in a British possession of a group to which this part of this Act applies, is or is suspected of being in or on his way to any other British possession of the same group, a judge, magistrate, or other officer who would have lawful authority to issue a summons, requiring the attendance of such witness, if the witness were within his jurisdiction, may issue a summons for the attendance of such witness, and a magistrate in any other British possession of the same group, if satisfied that the summons was issued by some judge, magistrate, or officer having lawful authority as aforesaid, may endorse the summons with his name; and the witness, on service in that possession of the summons, so endorsed, and on payment or tender of a reasonable amount for his expenses, shall obey the summons, and in default shall be liable to be tried and punished either in the possession in which he is served or in the possession in which the summons was issued, and shall be liable to the punishment imposed by the law of the possession in which he is tried for the failure of a witness to obey such a summons. The expression "summons" in this section includes any subpœna or other process for requiring the attendance of a witness.

Provisional warrant in group of

16. A MAGISTRATE in a British possession of a group to which this part of this Act applies, before the endorsement in pursuance of this part of this Act

British possessions.

of a warrant for the apprehension of any person, may issue a provisional warrant for the apprehension of that person, on such information and under such circumstances as would in his opinion justify the issue of a warrant if the offence of which such person is accused were an offence punishable by the law of the said possession, and had been committed within his jurisdiction, and such warrant may be backed and executed accordingly; provided that a person arrested under such provisional warrant shall be discharged unless the original warrant is produced and endorsed within such reasonable time as may under the circumstances seem requisite.

Discharge of prisoner not returned within one month to British possession of same group.

17. If a prisoner in a British possession whose return is authorised in pursuance of this part of this Act is not conveyed out of that possession within one month after the date of the warrant ordering his return, a magistrate or a superior court, upon application by or on behalf of the prisoner, and upon proof that reasonable notice of the intention to make such application has been given to the person holding the warrant and to the chief officer of the police of such possession or of the province or town where the prisoner is in custody, may, unless sufficient cause is shown to the contrary, order such prisoner to be discharged out of custody.

Any order or refusal to make an order of discharge by a magistrate under this section shall be subject to appeal to a superior court.

Sending back of prisoner not prosecuted or acquitted to British possession of same group.

18. Where a prisoner accused of an offence is returned in pursuance of this part of this Act to a British possession, and either is not prosecuted for the said offence within six months after his arrival in that possession or is acquitted of the said offence, the governor of that possession, if he thinks fit, may, on the requisition of such person, cause him to be sent back, free of cost, and with as little delay as possible, to the British possession in or on his way to which he was apprehended.

Refusal to return prisoner where offence too trivial.

19. Where the return of a prisoner is sought or ordered under this part of this Act, and it is made to appear to a magistrate or to a superior court that by reason of the trivial nature of the case, or by reason of the application for the return of such prisoner not being made in good faith in the interests of justice or otherwise, it would, having regard to the distance, to the facilities of communication, and to all the circumstances of the case, be unjust or oppressive, or too severe a punishment, to return the prisoner either at all or until the expiration of a certain period, the court or magistrate may discharge the prisoner either absolutely or on bail, or order that he shall not be returned until after the expiration of the period named in the order, or may make such other order in the premises as to the magistrate or court seems just.

Any order or refusal to make an order of discharge by a magistrate under this section shall be subject to an appeal to a superior court.

PART III.

Trial, etc., of offences.

20. Where two British possessions adjoin, a person accused of an offence committed on or within the distance of five hundred yards from the common boundary of such possession may be apprehended, tried, and punished in either of such possessions. Offences committed on boundary of two adjoining British possessions.

21. Where an offence is committed on any person or in respect of any property in or upon any carriage, cart, or vehicle whatsoever employed in a journey, or on board any vessel whatsoever employed in a navigable river, lake, canal, or inland navigation, the person accused of such offence may be tried in any British possession through a part of which such carriage, cart, vehicle, or vessel passed in the course of the journey or voyage during which the offence was committed; and where the side, bank, centre, or other part of the road, river, lake, canal, or inland navigation along which the carriage, cart, vehicle, or vessel passed in the course of such journey or voyage is the boundary of any British possession, a person may be tried for such offence in any British possession of which it is the boundary: Offences committed on journey between two British possessions.

Provided that nothing in this section shall authorise the trial for such offence of a person who is not a British subject, where it is not shown that the offence was committed in a British possession.

22. A person accused of the offence (under whatever name it is known) of swearing or making any false deposition, or of giving or fabricating any false evidence, for the purposes of this Act, may be tried either in the part of Her Majesty's dominions in which such deposition or evidence is used, or in the part in which the same was sworn, made, given, or fabricated, as the justice of the case may require. Trial of offence of false swearing or giving false evidence.

23. Where any part of this Act provides for the place of trial of a person accused of an offence, that offence shall, for all purposes of and incidental to the apprehension, trial, and punishment of such person, and of and incidental to any proceedings and matters preliminary, incidental to, or consequential thereon, and of and incidental to the jurisdiction of any court, constable, or officer with reference to such offence, and to any person accused of such offence, be deemed to have been committed in any place in which the person accused of the offence can be tried for it, and such person may be punished in accordance with the Courts Colonial Jurisdiction Act, 1874.[1] Supplemental provision as to trial of person in any place. & 38 Vict., 27.

24. Where a warrant for the apprehension of a person accused of an offence has been endorsed in pursuance of any part of this Act in any part of Her Majesty's dominions, or where any part of the Act provides for the place of Issue of search warrant.

[1] *See ante*, p. 556.

trial of a person accused of an offence, every court and magistrate of the part in which the warrant is endorsed or the person accused of the offence can be tried shall have the same power of issuing a warrant to search for any property alleged to be stolen or to be otherwise unlawfully taken or obtained by such person, or otherwise to be the subject of such offence, as that court or magistrate would have if the property had been stolen or otherwise unlawfully taken or obtained, or the offence had been committed wholly within the jurisdiction of such court or magistrate.

Removal of prisoner by sea from one place to another.

25. WHERE a person is in legal custody in a British possession either in pursuance of this Act or otherwise, and such person is required to be removed in custody to another place in or belonging to the same British possession, such person, if removed by sea in a vessel belonging to Her Majesty or any of Her Majesty's subjects, shall be deemed to continue in legal custody until he reaches the place to which he is required to be removed; and the provisions of this Act with respect to the retaking of a prisoner who has escaped, and with respect to the trial and punishment of a person guilty of the offence of escaping or attempting to escape, or aiding or attempting to aid a prisoner to escape, shall apply to the case of a prisoner escaping while being lawfully removed as aforesaid, in like manner as if he were being removed in pursuance of a warrant endorsed in pursuance of this Act.

PART IV.

SUPPLEMENTAL.

Warrants and Escape.

Endorsement of warrant.

26. AN endorsement of a warrant in pursuance of this Act shall be signed by the authority endorsing the same, and shall authorise all or any of the persons named in the endorsement, and of the persons to whom the warrant was originally directed, and also every constable, to execute the warrant within the part of Her Majesty's dominions or place within which such endorsement is by this Act made a sufficient authority, by apprehending the person named in it, and bringing him before some magistrate in the said part or place, whether the magistrate named in the endorsement or some other.

For the purposes of this Act every warrant, summons, subpœna and process, and every endorsement made in pursuance of this Act thereon, shall remain in force, notwithstanding that the person signing the warrant or such endorsement dies or ceases to hold office.

Conveyance of fugitives and witnesses.

27. WHERE a fugitive or prisoner is authorised to be returned to any part of Her Majesty's dominions in pursuance of Part One or Part Two of this Act, such fugitive or prisoner may be sent thither in any ship belonging to Her Majesty or to any of her subjects.

For the purpose aforesaid, the authority signing the warrant for the return may order the master of any ship belonging to any subject of Her Majesty bound to the said part of Her Majesty's dominions to receive and afford a passage and subsistence during the voyage to such fugitive or prisoner, and to the person having him in custody, and to the witnesses, so that such master be not required to receive more than one fugitive or prisoner for every hundred tons of his ship's registered tonnage, or more than one witness for every fifty tons of such tonnage.

The said authority shall endorse or cause to be endorsed upon the agreement of the ship such particulars with respect to any fugitive prisoner or witness sent in her as the Board of Trade from time to time require.

Every such master shall, on his ship's arrival in the said part of Her Majesty's dominions, cause such fugitive or prisoner, if he is not in the custody of any person, to be given into the custody of some constable, there to be dealt with according to law.

Every master who fails on payment or tender of a reasonable amount for expenses to comply with an order made in pursuance of this section, or to cause a fugitive or prisoner committed to his charge to be given into custody as required by this section, shall be liable on summary conviction to a fine not exceeding fifty pounds, which may be recovered in any part of Her Majesty's dominions in like manner as a penalty of the same amount under the Merchant Shipping Act, 1854,[1] and the Acts amending the same.

[17 & 18 Vict., c. 104.]

Escape of prisoner from custody.

28. If a prisoner escape, by breach of prison or otherwise, out of the custody of a person acting under a warrant issued or endorsed in pursuance of this Act, he may be retaken in the same manner as a person accused of a crime against the law of that part of Her Majesty's dominions to which he escapes may be retaken upon an escape.

A person guilty of the offence of escaping or of attempting to escape, or of aiding or attempting to aid a prisoner to escape, by breach of prison or otherwise, from custody under any warrant issued or endorsed in pursuance of this Act, may be tried in any of the following parts of Her Majesty's dominions, namely, the part to which and the part from which the prisoner is being removed, and the part in which the prisoner escapes, and the part in which the offender is found.

Evidence.

Depositions to be evidence and authentication of depositions and warrants.

29. A MAGISTRATE may take depositions for the purposes of this Act in the absence of a person accused of an offence in like manner as he might take the same if such person were present and accused of the offence before him.

---

[1] *See* now the Merchant Shipping Act, 1894 (57 & 58 Vict., c. 60), printed *post*, p. 971.

Depositions (whether taken in the absence of the fugitive or otherwise), and copies thereof, and official certificates of or judicial documents stating facts, may, if duly authenticated, be received in evidence in proceedings under this Act:

Provided that nothing in this Act shall authorise the reception of any such depositions, copies, certificates, or documents in evidence against a person upon his trial for an offence.

Warrants and depositions, and copies thereof, and official certificates of or judicial documents stating facts, shall be deemed duly authenticated for the purposes of this Act if they are authenticated in manner provided for the time being by law, or if they purport to be signed by or authenticated by the signature of a judge, magistrate, or officer of the part of Her Majesty's dominions in which the same are issued, taken, or made, and are authenticated either by the oath of some witness, or by being sealed with the official seal of a Secretary of State, or with the public seal of a British possession, or with the official seal of a governor of a British possession, or of a colonial secretary, or of some secretary or minister administering a department of the government of a British possession.

And all courts and magistrates shall take judicial notice of every such seal as is in this section mentioned, and shall admit in evidence without further proof the documents authenticated by it.

Miscellaneous.

Provision as to exercise of jurisdiction by magistrates.

30. The jurisdiction under Part One of this Act to hear a case and commit a fugitive to prison to await his return shall be exercised,—

(1) in England, by a chief magistrate of the metropolitan police courts or one of the other magistrates of the metropolitan police court at Bow Street; and

(2) in Scotland, by the sheriff or sheriff substitute of the county of Edinburgh; and

(3) in Ireland, by one of the police magistrates of the Dublin metropolitan police district; and

(4) in a British possession, by any judge, justice of the peace, or other officer having the like jurisdiction as one of the magistrates of the metropolitan police court in Bow Street, or by such other court, judge, or magistrate as may be from time to time provided by an Act or ordinance passed by the legislature of that possession.

If a fugitive is apprehended and brought before a magistrate who has no power to exercise the jurisdiction under this Act in respect of that fugitive, that magistrate shall order the fugitive to be brought before some magistrate having that jurisdiction, and such order shall be obeyed.

31. It shall be lawful for Her Majesty in Council from time to time to make Orders for the purposes of this Act, and to revoke and vary any Order so made; and every Order so made shall while it is in force have the same effect as if it were enacted in this Act.

Power as to making and revocation of Orders in Council.

An Order in Council made for the purposes of this Act shall be laid before Parliament as soon as may be after it is made if Parliament is then in session, or if not, as soon as may be after the commencement of the then next session of Parliament.

32. If the legislature of a British possession pass any Act or ordinance—

Power of legislature of British possession to pass laws for carrying into effect this Act.

(1) for defining the offences committed in that possession to which this Act or any part thereof is to apply; or

(2) for determining the court, judge, magistrate, officer, or person by whom and the manner in which any jurisdiction or power under this Act is to be exercised; or

(3) for payment of the costs incurred in returning a fugitive or a prisoner, or in sending him back if not prosecuted or if acquitted, or otherwise in the execution of this Act; or

(4) in any manner for the carrying of this Act or any part thereof into effect in that possession,

it shall be lawful for Her Majesty by Order in Council to direct, if it seems to Her Majesty in Council necessary or proper for carrying into effect the objects of this Act, that such Act or ordinance, or any part thereof, shall with or without modification or alteration be recognised and given effect to throughout Her Majesty's dominions and on the high seas as if it were part of this Act.

Application of Act.

33. Where a person accused of an offence can, by reason of the nature of the offence, or of the place in which it was committed, or otherwise, be under this Act or otherwise, tried for or in respect of the offence in more than one part of Her Majesty's dominions, a warrant for the apprehension of such person may be issued in any part of Her Majesty's dominions in which he can, if he happens to be there, be tried; and each part of this Act shall apply as if the offence had been committed in the part of Her Majesty's dominions where such warrant is issued, and such person may be apprehended and returned in pursuance of this Act, notwithstanding that in the place in which he is apprehended a court has jurisdiction to try him:

Application of Act to offences at sea or triable in several parts of Her Majesty's dominions.

Provided that if such person is apprehended in the United Kingdom a Secretary of State, and he if is apprehended in a British possession, the governor of such possession, may, if satisfied that, having regard to the place where the witnesses for the prosecution and for the defence are to be found, and to all the circumstances of the case, it would be conducive to the interests of justice so to do, order such person to be tried in the part of Her Majesty's dominions in which he is apprehended, and in such case any warrant previously issued for his return shall not be executed.

Application of Act to convicts.

34. Where a person convicted by a court in any part of Her Majesty's dominions of an offence committed either in Her Majesty's dominions or elsewhere, is unlawfully at large before the expiration of his sentence, each part of this Act shall apply to such person, so far as is consistent with the tenor thereof, in like manner as it applies to a person accused of the like offence committed in the part of Her Majesty's dominions in which such person was convicted.

Application of Act to removal of person triable in more than one part of Her Majesty's dominions.

35. Where a person accused of an offence is in custody in some part of Her Majesty's dominions, and the offence is one for or in respect of which, by reason of the nature thereof or of the place in which it was committed or otherwise, a person may under this Act or otherwise be tried in some other part of Her Majesty's dominions, in such case a superior court, and also if such person is in the United Kingdom a Secretary of State, and if he is in a British possession the governor of that possession, if satisfied that, having regard to the place where the witnesses for the prosecution and for the defence are to be found, and to all the circumstances of the case, it would be conducive to the interests of justice so to do, may by warrant direct the removal of such offender to some other part of Her Majesty's dominions in which he can be tried, and the offender may be returned, and, if not prosecuted or acquitted, sent back free of cost in like manner as if he were a fugitive returned in pursuance of Part One of this Act, and the warrant were a warrant for the return of such fugitive, and the provisions of this Act shall apply accordingly.

Application of Act to foreign jurisdiction.

36. It shall be lawful for Her Majesty from time to time by Order in Council to direct that this Act shall apply as if, subject to the conditions, exceptions, and qualifications (if any) contained in the Order, any place out of Her Majesty's dominions in which Her Majesty has jurisdiction, and which is named in the Order, were a British possession, and to provide for carrying into effect such application.

Application of Act to, and execution of warrant in, United Kingdom, Channel Islands, and Isle of Man.

37. This Act shall extend to the Channel Islands and Isle of Man as if they were part of England and of the United Kingdom, and the United Kingdom and those islands shall be deemed for the purpose of this Act to be one part of Her Majesty's dominions; and a warrant endorsed in pursuance of Part One of this Act may be executed in every place in the United Kingdom and the said islands accordingly.

38. THIS Act shall apply where an offence is committed before the commencement of this Act, or, in the case of Part Two of this Act, before the application of that part to a British possession or to the offence, in like manner as if such offence had been committed after such commencement or application. Application of Act to past offences.

Definitions and Repeal.

39. IN this Act, unless the context otherwise requires,— Definition of terms—

the expression "Secretary of State" means one of Her Majesty's Principal Secretaries of State: "Secretary of State":

the expression "British possession" means any part of Her Majesty's dominions, exclusive of the United Kingdom, the Channel Islands, and Isle of Man; all territories and places within Her Majesty's dominions which are under one legislature shall be deemed to be one British possession and one part of Her Majesty's dominions: "British possession":

the expression "legislature," where there are local legislatures as well as a central legislature, means the central legislature only: "Legislature":

the expression "governor" means any person or persons administering the government of a British possession, and includes the governor and lieutenant-governor of any part of India: "Governor":

the expression "constable" means, out of England, any policeman or officer having the like powers and duties as a constable in England: "Constable":

the expression "magistrate" means, except in Scotland, any justice of the peace, and in Scotland means a sheriff or sheriff substitute and in the Channel Islands, Isle of Man, and a British possession means any person having authority to issue a warrant for the apprehension of persons accused of offences and to commit such persons for trial: "Magistrate":

the expression "offence punishable on indictment" means, as regards India, an offence punishable on a charge or otherwise: "Offence punishable on indictment":

the expression "oath" includes affirmation or declaration in the case of persons allowed by law to affirm or declare instead of swearing, and the expression "swear" and other words relating to an oath or swearing shall be construed accordingly: "Oath":

the expression "deposition" includes any affidavit, affirmation, or statement made upon oath as above defined: "Deposition":

the expression "superior court" means: "Superior Court":

(1) in England, Her Majesty's Court of Appeal and High Court of Justice; and

(2) in Scotland, the High Court of Judiciary; and

(3) in Ireland, Her Majesty's Court of Appeal and Her Majesty's High Court of Justice at Dublin; and

(4) in a British possession, any court having in that possession the like criminal jurisdiction to that which is vested in the High Court of Justice in England, or such court or judge as may be determined by any Act or ordinance of that possession.

40 & 41. [*Rep. as to U. K. 57 & 58, Vict., c. 56 (S. L. R.). Omitted as being spent.*]

SCHEDULE.

[*Rep. as to U. K. 57 & 58 Vict., c. 56 (S. L. R.). Omitted as being spent.*]

---

[1]The Documentary Evidence Act, 1882.

(45 & 46 Vict., c. 9.)

An Act to amend the Documentary Evidence Act, 1868, and other enactments relating to the evidence of documents by means of copies printed by the Government Printers.

[*19th June, 1882.*]

Whereas by the Documentary Evidence Act, 1868, and enactments applying that Act, divers proclamations, orders, regulations, rules, and other documents may be proved by the production of copies thereof purporting to be printed by the Government Printer, and the Government Printer is thereby defined to mean and include the Printer to Her Majesty:

31 & 32 V. c. 37. 33 & 34 V. c. 75, s. 33 & 34 V. c. 79, s. 34 & 35 V. c. 70, s. 40 & 41 V. c. 21, s. 40 & 41 V. c. 53, s.

And whereas divers other enactments provide that copies of Acts of Parliament, regulations, warrants, circulars, gazettes, and other documents shall be admissible in evidence if purporting to be printed by the Government Printer, or the Queen's Printer, or a printer authorised by Her Majesty, or otherwise under the authority of Her Majesty:

And whereas it is expedient to make further provision respecting the printing of the copies aforesaid:

* * * * * * * * * * * * *

Short title. **1.** This Act may be cited as the Documentary Evidence Act, 1882.

---

[1] This Act may be cited, with 25 others, as the Evidence Act, 1806 to 1895, *see* the Short Titles Act, 1896 (59 & 60 Vict., c. 14), *post*, p. 722. *See*, too, *Chitty's Statutes*, Tit. Evidence, p. 41 *Taylor* on Evidence, §§ 523, 524, 527.

2. WHERE any enactment, whether passed before or after the passing of this Act, provides that a copy of any Act of Parliament, proclamation, order, regulation, rule, warrant, circular, list, gazette, or document shall be conclusive evidence, or be evidence, or have any other effect, when purporting to be printed by the Government Printer, or the Queen's Printer, or a printer authorised by Her Majesty, or otherwise under Her Majesty's authority, whatever may be the precise expression used, such copy shall also be conclusive evidence, or evidence, or have the said effect (as the case may be) if it purports to be printed under the superintendence or authority of Her Majesty's Stationery Office.

Documents printed under superintendence of Stationery Office receivable in evidence.

3. IF any person prints any copy of any Act, proclamation, order, regulation, royal warrant, circular, list, gazette, or document which falsely purports to have been printed under the superintendence or authority of Her Majesty's Stationery Office, or tenders in evidence any copy which falsely purports to have been printed as aforesaid, knowing that the same was not so printed, he shall be guilty of felony, and shall, on conviction, be liable to penal servitude for a term not exceeding seven years, or to be imprisoned for a term not exceeding two years, with or without hard labour.

Penalty for forgery.

4. THE Documentary Evidence Act, 1868, as amended by this Act, shall apply to proclamations, orders, and regulations issued by the Lord Lieutenant or other chief governor or governors of Ireland, either alone or acting with the advice of the Privy Council in Ireland, as fully as it applies to proclamations, orders, and regulations issued by Her Majesty.

Application of Act to Ireland.

In the same Act, the term "the Privy Council" shall include the Privy Council in Ireland, or any committee thereof.

In the same Act, and in this Act, the term "the Government Printer" shall include any printer to Her Majesty in Ireland and any printer printing in Ireland under the superintendence or authority of Her Majesty's Stationery Office.

THE BOMBAY CIVIL FUND ACT, 1882.

(45 & 46 Vict., c. 45.)

An Act to make provision for the transfer of the Assets and Liabilities of the Provident Branch of the Bombay Civil Fund and other Funds to the Secretary of State for India in Council.

[*18th August, 1882.*]

WHEREAS an institution known as the Provident Branch of the Bombay Civil Fund (founded on the Bombay Civil Fund of earlier date) was established in Bombay under the authority given by the Court of Directors of the East India Company in a public despatch to the Governor in Council at Bombay, dated the thirty-first of December one thousand eight hundred and twenty-four, the said Provident Branch having a separate capital for making provision for such of the civil servants of the said company as should be obliged by ill-health to leave India either temporarily or permanently, and for the granting of annuities to the widows and children of its members and of portions for the children of members, and the said fund was supported by the subscriptions of the civil servants of the said company and by certain contributions from the said company:

And whereas in a financial despatch to the Government of India, dated the twenty-first of July one thousand eight hundred and eighty-one, certain changes respecting the grant of annuities to widows were authorised by the Secretary of State for India in Council, and certain terms were stated on which the Secretary of State for India in Council was willing to take over the assets, liabilities, and management of the said institution:

And whereas in accordance with the instructions contained in the aforesaid despatch the Government of India caused the inquiry to be made, whether upon the terms offered by the Secretary of State for India in Council in the said despatch the subscribers to the said fund were willing to surrender the accumulated fund to the Secretary of State for India in Council, and the proposition so to make over the accumulated fund on the terms offered by the Secretary of State for India in Council was carried in the affirmative by the subscribers by a large majority of votes:

And whereas in order to avoid any doubt that may arise in regard to the legality of such transfer it is necessary to make provision by law for enabling the trustees of the said fund to transfer the assets and liabilities thereof to the Secretary of State for India in Council, and for enabling the Secretary of State for India in Council, to accept the same:

* * * * * *

Assets, etc., of Provident Branch of Bombay Civil Fund transferred to Secretary of State.

1. It shall be lawful for the trustees of the Provident Branch of the Bombay Civil Fund to transfer to the Secretary of State for India in Council the assets and liabilities of the fund, including any assets and liabilities to which the said trustees may have succeeded as representing the trustees of the earlier fund at Bombay, and for the Secretary of State for India in Council to accept the same.

Payments charged on said fund to be payable from revenues of India.

2. As soon as the assets and liabilities of the said fund, including as aforesaid, shall be transferred to the Secretary of State for India in Council, and the acceptance thereof by the Secretary of State for India in Council notified by the Government of India, all existing liabilities of the said fund

shall be deemed to be liabilities of the revenues of India, and all such liabilities may be enforced against the Secretary of State for India in Council in like manner as they might have been enforced against the trustees of the said fund if this Act had not been passed; and every civil servant, or widow or child of a civil servant, who shall at the date of such notification be an incumbent of an annuity from the said fund or from any earlier fund, the assets and liabilities of which shall have been transferred as aforesaid, shall be entitled to receive from time to time the amount of such annuity from the revenues of India; and every civil servant, and every widow or child of a civil servant, who shall be a subscriber to the said fund, or shall be an incumbent annuitant of the said fund at or after the date of such notification, shall be entitled to the benefits to which they are entitled under the existing rules at the date of the passing of this Act, with the additional benefit in the case of widows of a pension of sixty pounds per annum, such additional benefit to take effect as from the first of April one thousand eight hundred and eighty-two.

Provided that nothing in this Act contained shall be held to preclude the Secretary of State for India in Council from assigning to the incumbents on and subscribers to the said fund, or to any such widow or child as aforesaid, any benefits in addition to those secured to them by this Act, if on considering the assets and liabilities of the said fund the Secretary of State for India in Council shall deem it reasonable so to do.

How notifications, etc., to be given.

3. All notifications or applications on the part of the subscribers to or beneficiaries under the said fund which are required or prescribed by the rules of the said fund as existing at the date of this Act shall be given and made in such manner and to such person or persons as the Secretary of State for India in Council shall from time to time appoint.

Powers of trustees of fund vested in Secretary of State.

4. From and after the passing of this Act there shall vest in the Secretary of State for India in Council all powers and authorities, discretionary or otherwise, which were prior to the date of this Act vested in the trustees of the said fund, or the subscribers thereto in general meeting: Provided always, that notwithstanding anything herein contained, the Secretary of State for India in Council shall, as far as may be practicable, conform to and adopt the practice heretofore followed in the management of the said fund.

Saving for subscribers' claims.

5. Provided that nothing in this Act shall prejudice any claim which may be made by any subscriber to or beneficiary under the said fund, or by the representatives of any such subscriber or beneficiary upon the funds so transferred, and in case any question shall arise between any such subscriber, or the representatives of any deceased subscriber, or the widow or a child of any such subscriber, or the representatives of any such widow or child on the one hand, and the Secretary of State for India in Council on the other, as to any liability or alleged liability of the said fund such question shall be determined by Her Majesty's Court of Appeal in such manner as may be provided by any General Orders, or as the said Court may on special application think fit to prescribe, anything in the Statute of Limitations to the contrary notwithstanding.

Assets, etc., of Bengal and Madras Funds may be transferred to Secretary of State after vote.

6. And whereas it may be expedient that the Secretary of State for India in Council should have authority in like manner to accept the transfer of the assets, liabilities, and management of other institutions, known as the Bengal Civil Fund and the Madras Civil Fund, with the consent of the subscribers to the said institutions respectively: It shall be lawful for the managers or trustees to make over the assets, liabilities and management of both or either of the said funds, and for the Secretary of State for India in Council to take and assume the same upon such terms as the Secretary of State for India in Council may approve, if at any time hereafter it shall appear by a vote, specially taken for the purpose, that a majority of not less than three-fourths of the subscribers to those institutions who may vote upon the question are in favour of such transfer.

The Reserve Forces Act, 1882.[1]

(45 & 46 Vict., c. 48.)

An Act to consolidate the Acts relating to the Reserve Forces.

[*18th August, 1882.*]

* * * * * * *

Preliminary.

Short title.

1. This Act may be cited as the Reserve Forces Act, 1882.

Commencement of Act.

2. This Act shall come into operation on the first day of January one thousand eight hundred and eighty-three, which day is in this Act referred to as the commencement of this Act.

PART I.

Army Reserve.

Establishment of army reserve.

3. It shall be lawful for Her Majesty to keep up a force in the United Kingdom, called the army reserve, to consist of two classes, as follows:—

Class I.—The first class shall consist of such number of men as may from time to time be provided by Parliament, and shall be liable, when called out on permanent service, to serve either in the United Kingdom or elsewhere, and

[1] During the passage of this volume through the Press, ss. 3 & 10 (*4*) of this Act have been further amended by the Reserve Forces Act, 1900 (63 & 64 Vict., c. 42), *see* Gazette of India, 1900, for the month of November, Pt. I.

shall consist of men who, having served in any of Her Majesty's regular forces, may either be transferred to the reserve in pursuance of the Army Act, 1881, or be enlisted or re-engaged in pursuance of this Act.

[& 45 Vict., 8.]

For the purpose of establishing a supplemental reserve it shall be lawful for Her Majesty to direct that the first class of the army reserve shall consist of two divisions, and in the event of such direction being given men in the second division shall not be liable to be called out on permanent service until directions have been given for calling out the whole of the first division on such service.

Class II.—The second class shall consist of such number of men as may from time to time be provided by Parliament, and shall be liable, when called out on permanent service, to serve in the United Kingdom only, and shall consist of men who—

(*a*) being out-pensioners of Chelsea Hospital, or (on account of service in the Royal Marines) out-pensioners of Greenwich Hospital; or

(*b*) having served in any of Her Majesty's regular forces for not less than the full term of their original enlistment,

may be enlisted or re-engaged in pursuance of this Act.

Procedure and term of service on enlistment or re-engagement.

4. Every man who enters the army reserve—

(*a*) If he enters otherwise than by transfer to the reserve in pursuance of the Army Act, 1881,[1] shall be enlisted; and

[& 45 Vict., 8.]

(*b*) If he is re-engaged in the army reserve, shall be re-engaged, in such manner, and for a term of such length, and to begin at such date, as may be prescribed.

Calling out army reserve in aid of the civil power.

5. (*1*) It shall be lawful for a Secretary of State, at any time when occasion appears to require, to call out the whole or so many as he thinks necessary of the men belonging to the army reserve, to aid the civil power in the preservation of the public peace.

(*2*) It shall be lawful for any officer commanding Her Majesty's forces in any town or district, on the requisition in writing of any justice of the peace, to call out for the purpose aforesaid the men belonging to the army reserve who are resident in such town or district, or such of them as he may think necessary.

(*3*) Any power by this section vested in a Secretary of State may as regards men resident in Ireland be exercised also by the Lord Lieutenant.

Punishment of certain offences by army reserve men.

6. (*1*) Where a man belonging to the army reserve—

(*a*) Fails without reasonable excuse on two consecutive occasions to comply with the orders or regulations in force under this Act with respect to the payment of the army reserve; or

---

[1] Printed *ante*, p. 614.

(*Sec. 6.*)

(*b*) When required by or in pursuance of the orders or regulations in force under this Act to attend at any place, fails without reasonable excuse to attend in accordance with such requirement; or

(*c*) Uses threatening or insulting language, or behaves in an insubordinate manner, to any officer or warrant or non-commissioned officer who in pursuance of the orders or regulations in force under this Act is acting in the execution of his office, and who would be the superior officer of such man if such man were subject to military law; or

(*d*) By any fraudulent means obtains or is accessory to the obtaining of any pay or other sum contrary to the orders or regulations in force under this Act; or

(*e*) Fails without reasonable excuse to comply with the orders or regulations in force under this Act,

he shall be guilty of an offence.

(2) A man belonging to the army reserve who commits an offence under this section, whether otherwise subject to military law or not, shall be liable as follows; that is to say,

(*a*) be liable to be tried by court-martial, and on conviction to suffer imprisonment, or such less punishment as in the Army Act, 1881,[1] mentioned; or 44 & 45 Vict. c. 58.

(*b*) be liable to be convicted by a court of summary jurisdiction, and to be sentenced to a fine of not less than forty shillings and not more than twenty-five pounds, and in default of payment to imprisonment, with or without hard labour, for any term not less than seven days and not more than the maximum term allowed by law for non-payment of the fine;

and may in any case be taken into military custody.

(3) Where a man belonging to the army reserve commits in the presence of any officer any offence under this section, or any offence under sub-section two or sub-section three of section one hundred and forty-two of the Army Act, 1881 (relating to the punishment of personation), that officer may, if he thinks fit, order such man, in lieu of being taken into military custody, to be taken into custody by any constable, and brought before a court of summary jurisdiction for the purpose of being dealt with by that court. 44 & 45 Vict. c. 58.

(4) A certificate purporting to be signed by an officer who is therein mentioned as an officer appointed to pay a man belonging to the army reserve, and

[1] Printed *ante*, p. 614.

stating that such man has failed on two consecutive occasions to comply with the orders or regulations in force under this Act with respect to the payment of the army reserve, shall, without proof of the signature or appointment of such officer, be evidence of such failure.

(6) Where a man belonging to the army reserve is required by or in pursuance of the orders or regulations in force under this Act to attend at any place, a certificate purporting to be signed by an officer or person who is mentioned in such certificate as appointed to be present at such place for the purpose of inspecting men belonging to the army reserve, or for any other purpose connected with such reserve, and stating that the man failed to attend in accordance with the said requirement, shall, without proof of the signature or appointment of such officer or person, be evidence of such failure.

7. A MAN belonging to the army reserve shall not be liable to serve the office of constable, or any other parochial, township, or borough office. Men exempt from parish officers, etc.

PART II.

MILITIA RESERVE.

8. (*1*) IT shall be lawful for Her Majesty to keep up a force in the United Kingdom called the militia reserve, consisting of such number of men as may from time to time be provided by Parliament. Establishment of militia reserve.

(*2*) A Secretary of State may cause to be enlisted from time to time in the militia reserve such militiamen as are willing to enlist themselves, not exceeding the prescribed number (if any) out of any particular corps.

9. (*1*) EVERY man enlisted in the militia reserve shall be enlisted to serve either for six years or for the residue of the term of his militia engagement. Term of service, and re-engagement.

(*2*) A man in the militia reserve who is re-engaged as a militiaman may also be re-engaged in the militia reserve for the prescribed period, not exceeding the term for which he is re-engaged as a militiaman.

10. (*1*) A man belonging to the militia reserve shall, subject to the provisions of this Act, continue to be for all purposes a militiaman, and if he has enlisted in the militia reserve for a period which will expire subsequently to the expiration of his militia engagement he shall be deemed to have enlisted in the militia for such longer period. Effect of enlistment on position as militiaman.

(*2*) A Secretary of State may in his discretion at any time discharge a man belonging to the militia reserve from his engagement, and a man so discharged shall thenceforth for the remainder of his engagement in the militia reserve be a militiaman only, and may be discharged from the militia or otherwise dealt with accordingly.

(*3*) When a man has enlisted in the militia reserve, his place in the militia shall not be deemed vacant until directions are given for calling him out on permanent service, but when such directions are given his place shall be deemed vacant, and shall be filled in manner provided by law with respect to vacancies in the militia.

(*4*) When a man who has been so called out is released from permanent service on the ground of his services being no longer required, he shall again become for the remainder (if any) of his engagement a militiaman in the corps to which he previously belonged, with rank and pay not lower than he was entitled to before he entered on permanent service; and if there is no vacancy he shall be deemed to be a supernumerary until there is a vacancy.

PART III.

General.

Annual Training and Calling out on Permanent Service of Reserves.

Annual training of reserve forces.

11. (*1*) All or any of the men belonging to the army reserve and the militia reserve respectively may be called out for annual training at such time or times, and at such place or places within the United Kingdom, and for such period or periods, as may be prescribed, not exceeding in any one year, in the case of a man belonging to the army reserve twelve days or twenty drills, and in the case of a man belonging to the militia reserve fifty-six days.

(*2*) Every man so called out may during his annual training be attached to and trained with a body of the regular or auxiliary forces.

(*3*) The annual training under this section of a man belonging to the militia reserve shall be in substitution for the annual training to which he is liable as a militiaman.

Calling out reserve forces on permanent service.

12. (*1*) In case of imminent national danger or of great emergency, it shall be lawful for Her Majesty in Council by proclamation, the occasion being first communicated to Parliament, if Parliament be then sitting, or declared in Council and notified by the proclamation, if Parliament be not then sitting, to order that the army reserve and the militia reserve, or either of them, shall be called out on permanent service.

(*2*) It shall be lawful for Her Majesty by any such proclamation to order a Secretary of State from time to time to give, and when given to revoke or vary, such directions as may seem necessary or proper for calling out the forces or force mentioned in the proclamation, or all or any of the men belonging thereto.

(*3*) Every such proclamation and the directions given in pursuance thereof shall be obeyed as if enacted in this Act, and every man for the time being called out by such directions shall attend at the place and time fixed by those directions, and at and after that time shall be deemed to be called out on permanent service.

(*4*) A proclamation under this section shall for the purposes of the Army Act, 1881, be deemed to be a proclamation requiring soldiers in the reserve to re-enter upon army service.

44 & 45 Vict., c. 58.

Assembly of Parliament when reserve forces ordered to be called out on permanent service.

13. WHENEVER Her Majesty orders the army reserve and militia reserve, or either of them, to be called out on permanent service, if Parliament be then separated by such adjournment or prorogation as will not expire within ten days, a proclamation shall be issued for the meeting of Parliament within ten days, and Parliament shall accordingly meet and sit upon the day appointed by such proclamation, and shall continue to sit and act in like manner as if it had stood adjourned or prorogued to the same day.

Service of reserve men called out.

14. (*1*) A MAN belonging to either of the reserve forces when called out on permanent service shall be liable to serve until Her Majesty no longer requires his services, so, however, that he shall not be required to serve for a period exceeding in the whole the remainder unexpired of his term of service in the reserve force to which he belongs, and any further period not exceeding twelve months during which as a soldier of the regular forces he can, under section eighty-seven of the Army Act, 1881,[1] be detained in service after the time at which he would otherwise be entitled to be discharged.

(*2*) A man called out on permanent service shall during his service form part of the regular forces, and be subject to the Army Act, 1881,[1] accordingly, and the competent military authority within the meaning of Part Two of that Act may, if it seems proper, appoint him to any corps as a soldier of the regular forces, and the competent military authority within the meaning of the said Part Two may within three months after such appointment transfer him to any other corps of the regular forces, so, however, that he shall not without his consent be appointed or transferred to a corps which is not in the arm or branch in which he previously served.

44 & 45 Vict., c. 58.

(*3*) Nothing in this section shall render a man in the second class of the army reserve liable to serve out of the United Kingdom, and such man may from time to time be transferred from one corps to another for the purpose of securing his non-liability to serve out of the United Kingdom.

Punishment for non-attendance for annual training or permanent service, etc.

15. (*1*) WHEN a man belonging to the army or militia reserve is called out for annual training or on permanent service, or when a man belonging to the army reserve is called out in aid of the civil power, and such man, without leave lawfully granted or such sickness or other reasonable excuse as may be

[1] Printed *ante*, p. 614.

allowed in the prescribed manner, fails to appear at any time and place at which he is required upon such calling out to attend, he shall—

(*a*) If called out on permanent service, or in aid of the civil power, be guilty, according to the circumstances, of deserting within the meaning of section twelve, or of absenting himself without leave within the meaning of section fifteen, of the Army Act,[1] 1881, and 44 & 45 Vic. c. 58.

(*b*) If called out for annual training, be guilty of absenting himself without leave within the meaning of section fifteen of the Army Act,[1] 1881. 44 & 45 Vic. c. 58.

(*2*) A man belonging to the army or militia reserve who commits an offence under this section, or under section twelve or section fifteen of the Army Act,[1] 1881, whether otherwise subject to military law or not, shall be liable as follows; that is to say, 44 & 45 Vic. c. 58.

(*a*) be liable to be tried by court-martial, and convicted and punished accordingly; or

(*b*) be liable to be convicted by a court of summary jurisdiction, and to be sentenced to a fine of not less than forty shillings and not more than twenty-five pounds, and in default of payment to imprisonment, with or without hard labour, for any term not less than seven days and not more than the maximum term allowed by law for non-payment of the fine;

and may in any case be taken into military custody.

Supplemental provisions as to deserters and absentees.

16. (*1*) Section one hundred and fifty-four of the Army Act, 1881,[1] shall apply to a man who is a deserter or absentee without leave from the army or militia reserve within the meaning of this Act in like manner as it applies to a deserter in that section mentioned, and a man who under that section is delivered into military custody or committed for the purpose of being so delivered may be tried as provided by this Act. 44 & 45 Vic. c. 58.

(*2*) Any person who falsely represents himself to be a deserter or absentee without leave from the army or militia reserve shall be liable, on conviction by a court of summary jurisdiction, to imprisonment with or without hard labour, for a term not exceeding three months.

Punishment for inducing reserve man to desert or absent himself.

17. (*1*) Any person who by any means whatsoever—

(*a*) Procures or persuades any man belonging to the army or militia reserve to commit an offence of absence without leave within the meaning of this Act, or attempts to procure or persuade any man belonging to the army or militia reserve to commit such offence; or

[1] Printed *ante*, p. 614.

(*b*) Knowing that a man belonging to the army or militia reserve is about to commit an offence of absence without leave within the meaning of this Act, aids or assists him in so doing; or

(*c*) Knowing any man belonging to the army or militia reserve to be an absentee without leave within the meaning of this Act, conceals such man, or aids or assists him in concealing himself, or employs or continues to employ him, or aids or assists in his rescue;

shall be liable, on conviction by a court of summary jurisdiction, to a fine not exceeding twenty pounds.

44 & 45 Vict., c. 58. (2) Section one hundred and fifty-three of the Army Act, 1881,[1] shall apply as if a man belonging to the army or militia reserve were a soldier, and as if the word "desert" and other words referring to desertion included desertion within the meaning of this Act as well as desertion within the meaning of the 44 & 45 Vict., c. 58. Army Act, 1881[1]; and any person who, knowing any man belonging to the army or militia reserve to be a deserter within the meaning of this Act or of the 44 & 45 Vict., c. 58. Army Act, 1881,[1] employs or continues to employ such man, shall be deemed to aid him in concealing himself within the meaning of the said section.

Supplemental.

18. (*1*) SUBJECT to the provisions of this Act, and save as is otherwise prescribed, a man enlisting in the army or militia reserve shall be attested in the same manner as a recruit in the regular forces, and the following sections of the Army Act, 1881[1]; (that is to say)— Attestation of men enlisting in reserve forces. 44 & 45 Vict., c. 58.

Section eighty (relating to the mode of enlistment and attestation);

Section ninety-eight (imposing a fine for unlawful recruiting);

Section ninety-nine (making recruits punishable for false answers);

Section one hundred (relating to the validity of attestation and enlistment, or re-engagement);

Section one hundred and one (relating to the competent military authority); and

So much of section one hundred and sixty-three as relates to an attestation paper, or a copy thereof, or a declaration, being evidence, shall apply in like manner as if they were herein re-enacted, with the substitution—

(*a*) Of "man," or, if the context so requires, "reserve" man, for "soldier," and of "army reserve or militia reserve, as the case may be," for "regular forces"; and

(*b*) In section one hundred, so far as relates to the militia reserve, of "one whole period of annual training" for "three months."

---

[1] Printed *ante*, p. 614.

(2) A man so enlisting may be attested by a regular officer, or by a militia officer, and the sections of the Army Act, 1881, in this section mentioned, and also section thirty-three of the same Act, shall, as applied to the army or militia reserve, be construed as if a justice of the peace in those sections included such an officer.

Record of illegal absence of reserve man.

19. (*1*) WHERE a man belonging to the army reserve or militia reserve is subject to military law, and is illegally absent from his duty, a court of inquiry under section seventy-two of the Army Act, 1881,[1] may be assembled after the expiration of twenty-one days from the date of such absence, notwithstanding that the period during which such man was subject to military law is less than twenty-one days, or has expired before the expiration of twenty-one days; and the record mentioned in that section may be entered in manner thereby provided, or in such regimental books and by such officer as may be prescribed.

44 & 45 Vict, c. 58.

(2) Where a man belonging to the army reserve or militia reserve fails to appear at the time and place at which he is required upon being called out for annual training or on permanent service to attend, and his absence continues for not less than fourteen days, an entry of such absence shall be made by the prescribed officer in the prescribed manner and in the prescribed regimental books, and such entry shall be conclusive evidence of the fact of such absence.

Orders and regulations as to reserve forces.

20. (*1*) SUBJECT to the provisions of this Act it shall be lawful for Her Majesty, by order signified under the hand of a Secretary of State, from time to time to make, and when made revoke and vary, orders with respect to the government, discipline, and pay of the army reserve and the militia reserve or either of them, and with respect to other matters and things relating to the army reserve and the militia reserve or either of them, including any matter by this Act authorized to be prescribed, or expressed to be subject to orders or regulations.

(2) Subject to the provisions of any such order, a Secretary of State may from time to time make, and when made revoke and vary, general or special regulations with respect to any matter with respect to which Her Majesty may make orders under this section.

(3) Where a man entered the army or militia reserve before the date of any order or regulation made under this Act, nothing in such order or regulation shall render such man liable, without his consent, to be appointed, transferred, or attached to any military body to which he could not, without his consent, have been appointed, transferred, or attached if the said order or regulation had not been made.

---

[1] Printed *ante*, p. 614.

(*4*) All orders and general regulations made under this Act shall be laid before both Houses of Parliament as soon as practicable after they are made, if Parliament be then sitting, or if Parliament be not sitting, then as soon as practicable after the beginning of the then next session of Parliament.

Exercise powers vested in holder of military office.

21. (*1*) Any power or jurisdiction given to, and any act or thing to be done by, to, or before any person holding any military office may in relation to the reserve forces be exercised by or done by, to, or before any other person for the time being authorised in that behalf according to the custom of the service.

(*2*) Where by this Act, or by any order or regulation in force under this Act, any order is authorized to be made by any military authority, such order may be signified by an order, instruction, or letter under the hand of any officer authorized to issue orders on behalf of such military authority, and an order, instruction, or letter purporting to be signed by any officer appearing therein to be so authorized shall be evidence of his being so authorized.

Pensions of army reserve men.

22. Where, either before or after the passing of this Act, a man in the army reserve has been called out on permanent service, and at the termination of such service has been returned to the army reserve, and has become entitled to pension under any order or regulation in force under this Act (whether made before or after such calling out or return), the Commissioners of Chelsea Hospital shall have the same power to award and pay the said pension, and otherwise in relation to the said pension, as they would have if such man had been discharged from the army on reduction.

Application to reserve forces of enactments respecting exemptions from tolls and conveyance of regular forces.

[44] & 45 Vict., [c.] 58.

23. (*1*) For the purpose of section one hundred and forty-three of the Army Act, 1881,[1] and of all other enactments relating to such duties, tolls, and ferries as are in that section mentioned, officers and men belonging to the army or militia reserve, when going to or returning from any place at which they are required to attend, and for non-attendance at which they are liable to be punished, shall be deemed to be officers and soldiers of Her Majesty's regular forces on duty.

(*2*) All enactments for the time being in force concerning the conveyance by railway or otherwise of any part of the regular forces, and their baggage, stores, arms, ammunition, and other necessaries and things, shall apply as if the army and militia reserve were such part of the regular forces.

Notices.

24. With respect to notices required in pursuance of the orders or regulations in force under this Act to be given to men belonging to the army or militia reserve, the following provisions shall have effect:—

(1) A notice may be served on any such man either by being sent by

[1] Printed *ante*, p. 64.

post to his last registered place of abode, or by being served in the prescribed manner;

(2) Evidence of the delivery at the last registered place of abode of a man belonging to the army or militia reserve of a notice, or of a letter addressed to such man and containing a notice, shall be evidence that such notice was brought to the knowledge of such man;

(3) The publication of a notice in the prescribed manner in the parish in which the last registered place of abode of a man belonging to the army or militia reserve is situate shall be sufficient notice to such man, notwithstanding that a copy of such notice is not served on him;

(4) Every constable, overseer of the poor, and inspector of the poor shall, when so required by or on behalf of a Secretary of State, conform with the orders and regulations for the time being in force under this Act with respect to the publication and service of notices, and in default shall be liable, on conviction by a court of summary jurisdiction, to a fine not exceeding twenty pounds.

Trial of offences.

25. (*1*) Any offence which under this Act is punishable on conviction by court-martial shall for all purposes of and incidental to the arrest, trial, and punishment of the offender, including the summary dealing with the case by his commanding officer, be deemed to be an offence under the Army Act,[1] 1881, with this modification, that any reference in that Act to forfeitures and stoppages shall be construed to refer to such forfeitures and stoppages as may be prescribed.

44 & 45 Vict. c. 58.

(*2*) Any offence which under this Act is punishable on conviction by a court of summary jurisdiction may be prosecuted, and any fine recoverable on such conviction may be recovered, in manner provided by sections one hundred and sixty-six, one hundred and sixty-seven, and one hundred and sixty-eight of the Army Act, 1881,[1] in like manner as if those sections were herein re-enacted and in terms made applicable to this Act.

(*3*) Save as provided by the said section one hundred and sixty-six, the minimum fixed by this Act for the amount of any fine or for the term of any imprisonment shall be duly observed by courts of summary jurisdiction, and shall, notwithstanding anything contained in any other Act, not be reduced by way of mitigation or otherwise.

(*4*) For all purposes in relation to the arrest, trial, and punishment of a person for any offence punishable under this Act, including the summary

[1] Printed *ante*, p. 614.

dealing with the case by the commanding officer, this Act shall apply to the Channel Islands and the Isle of Man.

Provisions as to offences both by court-martial and by court of summary jurisdiction.

26. With respect to the trial and punishment of men charged with offences which in pursuance of this Act are cognizable both by a court-martial and by a court of summary jurisdiction, the following provisions shall have effect:—

(1) An alleged offender shall not be liable to be tried both by court-martial and by a court of summary jurisdiction, but may be tried by either of such courts, according as may be prescribed by orders or regulations under this Act.

(2) Proceedings against an alleged offender, before either a court-martial or his commanding officer or a court of summary jurisdiction, may be instituted whether the term of this reserve service has or has not expired, and may, notwithstanding anything in any other Act, be instituted at any time within two months after the time at which the offence becomes known to an officer who under the orders or regulations in force under this Act has power to direct the offender to be tried by a court-martial or by a court of summary jurisdiction, if the offender is apprehended at that time, or if he is not apprehended at that time, then within two months after the time at which he is apprehended, whether such apprehension is by a civil or military authority, and any limitation contained in any other Act with respect to the time for hearing and determining an offence shall not apply in the case of any proceedings so instituted.

(3) For the purposes of this section the expression "tried by court-martial" shall include "dealt with summarily by his commanding officer."

Evidence.

44 & 45 Vict., c. 58.

27. (*1*) Section one hundred and sixty-four of the Army Act, 1881[1] (which relates to evidence of the civil conviction or acquittal of a person subject to military law), shall apply to a man belonging to the army or militia reserve who is tried by a civil court, whether he is or is not at the time of such trial subject to military law.

(*2*) Section one hundred and sixty-three of the Army Act, 1881[1] (relating to evidence), shall apply to all proceedings under this Act.

Definitions.

28. In this Act, unless the context otherwise requires—

The expression "man" includes a warrant officer not holding an honorary commission, and a non-commissioned officer.

The expression "out-pensioners of Chelsea Hospital" includes all persons

[1] Printed *ante*, p. 614.

(*Sec. 29.*)

whose claims for prospective or deferred pension have been registered in virtue of any warrant of Her Majesty.

The expression "prescribed" means prescribed by orders or regulations in force under this Act.

Other expressions have the same meaning as they have in the Army Act, 1881.[1]

In the Army Act, 1881,[1] the expressions "army reserve force" and "militia reserve force" shall respectively mean the army reserve and militia reserve under this Act. 44 & 45 Vict. c. 58.

Repeal of Acts.

29. The Acts mentioned in the schedule to this Act are hereby repealed as from the commencement of this Act to the extent in the third column of that schedule mentioned:

Provided as follows—

(1) Such repeal shall not revive any enactment, and shall not, save as herein otherwise provided, affect anything previously done or suffered, or any existing right or title, or any remedy in respect thereof, or the proof of any past act.

(2) All orders, warrants, regulations, and directions in relation to the army reserve force or to the militia reserve force which exist at the commencement of this Act shall, so far as consistent with the tenor thereof, be of the same effect as if they were orders or regulations under this Act, and may be revoked or altered accordingly.

(3) Any man who at the commencement of this Act belongs to the first or second class of the army reserve force, or to the militia reserve force, shall continue to belong to the first or second class of the army reserve or to the militia reserve under this Act, as the case may be, in like manner as if he had entered the same in pursuance of this Act.

(4) Where a man belonging to either the army reserve force or the militia reserve force entered such force before the passing of the Regulation of the Forces Act, 1881,[1] or before the date of any regulation made under the said Act, nothing in the said Act or regulation or in this Act shall require such man without his consent to serve in or be appointed, transferred, or attached to any military body in or to which he could not have been required without his consent to serve or be appointed, transferred, or attached, if the Regulation of the Forces Act, 1881,[1] or this Act, or the said regulation, as the case may be, had not been passed or made, or to serve for any longer period than that for which he was, before the passing of the Regulation of the Forces Act, 1881,[1] or before the date of such regulation, as the case may be, liable to serve. 44 & 45 Vict. c. 57.

[1] Printed *ante*, p. 614.

(5) In the case of any offence committed before the commencement of this Act, if any proceeding for the trial or punishment of the offender has been commenced before the commencement of this Act, such proceeding may be carried on and completed, and the offender may be tried and punished, as if this Act had not passed; but, save as aforesaid, this Act shall apply to the arrest, trial, conviction, and punishment of a person accused of an offence committed before the commencement of this Act (including the dealing with the case by the commanding officer), so however that a person shall not be subject for any such offence to any greater punishment than that to which he was subject before the commencement of this Act, nor to any punishment for anything done before the commencement of this Act which at the time of it being done was not an offence punishable by law.

Where a proclamation has been issued, or any man belonging to the army or militia reserve has been called out before the commencement of this Act, this Act shall apply as if such proclamation had been issued, and men called out in pursuance of this Act.

SCHEDULE.

ENACTMENTS REPEALED.

A description or citation of an Act in this Schedule is inclusive of the word, section, or other part first and last mentioned or otherwise referred to as forming the beginning, or as forming the end, of the portion described in the description or citation.

30 & 31 Vict., c. 110 .	The Reserve Force Act, 1867.	The whole Act.
30 & 31 Vict., c. 111 .	The Militia Reserve Act, 1867.	The whole Act.
33 & 34 Vict., c. 67 .	The Army Enlistment Act, 1870.	Sections fourteen and fifteen, and section twenty, except so far as it relates to the militia, yeomanry, or volunteers.
34 & 35 Vict., c. 86 .	The Regulation of the Forces Act, 1871.	So much of sections seven and nineteen as relates to the army reserve or the militia reserve.
36 & 37 Vict., c. 68 .	An Act for extending the Period of Service in the Militia; and for other purposes.	Section six.
41 & 42 Vict., c. 10 .	An Act for punishing Mutiny and Desertion, and for the better Payment of the Army and their Quarters.	Sections forty-two, forty-seven, forty-eight, and one hundred and nine.

42 & 43 Vict., c. 32	The Army Discipline and Regulation (Commencement) Act, 1879.	Section five, from "Any reference in the Reserve Force" to the end of the section, and so much of the rest of the section as relates to the reserve forces or keeps in force any portion of the Army Mutiny Act relating to the reserve forces.
42 & 43 Vict., c. 33	The Army Discipline and Regulation Act, 1879.	So much as is unrepealed.
44 & 45 Vict., c. 57	The Regulation of the Forces Act, 1881.	Sections ten to thirteen and forty-five, and so much of section fifty-three as relates to the reserve forces.
44 & 45 Vict., c. 58	The Army Act, 1881.	Section one hundred and sixty-three, from "evidence of the delivery" to "knowledge of such man" (being paragraph (*f*) of sub-section one); section one hundred and ninety, from the expression "the army reserve force" to "Militia Reserve Act, 1867, and any Act amending the same"; and section one hundred and ninety-three from "so much of the Army Discipline and Regulation Act, 1879," to the end of the section.

The India (Home Charges Arrears) Act, 1882.

(45 & 46 Vict., c. 79.)

An Act to make provision for the arrangement of Accounts between the Commissioners of Her Majesty's Treasury and the Secretary of State in Council of India in respect of certain Home Charges for Her Majesty's Forces serving in India.

[*18th August, 1882.*]

Whereas certain home charges of Her Majesty's forces serving in India payable out of the revenues of India are defrayed in the first instance out of the Exchequer, and under an arrangement in force since the thirty-first day of March one thousand eight hundred and seventy advances were from time to time made out of the revenues of India to the Exchequer by way of repayment of those charges, and the actual expenditure was to be subsequently ascertained and adjusted:

And whereas differences have been pending between the Secretary of State for the War Department and the Secretary of State in Council of India which prevented such adjustment, and in consequence the accounts of the said actual expenditure fell into arrear; so that while the claim on the part of the Exchequer for the period from the thirty-first day of March one thousand eight hundred and seventy to the thirty-first day of March one thousand eight hundred and seventy-seven amounted to three million three hundred and two thousand two hundred and forty-six pounds eleven shillings and eightpence the total amount advanced by way of repayment to the Exchequer out of the revenues of India amounted only to two million eight hundred and ninety thousand pounds, and the balance claimed by the Commissioners of Her Majesty's Treasury as due to the Exchequer, but disputed in part by the Secretary of State in Council of India, amounted to four hundred and twelve thousand two hundred and forty-six pounds eleven shillings and eightpence, which balance was reduced by a subsequent settlement of twenty-one thousand six hundred and thirty-five pounds to a net claim of three hundred and ninety thousand six hundred and eleven pounds eleven shillings and eightpence as due to the Exchequer but in part disputed as before mentioned:

And whereas the Commissioners of Her Majesty's Treasury, by a Minute dated the second day of July one thousand eight hundred and seventy-eight, proposed as an arrangement of the said differences and accounts that the sums actually advanced out of the revenues of India to the Exchequer by way of repayment of the said charges during the years above mentioned should be taken in full discharge of all the claims of the Exchequer upon the revenues of India in respect of the aforesaid charges:

And whereas it is expedient to sanction the said arrangement:

* * * * * * *

1. This Act may be cited as the India (Home Charges Arrears) Act, 1882. Short title.

2. The arrangement of the above-recited differences and accounts proposed in the said Minute of the Commissioners of Her Majesty's Treasury, dated the second day of July one thousand eight hundred and seventy-eight, is hereby sanctioned. Sanction of arrangement of Treasury Minute of 2 July 1878.

The Companies (Colonial Registers) Act, 1883.[1]

(46 & 47 Vict., c. 30.)

An Act to authorise Companies registered under the Companies Act, 1862, to keep Local Registers of their Members in British Colonies.

[*20th August, 1883.*]

Whereas many companies registered under the Companies Act, 1862, carry on business in British colonies, and dealings in their shares are frequent in such colonies, but delay, inconvenience, and expense are occasioned by

---

[1] This Act may be cited with 12 others as the Companies Acts, 1862 to 1898: see the Short Titles Act, 1896 (59 & 60 Vict., c. 14), *post*, p. 1255. *See*, too, *Chitty's Statutes*, Tit. Companies, p. 117.

reason of the absence of any legal provision for keeping local registers of members, and it is expedient that such provisions as this Act contains be made in that behalf:

* * * * * * *

Short title and construction.

1. This Act may be cited for all purposes as the Companies (Colonial Registers) Act, 1883; and this Act shall, so far as is consistent with the tenor thereof, be construed as one with the Companies Acts, 1862 to 1880, and the said Acts and this Act may be referred to as the Companies Acts, 1862 to 1883.

Definitions.

2. In this Act the term "company" means a company registered under the Companies Act, 1862, and having a capital divided into shares; the term "shares" includes stock; the term "colony" does not include any place within the United Kingdom, the Isle of Man, or the Channel Islands, but includes such territories as may for the time being be vested in Her Majesty by virtue of an Act of Parliament for the government of India, and any plantation, territory, or settlement situate elsewhere within Her Majesty's dominions.

Power for companies to keep colonial registers.

3. (1) Any company whose objects comprise the transaction of business in a colony may, if authorised so to do by its regulations, as originally framed or as altered by special resolution, cause to be kept in any colony in which it transacts business a branch register or registers of members resident in such colony.

(2) The company shall give to the registrar of joint stock companies notice of the situation of the office where any such branch register (in this Act called a colonial register) is kept, and of any change therein, and of the discontinuance of any such office in the event of the same being discontinued.

(3) A colonial register shall, as regards the particulars entered therein, be deemed to be a part of the company's register of members, and shall be *primâ facie* evidence of all particulars entered therein. Any such register shall be kept in the manner provided by the Companies Acts, 1862 to 1880, with this qualification, that the advertisement mentioned in section thirty-three of the Companies Act, 1862, shall be inserted in some newspaper circulating in the district wherein the register to be closed is kept, and that any competent court in the colony where such register is kept shall be entitled to exercise the same jurisdiction of rectifying the same as is by section thirty-five of the Companies Act, 1862, vested, as respects a register, in England and Ireland in Her Majesty's superior courts of law or equity, and that all offences under section thirty-two of the Companies Act, 1862,[1] may, as 25 & 26 V. c. 89.

[1] Not reproduced in this volume.

regards a colonial register, be prosecuted summarily before any tribunal in the colony where such register is kept having summary criminal jurisdiction.

(4) The company shall transmit to its registered office a copy of every entry in its colonial register or registers as soon as may be after such entry is made, and the company shall cause to be kept at its registered office, duly entered up from time to time, a duplicate or duplicates of its colonial register or registers. The provisions of section thirty-two of the Companies Act, 1862, shall apply to every such duplicate, and every such duplicate shall, for all the purposes of the Companies Acts, 1862 to 1880, be deemed to be part of the register of members of the company.

(5) Subject to the provisions of this Act with respect to the duplicate register, the shares registered in a colonial register shall be distinguished from the shares registered in the principal register, and no transaction with respect to any shares registered in a colonial register shall, during the continuance of the registration of such shares in such colonial register, be registered in any other register.

(6) The company may discontinue to keep any colonial register, and thereupon all entries in that register shall be transferred to some other colonial register kept by the company in the same colony, or to the register of members kept at the registered office of the company.

(7) In relation to stamp duties the following provisions shall have effect:—

(*a*) An instrument of transfer of a share registered in a colonial register under this Act shall be deemed to be a transfer of property situated out of the United Kingdom, and unless executed in any part of the United Kingdom shall be exempt from British stamp duty.

(*b*) Upon the death of a member registered in a colonial register under this Act, the share or other interest of the deceased member shall for the purposes of this Act so far as relates to British duties be deemed to be part of his estate and effects situated in the United Kingdom for or in respect of which probate or letters of administration is or are to be granted, or whereof an inventory is to be exhibited and recorded in like manner as if he were registered in the register of members kept at the registered office of the company.[1]

---

[1] The provisions of s. 3 (7) have been amended by 52 & 53 Vict., c. 42, s. 18, which runs as follows:—

"18. Notwithstanding provision (*b*) in section 7 [*sic.*—section 3, sub-section (7)?] of the Companies (Colonial Registers) Act, 1883, the share or other interest of a deceased member registered in a Colonial Register under that Act, who shall have died domiciled elsewhere than in the United Kingdom, shall, so far as relates to British duties, not be deemed to be part of his estate and effects situated in the United Kingdom, for or in respect of which probate or letters of administration is or are to be granted or whereof an inventory is to be exhibited and recorded."

(8) Subject to the provisions of this Act, any company may, by its regulations as originally framed, or as altered by special resolution, make such provisions as it may think fit respecting the keeping of colonial registers.

The Bankruptcy Act, 1883.[1]

(46 & 47 Vict., c. 52.)

An Act to amend and consolidate the Law of Bankruptcy.

[*25th August, 1883.*]

* * * * * * *
* * * * * * *

Warrants of Bankruptcy Courts.

119.[2] (*1*) Any warrant of a Court having jurisdiction in bankruptcy in England may be enforced in Scotland, Ireland, the Isle of Man, the Channel Islands, and elsewhere in Her Majesty's Dominions in the same manner and subject to the same privileges in and subject to which a warrant issued by any justice of the peace against a person for an indictable offence against the laws of England may be executed in those parts of Her Majesty's Dominions respectively in pursuance of the Acts of Parliament in that behalf.

(*2*) A search warrant issued by a Court having jurisdiction in bankruptcy for the discovery of any property of a debtor may be executed in manner prescribed or in the same manner and subject to the same privileges in and subject to which a search warrant for property supposed to be stolen may be executed according to law.

* * * * * * *
* * * * * * *

The Colonial Attorneys Relief Act Amendment Act, 1884.

(47 & 48 Vict., c. 24.)

An Act to amend the Colonial Attorneys Relief Act.

[*3rd July, 1884.*]

20 & 21 Vict., c. 39. 37 & 38 Vict., c. 41.

Whereas it is expedient to extend the provisions of the Colonial Attorneys Relief Act as to certain colonies or dependencies :

* * * * * * *

Extension of 20 & 21 Vict., c. 39, to

1. Upon application made by the governor or person exercising the functions of governor of any of Her Majesty's colonies or dependencies,

[1] See *Chitty's Statutes*, Tit. Bankruptcy, p. 8.

[2] This is the only extant section of the Statute applicable to India.

and after it has been shown to the satisfaction of Her Majesty's Principal Secretary of State for the Colonies, that the system of jurisprudence as administered in such colony or dependency answers to and fulfils the conditions specified in section three of the Colonial Attorneys Relief Act, and also that the attorneys and solicitors of the superior courts of law or equity in England are admitted as attorneys and solicitors in the superior courts of law and equity of such colony or dependency, on production of their certificates of admission in the English courts, without service in the colony or dependency or examination, except in the laws of the colony or dependency in so far as they differ from the laws of England, Her Majesty may from time to time by Order in Council direct the Colonial Attorneys Relief Act to come into operation as to such colony or dependency, although persons may in certain cases be admitted as attorneys or solicitors in such colony or dependency without possessing all the qualifications for admission or having fulfilled the conditions specified in the said section three, and thereupon, but not otherwise, the provisions of the Colonial Attorneys Relief Act shall apply to persons duly admitted as attorneys and solicitors in such colony or dependency after service and examination; that is to say, no attorney or solicitor of any such colony or dependency shall be admitted as a solicitor of the Supreme Court in England unless, in addition to the requirements of the Colonial Attorneys Relief Act, he prove by affidavit that he has served for five years under articles of clerkship to a solicitor or attorney-at-law in such colony or dependency, and passed an examination to test his fitness and capacity, before he was admitted an attorney or solicitor in such colony or dependency, and further that he has since been in actual practice as attorney or solicitor in such colony or dependency for the period of seven years at the least.'

colony on application of governor, etc.

[...]8 Vict.,

2. This Act may be cited as the Colonial Attorneys Relief Act Amendment Act, 1884.

Short title.

THE COLONIAL PRISONERS REMOVAL ACT, 1884.[1]

(47 & 48 Vict., c. 31.)

An Act to make further provision respecting the removal of Prisoners and Criminal Lunatics from Her Majesty's possessions out of the United Kingdom. [*28th July, 1884.*]

WHEREAS it is expedient to provide for the removal of prisoners undergoing sentence, and of criminal lunatics from one British possession to another British possession, or to the United Kingdom:

* * * * * * *

[1] See *Chitty's Statutes*, Tit. Colonies, p. 18.

Preliminary.

Short title.

1. This Act may be cited as the Colonial Prisoners Removal Act, 1884.

Prisoners' Removal.

Removal of prisoners from British possessions in certain cases.

2. Where as regards a prisoner undergoing sentence of imprisonment in any British possession for any offence it appears to the removing authority herein-after mentioned either—

(*a*) that it is likely that the life of the prisoner will be endangered or his health permanently injured by further imprisonment in such British possession; or

(*b*) that the prisoner belonged, at the time of committing the said offence, to the Royal Navy or to Her Majesty's regular military forces; or

(*c*) that the offence was committed wholly or partly beyond the limits of the said British possession; or

(*d*) that by reason of there being no prison in the said British possession in which the prisoner can properly undergo his sentence or otherwise the removal of the prisoner is expedient for his safer custody or for more efficiently carrying his sentence into effect; or

(*e*) that the prisoner belongs to a class of persons who under the law of the said British possession are subject to removal under this Act;

in any such case the removing authority may, subject nevertheless to the regulations in force under this Act, order such prisoner to be removed to any British possession or to the United Kingdom to undergo his sentence or the residue thereof.

Return of removed prisoner.

3. (1) Where a prisoner has been removed in pursuance of this Act, a Secretary of State or the Government of a British possession to which the prisoner has been so removed, may order the prisoner, for the purpose of undergoing the residue of his sentence, to be returned to the British possession from which he was removed.

(2) If a Secretary of State or the Government of a British possession to which a prisoner is removed under this Act, requires the prisoner to be returned for discharge to the British possession from which he was removed, the prisoner shall, in accordance with the regulations under this Act, be returned to the said British possession for the purpose of being there discharged at the expiration of his sentence. In any other case a prisoner when discharged at the expiration of his sentence shall be entitled to be sent free of cost to the British possession from which he was removed:

Provided that where a prisoner at the date of his sentence belonged to the Royal Navy or to Her Majesty's regular military forces, nothing in this section shall require such prisoner to be returned to the British possession from which he was removed, or entitle him to be sent there free of cost.

4. (1) It shall be lawful for Her Majesty in Council from time to time to make, and when made, revoke and vary regulations as to the removal, return, and discharge of prisoners under this Act. Regulations as to removal.

(2) The regulations may provide for varying the conditions of a sentence of imprisonment passed in a British possession, where they differ from the conditions of a sentence of imprisonment in the part of Her Majesty's dominions to which the prisoner is removed, with a view to bringing them into conformity with the latter conditions, but the prisoner shall not by reason of such variation undergo an imprisonment of any longer duration; and where the latter conditions appear to a Secretary of State to be more severe than the former conditions, the Secretary of State may remit a portion of the imprisonment, so that the punishment undergone by the prisoner shall not in the opinion of the Secretary of State be more severe than the punishment to which the prisoner was originally sentenced, and the sentence of imprisonment shall, so long as the prisoner remains in the part of Her Majesty's dominions to which he is removed, be carried into effect as if the conditions thereof as so varied were the conditions of the original sentence.

(3) The regulations may also provide for the forms to be used under this Act and generally for the execution of this Act.

(4) All regulations made under this section shall be duly observed by all persons, and shall be laid before both Houses of Parliament as soon as may be after they are made.

5. The removing authority for the purposes of this Act shall be a Secretary of State acting with the concurrence of the Government of every British possession concerned. Removing authority.

6. (1) The concurrence of the Government of a British possession, and any requisition by the Government of a British possession, may be given or made by the Governor in Council or such other authority as may be from time to time provided by the law of that possession, but shall be signified by writing under the hand of the Governor or of the Colonial Secretary or of any other officer appointed in this behalf by the law of that possession. Evidence of act of government of British possession or Secretary of State.

(2) Any writing purporting to give such concurrence or make such requisition, and to be signed by the Governor or Colonial Secretary or other officer for the time being, shall be conclusive evidence that the concurrence of or requisition by the Government of the British possession has been duly given or made

according to law; and any writing purporting to be under the hand of a Secretary of State and to order the removal of a prisoner from a British possession shall be conclusive evidence that such order has been duly given by the Secretary of State, and every such writing as above in this section mentioned shall be admissible in evidence in any court in Her Majesty's dominions without further proof.

Warrant for removal of prisoner.

7. (1) Where the removal of a prisoner from a British possession is ordered in pursuance of this Act, a Secretary of State or the Governor of the British possession may by warrant under his hand direct the prisoner to be removed to the part of Her Majesty's dominions mentioned in the said order, and for that purpose to be delivered into the custody of the persons named or described in the warrant or some one or more of them, and to be held in custody and conveyed by sea or otherwise to the said part of Her Majesty's dominions, there to undergo his sentence, or the residue thereof, until returned in pursuance of this Act or discharged, and such warrant shall be forthwith executed according to the tenor thereof.

(2) Where a prisoner is to be returned to a British possession, a Secretary of State or the Governor of the possession in which he has been undergoing his sentence, shall issue a like warrant, which shall be duly executed according to the tenor thereof.

(3) Every warrant purporting to be issued in pursuance of this Act, and to be under the hand of a Secretary of State or Governor of a British possession, shall be received in evidence in every court of justice in Her Majesty's dominions without further proof, and shall be evidence of the facts therein stated, and all acts done in pursuance of such warrant shall be deemed to have been authorised by law.

Dealing with removed prisoner.

8. (1) Every prisoner removed in pursuance of this Act shall, until he is returned in pursuance of this Act, be dealt with in the part of Her Majesty's dominions to which he is removed, in like manner as if his sentence (with such variation, if any, of the conditions thereof as may have been duly made in pursuance of regulations under this Act) had been duly awarded in that part, and shall be subject accordingly to all laws and regulations in force in that part, with the following qualifications, that his conviction, judgment and sentence may be questioned in the part of Her Majesty's dominions from which he has been removed in the same manner as if he had not been removed, and that his sentence may be remitted and his discharge ordered in the same manner and by the same authority as if he had not been removed.

(2) The officer in charge of any prison, on request by any person having the custody of a prisoner under a warrant issued in pursuance of this Act, and

on payment or tender of a reasonable amount for expenses, shall receive such prisoner and detain him for such reasonable time as may be requested by the said person for the purpose of the proper execution of the warrant.

Escape of prisoner from custody.

9. (1) If a prisoner while in custody in pursuance of this Act, or under a warrant issued in pursuance of this Act, escapes by breach of prison or otherwise, out of custody, he may be retaken in the same manner as a person convicted of a crime against the law of the place to which he escapes may be retaken upon an escape.

(2) A person guilty of the offence of so escaping or of attempting so to escape, or of aiding or attempting to aid any such prisoner so to escape, may be tried in any of the following parts of Her Majesty's dominions, namely, the part to which and the part from which the prisoner is being removed or returned, and the part in which the prisoner escapes, and the part in which the offender is found, and such offence shall be deemed to be an offence against the law of the part of Her Majesty's dominions in which he may be so tried, and for all purposes of and incidental to the apprehension, trial, and punishment of the person accused of such offence, and of and incidental to any proceedings and matters preliminary, incidental to or consequential thereon, and of and incidental to the jurisdiction of any court constable or officer with reference to such offence, and to the person accused thereof, such offence shall be deemed to have been committed in the said part, and such person may be punished in accordance with the Courts (Colonial) Jurisdiction Act, 1874.[1]

& 38 Vict., 7.

Criminal Lunatics.

Application of Act to removal of criminal lunatics.

10. (1) The provisions of this Act shall apply to a person in custody as a criminal lunatic in like manner, so far as consistent with the tenor thereof, as they apply to a prisoner undergoing sentence of imprisonment; and separate regulations may be made by Her Majesty in Council under this Act in relation to criminal lunatics and (subject to those regulations) all laws and regulations in force in the part of Her Majesty's dominions in which a criminal lunatic removed or returned is for the time being in custody under a warrant issued in pursuance of this Act, shall apply to such criminal lunatic as if he had become a criminal lunatic in that part.

(2) Where a person, who is a criminal lunatic by reason of being unfit to be tried for an offence, is removed in pursuance of this Act, and a Secretary of State or the Government of the British possession to or from which such person was removed considers that such person has become sufficiently sane to be tried for the said offence, and requires him to be returned for trial to the British possession from which he was removed, he shall, in accordance with the regulations

[1] Printed *ante*, p. 556.

under this Act be returned as a prisoner to the said British possession for the purpose of being there tried for the said offence, and shall be removed thither in custody in like manner as if he had been arrested under a warrant on a charge for the said offence.

Miscellaneous.

Cost of removal.

11. (1) The cost of the removal of any prisoner or criminal lunatic under this Act and of his maintenance while in confinement, and of his return, and of his being sent after discharge to any place, shall be paid in such manner as may be arranged between the Governments of the British possessions concerned and the Secretary of State, subject, as regards any cost to be paid out of moneys provided by Parliament, to the consent of the Commissioners of Her Majesty's Treasury.

(2) Nothing in this Act shall affect any power to recover the expenses of removing or returning any prisoner or criminal lunatic from the property of such prisoner or criminal lunatic or otherwise.

Power of legislature of British possession to pass laws for carrying Act into effect.

12. If the legislature of a British possession pass any law—

(*a*) for determining the authority by whom and the manner in which any jurisdiction, power, or concurrence under this Act is to be exercised or given; or

(*b*) for payment of the costs incurred in the removal, maintenance, return, or sending back after discharge of a prisoner or criminal lunatic; or

(*c*) for dealing in such possession with prisoners or criminal lunatics removed thereto in pursuance of this Act; or

(*d*) for making any class of prisoners subject to removal under this Act; or

(*e*) otherwise in any manner for the carrying of this Act or any part thereof into effect as regards the said possession,

it shall be lawful for Her Majesty in Council to direct that such law or any part thereof shall with or without modification or alteration be recognised and given effect to throughout Her Majesty's dominions and on the high seas as if it were part of this Act.

Power as to making and revocation of Orders in Council.

13. (1) It shall be lawful for Her Majesty in Council from time to time to make Orders for the purposes of this Act, and to revoke and vary any Order so made, and every Order so made shall while it is in force have the same effect as if it were enacted in his Act.

(2) An Order in Council made for the purposes of this Act shall be laid before Parliament as soon as may be after it is made if Parliament is then in

session, or, if not, as soon as may be after the commencement of the then next session of Parliament.

14. This Act shall extend to the Channel Islands and Isle of Man as if they were part of England and the United Kingdom. Application of Act to Channel Islands and Isle of Man.

15. It shall be lawful for Her Majesty in Council from time to time to direct that this Act shall apply, as if, subject to the conditions, exceptions, and qualifications (if any) contained in the Order, any place out of Her Majesty's dominions in which Her Majesty has jurisdiction, and which is named in the Order, were a British possession and part of Her Majesty's dominions, and to provide for carrying into effect such application. Application of Act to place under foreign jurisdiction Acts. See 41 & 42 Vict., c. 67.

16. (1) Nothing in this Act shall affect the provisions of the Army Act,[1] 1881. Savings. [44] & 45 Vict., [c.] 58.

(2) This Act shall not affect any agreement made either before or after the passing of this Act under the Colonial Prisoners Removal Act, 1869,[2] nor any provisions contained in the Act of the session of the fourteenth and fifteenth years of the reign of Her present Majesty, chapter eighty-one, intituled "An Act to authorise the removal from India of insane persons charged with offences, and to give better effect to inquisitions of lunacy taken in India." [32] & 33 Vict., [c.] 10.

17. This Act shall apply to a prisoner who has been convicted, and to a criminal lunatic who has become a criminal lunatic, before the passing of this Act, in like manner as if he had been convicted and become a criminal lunatic after the commencement of this Act. Application of Act to existing and criminal lunatics.

18. In this Act, unless the context otherwise requires, the following expressions have the following meanings; that is to say, Definitions.

The expression "British possession" does not include any place within the United Kingdom, the Isle of Man, or the Channel Islands, but includes all other territories and places being part of Her Majesty's dominions, and all territories and places within Her Majesty's dominions which are not part of India and are under one legislature shall be deemed to be one British possession, and any part of India under a Governor or Lieutenant-Governor shall be deemed to be one British possession.

The expression "India" means[3] all territories and places within Her Majesty's dominions which are subject to the Governor General of India in Council.

The expression "legislature" where there are local legislatures, as well as a central legislature, means the central legislature only, and in every part of India means the Governor General in Council.

---

[1] Printed *ante*, p. 614.
[2] Not printed in these volumes.
[3] *Cf.* definition in Interpretation Act, 1889 (52 & 53 Vict., c. 63), s. 18 (5), *post*, p. 862.

The expression "Secretary of State" means one of Her Majesty's Principal Secretaries of State.

The expression "Governor" means any person or persons administering the government of a British possession, and includes the Governor General of India and also the Governor and Lieutenant-Governor of any part of India.

The expression "Colonial Secretary" includes a person performing the like duties as a Colonial Secretary, whether known as Government Secretary, Chief Secretary to the Government, or by any other title.

The expression "prison" includes any place for the confinement or detention of prisoners whether convicted or unconvicted.

The expression "sentence of imprisonment" means any sentence involving confinement in a prison, whether combined or not with labour, and whether known as penal servitude, imprisonment with hard labour, rigorous imprisonment, imprisonment, or otherwise, and includes a sentence awarded by way of commutation as well as an original sentence passed by the court.

The expression "criminal lunatic" means a person detained in custody by reason of his having been charged with an offence, and either found to have been insane at the time of such offence, or found or certified or otherwise lawfully proved to be unfit on the ground of his insanity to be tried for the same, and includes a person convicted of an offence and afterwards certified or otherwise lawfully proved to be insane.

The Indian Marine Service Act, 1884.[1]

(47 & 48 Vict., c. 38.)

An Act to provide for the regulation of Her Majesty's Indian Marine Service.

[*28th July, 1884.*]

Whereas a marine establishment, called Her Majesty's Indian Marine Service, is employed under the direction of the Governor General of India in Council for the transport of troops, the guarding of convict settlements, the suppression of piracy, the survey of coasts and harbours, the visiting of lighthouses, the relief of distressed or wrecked vessels, and other local objects, and is maintained out of the revenues of India:

And whereas the members of Her Majesty's Indian Marine Service are not subject either to the Naval Discipline Act, 1866, or to the Merchant Shipping Act, 1854, and Acts amending it, or to any corresponding law made, enacted, or in force under the authority of the Government of India; and it is

29 & 30 c. 109.
17 & 18 c. 104.

---

[1] For digest, see Ilbert's *Government of India*, p. 325.

expedient that the Governor General of India in Council should have power to make laws for the purpose of maintaining discipline in that service:

* * * * * * * *

1. This Act may be cited as the Indian Marine Service Act, 1884. **Short title.**

2. The Governor General of India in Council shall have power, subject to the provisions contained in the Indian Councils Act, 1861,[1] as amended by subsequent Acts, at meetings for the purpose of making laws and regulations, to make laws for all persons employed or serving in or belonging to Her Majesty's Indian Marine Service: **Power for Governor General in Council to make laws for Indian Marine Service.** 24 & 25 Vict., c. 67.

Provided as follows:

(*a*) A law made under this section shall not apply to any offence, unless the vessel to which the offender belongs is at the time of the commission of the offence within the limits of Indian waters as defined by this Act:

(*b*) The punishments imposed by any such law for offences shall be similar in character to and shall not be in excess of the punishments which may at the time of making the law be imposed for similar offences under the Acts relating to Her Majesty's Navy, except that in the case of persons other than Europeans or Americans imprisonment for any term not exceeding fourteen years, or transportation for life or any less term, may be substituted for penal servitude.[2]

3. For the purposes of this Act the expression "Indian waters" includes the high seas between the Cape of Good Hope on the west and the straits of Magellan on the east, and all territorial waters between those limits. **Definition of Indian waters.**

4. A law under this Act shall, until the Governor General makes known that he has received a notification of the disallowance thereof by Her Majesty or until the repeal thereof, be, subject to the provisions of this Act, of the same force and effect as an Act of Parliament, and shall be taken notice of by all courts of justice in the same manner as if it were a Public Act of Parliament. **Effect and judicial notice of laws made under Act.**

5. Nothing in this Act shall authorise the Governor General in Council, without the previous approval of the Secretary of State for India in Council, to make any law whereby power is given to any court other than the High Court established under the Act of the session held in the twenty-fourth and twenty-fifth years of Her Majesty, chapter one hundred and four "for establishing High Courts of Judicature in India," to sentence to the punishment of death any of Her Majesty's natural-born subjects born in Europe, or any child of any such subject. **Restriction on power to make law imposing sentence of death.**

[1] Printed in Vol. I of the Collection of Statutes relating to India, Ed. 1899, p. 389.

[2] See the Indian Marine Act, 1887 (XIV of 1887). Printed, Genl. Acts, Volume V, Ed. 1898.

Placing of vessels, officers and men of Indian Marine Service under Naval Discipline Acts in time of war.

6. In case a state of war exists between Her Majesty and any foreign power it shall be lawful for Her Majesty by Proclamation or Order in Council to direct that any vessel belonging to Her Majesty's Indian Marine Service and the men and officers from time to time serving thereon shall be under the command of the senior naval officer of the station where for the time being such ship may be. And while any such vessel is under such command such vessel shall be deemed to all intents a vessel of war of the Royal Navy, and the men and officers from time to time serving in such vessel shall be under such Naval Discipline Act [1] or Acts as may be in force for the time being and subject to such regulations as may be issued by the Lords Commissioners of the Admiralty, with the concurrence of the Secretary of State for India in Council.

THE NAVAL DISCIPLINE ACT, 1884.

(47 & 48 Vict., c. 39.)

An Act to amend the Naval Discipline Act, 1866.,

[*28th July, 1884.*]

Be it enacted by the Queen's most Excellent Majesty, by and with the advice and consent of the Lords Spiritual and Temporal, and Commons, in this present Parliament assembled, and by the authority of the same, as follows:

Amendment of Part III.

Amendment of 29 & 30 Vict., c. 109, s. 56, as to trial of offences by officer in command of a ship.

1. (*1*) In section fifty-six of the Naval Discipline Act, 1866, the following enactments shall be substituted for the provisions of that section relating to the trial of an offence by a commanding officer repealed by this Act, and shall be sub-sections two and three of that section, and sub-section three shall be numbered four: 29 & 30 Vict. c. 109.

(*2*) Any offence not capital which is triable under this Act, and (except in the cases by this Act expressly provided for) is not committed by an officer, may, under such regulations as the Admiralty from time to time issue, be summarily tried and punished by the officer in command of the ship to which the offender belongs at the time either of the commission or of the trial of the offence, subject to the restriction that the commanding officer shall not have power to award penal servitude or to award imprisonment for more than three months.

---

[1] The Naval Discipline Act now in force is 29 & 30 Vict., c. 109, printed in Vol. I, p. 408.

(*3*) The power by this section vested in an officer commanding a ship may,—

(*a*) as respects persons on board a tender to the ship, be exercised, when the tender is absent from the ship, by the officer in command of the tender; and

(*b*) as respects persons on board any boat or boats belonging to the ship, be exercised, when such boat or boats is or are absent on detached service, by the officer in command of the boat or boats; and

(*c*) as respects persons subject to this Act on shore on detached service, or such of those persons as are not for the time being made subject to military law by an order under section one hundred and seventy-nine of the Army Act, 1881, be exercised by the officer in immediate command on shore of those persons. 44 & 45 Vict., c. 58.

Amendment of Part IV.

Amendment of 29 & 30 Vict., c. 109, s. 58, as to holding or constitution of courts-martial.

2. In section fifty-eight of the Naval Discipline Act, 1866, the following amendments shall be made:—

(A) Whereas by sub-section three of section fifty-eight of the Naval Discipline Act, 1866, it is enacted that a court-martial shall not be held unless at least three of Her Majesty's ships, commanded as therein mentioned, are together at the time when such court-martial is held, and it is expedient to reduce the number, therefore 29 & 30 Vict., c. 109.

two shall be substituted for three in sub-section three of section fifty-eight.

(B) There shall be substituted for sub-section seven of section fifty-eight the following sub-section:—

(7) No court-martial for the trial of a person below the rank of captain in Her Majesty's navy shall be duly constituted unless the president is a captain or of higher rank, nor, if the person to be tried is of the rank of commander, unless, in addition to the president, two other members of the court are of the rank of commander or of higher rank.

Amendment of Part V.

Amendment of s. 70 as to sentence of penal servitude and imprisonment.

3. There shall be substituted for sections seventy and seventy-one of the Naval Discipline Act, 1866, the following section, which shall be numbered as section seventy:—

Where a person is in pursuance of this Act convicted by a court-martial and either is sentenced or has his sentence commuted to penal servitude, such conviction and sentence shall be of the same effect as if such person had been convicted by a civil court in the United Kingdom of an offence punishable by penal servitude and sentenced by that court to penal servitude, and all enactments relating to a convict so sentenced shall, so far as circumstances admit, apply accordingly; and the said convict shall be removed to some prison in which a convict so sentenced by a civil court in the United Kingdom can be confined either permanently or temporarily, and the order of the Admiralty or of the Commander-in-Chief, or of the officer ordering the court-martial by whom such person was convicted, shall be a sufficient warrant for the transfer of the said person to such prison to undergo his sentence according to law, and until he reaches such prison for his detention in naval custody, or in any civil prison or place of confinement.

Amendment of s. 73 as to cumulative sentences of imprisonment.

4. There shall be added at the end of section seventy-three of the Naval Discipline Act, 1866, the following proviso:— 29 & 30 Vict. c. 109.

Provided that nothing in this section shall cause a person to undergo imprisonment for any period exceeding two consecutive years, and so much of any term of imprisonment imposed on a person by a sentence in pursuance of this section as would prolong his imprisonment beyond that period shall be deemed to be remitted.

Amendment of s. 74 as to commencement of term of imprisonment.

5. There shall be added to section seventy-four of the Naval Discipline Act, 1866, the following sub-sections as sub-sections two and three thereof:—

(2) Where, by reason of a ship being at sea or off a place at which there is no proper prison, a sentence of imprisonment cannot be duly executed, then, subject as hereinafter mentioned, an offender under sentence of imprisonment may be sent with all reasonable speed to some place at which there is a proper prison in which the sentence can be duly executed, and on arrival there the offender shall undergo his sentence, in like manner as if the date of such arrival were the day on which the sentence was awarded, and that notwithstanding that in the meanwhile he has returned to his duty or become entitled to his discharge; and the term of imprisonment shall be reckoned accordingly, subject however to the deduction of any time during which he has been kept in confinement in respect of the said sentence.

(3) Where in pursuance of this Act a person is sentenced to imprisonment, the order of the Admiralty or of the Commander-in-Chief, or of the officer ordering the court-martial by which such person was sentenced, or, if he was sentenced by the commanding officer of a ship, the order of such commanding officer, shall be a sufficient warrant for the sending of such person to the place of imprisonment, there to undergo his sentence according to law, and until he reaches such place of imprisonment, for his detention in naval custody, or in any civil prison or place of confinement.

6. There shall be substituted for the portion of section eighty-one of the Naval Discipline Act, 1866, which is repealed by this Act, the following enactment, which shall be sub-section two thereof:— **Amendment of s. 81 as to the Admiralty setting apart buildings and ships as naval prisons.**

29 Vict.,

(*2*) The Admiralty shall have the same power and authority in respect to naval prisons as one of Her Majesty's Principal Secretaries of State has in relation to military prisons under section one hundred and thirty-three of the Army Act, 1881, and that section shall apply as if it were herein re-enacted with the substitution of "the Admiralty" for "a Secretary of State", and of "naval" for "military", and rules and regulations may be made accordingly by the Admiralty.

44 Vict.,

Supplemental.

7. (*1*) Every enactment and word of this Act which is expressed to be substituted for or added to any portion of the Naval Discipline Act, 1866, shall form part of that Act in the place assigned to it by this Act, and the Naval Discipline Act, 1866, and all Acts, including this Act, which refer thereto shall, after the commencement of and subject to the savings contained in this Act, be construed as if the said enactment or word had been originally enacted in the Naval Discipline Act, 1866, in the place so assigned, and, where it is substituted for another enactment or word, had been so enacted in lieu of that enactment or word; and the expression "this Act", as used in the Naval Discipline Act, 1866, or this Act, shall be construed accordingly. **Construction and printing of Naval Discipline Act.**

(*2*) A copy of the Naval Discipline Act, 1866, with every such enactment and word inserted in the place so assigned, and with the omission of the parts expressly repealed by this Act or by the Statute Law Revision Act, 1875, and with the sections and sub-sections numbered in manner directed by this Act, shall be prepared and certified by the Clerk of the Parliaments, and deposited with the rolls of Parliament; Her Majesty's printers shall print in accordance with the copy so certified all copies of the Naval Discipline Act, 1866, which are printed after the commencement of this Act.

Repeal, Commencement, and Short Title.

8. (*1*) The Acts mentioned in the schedule to this Act are hereby repealed, as from the commencement of this Act, to the extent in the third column of that schedule mentioned. **Repeal of Acts, and savings.**

(*2*) This Act, or the repeal enacted by this Act, shall not affect anything done or suffered or any right or liability acquired or incurred before the commencement of this Act, and shall not affect any legal proceeding in reference to any such thing, right, or liability, and any such legal proceeding may be instituted, carried on, and completed as if this Act had not passed.

(*3*) In the case of any offence committed before the commencement of this Act, if any proceeding for the trial or punishment of the offender has been commenced before the commencement of this Act, such proceeding may be carried on and completed and the offender may be tried and punished as if this Act had not passed, but, save as aforesaid, this Act shall apply to the trial and punishment of a person accused of such offence, and the section substituted for sections seventy and seventy-one of the Naval Discipline Act, 1866, and the addition to section seventy-four of that Act, with respect to the warrant for sending a person to a place of imprisonment, shall apply to a person sentenced, whether before or after the commencement of this Act. 29 & 30 Vic. c. 109.

(*4*) Any regulations in force in any naval prison at the commencement of this Act shall continue in force until revoked by regulations made in pursuance of this Act.

Commencement of Act.

9. This Act shall come into force at the expiration of six months from the passing thereof, or at any earlier date from time to time fixed by the Admiralty, and the Admiralty may fix different dates for different stations and places, and the day on which this Act comes into operation on any station or in any place shall as regards that station or place be deemed to be the commencement of this Act.

Short title.

10. This Act may be cited as the Naval Discipline Act, 1884.

SCHEDULE.

Acts Repealed.

A description or citation of a portion of an Act in this Schedule is inclusive of the word, section or other part first and last mentioned, or otherwise referred to as forming the beginning or as forming the end of the portion described in the description or citation.

Session and Chapter.	Title.	Extent of Repeal.
44 Geo. 3, c. 13	An Act to prevent the desertion and escape of petty officers, seamen, and others from His Majesty's service, by means or under colour of any civil or criminal process.	The whole Act.
5 Geo. 4, c. 83	An Act for the punishment of idle and disorderly persons, and rogues and vagabonds, in that part of Great Britain called England.	Section sixteen, from "other than a person" down "to England."

SCHEDULE—*continued.*

Session and Chapter.	Title.	Extent of Repeal.
29 & 30 Vict., c. 109 .	An Act to make provision for the discipline of the navy.	Section fifty-six from "and any offence" to the end of sub-section two; in section fifty-eight, sub-section seven; section seventy; section seventy-one; section seventy-seven; section eighty-one, from "and all powers and authorities with respect to" to the end of the section; in section eighty-four the date "1866."

The Criminal Lunatics Act, 1884.[1]

(47 & 48 Vict., c. 64.)

An Act to consolidate and amend the Law relating to Criminal Lunatics.

[*14th August, 1884.*]

* * * * * * *

* * * * * * *

10. (4)[2] When the criminal lunatic was a person removed from India in pursuance of the Lunatics Removal (India) Act, 1851,[3] all expenses attending the removal of any such person from India, and his safe custody and maintenance, shall continue to be defrayed in the same manner as if this Act had not been passed.

14 & 15 Vict., c. 81.

Provision as to expenses of maintenance of criminal lunatic.

* * * * * * *

* * * * * * *

[1] See *Chitty's Statutes*, Tit. Lunatics Criminal, p. 155.
[2] This is the only provision of the Act applicable to India.
[3] Printed, Vol. I, p. 278.

THE EAST INDIA UNCLAIMED STOCK ACT, 1885.[1]
(48 & 49 Vict., c. 25.)

An Act for making provision for the transfer to the Secretary of State in Council of India of Unclaimed India Stock and Dividends; and for amending the East Indian Railway Company Purchase Act, 1879, and the East Indian Railway (Redemption of Annuities) Act, 1881; and for other purposes. [*16th July, 1885.*]

* * * * * * *

Short title.
1. This Act may be cited as the East India Unclaimed Stock Act, 1885.

Interpretation.
2. In this Act, unless the context otherwise requires—

"Secretary of State" means the Secretary of State in Council of India.

"India stock" means and includes India five per cent. stock, India four per cent. stock, India three and a half per cent. stock, India three per cent. stock, East India four per cent. transfer loan, and any India stock from time to time raised in the United Kingdom and transferable at the Bank of England or Bank of Ireland.

"High Court" means Her Majesty's High Court of Justice in England, or, as the case may be, Her Majesty's High Court of Justice in Ireland.

"Bank of England" means the Governor and Company of the Bank of England, and includes their successors.

"Bank of Ireland" means the Governor and Company of the Bank of Ireland, and includes their successors.

"Government Directors" includes any ex officio or other director appointed by the Secretary of State.

"Indian railway company" means any railway company constructing or working railways in India.

"Person" includes a body of persons corporate or unincorporate.

Unclaimed Stock, etc., and Dividends.

Unclaimed moneys arising from redemption of stock.
3. (1) All principal sums of money which have become or may hereafter become payable to any holder of India stock, by reason of its redemption, and which have not been or shall not have been claimed for ten years or more, shall be paid to the Secretary of State; and all principal sums of money which have so become or may hereafter so become payable to any holder of India stock whereon dividend has not been or shall not have been claimed for ten years or more shall be paid to the Secretary of State.

(2) All such principal sums so paid may be applied by the Secretary of State as part of the revenues of India or otherwise as he may think fit, subject to the claims of the parties entitled thereto.

---

[1] This Act may be cited with eighteen others as the East India Loans Acts, 1859 to 1893, see the Short Titles Act, 1896 (59 & 60 Vict., c. 14), *post*, p. 1255.

(*Secs. 4-8.*)

(3) For the purposes of this Act relating to the application of dividends and the claims of parties entitled, and consequent proceedings, such principal sums of money shall be deemed to be included in the term " stock, " and payment thereof in the term " transfer," and repayment thereof in the term " re-transfer."

Unclaimed stock.

4. (1) All India stock whereon dividend has not or shall not have been claimed for ten years or more (except where payment of dividend has been restrained by a court of justice) shall be transferred in the books of the Bank of England, or (as the case may be) of the Bank of Ireland, to an account to be intituled " The Secretary of State in Council of India Unclaimed Stock Account, " to be held by the Secretary of State subject to the claims of the parties entitled thereto. The Bank of England, or (as the case may be) the Bank of Ireland, shall, during the six months next previous to such transfer, give notice in writing to the stockholder, at his registered address, of the impending transfer to the Secretary of State.

(2) In the event of any stock being redeemed while held by the Secretary of State under the foregoing enactment, the principal sums of money representing such stock shall, for the purposes of this Act relating to the application of dividends and the claims of parties entitled and consequent proceedings, be deemed to be included in the term " stock, " and repayment thereof in the term " re-transfer."

List of names from which stock transferred.

5. Immediately after every such transfer the name of the person in whose name the stock stood immediately before the transfer, the residence and description of such person, the amount transferred, and the date of transfer, shall be entered in a list to be kept for the purpose by the Bank in whose books the stock stands.

A duplicate of such list shall be kept at the India Office.

Mode of transfer.

6. Every such transfer shall be made and signed by the accountant general or deputy or assistant accountant general or secretary or deputy or assistant secretary of the Bank in whose books the stock stands at the time of transfer, and shall be as effectual to all intents as if signed by the person in whose name the stock was then standing.

Subsequent dividends on stock transferred.

7. Where stock is transferred under this Act all dividends accruing thereon after the transfer shall be paid to the Secretary of State, and applied by him as part of the revenues of India, subject to the claims of the parties entitled thereto.

Re-transfer and payment to person showing title.

8. The Governor or Deputy Governor of the Bank of England or Ireland may direct the accountant general or deputy or assistant accountant general or secretary or deputy or assistant secretary of that Bank to re-transfer any stock transferred under this Act to any person showing his right thereto to the

satisfaction of the Governor or Deputy Governor, and to pay the dividends due thereon, as if the same had not been transferred or paid to the Secretary of State.

But in case the Governor or Deputy Governor is not satisfied of the right of any person claiming to be entitled to any such stock or dividends, the claimant may, by petition in a summary way, state and verify his claim in the Chancery Division of the High Court.

The petition shall be served on the Secretary of State, or on one of his under secretaries, or on his assistant under secretary, at the India Office, and the Court shall make such order thereon (either for re-transfer of the stock to which the petition relates and payment of the dividends accrued thereon, or otherwise), and touching the costs of the application, as to the Court seems just.

All costs and expenses incurred by or on behalf of the Secretary of State in resisting or appearing on any such petition, if not ordered by the Court to be paid out of the stock and dividends thereby claimed, shall be paid by the Secretary of State out of the revenues of India.

Where any re-transfer or payment is made to any such claimant either with or without the authority of the Court, the Bank of England or of Ireland (as the case requires) shall give notice thereof to the Secretary of State, within three days after making the same.

Three months' notice before re-transfer or payment.

9. Stock exceeding the sum of twenty pounds shall not be re-transferred from the Secretary of State under this Act, nor shall dividends exceeding twenty pounds in the whole be paid to a claimant under this Act, until three months after application made for the same, nor until public notice has been given thereof as in this Act provided.

Advertisements before re-transfer or payment.

10. The Bank of England or of Ireland shall require the applicant to give such public notice as they think fit by advertisements, in the case of either Bank in one or more newspapers circulating in London and elsewhere, and in the case of the Bank of Ireland also in one or more newspapers circulating in Dublin and elsewhere in Ireland.

Every such notice shall state the name, residence, and description of the person in whose name the stock stood when transferred to the Secretary of State, the amount thereof, the name of the claimant, and the time at which the re-transfer thereof and payment of dividends will be made if no other claimant sooner appears and makes out his claim.

Where any such re-transfer or payment is ordered by the High Court the notice shall also state the purport of the order.

11. At any time before re-transfer of stock or payment of dividend as aforesaid to a claimant any person may apply to the Chancery Division of the High Court by motion or petition, to rescind or vary any order made for re-transfer or payment thereof.

Application to Court to rescind order.

12. Where any stock or dividends having been re-transferred or paid as aforesaid to a claimant by either Bank is or are afterwards claimed by another person, the Bank and their officers shall not be responsible for the same to such other claimant, but he may have recourse against the person to whom the re-transfer or payment was made. Provided that if in any case a new claimant establishes his title to any stock or dividends re-transferred or paid to a former claimant, and is unable to obtain transfer on payment thereof from the former claimant, the Court shall, on application by petition by the new claimant, verified as the Court requires, order the Secretary of State to transfer to him such sum in stock, and to pay to him such sum in money for dividend, as the Court thinks just.

Bank not responsible to second claimant.

Order in favour of second claimant showing title.

Such transfer shall be made from stock transferred to the Secretary of State under this Act; and such money for dividend shall be paid out of the revenues of India.

13. Where any dividend accrued due on any sum of stock is not claimed for ten years or more, the dividend so unclaimed, and all dividends subsequently accrued due in respect of the same sum of stock and unclaimed, shall be paid to the Secretary of State.

Payment of unclaimed dividends to Secretary of State.

All such dividends shall be dealt with in like manner, as nearly as may be, as stock transferred to the Secretary of State under the foregoing provisions of this Act or the dividends accruing thereon after the transfer, as the case may require; and the foregoing provisions of this Act shall accordingly have effect, in relation thereto, and to the application and payment of and claims to the same, as if the foregoing provisions of this Act were repeated and in terms made applicable thereto respectively.

14. The Secretary of State may from time to time empower the Bank of England or of Ireland to investigate the circumstances of any stock or dividends remaining unclaimed with a view to ascertain the owners thereof.

Investigation as to unclaimed stock or dividends.

15. All stock described in a stock certificate in respect of which no coupon is presented for payment for ten years or more shall be dealt with in like manner, as nearly as may be, as stock whereon dividend has not or shall not have been claimed for ten years or more.

Unclaimed stock in stock certificates and unclaimed coupons.

Sums due and unclaimed on coupons shall be dealt with in like manner, as nearly as may be, as unclaimed dividends due in respect of stock.

Indemnity to Banks.

16. The Banks of England and Ireland and their respective governors, deputy governors, and officers are hereby indemnified in respect of every transfer or re-transfer of stock or payment of dividends under this Act, and shall not be in any manner responsible to any person having or claiming any interest therein.

Unclaimed East Indian Railway Annuity and Unclaimed Railway Debentures.

Re-transfer to Secretary of State of unclaimed East Indian Railway annuity.

42 & 43 Vic. c. 206.

17. Whereas it is provided by section ten of the East Indian Railway Company Purchase Act, 1879 (in this section called the Purchase Act), that the annuity created by that Act (in this section referred to as the annuity) shall from time to time be paid by the Secretary of State to the East Indian Railway Company (in this section referred to as the Company), and shall be received and held by them for the purpose of distribution by them amongst the several persons entitled from time to time thereto under that Act, and shall not nor shall any part thereof at any time be paid or applied by the Company otherwise than for the purpose of such distribution:

And whereas at the time of the purchase of the East Indian Railway under the said Act the capital of the Company included a sum of twenty-three thousand eight hundred and eighty pounds capital stock in respect of which no person was registered in the books of the Company as the proprietor thereof, and the annuities representing the same now remain unpaid:

And whereas no distribution can at present be made of such unclaimed annuities, and it is expedient to authorise the Secretary of State to suspend payment of a portion of the annuity equal in amount to such unclaimed annuities:

And whereas it is also expedient to provide for the repayment by the Company to the Secretary of State of any annuities other than the said unclaimed annuities representing the said unclaimed capital stock already received by the Company which may remain in the hands of the Company unclaimed for ten years, and further to authorise the Secretary of State to suspend payment of a portion of the annuity equal in amount to such annuities so remaining unclaimed:

And whereas by section eighteen of the Purchase Act the Board of Directors of the Company were directed to divide the annuitants into two classes to be called respectively Class A and Class B, and provision was made by section twenty-three of the said Act for the creation of a sinking fund attached to annuities of Class B derived from the investment of certain deductions to be made from annuities of that class as thereby provided, and it is expedient that so much of the accumulations of the said sinking fund as may be attributable to unclaimed annuities should be repaid to the Secretary of State when the sinking fund shall be distributed according to the provisions of section twenty-five of the said Act :

And whereas it is expedient that the Purchase Act should be amended: It is hereby enacted as follows:

(1) Nothing in this section contained shall alter or affect the liability of the Company under the Purchase Act with regard to the moneys before the passing of this Act received by them in respect of the said unclaimed annuities representing the said sum of twenty-three thousand eight hundred and eighty pounds unclaimed capital stock of the Company.

(2) The Secretary of State may henceforth suspend payment to the Company of a portion of the annuity equal in amount to the said unclaimed annuities representing the said sum of twenty-three thousand eight hundred and eighty pounds.

(3) If and whenever any annuities (other than annuities before the passing of this Act paid by the Secretary of State to the Company in respect of the said unclaimed capital stock of the Company) shall have remained or shall remain after payment by the Secretary of State to the Company in the hands of the Company unclaimed for a period of ten years, such annuities shall be repaid to the Secretary of State by the Company less any sum by the Purchase Act authorised to be deducted by the Board of Directors of the Company in respect of the said sinking fund attached to annuities of the said Class B and in respect of expenses in relation to annuities of either class.

(4) The Secretary of State may, after any such repayment, suspend payment to the Company of a portion of the annuity equal in amount to the annuities which have so remained unclaimed for such period of ten years: Provided that if there be comprised in any such unclaimed annuities any annuities of the said Class B, the Secretary of State shall, at the times and in the manner by the Purchase Act prescribed for payment of the annuity, pay to the Company so much of such unclaimed annuities as represents the deduction by the Purchase Act authorised to be made by the said Board of Directors in respect of the said sinking fund attached to annuities of the said Class B.

(5) Notwithstanding anything in this section contained, the Secretary of State shall continue to pay to the Company in respect of any

annuities, the payment of which has been suspended, any sums which by the Purchase Act the Board of Directors of the Company are authorised to deduct from the annuities payable to the annuitants of both classes in respect of the expenses of the payment and management of the annuity.

(6) The Board of Directors of the Company, when the time for division of the moneys representing the accumulations of the said sinking fund shall arrive, shall pay to the Secretary of State such part of such accumulations as may be represented by any annuities of the said Class B at that time unclaimed.

(7) The Secretary of State shall hold any moneys representing unclaimed annuities at any time repaid to him by the Company and any moneys paid to him by the Board of Directors on the eventual division of the said sinking fund, and any annuities his obligation to pay which is under this Act at any time suspended, subject to the claim of any person who may at any time, in manner by this Act provided, establish his claim thereto, and subject to such claims the Secretary of State may apply such moneys as part of the revenues of India, or otherwise as he may think fit.

(8) The Secretary of State shall be bound to indemnify the Company against all claims in respect of any moneys representing unclaimed annuities at any time repaid to him by the Company, and of any moneys paid to him by the Board of Directors of the Company, on the eventual division of the said sinking fund, and of any annuities his obligation to pay which is under this Act at any time suspended; and the remedy of any person claiming to be entitled to any such moneys or annuities shall be against the Secretary of State in manner by this Act provided, and not against the Company.

(9) If and whenever any person claiming to be entitled to any moneys representing unclaimed annuities at any time repaid to the Secretary of State by the Company, or to any moneys paid to the Secretary of State by the Board of Directors of the Company on the eventual division of the said sinking fund, or to any unclaimed annuities the payment of which has under any provision of this Act been suspended, establishes his right thereto respectively to the satisfaction of the Secretary of State, the Secretary of State shall forthwith, free of all expense to the

(*Sec. 17.*)

claimant, pay to such person the moneys to which he has so established his claim, and shall, if the claim be in respect of unclaimed annuities, give notice in writing to the Board of Directors of the Company that such claim has been so established, and thereupon the said Board shall enter the name of such claimant in the proper register of annuitants, and the obligation of the Secretary of State to pay to the Company the portion of the annuity representing the unclaimed annuities in question shall revive. But in case the Secretary of State is not satisfied of the right of any person claiming to be entitled to any such moneys or unclaimed annuities, as the case may be, the claimant may, by petition in a summary way, state and verify his claim in the Chancery Division of Her Majesty's High Court of Justice, and the Court shall make such order thereon declaring the claimant entitled or not entitled to any such moneys or unclaimed annuities as the case may require, and touching the costs of the application as to the Court seems just, and upon any such order of the Court in favour of any claimant, he shall be entitled to the same rights in respect of the moneys or unclaimed annuities claimed by him as if he had established his right thereto to the satisfaction of the Secretary of State as in this sub-section before mentioned. All costs and expenses incurred by or on behalf of the Secretary of State in resisting or appearing on any such petition, if not ordered by the Court to be paid out of any moneys claimed or otherwise, shall be paid by the Secretary of State out of the revenues of India.

(10) The Secretary of State shall require the applicant to give such public notice as the Secretary of State thinks fit by advertisement in one or more newspapers circulating in London and elsewhere, and such notice shall contain such particulars as the case requires and as the Secretary of State directs.

(11) At any time before repayment of any moneys to any claimant or the entry of his name in either register of annuitants, any person may apply to the said Division of the Court, by motion or petition, to rescind or vary any order made for payment or entry. If in any case a new claimant establishes his right to any moneys repaid to the former claimant, or to any annuities in respect of which any former claimant has been entered in either register of annuitants as the holder thereof, and such new

claimant is unable to obtain repayment of such moneys from the former claimant, or to procure the entry of his name in the proper register as the holder of any of such annuities, the said Division of the Court shall, on application by petition by the new claimant, verified as the Court requires, order the Secretary of State to pay to such new claimant the sum of money to which he has established his claim, or to purchase for him annuities of the class to which he has established his claim, or (if such new claimant consent) to give him the current value of such annuities in India stock. All moneys which the Court may order the Secretary of State to pay to or on behalf of any such new claimant shall be paid out of the revenues of India.

Unclaimed railway debentures.

18. All sums of money already paid or which shall hereafter be paid by the Secretary of State to any Indian railway company for the discharge of any debentures, either before or after the passing of this Act, issued or authorised to be issued under his guarantee, in respect of which no claim has or shall have been made for one year or more after such payment by any party thereto entitled, shall (whether any person is or is not registered as entitled thereto) be repaid to the Secretary of State.

The said sums so repaid to the Secretary of State may be applied by him as part of the revenues of India or otherwise as the Secretary of State may think fit, subject to the claims of the parties entitled thereto.

Claims by parties entitled.

19. Where any person claims to be entitled to any sum repaid to the Secretary of State under the last preceding section, the Secretary of State may, on such person showing his right thereto to the satisfaction of the Secretary of State, pay such sum to such person; but in case the Secretary of State is not satisfied of the right of such person, then the person claiming to be entitled to any sum repaid to the Secretary of State may state and verify his claim by petition in the Chancery Division of the High Court in England in a summary way in manner provided by this Act with respect to petitions for stock or dividends; and the provisions of this Act with regard to such petitions and the proceedings consequent thereon shall, with any necessary modifications, apply to claims under this section.

Indemnity to railway companies.

20. Where any sum is retained by or repaid to the Secretary of State in respect of unclaimed annuity or unclaimed debentures as by this Act provided, the respective railway companies shall be and hereby are indemnified in respect thereof, and shall not be in any manner responsible to any person having or claiming any interest therein.

Miscellaneous.

21. No stamp duty shall be paid or chargeable in respect of the transfer of any stock or annuity to or from the Secretary of State pursuant to the provisions of this Act. Exemption from stamp duty.

22. Whereas provision has been made for the appointment of a Government director by the Secretary of State on the Boards of certain Indian railway companies; and in some cases the Secretary of State is empowered to appoint a person to represent the Government director at Board meetings and otherwise; and it is expedient that in all cases the Secretary of State should have such power: It is hereby enacted as follows: Deputy Government directors.

It shall be lawful for the Secretary of State, in the case of any Indian railway company, where under his contract with that company he has the power to appoint a Government director but not a person to represent him, from time to time to appoint a person to represent the Government director in his absence at the Board of any such Indian railway company, and any deputy so appointed shall have and may exercise (subject to any regulations of the Secretary of State) all or any of the powers of the Government director.

23. (1) Notwithstanding any provision in any Act of Parliament or deed of settlement or other instrument founding or regulating a company to the contrary, it shall be lawful for any Indian railway company, from time to time, with the sanction of the Secretary of State, and subject to such regulations and conditions as he may think fit to impose,— Issue of railway debentures to order or bearer.

(*a*) to issue debenture bonds payable to bearer, which shall be negotiable by delivery;

(*b*) to issue debenture bonds payable to order, which shall be negotiable by indorsement of the holder;

(*c*) to issue debenture bonds payable in rupee currency;

(*d*) to make provision for the exchange of debenture bonds on the application of the holder for debenture bonds of any other form or kind issued by the company.

(2) This section does not confer any additional or further borrowing powers on any Indian railway company, but applies only to the mode of exercise of borrowing powers conferred independently of this Act;

(3) Trustees (unless expressly authorised by the terms of their trust to hold securities payable to bearer) may not hold debenture bonds payable to bearer issued under this section.

24. For all or any of the purposes of this Act the Secretary of State may require any railway company to which this Act applies to furnish such returns and give such information as he may think expedient. Returns to Secretary of State.

Amendment o 44 & 45 Vict., c. 53.

25. Whereas provision has been made by the East Indian Railway Redemption of Annuities Act, 1881[1] (in this section referred to as the Redemption Act), for the redemption by the Secretary of State of annuities comprised in the annuity created by the East Indian Railway Company Purchase Act, 1879 (in this section referred to as the Purchase Act); and whereas the provisions of the Redemption Act are inapplicable to such of the said annuities as are annuities of the said Class B in section seventeen of this Act referred to, and it is expedient to make provision applicable to the redemption of such annuities, and also for the redemption of annuities of a similar character which have been or may be created for the purchase of Indian railways:

42 & 43 Vict., c. 206.

And whereas under certain contracts made with divers Indian railway companies before the passing of the Redemption Act, the Secretary of State is enabled on terms therein specified to purchase their undertakings either for a capital sum or by means of the creation and grant of an annuity; and whereas the power to create such annuities constitutes a liability contingently chargeable, though not actually charged, on the revenues of India at the date of the passing of the said Act; and whereas it is expedient that the provisions of the Redemption Act should apply to such annuities as and when created: It is hereby enacted as follows:

(1) When the Secretary of State redeems any annuities of the said Class B, he shall be liable in respect of his holding from time to time to contribute rateably with other annuitants to the sinking fund attached to annuities of the said Class B; and in other respects he shall be liable to, and shall have the benefit of, the provisions of sections forty-nine and fifty of the Purchase Act, and on the distribution of the sinking fund attached to annuities of the said Class B, he shall be entitled to receive such share of the sum then distributed as may be attributable to any annuities so redeemed; and any sums which he may contribute to the sinking fund created by the Purchase Act which may be attributable to any annuities redeemed by him shall (by reason of his contribution to the sinking fund) be deemed to have been invested in accordance with the provisions of section two of the Redemption Act, notwithstanding that they have not been set aside and invested in manner directed by section fifty-one of the Purchase Act; and the provisions of the foregoing enactment shall, with any necessary modifications, apply to any annuities

---

[1] Printed *ante*, p. 610.

similar to the annuities of the said Class B under the Purchase Act which have been or may be created for the purchase of any Indian railway.

(2) Section two of the Redemption Act shall be construed and have effect as if the words "now charged or contingently chargeable" were substituted therein for the words "now charged," so as to apply to any annuity which the Secretary of State has created or may create under any of the contracts above referred to.

The East India Loan Act, 1885.[1]

(48 & 49 Vict., c. 28.)

An Act to enable the Secretary of State in Council of India to raise Money in the United Kingdom for the Service of the Government of India.

[*22nd July, 1885.*]

Whereas the exigencies of the public service in India require that the Secretary of State in Council of India should be enabled to raise money in the United Kingdom on the credit of the revenues of India:

* * * * * * *

1. It shall be lawful for the Secretary of State in Council of India, at any time or times after the passing of this Act, to raise in the United Kingdom, for the service of the Government of India, any sum or sums of money not exceeding in the whole ten millions of pounds sterling, such sum or sums to be raised by the creation and issue of bonds, debentures, or capital stock bearing interest, or partly by one of such modes, and partly by another or others. *Power to the Secretary of State in Council of India to raise any sum not exceeding 10,000,000l.*

2. All bonds issued under the authority of this Act may be issued under the hands of two members of the Council of India, and countersigned by the Secretary of State for India, or one of his under secretaries, or his assistant under secretary, and shall be for such respective amounts, payable after such notice, and at such rate or rates of interest, as the said Secretary of State in Council may think fit. *As to issue of bonds.*

3. All debentures issued under the authority of this Act may be issued under the hands of two members of the Council, and countersigned as *As to issue of debentures.*

---

[1] This Act may be cited with eighteen others as the East India Loans Acts, 1859 to 1893—See the Short Titles Act, 1896 (59 & 60 Vict., c. 14), *post*, p. 1255.

aforesaid, for such respective amounts, and at such rate or rates of interest, as the Secretary of State in Council may think fit, and shall be issued at or for such prices and on such terms as may be determined by the Secretary of State in Council.

As to payment of principal and interest on debentures.

4. All debentures issued under the authority of this Act shall be paid off at par at a time or times to be mentioned in such debentures respectively; and the interest on all such debentures shall be paid half-yearly on such days as shall be mentioned therein; and the principal moneys and interest secured by such debentures shall be payable either at the treasury of the Secretary of State in Council in London or at the Bank of England.

Debentures and coupons for interest transferable by delivery.

5. All or any number of the debentures issued under the authority of this Act, and all right to and in respect of the principal and interest moneys secured thereby, shall be transferable by the delivery of such debentures; and the coupons for interest annexed to any debenture issued under the authority of this Act shall also pass by delivery.

Capital stock may be created and issued.

6. Any capital stock created under the authority of this Act shall bear such a rate of interest as the Secretary of State in Council may think fit; and such capital stock may be issued on such terms as may be determined by the Secretary of State in Council; and any such capital stock may bear interest during such period, and be paid off at par at such time, as the Secretary of State in Council may prescribe previously to the issue of such capital stock.

Transfer books of such capital stock to be kept.

7. In case of the creation and issue of any such capital stock there shall be kept, either at the office of the Secretary of State in Council in London or at the Bank of England, books wherein entries shall be made of the said capital stock, and wherein all assignments or transfers of the same, or any part thereof, shall be entered and registered, and shall be signed by the parties making such assignments or transfers, or, if such parties be absent, by his, her, or their attorney or attorneys thereunto lawfully authorized by writing under his, her, or their hands and seals, to be attested by two or more credible witnesses; and the person or persons to whom such transfer or transfers shall be made may respectively underwrite his, her, or their acceptance thereof; and no other mode of assigning or transferring the said capital stock or any part thereof, or any interest therein, shall be good and available in law, and no stamp duties whatsoever shall be charged on the said transfers or any of them.

Amount charged on revenues of India not to exceed 10,000,000*l*.

8. The whole amount of the principal moneys to be charged on the revenues of India under this Act shall not exceed ten millions.

9. Upon or for the repayment of any principal money secured under the authority of this Act, the Secretary of State in Council may at any time borrow or raise, by all or any of the modes aforesaid, all or any part of the amount of principal money repaid or to be repaid, and so from time to time as all or any part of any principal money under this Act may require to be repaid, but the amount to be charged upon the revenues of India shall not in any case exceed the principal moneys required to be repaid.

Power to raise money for payment of principal money.

10. All bonds and debentures to be issued under this Act, and the principal moneys and interest thereby secured, and all capital stock to be issued under this Act, and the interest thereon, shall be charged on and payable out of the revenues of India, in like manner as other liabilities incurred on account of the Government of India.

Securities, etc., to be charged on revenues of India.

11. The provisions contained in section four of the Act of the session holden in the fifth and sixth years of King William the Fourth, chapter sixty-four,[1] with respect to the composition and agreement for the payment by the East India Company of an annual sum in lieu of stamp duties on their bonds, and the exemption of their bonds from stamp duties, shall be applicable with respect to bonds and debentures to be issued under the authority of this Act, as if such provisions were here repeated and re-enacted with reference thereto.

Provisions as to composition for stamp duties on India bonds extended to bonds and debentures issued under this Act.

12. All provisions now in force in anywise relating to the offence of forging or altering, or offering, uttering, disposing of, or putting off, knowing the same to be forged or altered, any East India bond, with intent to defraud, shall extend and be applicable to and in respect of any debenture or bond issued under the authority of this Act.

Forgery of debentures and bonds to be punishable as forgery of East India bonds.

13. This Act shall not prejudice or affect any power of raising or borrowing money vested in the said Secretary of State in Council at the time of passing thereof.

Saving borrowing powers of Secretary of State in Council.

14. Any capital stock created under this Act shall be deemed to be East India stock, within the Act of the twenty-second and twenty-third Victoria,[2] chapter thirty-five, section thirty-two, unless and until Parliament shall otherwise provide; and any capital stock created under this Act shall be deemed to be and shall mean India stock within the Act of the twenty-sixth and twenty-seventh Victoria, chapter seventy-three, anything in the said last-mentioned Act to the contrary notwithstanding.

Stock created under this Act to be deemed East India stock.

---

[1] Printed, Vol. I, p. 192.
[2] Law of Property Amendment Act, not in force in India.

THE SUBMARINE TELEGRAPH ACT, 1885.[1]

(48 & 49 Vict., c. 49.)

An Act to carry into effect an International Convention for the Protection of Submarine Telegraph Cables.

[*6th August, 1885.*]

* * * * * *

Short title.

1. This Act may be cited as the Submarine Telegraph Act, 1885.

Confirmation of Convention.

2. The Convention of the fourteenth of March one thousand eight hundred and eighty-four mentioned in the schedule to this Act as set forth in that schedule is hereby confirmed, and subject to the provisions of this Act the articles of such Convention (referred to in this Act as the Convention) shall be of the same force as if they were enacted in the body of this Act.

Punishment for violation of Article 2 of Convention.

3. (1) A person shall not unlawfully and wilfully, or by culpable negligence, break or injure any submarine cable to which the Convention for the time being applies, in such manner as might interrupt or obstruct in whole or in part telegraphic communication.

(2) Any person who acts or attempts to act in contravention of this section shall be guilty of a misdemeanour, and on conviction—

(*a*) if he acted wilfully, shall be liable to penal servitude for a term not exceeding five years, or to imprisonment, with or without hard labour, for a term not exceeding two years and to a fine either in lieu of or in addition to such penal servitude or imprisonment; and

(*b*) if he acted by culpable negligence, shall be liable to imprisonment for a term not exceeding three months, without hard labour, and to a fine not exceeding one hundred pounds either in lieu of or in addition to such imprisonment.

(3) Where a person does any act with the object of preserving the life or limb of himself or of any other person, or of preserving the vessel to which he belongs or any other vessel, and takes all reasonable precautions to avoid injury to a submarine cable, such person shall not be deemed to have acted unlawfully and wilfully within the meaning of this section.

(4) A person shall not be deemed to have unlawfully and wilfully broken or injured any submarine cable, where in the *bonâ fide* attempt to repair another submarine cable injury has been done to such first-mentioned cable, or the same has been broken; but this shall not apply so as to exempt such

[1] See *Chitty's Statutes*, Tit. Telegraph, p. 42.

person from any liability under this Act or otherwise to pay the cost of repairing such breakage or injury.

(5) Any person who within or (being a subject of Her Majesty) without Her Majesty's dominions in any manner procures, counsels, aids, abets, or is accessory to the commission of any offence under this section, shall be guilty of a misdemeanour, and shall be liable to be tried and punished for the offence as if he had been guilty as a principal.

4. [*Rep. 50 Vict., c. 3, s. 3.*]

5. (1) It is hereby declared that the enactments of the Merchant Shipping Act, 1862,[1] and the enactments amending the same, touching regulations as to lights and to signals and for the avoiding of collisions, shall extend to authorise regulations for carrying into effect Articles five and six of the schedule to this Act, within as well as without the territorial waters of Her Majesty's dominions, and regulations may be made, applied, altered, and revoked, and the contravention thereof punished accordingly under the said enactments, and section six of the Sea Fisheries Act, 1883, shall extend to the enforcement of the said regulations as regards sea fishing boats within the limits of that Act.

25 & 26 Vict., c. 63.

Application of law as to lights and signals or carrying into effect Articles five and six of Convention.

(2) If any vessel engaged in the laying or repairing of a submarine cable to which the Convention for the time being applies, interferes contrary to the said regulations or articles with any vessel engaged in fishing, or if the operations of any vessel in connection with any such submarine cable are wilfully delayed so as to interfere with sea fishing, the master of the vessel, or the owner thereof, if it appear that he was in fault, shall be deemed guilty of a breach of the said regulations and may be punished accordingly.

6. (1) For the purpose of carrying into effect the Convention, a person commanding a ship of war of Her Majesty or of any foreign state for the time being bound by the Convention, or a ship specially commissioned for the purpose of the Convention by Her Majesty or by the government of such foreign state, may exercise and perform the powers and duties vested in and imposed on such officer by any article in the Schedule to this Act.

Powers of British and foreign officers.

(2) If any person obstructs any such officer in such exercise or performance, or refuses or neglects to comply with any demand or direction lawfully made or given by him in pursuance of this Act, such person shall be liable, on summary conviction, to a fine not exceeding fifty pounds or to be imprisoned for a term not exceeding two months, with or without hard labour.

(3) Any action, prosecution, or proceeding against any officer for any act done in pursuance or execution or intended execution of this Act, or in

[1] *See* now the Merchant Shipping Act, 1894 (57 & 58 Vict., c. 60), printed *post*, p. 971.

respect of any alleged neglect or default in the execution of this Act, shall not lie or be instituted unless it is commenced within twelve months next after the act, neglect, or default complained of.

(4) In any such action, tender of amends before the action was commenced may, in lieu of or in addition to any other plea, be pleaded. If the action was commenced after such tender, or is proceeded with after payment into court of any money in satisfaction of the plaintiff's claim, and the plaintiff does not recover more than the sum tended or paid, he shall not recover any costs incurred after such tender or payment, and the defendants shall be entitled to costs, to be taxed as between solicitor and client, as from the time of such tender or payment.

(5) Every such action shall be brought in one of Her Majesty's superior courts in the United Kingdom (which courts shall have jurisdiction to try the same wherever the matter complained of occurred) or in a supreme court in India or in a court exercising in a British possession the like authority as the High Court of Justice in England, but in no other court whatsoever.

Incorporation of Part X of 17 & 18 Vict., c. 104.

7. Part X of the Merchant Shipping Act, 1854[1] (which relates to legal procedure), and the enactments amending the same, so far as unrepealed, shall have effect as if enacted in this Act, and offences under this Act may be tried, and fines under this Act recovered accordingly, save that nothing in the said part shall authorise the award of any punishment not authorised by this Act, or the summary prosecution of any indictable offence under this Act.

Evidence.

8. (1) Any document drawn up in pursuance of Article seven or Article ten of the schedule to this Act shall be admissible in any proceeding, civil or criminal, as *primâ facie* evidence of the facts or matters therein stated.

(2) If evidence contained in any such document was taken on oath in the presence of the person charged in such evidence, and such person had an opportunity of cross-examining the person giving such evidence and of making his reply to such evidence, the officer drawing up such document may certify the said facts, or any of them.

(3) Any document or certificate in this section mentioned purporting to be signed by an officer authorised to act under the Schedule to this Act for carrying into effect the Convention, shall be admissible in evidence without proof of such signature, and, if purporting to be signed by any other person, shall, if certified by any such officer to have been so signed, be deemed until the contrary is proved to have been signed by such other person.

---

[1] *See* now the Merchant Shipping Act, 1894 (57 & 58 Vict., c. 60), printed *post*, p. 971.

(4) If any person forges the signature of any such officer to any such document as above mentioned, or makes use of any such document knowing the signature thereto to be forged, such person shall be guilty of a misdemeanour and liable on summary conviction to imprisonment for a term not exceeding three months with or without hard labour, and on conviction on indictment to imprisonment with or without hard labour for a term not exceeding two years.

Liability of masters of vessels.

9. Where any offence against this Act has been committed by means of a vessel, or of any boat belonging to a vessel, the master of such vessel shall, until some other person is shown to have been in charge of and navigating such vessel or boat, be deemed to have been in charge of and navigating the same, and be liable to be punished accordingly.

Savings.

10. The provisions of this Act shall be in addition to and not in derogation of any other provisions existing at common law or under Act of Parliament or under the law of a British possession for the protection of submarine cables; and nothing in this Act shall prevent any person being liable under any Act of Parliament, law of a British possession, or otherwise to any indictment, proceeding, punishment, or penalty other than is provided for any offence by this Act, so that no person shall be punished twice for the same offence; and nothing in this Act, nor any proceedings with respect to any matter, shall exempt a person from any liability in any action or suit with reference to the same matter so that no person shall be required to pay compensation twice in respect of the same injury.

Extent of Act.

11. This Act shall, so far as such extension is consistent with the tenor o this Act, extend to the whole of Her Majesty's dominions, and to all places within the jurisdiction of the Admiral of England, and to all places where Her Majesty has jurisdiction.

Definitions.

12. In this Act, unless the context otherwise requires,—

The expression "vessel" means every description of vessel used in navigation in whatever way it is propelled; and any reference to a vessel shall include a reference to a boat belonging to such vessel:

The expression "master" includes every person having command or charge of a vessel:

The expression "British possession" includes any part of Her Majesty's dominions exclusive of the United Kingdom:

The expression "person" includes a body of persons corporate or unincorporate.

Commencement and continuance of Act.

13. This Act shall come into force on such day as may be fixed by a notice in that behalf published in the London Gazette, and if the Convention ceases to be binding on Her Majesty, shall cease to be of any effect.

SCHEDULE.

Submarine Telegraphs Convention.

Convention for the preservation of telegraphic communications by means of submarine telegraphs made on the 14th of March, 1884, between Her Majesty the Queen of the United Kingdom of Great Britain and Ireland, Empress of India, His Majesty the German Emperor, King of Prussia, His Excellency the President of the Argentine Confederation, His Majesty the Emperor of Austria, King of Bohemia, etc., and Apostolic King of Hungary, His Majesty the King of the Belgians, His Majesty the Emperor of Brazil, His Excellency the President of the Republic of Costa Rica, His Majesty the King of Denmark, His Excellency the President of the Dominican Republic, His Majesty the King of Spain, His Excellency the President of the United States of America, His Excellency the President of the United States of Colombia, His Excellency the President of the French Republic, His Excellency the President of the Republic of Guatemala, His Majesty the King of the Hellenes, His Majesty the King of Italy, His Majesty the Emperor of the Ottomans, His Majesty the King of the Netherlands, Grand Duke of Luxemburg, His Majesty the Shah of Persia, His Majesty the King of Portugal and the Algarves, His Majesty the King of Roumania, His Majesty the Emperor of all the Russias, His Excellency the President of the Republic of Salvador, His Majesty the King of Servia, His Majesty the King of Sweden and of Norway, and His Excellency the President of the Oriental Republic of the Uruguay.

The following is an English translation of the Convention with the omission of the formal beginning and end :—

Article I.

The present Convention applies outside territorial waters to all legally established submarine cables landed on the territories, colonies, or possessions of one or more of the High Contracting Parties.

Article II.

It is a punishable offence to break or injure a submarine cable, wilfully or by culpable negligence, in such manner as might interrupt or obstruct telegraphic communication, either wholly or partially, such punishment being without prejudice to any civil action for damages.

(*Schedule.*)

This provision does not apply to cases where those who break or injure a cable do so with the lawful object of saving their lives or their ship, after they have taken every necessary precaution to avoid so breaking or injuring the cable.

ARTICLE III.

The High Contracting Parties undertake that, on granting a concession for landing a submarine cable, they will insist, so far as possible, upon proper measures of safety being taken, both as regards the track of the cable and its dimensions.

ARTICLE IV.

The owner of a cable who, on laying or repairing his own cable, breaks or injures another cable, must bear the cost of repairing the breakage or injury, without prejudice to the application, if need be, of Article II of the present Convention.

ARTICLE V.

Vessels engaged in laying or repairing submarine cables shall conform to the regulations as to signals which have been, or may be, adopted by mutual agreement among the High Contracting Parties, with the view of preventing collisions at sea.

When a ship engaged in repairing a cable exhibits the said signals, other vessels which see them, or are able to see them, shall withdraw to or keep beyond a distance of one nautical mile at least from the ship in question, so as not to interfere with her operations.

Fishing gear and nets shall be kept at the same distance.

Nevertheless, fishing vessels which see or are able to see a telegraph ship exhibiting the said signals shall be allowed a period of twenty-four hours at most within which to obey the notice so given, during which time they shall not be interfered with in any way.

The operations of the telegraph ships shall be completed as quickly as possible.

ARTICLE VI.

Vessels which see, or are able to see, the buoys showing the position of a cable when the latter is being laid, is out of order, or is broken, shall keep beyond a distance of one-quarter of a nautical mile at least from the said buoys.

Fishing nets and gear shall be kept at the same distance.

ARTICLE VII.

Owners of ships or vessels who can prove that they have sacrificed an anchor, a net, or other fishing gear in order to avoid injuring a submarine cable shall receive compensation from the owner of the cable.

In order to establish a claim to such compensation, a statement, supported by the evidence of the crew, should, whenever possible, be drawn up immediately after the occurrence; and the master must, within twenty-four hours after his return to, or next putting into port, make a declaration to the proper authorities.

The latter shall communicate the information to the consular authorities of the country to which the owner of the cable belongs.

Article VIII.

The tribunals competent to take cognizance of infractions of the present Convention are those of the country to which the vessel on board of which the offence was committed belongs.

It is, moreover, understood that, in cases where the provisions in the previous paragraph cannot apply, offences against the present Convention will be dealt with in each of the Contracting States in accordance, so far as the subjects and citizens of those States respectively are concerned, with the general rules of criminal jurisdiction prescribed by the laws of that particular State, or by international treaties.

Article IX.

Prosecutions for infractions provided against by Articles II, V and VI of the present Convention shall be instituted by the State, or in its name.

Article X.

Offences against the present Convention may be verified by all means of proof allowed by the legislation of the country of the court. When the officers commanding the ships of war, or ships specially commissioned for the purpose by one of the High Contracting Parties, have reason to believe that an infraction of the measures provided for in the present Convention has been committed by a vessel other than a vessel of war, they may demand from the captain or master the production of the official documents proving the nationality of the said vessel. The fact of such document having been exhibited shall then be endorsed upon it immediately. Further, formal statements of the facts may be prepared by the said officers, whatever may be the nationality of the vessel incriminated. These formal statements shall be drawn up in the form and in the language used in the country to which the officer making them belongs; they may be considered, in the country where they are adduced, as evidence in accordance with the laws of that country. The accused and the witnesses shall have the right to add, or to have added, thereto, in their own language, any explanations they may consider useful. These declarations shall be duly signed.

ARTICLE XI.

The proceedings and trial in cases of infraction of the provisions of the present Convention shall always take place as summarily as the laws and regulations in force will permit.

ARTICLE XII.

The High Contracting Parties engage to take or to propose to their respective Legislatures the necessary measures for insuring the execution of the present Convention, and especially for punishing, by either fine or imprisonment, or both, those who contravene the provisions of Articles V and VI.

ARTICLE XIII.

The High Contracting Parties will communicate to each other laws already made, or which may hereafter be made, in their respective countries relating to the object of the present Convention.

ARTICLE XIV.

States which have not signed the present Convention may adhere to it on making a request to that effect. This adhesion shall be notified through the diplomatic channel to the Government of the French Republic, and by the latter to the other Signatory Powers.

ARTICLE XV.

It is understood that the stipulations of the present Convention do not in any way restrict the freedom of action of belligerents.

ARTICLE XVI.

The present Convention shall be brought into force on a day to be agreed upon by the High Contracting Powers.

It shall remain in force for five years from that day, and unless any of the High Contracting Parties have announced, twelve months before the expiration of the said period of five years, its intention to terminate its operation, it shall continue in force for a period of one year, and so on from year to year.

If one of the Signatory Powers denounce the Convention, such denunciation shall have effect only as regards that Power.

ARTICLE XVII.

The present Convention shall be ratified, and the ratifications exchanged at Paris with as little delay as possible, and, at the latest, at the expiration of a year.

ADDITIONAL ARTICLE.

The stipulations of the Convention concluded under to-day's date for the protection of submarine cables shall be applicable, in conformity with Article I, to the colonies and possessions of Her Britannic Majesty, with the exception of those herein-after mentioned, namely :—

Canada.
Newfoundland.
The Cape.
Natal.
New South Wales.
Victoria.
Queensland.
Tasmania.
South Australia.
Western Australia.
New Zealand.

Provided always, that the stipulations of the said Convention shall be applicable to any of the above-named colonies or possessions on whose behalf notice to that effect shall have been given by Her Britannic Majesty's Representative at Paris to the French Minister for Foreign Affairs.

Each of the above-named colonies or possessions which may have acceded to the said Convention shall be at liberty to withdraw from it in the same manner as the powers parties to it. In the event of any of the said colonies or possessions desiring to withdraw from the Convention, a notification to that effect shall be made by Her Britannic Majesty's Representative at Paris to the French Minister for Foreign Affairs.

The Indian Army Pension Deficiency Act, 1885.

(48 & 49 Vict., c. 67.)

An Act to provide for the discharge of the liability of the Consolidated Fund in respect of certain Indian Army Pensions.

[*14th August, 1885.*]

Whereas pensions and other retiring allowances (in this Act referred to as pensions) granted to persons in respect of service in Her Majesty's military forces, are paid out of moneys provided by Parliament, and where such persons have served in India, a part of such pensions (in this Act referred to as Indian

Army pensions) proportionate to their period of service in India ought to be repaid out of the revenues of India;

And whereas under an arrangement with the Government of India in respect of Indian Army pensions, which first came into course of payment before the first day of April one thousand eight hundred and seventy, no sum has been since the thirty-first day of March one thousand eight hundred and seventy, or will be so repaid except as herein-after mentioned, whereby a large annual sum has become charged on and payable out of the Consolidated Fund of the United Kingdom;

And whereas in respect of the Indian Army pensions granted to men serving in regiments of the East India Company and transferred to Her Majesty's army, which first came into course of payment before the first day of April one thousand eight hundred and seventy, a sum was repaid out of the revenues of India, on account of the capital value thereof, but such sum is insufficient to cover the amount of such pensions, and thereby the deficiency has become charged on and is payable out of the Consolidated Fund of the United Kingdom;

And whereas under an arrangement with the Government of India as to repayments out of the revenues of India in respect of the Indian Army pensions which first came into course of payment during the period beginning on the first day of April one thousand eight hundred and seventy, the capital value thereof was to be ascertained and paid out of the revenues of India, but such arrangement in consequence of entailing a loss upon the Consolidated Fund of the United Kingdom has been determined and applies only to Indian Army pensions which first came into course of payment before the first day of April one thousand eight hundred and eighty-four;

And whereas a portion of the capital value due under the said arrangement, has been ascertained and paid out of the revenues of India, and the remainder thereof is in course of being ascertained, and, when ascertained, will be paid out of the revenues of India;

And whereas in several years ending on the thirty-first day of March (in this Act referred to as financial year) the whole amount so paid out of the revenues of India in respect of the said capital value of Indian Army pensions was paid into the Exchequer and applied as part of the annual revenue of the Consolidated Fund, although a portion thereof represented the capital value of the said pensions, and, by reason of such application, the Consolidated Fund is liable in future years to the payment of the said pensions without any further payment in respect thereof from the revenues of India;

And whereas in other financial years a portion of the amount so paid out of the revenues of India in respect of the said capital value of Indian Army pensions was paid into the Exchequer, and carried to the Consolidated Fund, and the residue thereof was paid into the Bank of England in the name of Her Majesty's Paymaster-General, and carried in his books to an account intituled "The Indian Army Non-effective Arrears";

And whereas the net liability of the Consolidated Fund on the thirty-first day of March one thousand eight hundred and eighty-four resulting from the causes above mentioned, after deducting the sums standing to the said "Indian Army Non-effective Arrears" account, and the sums which will be payable out of the revenues of India in respect of the capital value of Indian Army pensions has been estimated at a sum of four million two hundred thousand pounds or thereabouts,

And whereas it is expedient to provide for the gradual discharge of such liability

* * * * * * *

Short title.

1. This Act may be cited as the Indian Army Pension Deficiency Act, 1885.

Establishment of Indian Army Pension Deficiency Fund.

2. There shall be paid to the Commissioners for the Reduction of the National Debt (in this Act referred to as the National Debt Commissioners) the following moneys, that is to say,

(*a*) all sums now standing in the books of Her Majesty's Paymaster-General to the account of the Indian Army Non-effective Arrears;

(*b*) all sums from time to time paid out of the revenues of India to Her Majesty's Paymaster-General, in respect of the Indian Army pensions which first came into course of payment before the first day of April one thousand eight hundred and eighty-four, or in respect of any other Indian Army pensions mentioned in this Act; and

(*c*) the annuity created by this Act.

Such moneys are in this Act referred to as the Indian Army Pension Deficiency Fund.

Application of Indian Army Pension Deficiency Fund.

3. (1) The National Debt Commissioners shall pay out of the Indian Army Pension Deficiency Fund such sums as may from time to time be certified, by one of Her Majesty's Principal Secretaries of State, to be estimated to be required to repay the charge payable in any financial year in respect of Indian Army pensions which first came into course of payment during the period beginning on the first day of April one thousand eight hundred and seventy, and ending on the thirty-first of March one thousand eight hundred and eighty-four, and in respect of the Indian Army pensions which were granted

to men serving in regiments of the East India Company and transferred to Her Majesty's Army, and which first came into course of payment before the first day of April one thousand eight hundred and seventy.

(2) On the determination of all such pensions, all moneys standing to the account of the Indian Army Pension Deficiency Fund shall be applied by the National Debt Commissioners as if they were part of the old sinking fund.

Creation of annuity to meet deficiency.

4. (1) There shall be charged on and paid out of the Consolidated Fund to the National Debt Commissioners an annuity of one hundred and fifty thousand pounds, beginning on the first day of April one thousand eight hundred and eighty-five and payable by such periodical payments as the Commissioners of Her Majesty's Treasury from time to time fix.

(2) As soon as all charges on the Indian Army Pension Deficiency Fund cease, the annuity under this section shall determine.

Management of Indian Army Pension Deficiency Fund.

5. (1) The National Debt Commissioners shall from time to time invest any moneys forming part of the Indian Army Pension Deficiency Fund which are not for the time being required for the other purposes of this Act, in any securities in which they may invest moneys held by them on account of savings banks, and may from time to time sell the securities in which they have so invested. All money arising from the income or sale of such securities shall be carried to and form part of the Indian Army Pension Deficiency Fund, and may be invested and applied accordingly.

(2) The National Debt Commissioners may from time to time lend to the Indian Army Pension Deficiency Fund, on the security of that fund, any moneys held by them on account of savings banks or otherwise, which they have power to invest in Government securities, and any sum so lent shall be a charge on the Indian Army Pension Deficiency Fund, and be repaid out of that fund by an annuity of such amount, and for such term as may be certified by the Comptroller or Assistant Comptroller, and the Actuary of the National Debt Office, to be sufficient to repay the sum borrowed with interest at three and a quarter per cent. per annum.

(3) Such accounts of the Indian Army Pension Deficiency Fund shall annually be laid before Parliament as the Commissioners of Her Majesty's Treasury may direct.

THE EVIDENCE BY COMMISSION ACT, 1885.[1]

(48 & 49 Vict., c. 74.)

An Act to amend the Law relating to taking Evidence by Commission in India and the Colonies, and elsewhere in Her Majesty's Dominions.

[*14th August, 1885.*]

BE it enacted by the Queen's most Excellent Majesty, by and with the advice and consent of the Lords Spiritual and Temporal, and Commons, in this present Parliament assembled, and by the authority of the same, as follows:

Short title.

1. This Act may be cited as the Evidence by Commission Act, 1885.

Power to courts to nominate examiner in civil proceedings.

2. Where in any civil proceeding in any court of competent jurisdiction an order for the examination of any witness or person has been made, and a commission, mandamus, order, or request for the examination of such witness or person is addressed to any court, or to any judge of a court, in India or the Colonies, or elsewhere in Her Majesty's dominions, beyond the jurisdiction of the court ordering the examination, it shall be lawful for such court, or the chief judge thereof, or such judge, to nominate some fit person to take such examination, and any deposition or examination taken before an examiner so nominated shall be admissible in evidence to the same extent as if it had been taken by or before such court or judge.

Power in criminal proceedings to nominate judge or magistrate to take depositions.

3. Where in any criminal proceeding a mandamus or order for the examination of any witness or person is addressed to any court, or to any judge of a court, in India or the Colonies, or elsewhere in Her Majesty's dominions, beyond the jurisdiction of the court ordering the examination, it shall be lawful for such court, or the chief judge thereof, or such judge, to nominate any judge of such court, or any judge of an inferior court, or magistrate within the jurisdiction of such first-mentioned court, to take the examination of such witness or person, and any deposition or examination so taken shall be admissible in evidence to the same extent as if it had been taken by or before the court or judge to whom the mandamus or order was addressed.

Application of 22 Vict., c. 20, as to conduct

4. The provisions of the Act passed in the twenty-second year of Her Majesty, chapter twenty, intituled "An Act to provide for taking evidence in suits and proceedings pending before tribunals in Her Majesty's

---

[1] This Act may be cited with 25 others as the Evidence Acts, 1806 to 1895—*see* the Short Titles Act, 1896 (59 & 60 Vict., c. 14), *post*, p. 1255. See, too, *Chitty's Statutes*, Tit. Evidence, p. 42 Taylor on Evidence, §§ 13, 14.

dominions in places out of the jurisdiction of such tribunals" (which may be cited as the Evidence by Commission Act, 1859)[1], as amended by this Act, shall apply to proceedings under this Act. money, etc., to proceedings under this Act.

Amendment of 22 Vict., c. 20, as to costs.

5. The power to make rules conferred by section six of the Evidence by Commission Act, 1859, shall be deemed to include a power to make rules with regard to all costs of or incidental to the examination of any witness or person, including the remuneration of the examiner, if any, whether the examination be ordered pursuant to that Act or under this or any other Act for the time being in force relating to the examination of witnesses beyond the jurisdiction of the court ordering the examination.

Oath or affirmation of witness.

6. When pursuant to any such commission, mandamus, order, or request as in this Act referred to, any witness or person is to be examined in any place beyond the jurisdiction of the court ordering the examination, such witness or person may be examined on oath, affirmation, or otherwise, according to the law in force in the place where the examination is taken, and any deposition or examination so taken shall be as effectual for all purposes as if the witness or person had been examined on oath before a person duly authorised to administer an oath in the court ordering the examination.

The International Copyright Act, 1886[2].

(49 & 50 Vict., c. 33.)

An Act to amend the Law respecting International and Colonial Copyright.

[*25th June, 1886.*]

Whereas by the International Copyright Acts Her Majesty is authorised by Order in Council to direct that as regards literary and artistic works first published in a foreign country the author shall have copyright therein during the period specified in the order, not exceeding the period during which authors of the like works first published in the United Kingdom have copyright:

And whereas at an international conference held at Berne in the month of September one thousand eight hundred and eighty-five a draft of a convention was agreed to for giving to authors of literary and artistic works first published in one of the countries parties to the convention copyright in such works throughout the other countries parties to the convention:

---

[1] 22 Vict., c. 20, printed Vol. I, p. 317.

[2] This Act may be cited with four others as the International Copyright Acts—*see* the Short Titles Act, 1896 (59 & 60 Vict., c. 14), *post*, p. 1255. See, too, *Chitty's Statutes*, Tit. Copyright, p. 55; also Scrutton, p. 246.

And whereas, without the authority of Parliament, such convention cannot be carried into effect in Her Majesty's dominions and consequently Her Majesty cannot become a party thereto, and it is expedient to enable Her Majesty to accede to the convention.

* * * * * * *

Short titles and construction.

1. (1) This Act may be cited as the International Copyright Act, 1886.

(2) The Acts specified in the first part of the First Schedule to this Act are in this Act referred to and may be cited by the short titles in that schedule mentioned, and those Acts, together with the enactment specified in the second part of the said schedule, are in this Act collectively referred to as the International Copyright Acts.

The Acts specified in the Second Schedule to this Act may be cited by the short titles in that schedule mentioned, and those Acts are in this Act referred to, and may be cited collectively as the Copyright Acts.

(3) This Act and the International Copyright Acts shall be construed together, and may be cited together as the International Copyright Acts, 1844 to 1886.

Amendment as to extent and effect of order under International Copyright Acts.

2. The following provisions shall apply to an Order in Council under the International Copyright Acts:—

(1) The order may extend to all the several foreign countries named or described therein:

(2) The order may exclude or limit the rights conferred by the International Copyright Acts in the case of authors who are not subjects or citizens of the foreign countries named or described in that or any other order, and if the order contains such limitation and the author of a literary or artistic work first produced in one of those foreign countries is not a British subject, nor a subject or citizen of any of the foreign countries so named or described, the publisher of such work, unless the order otherwise provides, shall for the purpose of any legal proceedings in the United Kingdom for protecting any copyright in such work be deemed to be entitled to such copyright as if he were the author, but this enactment shall not prejudice the rights of such author and publisher as between themselves:

(3) The International Copyright Acts and an order made thereunder shall not confer on any person any greater right or longer term of copyright in any work than that enjoyed in the foreign country in which such work was first produced.

Simultaneous publication.

3. (1) An Order in Council under the International Copyright Acts may provide for determining the country in which a literary or artistic work first produced simultaneously in two or more countries, is to be deemed, for the purpose of copyright, to have been first produced, and for the purposes of this section "country" means the United Kingdom and a country to which an order under the said Acts applies.

(2) Where a work produced simultaneously in the United Kingdom, and in some foreign country or countries is by virtue of an Order in Council under the International Copyright Acts deemed for the purpose of copyright to be first produced in one of the said foreign countries and not in the United Kingdom, the copyright in the United Kingdom shall be such only as exists by virtue of production in the said foreign country, and shall not be such as would have been acquired if the work had been first produced in the United Kingdom.

Modification of certain provisions of International Copyright Acts.

4. (1) Where an order respecting any foreign country is made under the International Copyright Acts the provisions of those Acts with respect to the registry and delivery of copies of works shall not apply to works produced in such country except so far as provided by the order.

(2) Before making an Order in Council under the International Copyright Acts in respect of any foreign country, Her Majesty in Council shall be satisfied that that foreign country has made such provisions (if any) as it appears to Her Majesty expedient to require for the protection of authors of works first produced in the United Kingdom.

Restriction on translation.

5. (1) Where a work being a book or dramatic piece is first produced in a foreign country to which an Order in Council under the International Copyright Acts applies, the author or publisher, as the case may be, shall, unless otherwise directed by the order, have the same right of preventing the production in and importation into the United Kingdom of any translation not authorised by him of the said work as he has of preventing the production and importation of the original work.

(2) Provided that if after the expiration of ten years, or any other term prescribed by the order, next after the end of the year in which the work, or in the case of a book published in numbers each number of the book, was first produced, an authorised translation in the English language of such work or number has not been produced, the said right to prevent the production in and importation into the United Kingdom of an unauthorised translation of such work shall cease.

(3) The law relating to copyright, including this Act, shall apply to a lawfully produced translation of a work in like manner as if it were an original work.

(*Secs. 6-8.*)

(4) Such of the provisions of the International Copyright Act, 1852,[1] relating to translations as are unrepealed by this Act shall apply in like manner as if they were re-enacted in this section. 15 & 16 Vict. c. 12.

Application of Act to existing works.

6. Where an Order in Council is made under the International Copyright Acts with respect to any foreign country, the author and publisher of any literary or artistic work first produced before the date at which such order comes into operation shall be entitled to the same rights and remedies as if the said Acts and this Act and the said order had applied to the said foreign country at the date of the said production: Provided that where any person has before the date of the publication of an Order in Council lawfully produced any work in the United Kingdom, nothing in this section shall diminish or prejudice any rights or interests arising from or in connection with such production which are subsisting and valuable at the said date.

Evidence of foreign copyright.

7. Where it is necessary to prove the existence or proprietorship of the copyright of any work first produced in a foreign country to which an Order in Council under the International Copyright Acts applies, an extract from a register or a certificate, or other document stating the existence of the copyright, or the person who is the proprietor of such copyright, or is for the purpose of any legal proceedings in the United Kingdom deemed to be entitled to such copyright, if authenticated by the official seal of a Minister of State of the said foreign country, or by the official seal or the signature of a British diplomatic or consular officer acting in such country, shall be admissible as evidence of the facts named therein, and all courts shall take judicial notice of every such official seal and signature as is in this section mentioned, and shall admit in evidence, without proof, the documents authenticated by it.

Application of Copyright Acts to colonies.

8. (1) The Copyright Acts shall, subject to the provisions of this Act, apply to a literary or artistic work first produced in a British possession in like manner as they apply to a work first produced in the United Kingdom:

Provided that—

(*a*) the enactments respecting the registry of the copyright in such work shall not apply if the law of such possession provides for the registration of such copyright; and

(*b*) where such work is a book the delivery to any persons or body of persons of a copy of any such work shall not be required.

(2) Where a register of copyright in books is kept under the authority of the government of a British possession, an extract from that register purporting to be certified as a true copy by the officer keeping it, and authenticated by the public seal of the British possession, or by the official seal or the

[1] 15 & 16 Vict., c. 12, printed Vol. I, p. 281.

signature of the governor of a British possession, or of a colonial secretary, or of some secretary or minister administering a department of the government of a British possession, shall be admissible in evidence of the contents of that register, and all courts shall take judicial notice of every such seal and signature, and shall admit, in evidence, without further proof, all documents authenticated by it.

(3) Where before the passing of this Act an Act or ordinance has been passed in any British possession respecting copyright in any literary or artistic works, Her Majesty in Council may take an Order modifying the Copyright Acts and this Act, so far as they apply to such British possession, and to literary and artistic works first produced therein, in such manner as to Her Majesty in Council seems expedient.

(4) Nothing in the Copyright Acts or this Act shall prevent the passing in a British possession of any Act or ordinance respecting the copyright within the limits of such possession of works first produced in that possession.

Application of International Copyright Acts to colonies.

9. Where it appears to Her Majesty expedient that an Order in Council under the International Copyright Acts made after the passing of this Act as respects any foreign country, should not apply to any British possession, it shall be lawful for Her Majesty by the same or any other Order in Council to declare that such Order and the International Copyright Acts and this Act shall not, and the same shall not, apply to such British possession, except so far as is necessary for preventing any prejudice to any rights acquired previously to the date of such Order; and the expressions in the said Acts relating to Her Majesty's dominions shall be construed accordingly; but save as provided by such declaration the said Acts and this Act shall apply to every British possession as if it were part of the United Kingdom.

Making of Orders in Council.

10. (1) It shall be lawful for Her Majesty from time to time to make Orders in Council for the purposes of the International Copyright Acts and this Act, for revoking or altering any Order in Council previously made in pursuance of the said Acts, or any of them.

(2) Any such Order in Council shall not affect prejudicially any rights acquired or accrued at the date of such Order coming into operation, and shall provide for the protection of such rights.

Definitions.

11. In this Act, unless the context otherwise requires—

The expression "literary and artistic work" means every book, print, lithograph, article of sculpture, dramatic piece, musical composition, painting, drawing, photograph, and other work of literature and art to which the Copyright Acts or the International Copyright Acts, as the case requires, extend.

The expression "author" means the author, inventor, designer, engraver, or maker of any literary or artistic work, and includes any person claiming through the author; and in the case of a posthumous work means the proprietor of the manuscript of such work and any person claiming through him; and in the case of an encyclopædia, review, magazine, periodical work, or work published in a series of books or parts, includes the proprietor, projector, publisher, or conductor.

The expressions "performed" and "performance" and similar words include representation and similar words.

The expression "produced" means, as the case requires, published or made, or performed or represented, and the expression "production" is to be construed accordingly.

The expression "book published in numbers" includes any review, magazine, periodical work, work published in a series of books or parts, transactions of a society or body, and other books of which different volumes or parts are published at different times.

The expression "treaty" includes any convention or arrangement.

The expression "British possession" includes any part of Her Majesty's dominions exclusive of the United Kingdom; and where parts of such dominions are under both a central and a local legislature, all parts under one central legislature are for the purposes of this definition deemed to be one British possession.

Repeal of Acts.

12. The Acts specified in the Third Schedule to this Act are hereby repealed as from the passing of this Act to the extent in the third column of that schedule mentioned:

Provided as follows:

(*a*) Where an Order in Council has been made before the passing of this Act under the said Acts as respects any foreign country the enactments hereby repealed shall continue in full force as respects that country until the said Order is revoked.

(*b*) The said repeal and revocation shall not prejudice any rights acquired previously to such repeal or revocation, and such rights shall continue and may be enforced in like manner as if the said repeal or revocation had not been enacted or made.

FIRST SCHEDULE.

International Copyright Acts.

Part I.

Session and Chapter.	Title.	Short Title.
7 & 8 Vict., c. 12	An Act to amend the law relating to International Copyright.	The International Copyright Act, 1844.
15 & 16 Vict., c. 12	An Act to enable Her Majesty to carry into effect a convention with France on the subject of copyright, to extend and explain the International Copyright Acts, and to explain the Acts relating to copyright in engravings.	The International Copyright Act, 1852.
38 & 39 Vict., c. 12	An Act to amend the law relating to International Copyright.	The International Copyright Act, 1875.

Part II.

Session and Chapter.	Title.	Enactment referred to.
25 & 26 Vict., c. 68	An Act for amending the law relating to copyright in works of the fine arts, and for repressing the commission of fraud in the production and sale of such works.	Section twelve.

SECOND SCHEDULE.

Copyright Acts.

Session and Chapter.	Title.	Short Title.
8 Geo. 2, c. 13	An Act for the encouragement of the arts of designing, engraving, and etching, historical and other prints, by vesting the properties thereof in the inventors and engravers during the time therein mentioned.	The Engraving Copyright Act, 1734.
7 Geo. 3, c. 38	An Act to amend and render more effectual an Act made in the eighth year of the reign of King George the Second, for encouragement of the arts of designing, engraving, and etching, historical and other prints, and for vesting in and securing to Jane Hogarth, widow, the property in certain prints.	The Engraving Copyright Act, 1766.

SECOND SCHEDULE—*contd.*

Copyright Acts—*contd.*

Session and Chapter.	Title.	Short Title.
15 Geo. 3, c. 53 .	An Act for enabling the two Universities in England, the four Universities in Scotland, and the several Colleges of Eton, Westminster, and Winchester, to hold in perpetuity their copyright in books given or bequeathed to the said universities and colleges for the advancement of useful learning and other purposes of education; and for amending so much of an Act of the eighth year of the reign of Queen Anne, as relates to the delivery of books to the warehouse keeper of the Stationers' Company for the use of the several libraries therein mentioned.	The Copyright Act, 1775.
17 Geo. 3, c. 57 .	An Act for more effectually securing the property of prints to inventors and engravers by enabling them to sue for and recover penalties in certain cases.	The Prints Copyright Act, 1777.
54 Geo. 3, c. 56 .	An Act to amend and render more effectual an Act of His present Majesty for encouraging the art of making new models and casts of busts and other things therein mentioned, and for giving further encouragement to such arts.	The Sculpture Copyright Act, 1814.
3 Will. 4, c. 15 .	An Act to amend the laws relating to Dramatic Literary Property.	The Dramatic Copyright Act, 1833.
5 & 6 Will. 4, c. 65	An Act for preventing the publication of Lectures without consent.	The Lectures Copyright Act, 1835.
6 & 7 Will. 4, c. 59	An Act to extend the protection of copyright in prints and engravings to Ireland.	The Prints and Engravings Copyright Act, 1836.
6 & 7 Will. 4, c. 110	An Act to repeal so much of an Act of the fifty-fourth year of King George the Third, respecting copyrights, as requires the delivery of a copy of every published book to the libraries of Sion College, the four Universities of Scotland, and of the King's Inns in Dublin.	The Copyright Act, 1836.
5 & 6 Vict., c. 45	An Act to amend the law of copyright.	The Copyright Act, 1842.

(Second and Third Schedules.)

SECOND SCHEDULE—*contd.*

COPYRIGHT ACTS—*contd.*

Session and Chapter.	Title.	Short Title.
10 & 11 Vict., c. 95	An Act to amend the law relating to the protection in the Colonies of works entitled to copyright in the United Kingdom.	The Colonial Copyright Act, 1847.
25 & 26 Vict., c. 68	An Act for amending the law relating to copyright in works of the fine arts, and for repressing the commission of fraud in the production and sale of such works.	The Fine Arts Copyright Act, 1862.

THIRD SCHEDULE.

ACTS REPEALED.

Session and Chapter.	Title.	Extent of repeal.
7 & 8 Vict., c. 12	An Act to amend the law relating to international copyright.	Sections fourteen, seventeen and eighteen.
15 & 16 Vict., c. 12	An Act to enable Her Majesty to carry into effect a convention with France on the subject of copyright to extend and explain the International Copyright Acts, and to explain the Acts relating to copyright engravings.	Sections one to five, both inclusive, and sections eight and eleven.
25 & 26 Vict., c. 68	An Act for amending the law relating to copyright in works of the fine arts, and for repressing the commission of fraud in the production and sale of such works.	So much of section twelve as incorporates any enactment repealed by this Act.

The Medical Act, 1886.[1]

(49 & 50 Vict., c. 48.)

An Act to amend the Medical Acts.

[*25th June, 1886.*]

* * * * * * *

Short title and construction.

1. This Act may be cited as the Medical Act, 1886, and shall be construed as one with the Medical Acts.

PART I.

Admission to Medical Practice and Constitution of General Council.

Qualifying Examinations.

Examination before registration.

2. On and after the appointed day a person shall not be registered under the Medical Acts in respect of any qualification referred to in any of those Acts, unless he has passed such qualifying examination in medicine, surgery, and midwifery, as is in this Act mentioned.

Qualifying examinations held by medical authorities.

3. (1) A qualifying examination shall be an examination in medicine, surgery, and midwifery held, for the purpose of granting a diploma or diplomas conferring the right of registration under the Medical Acts, by any of the following bodies, that is to say:—

(*a*) Any university in the United Kingdom or any medical corporation, legally qualified at the passing of this Act to grant such diploma or diplomas in respect of medicine and surgery; or

(*b*) Any combination of two or more medical corporations in the same part of the United Kingdom who may agree to hold a joint examination in medicine, surgery, and midwifery, and of whom one at least is capable of granting such diploma as aforesaid in respect of medicine, and one at least is capable of granting such diploma in respect of surgery; or

(*c*) Any combination of any such university as aforesaid with any other such university or universities or of any such university or universities with a medical corporation or corporations, the bodies forming such combination being in the same part of the United Kingdom.

---

[1] This Act may be cited with five others as the Medical Acts—*see* the Short Titles Act, 1896 (59 & 60 Vict., c. 14), *post*, p. 1255. See, too, *Chitty's Statutes*, Tit. Medical, etc., Acts, p. 68.

(2) The standard of proficiency required from candidates at the said qualifying examinations shall be such as sufficiently to guarantee the possession of the knowledge and skill requisite for the efficient practice of medicine, surgery and midwifery; and it shall be the duty of the General Council to secure the maintenance of such standard of proficiency as aforesaid; and for that purpose such number of inspectors as may be determined by the General Council shall be appointed by the General Council and shall attend, as the General Council may direct, at all or any of the qualifying examinations held by any of the bodies aforesaid.

(3) Inspectors of examinations appointed under this section shall not interfere with the conduct of any examinations, but it shall be their duty to report to the General Council their opinion as to the sufficiency or insufficiency of every examination which they attend, and any other matters in relation to such examination which the General Council may require them to report; and the General Council shall forward a copy of every such report to the body or to each of the bodies which held the examination in respect of which the said report was made, and shall also forward a copy of such report, together with any observations thereon made by the said body or bodies, to the Privy Council.

(4) An inspector of examinations appointed under this section shall receive such remuneration, to be paid as part of the expenses of the General Council, as the General Council, with the sanction of the Privy Council, may determine.

4. (1) If at any time it appears to the General Council that the standard of proficiency in medicine, surgery and midwifery, or in any of those subjects or any branch thereof, required from candidates at the qualifying examinations held by any of the bodies for the time being holding such examinations is insufficient, the General Council shall make a representation to that effect to the Privy Council, and the Privy Council, if they think fit, after considering such representation, and also any objections thereto made by any body or bodies to which such representation relates, may by order declare that the examinations of any such body or bodies shall not be deemed to be qualifying examinations for the purpose of registration under the Medical Acts; and Her Majesty, with the advice of Her Privy Council, if upon further representation from the General Council or from any body or bodies to which such order relates it seems to Her expedient so to do, shall have power at any time to revoke any such order.

Withdrawal from medical authorities of right to hold qualifying examinations.

(2) During the continuance of any such order the examinations held by the body or bodies to which it relates shall not be deemed qualifying examinations under this Act, and any diploma granted to persons on passing such

examinations shall not entitle such persons to be registered under the Medical Acts, and any such body shall not choose either separately or collectively with any other body a member of the General Council; and the member (if any) for the time being representing such body in the General Council shall, unless he was chosen by such body collectively with any other body not subject to an order under this section, be suspended from taking part in the proceedings of the General Council.

Qualifying examinations held by medical corporation with assistant examiners.

5. (1) If a medical corporation represents to the General Council that it is unable to enter into such combination as is in this Act mentioned for the purpose of holding qualifying examinations, and the General Council are satisfied that the said medical corporation has used its best endeavours to enter into such combination as aforesaid, and is unable to do so on reasonable terms, it shall be lawful for the General Council from time to time, if they think fit, on the application of such corporation, to appoint any number of examiners to assist at the examinations which are held by such corporation for the purpose of granting any diploma or diplomas conferring on the holders thereof, if they have passed a qualifying examination, the right of registration under the Medical Acts.

(2) It shall be the duty of the said assistant examiners to secure at the said examinations the maintenance of such standard of proficiency in medicine, surgery, and midwifery as is required under the foregoing provisions of this Act from candidates at qualifying examinations, and for that purpose the said assistant examiners shall have such powers and perform such duties in the conduct of those examinations as the General Council may from time to time by order prescribe; and any examination held subject to the provisions of this section shall be deemed to be a qualifying examination within the meaning of this Act.

(3) Assistant examiners appointed under this section shall receive such remuneration, to be paid by the medical corporation at whose examinations they take part, as the General Council determine.

(4) A medical corporation shall have power to admit to its examinations assistant examiners appointed under this section, and to conduct its examinations in accordance with the requirements of this section and of any orders made thereunder, anything in any Act or charter relating to such corporation to the contrary notwithstanding.

Effect of Registration.

Privileges of registered persons.

6. On and after the appointed day a registered medical practitioner shall, save as in this Act mentioned, be entitled to practise medicine, surgery, and

midwifery in the United Kingdom, and (subject to any local law) in any other part of Her Majesty's dominions, and to recover in due course of law in respect of such practice any expenses, charges in respect of medicaments or other appliances, or any fees to which he may be entitled, unless he is a fellow of a college of physicians, the fellows of which are prohibited by byelaw from recovering at law their expenses, charges, or fees, in which case such prohibitory byelaw, so long as it is in force, may be pleaded in bar of any legal proceeding instituted by such fellow for the recovery of expenses, charges, or fees.

Constitution of General Council.

Members of General Council.

7. (1) After the passing of this Act the General Council shall consist of the following members, that is to say:—

Five persons nominated from time to time by Her Majesty, with the advice of Her Privy Council, three of whom shall be nominated for England, one for Scotland, and one for Ireland:

One person chosen from time to time by each of the following bodies;—

The Royal College of Physicians of London;
The Royal College of Surgeons of England;
The Apothecaries Society of London;
The University of Oxford;
The University of Cambridge;
The University of London;
The University of Durham;
The Victoria University, Manchester;
The Royal College of Physicians of Edinburgh;
The Royal College of Surgeons of Edinburgh;
The Faculty of Physicians and Surgeons of Glasgow;
The University of Edinburgh;
The University of Glasgow;
The University of Aberdeen;
The University of St. Andrews;
The King's and Queen's College of Physicians in Ireland;
The Royal College of Surgeons in Ireland;
The Apothecaries Hall of Ireland;
The University of Dublin;
The Royal University of Ireland:

Three persons elected from time to time by the registered medical practitioners resident in England:

One person elected from time to time by the registered medical practitioners resident in Scotland:

One person elected from time to time by the registered medical practitioners resident in Ireland;

(2) The provisions of this section relating to the representation of the Universities of Edinburgh and Aberdeen shall take effect on the occurrence of the first vacancy in the office of the person representing those Universities at the time of the passing of this Act, and the provisions of this section relating to the representation of the Universities of Glasgow and St. Andrews shall take effect on the occurrence of the first vacancy in the office of the person representing such last-mentioned Universities at the time of the passing of this Act; but nothing in this section shall affect the duration of the term of office of any person who at the time of the passing of this Act is a member of the General Council.

Regulations as to election of representatives of the medical profession.

8. (1) The members of the General Council representing the registered medical practitioners resident in the several parts of the United Kingdom (in this section referred to as "direct representatives") shall themselves be registered medical practitioners; they shall be elected to hold office for the term of five years, and shall be capable of re-election, and any of them may at any time resign his office by letter addressed to the president of the General Council, and upon the death or resignation of any one of them, some other person shall be elected in his place, but the proceedings of the General Council shall not be questioned on account of a vacancy or vacancies among the direct representatives.

(2) Each direct representative shall be a member of the branch council for the part of the United Kingdom in which he is elected; he shall also be entitled to fees for attendance and travelling expenses to the same extent as other members of the General Council are entitled to the same.

(3) The president of the General Council, or any other person whom the General Council may from time to time appoint, shall be the returning officer for the purpose of elections of direct representatives, and such returning officer shall, some time not less than six weeks nor more than two months before the day on which the term of office of any such representative will expire, and as soon as conveniently may be after the occurrence of any vacancy arising from the death or resignation of any such representative, issue his precept to the branch council for that part of the United Kingdom in which such representative was elected, requiring the said branch council to cause a representative to be elected by the registered medical practitioners resident in that part of the United Kingdom within twenty-one days after the receipt of the precept of the returning officer.

(4) The election shall be conducted in such manner as may be provided by regulations to be made by the Privy Council, provided as follows :—

(*a*) The nomination shall be in writing, and the nomination paper of each candidate shall be signed by not fewer than twelve registered medical practitioners; and

(*b*) The election shall be conducted by voting papers, and it shall be the duty of the branch council in any part of the United Kingdom in which an election is to be held, to cause a voting paper to be forwarded by post to each registered medical practitioner resident in that part at his registered address, but the election shall not be rendered void by reason of the omission of the branch council to cause such voting paper to be forwarded in any particular case or cases, and any registered medical practitioner to whom a voting paper has not been sent in pursuance of this Act may on application to the registrar of the said branch council obtain one from him; and

(*c*) Any registered medical practitioner entitled to vote at such election may vote for as many candidates as there are representatives to be elected.

(5) Each branch council shall certify to the returning officer the person or persons elected by the registered medical practitioners resident in the part of the United Kingdom to which such branch council belongs.

(6) A direct representative elected in place of any such representative retiring on the expiration of the period for which he was elected shall come into office at the expiration of that period, and a direct representative elected to fill a vacancy caused by the death or resignation of any such representative shall come into office on the day on which he is certified by the branch council to the returning officer to have been elected.

(7) The expenses attending the election of a direct representative shall be defrayed as part of the expenses of the branch council for that part of the United Kingdom in which such representative is elected.

(8) For the purpose of the first election of direct representatives the returning officer shall, in the course of such period of seven days (ending not later than the fifteenth day of November next succeeding the passing of this Act) as the Privy Council may appoint, issue his precept to the branch council in each part of the United Kingdom, requiring such branch council to cause the proper number of representatives to be elected in the part of the United Kingdom to which such branch council belongs, within twenty-one days after the receipt of the said precept; and the said representatives shall

come into office on the first day of January one thousand eight hundred and eighty-seven.

Election of president of General Council.

9. The General Council from time to time, on the occurrence of a vacancy in the office of president of the General Council, shall elect one of their number to be president for a term not exceeding five years, and not extending beyond the expiration of the term for which he has been made a member of the said Council, but nothing in this Act shall affect the duration of the term of office of the person who at the time of the passing of this Act is president of the General Council.

Revision of constitution of General Council.

10. (1) The General Council may at any time represent to the Privy Council all or any of the following matters:—

(*a*) That it is expedient to confer on any university or other body in the United Kingdom capable of granting a medical diploma, not being one of the constituent bodies for the time being of the General Council, and being, in the opinion of the General Council, of sufficient importance to be worthy of such a privilege, the power of returning a member to the General Council, either separately or collectively with any other body or bodies in the same part of the United Kingdom capable of granting a medical diploma:

(*b*) That it is expedient to confer on any constituent body for the time being returning a member to the General Council collectively with any other body or bodies, and being, in the opinion of the General Council, of sufficient importance to be worthy of such a privilege, the power of returning a member to such council separately:

(*c*) That it is expedient to confer on the registered medical practitioners resident in any part of the United Kingdom the power of returning an additional member to the General Council:

(*d*) That it is expedient that any constituent body having, in the opinion of the General Council, so diminished in importance as not to be entitled to such privilege, should either be wholly deprived of the power of returning a member to the General Council, or be deprived of the power of returning a member separately, and permitted to return a member collectively with some other body or bodies.

(2) The Privy Council, before considering such representation, shall cause the same to be laid before both Houses of Parliament.

(3) If either House of Parliament, within forty days (exclusive of any period of adjournment for more than one week) next after any such representation has been laid before such House, present an address to Her Majesty declaring that such representation or any part thereof ought not to be carried into effect, no further proceedings shall be taken in respect of the representation in regard to which such address has been presented, but if no such address is presented by either House of Parliament within such forty days as aforesaid, the Privy Council may, if they think fit, report to Her Majesty that it is expedient to give effect to such representation, and it shall be lawful for Her Majesty by Order in Council to give effect to the same, and any Order in Council so made shall be of the same validity as if it had been enacted in this Act.

PART II.

Colonial and Foreign Practitioners.

Registration of colonial practitioner with recognised diploma.

11. On and after the prescribed day where a person shows to the satisfaction of the registrar of the General Council that he holds some recognised colonial medical diploma or diplomas (as herein-after defined) granted to him in a British possession to which this Act applies, and that he is of good character, and that he is by law entitled to practise medicine, surgery, and midwifery in such British possession, he shall, on application to the said registrar, and on payment of such fee not exceeding five pounds as the General Council may from time to time determine, be entitled, without examination in the United Kingdom, to be registered as a colonial practitioner in the medical register:

Provided that he proves to the satisfaction of the registrar any of the following circumstances:—

(1) That the said diploma or diplomas was or were granted to him at a time when he was not domiciled in the United Kingdom, or in the course of a period of not less than five years during the whole of which he resided out of the United Kingdom; or

(2) That he was practising medicine or surgery or a branch of medicine or surgery in the United Kingdom on the said prescribed day, and that he has continuously practised the same either in the United Kingdom or elsewhere for a period of not less than ten years immediately preceding the said prescribed day.

Registration of foreign practitioner with recognised diploma.

12. On and after the said prescribed day where a person shows to the satisfaction of the registrar of the General Council that he holds some recognised foreign medical diploma or diplomas (as herein-after defined) granted in a foreign country to which this Act applies, and that he is of good character, and that he is by law entitled to practise medicine, surgery, and midwifery in such foreign country, he shall, on application to the said registrar, and on payment of such fee not exceeding five pounds as the General Council may from time to time determine, be entitled, without examination in the United Kingdom, to be registered as a foreign practitioner in the medical register:

Provided that he proves to the satisfaction of the registrar any of the following circumstances:—

(1) That he is not a British subject; or

(2) That, being a British subject, the said diploma or diplomas was or were granted to him at a time when he was not domiciled in the United Kingdom, or in the course of a period of not less than five years during the whole of which he resided out of the United Kingdom; or

(3) That, being a British subject, he was practising medicine or surgery, or a branch of medicine or surgery, in the United Kingdom on the said prescribed day, and that he has continuously practised the same in the United Kingdom or elsewhere for a period of not less than ten years immediately preceding the said prescribed day.

Medical diploma of colonial and foreign practitioner when deemed to be recognised.

13. (1) The medical diploma or diplomas granted in a British possession or foreign country to which this Act applies, which is or are to be deemed such recognised colonial or foreign medical diploma or diplomas as is or are required for the purposes of this Act, shall be such medical diploma or diplomas as may be recognised for the time being by the General Council as furnishing a sufficient guarantee of the possession of the requisite knowledge and skill for the efficient practice of medicine, surgery, and midwifery.

(2) Where the General Council have refused to recognise as aforesaid any colonial or foreign medical diploma, the Privy Council, on application being made to them, may, if they think fit, after considering such application, and after communication with the General Council, order the General Council to recognise the said diploma, and such order shall be duly obeyed.

(3) If a person is refused registration as a colonial or foreign practitioner on any other ground than that the medical diploma or diplomas held by such

person is or are not such recognised medical diploma or diplomas as above defined, the registrar of the General Council shall, if required, state in writing the reason for such refusal, and the person so refused registration may appeal to the Privy Council, and the Privy Council, after communication with the General Council, may dismiss the appeal or may order the General Council to enter the name of the appellant on the register.

(4) A person may, if so entitled under this Act, be registered both as a colonial and a foreign practitioner.

Separate list of colonial and foreign practitioners in medical register.

14. The medical register shall contain a separate list of the names and addresses of the colonial practitioners, and also a separate list of the names and addresses of the foreign practitioners registered under this Act; each list shall be made out alphabetically according to the surnames; and the provisions of the Medical Act, 1858, relating to persons registered under that Act, and relating to the medical register and to offences in respect thereof, shall, so far as may be, apply in the case of colonial and foreign practitioners registered under this Act and of the said lists of those practitioners, in the same way as such provisions apply in the case of persons registered under the said Medical Act, 1858, and of the register as kept under that Act.

Medical titles of colonial and foreign practitioners.

15. On and after the appointed day it shall be lawful for any registered medical practitioner who being on the list of colonial or of foreign practitioners is on that day in possession of or thereafter obtains any recognised colonial or foreign medical diploma granted in a British possession or foreign country to which this Act applies to cause a description of such diploma to be added to his name in the medical register.

Registration of foreign degrees held by registered medical practitioners.

16. On and after the appointed day it shall be lawful for any registered medical practitioner who, being on the medical register by virtue of English, Scotch, or Irish qualifications, is in possession of a foreign degree in medicine, to cause a description of such foreign medical degree to be added to his name as an additional title in the medical register, provided he shall satisfy the General Council that he obtained such degree after proper examination and prior to the passing of this Act.

Power of Her Majesty in Council to define colonies and foreign countries to which this part of the Act applies.

17. (1) Her Majesty may from time to time by Order in Council declare that this part of this Act shall be deemed on and after a day to be named in such Order to apply to any British possession or foreign country which in the opinion of Her Majesty affords to the registered medical practitioners of the United Kingdom such privileges of practising in the said British possession or foreign country as to Her Majesty may seem just; and from and after the day named in such Order in Council such British possession or foreign country shall be deemed to be a British possession or foreign country to which this Act applies within the meaning of this part thereof; but until such Order in Council has been made in respect of any British possession or foreign country, this part of this Act shall not be deemed to apply to any such possession or country; and the expression "the prescribed day" as used in this part of this Act means, as respects any British possession or foreign country, the day on and after which this part of this Act is declared by Order in Council to apply to such British possession or foreign country.

(2) Her Majesty may from time to time by Order in Council revoke and renew any Order made in pursuance of this section; and on the revocation of such Order as respects any British possession or foreign country, such possession or foreign country shall cease to be a possession or country to which this part of this Act applies, without prejudice nevertheless to the right of any persons whose names have been already entered on the register.

Amendment of 21 & 22 Vict., c. 90, s. 36, as to medical officers in ships.

18. Nothing in the Medical Act, 1858, shall prevent a person holding a medical diploma entitling him to practise medicine or surgery in a British possession to which this Act applies from holding an appointment as a medical officer in any vessel registered in that possession.

PART III.

Miscellaneous Provisions.

Default of General Council.

19. If at any time it appears to the Privy Council that the General Council has failed to secure the maintenance of a sufficient standard of proficiency at any qualifying examinations, or that occasion has arisen for the General Council to appoint assistant examiners under this Act for the purpose of examinations held by any medical corporation, or to exercise any power or perform any duty or do any act or thing vested in or imposed on or authorised to be done by the General Council under the Medical Acts or this Act, the Privy Council may notify their opinion to the General Council; and if the General Council fail to comply with any directions of the Privy Council relating to such notification, the Privy Council may themselves give effect to such directions, and for that purpose may exercise any power or do any act or thing vested in or authorised to be done by the General Council, and may of their own motion do any act or thing which, under the Medical Acts or this Act, they are authorised to do in pursuance of a representation or suggestion from the General Council.

20. The diploma of member of the King's and Queen's College of Physicians in Ireland, and the degree of Master in Obstetrics of any university in the United Kingdom, shall be deemed to be added to the qualifications prescribed in Schedule A to the Medical Act, 1858.

Addition to qualifications under 21 & 22 Vict., c. 90.

21. Every registered medical practitioner to whom a diploma for proficiency in sanitary science, public health, or state medicine, has after special examination been granted by any college or faculty of physicians or surgeons or university in the United Kingdom, or by any such bodies acting in combination, shall, if such diploma appears to the Privy Council or to the General Council to deserve recognition in the medical register, be entitled, on payment of such fee as the General Council may appoint, to have such diploma entered in the said register, in addition to any other diploma or diplomas in respect of which he is registered.

Registration of diploma in sanitary science.

22. (1) All powers vested in the Privy Council by the Medical Acts or this Act may be exercised by any two or more of the Lords and others of Her Majesty's most honourable Privy Council.

Exercise of powers of Privy Council.

(2) Any act of the Privy Council under the Medical Acts or this Act shall be sufficiently signified by an instrument signed by the Clerk of the Council, and every order and act signified by an instrument purporting to be signed by the Clerk of the Council shall be deemed to have been duly made and done by the Privy Council, and every instrument so signed shall be received in evidence in all courts and proceedings without proof of the authority or signature of the Clerk of the Council, or other proof.

23. The following copies of any orders made in pursuance of the Medical Acts or this Act, or the Dentists Act, 1878,[1] shall be evidence; that is to say,—

Evidence of orders.

(1) Any copy purporting to be printed by the Queen's printer, or by any other printer in pursuance of an authority given by the General Council:

(2) Any copy of an order certified to be a true copy by the registrar of the General Council, or by any other person appointed by the General Council either in addition to or in exclusion of the registrar to certify such orders.

Saving Clauses.

24. This Act shall not increase or diminish the privileges in respect of his practice of any person who, on the day preceding the appointed day, is a

Saving as to practice of existing practitioners.

[1] 41 & 42 Vict., c. 33, printed *ante*, p. 578.

registered medical practitioner, and such person shall be entitled on and after the said appointed day to practise, in pursuance of the qualification possessed by him before the said appointed day, in medicine, surgery, and midwifery, or any of them, or any branch of medicine or surgery, according as he was entitled to practise the same before the said appointed day, but not further or otherwise.

Saving as to local law.

25. Any person who at the time of the repeal of any enactment repealed by this Act was, in pursuance of such enactment, legally entitled to practise as a medical practitioner in any colony or part of Her Majesty's dominions other than the United Kingdom, shall after the date of such repeal continue to be so entitled if he would have been entitled if no such repeal had taken place.

Dentists.

Provisions as to 41 & 42 Vict., c. 33.

26. It is hereby declared that the words "title, addition, or description," where used in the Dentists Act, 1878,[1] include any title, addition to a name, designation, or description, whether expressed in words or by letters, or partly in one way and partly in the other.

There shall be repealed so much of section four of the Dentists Act, 1878,[1] as provides that a prosecution for any of the offences above in that Act mentioned shall not be instituted by a private person, except with the consent of the General Council or of a branch council, and a prosecution for any such offences may be instituted by a private person accordingly.

Notwithstanding anything in section five of the Dentists Act, 1878,[1] the rights of any person registered under the Dentists Act, 1878,[1] to practise dentistry or dental surgery in any part of Her Majesty's dominions other than the United Kingdom shall be subject to any local law in force in that part.

It shall be lawful for Her Majesty at any time after the said appointed day to declare by Order in Council that section twenty-eight of the said Dentists Act, 1878,[1] shall be in force on and after a day to be named in such Order, but in the meantime and until such order has been made, and before such day as last aforesaid, such section shall not be deemed to be in force.

Save as in this Act mentioned the Dentists Act, 1878,[1] shall not be affected by this Act.

Definitions.

Definitions.

27. In this Act, unless the context otherwise requires,—

The expression "part of the United Kingdom" means, according to circumstances, England, Scotland, or Ireland :

---

[1] 41 & 42 Vict., c. 33, printed *ante*, p. 573.

(Sec. 28.)

The expression "British possession" means any part of Her Majesty's dominions exclusive of the United Kingdom, but inclusive of the Isle of Man and the Channel Islands; and where parts of such dominions are under both a central and a local legislature, all parts under one central legislature are for the purposes of this definition deemed to be one British possession:

The expression "local law" means an Act or Ordinance passed by the legislature of a British possession:

The expression "the appointed day" means the first of June one thousand eight hundred and eighty-seven, or such other day in June one thousand eight hundred and eighty-seven as may be appointed by the Privy Council:

The expression "medical corporation" means any body in the United Kingdom, other than a university, for the time being competent to grant a diploma or diplomas conferring on the holder thereof, if he has passed a qualifying examination, the right of registration under the Medical Acts:

The expression "registered medical practitioner" means any person for the time being registered under the Medical Acts:

The word "diploma" means any diploma, degree, fellowship, membership, license, authority to practise, letters, testimonial, certificate, or other status or document granted by any university, corporation, college, or other body, or by any departments of or persons acting under the authority of the government of any country or place within or without Her Majesty's dominions:

The expression "medical diploma" means a diploma granted in respect of medicine, surgery, and midwifery, or any of them, or any branch of medicine or surgery:

The word "person" includes a body of persons, corporate or not corporate:

& 22 Vict., c. 90. The expression "the Medical Acts" means the Medical Act, 1858, and any Acts amending the same, passed before the passing of this Act.

Repeal.

28. The Acts mentioned in the first part of the schedule to this Act are hereby repealed to the extent mentioned in the third column of the said part; and the Acts mentioned in the second part of the said schedule shall be repealed on and after the appointed day to the extent mentioned in the third column of the said last-mentioned part; provided that the repeal enacted by this

Repeal of enactments in Schedule.

section shall not affect anything done or suffered, or any right or title acquired, or accrued, before such repeal takes effect, or any remedy, penalty, or proceeding in respect thereof.

THE SCHEDULE.

First Part.

Session and Chapter.	Title or short title of Act.	Extent of Repeal
21 & 22 Vict., c. 90 .	The Medical Act, 1858.	Sections four and five. Section twenty-four.
46 & 47 Vict., c. 19 .	The Medical Act (1858) Amendment Act, 1883.	The whole Act.

Second Part.

Session and Chapter.	Title or short title of Act.	Extent of Repeal
21 & 22 Vict., c. 90 .	The Medical Act, 1858.	Section thirty-one.
31 & 32 Vict., c. 29 .	The Medical Act Amendment Act, 1868.	The whole Act.

The Submarine Telegraph Act, 1886.[1]

(50 Vict., c. 3.)

An Act to amend the Submarine Telegraph Act, 1885.

[*25th September, 1886.*]

Whereas the delegates of the States, parties to the convention of the fourteenth day of March one thousand eight hundred and eighty-four, mentioned in the schedule to the Submarine Telegraph Act, 1885, have recommended for adoption by their respective States a declaration respecting the interpretation of such convention, and it is expedient to provide for giving effect to such declaration when adopted.

* * * * - - -

---

[1] See *Chitty's Statutes*, Tit. Telegraphs, p. 40.

48 & 49 Vict., c. 49. 1. This Act shall be construed as one with the Submarine Telegraph Act, 1885,[1] and that Act and this Act may be cited together as the Submarine Telegraph Acts, 1885[1] and 1886, and this Act may be cited separately as the Submarine Telegraph Act, 1886. Short title and construction.

2. It shall be lawful for Her Majesty in Council at any time after the passing of this Act to order that the declaration mentioned in the schedule to this Act, as set forth in that schedule, shall be of the same force, and the same shall accordingly be of the same force, as the articles of the convention set forth in the schedule to the Submarine Telegraph Act, 1885.[1] Confirmation of declaration.

3. Section four of the Submarine Telegraph Act, 1885,[1] is hereby repealed. Repeal of 48 & 49 Vict., c. 49, s. 4.

SCHEDULE.

Submarine Telegraph Declaration.

Certain doubts having been raised as to the meaning of the word "wilfully" used in article two of the convention of the fourteenth of March one thousand eight hundred and eighty-four, it is understood that the provision in respect of penal responsibility contained in the said article does not apply to cases of breakage or injury caused accidentally or of necessity in the repair of a cable when all precautions have been taken to avoid such breakage or injury.

It is equally understood that article four of the convention had no other object, and is to have no other effect, than to empower the competent tribunals of each country to decide in conformity with their laws and according to the circumstances the question of the civil responsibility of the owner of a cable, who in laying or repairing his own cable breaks or injures another cable, as well as the consequences of such responsibility if it is recognised as existing.

The Conversion of India Stock Act, 1887.

(50 & 51 Vict., c. 11.)

An Act for giving facilities for the conversion of India Four per Cent. Stock into India Three and a half per Cent. Stock, and for other purposes relating thereto.

[*23rd May, 1887.*]

Whereas, in accordance with the conditions under which India Four per Cent. Stock has been issued, the Secretary of State in Council of India has

[1] Printed *ante*, p. 800.

power to give notice of his intention to redeem that stock at par on the tenth day of October one thousand eight hundred and eighty-eight:

And whereas the said Secretary of State has offered to holders of India Four per Cent. Stock in exchange for such stock and in lieu of repayment in cash, a like amount of India Three and a half per Cent. Stock, bearing interest from the fifth day of July one thousand eight hundred and eighty-seven, together with the payment on the sixth day of July one thousand eight hundred and eighty-seven of one pound twelve shillings and sixpence per cent. on the amount of stock exchanged, to be treated as interest so as to make up a sum equal to interest thereon at the rate of four pounds per cent. per annum to the tenth day of October one thousand eight hundred and eighty-eight:

* * * * * * *

Short title.

1. This Act may be cited as the Conversion of India Stock Act, 1887.

Power of holders, trustees, etc., in relation to exchange of India Four per Cent. Stock for India Three and a half per Cent. Stock.

2. Where any India Four per Cent. Stock is standing in the name of any person, such person (in this section referred to as the holder) may, with the consent of the Secretary of State, exchange such stock or any part thereof for India Three and a half per Cent. Stock: Provided that when the consent of any person other than the holder is required for a change of investment by such holder, such consent shall be required for the purpose of an exchange in pursuance of this section; and when the holder is a trustee and has not power under the terms of his trust to vary investments, the consent either of every person interested in the stock, or when any such person is an infant or a person of unsound mind the consent of his guardian or guardians or of the committee of his estate or curator bonis (as the case may be), or the consent of a judge of the High Court of Justice in England and Ireland or in Scotland of a judge of the Court of Session, shall be required for the purpose of an exchange in pursuance of this section; and when the holder in a joint account is an infant, or a person of unsound mind, or is under any other disability, or is beyond the seas, the other holders or holder may, with the consent of a judge of the High Court of Justice in England and Ireland, or in Scotland of a judge of the Court of Session, exchange in pursuance of this section, such stock or any part thereof for India Three and a half per Cent. Stock; and such consents having been obtained, holders shall not be liable for any loss resulting from any exchange in pursuance of this section. Subject to rules of court, any jurisdiction given by this Act to a judge of the High Court of Justice shall be exercised by a judge of the Chancery Division.

The Bank shall not be bound to inquire as to whether any such consent as aforesaid is given to any exchange, nor be responsible in the event of any consent not having been given.

3. A power, whether subject or not to any restrictions or conditions, to invest in India Four per Cent. Stock shall extend to authorise an investment, subject to the same conditions and restrictions (if any) in India Three and a half per Cent. Stock.

Powers of investment.

4. Where stock is exchanged under this Act, the stock taken in exchange, and the interest thereon, shall be subject to the same trusts, charges, rights, distringas, and restraints as affect the stock cancelled on the exchange, and the interest thereon respectively.

Stock taken in exchange to be held subject to same provisions as former stock.

5. Every power of attorney in force for the sale and transfer of any India Four per Cent. Stock shall, unless it be legally revoked or become void, remain in force for the purpose of enabling the attorney or attorneys therein named or referred to to receive and give receipts for the money which will become payable for the redemption of any principal sum of such India Four per Cent. Stock, and to sell and transfer any India Three and a half per Cent. Stock that may be accepted in exchange for such India Four per Cent. Stock, or into which such India Four per Cent. Stock may be converted and to receive the consideration money and give receipts for the same.

Powers of attorney for sale and transfer of India Four per Cent. Stock to apply to India Three and a half per Cent. Stock.

6. Every power of attorney in force for the receipt of dividends on any India Four per Cent. Stock shall, unless it be legally revoked or become void, remain in force for the purpose of enabling the attorney or attorneys therein named or referred to to receive the dividends to accrue on India Three and a half per Cent. Stock, and also to receive the said payment of one pound twelve shillings and sixpence per cent. on India Four per Cent. Stock which will become payable on the sixth day of July one thousand eight hundred and eighty-seven.

Powers of attorney for receipt of dividends on India Four per Cent. Stock to apply to India Three and a half per Cent. Stock.

7. Every request for the transmission of dividend warrants by post relating to India Four per Cent. Stock in force at the time of the passing of this Act, or which may hereafter be made in pursuance of the Act of the thirty-fourth and thirty-fifth Victoria, chapter twenty-nine, shall, unless it be legally revoked or become void, extend and apply to India Three and a half per Cent. Stock as if the stock mentioned in such request were therein described as India Three and a half per Cent. Stock.

Requests for post dividend warrants in respect of India Four per Cent. Stock to apply to India Three and a half per Cent. Stock.

8. Where the holder of India Four per Cent. Stock to the amount of one thousand pounds nominal value or less is an infant or a person of unsound mind, and no steps are taken on or before the first day of July one thousand eight hundred and eighty-seven for the exchange of such stock for India Three and a half per Cent. Stock, such exchange shall be made, notwithstanding that no consent may have been given by his guardian or guardians, or by the committee of his estate or curator bonis (as the case may be). For the purpose

Power to exchange stock up to 1,000*l.* value standing in name of infant or of person of unsound mind.

of effecting such exchange the Bank shall, by the direction of the Secretary of State, cancel in their books as from the first day of July one thousand eight hundred and eighty-seven the amount to be exchanged of India Four per Cent. Stock standing in the name of any such holder, and shall inscribe in their books in the name of such holder the amount of India Three and a half per Cent. Stock to be given in exchange for the India Four per Cent. Stock so cancelled. The Secretary of State may provide as to the evidence of title, unsoundness of mind, or other matter which the Bank may require. A direction from the Secretary of State shall be a sufficient authority for anything done by the Bank in pursuance of such direction for the purposes of this section.

Definitions.

9. In this Act,—

"The Secretary of State" means the Secretary of State in Council of India.

"The Bank" means the Governor and Company of the Bank of England, or the Governor and Company of the Bank of Ireland, as the case may be, and includes their successors.

"Person" includes a body of persons corporate or unincorporate.

The British Settlements Act, 1887.

(50 & 51 Vict., c. 54.)

An Act to enable Her Majesty to provide for the Government of Her Possessions acquired by Settlement.

[*16th September, 1887.*]

Whereas divers of Her Majesty's subjects have resorted to and settled in, and may hereafter resort to and settle in, divers places where there is no civilized government, and such settlements have become or may hereafter become possessions of Her Majesty, and it is expedient to extend the power of Her Majesty to provide for the government of such settlements, and for that purpose to repeal and re-enact with amendments the existing Acts enabling Her Majesty to provide for such government:

* * * * * * *

Short title.

1. This Act may be cited as the British Settlements Act, 1887.

Power of the Queen in Council to make laws and establish courts.

2. It shall be lawful for Her Majesty the Queen in Council from time to time to establish all such laws and institutions, and constitute such courts and officers, and make such provisions and regulations for the proceedings in the said courts and for the administration of justice, as may appear to Her

Majesty in Council to be necessary for the peace, order, and good government of Her Majesty's subjects and others within any British settlement.

3. It shall be lawful for Her Majesty the Queen from time to time, by any instrument passed under the Great Seal of the United Kingdom, or by any instructions under Her Majesty's Royal Sign Manual referred to in such instrument as made, or to be made, as respects any British settlement, to delegate to any three or more persons within the settlement all or any of the powers conferred by this Act on Her Majesty in Council, either absolutely or subject to such conditions, provisions, and limitations as may be specified in such instrument or instructions.

Delegation of power by the Queen.

Provided that, notwithstanding any such delegation, the Queen in Council may exercise all or any of the powers under this Act: Provided always, that every such instrument or instruction as aforesaid shall be laid before both Houses of Parliament as soon as conveniently may be after the making and enactment thereof respectively.

4. It shall be lawful for Her Majesty the Queen in Council to confer on any court in any British possession any such jurisdiction, civil or criminal, original or appellate, in respect of matters occurring or arising in any British settlement, as might be conferred by virtue of this Act upon a court in the settlement, and to make such provisions and regulations as Her Majesty in Council may think fit respecting the exercise of the jurisdiction conferred under this section on any court, and respecting the enforcement and execution of the judgments, decrees, orders, and sentences of such court, and respecting appeals therefrom; and every Order of Her Majesty in Council under this section shall be effectual to vest in the court the jurisdiction expressed to be thereby conferred, and the court shall exercise the same in accordance with and subject to the said provisions and regulations: Provided always, that every Order in Council made in pursuance of this Act shall be laid before both Houses of Parliament as soon as conveniently may be after the making thereof.

Power to the Queen in Council to confer jurisdiction on certain courts.

5. It shall be lawful for Her Majesty the Queen in Council from time to time to make, and when made to alter and revoke, Orders for the purposes of this Act.

Making of Orders in Council, etc.

6. For the purposes of this Act the expression "British possession" means any part of Her Majesty's possessions out of the United Kingdom, and the expression "British settlement" means any British possession which has not been acquired by cession or conquest, and is not for the time being within the jurisdiction of the Legislature, constituted otherwise than by virtue of this Act or of any Act repealed by this Act, of any British possession.

Definitions.

Repeal.

7. The Acts mentioned in the schedule to this Act are hereby repealed: Provided that—

(*a*) Such repeal shall not affect anything done or suffered previously to such repeal in pursuance of any such Act, or in pursuance of any Order in Council, commission, instructions, law, ordinance, or other thing made or done in pursuance of any such Act; and

(*b*) All Orders in Council, commissions, and instructions purporting to be made or given in pursuance of the Acts hereby repealed, or either of them, shall continue in force in like manner as if they had been made and given in pursuance of this Act, and such commissions had originally been instruments authorised by this Act, and shall be subject to be revoked or recalled accordingly.

SCHEDULE.

Session and Chapter.	Title.
6 & 7 Vict., c. 13 .	An Act to enable Her Majesty to provide for the Government of Her Settlements on the Coast of Africa and in the Falkland Islands.
23 & 24 Vict., c. 121	An Act to amend an Act passed in the sixth year of Her Majesty Queen Victoria intituled An Act to enable Her Majesty to provide for the Government of Her Settlements on the Coast of Africa and in the Falkland Islands.

THE SUPERANNUATION ACT, 1887.

(50 & 51 Vict., c. 67.)

An Act to amend the Superannuation Acts, 1834 and 1859; and for other purposes. [*16th September, 1887.*]

* * * * * * *

Grant of gratuity or allowance to injured civil servant.

1. (1) Where a person employed in the civil service of the State is injured—

(*a*) in the actual discharge of his duty; and

(*b*) without his own default; and

(*c*) by some injury specifically attributable to the nature of his duty, the Treasury may grant to him, or, if he dies from the injury, to his widow, his mother, if wholly dependent on him at the time of his death, and to his children, or to any of them, such gratuity or annual allowance as the Treasury may consider reasonable, and as may be permitted by the terms of a warrant under this section.

(2) The Treasury shall forthwith after the passing of this Act frame a warrant regulating the grant of gratuities and annual allowances under this section, and the warrant so framed shall be laid before Parliament.

(3) Provided that a gratuity under this section shall not exceed one year's salary of the person injured, and an allowance under this section shall not, together with any superannuation allowance to which he is otherwise entitled, exceed the salary of the person injured, or three hundred pounds a year, whichever is less.

2. (1) Where a civil servant is removed from his office on the ground of his inability to discharge efficiently the duties of his office, and a superannuation allowance cannot lawfully be granted to him under the Superannuation Acts, 1834[1] and 1859, and the Treasury think that the special circumstances of the case justify the grant to him of a retiring allowance, they may grant to him such retiring allowance as they think just and proper, but in no case exceeding the amount for which his length of service would qualify him under sections two and four of the Superannuation Act, 1859, without any additions under section seven of that Act. Power to grant retiring allowance to persons removed.

(2) A minute of the Treasury granting an allowance under this section to any civil servant shall set forth the amount of the allowance granted to him, and the reasons for such allowance, and shall be laid before Parliament: Provided that the Treasury before making the grant shall consider any representation which the civil servant removed may have submitted to them.

3. Where a person at the time he becomes a civil servant within the meaning of this Act is serving the State in a temporary capacity, the Treasury may, if in their opinion any special circumstances of the case warrant such a course, direct that his service in that capacity may be reckoned for the purposes of the Superannuation Acts, 1834[1] and 1859, and this Act, as service in the capacity of a civil servant, and it shall be so reckoned accordingly. Reckoning of temporary services.

4 Will. 4. c. 24.

4. If a person employed in any public department in a capacity in respect of which a superannuation allowance cannot be granted under the Superannuation Act, 1859, retires, or is removed from his employment, and Compassionate gratuity on retirement of person not entitled to superannuation.

(*a*) the employment is one to which he was required to devote his whole time, and

[1] Printed, Vol I, p. 183.

(*b*) the remuneration for the employment was paid entirely out of moneys provided by Parliament, and

(*c*) he has served in the employment for not less than seven years, if he is removed in consequence of the abolition of his employment, or for the purpose of facilitating improvements in the organisation of the department by which economy can be effected, or for not less than fifteen years if his retirement is caused from infirmity of mind or body, permanently incapacitating him from the duties of his employment,

the Treasury may, if they think fit, grant to him a compassionate gratuity not exceeding one pound or one week's pay, whichever is the greater, for each year of his service in his employment.

Provision against double pensions.

5. A person shall not be entitled to reckon the same period of time both for the purpose of a superannuation allowance under the Superannuation Acts, 1834 and 1859, and this Act, and also for the purpose of naval or military non-effective pay.

Regulations as to officers receiving half-pay or retired pay.

6. (1) The Treasury may, within one month after the passing of this Act, frame rules as to the conditions on which any civil employment of profit under any public department as defined by this Act, or any employment of profit under the Government of any British possession, or any employment under the Government of any Foreign State, may be accepted or held by any person who is in receipt of or has received any sum granted by Parliament for the pay, half-pay, or retired pay of officers of Her Majesty's naval or land forces, or otherwise for payment for past service in either of such forces, or who has commuted the right to receive the same, and as to the effect of such acceptance or holding on the said pay or sum, and the Treasury may in such rules provide for the enforcement thereof by the forfeiture, suspension, or reduction of any such pay or sum as aforesaid, or of any commutation money or remuneration for such employment.

(2) Such rules shall also provide for the returns to be laid before Parliament of such officers accepting employment as are affected by the rules, and shall come into operation at the date of the passing of this Act.

(3) The rules shall be laid before both Houses of Parliament forthwith.

(4) For the purposes of this section "British possession" means any part of Her Majesty's dominions out of the United Kingdom, and this section shall apply to Cyprus as if it were a British possession.

7. (1) * * * * * [1] Provision as to lunatics.

(2) Where any annuity, whether pension, superannuation, or other allowance, is payable out of moneys provided by Parliament to a person in respect either of service as a civil servant or of military or naval service, and such person is or becomes a lunatic towards whose maintenance a contribution is made out of money provided by Parliament, then as long as the contribution is made his annuity shall be reduced by an amount equal to that contribution, and if the amount of the contribution exceeds the amount of the annuity, the annuity shall cease to be payable.

8. On the death of a person to whom any sum not exceeding one hundred pounds is due from a public department in respect of any civil pay, superannuation, or other allowance, annuity or gratuity, then, if the prescribed public department so direct, but subject to the regulations (if any) made by the Treasury, probate or other proof of the title of the personal representative of the deceased person may be dispensed with, and the said sum may be paid or distributed to or among the persons appearing to the public department to be beneficially entitled to the personal estate of the deceased person, or to or among any one or more of those persons, or in case of the illegitimacy of the deceased person or his children, to or among such persons as the department may think fit, and the department shall be discharged from all liability in respect of any such payment or distribution. Distribution of money not exceeding 100*l.* without probate.

9. The decision of the Treasury on any question which arises as to the application of any section of this Act to any person, or as to the amount of any allowance or gratuity under this Act, or as to the reckoning of any service for such allowance or gratuity, shall be final. Decision of Treasury.

10. Nothing in this Act shall be construed so as in any way to interfere with the rights existing at the passing of this Act of any civil servant then holding office. Saving for existing interests.

11. Every warrant and minute under this Act which is required to be laid before Parliament shall be laid before both Houses of Parliament in manner provided by section thirteen of the Superannuation Act, 1859. Laying of warrant and minutes before Parliament.

12. In this Act, unless the context otherwise requires,— Definations.

The expression "civil servant" means a person who has served in an established capacity in the permanent civil service of the State within the meaning of section seventeen of the Superannuation Act, 1859 : Vict., 9.

[1] Sub-section (1), which was repealed by 53 & 58 Vict., c. 41, s. 94, has been omitted.

The expression "Treasury" means the Commissioners of Her Majesty's Treasury.

The expression "public department" means the Treasury, the Commissioners for executing the office of Lord High Admiral, and any of Her Majesty's Principal Secretaries of State, and any other public department of the Government; and the expression "prescribed public department" means, as respects any matter, the department prescribed for the purpose of that matter by the Treasury.

Short titles.

13. The Act of the session of the fourth and fifth years of the reign of King William the Fourth, chapter twenty-four, intituled "An Act to alter, amend, and consolidate the laws for regulating the pensions, compensations, and allowances to be made to persons in respect of their having held civil offices in His Majesty's service," is in this Act referred to and may be cited as the Superannuation Act, 1834,[1] and that Act and the Superannuation Act, 1859, are together in this Act referred to as the Superannuation Acts, 1834[1] and 1859.

The said Acts and this Act may be cited together as the Superannuation Acts, 1834[1] to 1887, and this Act may be cited separately as the Superannuation Act, 1887.

Repeal.

14. The Acts set forth in the schedule to this Act are hereby repealed to the extent in the third column of that schedule mentioned as from the passing of this Act, without prejudice to anything previously done or suffered in pursuance of the enactments hereby repealed.

SCHEDULE.

Section 14.

ACTS REPEALED.

Session and Chapter.	Title or Short Title.	Extent of Repeal.
4 & 5 Will. 4, c. 24	An Act to alter, amend, and consolidate the laws for regulating pensions, compensations, and allowances to be made to persons in respect of their having held civil offices in His Majesty's service.	Section sixteen.
6 & 7 Will. 4, c. 13	An Act to consolidate the laws relating to the constabulary force in Ireland.	Section thirty.
7 Will. 4, & 1 Vict., c. 25.	An Act to make more effectual provisions relating to the police in the district of Dublin metropolis.	Section nineteen.

[1] Printed, Vol. I, p. 183.

(Schedule.)

50 & 51 Vict., c. 70.] *The Appellate Jurisdiction Act, 1887.*

SCHEDULE.

ACTS REPEALED.

Session and Chapter.	Title or Short Title.	Extent of Repeal.
2 & 3 Vict., c. 47 . .	An Act for further improving the police in and near the metropolis.	Section nineteen.
2 & 3 Vict., c. 93 . .	An Act for the establishment of county and district constables by the authority of justices of the peace.	Section eleven.
22 Vict., c. 26 . .	The Superannuation Act, 1859 . .	Section five.
22 & 23 Vict., c. 32 .	An Act to amend the law concerning the police in counties and boroughs in England and Wales.	Section twenty-seven.
31 & 32 Vict., c. 90 .	An Act to empower certain public departments to pay otherwise than to executors or administrators small sums due on account of pay or allowances to persons deceased.	The whole Act.
33 & 34 Vict., c. 96 .	An Act to apply a sum out of the Consolidated Fund to the service of the year ending the thirty-first day of March one thousand eight hundred and seventy-one, and to appropriate the supplies granted in this session of Parliament.	Sub-sections four, five and six of section six.
35 & 36 Vict., c. 12 .	The Superannuation Act, 1872 .	The whole Act.

THE APPELLATE JURISDICTION ACT, 1887.[1]

(50 & 51 Vict., c. 70.)

An Act to amend the Appellate Jurisdiction Act, 1876.

[*16th September, 1887.*]

39 & 40 Vict., c. 59. WHEREAS it is expedient to amend the Appellate Jurisdiction Act, 1876:

* * * * * * *

[1] See *Chitty's Statutes*, Tit. Judicature, p. 111.

(*Secs. 1-6.*)

Lord of Appeal may take his seat during prorogation.

1. Whereas it is expedient that any Lord of Appeal, as defined by the Appellate Jurisdiction Act, 1876, notwithstanding that he may not be a Lord of Appeal in Ordinary within the meaning of that Act, should be empowered to take his seat and the oaths at the sittings of the House of Lords for hearing and determining appeals during the prorogation of Parliament: Be it enacted that, notwithstanding anything in the eighth section of the said Act contained, every Lord of Appeal shall be empowered to take his seat and the oaths at any such sitting of the House of Lords during prorogation.

Retired Lord of Appeal in Ordinary may sit in House of Lords.

2. The sixth section of the Appellate Jurisdiction Act, 1876, shall be construed and take effect, as well in respect of any Lord of Appeal in Ordinary heretofore appointed under that Act, as of any such Lord hereafter appointed, so as to entitle any person so appointed to sit and vote as a member of the House of Lords during his life as fully as if the words "during the time that he continues in his office as a Lord of Appeal in Ordinary, and no longer" had been omitted from the said section.

Amendment of 3 & 4 Will. 4, c. 41.

3. The Judicial Committee of the Privy Council as formed under the provisions of the first section of the Act of the third and fourth William the Fourth, chapter forty-one, intituled "An Act for the better administration of Justice in His Majesty's Privy Council," shall include such members of Her Majesty's Privy Council as are for the time being holding or have held any of the offices in the Appellate Jurisdiction Act, 1876, and this Act, described as high judicial offices.

Remuneration in Judicial Committee.

4. Any person who shall in virtue of the thirtieth section of the Act of the third and fourth William the Fourth, chapter forty-one, attend the sittings of the Judicial Committee of the Privy Council, shall be deemed to be included as a member of the said Committee for all purposes, and shall, if there be only one such person, be entitled to receive the whole amount of the sums by the said section provided, that is to say, eight hundred pounds for every year during which he shall so attend; but if there shall at any time be two such persons, they shall severally be entitled to the sums provided in the said section.

Amendment of 39 & 40 Vict., c. 59, s. 25.

5. The expression "high judicial office" as defined in the twenty-fifth section of the Appellate Jurisdiction Act, 1876, shall be deemed to include the office of a Lord of Appeal in Ordinary and the office of a member of the Judicial Committee of the Privy Council.

Short title.

6. This Act may be cited as the Appellate Jurisdiction Act, 1887.

THE OUDE AND ROHILKUND RAILWAY PURCHASE ACT, 1888.

(51 & 52 Vict., c. 5.)

An Act to empower the Secretary of State in Council of India to raise money in the United Kingdom for the purchase of the Oude and Rohilkund Railway, and for the construction, extension, and equipment of Railways in India, through the Agency of Companies, and for other purposes relating thereto.

[*27th April, 1888.*]

WHEREAS the Secretary of State in Council, by virtue of the power vested in him under the contracts between him and the Company, on the second day of January, one thousand eight hundred and eighty-eight, gave to the Oude and Rohilkund Company, Limited, notice of his intention to purchase the undertaking of the Company:

And whereas, in consequence of such notice, the Secretary of State in Council has become liable to pay to the Company in London on the thirty-first day of December, one thousand eight hundred and eighty-eight, the amount of five million thirty-six thousand and forty-eight pounds sixteen shillings and eight pence for the said purchase, and has also become liable to pay the sum of five million three hundred thousand pounds borrowed by the Company on the debentures and debenture stock specified in the schedule to this Act annexed, as and when the same respectively shall become redeemable:

And whereas it is expedient that the Secretary of State in Council of India should be empowered to raise money in manner in this Act mentioned for the purchase on behalf of Her Majesty for the purposes of the Government of India of the undertaking of the said Company, and for the redemption and discharge of the said debentures and debenture stock as and when the same respectively shall fall due and become redeemable:

And whereas large sums of money have been from time to time raised on bonds or debentures for the purposes of constructing, extending, and equipping various railways in India by companies under the guarantee, as respects both interest and principal, of the Secretary of State in Council of India:

And whereas the Secretary of State in Council is advised that the charge on the revenues of India on account of the moneys from time to time required for the said last-mentioned purposes, through the agency of such companies, might be less if such moneys were raised by the Secretary of State in Council of India in the United Kingdom, on the credit of the revenues of India, than if such moneys were raised through the agency of such companies:

And whereas it is expedient that the Secretary of State in Council of India be empowered to raise such moneys in manner in this Act mentioned:

Be it therefore enacted by the Queen's most Excellent Majesty by and with the advice and consent of the Lords Spiritual and Temporal, and Commons, in this present Parliament assembled, and by the authority of the same, as follows:

Short title. 1. This Act may be cited as the Oude and Rohilkund Railway Purchase Act, 1888.

Definition. 2. In this Act the expression "Secretary of State" means the Secretary of State in Council of India, unless the context otherwise requires.

Power to raise 10,336,048*l.* 16*s.* 8*d.* for purchase of Oude and Rohilkund Railway. 3. It shall be lawful for the Secretary of State at any time or times after the passing of this Act to raise in the United Kingdom, for the purchase of the railways, works, stations, telegraphs, engines, carriages, stock, plant, and machinery belonging to or forming the undertaking of the Oude and Rohilkund Railway Company, Limited, and as and when necessary for the discharge and redemption of debentures and debenture stock issued by the Company, any sum or sums of money not exceeding in the whole the sum of ten million three hundred and thirty-six thousand and forty-eight pounds sixteen shillings and eight pence.

Power to raise 10,000,000*l.* for constructing, extending, and equipping railways in India. 4. It shall further be lawful for the Secretary of State to raise in the United Kingdom any sum or sums of money not exceeding in the whole ten millions of pounds sterling to be applied, from time to time, in such manner and under such conditions as the Secretary of State may determine for the purposes of constructing, extending, and equipping railways in India through the agency of a company or companies under engagement with the Secretary of State, or in the repayment or discharge of the principal of any bonds or debentures issued by any such company under the guarantee of the Secretary of State.

Mode of raising moneys. 5. All moneys raised under the authority of this Act shall be raised either by the creation and issue of bonds, debentures, or capital stock bearing interest, or partly by one of such modes and partly by another or others.

Securities, etc., to be charged on revenues of India. 6. All bonds and debentures issued under this Act, and the principal moneys and interest thereby secured, and all capital stock issued under this Act, and the interest thereon, shall be charged on and payable out of the revenues of India, in like manner as other liabilities incurred on account of the Government of India.

Limit of charge on revenues of India. 7. The whole amount of principal moneys to be charged on the revenues of India under this Act shall not exceed ten millions of pounds sterling, beyond the amount required to be charged for the purchase of the Oude and Rohilkund Railway, and for the discharge of the debentures and debenture stock mentioned in the schedule to this Act annexed.

8. Upon or for the repayment of any principal moneys secured under the authority of this Act, the Secretary of State may at any time borrow or raise, by all or any of the modes aforesaid, all or any part of the amount of principal money repaid or to be repaid, and so from time to time as all or any part of any principal moneys under this Act may require to be repaid, but the whole amount to be charged on the revenues of India shall not in any case exceed the principal moneys required to be repaid. Power to re-borrow.

9. All bonds issued under the authority of this Act may be issued under the hands of two members of the Council of India, and countersigned by the Secretary of State for India or one of his under secretaries, or his assistant under secretary, and shall be for such respective amounts, payable after such notice, and at such rate or rates of interest, as the Secretary of State may think fit. As to issue of bonds.

10. All debentures issued under the authority of this Act may be issued under the hands of two members of the Council of India, and countersigned as aforesaid, for such respective amounts, and at such rate or rates of interest, as the Secretary of State may think fit, and shall be issued at or for such price and on such terms as may be determined by the Secretary of State. As to issue of debentures.

11. All debentures issued under the authority of this Act shall be paid off at par at a time or times to be mentioned in such debentures respectively; and the interest on all such debentures shall be paid on such days as shall be mentioned therein; and the principal moneys and interest secured by such debentures shall be payable either at the treasury of the Secretary of State in London or at the Bank of England. As to payment of principal and interest on debentures.

12. Debentures issued under the authority of this Act, and all right to and in respect of the principal and interest moneys secured thereby, shall be transferable by the delivery of such debentures, or, at the discretion of the Secretary of State, by deed; provided that the coupons for interest annexed to any debenture issued under the authority of this Act shall pass by delivery. Mode of transfer of debentures.

13. Any capital stock created under the authority of this Act shall bear such rate of interest as the Secretary of State may think fit; and such capital stock may be issued on such terms as may be determined by the Secretary of State; and any such capital stock may bear interest during such period, and be paid off at par at such time, as the Secretary of State may prescribe previously to the issue of such capital stock. Capital stock.

14. In case of the creation and issue of any such capital stock, there shall be kept, either at the office of the Secretary of State in London or at the Bank of England, books wherein entries shall be made of the said capital stock, and wherein all assignments or transfers of the same, or any part thereof, shall be entered and registered, and shall be signed by the parties making such assign- Transfer books of capital stock.

ments or transfers, or, if such parties be absent, by his, her, or their attorney or attorneys thereunto lawfully authorised by writing under his, her, or their hands and seals, to be attested by two or more credible witnesses; and the person or persons to whom such transfer or transfers shall be made may respectively underwrite his, her, or their acceptance thereof; and no other mode of assigning or transferring the said capital stock or any part thereof, or any interest therein, shall be good and available in law, and no stamp duties whatsoever shall be charged on the said transfers or any of them.

5 & 6 Will. 4, c. 64, s. 4, extended to bonds and debentures under Act.

15. The provisions contained in section four of the Act of the session holden in the fifth and sixth years of King William the Fourth, chapter sixty-four, with respect to the composition and agreement for the payment by the East India Company of an annual sum in lieu of stamp duties on their bonds, and the exemption of their bonds from stamp duties, shall be applicable with respect to the bonds and debentures to be issued under the authority of this Act, as if such provisions were here repeated and re-enacted with reference thereto.

Punishment of forgery of bonds and debentures.

16. All provisions now in force in anywise relating to the offence of forging or altering, or offering, uttering, disposing of, or putting off, knowing the same to be forged or altered, any East India bond, with intent to defraud, shall extend and be applicable to and in respect of any bond or debenture issued under the authority of this Act.

Saving existing borrowing powers.

17. This Act shall not prejudice or affect any power of raising or borrowing money vested in the said Secretary of State at the time of passing thereof.

Extension of 22 & 23 Vict., c. 35, s. 32, 26 & 27 Vict., c. 73, to capital stock under Act.

18. Any capital stock created under this Act shall be deemed to be East India stock, within the Act of the twenty-second and twenty-third Victoria, chapter thirty-five, section thirty-two, unless and until Parliament shall otherwise provide; and any capital stock created under this Act shall be deemed to be and shall mean India stock within the Act of the twenty-sixth and twenty-seventh Victoria, chapter seventy-three, anything in the said last-mentioned Act to the contrary notwithstanding.

Amount, etc., of moneys raised under Act to be shown in parliamentary return.

19. The amount of all moneys raised under this Act and the manner in which the same shall have been applied shall be shown in the half-yearly returns of all loans raised in England to be prepared by the Secretary of State and presented to both Houses of Parliament under the provisions of section fifteen of the Act forty-two and forty-three Victoria, chapter sixty.[1]

[1] Printed *ante*, p. 599.

SCHEDULE.

DEBENTURES OF THE OUDE AND ROHILKUND RAILWAY COMPANY.

Amounts.	Dates of Redemption.	Rates of Interest per Annum.
£		
300,000	1 May, 1888	4 per cent.
345,000	16 May, 1888	" "
500,000	1 June, 1888	" "
740,000	1 August, 1888	3½ "
500,000	1 December, 1890	" "
31,000	16 August, 1891	" "
1,000,000	1 April, 1892	" "
155,000	16 May, 1892	" "
615,800	4 June, 1892	" "
308,000	16 August, 1893	" "
426,000	1 October, 1893	" "
4,916,300		

DEBENTURE STOCK CREATED BY THE COMPANY.

384,700*l.*, bearing interest at 4 per cent., redeemable at par at the option of the Secretary of State at any time after 6th May, 1898, upon six months' notice being published in the "London Gazette."

THE COMMISSIONERS FOR OATHS ACT, 1889.[1]

(52 & 53 Vict., c. 10.)

An Act for amending and consolidating enactments relating to the administration of Oaths.

[*31st May, 1889.*]

* * * * * *

1. (1) The Lord Chancellor may from time to time, by commission signed by him, appoint persons being practising solicitors or other fit and proper persons to be commissioners for oaths, and may revoke any such appointment. *Appointment and powers of commissioners for oaths.*

(2) A commissioner for oaths may, by virtue of his commission, in England or elsewhere, administer any oath or take any affidavit for the purposes of any court or matter in England, including any of the ecclesiastical courts or jurisdictions, matters ecclesiastical, matters relating to application for notarial faculties, and matters relating to the registration of any instrument, whether under an Act of Parliament or otherwise, and take any bail of

[1] Explained and amended by 53 & 54 Vict., c. 7, and 54 & 55 Vict., c. 50, *post*, p. 879 and p. 906. See *Chitty's Statutes*, Tit. Oaths, etc., p. 18; *Taylor on Evidence*, §§ 11, 12.

recognisance in or for the purpose of any civil proceeding in the Supreme Court, including all proceedings on the revenue side of the Queen's Bench Division.

(3) Provided that a commissioner for oaths shall not exercise any of the powers given by this section in any proceeding in which he is solicitor to any of the parties to the proceeding, or clerk to any such solicitor, or in which he is interested.

Powers of certain officers of court, etc., to administer oath.

2. Every person who, being an officer of or performing duties in relation to any court, is for the time being so authorised by a judge of the court, or by or in pursuance of any rules or orders regulating the procedure of the court, and every person directed to take an examination in any cause or matter in the Supreme Court, shall have authority to administer any oath or take any affidavit required for any purpose connected with his duties.

Taking of oaths out of England.

3. (1) Any oath or affidavit required for the purpose of any court or matter in England, or for the purpose of the registration of any instrument in any part of the United Kingdom, may be taken or made in any place out of England before any person having authority to administer an oath in that place.

(2) In the case of a person having such authority otherwise than by the law of a foreign country, judicial and official notice shall be taken of his seal or signature affixed, impressed, or subscribed to or on any such oath or affidavit.

Appointment of persons to administer oaths for prize proceedings.

4. The Lord Chancellor may, whenever it appears to him necessary to do so, authorise any person to administer oaths and take affidavits for any purpose relating to prize proceedings in the Supreme Court, whilst that person is on the high seas or out of Her Majesty's dominions, and it shall not be necessary to affix any stamp to the document by which he is so authorised.

Jurat to state where and when oath is taken

5. Every commissioner before whom any oath or affidavit is taken or made under this Act shall state truly in the jurat or attestation at what place and on what date the oath or affidavit is taken or made.

Powers as to oaths and notarial acts abroad.

6. (1) Every British ambassador, envoy, minister, charge d'affaires and secretary of embassy or legation exercising his functions in any foreign country, and every British consul-general, consul, vice-consul, acting consul, pro-consul, and consular agent [acting consul-general, acting vice-consul, and acting consular agent][1] exercising his functions in any foreign place, may, in that country or place, administer any oath and take any affidavit, and also do any notarial act which any notary public can do within the United Kingdom; and every oath, affidavit, and notarial act administered, sworn, or done

[1] The words in square brackets were inserted by 54 & 55 Vict., c. 50, s. 2, *post*, p. 906.

by or before any such person shall be as effectual as if duly administered sworn, or done by or before any lawful authority in any part of the United Kingdom.

(2) Any document purporting to have affixed, impressed, or subscribed thereon or thereto the seal and signature of any person authorised by this section to administer an oath in testimony of any oath, affidavit, or act being administered, taken, or done by or before him, shall be admitted in evidence without proof of the seal or signature being the seal or signature of that person, or of the official character of that person.

7. Whoever wilfully and corruptly swears falsely in any oath or affidavit taken or made in accordance with the provisions of this Act, shall be guilty of perjury in every case where if he had so sworn in a judicial proceeding before a court of competent jurisdiction he would be guilty of perjury. Perjury.

8. Whoever forges, counterfeits, or fraudulently alters the seal or signature of any person authorized by or under this Act to administer an oath, or tenders in evidence, or otherwise uses, any affidavit having any seal or signature so forged or counterfeited or fraudulently altered, knowing the same to be forged, counterfeited, or fraudulently altered, shall be guilty of felony, and liable on conviction to penal servitude for any term not exceeding seven years and not less than five years, or to imprisonment with or without hard labour for any term not exceeding two years. Forgery.

9. Any offence under this Act, whether committed within or without Her Majesty's dominions, may be inquired of, dealt with, tried, and punished in any county or place in the United Kingdom in which the person charged with the offence was apprehended or is in custody, and for all purposes incidental to or consequential on the trial or punishment the offence shall be deemed to have been committed in that county or place. Trial of offences.

10. Where any offence under this Act is alleged to have been committed with respect to any affidavit, a judge of any court before which the affidavit is produced may order the affidavit to be impounded and kept in such custody and for such time and on such conditions as he thinks fit. Impounding of documents.

11. In this Act, unless the context otherwise requires,— Definitions.

"Oath" includes affirmation and declaration:

"Affidavit" includes affirmation, statutory or other declaration, acknowledgment, examination, and attestation or protestation of honour:

"Swear" includes affirm, declare, and protest;

"Supreme Court" means the Supreme Court of Judicature in England.

12. The enactments specified in the schedule to this Act are hereby repealed to the extent specified in that schedule: Repeal.

Provided that this repeal shall not affect—

(*a*) anything done or suffered under any enactment repealed by this Act; nor

(*b*) any appointment made under or authority given by or in pursuance of any enactment so repealed; nor

(*c*) any punishment incurred or to be incurred in respect of any offence committed before the commencement of this Act against any enactment so repealed; nor

(*d*) any legal proceeding for enforcing any such punishment;

and any such legal proceeding may be instituted or continued and any such punishment may be imposed as if this Act had not been passed.

Commissions issued before commencement of Act.

13. A commissioner authorised before the commencement of this Act to administer oaths in the Supreme Court shall be deemed to be a commissioner for oaths within the meaning of this Act.

Commencement.

14. This Act shall commence and come into operation on the first day of January one thousand eight hundred and ninety.

Short title.

15. This Act may be cited as the Commissioners for Oaths Act, 1889.

SCHEDULE.

A description or citation of a portion of an Act is inclusive of the words, sections, or other parts, first and last mentioned, or otherwise referred to as forming the beginning, or as forming the end respectively, of the portion comprised in the description or citation.

Session and Chapter.	Title.	Extent of Repeal.
16 & 17 Chas. 2, c. 9 .	An Act to empower the Chancellor of the duchy to grant commissions for taking affidavits within the duchy liberty.	The whole Act.
17 Geo. 2, c. 7. . .	An Act for taking and swearing affidavits to be made use of in any of the courts of the county palatine of Lancaster.	Ditto ditto.
4 Geo. 3, c. 21. . .	An Act for taking and swearing affidavits to be made use of in any of the courts of the county palatine of Durham.	Ditto ditto.
6 Geo. 4, c. 87 . .	An Act to regulate the payment of salaries and allowances to British consuls at foreign ports, and the disbursements at such ports for certain public purposes.	Section twenty.

SCHEDULE—*contd.*

Sessions and Chapter.	Title.	Extent of Repeal.
3 & 4 Will. 4, c. 42	An Act for the further amendment of the law and the better advancement of justice	Section forty-two.
4 & 5 Will. 4, c. 42	An Act to facilitate the taking of affidavits and affirmations in the court of the Vice Warden of the Stannaries of Cornwall.	The whole Act.
2 & 3 Vict., c. 58	An Act to make further provision for the administration of justice and for improving the practice and proceedings in the courts of the Stannaries of Cornwall.	Section six from "and that any commissioner."
5 & 6 Vict., c. 103	An Act for abolishing certain offices of the High Court of Chancery in England.	Sections seven and eight.
6 & 7 Vict., c. 82	An Act the title of which begins with the words "An Act for extending," and ends with the words "examination of witnesses."	Sections one to four.
11 & 12 Vict., c. 10	An Act for empowering certain officers of the High Court of Chancery to administer oaths and take declarations and affirmations.	The whole Act.
15 & 16 Vict., c. 76	The Common Law Procedure Act, 1852.	Sections twenty-three.
15 & 16 Vict., c. 86	An Act to amend the practice and course of proceeding in the High Court of Chancery.	Section twenty-two, twenty-three, and twenty-four.
16 & 17 Vict., c. 70	The Lunacy Regulation Act, 1853	Section fifty-seven.
16 & 17 Vict., c. 78	An Act relating to the appointment of persons to administer oaths in Chancery, and to affidavits made for purposes connected with registration.	The whole Act.
17 & 18 Vict., c. 78	The Admiralty Court Act, 1854	Section six from "and any examiner" to the end of the section. Sections seven to eleven.
18 & 19 Vict., c. 42	An Act to enable British diplomatic and consular agents abroad to administer oaths and do notarial acts.	The whole Act.

SCHEDULE—*concld.*

Sessions and Chapter.	Title.	Extent of Repeal.
18 & 19 Vict., c. 134	An Act the title of which begins with the words "An Act to make further provision," and ends with the words "leasing and sale thereof."	Section fifteen.
20 & 21 Vict., c. 77	An Act to amend the law relating to probates and letters of administration in England.	Section twenty-seven to "Provided that" and from "and any person who" to end of section.
21 & 22 Vict., c. 95	An Act to amend the Act of the twentieth and twenty-first Victoria, chapter seventy-seven.	Sections thirty to thirty-four.
21 & 22 Vict., c. 108	An Act to amend the Act of the twentieth and twenty-first Victoria, chapter eighty-five.	Sections twenty to twenty-three.
22 Vict., c. 16	An Act the title of which begins with the words "An Act to enable," and ends with the words "of the Exchequer."	The whole Act, except section five.
28 & 29 Vict., c. 104	The Crown Suits, etc., Act, 1865	Sections eighteen, nineteen, forty-three, and forty-four.
32 & 33 Vict., c. 38	The Bails Act, 1869	The whole Act.
40 & 41 Vict., c. 25	The Solicitors Act, 1877	Section eighteen.

The Official Secrets Act, 1889.[1]

(52 & 53 Vict., c. 52.)

An Act to prevent the Disclosure of Official Documents and information.

[*26th August, 1889.*]

* * * * * * *

Disclosure of information.

1. (*1*) (*a*) Where a person for the purpose of wrongfully obtaining information—

(i) enters or is in any part of a place belonging to Her Majesty the Queen, being a fortress, arsenal, factory, dockyard, camp, ship, office, or other like place, in which part he is not entitled to be; or

[1] See *Chitty's Statutes*, Tit. Criminal Law, p. 364.

(ii) when lawfully or unlawfully in any such place as aforesaid, either obtains any document, sketch, plan, model, or knowledge of anything which he is not entitled to obtain, or takes without lawful authority any sketch or plan; or

(iii) when outside any fortress, arsenal, factory, dockyard or camp belonging to Her Majesty the Queen, takes or attempts to take without authority given by or on behalf of Her Majesty, any sketch or plan of that fortress, arsenal, factory, dockyard, or camp; or

(*b*) where a person knowingly having possession of, or control over, any such document, sketch, plan, model, or knowledge as has been obtained or taken by means of any act which constitutes an offence against this Act at any time wilfully and without lawful authority communicates or attempts to communicate the same to any person to whom the same ought not, in the interest of the State, to be communicated at that time; or

(*c*) where a person after having been entrusted in confidence by some officer under Her Majesty the Queen with any document, sketch, plan, model, or information relating to any such place as aforesaid, or to the naval or military affairs of Her Majesty, wilfully and in breach of such confidence communicates the same when, in the interest of the State, it ought not to be communicated;

he shall be guilty of a misdemeanour, and on conviction be liable to imprisonment, with or without hard labour, for a term not exceeding one year, or to a fine, or to both imprisonment and a fine.

(2) Where a person having possession of any document, sketch, plan, model, or information relating to any fortress, arsenal, factory, dockyard, camp, ship, office, or other like place belonging to Her Majesty, or to the naval or military affairs of Her Majesty, in whatever manner the same has been obtained or taken, at any time wilfully communicates the same to any person to whom he knows the same ought not, in the interest of the State, to be communicated at that time, he shall be guilty of a misdemeanour, and be liable to the same punishment as if he committed an offence under the foregoing provisions of this section.

Where a person commits any act declared by this section to be a misdemeanour, he shall, if he intended to communicate to a foreign State any information, document, sketch, plan, model, or knowledge obtained or taken by him, or entrusted to him as aforesaid, or if he communicates the same to any agent of a foreign State, be guilty of felony, and on conviction be liable at the discretion of the court to penal servitude for life, or for any term not less than five years, or to imprisonment for any term not exceeding two years with or without hard labour.

Breach of official trust.

2. (*1*) Where a person, by means of his holding or having held an office under Her Majesty the Queen, has lawfully or unlawfully either obtained possession of or control over any document, sketch, plan, or model, or acquired any information, and at any time corruptly or contrary to his official duty communicates or attempts to communicate that document, sketch, plan, model, or information to any person to whom the same ought not, in the interest of the State, or otherwise in the public interest, to be communicated at that time, he shall be guilty of a breach of official trust.

(*2*) A person guilty of a breach of official trust shall—

(*a*) if the communication was made or attempted to be made to a foreign State, be guilty of felony, and on conviction be liable at the discretion of the court to penal servitude for life, or for any term not less than five years, or to imprisonment for any term not exceeding two years, with or without hard labour; and

(*b*) in any other case be guilty of a misdemeanour, and on conviction be liable to imprisonment, with or without hard labour, for a term not exceeding one year, or to a fine, or to both imprisonment and a fine.

(*3*) This section shall apply to a person holding a contract with any department of the Government of the United Kingdom, or with the holder of any office under Her Majesty the Queen as such holder, where such contract involves an obligation of secrecy, and to any person employed by any person or body of persons holding such a contract, who is under a like obligation of secrecy, as if the person holding the contract and the person so employed were respectively holders of an office under Her Majesty the Queen.

Punishment for incitement or counselling to commit offence.

3. Any person who incites or counsels, or attempts to procure, another person to commit an offence under this Act, shall be guilty of a misdemeanour, and on conviction be liable to the same punishment as if he had committed the offence.

Expenses of prosecution.

4. The expenses of the prosecution of a misdemeanour under this Act shall be defrayed in like manner as in the case of a felony.

Saving for laws of British possessions.

5. If by any law made before or after the passing of this Act by the legislature of any British possession[1] provisions are made which appear

[1] See the Indian Official Secrets Act, 1889 (XV of 1889). The English Statute has, however, not yet been suspended in British India. For Act XV of 1889, *see* Vol. V of the General Acts of the Governor General of India in Council, Ed. 1898, p. 353.

to Her Majesty the Queen to be of the like effect as those contained in this Act, Her Majesty may, by Order in Council, suspend the operation within such British possession of this Act, or of any part thereof, so long as such law continues in force there, and no longer, and such order shall have effect as if it were enacted in this Act:

Provided that the suspension of this Act, or of any part thereof, in any British possession shall not extend to the holder of an office under Her Majesty the Queen who is not appointed to that office by the Government of that possession.

The expression "British possession" means any part of Her Majesty's dominions not within the United Kingdom.

6. (*1*) This Act shall apply to all acts made offences by this Act when committed in any part of Her Majesty's dominions, or when committed by British officers or subjects elsewhere. Extent of Act and place of trial of offence.

(*2*) An offence under this Act, if alleged to have been committed out of the United Kingdom, may be inquired of, heard, and determined, in any competent British court in the place where the offence was committed, or in Her Majesty's High Court of Justice in England or the Central Criminal Court, and the Act of the forty-second year of the reign of King George the Third, chapter eighty-five, shall apply in like manner as if the offence were mentioned in that Act, and the Central Criminal Court as well as the High Court possessed the jurisdiction given by that Act to the Court of King's Bench.

(*3*) An offence under this Act shall not be tried by any court of general or quarter sessions, nor by the sheriff court in Scotland, nor by any court out of the United Kingdom which has not jurisdiction to try crimes which involve the greatest punishment allowed by law.

50 & 51 Vict. c. 20. (*4*) The provisions of the Criminal Law and Procedure (Ireland) Act, 1887, shall not apply to any trial under the provisions of this Act.

7. (*1*) A prosecution for an offence against this Act shall not be instituted except by or with the consent of the Attorney-General. Restriction on prosecution.

(*2*) In this section the expression "Attorney-General" means the Attorney or Solicitor General for England; and as respects Scotland, means the Lord Advocate; and as respects Ireland, means the Attorney or Solicitor General for Ireland; and if the prosecution is instituted in any court out of the United Kingdom, means the person who in that court is Attorney General, or exercises the like functions as the Attorney-General in England.

8. In this Act, unless the context otherwise requires— Interpretations.

Any reference to a place belonging to Her Majesty the Queen includes a place belonging to any department of the Government of the United Kingdom or of any of Her Majesty's possessions, whether the place is or is not actually vested in Her Majesty:

Expressions referring to communications include any communication, whether in whole or in part, and whether the document, sketch, plan, model, or information itself or the substance or effect thereof only be communicated:

The expression "document" includes part of a document:

The expression "model" includes design, pattern, and specimen:

The expression "sketch" includes any photograph or other mode of representation of any place or thing:

The expression "office under Her Majesty the Queen" includes any office or employment in or under any department of the Government of the United Kingdom, and so far as regards any document, sketch, plan, model, or information relating to the naval or military affairs of Her Majesty, includes any office or employment in or under any department of the Government of any of Her Majesty's possessions.

Saving. 9. This Act shall not exempt any person from any proceeding for an offence which is punishable at common law, or by military or naval law, or under any Act of Parliament other than this Act, so, however, that no person be punished twice for the same offence.

Short title. 10. This Act may be cited as the Official Secrets Act, 1889.

The Interpretation Act, 1889.[1]

(52 & 53 Vict., c. 63.)

An Act for consolidating enactments relating to the Construction of Acts of Parliament and for further shortening the Language used in Acts of Parliament.

[30th August, 1889.]

* * * * * * *

Re-enactment of existing Rules.

Rules as to gender and number. 1. (1) In this Act and in every Act passed after the year one thousand eight hundred and fifty, whether before or after the commencement of this Act, unless the contrary intention appears,—

(*a*) words importing the masculine gender shall include females; and

---

1 See *Chitty's Statutes*, Tit. Act of Parliament, p. 8.
Compare the General Clauses Act, 1897 (X of 1897). Printed General Acts, Vol. VI, Ed. 1898

(*b*) words in the singular shall include the plural, and words in the plural shall include the singular.

(2) The same rules shall be observed in the construction of every enactment relating to an offence punishable on indictment or on summary conviction, when the enactment is contained in an Act passed in or before the year one thousand eight hundred and fifty.

2. (1) In the construction of every enactment relating to an offence punishable on indictment or on summary conviction, whether contained in an Act passed before or after the commencement of this Act, the expression "person" shall, unless the contrary intention appears, include a body corporate. **Application of penal Acts to bodies corporate.**

(2) Where under any Act, whether passed before or after the commencement of this Act, any forfeiture or penalty is payable to a party aggrieved, it shall be payable to a body corporate in every case where that body is the party aggrieved.

3. In every Act passed after the year one thousand eight hundred and fifty, whether before or after the commencement of this Act, the following expressions shall, unless the contrary intention appears, have the meanings hereby respectively assigned to them, namely,— **Meanings of certain words in Acts since 1850.**

The expression "month" shall mean calendar month:

The expression "land" shall include messuages, tenements, and hereditaments, houses, and buildings of any tenure:

The expressions "oath" and "affidavit" shall, in the case of persons for the time being allowed by law to affirm or declare instead of swearing, include affirmation and declaration, and the expression "swear" shall, in the like case, include affirm and declare.

4. In every Act passed after the year one thousand eight hundred and fifty, and before the commencement of this Act, the expression "county" shall, unless the contrary intention appears, be construed as including a county of a city and a county of a town. **Meaning of "county" in past Acts.**

5. In every Act passed after the year one thousand eight hundred and sixty-six, whether before or after the commencement of this Act, the expression "parish" shall, unless the contrary intention appears, mean, as respects England and Wales, a place for which a separate poor rate is or can be made, or for which a separate overseer is or can be appointed. **Meaning of "parish."**

6. In this Act, and in every Act and Order of Council passed or made after the year one thousand eight hundred and forty-six, whether before or after the commencement of this Act, the expression "county court" shall, **Meaning of "county court."**

unless the contrary intention appears, mean as respects England and Wales a court under the County Courts Act, 1888.

Meaning of "sheriff clerk," etc., in Scotch Acts.

7. In every Act relating to Scotland, whether passed before or after the commencement of this Act, unless the contrary intention appears— 51 & 52 Vict., c. 43.

The expression, "sheriff clerk" shall include steward clerk;

The expressions "shire," "sheriffdom," and "county" shall include any stewartry in Scotland.

Sections to be substantive enactments.

8. Every section of an Act shall have effect as a substantive enactment without introductory words.

Acts to be public Acts.

9. Every Act passed after the year one thousand eight hundred and fifty, whether before or after the commencement of this Act, shall be a public Act and shall be judicially noticed as such, unless the contrary is expressly provided by the Act.

Amendment or repeal of Acts in same session.

10. Any Act may be altered, amended, or repealed in the same session of Parliament.

Effect of repeal in Acts passed since 1850.

11. (1) Where an Act passed after the year one thousand eight hundred and fifty, whether before or after the commencement of this Act, repeals a repealing enactment, it shall not be construed as reviving any enactment previously repealed, unless words are added reviving that enactment.

(2) Where an Act passed after the year one thousand eight hundred and fifty, whether before or after the commencement of this Act, repeals wholly or partially any former enactment and substitutes provisions for the enactment repealed, the repealed enactment shall remain in force until the substituted provisions come into operation.

New General Rules of Construction.

Official definitions in past and future Acts.

12. In this Act, and in every other Act whether passed before or after the commencement of this Act, the following expressions shall, unless the contrary intention appears, have the meanings hereby respectively assigned to them, namely :—

(1) The expression "the Lord Chancellor" shall, except when used with reference to Ireland only, mean the Lord High Chancellor of Great Britain for the time being, and when used with reference to Ireland only, shall mean the Lord Chancellor of Ireland for the time being.

(2) The expression "the Treasury" shall mean the Lord High Treasurer for the time being of the Commissioners for the time being of Her Majesty's Treasury.

(3) The expression "Secretary of State" shall mean one of Her Majesty's Principal Secretaries of State for the time being.

(4) The expression "the Admiralty" shall mean the Lord High Admiral of the United Kingdom for the time being, or the Commissioners for the time being for executing the office of Lord High Admiral of the United Kingdom.

(5) The expression "the Privy Council" shall, except when used with reference to Ireland only, mean the Lords and others for the time being of Her Majesty's Most Honourable Privy Council, and when used with reference to Ireland only, shall mean the Privy Council of Ireland for the time being.

(6) The expression "the Education Department" shall mean the Lords of the Committee for the time being of the Privy Council appointed for Education.

(7) The expression "the Scotch Education Department" shall mean the Lords of the Committee for the time being of the Privy Council appointed for Education in Scotland.

(8) The expression "the Board of Trade" shall mean the Lords of the Committee for the time being of the Privy Council appointed for the consideration of matters relating to trade and foreign plantations.

(9) The expression "Lord Lieutenant," when used with reference to Ireland, shall mean the Lord Lieutenant of Ireland or other Chief Governors or Governor of Ireland for the time being.

(10) The expression "Chief Secretary," when used with reference to Ireland, shall mean the Chief Secretary to the Lord Lieutenant for the time being.

(11) The expression "Postmaster General" shall mean Her Majesty's Postmaster General for the time being.

(12) The expression "Commissioners of Woods" or "Commissioners of Woods and Forests" shall mean the Commissioners of Her Majesty's Woods, Forests, and Land Revenues for the time being.

(13) The expression "Commissioners of Works" shall mean the Commissioners of Her Majesty's Works and Public Buildings for the time being.

(14) The expression "Charity Commissioners" shall mean the Charity Commissioners for England and Wales for the time being.

(15) The expression "Ecclesiastical Commissioners" shall mean the Ecclesiastical Commissioners for England for the time being.

(16) The expression "Queen Anne's Bounty" shall mean the Governors of the Bounty of Queen Anne for the augmentation of the maintenance of the poor clergy.

(17) The expression "National Debt Commissioners" shall mean the Commissioners for the time being for the Reduction of the National Debt.

(18) The expression "the Bank of England" shall mean, as circumstances require, the Governor and Company of the Bank of England or the bank of the Governor and Company of the Bank of England.

(19) The expression "the Bank of Ireland" shall mean, as circumstances require, the Governor and Company of the Bank of Ireland, or the bank of the Governor and Company of the Bank of Ireland.

(20) The expression "consular officer" shall include consul-general, consul, vice-consul, consular agent, and any person for the time authorised to discharge the duties of consul-general, consul, or vice-consul.

Judicial definitions in past and future Acts.

13. In this Act and in every other Act whether passed before or after the commencement of this Act, the following expressions shall, unless the contrary intention appears, have the meanings hereby respectively assigned to them, namely :—

(1) The expression "Supreme Court," when used with reference to England or Ireland, shall mean the Supreme Court of Judicature in England or Ireland, as the case may be, or either branch thereof.

(2) The expression "Court of Appeal," when used with reference to England or Ireland, shall mean Her Majesty's Court of Appeal in England or Ireland, as the case may be.

(3) The expression "High Court," when used with reference to England or Ireland, shall mean Her Majesty's High Court of Justice in England or Ireland, as the case may be.

(4) The expression "court of assize" shall, as respects England, Wales, and Ireland, mean a court of assize, a court of oyer and terminer, and a court of gaol delivery, or any of them, and shall, as respects England and Wales, include the Central Criminal Court.

(5) The expression "assizes," as respects England, Wales, and Ireland, shall mean the courts of assize usually held in every year, and shall include the sessions of the Central Criminal Court, but shall not include any court of assize held by virtue of any special commission, or, as respects Ireland, any court held by virtue of the powers conferred by section sixty-three of the Supreme Court of Judicature Act (Ireland), 1877.

(6) The expression "the Summary Jurisdiction Act, 1848," shall mean the Act of the session of the eleventh and twelfth years of the reign of Her present Majesty, chapter forty-three, intituled "An Act to facilitate the performance of the duties of justices of the peace out of sessions within England and Wales with respect to summary convictions and orders." 40 & 41 Vict., c. 57.

(7) The expression "the Summary Jurisdiction (England) Acts" and the expression "the Summary Jurisdiction English Acts," shall respectively

12 Vict., mean the Summary Jurisdiction Act, 1848, and the Summary Jurisdiction
43 Vict., Act, 1879, and any Act, past or future, amending those Acts or either of them.

28 Vict., (8) The expression "the Summary Jurisdiction (Scotland) Acts" shall
45 Vict., mean the Summary Jurisdiction (Scotland) Acts, 1864 and 1881, and any Act, past or future, amending those Acts or either of them.

(9) The expression "the Summary Jurisdiction (Ireland) Acts" shall mean, as respects the Dublin Metropolitan Police District, the Acts regulating the powers and duties of justices of the peace or of the police of that district, and as respects any other part of Ireland, the Petty Sessions (Ireland) Act,
15 Vict., 1851, and any Act, past or future, amending the same.

(10) The expression "the Summary Jurisdiction Acts" when used in relation to England or Wales shall mean the Summary Jurisdiction (England) Acts, and when used in relation to Scotland the Summary Jurisdiction (Scotland) Acts, and when used in relation to Ireland the Summary Jurisdiction (Ireland) Acts.

(11) The expression "court of summary jurisdiction" shall mean any justice or justices of the peace, or other magistrate, by whatever name called, to whom jurisdiction is given by, or who is authorised to act under, the Summary Jurisdiction Acts, whether in England, Wales, or Ireland, and whether acting under the Summary Jurisdiction Acts or any of them, or under any other Act, or by virtue of his commission, or under the common law.

(12) The expression "petty sessional court" shall, as respects England or Wales, mean a court of summary jurisdiction consisting of two or more justices when sitting in a petty sessional court-house, and shall include the Lord Mayor of the city of London, and any alderman of that city, and any metropolitan or borough police magistrate or other stipendiary magistrate when sitting in a court-house or place at which he is authorised by law to do alone any act authorised to be done by more than one justice of the peace.

(13) The expression "petty sessional court-house" shall, as respects England or Wales, mean a court-house or other place at which justices are accustomed to assemble for holding special or petty sessions, or which is for the time being appointed as a substitute for such a court-house or place, and where the justices are accustomed to assemble for either special or petty sessions at more than one court-house or place in a petty sessional division, shall mean any such court-house or place. The expression shall also include any court-house or place at which the Lord Mayor of the city of London or any alderman of that city, or any metropolitan or borough police magistrate or other stipendiary magistrate is authorised by law to do alone any act authorised to be done by more than one justice of the peace.

(14) The expression "court of quarter sessions" shall mean the justices of any county, riding, parts, division, or liberty of a county, or of any county of a city, or county of a town, in general or quarter sessions assembled, and shall include the court of the recorder of a municipal borough having a separate court of quarter sessions.

Meaning of "rules of court."

14. In every Act passed after the commencement of this Act, unless the contrary intention appears, the expression "rules of court" when used in relation to any court shall mean rules made by the authority having for the time being power to make rules or orders regulating the practice and procedure of such court, and as regards Scotland shall include acts of adjournal and acts of sederunt.

The power of the said authority to make rules of court as above defined shall include a power to make rules of court for the purpose of any Act passed after the commencement of this Act, and directing or authorising anything to be done by rules of court.

Meaning of borough.

15. In this Act and in every Act passed after the commencement of this Act the following expressions shall, unless the contrary intention appears, have the meanings hereby respectively assigned to them, namely:—

(1) The expression "municipal borough" shall mean, as respects England and Wales, any place for the time bieng subject to the Municipal Corporations Act, 1882, and any reference to the mayor, aldermen and burgesses of a borough shall include a reference to the mayor, aldermen and citizens of a city, and any reference to the powers, duties, liabilities or property of the council of a borough shall be construed as a reference to the powers, duties, liabilities, or property of the mayor, aldermen, and burgesses of the borough acting by the council. 45 & 46 Vict. c. 50.

(2) The expression "municipal borough" shall mean, as respects Ireland, any place for the time being subject to the Act of the session of the third and fourth years of the reign of Her present Majesty, chapter one hundred and eight, intituled "An Act for the regulation of municipal corporations in Ireland."

(3) The expression "parliamentary borough" shall mean any borough, burgh, place or combination of places returning a member or members to serve in Parliament, and not being either a county or division of a county, or a university, or a combination of universities.

(4) The expression "borough" when used in relation to local government shall mean a municipal borough as above defined, and when used in relation to parliamentary elections or the registration of parliamentary electors shall mean a parliamentary borough as above defined.

Meaning of guardians and union.

16. In this Act, and in every Act passed after the commencement of this Act, the following expressions shall, unless the contrary intention appears, have the meanings hereby respectively assigned to them, namely:—

; 5 Will. 4, '6.

(1) The expression "board of guardians" shall, as respects England and Wales, mean a board of guardians elected under the Poor Law Amendment Act, 1834, and the Acts amending the same, and shall include a board of guardians or other body of persons performing under any local Act the like functions to a board of guardians under the Poor Law Amendment Act, 1834.

(2) The expression "poor law union" shall, as respects England and Wales, mean any parish or union of parishes for which there is a separate board of guardians.

(3) The expression "board of guardians" shall, as respects Ireland, mean a board of guardians elected under the Act of the session of the first and second years of the reign of Her present Majesty, chapter fifty-six, intituled "An Act for the more effectual relief o the destitute poor in Ireland", and the Acts amending the same, and shall include any body of persons appointed by the Local Government Board for Ireland to carry into execution the provisions of those Acts.

(4) The expression "poor law union" shall, as respects Ireland, mean any townland or place or union, or townlands or places, for which there is a separate board of guardians.

Definitions relating to elections.

17. In every Act passed after the commencement of this Act the following expressions shall, unless the contrary intention appears, have the meanings hereby respectively assigned to them, namely:—

(1) The expression "parliamentary election" shall mean the election of a member or members to serve in Parliament for a county or division of a county, or parliamentary borough or division of a parliamentary borough, or for a university or combination of universities.

(2) The expression "parliamentary register of electors" shall mean a register of persons entitled to vote at any parliamentary election.

(3) The expression "local government register of electors" shall mean, as respects an administrative county in England or Wales other than a county borough, the county register, and as respects a county borough or other municipal borough, the burgess roll.

Geographical and colonial definitions in future Acts.

18. In this Act, and in every Act passed after the commencement of this Act, the following expressions shall, unless the contrary intention appears, have the meanings hereby respectively assigned to them, namely:—

(1) The expression "British Islands" shall mean the United Kingdom, the Channel Islands, and the Isle of Man.

(2) The expression "British possession" shall mean any part of Her Majesty's dominions, exclusive of the United Kingdom, and where parts of such dominions are under both a central and a local legislature, all parts under the central legislature shall, for the purposes of this definition, be deemed to be one British possession.

(3) The expression "colony" shall mean any part of Her Majesty's dominions, exclusive of the British Islands and of British India, and where parts of such dominions are under both a central and a local legislature, all parts under the central legislature shall, for the purposes of this definition, be deemed to be one colony.

(4) The expression "British India" shall mean all territories and places within Her Majesty's dominions which are for the time being governed by Her Majesty through the Governor General of India, or through any governor or other officer subordinate to the Governor General of India.

(5) The expression "India" shall mean British India, together with any territories of any native prince or chief under the suzerainty of Her Majesty exercised through the Governor General of India, or through any governor or other officer subordinate to the Governor General of India.

(6) The expression "Governor" shall, as respects Canada and India, mean the Governor General, and include any person who for the time being has the powers of the Governor General, and as respects any other British possession, shall include the officer for the time being administering the government of that possession.

(7) The expression "colonial legislature" and the expression "legislature," when used with reference to a British possession, shall respectively mean the authority other than the Imperial Parliament or Her Majesty the Queen in Council, competent to make laws for a British possession.

Meaning of "person" in future Acts.

19. In this Act, and in every Act passed after the commencement of this Act, the expression "person" shall, unless the contrary intention appears, include any body of persons corporate or unincorporate.

Meaning of "writing" in past and future Acts.

20. In this Act, and in every other Act whether passed before or after the commencement of this Act, expressions referring to writing shall, unless the contrary intention appears, be construed as including references to printing, lithography, photography, and other modes of representing or reproducing words in a visible form.

Meaning of "statutory declaration" in past and future Acts.

21. In this Act, and in every other Act whether passed before or after the commencement of this Act, the expression "statutory declaration" shall, unless the contrary intention appears, mean a declaration made by virtue of the Statutory Declarations Act, 1835.[1] 5 & 6 Will. 4 c. 62.

[1] 5 & 6 Will. 4, c. 62, printed, Vol. I, p. 187.

Meaning of "financial year" in future Acts.

22. In this Act, and in every Act passed after the commencement of this Act, the expression "financial year" shall, unless the contrary intention appears, mean as respects any matters relating to the Consolidated Fund or moneys provided by Parliament, or to the Exchequer, or to Imperial taxes or finance, the twelve months ending the thirty-first day of March.

Definition of Lands Clauses Acts.

23. In any Act passed after the commencement of this Act unless the contrary intention appears,—

The expression "Lands Clauses Acts" shall mean—

9 Vict., 18. & 24 Vict., 06. & 32 Vict., 18. & 47 Vict., 5.

(*a*) as respects England and Wales, the Lands Clauses Consolidation Act, 1845, the Lands Clauses Consolidation Acts Amendment Act, 1860, the Lands Clauses Consolidation Act, 1869, and the Lands Clauses (Umpire) Act, 1883, and any Acts for the time being in force amending the same; and

9 Vict., 19. & 24 Vict., 06.

(*b*) as respects Scotland, the Lands Clauses Consolidation (Scotland) Act, 1845, and the Lands Clauses Consolidation Acts Amendment Act, 1860, and any Acts for the time being in force amending the same; and

9 Vict., 18. & 24 Vict., 7. & 15 Vict., 0. & 28 Vict., 1. & 33 Vict., 0.

(*c*) as respects Ireland, the Lands Clauses Consolidation Act, 1845, the Lands Clauses Consolidation Acts Amendment Act, 1860, the Railways Act (Ireland), 1851, the Railways Act (Ireland), 1860, the Railways Act (Ireland), 1864, and the Railways Traverse Act, and any Acts for the time being in force amending the same.

Meaning of Irish Valuation Acts.

24. In any Act passed before or after the commencement of this Act, the expression "Irish Valuation Acts" shall mean the Acts relating to the valuation of rateable property in Ireland.

Meaning of "ordnance map."

25. In this Act, and in every other Act whether passed before or after the commencement of this Act, the expression "ordnance map" shall, unless the contrary intention appears, mean a map made under the powers conferred by the Survey (Great Britain) Acts, 1841 to 1870, or by the Survey (Ireland) Acts, 1825 to 1870, and the Acts amending the same respectively.

Meaning of service by post.

26. Where an Act passed after the commencement of this Act authorises or requires any document to be served by post, whether the expression "serve" or the expression "give" or "send", or any other expression is used, then, unless the contrary intention appears, the service shall be deemed to be effected by properly addressing, prepaying, and posting a letter containing the document, and unless the contrary is proved to have been effected at the time at which the letter would be delivered in the ordinary course of post.

Meaning of "committed for trial."

27. In every Act passed after the commencement of this Act, the expression "committed for trial" used in relation to any person shall, unless the contrary intention appears, mean, as respects England and Wales, committed to prison with the view of being tried before a judge and jury, whether the person is committed in pursuance of section twenty-two or of section twenty-five of the Indictable Offences Act, 1848, or is committed by a court, judge, coroner or other authority having power to commit a person to any prison with a view to his trial, and shall include a person who is admitted to bail upon a recognizance to appear and take his trial before a judge and jury.

11 & 12 Vict. c. 42.

Meanings of "sheriff," "felony," and "misdemeanour" in future Scotch Acts.

28. In this Act, and in every Act passed after the commencement of this Act, unless the contrary intention appears—

The expression "sheriff" shall, as respects Scotland, include a sheriff substitute:

The expression "felony" shall, as respects Scotland, mean a high crime and offence:

The expression "misdemeanour" shall, as respects Scotland, mean an offence.

Meaning of "county court" in future Irish Acts.

29. In every Act passed after the commencement of this Act, unless the contrary intention appears, the expression "county court" shall, as respects Ireland, mean a civil bill court within the meaning of the County Officers and Courts (Ireland) Act, 1877.

40 & 41 Vict. c. 56.

References to the Crown.

30. In this Act, and in every other Act, whether passed before or after the commencement of this Act, references to the Sovereign reigning at the time of the passing of the Act or to the Crown shall, unless the contrary intention appears, be construed as references to the Sovereign for the time being, and this Act shall be binding on the Crown.

Construction of statutory rules, etc.

31. Where any Act, whether passed before or after the commencement of this Act, confers power to make, grant, or issue any instrument, that is to say, any Order in Council, order, warrant, scheme, letters patent, rules, regulations, or byelaws, expressions used in the instrument, if it is made after the commencement of this Act, shall, unless the contrary intention appears, have the same respective meanings as in the Act conferring the power.

Construction of provisions as to exercise of powers and duties.

32. (1) Where an Act passed after the commencement of this Act confers a power or imposes a duty, then, unless the contrary intention appears, the power may be exercised and the duty shall be performed from time to time as occasion requires.

(2) Where an Act passed after the commencement of this Act confers a power or imposes a duty on the holder of an office, as such, then, unless the contrary intention appears, the power may be exercised and the duty shall be performed by the holder for the time being of the office.

(3) Where an Act passed after the commencement of this Act confers a power to make any rules, regulations, or byelaws, the power shall, unless the contrary intention appears, be construed as including a power, exerciseable in the like manner and subject to the like consent and conditions, if any, to rescind, revoke, amend, or vary the rules, regulations, or byelaws.

33. Where an act or omission constitutes an offence under two or more Acts, or both under an Act and at common law, whether any such Act was passed before or after the commencement of this Act, the offender shall, unless the contrary intention appears, be liable to be prosecuted and punished under either or any of those Acts or at common law, but shall not be liable to be punished twice for the same offence. **Provisions as to offences under two or more laws.**

34. In the measurement of any distance for the purposes of any Act passed after the commencement of this Act, that distance shall, unless the contrary intention appears, be measured in a straight line on a horizontal plane. **Measurement of distances.**

35. (1) In any Act, instrument, or document, an Act may be cited by reference to the short title, if any, of the Act, either with or without a reference to the chapter, or by reference to the regnal year in which the Act was passed, and where there are more statutes or sessions than one in the same regnal year, by reference to the statute or the session, as the case may require, and where there are more chapters than one, by reference to the chapter, and any enactment may be cited by reference to the section or sub-section of the Act in which the enactment is contained. **Citation of Acts.**

(2) Where any Act passed after the commencement of this Act contains such reference as aforesaid, the reference shall, unless a contrary intention appears, be read as referring, in the case of statutes included in any revised edition of the statutes purporting to be printed by authority, to that edition, and in the case of statutes not so included, and passed before the reign of King George the First, to the edition prepared under the direction of the Record Commission; and in other cases to the copies of the statutes purporting to be printed by the Queen's Printer, or under the superintendence or authority of Her Majesty's Stationery Office.

(3) In any Act passed after the commencement of this Act a description or citation of a portion of another Act shall, unless the contrary intention appears, be construed as including the word, section, or other part mentioned or referred to as forming the beginning and as forming the end of the portion comprised in the description or citation.

36. (1) In this Act, and in every Act passed either before or after the commencement of this Act, the expression "commencement," when used with reference to an Act, shall mean the time at which the Act comes into operation. **"Commencement."**

(2) Where an Act passed after the commencement of this Act, or any Order in Council, order, warrant, scheme, letters patent, rules, regulations, or bye-laws made, granted, or issued, under a power conferred by any such Act, is expressed to come into operation on a particular day, the same shall be construed as coming into operation immediately on the expiration of the previous day.

Exercise of statutory powers between passing and commencement of Act.

37. Where an Act passed after the commencement of this Act is not to come into operation immediately on the passing thereof, and confers power to make any appointment, to make, grant, or issue any instrument, that is to say, any Order in Council, order, warrant, scheme, letters patent, rules, regulations, or byelaws, to give notices, to prescribe forms, or to do any other thing for the purposes of the Act, that power may, unless the contrary intention appears, be exercised at any time after the passing of the Act, so far as may be necessary or expedient for the purpose of bringing the Act into operation at the date of the commencement thereof, subject to this restriction, that any instrument made under the power shall not, unless the contrary intention appears in the Act, or the contrary is necessary for bringing the Act into operation, come into operation until the Act comes into operation.

Effect of repeal in future Acts.

38. (1) Where this Act or any Act passed after the commencement of this Act repeals and re-enacts, with or without modification, any provisions of a former Act, references in any other Act to the provisions so repealed, shall, unless the contrary intention appears, be construed as references to the provisions so re-enacted.

(2) Where this Act or any Act passed after the commencement of this Act repeals any other enactment, then, unless the contrary intention appears, the repeal shall not—

(*a*) revive anything not in force or existing at the time at which the repeal takes effect; or

(*b*) affect the previous operation of any enactment so repealed or anything duly done or suffered under any enactment so repealed; or

(*c*) affect any right, privilege, obligation, or liability acquired, accrued, or incurred under any enactment so repealed; or

(*d*) affect any penalty, forfeiture, or punishment incurred in respect of any offence committed against any enactment so repealed; or

(*e*) affect any investigation, legal proceeding, or remedy in respect of any such right, privilege, obligation, liability, penalty, forfeiture or punishment as aforesaid,

and any such investigation, legal proceeding, or remedy may be instituted, continued, or enforced, and any such penalty, forfeiture, or punishment may be imposed, as if the repealing Act had not been passed.

Supplemental.

39. In this Act the expression "Act" shall include a local and personal Act and a private Act. Definition of "Act" in this Act.

40. The provisions of this Act respecting the construction of Acts passed after the commencement of this Act shall not affect the construction of any Act passed before the commencement of this Act, although it is continued or amended by an Act passed after such commencement. Saving for past Acts.

41. The Acts described in the Schedule to this Act are hereby repealed to the extent appearing in the third column of the Schedule. Repeal.

42. This Act shall come into operation on the first day of January one thousand eight hundred and ninety. Commencement of Act.

43. This Act may be cited as the Interpretation Act, 1889. Short title.

SCHEDULE.

ENACTMENTS REPEALED.

Session and Chapter.	Title or Short Title.	Extent of Repeal.
7 & 8 Geo. 4, c. 28	An Act for further improving the administration of justice in criminal cases in England.	Section fourteen.
9 Geo. 4, c. 54	An Act for improving the administration of justice in criminal cases in Ireland.	Section thirty-five.
7 Will. 4, & 1 Vict., c. 39.	An Act to interpret the words "sheriff," "sheriff clerk," "shire," sheriffdom," and "county," occurring in Acts of Parliament relating to Scotland.	The whole Act.
13 & 14 Vict., c. 21	An Act for shortening the language used in Acts of Parliament.	The whole Act.
29 & 30 Vict., c. 113	The Poor Law Amendment Act of 1866.	Section eighteen, from the beginning to "can be appointed, and".
42 & 43 Vict., c. 49	The Summary Jurisdiction Act, 1879	In section twenty the sub-sections numbered (3) and (6). Section fifty.
47 & 48 Vict., c. 43	The Summary Jurisdiction Act, 1884	Section seven.
51 & 52 Vict., c. 43	The County Courts Act, 1888	Section one hundred and eighty-seven, from the beginning to "is meant, and".

The Council of India Reduction Act, 1889.[1]

(52 & 53 Vict., c. 65.)

An Act to amend the Law as to the Council of India.

[*30th August, 1889.*]

* * * * * *

Power to reduce number of Council.

1. The Secretary of State may, if and whenever he thinks fit, and provided that the total number of the Council be not thereby reduced below ten, record his intention to abstain from filling any vacancy in the Council of India, and such vacancy shall thenceforward remain unfilled.

Short title.

2. This Act may be cited as the Council of India Reduction Act, 1889.

The South Indian Railway Purchase Act, 1890.

(53 & 54 Vict., c. 6.)

An Act to empower the Secretary of State in Council of India to raise Money in the United Kingdom for the Purchase of the South Indian Railway, and for other purposes relating thereto.

[*2nd May, 1890.*]

Whereas the Secretary of State in Council, by virtue of the power vested in him under the contract between him and the Company, gave notice on the third day of March, one thousand eight hundred and ninety, to the South Indian Railway Company, of his intention to purchase the undertaking of the Company:

And whereas, in consequence of such notice, the Secretary of State in Council has become liable to pay to the Company in London, on the thirty-first day of December, one thousand eight hundred and ninety, the amount of four million one hundred and ninety-seven thousand five hundred and fifty-six pounds eleven shillings and twopence for the said purchase, and has also become liable to pay the sum of one million and seventy thousand pounds borrowed by the Company on the debentures specified in the schedule to this Act annexed, as and when the same respectively shall become redeemable.

And whereas it is expedient that the Secretary of State in Council should be empowered to raise money in manner in this Act mentioned for the purchase on behalf of Her Majesty for the purposes of the Government of India of the undertaking of the said Company, and for the redemption and discharge of the

---

[1] For digest, see Ilbert's *Government of India*, p. 325.

said debentures as and when the same respectively shall fall due and become redeemable:

* * * * * *

1. This Act may be cited as the South Indian Railway Purchase Act, 1890. **Short title.**

2. In this Act the expression "Secretary of State" means the Secretary of State in Council of India, unless the context otherwise requires. **Definition.**

3. It shall be lawful for the Secretary of State at any time or times after the passing of this Act to raise in the United Kingdom, for the purchase of the railways, works, stations, telegraphs, engines, carriages, stock, plant, and machinery, belonging to or forming the undertaking of the South Indian Railway Company, and as and when necessary for the discharge and redemption of debentures issued by the Company, any sum or sums of money not exceeding in the whole the sum of five million two hundred and sixty-seven thousand five hundred and fifty-six pounds eleven shillings and twopence. **Power to raise 5,267,556*l.* 11*s.* 2*d.* for purchase of South Indian Railway.**

4. All moneys raised under the authority of this Act shall be raised either by the creation and issue of bonds, debentures, or capital stock bearing interest, or partly by one of such modes and partly by another or others. **Mode of raising moneys.**

5. All bonds and debentures issued under this Act, and the principal moneys and interest thereby secured, and all capital stock issued under this Act, and the interest thereon, shall be charged on and payable out of the revenues of India, in like manner as other liabilities incurred on account of the Government of India. **Securities, etc., to be charged on revenues of India.**

6. The whole amount of principal moneys to be charged on the revenues of India under this Act shall not exceed the amount required to be charged for the purchase of the South Indian Railway, and for the discharge of the debentures mentioned in the schedule to this Act annexed. **Limit of charge on revenues of India.**

7. Upon or for the repayment of any principal moneys secured under the authority of this Act, the Secretary of State may at any time borrow or raise, by all or any of the modes aforesaid, all or any part of the amount of principal money repaid or to be repaid, and so from time to time as all or any part of any principal moneys under this Act may require to be repaid, but the whole amount to be charged on the revenues of India shall not in any case exceed the principal moneys required to be repaid. **Power to re-borrow.**

8. All bonds issued under the authority of this Act may be issued under the hands of two members of the Council of India, and countersigned by the Secretary of State for India or one of his under secretaries, or his assistant under secretary, and shall be for such respective amounts, payable after such notice, and at such rate or rates of interest, as the Secretary of State may think fit. **As to issue of bonds.**

9. All debentures issued under the authority of this Act may be issued under the hands of two members of the Council of India, and countersigned as **As to issue of debentures.**

aforesaid for such respective amounts, and at such rate or rates of interest, as the Secretary of State may think fit, and shall be issued at or for such prices and on such terms as may be determined by the Secretary of State.

As to payment of principal and interest on debentures.

10. All debentures issued under the authority of this Act shall be paid off at par at a time or times to be mentioned in such debentures respectively; and the interest on all such debentures shall be paid on such days as shall be mentioned therein; and the principal moneys and interest secured by such debentures shall be payable either at the treasury of the Secretary of State in London or at the Bank of England.

Mode of transfer of debentures.

11. Debentures issued under the authority of this Act, and all right to and in respect of the principal and interest moneys secured thereby, shall be transferable by the delivery of such debentures, or at the discretion of the Secretary of State, by deed: provided that the coupons for interest annexed to any debenture issued under the authority of this Act shall pass by delivery.

Capital stock.

12. Any capital stock created under the authority of this Act shall bear such rate of interest as the Secretary of State may think fit; and such capital stock may be issued on such terms as may be determined by the Secretary of State; and any such capital stock may bear interest during such period, and be paid off at par at such time, as the Secretary of State may prescribe previously to the issue of such capital stock.

Transfer books of capital stock.

13. In case of the creation and issue of any such capital stock, there shall be kept, either at the office of the Secretary of State in London, or at the Bank of England, books wherein entries shall be made of the said capital stock, and wherein all assignments or transfers of the same, or any part thereof, shall be entered and registered, and shall be signed by the parties making such assignments or transfers, or, if such parties be absent, by his, her, or their attorney or attorneys thereunto lawfully authorised by writing under his, her, or their hands and seals, to be attested by two or more credible witnesses; and the person or persons to whom such transfer or transfers shall be made may respectively underwrite his, her, or their acceptance thereof; and no other mode of assigning or transferring the said capital stock or any part thereof, or any interest therein, shall be good and available in law, and no stamp duties whatsoever shall be charged on the said transfers or any of them.

5 & 6 Will. 4, c. 64, s. 4, extended to bonds and debentures under Act.

14. The provisions contained in section four of the Act of the session holden in the fifth and sixth years of King William the Fourth, chapter sixty-four, with respect to the composition and agreement for the payment by the East India Company of an annual sum in lieu of stamp duties on their bonds, and the exemption of their bonds from stamp duties, shall be applicable with respect to the bonds and debentures to be issued under the authority of this Act, as if such provisions were here repeated and re-enacted with reference thereto.

15. All provisions now in force in anywise relating to the offence of forging or altering, or offering, uttering, disposing of, or putting off, knowing the same to be forged or altered, any East India bond, with intent to defraud, shall extend and be applicable to and in respect of any bond or debenture issued under the authority of this Act. Punishment of forgery of bonds and debentures.

16. This Act shall not prejudice or affect any power of raising or borrowing money vested in the said Secretary of State at the time of passing thereof. Saving existing borrowing powers.

17. Any capital stock created under this Act shall be deemed to be and shall mean India stock within the Act of the twenty-sixth and twenty-seventh Victoria, chapter seventy-three, anything in the said last-mentioned Act to the contrary notwithstanding. Extension of 26 & 27 Vict., c. 73, to capital stock under Act.

18. The amount of all moneys raised under this Act and the manner in which the same shall have been applied shall be shown in the half-yearly returns of all loans raised in England to be prepared by the Secretary of State, and presented to both Houses of Parliament under the provisions of section fifteen of the Act forty-two and forty-three Victoria, chapter sixty.[1] Amount, etc., of moneys raised under Act to be shown in Parliamentary return.

SCHEDULE.

Debenture of the South Indian Railway Company.

Amounts.	Dates of Redemption.	Rates of Interest per Annum.
£		
86,100	1 July, 1891	3½ per cent.
150,000	1 July, 1892	" "
520,200	1 July, 1893	" "
313,700	1 July, 1896	3¼ "
1,070,000		

The Commissioners for Oaths Amendment Act, 1890.

(53 & 54 Vict., c. 7.)

An Act to amend the Commissioners for Oaths Act, 1889.

[*22nd May, 1890.*]

* * * * * * *

1. An affidavit to be used in a county court may be sworn before any Commissioner to administer oaths in the Court of Chancery of the county palatine of Lancaster not being a registrar of a county court. Swearing of affidavit.

[1] The East India Loan Act, 1879 (42 & 43 Vict., c. 60), printed *ante*, p. 580.

Short title. 2. This Act may be cited as the Commissioners for Oaths Amendment Act, 1890.

THE COLONIAL COURTS OF ADMIRALTY ACT, 1890.[1]

(53 & 54 Vict., c. 27.)

An Act to amend the Law respecting the exercise of Admiralty Jurisdiction in Her Majesty's Dominions and elsewhere out of the United Kingdom.

[25th July, 1890.]

* * * * * * *

Short title. 1. This Act may be cited as the Colonial Courts of Admiralty Act, 1890.

Colonial Courts of Admiralty. 2. (1) Every court of law in a British possession, which is for the time being declared in pursuance of this Act to be a court of Admiralty, or which, if no such declaration is in force in the possession, has therein original unlimited civil jurisdiction, shall be a court of Admiralty, with the jurisdiction in this Act mentioned, and may for the purpose of that jurisdiction exercise all the powers which it possesses for the purpose of its other civil jurisdiction, and such court in reference to the jurisdiction conferred by this Act is in this Act referred to as a Colonial Court of Admiralty. Where in a British possession the Governor is the sole judicial authority, the expression "court of law" for the purposes of this section includes such Governor.

(2) The jurisdiction of a Colonial Court of Admiralty shall, subject to the provisions of this Act, be over the like places, persons, matters, and things, as the Admiralty jurisdiction of the High Court in England, whether existing by virtue of any statute or otherwise, and the Colonial Court of Admiralty may exercise such jurisdiction in like manner and to as full an extent as the High Court in England, and shall have the same regard as that Court to international law and the comity of nations.

(3) Subject to the provisions of this Act any enactment referring to a Vice-Admiralty Court, which is contained in an Act of the Imperial Parliament or in a Colonial law, shall apply to a Colonial Court of Admiralty, and be read as if the expression "Colonial Court of Admiralty" were therein substituted for "Vice-Admiralty Court" or for other expressions respectively referring to such Vice-Admiralty Courts or the judge thereof, and the Colonial Court of Admiralty shall have jurisdiction accordingly:

---

[1] See *Chitty's Statutes*, Tit. Admiralty, p. 33.

Provided as follows:—

(*a*) Any enactment in an Act of the Imperial Parliament referring to the Admiralty jurisdiction of the High Court in England, when applied to a Colonial Court of Admiralty in a British possession, shall be read as if the name of that possession were therein substituted for England and Wales; and

[27] & 28 Vict., [c.] 25. [36] & 37 Vict., [c.] 88.

(*b*) A Colonial Court of Admiralty shall have under the Naval Prize Act,[1] 1864, and under the Slave Trade Act, 1873,[2] and any enactment relating to prize or the slave trade, the jurisdiction thereby conferred on a Vice-Admiralty Court and not the jurisdiction thereby conferred exclusively on the High Court of Admiralty or the High Court of Justice; but, unless for the time being duly authorised, shall not by virtue of this Act exercise any jurisdiction under the Naval Prize Act, 1864,[1] or otherwise in relation to prize; and

(*c*) A Colonial Court of Admiralty shall not have jurisdiction under this Act to try or punish a person for an offence which according to the law of England is punishable on indictment; and

(*d*) A Colonial Court of Admiralty shall not have any greater jurisdiction in relation to the laws and regulations relating to Her Majesty's Navy at sea, or under any Act providing for the discipline of Her Majesty's Navy, than may be from time to time conferred on such court by Order in Council.

(4) Where a Court in a British possession exercises in respect of matters arising outside the body of a county or other like part of a British possession any jurisdiction exerciseable under this Act, that jurisdiction shall be deemed to be exercised under this Act and not otherwise.

Power of Colonial legislature as to Admiralty jurisdiction.

3. The legislature of a British possession may by any Colonial law—

(*a*) declare any court of unlimited civil jurisdiction, whether original or appellate, in that possession to be a Colonial Court of Admiralty, and provide for the exercise by such court of its jurisdiction under this Act, and limit territorially, or otherwise, the extent of such jurisdiction; and

(*b*) confer upon any inferior or subordinate court in that possession such partial or limited Admiralty jurisdiction under such regulations and with such appeal (if any) as may seem fit:

Provided that any such Colonial law shall not confer any jurisdiction which is not by this Act conferred upon a Colonial Court of Admiralty.

Reservation of Colonial law for Her Majesty's assent.

4. Every Colonial law which is made in pursuance of this Act, or affects the jurisdiction of or practice or procedure in any court of such possession in

---

[1] 27 & 28 Vict., c. 25, printed Vol. I, p. 879.

[2] 36 & 37 Vict. c. 88, printed *ante*, p. 540.

respect of the jurisdiction conferred by this Act, or alters any such Colonial law as above in this section mentioned, which has been previously passed, shall, unless previously approved by Her Majesty through a Secretary of State, either be reserved for the signification of Her Majesty's pleasure thereon, or contain a suspending clause providing that such law shall not come into operation until Her Majesty's pleasure thereon has been publicly signified in the British possession in which it has been passed.

Local Admiralty appeal.

5. Subject to rules of court under this Act, judgments of a court in a British possession given or made in the exercise of the jurisdiction conferred on it by this Act, shall be subject to the like local appeal, if any, as judgments of the court in the exercise of its ordinary civil jurisdiction, and the court having cognizance of such appeal shall for the purpose thereof possess all the jurisdiction by this Act conferred upon a Colonial Court of Admiralty.

Admiralty appeal to the Queen in Council.

6. (1) The appeal from a judgment of any court in a British possession in the exercise of the jurisdiction conferred by this Act, either where there is as of right no local appeal or after a decision on local appeal, lies to Her Majesty the Queen in Council.

(2) Save as may be otherwise specially allowed in a particular case by Her Majesty the Queen in Council, an appeal under this section shall not be allowed—

(*a*) from any judgment not having the effect of a definitive judgment unless the court appealed from has given leave for such appeal, nor

(*b*) from any judgment unless the petition of appeal has been lodged within the time prescribed by rules, or if no time is prescribed within six months from the date of the judgment appealed against, or if leave to appeal has been given then from the date of such leave.

(3) For the purpose of appeals under this Act, Her Majesty the Queen in Council and the Judicial Committee of the Privy Council shall, subject to rules under this section, have all such powers for making and enforcing judgments, whether interlocutory or final, for punishing contempts, for requiring the payment of money into court, or for any other purpose, as may be necessary, or as were possessed by the High Court of Delegates before the passing of the Act transferring the powers of such court to Her Majesty in Council, or as are for the time being possessed by the High Court in England or by the court appealed from in relation to the like matters as those forming the subject of appeals under this Act.

(4) All Orders of the Queen in Council or the Judicial Committee of the Privy Council for the purposes aforesaid or otherwise in relation to appeals

under this Act shall have full effect throughout Her Majesty's dominions and in all places where Her Majesty has jurisdiction.

(5) This section shall be in addition to and not in derogation of the authority of Her Majesty in Council or the Judicial Committee of the Privy Council arising otherwise than under this Act, and all enactments relating to appeals to Her Majesty in Council or to the powers of Her Majesty in Council or the Judicial Committee of the Privy Council in relation to those appeals, whether for making rules and orders or otherwise, shall extend, save as otherwise directed by Her Majesty in Council, to appeals to Her Majesty in Council under this Act.

Rules of court.

7. (1) Rules of court for regulating the procedure and practice (including fees and costs) in a court in a British possession in the exercise of the jurisdiction conferred by this Act, whether original or appellate, may be made by the same authority and in the same manner as rules touching the practice, procedure, fees, and costs in the said court in the exercise of its ordinary civil jurisdiction respectively are made:

Provided that the rules under this section shall not, save as provided by this Act, extend to matters relating to the slave trade, and shall not (save as provided by this section) come into operation until they have been approved by Her Majesty in Council, but on coming into operation shall have full effect as if enacted in this Act, and any enactment inconsistent therewith shall, so far as it is so inconsistent, be repealed.

(2) It shall be lawful for Her Majesty in Council, in approving rules made under this section, to declare that the rules so made with respect to any matters which appear to Her Majesty to be matters of detail or of local concern may be revoked, varied, or added to without the approval required by this section.

(3) Such rules may provide for the exercise of any jurisdiction conferred by this Act by the full court, or by any judge or judges thereof, and subject to any rules, where the ordinary civil jurisdiction of the court can in any case be exercised by a single judge, any jurisdiction conferred by this Act may in the like case be exercised by a single judge.

Droits of Admiralty and of the Crown.

8. (1) Subject to the provisions of this section nothing in this Act shall alter the application of any droits of Admiralty or droits of or forfeitures to the Crown in a British possession; and such droits and forfeitures, when condemned by a court of a British possession in the exercise of the jurisdiction conferred by this Act, shall, save as is otherwise provided by any other Act, be notified, accounted for, and dealt with in such manner as the Treasury from time to time direct, and the officers of every Colonial Court of Admiralty and of every other court in a British possession exercising Admiralty jurisdiction shall obey such directions in respect of the said droits and forfeitures as may be from time to time given by the Treasury.

(2) It shall be lawful for Her Majesty the Queen in Council by Order to direct that, subject to any conditions, exceptions, reservations, and regulations contained in the Order, the said droits and forfeitures condemned by a court in a British possession shall form part of the revenues of that possession either for ever or for such limited term or subject to such revocation as may be specified in the Order.

(3) If and so long as any of such droits or forfeitures by virtue of this or any other Act form part of the revenues of the said possession the same shall, subject to the provisions of any law for the time being applicable thereto, be notified, accounted for, and dealt with in manner directed by the Government of the possession, and the Treasury shall not have any power in relation thereto.

Power to establish Vice-Admiralty Court.

9. (1) It shall be lawful for Her Majesty, by commission under the Great Seal, to empower the Admiralty to establish in a British possession any Vice-Admiralty Court or Courts.

(2) Upon the establishment of a Vice-Admiralty Court in a British possession, the Admiralty, by writing under their hands and the seal of the office of Admiralty, in such form as the Admiralty direct, may appoint a judge, registrar, marshal, and other officers of the court, and may cancel any such appointment; and in addition to any other jurisdiction of such court, may (subject to the limits imposed by this Act or the said commission from Her Majesty) vest in such court the whole or any part of the jurisdiction by or by virtue of this Act conferred upon any Courts of that British possession, and may vary or revoke such vesting, and while such vesting is in force the power of such last-mentioned courts to exercise the jurisdiction so vested shall be suspended.

Provided that—

(*a*) nothing in this section shall authorise a Vice-Admiralty Court so established in India or in any British possession having a representative legislature, to exercise any jurisdiction, except for some purpose relating to prize, to Her Majesty's Navy, to the slave trade, to the matters dealt with by the Foreign Enlistment Act, 1870,[1] or the Pacific Islanders Protection Acts, 1872 and 1875, or to matters in which questions arise relating to treaties or conventions with foreign countries, or to international law; and

33 & 34 V. c. 90.
35 & 36 V. c. 19.
38 & 39 V. c. 51.

(*b*) in the event of a vacancy in the office of judge, registrar, marshal, or other officer of any Vice-Admiralty Court in a British

[1] Printed Vol. I, p. 472.

possession, the Governor of that possession may appoint a fit person to fill the vacancy until an appointment to the office is made by the Admiralty.

(3) The provisions of this Act with respect to appeals to Her Majesty in Council from courts in British possessions in the exercise of the jurisdiction conferred by this Act shall apply to appeals from Vice-Admiralty Courts, but the rules and orders made in relation to appeals from Vice-Admiralty Courts may differ from the rules made in relation to appeals from the said courts in British possessions.

(4) If Her Majesty at any time by commission under the Great Seal so directs, the Admiralty shall by writing under their hands and the seal of the office of Admiralty abolish a Vice-Admiralty Court established in any British possession under this section, and upon such abolition the jurisdiction of any Colonial Court of Admiralty in that possession which was previously suspended shall be revived.

Power to appoint a vice-admiral.

10. Nothing in this Act shall affect any power of appointing a vice-admiral in and for any British possession or any place therein; and whenever there is not a formally appointed vice-admiral in a British possession or any place therein, the Governor of the possession shall be *ex officio* vice-admiral thereof.

Exception of Channel Islands and other possessions.

11. (1) The provisions of this Act with respect to Colonial Courts of Admiralty shall not apply to the Channel Islands.

(2) It shall be lawful for the Queen in Council by Order to declare, with respect to any British possession which has not a representative legislature, that the jurisdiction conferred by this Act on Colonial Courts of Admiralty shall not be vested in any court of such possession, or shall be vested only to the partial or limited extent specified in the Order.

Application of Act to courts under Foreign Jurisdiction Acts.

12. It shall be lawful for Her Majesty the Queen in Council by Order to direct that this Act shall, subject to the conditions, exceptions, and qualifications (if any) contained in the Order, apply to any Court established by Her Majesty for the exercise of jurisdiction in any place out of Her Majesty's dominions which is named in the Order as if that Court were a Colonial Court of Admiralty, and to provide for carrying into effect such application.

Rules for procedure in slave trade matters.

13. (1) It shall be lawful for Her Majesty the Queen in Council by Order to make rules as to the practice and procedure (including fees and costs) to be observed in and the returns to be made from Colonial Courts of Admiralty and Vice-Admiralty Courts in the exercise of their jurisdiction in matters relating to the slave trade, and in and from East African Courts as defined by the Slave Trade (East African Courts) Acts, 1873 and 1879.

& 37 Vict., 59.
& 43 Vict., 38.

(2) Except when inconsistent with such Order in Council, the rules of court for the time being in force in a Colonial Court of Admiralty or Vice-Admiralty Court shall, so far as applicable, extend to proceedings in such court in matters relating to the slave trade.

(3) The provisions of this Act with respect to appeals to Her Majesty in Council, from courts in British possessions in the exercise of the jurisdiction conferred by this Act, shall apply, with the necessary modifications, to appeals from judgments of any East African Court made or purporting to be made in exercise of the jurisdiction under the Slave Trade (East African Courts) Acts, 1873 and 1879. 36 & 37 V. c. 59. 42 & 43 V.

Orders in Council.

14. It shall be lawful for Her Majesty in Council from time to time to make Orders for the purposes authorised by this Act, and to revoke and vary such Orders, and every such Order while in operation shall have effect as if it were part of this Act.

Interpretation.

15. In the construction of this Act, unless the context otherwise requires,—

The expression "representative legislature" means, in relation to a British possession, a legislature comprising a legislative body of which at least one-half are elected by inhabitants of the British possession.

The expression "unlimited civil jurisdiction" means civil jurisdiction unlimited as to the value of the subject-matter at issue, or as to the amount that may be claimed or recovered.

The expression "judgment" includes a decree, order, and sentence.

The expression "appeal" means any appeal, rehearing, or review; and the expression "local appeal" means an appeal to any court inferior to Her Majesty in Council.

The expression "Colonial law" means any Act, ordinance, or other law having the force of legislative enactment in a British possession and made by any authority, other than the Imperial Parliament of Her Majesty in Council, competent to make laws for such possession.

Commencement of Act.

16. (1) This Act shall, save as otherwise in this Act provided, come into force in every British possession on the first day of July, one thousand eight hundred and ninety-one.

Provided that—

(*a*) This Act shall not come into force in any of the British possessions named in the First Schedule to this Act until Her Majesty so directs by Order in Council, and until the day named in that behalf in such Order; and (*b*) If before any day above mentioned rules of court for the Colonial Court of Admiralty in any British possession have been approved by Her Majesty in Council, this Act may be proclaimed in that possession by the Governor thereof, and on such proclamation shall come into force on the day named in the proclamation.

(2) The day upon which this Act comes into force in any British possession shall, as regards that British possession, be deemed to be the commencement of this Act.

(3) If, on the commencement of this Act in any British possession, rules of court have not been approved by Her Majesty in pursuance of this Act, the rules in force at such commencement under the Vice-Admiralty Courts Act, 1863, and in India the rules in force at such commencement regulating the respective Vice-Admiralty Courts or Courts of Admiralty in India, including any rules made with reference to proceedings instituted on behalf of Her Majesty's ships, shall, so far as applicable, have effect in the Colonial Court or Courts of Admiralty of such possession, and in any Vice-Admiralty Court established under this Act in that possession, as rules of court under this Act, and may be revoked and varied accordingly; and all fees payable under such rules may be taken in such manner as the Colonial Court may direct, so however that the amount of each such fee shall so nearly as practicable be paid to the same officer or person who but for the passing of this Act would have been entitled to receive the same in respect of like business. So far as any such rules are inapplicable or do not extend, the rules of court for the exercise by a court of its ordinary civil jurisdiction shall have effect as rules for the exercise by the same court of the jurisdiction conferred by this Act.

& 27 Vict., 24.

(4) At any time after the passing of this Act any Colonial law may be passed, and any Vice-Admiralty Court may be established and jurisdiction vested in such Court, but any such law, establishment, or vesting shall not come into effect until the commencement of this Act.

17. On the commencement of this Act in any British possession, but subject to the provisions of this Act, every Vice-Admiralty Court in that possession shall be abolished; subject as follows,—

Abolition of Vice-Admiralty Courts.

(1) All judgments of such Vice-Admiralty Court shall be executed and may be appealed from in like manner as if this Act had not passed, and all appeals from any Vice-Admiralty Court pending at the commencement of this Act shall be heard and determined, and the judgment thereon executed as nearly as may be in like manner as if this Act had not passed:

(2) All proceedings pending in the Vice-Admiralty Court in any British possession at the commencement of this Act shall, notwithstanding the repeal of any enactment by this Act, be continued in a Colonial Court of Admiralty of the possession in manner directed by rules of court, and, so far as no such rule extends, in like manner, as nearly as may be, as if they had been originally begun in such court:

(3) Where any person holding an office, whether that of judge, registrar, or marshal, or any other office in any such Vice-Admiralty Court in a British possession, suffers any pecuniary loss in consequence of the abolition of such court, the Government of the British possession, on complaint of such person, shall provide that such person shall receive reasonable compensation (by way of an increase of salary or a capital sum, or otherwise) in respect of his loss, subject nevertheless to the performance, if required by the said Government, of the like duties as before such abolition.

(4) All books, papers, documents, office furniture, and other things at the commencement of this Act belonging, or appertaining to any Vice-Admiralty Court, shall be delivered over to the proper officer of the Colonial Court of Admiralty, or be otherwise dealt with in such manner as, subject to any directions from Her Majesty, the Governor may direct.

(5) Where, at the commencement of this Act in a British possession, any person holds a commission to act as advocate in any Vice-Admiralty Court abolished by this Act, either for Her Majesty or for the Admiralty, such commission shall be of the same avail in every court of the same British possession exercising jurisdiction under this Act, as if such court were the court mentioned or referred to in such commission.

Repeal. **18.** The Acts specified in the Second Schedule to this Act shall, to the extent mentioned in the third column of that schedule, be repealed as respects any British possession as from the commencement of this Act in that possession, and as respects any courts out of Her Majesty's dominions as from the date of any Order applying this Act:

Provided that—

(*a*) Any appeal against a judgment made before the commencement of this Act may be brought and any such appeal and any proceedings or appeals pending at the commencement of this Act may be carried on and completed and carried into effect as if such repeal had not been enacted; and

(*b*) All enactments and rules at the passing of this Act in force touching the practice, procedure, fees, costs, and returns in matters relating to the slave trade, in Vice-Admiralty Courts and in East African courts shall have effect as rules made in pursuance of this Act, and shall apply to Colonial Courts of Admiralty, and may be altered and revoked accordingly.

SCHEDULES.

FIRST SCHEDULE.

BRITISH POSSESSIONS IN WHICH OPERATION OF ACT IS DELAYED. Section 16.

New South Wales.
Victoria.
St. Helena.
British Honduras.

SECOND SCHEDULE.

ENACTMENTS REPEALED. Section 18.

Session and Chapter.	Title of Act.	Extent of Repeal.
56 Geo. 3, c. 82	An Act to render valid the judicial Acts of Surrogates of Vice-Admiralty Courts abroad, during vacancies in office of Judges of such courts.	The whole Act.
2 & 3 Will. 4, c. 51	An Act to regulate the practice and the fees in the Vice-Admiralty Courts abroad, and to obviate doubts as to their jurisdiction.	The whole Act.
3 & 4 Will. 4, c. 41	An Act for the better administration of justice in His Majesty's Privy Council.	Section two.
6 & 7 Vict., c. 38	An Act to make further regulations for facilitating the hearing appeals and other matters by the Judicial Committee of the Privy Council.	In section two, the words "or from any Admiralty or Vice-Admiralty Courts," and the words "or the Lords Commissioners of Appeals in prize causes or their surrogates."

SECOND SCHEDULE—*continued.*

ENACTMENTS REPEALED—*continued.*

Session and Chapter.	Title of Act.	Extent of Repeal.
6 & 7 Vict., c. 38—*contd.*	An Act to make further regulations for facilitating the hearing appeals and other matters by the Judicial Committee of the Privy Council—*contd.*	In section three, the words "and the High Court of Admiralty of England," and the words "and from any Admiralty or Vice-Admiralty Courts." In section five, from the first "the High Court of Admiralty" to the end of the section. In section seven, the words "and from Admiralty or Vice-Admiralty Courts." Sections nine and ten, so far as relates to maritime causes. In section twelve, the words "or maritime." In section fifteen, the words "and Admiralty and Vice-Admiralty."
7 & 8 Vict., c. 69	An Act for amending an Act passed in the fourth year of the reign of His late Majesty, intituled, "An Act for the better administration of justice in His Majesty's Privy Council," and to extend its jurisdiction and powers.	In section twelve, the words "and from Admiralty and Vice-Admiralty Courts," and so much of the rest of the section as relates to maritime causes.
26 Vict., c. 24	The Vice-Admiralty Courts Act, 1863.	The whole Act.
30 & 31 Vict., c. 45	The Vice-Admiralty Courts Act Amendment Act, 1867.	The whole Act.
36 & 37 Vict., c. 59	The Slave Trade (East African Courts) Act, 1873.	Sections four and five.
36 & 37 Vict., c. 88	The Slave Trade Act, 1873	Section twenty as far as relates to the taxation of any costs, charges, and expenses which can be taxed in pursuance of this Act. In section twenty-three the words "under the Vice-Admiralty Courts Act, 1863."

SECOND SCHEDULE—*concluded.*

ENACTMENTS REPEALED—*concluded.*

Session and Chapter.	Title of Act.	Extent of Repeal.
38 & 39 Vict., c. 51	The Pacific Islanders Protection Act, 1875.	So much of section six as authorises Her Majesty to confer Admiralty jurisdiction on any court.

THE FOREIGN JURISDICTION ACT, 1890.[1]

(53 & 54 Vict., c. 37.)

An Act to consolidate the Foreign Jurisdiction Acts.

[*4th August, 1890.*]

WHEREAS by treaty, capitulation, grant, usage, sufferance, and other lawful means, Her Majesty the Queen has jurisdiction within divers foreign countries, and it is expedient to consolidate the Acts relating to the exercise of Her Majesty's jurisdiction out of Her dominions :

* * * * * * *

Exercise of jurisdiction in foreign country.

1. It is and shall be lawful for Her Majesty the Queen to hold, exercise, and enjoy any jurisdiction which Her Majesty now has or may at any time hereafter have within a foreign country in the same and as ample a manner as if Her Majesty had acquired that jurisdiction by the cession or conquest of territory.

Exercise of jurisdiction over British subjects in countries without regular governments.

2. Where a foreign country is not subject to any government from whom Her Majesty the Queen might obtain jurisdiction in the manner recited by this Act, Her Majesty shall by virtue of this Act have jurisdiction over Her Majesty's subjects for the time being resident in or resorting to that country, and that jurisdiction shall be jurisdiction of Her Majesty in a foreign country within the meaning of the other provisions of this Act.

Validity of acts done in pursuance of jurisdiction.

3. Every act and thing done in pursuance of any jurisdiction of Her Majesty in a foreign country shall be as valid as if it had been done according to the local law then in force in that country.

Evidence as to existence or extent of jurisdiction in foreign country.

4. If in any proceeding, civil or criminal, in a court in Her Majesty's dominions or held under the authority of Her Majesty any question arises as to the existence or extent of any jurisdiction of Her Majesty in a foreign

[1] See *Chitty's Statutes*, Tit. Foreign Jurisdiction, p. 1.
Cf. the Foreign Jurisdiction and Extradition Act, 1879 (XXI of 1879).

country, a Secretary of State shall, on the application of the court, send to the court within a reasonable time his decision on the question, and his decision shall for the purposes of the proceeding be final.

(2) The court shall send to the Secretary of State, in a document under the seal of the court, or signed by a judge of the court, questions framed so as properly to raise the question, and sufficient answers to those questions shall be returned by the Secretary of State to the court, and those answers shall, on production thereof, be conclusive evidence of the matters therein contained.

Power to extend enactments in First Schedule.

5. (1) It shall be lawful for Her Majesty the Queen in Council, if She thinks fit, by Order to direct that all or any of the enactments described in the First Schedule to this Act, or any enactments for the time being in force amending or substituted for the same, shall extend, with or without any exceptions, adaptations, or modifications in the Order mentioned, to any foreign country in which for the time being Her Majesty has jurisdiction.

(2) Thereupon those enactments shall, to the extent of that jurisdiction, operate as if that country were a British possession, and as if Her Majesty in Council were the Legislature of that possession.

Power to send persons charged with offences for trial to a British possession.

6. (1) Where a person is charged with an offence cognizable by a British court in a foreign country, any person having authority derived from Her Majesty in that behalf may, by warrant, cause the person so charged to be sent for trial to any British possession for the time being appointed in that behalf by Order in Council, and upon the arrival of the person so charged in that British possession, such criminal court of the possession as is authorised in that behalf by Order in Council, or if no court is so authorised, the supreme criminal court of that possession, may cause him to be kept in safe and proper custody, and so soon as conveniently may be may inquire of, try, and determine the offence, and on conviction punish the offender according to the laws in force in that behalf within that possession in the same manner as if the offence had been committed within the jurisdiction of that criminal court.

Provided that—

(*a*) A person so charged may, before being so sent for trial, tender for examination to a British court in the foreign country where the offence is alleged to have been committed any competent witness whose evidence he deems material for his defence and whom he alleges himself unable to produce at the trial in the British possession:

(*b*) In such case the British court in the foreign country shall proceed in the examination and cross-examination of the witness as though he had been tendered at a trial before that court, and shall cause the evidence so taken to be reduced into writing, and shall transmit to the criminal court of the British possession by which the person charged is to be tried a copy of the evidence, certified as correct under the seal of the court before which the evidence was taken, or the signature of a judge of that court:

(*c*) Thereupon the court of the British possession before which the trial takes place shall allow so much of the evidence so taken as would have been admissible according to the law and practice of that court, had the witness been produced and examined at the trial, to be read and received as legal evidence at the trial:

(*d*) The court of the British possession shall admit and give effect to the law by which the alleged offender would have been tried by the British court in the foreign country in which his offence is alleged to have been committed, so far as that law relates to the criminality of the act alleged to have been committed, or the nature or degree of the offence, or the punishment thereof, if the law differs in those respects from the law in force in that British possession.

(2) Nothing in this section shall alter or repeal any law, statute, or usage by virtue of which any offence committed out of Her Majesty's dominions may, irrespectively of this Act, be inquired of, tried, determined, and punished within Her Majesty's dominions, or any part thereof.

Provision as to place of punishment of persons convicted.

7. Where an offender convicted before a British court in a foreign country has been sentenced by that court to suffer death, penal servitude, imprisonment, or any other punishment, the sentence shall be carried into effect in such place as may be directed by Order in Council or be determined in accordance with directions given by Order in Council, and the conviction and sentence shall be of the same force in the place in which the sentence is so carried into effect as if the conviction had been made and the sentence passed by a competent court in that place.

Validity of acts done under Order in Council.

8. Where, by Order in Council made in pursuance of this Act, any British court in a foreign country is authorised to order the removal or deportation of any person from that country, that removal or deportation, and any detention for the purposes thereof, according to the provisions of the Order in Council, shall be as lawful as if the order of the court were to have effect wholly within that country.

Power to assign jurisdiction to

9. It shall be lawful for Her Majesty the Queen in Council, by Order, to assign to or confer on any court in any British possession, or held under the

British courts in cases within Foreign Jurisdiction Act.

authority of Her Majesty, any jurisdiction, civil or criminal, original or appellate, which may lawfully by Order in Council be assigned to or conferred on any British court in any foreign country, and to make such provisions and regulations as to Her Majesty in Council seem meet respecting the exercise of the jurisdiction so assigned or conferred, and respecting the enforcement and execution of the judgments, decrees, orders, and sentences of any such court, and respecting appeals therefrom.

Power to amend Orders in Council.

10. It shall be lawful for Her Majesty the Queen in Council to revoke or vary any Order in Council made in pursuance of this Act.

Laying before Parliament, and effect of Orders in Council.

11. Every Order in Council made in pursuance of this Act shall be laid before both Houses of Parliament forthwith after it is made, if Parliament be then in session, and if not, forthwith after the commencement of the then next session of Parliament, and shall have effect as if it were enacted in this Act.

In what cases Orders in Council void for repugnancy.

12. (1) If any Order in Council made in pursuance of this Act as respects any foreign country is in any respect repugnant to the provisions of any Act of Parliament extending to Her Majesty's subjects in that country, or repugnant to any order or regulation made under the authority of any such Act of Parliament or having in that country the force and effect of any such Act, it shall be read subject to that Act, order, or regulation, and shall, to the extent of such repugnancy, but not otherwise, be void.

(2) An Order in Council made in pursuance of this Act shall not be, or be deemed to have been, void on the ground of repugnancy to the law of England unless it is repugnant to the provisions of some such Act of Parliament, order, or regulation as aforesaid.

Provisions for protection of persons acting under Foreign Jurisdiction Acts.

13. (1) An action, suit, prosecution, or proceeding against any person for any act done in pursuance or execution or intended execution of this Act, or of any enactment repealed by this Act, or of any Order in Council made under this Act, or of any such jurisdiction of Her Majesty as is mentioned in this Act, or in respect of any alleged neglect or default in the execution of this Act, or of any such enactment, Order in Council, or jurisdiction as aforesaid, shall not lie or be instituted—

(*a*) in any court within Her Majesty's dominions, unless it is commenced within six months next after the act, neglect, or default complained of, or in case of a continuance of injury or damage within six months next after the ceasing thereof, or where the cause of action arose out of Her Majesty's dominions within six months after the parties to the action, suit, prosecution, or proceeding have been within the jurisdiction of the court in which the same is instituted; nor (*b*) in any of Her Majesty's courts without Her Majesty's dominions, unless the cause of action arose within the jurisdiction of that court, and the action is commenced within six months next after the act, neglect, or default complained of, or, in case of a continuance of injury or damage, within six months next after the ceasing thereof.

(2) In any such action, suit, or proceeding, tender of amends before the same was commenced may be pleaded in lieu of or in addition to any other plea. If the action, suit, or proceeding was commenced after such tender, or is proceeded with after payment into court of any money in satisfaction of the plaintiff's claim, and the plaintiff does not recover more than the sum tendered or paid, he shall not recover any costs incurred after such tender or payment, and the defendant shall be entitled to costs, to be taxed as between solicitor and client, as from the time of such tender or payment; but this provision shall not affect costs on any injunction in the action, suit, or proceeding.

Jurisdiction over ships in certain Eastern seas.

14. It shall be lawful for Her Majesty the Queen in Council to make any law that may seem meet for the government of Her Majesty's subjects being in any vessel at a distance of not more than one hundred miles from the coast of China or of Japan, as fully and effectually as any such law might be made by Her Majesty in Council for the government of Her Majesty's subjects being in China or in Japan.

Provision as to subjects of Indian princes.

15. Where any Order in Council made in pursuance of this Act extends to persons enjoying Her Majesty's protection, that expression shall include all subjects of the several princes and states in India.

Definitions.

16. In this Act,—

The expression "foreign country" means any country or place out of Her Majesty's dominions:

The expression "British court in a foreign country" means any British court having jurisdiction out of Her Majesty's dominions in pursuance of an Order in Council whether made under any Act or otherwise:

The expression "jurisdiction" includes power.

Power to repeal or vary Acts in Second Schedule.

17. The Acts mentioned in the Second Schedule to this Act may be revoked or varied by Her Majesty by Order in Council.

Repeal.

18. The Acts mentioned in the Third Schedule to this Act are hereby repealed to the extent in the third column of that schedule mentioned: Provided that,—

(1) Any Order in Council, commission, or instructions made or issued in pursuance of any enactment repealed by this Act, shall, if

in force at the passing of this Act, continue in force, until altered or revoked by Her Majesty as if made in pursuance of this Act; and shall, for the purposes of this Act, be deemed to have been made or issued under and in pursuance of this Act; and

(2) Any enactment, Order in Council, or document referring to any enactment repealed by this Act shall be construed to refer to the corresponding enactment of this Act.

Short title. **19.** (1) This Act may be cited as the Foreign Jurisdiction Act, 1890.

(2) The Acts whereof the short titles are given in the First Schedule to this Act may be cited by the respective short titles given in that schedule.

SCHEDULES.

Sections 5, 19.

FIRST SCHEDULE.

Session and Chapter.	Title.	Enactments which may be extended by Order in Council.	Short Title.
12 & 13 Vict., c. 96.	An Act to provide for the prosecution and Trial in Her Majesty's Colonies of Offences committed within the jurisdiction of the Admiralty.	The whole Act .	Admiralty Offences (Colonial) Act, 1849.
14 & 15 Vict., c. 99.	An Act to amend the law of evidence.	Sections seven and eleven.	Evidence Act, 1851.
17 & 18 Vict., c. 104.	The Merchant Shipping Act, 1854.	Part X.	
19 & 20 Vict., c. 113.	An Act to provide for taking evidence in Her Majesty's Dominions in relation to civil and commercial matters pending before Foreign tribunals.	The whole Act .	Foreign Tribunals Evidence Act, 1856.
22 Vict., c. 20.	An Act to provide for taking evidence in Suits and Proceedings pending before Tribunals in Her Majesty's dominions, in places out of the jurisdiction of such tribunals.	The whole Act .	Evidence by Commission Act, 1859.
22 & 23 Vict., c. 63.	An Act to afford Facilities for the more certain Ascertainment of the Law administered in one Part of Her Majesty's Dominions, when pleaded in the Courts of another Part thereof.	The whole Act .	British Law Ascertainment Act, 1859.

FIRST SCHEDULE—*contd.*

Sections 5, 19.

Session and Chapter.	Title.	Enactments which may be extended by Order in Council.	Short Title.
23 & 24 Vict., c. 122.	An Act to enable the Legislatures of Her Majesty's Possessions Abroad to make Enactments similar to the Enactment of the Act ninth George the Fourth, chapter thirty-one, section eight.	The whole Act .	Admiralty Offences (Colonial) Act, 1860.
24 & 25 Vict., c. 11.	An Act to afford facilities for the better ascertainment of the Law of Foreign Countries when pleaded in Courts within Her Majesty's Dominions.	The whole Act .	Foreign Law Ascertainment Act, 1861.
30 & 31 Vict., c. 124.	The Merchant Shipping Act, 1867.	Section eleven.	
37 & 38 Vict., c. 94.	The Conveyancing (Scotland) Act, 1874.	Section fifty-one.	
44 & 45 Vict., c. 69.	The Fugitive Offenders Act, 1881.	The whole Act.	
48 & 49 Vict., c. 74.	The Evidence by Commission Act, 1885.	The whole Act.	

SECOND SCHEDULE.

Section 17.

Acts which may be revoked or varied by Order in Council.

Session and Chapter.	Title.	Extent of Repeal.
24 & 25 Vict., c. 31 .	An Act for the prevention and punishment of offences committed by Her Majesty's subjects within certain territories adjacent to the colony of Sierra Leone.	The whole Act.
26 & 27 Vict., c. 35 .	An Act for the prevention and punishment of offences committed by Her Majesty's subjects in South Africa.	The whole Act.

THIRD SCHEDULE.

Section 18.

Enactments repealed.

Session and Chapter.	Title or Short Title.	Extent of Repeal.
6 & 7 Vict., c. 94	The Foreign Jurisdiction Act, 1843	The whole Act.
20 & 21 Vict., c. 75	An Act to confirm an Order in Council concerning the exercise of jurisdiction in matters arising within the kingdom of Siam.	The whole Act.
28 & 29 Vict., c. 116	The Foreign Jurisdiction Act Amendment Act, 1865.	The whole Act.
29 & 30 Vict., c. 87	The Foreign Jurisdiction Act Amendment Act, 1866.	The whole Act.
33 & 34 Vict., c. 55	The Siam and Straits Settlements Jurisdiction Act, 1870.	The whole Act.
38 & 39 Vict., c. 85	The Foreign Jurisdiction Act, 1875	The whole Act.
39 & 40 Vict., c. 46	An Act for more effectually punishing offences against the laws relating to the slave trade.	Sections four and six.
41 & 42 Vict., c. 67	The Foreign Jurisdiction Act, 1878	The whole Act.

The Mail Ships Act, 1891.[1]

(54 & 55 Vict., c. 31.)

An Act to enable Her Majesty in Council to carry into effect Conventions which may be made with Foreign Countries respecting Ships engaged in Postal service.

[*21st July, 1891.*]

Be it enacted by the Queen's most Excellent Majesty, by and with the advice and consent of the Lords Spiritual and Temporal, and Commons, in this present Parliament assembled, and by the authority of the same, as follows:

Application of Act by Order in Council.

1. (1) Where Her Majesty the Queen has made a Convention with a Foreign State respecting the postal service between such Foreign State and the United Kingdom, or respecting the privileges of mail ships, that is to say, ships engaged in any postal service of such Foreign State or of any part of Her

[1] See *Chitty's Statutes*, Tit. Post Office, p. 85.

Majesty's dominions, it shall be lawful for Her Majesty in Council to order that this Act shall, and this Act shall accordingly, subject to any conditions, exceptions, and qualifications contained in the Order, apply, during the continuance of the Order, as regards such Convention and Foreign State, and the postal service and mail ships described in the Convention; and where by virtue of any such Order this Act or any section thereof applies as regards any Convention, Foreign State, postal service, or mail ship, the same is in this Act referred to as a Convention, Foreign State, postal service, or mail ship to which this Act or section applies.

(2) The Order shall recite or embody the terms of the Convention, and may be varied or revoked by Order in Council, but shall not continue in force for any longer period than the Convention.

(3) Every Order in Council under this Act shall be laid before both Houses of Parliament forthwith after it is made, or, if Parliament be not then sitting, after the then next meeting of Parliament, and shall also be notified in the London Gazette and published under the authority of Her Majesty's Stationery Office.

Conveyance of letters by crew or passengers of mail ships forbidden.

2. (1) Where this section applies to a Convention with a Foreign State, the master of a British mail ship to which this section applies when carrying mails to or from any port of the Foreign State, and the master of a mail ship of the foreign State, to which this section applies when carrying mails to or from any port of the United Kindom, shall not, nor shall any person on board the ship, whether a passenger or belonging to the ship or any other person, convey in the ship for delivery to another person in the Foreign State or United Kingdom, as the case may be, any letter, other than the letters contained in mail bags entrusted to the master by a postal officer of the United Kingdom or of any Foreign State, or than the despatches sent by the Government either of the United Kingdom or of any Foreign State.

(2) If a person on board such ship acts in contravention of this section, or refuses or fails on demand to give up to a postal officer, or, if such person is not the master, to the master, any letter so conveyed by him, he shall be liable, on summary conviction, to a fine not exceeding five pounds.

(3) It shall be the duty of the master of the ship to secure the observance of this section by all persons on board the ship, and to inform the proper authorities at the port at which the ship arrives of any breach of this section by any of those persons, and if he wilfully fails to perform that duty he shall be liable to a fine not exceeding five pounds.

(4) Provided that a person shall not be liable under this section to a fine for any offence for which he has been punished by the law of the Foreign State.

(5) Nothing in this section shall apply to any letters which if sent from the United Kingdom would be exempted from the exclusive privilege of the Postmaster-General under the Act of the session of the seventh year of King William the Fourth and the first of Her present Majesty, chapter thirty-three, intituled "An Act for the management of the Post Office." 7 Will. 4 & 1 Vict., c. 33.

Regulation as to giving of security for ships engaged in postal service.

3. (1) Where the owner of any ships, British or foreign, applies to the High Court in England, and

(*a*) produces a certificate of a Secretary of State that such owner is subsidised for the execution of any postal service within the meaning of a Convention with a Foreign State to which this Act applies, by reason of receiving from the Foreign State, or from the Government of the United Kingdom or of a British possession, a *bonâ fide* subsidy for the postal service mentioned in the certificate, and

(*b*) produces sufficient evidence of the nature of the said service and the number of and the prescribed particulars respecting the ships engaged therein, and

(*c*) gives notice of the application to the Board of Trade,

the High Court, after hearing the owner, and the Board of Trade if they wish to be heard, shall fix the nature and amount of the security which the owner ought to place under the control of the court for the purposes of this Act as respects the ships engaged in that postal service, and fix the maximum number and tonnage of the ships to which the security is to apply.

(2) The security shall be the bond of the owner guaranteed either—

(*a*) by the personal security of a surety, accompanied by an adequate real security given by the surety; or,

(*b*) by the payment or transfer into court of cash, or of securities of the Government of the United Kingdom.

(3) If the owner gives such security to the satisfaction of the High Court, then so long as the security is maintained and is sufficient to the satisfaction of the Court, and the number and tonnage of the ships for the time being actually engaged in carrying mails for the postal service in respect of which the security is given does not exceed the number and tonnage of the ships to which the security applies, the ships actually engaged in carrying mails for the said service shall be deemed to be exempted mail ships, and be entitled to the exemptions and privileges given by this Act to exempted mail ships; and the Board of Trade shall give the prescribed notices for informing the arresting authorities that the ships actually engaged in carrying the mails for the said postal service are exempted mail ships.

(4) Notice of every application respecting any security given in pursuance of this section shall be given to the Board of Trade.

(5) If at any time it appears to the Board of Trade that a security given as respects ships engaged in any postal service, is from any cause (whether pending claims, variation of the conditions of the service, or otherwise) insufficient, the Board of Trade shall apply to the High Court, and that Court, if satisfied of such insufficiency, shall require the security to be made sufficient to the satisfaction of the Court within a reasonable time, and direct that in default the ships engaged in the postal service shall cease to be exempted mail ships, and that the Board of Trade shall give the prescribed notices for informing the arresting authorities of such cesser.

(6) The amount and nature of the security may be varied and the whole security may be withdrawn, and the income of the security may be disposed of, by order of the High Court from time to time on such application either of the shipowners, or of the Board of Trade, or of any person appearing to be interested, and in such manner, and after such notice, and upon such terms and conditions as may be prescribed by rules of court, or, so far as the rules do not extend, as the Court may think just.

(7) Provided that before the security is actually withdrawn, the High Court shall be satisfied—

(*a*) that the prescribed notice of the order for withdrawal has been given to the arresting authorities; and

(*b*) that there is no pending claim for the purposes of which the security may be required;

and upon the prescribed notice of the order for withdrawal being given to an arresting authority, the ships shall, as respects that authority, cease, after the date specified in the notice, to be exempted ships.

(8) Rules of court may be made for carrying this section into effect, and in particular for regulating the nature, amount, and value of the security to be given, and the mode of giving security, and of giving notices to the arresting authorities, and for providing for the evidence of the exemption of ships under this section, and for the information to be given from time to time to the High Court respecting the ships to which the security applies, and for the jurisdiction of the High Court under this Act being exercised in chambers.

Arrest and execution of process on board exempted mail ships.

4. (1) Where this section applies to a Convention with a Foreign State, and an exempted mail ship to which this section applies is in a port in the United Kingdom, no person shall be arrested without warrant on board such ship, and before any process, civil or criminal, authorising the arrest of any person who is on board such ship is executed against that person the following provisions of this section shall be observed; that is to say,—

(*a*) written notice of the intention to arrest a person, who is, or is suspected to be, on board the ship, stating the hour at which, if necessary, the ship will be searched, shall, if it is a ship of a Foreign State and there is at the port a consulate of that State, be left at the consulate, addressed to the consular officer:

(*b*) it shall be the duty of the master upon demand, if the said person is on board his ship, to enable the proper officer to arrest him:

(*c*) if the officer is unable to arrest the said person he may, but if it is a foreign ship only after the expiration of such time after notice was left at the consulate as is specified in the convention, search the ship for such person, and if he is found may arrest him.

(2) The ship may be delayed for the purposes of this section for the time specified in the Convention, but not for any longer time.

(3) If the master of a ship refuses to permit a search of the ship in accordance with this section, any officer of customs may detain the ship, and such master shall be liable to a fine of five hundred pounds.

(4) This section shall apply to the arrest of the master in like manner as in the case of any other person.

Exemption from seizure of exempted mail ships.

5. (1) An exempted mail ship to which this section applies shall not, subject as in this Act mentioned, be liable to be arrested or detained by any arresting authority either for the purpose of founding jurisdiction in any Court of Admiralty, or of enforcing the payment of any damages, fine, debt or other claim or sum, or enforcing any forfeiture, whether arising from the misconduct of the master or any of the crew or otherwise, but every court of the United Kingdom by the process of which the ship could have been under the circumstances arrested or detained shall have the same jurisdiction as if the ship had been so arrested or detained, and any legal proceeding in relation to any such matter as aforesaid may be commenced by such service in the United Kingdom of any writ or process as may be prescribed by rules of court, and the High Court, on application, shall, in accordance with rules of court, cause the security to be applied in discharge of any such damages, fine, debt, claim, sum, or forfeiture.

(2) Provided that nothing in this section shall render invalid the arrest or detention of a ship before the prescribed notice has been given to the arresting authority, but such authority, on proof that the ship is an exempted mail ship, shall release the ship. Where the Commissioners of Customs, in pursuance of any Act or as a condition of waiving any forfeiture, require a deposit

to be made by any exempted mail ship to which this section applies, the amount of such deposit shall, on notice from the Commissioners of Customs, and without any further proceeding, be set apart out of the security as money belonging to the said Commissioners, and shall be paid and applied as they direct, and any rules of court relating to such notice, payment, or application shall be made with the consent of the Treasury.

Application of Act to public ships.

6. (1) Where the convention with a Foreign State provides that any provisions of the convention similar to those contained in this Act shall in any case apply to a public ship of a Foreign State when employed as a mail ship, it shall be lawful for Her Majesty the Queen to agree that the like provision shall apply to a public ship of Her Majesty in the like cases when employed as a mail ship, and to give effect to such agreement.

(2) An Order in Council applying this Act as regards a Convention with a Foreign State may, if it seems to Her Majesty in Council to be consistent with the Convention so to do, apply this Act as regards a public ship of that Foreign State when employed as a mail ship in the cases authorised by the Convention, and this Act shall apply accordingly, as if such ship were an exempted mail ship belonging to a private owner, and any person may be arrested on board such ship accordingly.

Legal proceedings.

7. (1) Every fine under this Act, if exceeding fifty pounds, may be recovered by action in the High Court in England or Ireland or in the Court of Session in Scotland, and the court in which it is recovered may reduce the amount of such fine, and a fine under this Act not exceeding fifty pounds may be recovered on summary conviction, provided that every offence for which a fine exceeding fifty pounds can be imposed under this Act may be prosecuted on summary conviction, but the fine imposed on such conviction shall not exceed fifty pounds.

(2) In the case of a summary conviction, any person who thinks himself aggrieved by such conviction may appeal to quarter sessions. In Scotland such person may appeal in manner provided by the Summary Prosecutions Appeals (Scotland) Act, 1875.

& 39 Vict., c. 62.

(3) Service of any summons or other matter in any legal proceeding under this Act shall be good service if made by leaving the summons for the person to be served on board the ship to which he belongs with the person being or appearing to be master of the ship.

(4) If a fine under this Act imposed on the master of a ship is not paid, and cannot be recovered out of any security given in pursuance of this Act, the Court may, in addition to any other power for enforcing payment of the fine, direct the amount to be levied by distress or poinding and sale of the

ship, her tackle, furniture, or apparel. An officer of customs in detaining a ship or releasing a ship after detention in pursuance of this Act shall act upon such requisition or authority and under such regulations as the Commissioners of Customs may make with the consent of the Treasury.

Application of Act to British Possessions.

8. (1) An Order in Council may for the purpose of a Convention with a Foreign State apply this Act, subject to any exceptions or modifications not inconsistent with the provisions of this Act, to any British Possession, and this Act when so applied shall, subject to those exceptions and modifications, and subject as hereinafter mentioned, have effect as if it were re-enacted with the substitution of such British Possession for the United Kingdom:

Provided that before it is applied to any British Possession named in the schedule to this Act the Government of such possession shall have adhered to the Convention.

(2) Where this ct applies to a British possession, it shall not be necessary for the owner of any mail ship to give security in any court in that possession, and the provisions of this Act with respect to the jurisdiction of any court of the United Kingdom, other than any jurisdiction relating to the application of the security, shall apply as if a court in the British Possession were subtituted for a court of the United Kingdom.

(3) It shall be lawful for Her Majesty in Council to make rules for carrying into effect, as respects British Possessions, the provisions of this Act with respect to the security given by mail ships, and in particular with respect to the commencement of a legal proceeding by service of a writ or process in the Possession, and to the notices to be given to arresting authorities in the Possession, and the evidence to be receivable by such authorities of the security having been given or withdrawn, and the application of the security in discharge of any damages, fine, debt, claim, sum, or forfeiture, where the same are or is recovered or payable either in the British Possession, or under proceedings pending concurrently in that British Possession and in any other British Possession or the United Kingdom.

(4) If by any law made either before or after the passing of this Act by the Legislature of any British Possession[1] provision is made for carrying into effect within such Possession any convention to which this Act applies, Her Majesty in Council may suspend the operation within such Possession of this Act or of any part thereof so far as it relates to such convention, and so long as such law continues in force there, or direct that such law or any part thereof shall have effect in such British Possession with or without modifications and alterations as if it were part of this Act.

---

[1] See the Indian Post Office Act, 1818 (VI of 1898), s. 10. General Acts, Ed. 1898, Vol. VI.

9. In this Act— Definitions.

The expression "mail bag" means a mail of letters, or a box, or parcel, or any other envelope in which post letters within the meaning of the Acts relating to the Post Office, are conveyed;

The expression "subsidy" includes a payment for the performance of a contract;

The expression "master of a ship" includes any person in charge of a ship, whether commander, mate, or any other person;

The expression "ship of a Foreign State" means a ship entitled to sail under the flag of a Foreign State;

The expression "arrresting authority" means any court, authority, or officer having power to arrest or detain a ship or to arrest a person on board a ship, or to order such arrest or detention, or to order the execution of any process, civil or criminal, for the arrest of a person on board any ship;

The expression "postal officer" means any person employed in the business of the Post Office of the United Kingdom or a British Possession or Foreign State, as the case may be, whether employed by the Postmaster General, or the chief of the Post Office of the British Possession, or the chief of the Post Office of the Foreign State, or by any person under him, or on behalf of any such Post Office.

10. This Act may be cited as the Mail Ships Act, 1891. Short title.

SCHEDULE.

British Possessions to which Act is applicable only upon the Government adhering to Convention.

British India.	Western Australia.
Dominion of Canada.	Queensland.
Newfoundland.	Tasmania.
New South Wales.	New Zealand.
Victoria.	Cape of Good Hope.
South Australia.	Natal.

The Commissioners for Oaths Act, 1891.[1]

(54 & 55 Vict., c. 50.)

An Act to amend the Commissioners for Oaths Act, 1889.

[*5th August, 1891.*]

Whereas doubts have been entertained whether the powers to administer oaths and take affidavits conferred on a commissioner for oaths by the Commissioners for Oaths Act, 1889,[2] extend to oaths and affidavits required by special provisions to be made before a justice of the peace, or any particular person or officer, and it is expedient to remove such doubts: 52 & 53 Vict. c. 10.

* * * * * * *

Affidavit, etc., may be made before commissioner at any place.

1. Where by or under the Merchant Shipping Acts, 1854 to 1889, or the Customs Consolidation Act, 1876, or the Patents, Designs, and Trade Marks Acts, 1883 to 1888, or the Pawnbrokers Act, 1872, or Acts amending the same respectively, any oath or affidavit is required to be taken or made before any particular person or officer, whether having special authority or otherwise, and whether at any particular place, or within any specified limits or otherwise, such oath or affidavit may be taken or made before a commissioner for oaths, at any place, and shall be as effectual to all intents and purposes as if taken or made before such person or officer, and at any particular place or within specified limits.

Amendment of 52 & 53 Vict., c. 10, s. 6, as to acting consular agent.

2. In section six of the Commissioners for Oaths Act, 1889, after the words "consular agent" shall be inserted the words "acting consul general, acting vice-consul, and acting consular agent."

Construction and short title.

3. This Act shall be read with the Commissioners for Oaths Act, 1889, and may be cited as the Commissioners for Oaths Act, 1891, and the Commissioners for Oaths Act, 1889,[2] and this Act may be cited together as the Commissioners for Oaths Acts, 1889 and 1891.

The Coinage Act, 1891.[3]

(54 & 55 Vict., c. 72.)

An Act to amend the Coinage Act, 1870.

[*5th August, 1891.*]

* * * * * * * *

Provision as to exchange of light gold coins.

1. (1) It shall be lawful for Her Majesty, by Order in Council, to direct that gold coins of the realm which have not been called in by proclamation

---

[1] See *Chitty's Statutes*, tit. Oaths, p. 22.
[2] Printed *ante*, p. 853.
[3] See Appendix, *post*, p. 1263.

33 & 34 Vict., c. 10. and are below the least current weight as provided by the Coinage Act, 1870,[1] shall, if they have not been illegally dealt with, and subject to such conditions as to time, manner, and order of presentation, as may be mentioned in the Order, be exchanged or paid for by or on behalf of the Mint at their nominal value.

(2) For the purposes of this Act a gold coin shall be deemed to have been illegally dealt with where the coin has been impaired, diminished, or lightened otherwise than by fair wear and tear, or has been defaced by having any name, word, device, or number stamped thereon, whether the coin has or has not been thereby diminished or lightened.

(3) In a sovereign or half sovereign loss of weight exceeding three grains from the standard weight shall, for the purposes of this Act, be *primâ facie* evidence that the coin has been impaired, diminished, or lightened otherwise than by fair wear and tear.

(4) Towards meeting the expenses to be incurred in pursuance of this section the sum of four hundred thousand pounds shall be charged on and issued from the Consolidated Fund in the year ending the thirty-first day of March, one thousand eight hundred and ninety-two, and, so far as not immediately required, may be invested in such manner as the Treasury direct; and any interest thereon shall be applied for the purposes of this section.

Remedy allowances for coin.

2. The remedy allowances for gold, silver, and bronze coins shall be such as are specified in the schedule to this Act: and in all copies of the Coinage Act, 1870,[1] printed after the passing of this Act, the First Schedule to that Act shall be printed so as to give effect to the amendments made by this section.

Short titles and construction.

3. (1) This Act may be cited as the Coinage Act, 1891.

(2) This Act and the Coinage Act, 1870,[1] may be cited together as the Coinage Acts, 1870 and 1891.

(3) Expressions used in this Act have the same meaning as in the Coinage Act, 1870.[1]

[1] See Appendix, *post*, p. 1203.

SCHEDULE.

Denomination of Coin.	Standard Fineness.	Remedy Allowance. Weight per Piece. Imperial Grains.	Metric Grams.	Millesimal Fineness.
GOLD:				
Five-pound	Eleven-Twelfths fine gold, one-twelfth alloy; or millesimal fineness 916·6.	1·00	0·06479	2
Two-pound		0·40	0·02592	
Sovereign		0·20	0·01296	
Half-sovereign		0·15	0·00972	
SILVER:				
Crown	Thirty-seven-fortieths fine silver, three-fortieths alloy; or millesimal fineness 925.	2·000	0·1296	4
Double-florin		1·678	0·1087	
Half-Crown		1 264	0·0783	
Florin		0·997	0·0646	
Shilling		0·578	0·0375	
Six pence		0·346	0·0224	
Groat or Four pence		0·262	0·0170	
Three pence		0·212	0·0138	
Two pence		0·144	0·0093	
Penny		0·087	0·0056	
BRONZE:				
Penny	Mixed metal, copper, tin and zinc.	2·91666	0·18899	None.
Halfpenny		1·75000	0·11339	
Farthing		0·87500	0·05669	

THE COLONIAL PROBATES ACT, 1892.[1]

(55 & 56 Vict., c. 6.)

An Act to provide for the Recognition in the United Kingdom of Probates and Letters of Administration granted in British Possessions.

[*20th May, 1892.*]

* * * * * * * *

Application of Act by Order in Council.

1. Her Majesty the Queen may, on being satisfied that the legislature of any British possession has made adequate provision for the recognition in

[1] See *Chitty's Statutes*, Tit. Executors, p. 94.

that possession of probates and letters of administration granted by the courts of the United Kingdom, direct by Order in Council that this Act shall, subject to any exceptions and modifications specified in the Order, apply to that possession, and thereupon, while the Order is in force, this Act shall apply accordingly.

2. (1) Where a court of probate in a British possession to which this Act applies has granted probate or letters of administration in respect of the estate of a deceased person, the probate or letters so granted may, on being produced to, and a copy thereof deposited with, a court of probate in the United Kingdom, be sealed with the seal of that court, and, thereupon, shall be of the like force and effect, and have the same operation in the United Kingdom, as if granted by that court.

Sealing in United Kingdom of colonial probates and letters of administration.

(2) Provided that the court shall, before sealing a probate or letters of administration under this section, be satisfied—

(*a*) that probate duty has been paid in respect of so much (if any) o the estate as is liable to probate duty in the United Kingdom; and

(*b*) in the case of letters of administration, that security has been given in a sum sufficient in amount to cover the property (if any) in the United Kingdom to which the letters of administration relate;

and may require such evidence, if any, as it thinks fit as to the domicile of the deceased person.

(3) The court may also, if it thinks fit, on the application of any creditor, require, before sealing, that adequate security be given for the payment of debts due from the estate to creditors residing in the United Kingdom.

(4) For the purposes of this section, a duplicate of any probate or letters of administration sealed with the seal of the court granting the same, or a copy thereof certified as correct by or under the authority of the court granting the same, shall have the same effect as the original.

(5) Rules of court may be made for regulating the procedure and practice, including fees and costs, in courts of the United Kingdom, on and incidental to an application for sealing a probate or letters of administration granted in a British possession to which this Act applies. Such rules shall, so far as they relate to probate duty, be made with the consent of the Treasury, and, subject to any exceptions and modifications made by such rules, the enactments for the time being in force in relation to probate duty (including the penal provisions thereof) shall apply as if the person who applies for sealing under this section were a person applying for probate or letters of administration.

Application of Act to British courts in foreign countries.

3. This Act shall extend to authorise the sealing in the United Kingdom of any probate or letters of administration granted by a British court in a foreign country, in like manner as it authorises the sealing of a probate or letters of administration granted in a British possession to which this Act applies, and the provisions of this Act shall apply accordingly with the necessary modifications.

Orders in Council.

4. (1) Every Order in Council made under this Act shall be laid before both Houses of Parliament as soon as may be after it is made, and shall be published under the authority of Her Majesty's Stationery Office.

(2) Her Majesty the Queen in Council may revoke or alter any Order in Council previously made under this Act.

(3) Where it appears to Her Majesty in Council that the legislature of part of a British possession has power to make the provision requisite for bringing this Act into operation in that part, it shall be lawful for Her Majesty to direct by Order in Council that this Act shall apply to that part as if it were a separate British possession, and thereupon, while the Order is in force, this Act shall apply accordingly.

Application of Act to probates, etc., already granted.

5. This Act when applied by an Order in Council to a British possession shall, subject to the provisions of the Order, apply to probates and letters of administration granted in that possession either before or after the passing of this Act.

Definitions.

6. In this Act—

The expression "court of probate" means any court or authority, by whatever name designated, having jurisdiction in matters of probate, and in Scotland means the sheriff court of the county of Edinburgh:

The expressions "probate" and "letters of administration" include confirmation in Scotland, and any instrument having in a British possession the same effect which under English law is given to probate and letters of administration respectively:

The expression "probate duty" includes any duty payable on the value of the estate and effects for which probate or letters of administration is or are granted:

The expression "British court in a foreign country" means any British court having jurisdiction out of the Queen's dominions in pursuance of an Order in Council, whether made under any Act or otherwise.

Short title.

7. This Act may be cited as the Colonial Probates Act, 1892.

THE INDIAN COUNCILS ACT, 1892.[1]

(55 & 56 Vict., c. 14.)

An Act to amend the Indian Councils Act, 1861.

[*20th June, 1892.*]

*   *   *   *   *   *   *

Provisions for increase of number of members of Indian councils for making law and regulations.

1. (1) The number of additional members of Council nominated by the Governor General under the provisions of section ten of the Indian Councils Act, 1861, shall be such as to him may seem from time to time expedient, but shall not be less than ten nor more than sixteen; and the number of additional members of Council nominated by the governors of the presidencies of Fort St. George and Bombay respectively under the provisions of section twenty-nine of the Indian Councils Act, 1861,[2] shall (besides the advocate general of the presidency or officer acting in that capacity) be such as to the said governors respectively may seem from time to time expedient, but shall not be less than eight nor more than twenty.

& 25 Vict., 7.

(2) It shall be lawful for the Governor General in Council by proclamation from time to time to increase the number of councillors whom the lieutenant governors of the Bengal Division of the presidency of Fort William and of the North-Western Provinces and Oudh respectively may nominate for their assistance in making laws and regulations: Provided always, that not more than twenty shall be nominated for the Bengal Division, and not more than fifteen for the North-Western Provinces and Oudh.

(3) Any person resident in India may be nominated an additional member of Council under sections ten and twenty-nine of the Indian Councils Act, 1861, and this Act, or a member of the Council of the lieutenant governor of any province to which the provisions of the Indian Councils Act, 1861,[1] touching the making of laws and regulations, have been or are hereafter extended or made applicable.

(4) The Governor General in Council may from time to time, with the approval of the Secretary of State in Council, make regulations as to the conditions under which such nominations, or any of them, shall be made by the Governor General, Governors, and Lieutenant-Governors respectively, and prescribe the manner in which such regulations shall be carried into effect.

Modification of provisions of 24 & 25 Vict., c. 67, as to business at legislative meetings.

2. Notwithstanding any provisions in the Indian Councils Act, 1861,[1] the Governor General of India in Council may from time to time make rules authorising at any meeting of the Governor General's Council for the purpose of making laws and regulations the discussion of the annual financial statement of the Governor General in Council and the asking of questions, but

[1] For digest, see Ilbert's *Government of India*, p. 325.
[2] Printed Vol. I, p. 339.

under such conditions and restrictions as to subject or otherwise as shall be in the said rules prescribed or declared: And notwithstanding any provisions in the Indian Councils Act, 1861,[1] the Governors in Council of Fort St. George and Bombay, respectively, and the lieutenant governor of any province to which the provisions of the Indian Councils Act, 1861,[1] touching the making of laws and regulations, have been or are hereafter extended or made applicable, may from time to time make rules for authorising at any meeting of their respective councils for the purpose of making laws and regulations the discussion of the annual financial statement of their respective local governments, and the asking of questions, but under such conditions and restrictions, as to subject or otherwise, as shall in the said rules applicable to such councils respectively be prescribed or declared. But no member at any such meeting of any council shall have power to submit or propose any resolution, or to divide the council in respect of any such financial discussion, or the answer to any question asked under the authority of this Act, or the rules made under this Act: Provided that any rule made under this Act by a governor in council, or by a lieutenant governor, shall be submitted for and shall be subject to the sanction of the Governor General in Council, and any rule made under this Act by the Governor General in Council shall be submitted for and shall be subject to the sanction of the Secretary of State in Council: Provided also that rules made under this Act shall not be subject to alteration or amendment at meetings for the purpose of making laws and regulations.

Meaning of 24 & 25 Vict., c. 67, s. 22. 3 & 4, Will. 4, c. 85, and 16 & 17 Vict., c. 95.

3. It is hereby declared that in the twenty-second section of the Indian Councils Act, 1861,[1] it was and is intended that the words "Indian territories now under the dominion of Her Majesty" should be read and construed as if the words "or hereafter" were and had at the time of the passing of the said Act been inserted next after the word "now"; and further, that the Acts third and fourth William the Fourth, chapter eighty-five, and sixteenth and seventeenth Victoria, chapter ninety-five, respectively shall be read and construed as if at the date of the enactment thereof respectively it was intended and had been enacted that the said Acts respectively should extend to and include the territories acquired after the dates thereof respectively by the East India Company, and should not be confined to the territories at the dates of the said enactments respectively in the possession and under the government of the said company.

Repeal. Power to fill up vacancy in number of additional members.

4. Sections thirteen and thirty-two of the Indian Councils Act, 1861,[1] are hereby repealed, and it is enacted that—

(1) If any additional member of Council, or any member of the council of a lieutenant governor, appointed under the said Act or this

[1] 24 & 25 Vict., c. 67, printed, Vol. I, p. 339.

Act, shall be absent from India or unable to attend to the duties of his office for a period of two consecutive months, it shall be lawful for the Governor general, the governor, or the lieutenant governor to whose council such additional member or member may have been nominated (as the case may be) to declare, by a notification published in the Government Gazette, that the seat in Council of such person has become vacant:

(2) In the event of a vacancy occurring by the absence from India, inability to attend to duty, death, acceptance of office, or resignation duly accepted, of any such additional member or member of the council of a lieutenant governor, it shall be lawful for the Governor General, for the governor, or for the lieutenant governor, as the case may be, to nominate any person as additional member or member, as the case may be, in his place; and every member so nominated shall be summoned to all meetings held for the purpose of making laws and regulations for the term of two years from the date of such nomination: Provided always that it shall not be lawful by such nomination, or by any other nomination made under this Act, to diminish the proportion of non-official members directed by the Indian Councils Act, 1861,[1] to be nominated.

Powers of Indian provincial legislatures.

5. The local legislature of any province in India may from time to time, by Acts passed under and subject to the provisions of the Indian Councils Act, 1861, and with the previous sanction of the Governor General, but not otherwise, repeal or amend as to that province any law or regulation made either before or after the passing of this Act by any authority in India other than that local legislature: Provided that an Act or a provision of an Act made by a local legislature, and subsequently assented to by the Governor General in pursuance of the Indian Councils Act, 1861,[1] shall not be deemed invalid by reason only of its requiring the previous sanction of the Governor General under this section.

Definitions.

6. In this Act—

The expression "local legislature" means—

(1) The Governor in Council for the purpose of making laws and regulations of the respective provinces of Fort St. George and Bombay; and

---

[1] 24 & 25 Vict., c. 67, printed, Vol. I, p. 339.

(2) The council for the purpose of making laws and regulations of the lieutenant governor of any province to which the provisions of the Indian Councils Act, 1861, touching the making of laws or regulations have been or are hereafter extended or made applicable.

The expression "province" means any presidency, division, province, or territory over which the powers of any local legislature for the time being extend.

Saving of powers of Governor General in Council.

7. Nothing in this Act shall detract from or diminish the powers of the Governor General in Council at meetings for the purpose of making laws and regulations.

Short title.

8. This Act may be cited as the Indian Councils Act, 1892; and the Indian Councils Act, 1861, and this Act may be cited together as the Indian Councils Acts, 1861 and 1892.

The Foreign Marriage Act, 1892.[1]

(55 & 56 Vict., c. 23.)

An Act to consolidate Enactments relating to the Marriage of British Subjects outside the United Kingdom.

[*27th June, 1892.*]

* * * * * * * *

Validity of marriages solemnized abroad in manner provided by Act.

1. All marriages between parties of whom one at least is a British subject solemnized in the manner in this Act provided in any foreign country or place by or before a marriage officer within the meaning of this Act shall be as valid in law as if the same had been solemnized in the United Kingdom with a due observance of all forms required by law.

Notice to marriage officer of intended marriage.

2. In every case of a marriage intended to be solemnized under this Act, one of the parties intending marriage shall sign a notice stating the name, surname, profession, condition, and residence of each of the parties, and whether each of the parties is or is not a minor, and give the notice to the marriage officer within whose district both of the parties have had their residence not less than one week then next preceding, and the notice shall state that they have so resided.

---

[1] See *Chitty's Statutes*, Tit. Marriage, p. 63.

3. (1) The marriage officer shall file every such notice, and keep it with the archives of his office, and shall also, on payment of the proper fee, forthwith enter in a book of notices to be kept by him for the purpose, and post up in some conspicuous place in his office, a true copy of every such notice, and shall keep the same so posted up during fourteen consecutive days before the marriage is solemnized under the notice.

Filing in registry and posting up of notice.

(2) The said book and copy posted up shall be open at all reasonable times, without fee, to the inspection of any person.

4. (1) The like consent shall be required to a marriage under this Act as is required by law to marriages solemnized in England.

Requirement of like consent to marriage as in England, and power to forbid marriage.

(2) Every person whose consent to a marriage is so required may, at any time before the solemnization thereof under this Act, forbid it by writing the word "forbidden" opposite to the entry of the intended marriage in the book of notices, and by subscribing thereto his name and residence, and the character by reason of which he is authorised to forbid the marriage; and if a marriage is so forbidden the notice shall be void, and the intended marriage shall not be solemnized under that notice.

5. (1) Any person may on payment of the proper fee enter with the marriage officer a caveat signed by him or on his behalf, and stating his residence and the ground of his objection against the solemnization of the marriage of any person named therein, and thereupon the marriage of that person shall not be solemnized until either the marriage officer has examined into the matter of the caveat and is satisfied that it ought not to obstruct the solemnization of the marriage, or the caveat is withdrawn by the person entering it.

Caveat against marriages may be lodged with marriage officer.

(2) In a case of doubt the marriage officer may transmit a copy of the caveat, with such statement respecting it as he thinks fit, to a Secretary of State, who shall refer the same to the Registrar-General, and the Registrar-General shall give his decision thereon in writing to the Secretary of State, who shall communicate it to the marriage officer.

(3) If the marriage officer refuses to solemnize or to allow to be solemnized in his presence the marriage of any person requiring it to be solemnized, that person may appeal to a Secretary of State, who shall give the marriage officer his decision thereon.

(4) The marriage officer shall forthwith inform the parties of and shall conform to any decision given by the Registrar-General or Secretary of State.

6. Where a marriage is not solemnized within three months next after the latest of the following dates—

When marriage not solemnized within three months a new notice required.

(a) the date on which the notice for it has been given to and entered by the marriage officer under this Act, or (*b*) if on a caveat being entered a statement has been transmitted to a Secretary of State, or if an appeal has been made to a Secretary of State, then the date of the receipt from the Secretary of State of a decision directing the marriage to be solemnized,

the notice shall be void, and the intended marriage shall not be solemnized under that notice.

Oath before marriage.

7. Before a marriage is solemnized under this Act, each of the parties intending marriage shall appear before the marriage officer, and make, and subscribe in a book kept by the officer for the purpose, an oath—

(*a*) that he or she believes that there is not any impediment to the marriage by reason of kindred or alliance, or otherwise; and

(*b*) that both of the parties have for three weeks immediately preceding had their usual residence within the district of the marriage officer; and

(*c*) where either of the parties, not being a widower or widow, is under the age of twenty-one years, that the consent of the persons whose consent to the marriage is required by law has been obtained thereto, or as the case may be, that there is no person having authority to give such consent.

Solemnization of marriage at office in presence of marriage officer and two witnesses.

8. (1) After the expiration of fourteen days after the notice of an intended marriage has been entered under this Act, then, if no lawful impediment to the marriage is shown to the satisfaction of the marriage officer, and the marriage has not been forbidden in manner provided by this Act, the marriage may be solemnized under this Act.

(2) Every such marriage shall be solemnized at the official house of the marriage officer, with open doors, between the hours of eight in the forenoon and three in the afternoon, in the presence of two or more witnesses, and may be solemnized by another person in the presence of the marriage officer, according to the rites of the Church of England, or such other form and ceremony as the parties thereto see fit to adopt, or may, where the parties so desire, be solemnized by the marriage officer.

(3) Where such marriage is not solemnized according to the rites of the Church of England, then in some part of the ceremony, and in the presence of the marriage officer and witnesses, each of the parties shall declare,

"I solemnly declare that I know not of any lawful impediment why I *A. B.* [*or C. D.*] may not be joined in matrimony to *C. D.* [*or A. B.*]"

And each of the parties shall say to the other,

"I call upon these persons here present to witness that I *A.B.* [*or C. D.*] take thee *C.D.* [*or A.B.*] to be my lawful wedded wife [or husband.]"

Marriage fees to marriage officer and registration of marriages.

9. (1) The marriage officer shall be entitled, for every marriage solemnized under this Act by him or in his presence, to have from the parties married the proper fee.

(2) He shall forthwith register in duplicate every such marriage in two marriage register books, which shall be furnished to him from time to time for that purpose by the Registrar-General (through a Secretary of State), according to the form provided by law for the registration of marriages in England, or as near to that form as the difference of the circumstances admits.

(3) The entry in each book of every such marriage shall be signed by the marriage officer, by the person solemnizing the marriage, if other than the marriage officer, by both the parties married, and by two witnesses of the marriage.

(4) All such entries shall be made in regular order from the beginning to the end of each book, and the number of the entry in each duplicate shall be the same.

(5) The marriage officer by whom or in whose presence a marriage is solemnized under this Act may ask of the parties to be married the several particulars required to be registered touching the marriage.

Annual forwarding of copies of registered book to Secretary of State.

10. (1) In January in every year every marriage officer shall make and send to a Secretary of State, to be transmitted by him to the Registrar General, a copy, certified by him to be a true copy, of all the entries of marriages during the preceding year in the register book kept by him, and if there has been no such entry, a certificate of that fact; and every such copy shall be certified, and certificate given, under his hand and official seal.

(2) The marriage officer shall keep the duplicate marriage register books safely until they are filled, and then send one of them to a Secretary of State, to be transmitted by him to the Registrar General.

Marriage officers and their districts.

11. (1) For the purposes of this Act the following officers shall be marriage officers, that is to say:—

(*a*) Any officer authorised in that behalf by a Secretary of State by authority in writing under his hand (in this Act referred to as a marriage warrant); and

(*b*) Any officer who under the marriage regulations herein-after mentioned is authorised to act as marriage officer without any marriage warrant,

and the district of a marriage officer shall be the area within which the duties of his office are exerciseable, or any such less area as is assigned by the marriage warrant or any other warrant of a Secretary of State, or is fixed by the marriage regulations.

(2) Any marriage warrant of a Secretary of State may authorize to be a marriage officer—

(*a*) a British ambassador residing in a foreign country to the government of which he is accredited and also any officer prescribed as an officer for solemnizing marriages in the official house of such ambassador;

(*b*) the holder of the office of British consul in any foreign country or place specified in the warrant; and

(*c*) a governor, high commissioner, resident, consular or other officer, or any person appointed in pursuance of the marriage regulations to act in the place of a high commissioner or resident, and this Act shall apply with the prescribed modifications to a marriage by or before a governor, high commissioner, resident, or officer so authorised by the warrant, and in such application shall not be limited to places outside Her Majesty's dominions.

(3) If a marriage warrant refers to the office without designating the name of any particular person holding the office, then, while the warrant is in force, the person for the time being holding or acting in such office shall be a marriage officer.

(4) A Secretary of State may, by warrant under his hand, vary or revoke any marriage warrant previously issued under this Act.

(5) Where a marriage officer has no seal of his office, any reference in this Act to the official seal shall be construed to refer to any seal ordinarily used by him, if authenticated by his signature with his official name and description.

Marriages on board Her Majesty's ships on foreign stations.

12. A marriage under this Act may be solemnized on board one of Her Majesty's ships on a foreign station, and with respect to such marriage—

(*a*) subject to the marriage regulations a marriage warrant of a Secretary of State may authorise the commanding officer of the ship to be a marriage officer;

(*b*) the provisions of this Act shall apply with the prescribed modifications.

Avoidance of objections to marriages on account of want of formalities or

13. (1) After a marriage has been solemnized under this Act it shall not be necessary, in support of the marriage, to give any proof of the residence for the time required by or in pursuance of this Act of either of the parties previous to the marriage, or of the consent of any person whose consent thereto is required by law, nor shall any evidence to prove the contrary be given in any legal proceeding touching the validity of the marriage. authority of officer.

(2) Where a marriage purports to have been solemnized and registered under this Act in the official house of a British ambassador or consul, or on board one of Her Majesty's ships, it shall not be necessary, in support of the marriage, to give any proof of the authority of the marriage officer by or before whom the marriage was solemnized and registered, nor shall any evidence to prove his want of authority, whether by reason of his not being a duly authorised marriage officer or of any prohibitions or restrictions under the marriage regulations or otherwise, be given in any legal proceeding touching the validity of the marriage.

Forfeiture of property in case of fraudulent marriage.

14. If a marriage is solemnized under this Act by means of any wilfully false notice signed, or oath made by either party to the marriage, as to any matter for which a notice, or oath, is by this Act required, the Attorney General may sue for the forfeiture of all estate and interest in any property in England accruing to the offending party by the marriage; and the proceedings thereupon, and the consequences thereof, shall be the same as are provided by law in the like case with regard to marriages solemnized in England according to the rites of the Church of England.

Punishment of false oath or notice.

15. If a person—

(*a*) knowingly and wilfully makes a false oath or signs a false notice, under this Act, for the purpose of procuring a marriage, or

(*b*) forbids a marriage under this Act by falsely representing himself to be a person whose consent to the marriage is required by law; knowing such representation to be false,

such person shall suffer the penalties of perjury, and may be tried in any county in England and dealt with in the same manner in all respects as if the offence had been committed in that county.

Evidence.

16. (1) Any book, notice, or document directed by this Act to be kept by the marriage officer or in the archives of his office, shall be of such a public nature as to be admissible in evidence on its mere production from the custody of the officer.

(2) A certificate of a Secretary of State as to any house, office, chapel, or other place being, or being part of, the official house of a British ambassador or consul shall be conclusive.

Application of Registration Acts to this Act.

17. All the provisions and penalties of the Marriage Registration Acts, relating to any registrar or register of marriages or certified copies thereof, shall extend to every marriage officer, and to the registers of marriages under this Act, and to the certified copies thereof (so far as the same are applicable thereto), as if herein re-enacted and in terms made applicable to this Act, and as if every marriage officer were a registrar under the said Acts.

Registration of marriages solemnized under local law.

18. Subject to the marriage regulations, a British consul, or person authorised to act as British consul, on being satisfied by personal attendance that a marriage between parties, of whom one at least is a British subject, has been duly solemnized in a foreign country, in accordance with the local law of the country, and on payment of the proper fee, may register the marriage in accordance with the marriage regulations as having been so solemnized, and thereupon this Act shall apply as if the marriage had been registered in pursuance of this Act, except that nothing in this Act shall affect the validity of the marriage so solemnized.

Power to refuse solemnization of marriage where marriage inconsistent with international law.

19. A marriage officer shall not be required to solemnize a marriage, or to allow a marriage to be solemnized in his presence, if in his opinion the solemnization thereof would be inconsistent with international law or the comity of nations:

Provided that any person requiring his marriage to be solemnized shall, if the officer refuses to solemnize it or allow it to be solemnized in his presence, have the right of appeal to the Secretary of State given by this Act.

Fees.

20. The proper fee under this Act shall be such fee as may for the time being be fixed under the Consular Salaries and Fees Act, 1891; and the fee so fixed as respects a consul shall be the fee which may be taken by any marriage officer; and the provisions relating to the levying, application, and remission of and accounting for fees under that Act shall apply to the same when taken by any marriage officer who is not a consul. 54 & 55 V. c. 36.

Power to make marriage regulations.

21. (1) Her Majesty the Queen in Council may make regulations (in this Act referred to as the marriage regulations)—

(*a*) Prohibiting or restricting the exercise by marriage officers of their powers under this Act in cases where the exercise of those powers appears to Her Majesty to be inconsistent with international law or the comity of nations or in places where sufficient facilities appear to Her Majesty to exist without the exercise of those powers, for the solemnization of marriages to which a British subject is a party; and

(*b*) Determining what offices, chapels, or other places are, for the purposes of marriages under this Act, to be deemed to be part of the official house or the office of a marriage officer; and (*c*) Modifying in special cases or classes of cases the requirements of this Act as to residence and notice, so far as such modification appears to Her Majesty to be consistent with the observance of due precautions against clandestine marriages; and

(*d*) Prescribing the forms to be used under this Act; and

(*e*) Adapting this Act to marriages on board one of Her Majesty's ships; and to marriages by or before a governor, high commissioner, resident, or other officer, and authorising the appointment of a person to act under this Act in the place of a high commissioner or resident; and

(*f*) Determining who is to be the marriage officer for the purpose of a marriage in the official house of a British ambassador, or on board one of Her Majesty's ships, whether such officer is described in the regulations or named in pursuance thereof, and authorising such officer to act without any marriage warrant; and

(*g*) Determining the conditions under which and the mode in which marriages solemnized in accordance with the local law of a foreign country may be registered under this Act; and

(*h*) Making such provisions as seem necessary or proper for carrying into effect this Act or any marriage regulations; and

(*i*) Varying or revoking any marriage regulations previously made.

(2) All regulations purporting to be made in pursuance of this section may be made either generally or with reference to any particular case or class of cases, and shall be published under the authority of Her Majesty's Stationery Office, and laid before both Houses of Parliament, and deemed to be within the powers of this Act, and shall while in force have effect as if enacted by this Act.

(3) Any marriage regulations which dispense for any reason, whether residence out of the district or otherwise, with the requirements of this Act, as to residence and notice, may require as a condition or consequence of the dispensation, the production of such notice, certificate, or document, and the taking of such oath, and may authorise the publication or grant of such notice, certificate, or document, and the charge of such fees as may be prescribed by the regulations; and the provisions of this Act, including those enacting punishments with reference to any false notice or oath, shall apply as if the said notice, certificate, or document were a notice, and such oath were an oath within the meaning of those provisions.

22. It is hereby declared that all marriages solemnized within the British lines by any chaplain or officer or other person officiating under the orders of *Validity of marriages solemnized*

Within British lines. the commanding officer of a British army serving abroad, shall be as valid in law as if the same had been solemnized within the United Kingdom, with a due observance of all forms required by law.

Saving. **23.** Nothing in this Act shall confirm or impair or in anywise affect the validity in law of any marriage solemnized beyond the seas, otherwise than as herein provided, and this Act shall not extend to the marriage of any of the Royal family.

Definitions. **24.** In this Act, unless the context otherwise requires,—

The expression "Registrar-General" means the Registrar-General of Births, Deaths, and Marriages in England:

The expression "Attorney General" means Her Majesty's Attorney General, or if there is no such Attorney General, or the Attorney General is unable or incompetent to act, Her Majesty's Solicitor General, for England:

The expression "the Marriage Registration Acts" means the Act of the session of the sixth and seventh years of the reign of King William the Fourth, chapter eighty-six, intituled "An Act for registering births, deaths, and marriages in England" and the enactments amending the same:

The expression "official house of a marriage officer" means, subject to the provisions of any marriage regulations, the office at which the business of such officer is transacted, and the official house of residence of such officer, and, in the case of any officer, who is an officer for solemnizing marriages in the official house of an ambassador, means the official house of the ambassador:

The expression "consul" means a consul-general, consul, vice-consul, pro-consul, or consular agent:

The expression "ambassador" includes a minister and a chargè d'affaires:

The expression "prescribed" means prescribed by marriage regulations under this Act.

Commencement of Act. **25.** This Act shall come into operation on the first day of January next after the passing thereof.

Repeal and savings. **26.** (1) The Acts specified in the schedule to this Act are hereby repealed to the extent in the third column of that Schedule mentioned.

Provided that—

(*a*) any Order in Council in force under any Act so repealed shall continue in force as if made in pursuance of this Act; and

(*b*) any proceedings taken with reference to a marriage, any register book kept, and any warrant issued in pursuance of the Acts hereby repealed, shall have effect as if taken, kept, and issued in pursuance of this Act; and (*c*) The fees which can be taken in pursuance of the Acts hereby repealed may continue to be taken in like manner as if fixed in pursuance of the Consular Salaries and Fees Act, 1891, and may be altered accordingly; and

(*d*) The forms prescribed by or in pursuance of the Acts hereby repealed may continue to be used as if prescribed by an Order in Council under this Act.

(2) Every marriage in fact solemnized and registered by or before a British consul or other marriage officer in intended pursuance of any Act hereby repealed shall, notwithstanding such repeal or any defect in the authority of the consul or the solemnization of the marriage elsewhere than at the consulate, be as valid as if the said Act had not been repealed, and the marriage had been solemnized at the consulate by or before a duly authorised consul:

Provided that this enactment shall not render valid any marriage declared invalid before the passing of this Act by any competent court, or render valid any marriage either of the parties to which has, before the passing of this Act, lawfully intermarried with any other person.

Short title.

27. This Act may be cited as the Foreign Marriage Act, 1892.

SCHEDULE.

ENACTMENTS REPEALED.

Session and Chapter.	Title.	Extent of Repeal.
4 Geo. 4, c. 91	An Act to relieve His Majesty's subjects from all doubt concerning the validity of certain marriages solemnized abroad.	The whole Act, so far as unrepealed.
12 & 13 Vict., c. 68	The Consular Marriage Act, 1849	The whole Act.
31 & 32 Vict., c. 61	The Consular Marriage Act, 1868	The whole Act.
33 & 34 Vict., c. 14	The Naturalization Act, 1870	In section eleven, the words, "and of the "marriages of persons "married at any of "Her Majesty's em- "bassies or legations."
53 & 54 Vict., c. 47	The Marriage Act, 1890	The whole Act.
54 & 55 Vict., c. 47	The Foreign Marriage Act, 1891	The whole Act.

The Superannuation Act, 1892.[1]

(55 & 56 Vict., c. 40.)

An Act to amend the Acts relating to Superannuation Allowances and Gratuities to Persons in the Public Service so far as respects the computation of successive Service in different Offices where not all subject to the Superannuation Acts, 1834 to 1887, and as respects the application of Section Six of the Superannuation Act, 1887, to Employments of Profit under the Government of India.

[*27th June, 1892.*]

* * * * * * *

Reckoning of service in one or more public offices.

1. (1) The Treasury may, within one month after the passing of this Act, frame rules regulating the superannuation allowance or gratuity which may be granted to persons who have served continuously and successively in two or more public offices as defined by this Act, but are not entitled to reckon for such grant service in all those offices.

(2) The said rules shall provide for reckoning service according to the rules under the Superannuation Acts, 1834[2] to 1887, and subject to such reckoning of service, for granting the same superannuation allowance or gratuity to any person as might have been granted to him, if his whole service had been in the public office from which he ultimately retires.

(3) The Treasury may determine in each case the funds or accounts out of which the superannuation allowance or gratuity is to be paid, and where it is to be paid out of more than one fund or account, may apportion the amounts to be paid out of each fund or account: Provided that in cases affecting the revenue of India the Secretary of State in Council of India shall determine the amount to be paid therefrom.

Extension to Indian employments of rules under 50 & 51 Vict., c. 67, s. 6.

2. The Treasury may, within one month after the passing of this Act, frame rules for the purpose of extending to employments of profit under the department of the Secretary of State in Council of India, or the Government of India, such of the existing rules under section six of the Superannuation Act, 1887,[3] as do not extend to those employments, and may consolidate the existing rules with the rules so framed.

Rules to be laid before Parliament.

3. A copy of any rules made under this Act shall forthwith be laid before Parliament, and the rules shall not come into operation until three months after such copy is so laid, nor if within those three months either

[1] This Act may be cited with eight others as the Superannuation Acts, 1834 to 1892. See, too, *Chitty's Statutes*, Tit. Pensions, p. 19.

[2] Printed Vol. I, p. 183.

[3] Printed *ante*, p. 842.

House passes a resolution objecting to them, but if such resolution is passed the Treasury may frame new rules, and this section shall apply as if the passing of the said resolution were substituted for the passing of this Act, and so on as often as occasion may require.

4. In this Act, unless the context otherwise requires— Definitions.

The expression "public office" means any office or employment (other than any office or employment in Her Majesty's naval or land forces) service in which qualifies for the grant of a superannuation allowance or gratuity, and the remuneration of which is paid out of—

(*a*) the Consolidated Fund of the United Kingdom; or

(*b*) moneys provided by Parliament, or dealt with as appropriations in aid; or

(*c*) the revenue of India; or

(*d*) the revenue of the Isle of Man; or

(*e*) any fund which, from its being administered by a public department, the Treasury may determine to be a public fund;

41 Vict., and includes the office of any existing prison officer within the meaning of
41 Vict., the Prisons Act, 1877, the General Prisons (Ireland) Act, 1877, and the
41 Vict., Prisons (Scotland) Act, 1877:

The expression "superannuation allowance" includes any pension or superannuation or other retiring allowance.

5. This Act shall take effect as from the first day of January one thousand eight hundred and ninety-one. Commencement of Act.

6. This Act may be cited as the Superannuation Act, 1892.

Will. 4, This Act shall be read as one with the Superannuation Acts, 1834 to 1887, and those Acts and this Act may be cited together as the Superannuation Acts, 1834 to 1892. Short title and construction.

The Regimental Debts Act, 1893.[1]

(56 & 57 Vict., c. 5.)

An Act to consolidate and amend the Law relating to the Payment of Regimental Debts, and the Collection and Disposal of the Effects of Officers and Soldiers in case of Death, Desertion, Insanity, and other cases.

[29th April, 1893.]

* * * * * * * * * * * * *

Collection of Effects and Payment of Preferential Charges.

On death of person subject to military law, committee of adjustment to secure effects and pay charges.

1. On the death of a person while subject to military law the prescribed committee of adjustment shall, as soon as may be, in accordance with the prescribed regulations and subject to any exceptions made thereby,—

(1) secure and make an inventory of all such of the effects of the deceased as are in camp or quarters, and, if the death occurs out of the United Kingdom, are within the prescribed area whether station, colony, or command, or other, (which area is in this Act referred to as the regulation area); and

(2) ascertain the amount and provide for the payment of the preferential charges on the property of the deceased.

Preferential charges.

2. The following shall be the preferential charges on the property of a person dying while subject to military law, and shall, except so far as other provision may be made for them or any of them, be payable in preference to all other debts and liabilities, and, as among themselves, in the following order:—

(1) Expenses of last illness and funeral:

(2) Military debts, namely, sums due in respect of, or of any advance in respect of—

(*a*) Quarters;

(*b*) Mess, band, and other regimental accounts;

(*c*) Military clothing, appointments and equipments, not exceeding a sum equal to six months' pay of the deceased, and having become due within eighteen months before his death;

to which shall be added, where the death occurs out of the United Kingdom,—

(3) Servants' wages, not exceeding two months wages to each servant; and

(4) Household expenses incurred within a month before the death, or after the last issue of pay to the deceased, whichever is the shorter period.

---

[1] See *Chitty's Statutes*, Tit. Army, p. 112.

Surplus only of personal estate to be deemed personal estate.

3. So much only of the personal property of a person dying while subject to military law as remains after payment of the preferential charges shall be considered personal estate of the deceased with reference to the calculation of probate duty, or of any other duty, tax, or percentage, or for any of the purposes of administration.

Decision of questions as to preferential charges.

4. If in any case a doubt or difference arises in relation to any preferential charge or the payment thereof, the decision of the Secretary of State, or of such officer or person as the Secretary of State deputes by writing to act in this behalf, shall be final, and shall be binding on all persons for all purposes.

Payment of preferential charges by representatives or other persons.

5. Subject to the prescribed regulations, if any person pays or secures the payment of the preferential charges in full, the committee of adjustment shall not further interfere in relation to the property, except, so far as they may be requested so to do by or on behalf of that person.

Powers and duties of committee where preferential charges are not paid.

6. (1) If within one month after the death or such further time not exceeding the prescribed time as the committee of adjustment allow, the preferential charges are not paid or secured to their satisfaction, the committee shall proceed to pay those charges.

(2) If the death occurs out of the United Kingdom, the committee of adjustment, save as may be prescribed, shall, if it appears to them necessary for the payment of the preferential charges, and in any case may, collect all the personal property of the deceased in the regulation area.

(3) The committee, save as may be prescribed, shall, for the purpose of paying the preferential charges and their expenses, and in any case may, at such time as, subject to the prescribed regulations, they think expedient, sell and convert into money such of the personal property of the deceased as does not consist of money.

(4) If the death occurs out of the United Kingdom they may also, save as otherwise prescribed, pay all debts which appear to them to be legally payable out of the personal estate of the deceased.

(5) For the purpose of the exercise of their duties the committee shall, to the exclusion of all authorities and persons whomsoever, have the same rights and powers as if they had taken out representation to the deceased, and also if in a colony the powers which any official administrator has by the law of that colony; and any receipt given by the committee shall have the like effect as if it had been given by the legal personal representative of the deceased.

(6) The committee of adjustment shall lodge the surplus remaining in their hands after payment of the said charges and expenses and debts with uch person (in this Act referred to as the paymaster), at such times, in such

manner, and together with such inventory, accounts, vouchers, and information, as may be prescribed.

Disposal of Surplus and Residue.

Disposal of surplus by paymaster.

7. The paymaster shall pay the surplus in the prescribed manner, and subject to the prescribed provisions and exceptions, as follows:

(1) If out of the United Kingdom he may pay thereout any expenses which under the prescribed regulations are chargeable against the surplus, and any debts which are legally payable out of the personal estate of the deceased;

(2) If he knows of a representative of the deceased in the same part of Her Majesty's dominons, he shall pay the surplus to that representative;

(3) If he does not know of such a representative as above mentioned, and the amount does not exceed one hundred pounds, he may pay or apply all or any part thereof to or for the benefit of such persons in the same part of Her Majesty's dominions as he knows of and appear to be beneficially entitled to the personal estate of the deceased, or to or for the benefit of any of such persons;

(4) He shall remit the surplus or so much thereof as is not paid or applied in pursuance of this section to the Secretary of State.

Disposal of residue by Secretary of State.

8. The Secretary of State, on being informed of the death of a person subject to military law, shall proceed with all reasonable speed as follows:

(1) He shall cause to be ascertained the total amount to the credit of the deceased, including any surplus or part of a surplus remitted by a paymaster as mentioned in this Act, and all arrears of pay, batta, grants, and other allowances in the nature thereof; which total amount so ascertained is in this Act referred to as the residue;

(2) If he has notice of a representative of the deceased, he shall pay the residue to that representative;

(3) He may, and if it is so prescribed shall, before such payment, publish the prescribed notice stating the amount of the residue and such other particulars respecting the deceased and his property as may seem fit, and also the mode in which any application respecting the residue is to be made to the Secretary of State: Provided that the Secretary of State may pay out of any money in his hands to the credit of the deceased any preferential charges appearing to him to have been left unpaid by the committee of adjustment.

9. Where the residue does not exceed one hundred pounds, the Secretary of State may, if he thinks fit, require representation to be taken out; but if he does not, and has no notice of a representative of the deceased, then, after the expiration of the prescribed time and the publication of the prescribed notice (if any), the residue shall be disposed of as follows:

Disposals by Secretary of State of residue where residue does not exceed one hundred pounds, and no representation.

(1) The Secretary of State may, if he thinks fit, pay or apply the residue or any part thereof, in accordance with the prescribed regulations to or for the benefit of any of the persons appearing to be beneficially entitled to the personal estate of the deceased, or any of them, and may for that purpose invest the same by deposit in a military or other savings bank or otherwise, and, if necessary, in the name or names of a trustee or trustees for any such person.

(2) Any part thereof remaining in the hands of the Secretary of State, and not irrevocably appropriated, shall be applied in paying any debt of the deceased which—

(*a*) accrued due within three years before the death; and

(*b*) is claimed from the Secretary of State within two years after the death; and

(*c*) is proved by the claimant to the satisfaction of the Secretary of State.

(3) Except as above in this section provided, a person shall not be entitled to obtain payment out of any residue in the hands of the Secretary of State of any sum due from the deceased.

10. (1) Where any residue or any part thereof remains undisposed of and unappropriated, the prescribed notice thereof shall be published, and during six years next after the publication of that notice, the like notice with any necessary modifications shall be annually published.

Application of residue undisposed of.

(2) So much of the residue as remains undisposed of and unappropriated for six months after the publication of the last of such notices shall, together with any income or accumulations of income accrued therefrom, be applied in the prescribed manner in or towards the creation or maintenance of such compassionate or other fund for the benefit of widows and children or other near relatives, of soldiers dying on service, or within six months after discharge as may be prescribed.

(3) Provided that the application under this section of any residue, or part of a residue, shall not bar any claim of any person to the same, or any part thereof.

Supplemental provisions.

Disposal of medals and decorations.

11. Medals and decorations shall not be considered to be comprised in the personal estate of the deceased with reference to the claims of creditors or for any of the purposes of administration under this Act or otherwise; and, notwithstanding anything in this or any other Act, the same, when secured by the committee of adjustment, shall be held and disposed of according to regulations laid down by royal warrant.

Disposal of effects not money.

12. Where any part of the personal estate of the deceased consists of effects, securities, or other property not converted into money, the provisions of this Act with respect to paying or remitting the surplus shall, save as may be prescribed, extend to the delivery, transmission, or transfer of such effects, securities or property, and the paymaster and Secretary of State shall respectively have the same power of converting the same into money as the representative of the deceased.

Regulations by royal warrant.

13. (1) Her Majesty the Queen may, by warrant under the royal sign manual, make regulations for all such things as are by this Act directed or authorised to be prescribed or made subject to regulations, and also such regulations as may seem fit for the better execution of this Act or any part thereof; and may by such regulations make different provisions to meet different cases or different circumstances.

(2) Every royal warrant made under this Act shall be printed by the Queen's printer, and published under the authority of Her Majesty's Stationery Office and laid before both Houses of Parliament as soon as may be after the making thereof.

Restriction on interposition of official administrators.

14. (1) An official administrator, notwithstanding any law, regulating his office independently of this Act, shall not interpose in any manner in relation to any property of a person dying while subject to military law, except in the prescribed cases, or except when and so far as he is expressly required to do so by a committee of adjustment, or paymaster or Secretary of State.

(2) The committee of adjustment in such cases, under such circumstances and at such times as may be prescribed, may request an official administrator to exercise his official powers either on behalf of the committee or otherwise, and the administrator shall comply with the request. The committee may also lodge any property secured or collected by them with any official administrator.

(3) Where under this Act any property comes to the hands of any official administrator, he shall administer the same as regards preferential charges and otherwise in accordance with this Act, and, subject thereto, according to the law regulating his office independently of this Act.

(4) The official administrator shall remit any surplus remaining in his hands after discharge of all debts and his charges to the Secretary of State at such time and in such manner as may be prescribed, to be disposed of according to the provisions of this Act as if remitted by a paymaster.

(5) An official administrator shall not take a percentage on the property exceeding three per cent. on the gross amount coming to or remaining in his hands after payment of preferential charges.

Money remitted not to be assets in place where remitted to.

15. Any property coming under this Act to the hands of any committee of adjustment or paymaster shall not, by reason of so coming, be deemed assets or effects at the place in which that committee or paymaster is stationed or resides, and it shall not be necessary by reason thereof that representation be taken out in respect of that property for that place.

Duty and representation where sums under 100*l*.

16. Where any surplus or residue, as the case may be, does not exceed one hundred pounds, no duty shall be payable in the United Kingdom or India in respect thereof, and it shall not be necessary that representation to any deceased person be taken out for the purpose of obtaining payment thereof or of any part thereof under this Act from a paymaster or a Secretary of State, except in any prescribed case, or in any case where the Secretary of State requires it.

Discharge of paymaster and Secretary of State.

17. Compliance with the regulations under this Act with respect to the mode of payment of any surplus or residue or any part thereof to any person (whether by transmission or remission to another place or person or otherwise) shall discharge the Secretary of State, or paymaster or other person complying with the regulations, and he shall not be liable by reason of the surplus or residue or part which may be in his hands having been paid, transmitted, remitted or otherwise dealt with in accordance with the regulations.

Validity of payments, sales, etc., under this Act.

18. Every payment, application, sale, or other disposition of property made by the Secretary of State, or by any committee of adjustment or by any paymaster, when acting in execution or supposed execution of this Act, or of any royal warrant for carrying this Act into effect, shall be valid as against all persons whomsoever; and the Secretary of State, and every officer belonging to any such committee, and every such paymaster as aforesaid shall, by virtue of this Act, be absolutely discharged from all liability in respect of the property so paid, applied, sold or disposed of.

Saving for rights of representative.

19. After the committee of adjustment have lodged with the paymaster the surplus of the property of any deceased person, any representative of that person and any official administrator shall, as regards any property of a deceased person not collected by the committee of adjustment and not forming part of the surplus or residue in this Act mentioned, have the same rights and duties as if this Act had not passed.

Creditor administering not entitled to claim property.

20. A creditor as such shall not be deemed a person entitled to take out representation to the deceased within the meaning of this Act or to pay or secure the preferential charges; nor shall a creditor taking out representation be entitled as representative of the deceased to claim from a paymaster or the Secretary of State any part of the property of the deceased.

Deposit in court of probate, etc., or original wills in hands of Secretary of State, and declaration of intestacy.

21. (1) Where any original will of a person dying while subject to military law, whether he died before or after the commencement of this Act, comes to the hands of a Secretary of State, and representation under the same is not taken out, then the Secretary of State may cause the same to be deposited as follows:

(*a*) Where the domicile of the testator appears to the Secretary of State to have been in Scotland, then in the office of the commissary clerk of the commissary court of the county of Edinburgh:

(*b*) Where the domicile of the testator appears to the Secretary of State to have been in Ireland, then in the place for the time being appointed in Dublin for the deposit of original wills brought into the High Court in Ireland:

(*c*) In any other case, in the place for the time being appointed in London for the deposit of original wills brought into the High Court in England.

(2) Where a person dies while subject to military law intestate and under this Act any residue of his property comes to the hands of the Secretary of State, and representation to the deceased is not taken out, then the Secretary of State may, if it seems fit, cause a declaration of his intestacy to be deposited in the place or office where his original will (if any) would be deposited as aforesaid.

(3) In every such case the Secretary of State may cause to be deposited, together with the original will or declaration of intestacy, an inventory showing the personal property of the deceased, and the application thereof, as far as the same is known.

(4) Every such original will, declaration of intestacy, and inventory shall be preserved and dealt with, and may be inspected, subject and according to the same rules or orders and on payment of the same fees as any other like documents deposited in that office or place, or subject and according to such other rules or orders and on payment of such other fees, as may be made or fixed in that behalf by the court, judge or other authority empowered to make

rules or orders in relation to other documents deposited in the same place or office.

Application of Act to special cases.

22. In the application of this Act to an army paymaster, the following modifications shall be made: Special provision as to an army paymaster.

(1) The powers and duties of the committee of adjustment shall arise immediately on his death, and shall continue notwithstanding that the professional charges are paid or secured:

(2) Money in the possession or under the control of an army paymaster at his death shall not be considered to be comprised in his effects for the purposes of this Act:

(3) The surplus in the hands of the committee of adjustment and the residue in the hands of a Secretary of State shall be dealt with and disposed of as may be prescribed and not according to the foregoing provisions of this Act.

23. Where a person subject to military law deserts, or is absent without leave for twenty-one days, or is convicted by a civil court of any offence which by the law of England is felony, or is delivered up as an apprentice, whether in pursuance of an order of a court, or otherwise, the provisions of this Act shall apply as if the person were dead, subject to the following modifications: Application of Act to deserters, felons, etc.

(1) The powers of the committee of adjustment shall arise and continue notwithstanding that the preferential charges are paid or secured:

(2) The committee of adjustment shall dispose of the surplus in the prescribed manner, and the same when so disposed of shall be free from all claim on the part of the said person or any one claiming through him.

24. Where a person subject to military law is ascertained in the prescribed manner to be insane, the provisions of this Act shall apply as if he had died at the time of his insanity being so ascertained, subject nevertheless to the prescribed exceptions, and to the following modifications: Application of Act to case of insanity.

(*a*) The preferential charges may be paid by the wife of the insane person, or by any person who, subject to the prescribed regulations, appears to be a relative of or person undertaking the care of the insane person or of his property:

(*b*) The committee of adjustment shall dispose of the surplus in the prescribed manner with a view to its being applied for the benefit of the insane person.

Application of Act to India.

General application of Act to India.

25. This Act shall apply to India as if it were a colony, subject to the modifications in this Act mentioned, and to this exception, that it shall not, save so far as may be prescribed, apply to any native of India within the meaning of Indian military law.

Provision where death occurs in India, the deceased not being a soldier.

26. In the case of the death of a person who dies while in India or while on service with any force under the command of the commander-in-chief in India, or of any provincial commander-in-chief in India, and who is not a soldier of Her Majesty's regular forces, this Act shall apply with the following modifications:

(1) The paymaster shall, after the prescribed notice, pay all debts of which he has notice within the prescribed time, and which appear to him to be lawfully payable out of the estate of the deceased: Provided that if under the special circumstances of the case of the deceased it appears to the paymaster inexpedient or unjust to pay any claims out of the estate, or if the claims lodged exceed in the whole the prescribed amount, the paymaster shall, without discharging those claims, or any of them, transfer the surplus aforesaid to the official administrator:

(2) Where the paymaster does not so transfer the surplus, he shall dispose thereof, or of so much thereof as remains after the discharge of any claims, in manner directed by this Act:

(3) The foregoing provisions of this section shall not apply to an army paymaster:

(4) The secretary to the Government of India in the military department shall have the same power as the Secretary of State to decide any doubt or difference as to preferential charges, and his decision shall have the same effect as if it were given by the Secretary of State.

Deduction of arrears of subscription to military and orphan funds.

27. Nothing in this Act shall prevent the Secretary of State from deducting in the pay office from any arrears of pay due to the deceased the amount of any arrears of subscription due by the deceased to the Indian military and orphan funds, or either of them.

Provision as to Secretary of State for India.

28. Anything authorised or required by this Act to be done by, to, or before a Secretary of State may, in the prescribed cases, be done by, to, or before the Secretary of State in Council of India.

Definitions ; Extent ; Commencement ; Repeal ; Short Title.

29. In this Act, unless the context otherwise requires,— Definitions.

The expression "officer" includes a warrant officer, although not holding an honorary commission:

The expression "representation" includes probate and letters of administration, with or without will annexed, and in Scotland confirmation, and in India or a colony the corresponding documents in use according to the law of India or the colony:

The expression "representative" means any person taking out representation, but does not include an official administrator:

The expression "official administrator" means in India the administrator general of any presidency or province, and in a colony means any public officer who has by law any powers or duties in relation to the collection or distribution of the estate of any deceased person :

The expression "prescribed" means prescribed by Royal Warrant.

Save as aforesaid expressions in this Act have the same meaning as in the Army Act.

30. (1) This Act shall apply to all persons subject to military law, whether within or without Her Majesty's dominions. Extent of Act.

(2) This Act shall be registered by the Royal Courts of the Channel Islands, and shall apply to those Islands and to the Isle of Man as if they were parts of the United Kingdom. 54 Vict., 7.

(3) This Act shall apply to a place in which Her Majesty exercises jurisdiction under the Foreign Jurisdiction Act, 1890,[1] as if that place were a colony.

31. This Act shall come into operation on the first day of October one thousand eight hundred and ninety-three, or any earlier day appointed either generally or with reference to any place or places by royal warrant. Commencement of Act.

32. The Regimental Debts Act, 1863, and section fifty-one of the Regulation of the Forces Act, 1881, are hereby repealed. Repeal.

33. This Act may be cited as the Regimental Debts Act, 1893. Short title.

---

[1] Printed *ante*, p. 891.

THE TRUSTEE ACT, 1893.[1]

(56 & 57 Vict., c. 53.)

An Act to consolidate Enactments relating to Trustees.

[*22nd September, 1893.*]

* * * * * * * *

PART I.

INVESTMENTS.

Authorised investments. 1. A trustee may, unless expressly for bidden by the instrument (if any) creating the trust, invest any trust funds in his hands, whether at the time in a state of investment or not, in manner following, that is to say:

(*a*) In any of the parliamentary stocks or public funds or Government securities of the United Kingdom:

(*b*) On real or heritable securities in Great Britain or Ireland:

(*c*) In the stock of the Bank of England or the Bank of Ireland:

(*d*) In India Three and a half per cent. stock and India Three per cent. stock, or in any other capital stock which may at any time hereafter be issued by the Secretary of State in Council of India under the authority of Act of Parliament, and charged on the revenues of India:

(*e*) In any securities the interest of which is for the time being guaranteed by Parliament:

(*f*) In consolidated stock created by the Metropolitan Board of Works, or by the London County Council, or in debenture stock created by the Receiver for the Metropolitan Police District:

(*g*) In the debenture or rent charge, or guaranteed or preference stock of any railway company in Great Britain or Ireland incorporated by special Act of Parliament, and having during each of the ten years last past before the date of investment paid a dividend at the rate of not less than three per centum per annum on its ordinary stock:

(*h*) In the stock of any railway or canal company in Great Britain or Ireland whose undertaking is leased in perpetuity or for a term of not less than two hundred years at a fixed rental to any such railway company as is mentioned in sub-section (*g*), either alone or jointly with any other railway company:

(*i*) In the debenture stock of any railway company in India the interest on which is paid or guaranteed by the Secretary of State in Council of India:

---

[1] Amended 57 & 58 Vict., c. 10, *post*, p. 965. See *Chitty's Statutes*, Tit. Trustees, p. 4.

(*Sec. 1.*)

(*j*) In the "B" annuities of the Eastern Bengal, the East Indian and the Scinde, Punjaub and Delhi Railways, and any like annuities which may at any time hereafter be created on the purchase of any other railway by the Secretary of State in Council of India, and charged on the revenues of India, and which may be authorised by Act of Parliament to be accepted by trustees in lieu of any stock held by them in the purchased railway; also in deferred annuities comprised in the register of holders of annuity Class D and annuities comprised in the register of annuitants Class C of the East Indian Railway Company:

(*k*) In the stock of any railway company in India upon which a fixed or minimum dividend in sterling is paid or guaranteed by the Secretary of State in Council of India, or upon the capital of which the interest is so guaranteed:

(*l*) In the debenture or guaranteed or preference stock of any company in Great Britain or Ireland, established for the supply of water for profit, and incorporated by special Act of Parliament or by Royal Charter, and having during each of the ten years last past before the date of investment paid a dividend of not less than five pounds per centum on its ordinary stock:

(*m*) In nominal or inscribed stock issued, or to be issued, by the corporation of any municipal borough having, according to the returns of the last census prior to the date of investment, a population exceeding fifty thousand, or by any county council, under the authority of any Act of Parliament or Provisional Order:

(*n*) In nominal or inscribed stock issued or to be issued by any commissioners incorporated by Act of Parliament for the purpose of supplying water, and having a compulsory power of levying rates over an area having, according to the returns of the last census prior to the date of investment, a population exceeding fifty thousand, provided that during each of the ten years last past before the date of investment the rates levied by such commissioners shall not have exceeded eighty per centum of the amount authorised by law to be levied:

(*o*) In any of the stocks, funds, or securities for the time being authorised for the investment of cash under the control or subject to the order of the High Court,

and may also from time to time vary any such investment.

Purchase at a premium of redeemable stocks.

2. (1) A trustee may under the powers of this Act invest in any of the securities mentioned or referred to in section one of this Act, notwithstanding that the same may be redeemable, and that the price exceeds the redemption value.

(2) Provided that a trustee may not under the powers of this Act purchase at a price exceeding its redemption value any stock mentioned or referred to in sub-sections (*g*), (*i*), (*k*), (*l*), and (*m*) of section one, which is liable to be redeemed within fifteen years of the date of purchase at par or at some other fixed rate, or purchase any such stock as is mentioned or referred to in the sub-sections aforesaid, which is liable to be redeemed at par or at some other fixed rate, at a price exceeding fifteen per centum above par or such other fixed rate.

(3) A trustee may retain until redemption any redeemable stock, fund, or security which may have been purchased in accordance with the powers of this Act.

Discretion of trustees.

3. Every power conferred by the preceding sections shall be exercised according to the discretion of the trustee, but subject to any consent required by the instrument, if any, creating the trust with respect to the investment of the trust funds.

Application of preceding sections.

4. The preceding sections shall apply as well to trusts created before as to trusts created after the passing of this Act, and the powers thereby conferred shall be in addition to the powers conferred by the instrument, if any, creating the trust.

Enlargement of express powers of investment.

5. (1) A trustee having power to invest in real securities, unless expressly forbidden by the instrument creating the trust, may invest and shall be deemed to have always had power to invest—

(*a*) on mortgage of property held for an unexpired term of not less than two hundred years, and not subject to a reservation of rent greater than a shilling a year, or to any right of redemption or to any condition for re-entry, except for non-payment of rent; and

(*b*) on any charge, or upon mortgage of any charge, made under the Improvement of Land Act, 1864. 27 & 28 c. 114.

(2) A trustee having power to invest in the mortgages or bonds of any railway company or of any other description of company may, unless the contrary is expressed in the instrument authorising the investment, invest in the debenture stock of a railway company or such other company as aforesaid.

(3) A trustee having power to invest money in the debentures or debenture stock of any railway or other company may, unless the contrary is expressed in the instrument authorising the investment, invest in any nominal debentures or nominal debenture stock issued under the Local Loans Act, 1875.

& 39 Vict., 8.

(4) A trustee having power to invest money in securities in the Isle of Man, or in securities of the government of a colony, may, unless the contrary is expressed in the instrument authorising the investment, invest in any securities of the Government of the Isle of Man, under the Isle of Man Loans Act, 1880.

& 44 Vict.,

(5) A trustee having a general power to invest trust moneys in or upon the security of shares, stock, mortgages, bonds, or debentures of companies incorporated by or acting under the authority of an Act of Parliament, may invest in, or upon the security of, mortgage debentures duly issued under and in accordance with the provisions of the Mortgage Debenture Act, 1865.

& 29 Vict., 8.

Power to invest, notwithstanding drainage charges.

6. A trustee having power to invest in the purchase of land or on mortgage of land may invest in the purchase, or on mortgage of any land, notwithstanding the same is charged with a rent under the powers of the Public Money Drainage Acts, 1846 to 1856, or the Landed Property Improvement (Ireland) Act, 1847, or by an absolute order made under the Improvement of Land Act, 1864, unless the terms of the trust expressly provide that the land to be purchased or taken in mortgage shall not be subject to any such prior charge.

11 Vict., 2.

Trustees not to convert inscribed stock into certificates to bearer.

7. (1) A trustee, unless authorised by the terms of his trust, shall not apply for or hold any certificate to bearer issued under the authority of any of the following Acts, that is to say:—

27 Vict., (*a*) The India-Stock Certificate, 1863;

34 Vict., (*b*) The National Debt Act, 1870;

39 Vict., (*c*) The Local Loans Act, 1875;

41 Vict., (*d*) The Colonial Stock Act, 1877.

(2) Nothing in this section shall impose on the Bank of England or of Ireland, or on any person authorised to issue any such certificates, any obligation to inquire whether a person applying for such a certificate is or is not a trustee, or subject them to any liability in the event of their granting any such certificate to a trustee, nor invalidate any such certificate if granted.

Loans and investments by trustees not chargeable as

8. (1) A trustee lending money on the security of any property in which he can lawfully lend shall not be chargeable with breach of trust by reason only of the proportion borne by the amount of the loan to the value of

breaches of trust.

the property at the time when the loan was made, provided that it appears to the court that in making the loan the trustee was acting upon a report as to the value of the property made by a person whom he reasonably believed to be an able practical surveyor or valuer instructed and employed independently of any owner of the property, whether such surveyor or valuer carried on business in the locality where the property is situate or elsewhere, and that the amount of the loan does not exceed two equal third parts of the value of the property as stated in the report, and that the loan was made under the advice of the surveyor or valuer expressed in the report.

(2) A trustee lending money on the security of any leasehold property shall not be chargeable with breach of trust only upon the ground that in making such loan he dispensed either wholly or partly with the production or investigation of the lessor's title.

(3) A trustee shall not be chargeable with breach of trust only upon the ground that in effecting the purchase of or in lending money upon the security of any property he has accepted a shorter title than the title which a purchaser is, in the absence of a special contract, entitled to require, if in the opinion of the court the title accepted be such as a person acting with prudence and caution would have accepted.

(4) This section applies to transfers of existing securities as well as to new securities, and to investments made as well before as after the commencement of this Act, except where an action or other proceeding was pending with reference thereto on the twenty-fourth day of December one thousand eight hundred and eighty-eight.

Liability or loss by reason of improper investments.

9. (1) Where a trustee improperly advances trust money on a mortgage security which would at the time of the investment be a proper investment in all respects for a smaller sum than is actually advanced thereon the security shall be deemed an authorised investment for the smaller sum, and the trustee shall only be liable to make good the sum advanced in excess thereof with interest.

(2) This section applies to investments made as well before as after the commencement of this Act except where an action or other proceeding was pending with reference thereto on the twenty-fourth day of December one thousand eight hundred and eighty-eight.

PART II.

Various Powers and Duties of Trustees.

Appointment of New Trustees.

Power of appointing new trustees.

10. (1) Where a trustee, either original or substituted, and whether appointed by a court or otherwise, is dead, or remains out of the United King-

dom for more than twelve months, or desires to be discharged from all or any of the trusts or powers reposed in or conferred on him, or refuses or is unfit to act therein, or is incapable of acting therein, then the person or persons nominated for the purpose of appointing new trustees by the instrument, if any, creating the trust, or if there is no such person, or no such person able and willing to act, then the surviving or continuing trustees or trustee for the time being, or the personal representatives of the last surviving or continuing trustee, may, by writing, appoint another person or other persons to be a trustee or trustees in the place of the trustee dead, remaining out of the United Kingdom, desiring to be discharged, refusing, or being unfit or being incapable, as aforesaid.

(2) On the appointment of a new trustee for the whole or any part of trust property—

(*a*) the number of trustees may be increased; and

(*b*) a separate set of trustees may be appointed for any part of the trust property held on trusts distinct from those relating to any other part or parts of the trust property, notwithstanding that no new trustees or trustee are or is to be appointed for other parts of the trust property, and any existing trustee may be appointed or remain one of such separate set of trustees; or, if only one trustee was originally appointed, then one separate trustee may be so appointed for the first-mentioned part; and

(*c*) it shall not be obligatory to appoint more than one new trustee where only one trustee was originally appointed, or to fill up the original number of trustees where more than two trustees were originally appointed; but, except where only one trustee was originally appointed, a trustee shall not be discharged under this section from his trust unless there will be at least two trustees to perform the trust; and

(*d*) any assurance or thing requisite for vesting the trust property, or any part thereof, jointly in the person who are the trustees, shall be executed or done.

(3) Every new trustee so appointed, as well before as after all the trust property becomes by law, or by assurance, or otherwise, vested in him, shall have the same powers, authorities, and discretions, and may in all respects act, as if he had been originally appointed a trustee by the instrument, if any, creating the trust.

(4) The provisions of this section relative to a trustee who is dead include the case of a person nominated trustee in a will but dying before the testator,

and those relative to a continuing trustee include a refusing or retiring trustee, if willing to act in the execution of the provisions of this section.

(5) This section applies only if and as far as a contrary intention is not expressed in the instrument, if any, creating the trust, and shall have effect subject to the terms of that instrument and to any provisions therein contained.

(6) This section applies to trusts created either before or after the commencement of this Act.

Retirement of trustee.

11. (1) Where there are more than two trustees, if one of them by deed declares that he is desirous of being discharged from the trust, and if his co-trustees and such other person, if any, as is empowered to appoint trustees, by deed consent to the discharge of the trustee, and to the vesting in the co-trustees alone of the trust property, then the trustee desirous of being discharged shall be deemed to have retired from the trust, and shall, by the deed, be discharged therefrom under this Act, without any new trustee being appointed in his place.

(2) Any assurance or th ng requisite for vesting the trust property in the continuing trustees alone shall be executed or done.

(3) This section applies only if and as far as a contrary intention is not expressed in the instrument, if any, creating the trust, and shall have effect subject to the terms of that instrument and to any provisions therein contained.

(4) This section applies to trusts created either before or after the commencement of this Act.

Vesting of trust property in new or continuing trustees.

12. (1) Where a deed by which a new trustee is appointed to perform any trust contains a declaration by the appointor to the effect that any estate or interest in any land subject to the trust, or in any chattel so subject, or the right to recover and receive any debt or other thing in action so subject, shall vest in the persons who by virtue of the deed become and are the trustees for performing the trust, that declaration shall, without any conveyance or assignment, operate to vest in those persons, as joint tenants, and for the purposes of the trust, that estate, interest, or right.

(2) Where a deed by which a retiring trustee is discharged under this Act contains such a declaration as is in this section mentioned by the retiring and continuing trustees, and by the other person, if any, empowered to appoint trustees, that declaration shall, without any conveyance or assignment, operate to vest in the continuing trustees alone, as joint tenants, and for the purpose of the trust, the estate, interest, or right to which the declaration relates.

(3) This section does not extend to any legal estate or interest in copyhold or customary land, or to land conveyed by way of mortgage for securing

money subject to the trust, or to any such share, stock, annuity, or property as is only transferable in books kept by a company or other body, or in manner directed by or under Act of Parliament.

(4) For purposes of registration of the deed in any registry, the person or persons making the declaration shall be deemed the conveying party or parties, and the conveyance shall be deemed to be made by him or them under a power conferred by this Act.

(5) This section applies only to deeds executed after the thirty-first of December one thousand eight hundred and eighty-one.

Purchase and Sale.

Power of trustee for sale to sell by auction, etc.

13. (1) Where a trust for sale or a power of sale of property is vested in a trustee, he may sell or concur with any other person in selling all or any part of the property, either subject to prior charges or not, and either together or in lots, by public auction or by private contract, subject to any such conditions respecting title or evidence of title or other matter as the trustee thinks fit, with power to vary any contract for sale, and to buy in at any auction, or to rescind any contract for sale and to re-sell, without being answerable for any loss.

(2) This section applies only if and as far as a contrary intention is not expressed in the instrument creating the trust or power, and shall have effect subject to the terms of that instrument and to the provisions therein contained.

(3) This section applies only to a trust or power created by an instrument coming into operation after the thirty-first of December one thousand eight hundred and eighty-one.

Power to sell subject to depreciatory conditions.

14. (1) No sale made by a trustee shall be impeached by any beneficiary upon the ground that any of the conditions subject to which the sale was made may have been unnecessarily depreciatory, unless it also appears that the consideration for the sale was thereby rendered inadequate.

(2) No sale made by a trustee shall, after the execution of the conveyance, be impeached as against the purchaser upon the ground that any of the conditions subject to which the sale was made may have been unnecessarily depreciatory, unless it appears that the purchaser was acting in collusion with the trustee at the time when the contract for sale was made.

(3) No purchaser, upon any sale made by a trustee, shall be at liberty to make any objection against the title upon the ground aforesaid.

(4) This section applies only to sales made after the twenty-fourth day of December one thousand eight hundred and eighty-eight.

Power to sell und 37 & 38 Vict., c. 78.

15. A trustee who is either a vendor or a purchaser may sell or buy without excluding the application of section two of the Vendor and Purchaser Act, 1874.

Married woman as bare trustee may convey.

16. When any freehold or copyhold hereditament is vested in a married woman as a bare trustee, she may convey or surrender it as if she were a emmesole.

Various Powers and Liabilities.

Power to authorise receipt of money by banker or solicitor.

17. (1) A trustee may appoint a solicitor to be his agent to receive and give a discharge for any money or valuable consideration or property receivable by the trustee under the trust, by permitting the solicitor to have the custody of, and to produce, a deed containing any such receipt as is referred to in section fifty-six of the Conveyancing and Law of Property Act, 1881; 44 & 45 Vict. c. 41.
and a trustee shall not be chargeable with breach of trust by reason only of his having made or concurred in making any such appointment; and the producing of any such deed by the solicitor shall have the same validity and effect under the said section as if the person appointing the solicitor had not been a trustee.

(2) A trustee may appoint a banker or solicitor to be his agent to receive and give a discharge for any money payable to the trustee under or by virtue of a policy of assurance by permitting the banker or solicitor to have the custody of and to produce the policy of assurance with a receipt signed by the trustee, and a trustee shall not be chargeable with a breach of trust by reason only of his having made or concurred in making any such appointment.

(3) Nothing in this section shall exempt a trustee from any liability which he would have incurred if this Act had not been passed, in case he permits any such money, valuable consideration, or property to remain in the hands or under the control of the banker or solicitor for a period longer than is reasonably necessary to enable the banker or solicitor (as the case may be) to pay or transfer the same to the trustee.

(4) This section applies only where the money or valuable consideration or property is received after the twenty-fourth day of December one thousand eight hundred and eighty-eight.

(5) Nothing in this section shall authorise a trustee to do anything which he is in express terms forbidden to do, or to omit anything which he is in express terms directed to do, by the instrument creating the trust.

Power to insure building.

18. (1) A trustee may insure against loss or damage by fire any building or other insurable property to any amount (including the amount of any insurance already on foot) not exceeding three equal fourth parts of the full value of such building or property, and pay the premiums for such insurance

out of the income thereof or out of the income of any other property subject to the same trusts, without obtaining the consent of any person who may be entitled wholly or partly to such income.

(2) This section does not apply to any building or property which a trustee is bound forthwith to convey absolutely to any beneficiary upon being requested to do so.

(3) This section applies to trusts created either before or after the commencement of this Act, but nothing in this section shall authorise any trustee to do anything which he is in express terms forbidden to do, or to omit to do anything which he is in express terms directed to do, by the instrument creating the trust.

Power of trustees of renewable leaseholds to renew and raise money for the purpose.

19. (1) A trustee of any leasehold for lives or years which are renewable from time to time either under any covenant or contract, or by custom or usual practice, may, if he thinks fit, and shall, if thereto required by any person having any beneficial interest, present or future, or contingent in the leaseholds, use his best endeavours to obtain from time to time a renewed lease of the same hereditaments on the accustomed and reasonable terms, and for that purpose may from time to time make or concur in making a surrender of the lease for the time being subsisting, and do all such other acts as are requisite: Provided that, where by the terms of the settlement or will the person in possession for his life or other limited interest is entitled to enjoy the same without any obligation to renew or to contribute to the expense of renewal, this section shall not apply unless the consent in writing of that person is obtained to the renewal on the part of the trustee.

(2) If money is required to pay for the renewal, the trustee effecting the renewal may pay the same out of any money then in his hands in trust for the persons beneficially interested in the lands to be comprised in the renewed lease, and if he has not in his hands sufficient money for the purpose, he may raise the money required by mortgage of the hereditaments to be comprised in the renewed lease, or of any other hereditaments for the time being subject to the uses or trusts to which those hereditaments are subject, and no person advancing money upon a mortgage purporting to be under this power shall be bound to see that the money is wanted or that no more is raised than is wanted for the purpose.

(3) This section applies to trusts created either before or after the commencement of this Act, but nothing in this section shall authorise any trustee to do anything which he is in express terms forbidden to do, or to omit to do anything which he is in express terms directed to do, by the instrument creating the trust.

Power of trustee to give receipts.

20. (1) The receipt in writing of any trustee for any money, securities or other personal property or effects payable, transferable or deliverable to him under any trust or power shall be a sufficient discharge for the same, and shall effectually exonerate the person paying, transferring, or delivering the same from seeing to the application or being answerable for any loss or misapplication thereof.

(2) This section applies to trusts created either before or after the commencement of this Act.

Power for executors and trustees to compound, etc.

21. (1) An executor or administrator may pay or allow any debt or claim on any evidence that he thinks sufficient.

(2) An executor or administrator, or two or more trustees acting together, or a sole acting trustee where by the instrument, if any, creating the trust a sole trustee is authorised to execute the trusts and powers thereof, may, if and as he or they may think fit, accept any composition or any security, real or personal, for any debt or for any property, real or personal, claimed, and may allow any time for payment for any debt, and may compromise, compound, abandon, submit to arbitration, or otherwise settle any debt, account, claim, or thing whatever relating to the testator's or intestate's estate or to the trust, and for any of those purposes may enter into, give, execute, and do such agreements, instruments of composition or arrangement, releases, and other things as to him or them seem expedient, without being responsible for any loss occasioned by any act or thing so done by him or them in good faith.

(3) This section applies only if and as far as a contrary intention is not expressed in the instrument, if any, creating the trust, and shall have effect subject to the terms of that instrument, and to the provisions therein contained.

(4) This section applies to executorships, administratorships and trusts constituted or created either before or after the commencement of this Act.

Powers of two or more trustees.

22. (1) Where a power or trust is given to or vested in two or more trustees jointly, then, unless the contrary is expressed in the instrument, if any, creating the power or trust, the same may be exercised or performed by the survivor or survivors of them for the time being.

(2) This section applies only to trusts constituted after or created by instruments coming into operation after the thirty-first day of December one thousand eight hundred and eighty-one.

Exoneration of trustees in respect of certain powers of attorney.

23. A trustee acting or paying money in good faith under or in pursuance of any power of attorney shall not be liable for any such act or payment by reason of the fact that at the time of the payment or act the person who gave the power of attorney was dead or had done some act to avoid the power if this fact was not known to the trustee at the time of his so acting or paying:

Provided that nothing in this section shall affect the right of any person entitled to the money against the person to whom the payment is made, and that the person so entitled shall have the same remedy against the person to whom the payment is made as he would have had against the trustee.

24. A trustee shall, without prejudice to the provisions of the instrument, if any, creating the trust, be chargeable only for money and securities actually received by him notwithstanding his signing any receipt for the sake of conformity, and shall be answerable and accountable only for his own acts, receipts, neglects or defaults, and not for those of any other trustee, nor for any banker, broker, or other person with whom any trust moneys, or securities may be deposited, nor for the insufficiency or deficiency of any securities, nor for any other loss, unless the same happens through his own wilful default; and may reimburse himself, or pay or discharge out of the trust premises, all expenses incurred in or about the execution of his trusts or powers. **Implied indemnity of trustees.**

PART III.

Powers of the Court.

Appointment of New Trustees and Vesting Orders.

25. (1) The High Court may, whenever it is expedient to appoint a new trustee or new trustees, and it is found inexpedient, difficult, or impracticable so to do without the assistance of the Court, make an order for the appointment of a new trustee or new trustees either in substitution for or in addition to any existing trustee or trustees, or although there is no existing trustee. In particular and without prejudice to the generality of the foregoing provision, the Court may make an order for the appointment of a new trustee in substitution for a trustee who is convicted of felony, or is a bankrupt. **Power of the Court to appoint new trustees.**

(2) An order under this section, and any consequential vesting order or conveyance, shall not operate further or otherwise as a discharge to any former or continuing trustee than an appointment of new trustees under any power for that purpose contained in any instrument would have operated.

(3) Nothing in this section shall give power to appoint an executor or administrator.

26. In any of the following cases, namely:— **Vesting orders as to land.**

(i) Where the High Court appoints or has appointed a new trustee; and

(ii) Where a trustee entitled to or possessed of any land, or entitled to a contingent right therein, either solely or jointly with any other person,—

(*a*) is an infant, or

(*Sec. 27.*)

(*b*) is out of the jurisdiction of the High Court, or

(*c*) cannot be found; and

(iii) Where it is uncertain who was the survivor of two or more trustees jointly entitled to or possessed of any land; and

(iv) Where, as to the last trustee known to have been entitled to or possessed of any land, it is uncertain whether he is living or dead; and

(v) Where there is no heir or personal representative to a trustee who was entitled to or possessed of land and has died intestate as to that land, or where it is uncertain who is the heir or personal representative or devisee of a trustee who was entitled to or possessed of land and is dead; and

(vi) Where a trustee jointly or solely entitled to or possessed of any land, or entitled to a contingent right therein, has been require by or on behalf of a person entitled to require a conveyance of the land or a release of the right, to convey the land or to release the right, and has wilfully refused or neglected to convey the land or release the right for twenty-eight days after the date of the requirement;

the High Court may make an order (in this Act called a vesting order) vesting the land in any such person in any such manner and for any such estate as the Court may direct, or releasing or disposing of the contingent right to such person as the Court may direct.

Provided that—

(*a*) Where the order is consequential on the appointment of a new trustee the land shall be vested for such estate as the Court may direct in the persons who on the appointment are the trustees; and

(*b*) Where the order relates to a trustee entitled jointly with another person, and such trustee is out of the jurisdiction of the High Court or cannot be found, the land or right shall be vested in such other person, either alone or with some other person.

Orders as to contingent rights of unborn person.

27. Where any land is subject to a contingent right in an unborn person or class of unborn persons who, on coming into existence would, in respect thereof, become entitled to or possessed of the land on any trust, the High Court may make an order releasing the land from the contingent right, or may make an order vesting in any person the estate to or of which the unborn person or class of unborn persons would, on coming into existence, be entitled or possessed in the land.

28. Where any person entitled to or possessed of land, or entitled to a contingent right in land, by way of security for money, is an infant, the High Court may make an order vesting or releasing or disposing of the land or right in like manner as in the case of an infant trustee.

Vesting order in place of conveyance by infant mortgagee.

29. Where a mortgagee of land has died without having entered into the possession or into the receipt of the rents and profits thereof, and the money due in respect of the mortgage has been paid to a person entitled to receive the same, or that last-mentioned person consents to any order for the reconveyance of the land, then the High Court may make an order vesting the land in such person or persons in such manner and for such estate as the Court may direct in any of the following cases, namely,—

Vesting order in place of conveyance by heir, or devisee of heir, etc., or personal representative of mortgagee.

(*a*) Where an heir or personal representative or devisee of the mortgagee is out of the jurisdiction of the High Court or cannot be found; and

(*b*) Where an heir or personal representative or devisee of the mortgagee on demand made by or on behalf of a person entitled to require a conveyance of the land has stated in writing that he will not convey the same or does not convey the same for the space of twenty-eight days next after a proper deed for conveying the land has been tendered to him by or on behalf of the person so entitled; and

(*c*) Where it is uncertain which of several devisees of the mortgagee was the survivor; and

(*d*) Where it is uncertain as to the survivor of several devisees of the mortgagee or as to the heir or personal representative of the mortgagee whether he is living or dead; and

(*e*) Where there is no heir or personal representative to a mortgagee who has died intestate as to the land, or where the mortgagee has died and it is uncertain who is his heir or personal representative or devisee.

30. Where any court gives a judgment or makes an order directing the sale or mortgage of any land, every person who is entitled to or possessed of the land, or entitled to a contingent right therein * * * * * * *[1] and is a party of the action or proceeding in which the judgment or order is given or made or is otherwise bound by the judgment or order, shall be deemed to be so entitled or possessed, as the case may be, as a trustee within the meaning of this Act; and the High Court may, if it thinks expedient, make an order vesting the land or

Vesting order consequential on judgment for sale or mortgage of land.

---

[1] Words repealed by 57 & 58 Vict., c. 10, s. 1, have been omitted. Printed *post*, p. 965.

any part thereof for such estate as that Court thinks fit in the purchaser or mortgagee or in any other person.

Vesting order consequential on judgment for specific performance, etc.

31. Where a judgment is given for the specific performance of a contract concerning any land, or for the partition, or sale in lieu of partition, or exchange, of any land, or generally where any judgment is given for the conveyance of any land either in cases arising out of the doctrine of election or otherwise, the High Court may declare that any of the parties to the action are trustees of the land or any part thereof within the meaning of this Act, or may declare that the interests of unborn persons who might claim under any party to the action, or under the will or voluntary settlement of any person deceased who was during his lifetime a party to the contract or transactions concerning which the judgment is given, are the interests of persons who, on coming into existence, would be trustees within the meaning of this Act, and thereupon the High Court may make a vesting order relating to the rights of those persons, born and unborn, as if they had been trustees.

Effect of vesting order.

32. A vesting order under any of the foregoing provisions shall in the case of a vesting order consequential on the appointment of a new trustee, have the same effect as if the persons who before the appointment were the trustees (if any) had duly executed all proper conveyances of the land for such estate as the High Court directs, or if there is no such person, or no such person of full capacity, then as if such person had existed and been of full capacity and had duly executed all proper conveyances of the land for such estate as the Court directs, and shall in every other case have the same effect as if the trustee or other person or description or class of persons to whose rights or supposed rights the said provisions respectively relate had been an ascertained and existing person of full capacity, and had executed a conveyance or release to the effect intended by the order.

Power to appoint person to convey.

33. In all cases where a vesting order can be made under any of the foregoing provisions, the High Court may, if it is more convenient, appoint a person to convey the land or release the contingent right, and a conveyance or release by that person in conformity with the order shall have the same effect as an order under the appropriate provision.

Effect of vesting order as to copyhold.

34. (1) Where an order vesting copyhold land in any person is made under this Act with the consent of the lord or lady of the manor, the land shall vest accordingly without surrender of admittance.

(2) Where an order is made under this Act appointing any person to convey any copyhold land, that person shall execute and do all assurances and things for completing the assurance of the land; and the lord and lady of the manor and every other person shall, subject to the customs of the manor and

the usual payments, be bound to make admittance to the land and to do all other acts for completing the assurance thereof, as if the persons in whose place an appointment is made were free from disability and had executed and done those assurances and things.

Vesting orders as to stock and choses in action.

35. (1) In any of the following cases, namely:—

(i) Where the High Court appoints or has appointed a new trustee; and

(ii) Where a trustee entitled alone or jointly with another person to stock or to a chose in action—

(*a*) is an infant, or

(*b*) is out of the jurisdiction of the High Court, or

(*c*) cannot be found; or

(*d*) neglects or refuses to transfer stock or receive the dividends or income thereof, or to sue for or recover a chose in action, according to the direction of the person absolutely entitled thereto for twenty-eight days next after a request in writing has been made to him by the person so entitled, or

(*e*) neglects or refuses to transfer stock or receive the dividends or income thereof, or to sue for or recover a chose in action for twenty-eight days next after an order of the High Court for that purpose has been served on him; or

(iii) Where it is uncertain whether a trustee entitled alone or jointly with another person to stock or to a chose in action is alive or dead,

the High Court may make an order vesting the right to transfer or call for a transfer of stock, or to receive the dividends or income thereof, or to sue for or recover a chose in action, in any such person as the Court may appoint:

Provided that—

(*a*) Where the order is consequential on the appointment by the Court of a new trustee, the right shall be vested in the persons who, on the appointment, are the trustees; and

(*b*) Where the person whose right is dealt with by the order was entitled jointly with another person, the right shall be vested in that last-mentioned person either alone or jointly with any other person whom the Court may appoint.

(2) In all cases where a vesting order can be made under this section, the Court may, if it is more convenient, appoint some proper person to make or join in making the transfer.

(3) The person in whom the right to transfer or call for the transfer o any stock is vested by an order of the Court under this Act, may transfer the stock to himself or any other person, according to the order, and the Banks of England and Ireland and all other companies shall obey every order under this section according to its tenor.

(4) After notice in writing of an order under this section it shall not be lawful for the Bank of England or of Ireland or any other company to transfer any stock to which the order relates or to pay any dividends thereon except in accordance with the order.

(5) The High Court may make declarations and give directions concerning the manner in which the right to any stock or chose in action vested under the provisions of this Act is to be exercised.

(6) The provisions of this Act as to vesting orders shall apply to shares in ships registered under the Acts relating to merchant shipping as if they were stock.

Persons entitled to apply for orders.

36. (1) An order under this Act for the appointment of a new trustee or concerning any land, stock, or chose in action subject to a trust, may be made on the application of any person beneficially interested in the land, stock, or chose in action, whether under disability or not, or on the application of any person duly appointed trustee thereof.

(2) An order under this Act concerning any land, stock, or chose in action subject to mortgage may be made on the application of any person beneficially interested in the equity of redemption, whether under disability or not, or of any person interested in the money secured by the mortgage.

Powers of new trustee appointed by Court.

37. Every trustee appointed by a court of competent jurisdiction shall, as well before as after the trust property becomes by law, or by assurance, or otherwise, vested in him, have the same powers, authorities, and discretions and may in all respects act as if he had been originally appointed a trustee by the instrument, if any, creating the trust.

Power to charge costs on trust estate.

38. The High Court may order the costs and expenses of and incident to any application for an order appointing a new trustee, or for a vesting order, or of and incident to any such order, or any conveyance or transfer in pursuance thereof, to be paid or raised out of the land or personal estate in respect whereof the same is made, or out of the income thereof, or to be borne and paid in such manner and by such persons as to the Court may seem just.

Trustees of charities.

39. The powers conferred by this Act as to vesting orders may be exercised for vesting any land, stock or chose in action in any trustee of a charity or society over which the High Court would have jurisdiction upon action duly instituted, whether the appointment of the trustee was made by instrument under a power or by the High Court under its general or statutory jurisdiction.

Orders made upon certain allegations to be conclusive evidence.

53 & 54 Vict. c. 5.

40. Where a vesting order is made as to any land under this Act or under the Lunacy Act, 1890, or under any Act relating to lunacy in Ireland, founded on an allegation of the personal incapacity of a trustee or mortgagee, or on an allegation that a trustee or the heir or personal representative or devisee of a mortgagee is out of the jurisdiction of the High Court or cannot be found, or that it is uncertain which of several trustees or which of several devisees of a mortgagee was the survivor, or whether the last trustee or the heir or personal representative or last surviving devisee of a mortgagee is living or dead, or on an allegation that any trustee or mortgagee has died intestate without an heir or has died and it is not known who is his heir or personal representative or devisee, the fact that the order has been so made shall be conclusive evidence of the matter so alleged in any court upon any question as to the validity of the order; but this section shall not prevent the High Court from directing a reconveyance or the payment of costs occasioned by any such order if improperly obtained.

Application of vesting order to land out of England.

41. The powers of the High Court in England to make vesting orders under this Act shall extend to all land and personal estate in Her Majesty's dominions, except Scotland.[1]

Payment into Court by Trustees.

Payment into Court by trustees.

42. (1) Trustees, or the majority of trustees, having in their hands or under their control money or securities belonging to a trust, may pay the same into the High Court; and the same shall, subject to the rules of Court, be dealt with according to the orders of the High Court.

(2) The receipt or certificate of the proper officer shall be a sufficient discharge to trustees for the money or securities so paid into Court.

(3) Where any moneys or securities are vested in any persons as trustees, and the majority are desirous of paying the same into court, but the concurrence of the other or others cannot be obtained, the High Court may order the payment into court to be made by the majority without the concurrence of the other or others; and where any such moneys or securites are deposited with any banker, broker, or other depositary, the Court may order payment or delivery of the moneys or securities to the majority of the trustees for the purpose of payment into court, and every transfer, payment and delivery made in pursuance of any such order shall be valid and take effect as if the same had been made on the authority or by the act of all the persons entitled to the moneys and securities so transferred, paid, or delivered.

---

[1] Ext. to Ireland by 57 & 58 Vict., c. 10, s. 2, *post*, p. 965.

Miscellaneous.

Power to give judgment in absence of a trustee.

43. Where in any action the High Court is satisfied that diligent search has been made for any person who, in the character of trustee, is made a defendant in any action, to serve him with a process of the Court, and that he cannot be found, the Court may hear and determine the action and give judgment therein against that person in his character of a trustee, as if he had been duly served, or had entered an appearance in the action and had also appeared by his counsel and solicitor at the hearing, but without prejudice to any interest he may have in the matters in question in the action in any other character.

Power to sanction sale of land or minerals separately.

44. (1) Where a trustee [or other person][1] is for the time being authorised to dispose of land by way of sale, exchange, partition, or enfranchisement, the High Court may sanction his so disposing of the land with an exception or reservation of any minerals, and with or without rights and powers of or incidental to the working, getting, or carrying away of the minerals, or so disposing of the minerals, with or without the said rights or powers, separately from the residue of the land.

(2) Any such trustee [or other person][1] with the said sanction previously obtained, may, unless forbidden by the instrument creating the trust or direction, from time to time, without any further application to the Court, so dispose of any such land or minerals.

(3) Nothing in this section shall derogate from any power which a trustee may have under the Settled Land Acts, 1882 to 1890, or otherwise.

Power to make beneficiary indemnity for breach of trust.

45. (1) Where a trustee commits a breach of trust at the instigation or request or with the consent in writing of a beneficiary, the High Court may, if it thinks fit, and notwithstanding that the beneficiary may be a married woman entitled for her separate use and restrained from anticipation, make such order as to the Court seems just, for impounding all or any part of the interest of the beneficiary in the trust estate by way of indemnity to the trustee or person claiming through him.

(2) This section shall apply to breaches of trust committed as well before as after the passing of this Act, but shall not apply so as to prejudice any question in an action or other proceeding which was pending on the twenty-fourth day of December one thousand eight hundred and eighty-eight, and is pending at the commencement of this Act.

Jurisdiction of palatine and county courts.

46. The provisions of this Act with respect to the High Court shall, in their application to cases within the jurisdiction of a palatine court or county court, include that court, and the procedure under this Act in palatine courts,

---

[1] Added by 57 & 58 Vict., c. 10, s. 3, *post*, p. 965.

and county courts shall be in accordance with the Acts and rules regulating the procedure of those courts.

PART IV.

Miscellaneous and Supplemental.

47. (1) All the powers and provisions contained in this Act with reference to the appointment of new trustees, and the discharge and retirement of trustees, are to apply to and include trustees for the purposes of the Settled Land Acts, 1882 to 1890, whether appointed by the Court or by the settlement, or under provisions contained in the settlement. Application to trustees under Settled Land Acts of provisions as to appointment of trustees.

(2) This section applies and is to have effect with respect to an appointment or a discharge and retirement of trustees taking place before as well as after the commencement of this Act.

(3) This section is not to render invalid or prejudice any appointment or any discharge and retirement of trustees effected before the passing of this Act, otherwise than under the provisions of the Conveyancing and Law of Property Act, 1881. 44 & 45 Vict., c. 41.

48. Property vested in any person on any trust or by way of mortgage shall not, in case of that person becoming a convict within the meaning of the Forfeiture Act, 1870, vest in any such administrator as may be appointed under that Act, but shall remain in the trustee or mortgagee, or survive, to his co-trustee or descend to his representative as if he had not become a convict; provided that this enactment shall not affect the title to the property so far as relates to any beneficial interest therein of any such trustee or mortgagee. Trust estates not affected by trustee becoming a convict. 33 & 34 Vict., c. 23.

49. This Act, and every order purporting to be made under this Act, shall be a complete indemnity to the Banks of England and Ireland, and to all persons for any acts done pursuant thereto; and it shall not be necessary for the Bank or for any person to inquire concerning the propriety of the order, or whether the Court by which it was made had jurisdiction to make the same. Indemnity.

50. In this Act, unless the context otherwise requires,— Definitions.

The expression "bankrupt" includes, in Ireland, insolvent:

The expression "contingent right," as applied to land, includes a contingent or executory interest, a possibility coupled with an interest, whether the object of the gift or limitation of the interest or possibility is or is not ascertained, also a right of entry, whether immediate or future, and whether vested or contingent:

(*Sec. 50.*)

The expressions "convey" and "conveyance" applied to any person include the execution by that person of every necessary or suitable assurance for conveying, assigning, appointing, surrendering, or otherwise transferring or disposing of land, whereof he is seised or possessed, or wherein he is entitled to a contingent right, either for his whole estate or for any less estate, together with the performance of all formalities required by law to the validity of the conveyance, including the acts to be performed by married women and tenants in tail in accordance with the provisions of the Acts for abolition of fines and recoveries in England and Ireland respectively, and also including surrenders and other acts which a tenant of customary or copyhold lands can himself perform preparatory to or in aid of a complete assurance of the customary or copyhold land:

The expression "devisee" includes the heir of a devisee and the devisee of an heir, and any person who may claim right by devolution of title of a similar description:

The expression "instrument" includes Act of Parliament:

The expression "land" includes manors and lordships, and reputed manors and lordships, and incorporeal as well as corporeal hereditaments, and any interest therein, and also an undivided share of land:

The expressions "mortgage" and "mortgagee" include and relate to every estate and interest regarded in equity as merely a security for money, and every person deriving title under the original mortgagee:

The expressions "pay" and "payment" as applied in relation to stocks and securities, and in connexion with the expression "into court" include the deposit or transfer of the same in or into court:

The expression "possessed" applies to receipt of income of, and to any vested estate less than a life estate, legal or equitable, in possession or in expectancy, in, any land:

The expression "property" includes real and personal property, and any estate and interest in any property, real or personal, and any debt, and any thing in action, and any other right or interest, whether in possession or not:

The expression "rights" includes estates and interests:

The expression "securities" includes stocks, funds, and shares; and so far as relates to payments into court has the same meaning as in the Court of Chancery (Funds) Act, 1872: 35 & 36 Vict. c. 44.

The expression "stock" includes fully paid up shares; and, so far as relates to vesting orders made by the Court under this Act, includes any fund, annuity, or security transferable in books kept by any company or society, or by instrument of transfer either alone or accompanied by other formalities, and any share or interest therein:

The expression "transfer," in relation to stock, includes the performance and execution of every deed, power of attorney, act, and thing on the part of the transferor to effect and complete the title in the transferee:

The expression "trust" does not include the duties incident to an estate conveyed by way of mortgage; but with this exception the expressions "trust" and "trustee" include implied and constructive trusts, and cases where the trustee has a beneficial interest in the trust property, and the duties incident to the office of personal representative of a deceased person.

51. The Acts mentioned in the schedule to this Act are hereby repealed except as to Scotland to the extent mentioned in the third column of that schedule. Repeal.

52. This Act does not extend to Scotland. Extent of Act.

53. This Act may be cited as the Trustee Act, 1893. Short title.

54. This Act shall come into operation on the first day of January one thousand eight hundred and ninety-four. Commencement.

SCHEDULE.

Session and Chapter.	Title or Short Title.	Extent of Repeal.
36 Geo. 3, c. 52	The Legacy Duty Act, 1796	Section thirty-two.
9 & 10 Vict., c. 101	The Public Money Drainage Act, 1846.	Section thirty-seven.
10 & 11 Vict., c. 32	The Landed Property Improvement (Ireland) Act, 1847.	Section fifty-three.
10 & 11 Vict., c. 96	An Act for better securing trust funds, and for the relief of trustees.	The whole Act.
11 & 12 Vict. c. 68	An Act for extending to Ireland an Act passed in the last session of Parliament, entitled "An Act for "better securing trust funds, and "for the relief of trustees."	The whole Act.

(*Schedule.*)

SCHEDULE—*continued.*

Session and Chapter.	Title or Short Title.	Extent of Repeal.
12 & 13 Vict., c. 74 .	An Act for the further relief of trustees.	The whole Act.
13 & 14 Vict., c. 60 .	The Trustee Act, 1850 . . .	Sections seven to nineteen, twenty-two to twenty-five, twenty-nine, thirty-two to thirty-six, forty-six, forty-seven, forty-nine, fifty-four and fifty-five; also the residue of the Act except so far as relates to the Court exercising jurisdiction in lunacy in Ireland.
15 & 16 Vict., c. 55 .	The Trustee Act, 1852 . . .	Sections one to five, eight, and nine; also the residue of the Act except so far as relates to the Court exercising jurisdiction in lunacy in Ireland.
17 & 18 Vict., c. 82 .	The Court of Chancery of Lancaster Act, 1854.	Section eleven.
18 & 19 Vict., c. 91 .	The Merchant Shipping Act Amendment Act, 1855.	Section ten, except so far as relates to the Court exercising jurisdiction in lunacy in Ireland.
20 & 21 Vict., c. 60 .	The Irish Bankrupt and Insolvent Act, 1857.	Section three hundred and twenty-two.
22 & 23 Vict., c. 35 .	The Law of Property Amendment Act, 1859.	Sections twenty-six, thirty and thirty-one.
23 & 24 Vict., c. 38 .	The Law of Property Amendment Act, 1860.	Section nine.
25 & 26 Vict., c. 108 .	An Act to confirm certain sales, exchanges, partitions, and enfranchisements by trustees and others.	The whole Act.
26 & 27 Vict., c. 73 .	An Act to give further facilities to the holders of Indian stock.	Section four.
27 & 28 Vict., c. 114 .	The Improvement of Land Act, 1864.	Section sixty so far as it relates to trustees; and section sixty-one.
28 & 29 Vict., c. 78 .	The Mortgage Debenture Act, 1865.	Section forty.

SCHEDULE—*concluded.*

Session and Chapter.	Title or Short Title.	Extent of Repeal.
31 & 32 Vict., c. 40	The Partition Act, 1868	Section seven.
33 & 34 Vict., c. 71	The National Debt Act, 1870	Section twenty-nine.
34 & 35 Vict., c. 27	The Debenture Stock Act, 1871	The whole Act.
37 & 38 Vict., c. 78	The Vendor and Purchaser Act, 1874.	Sections three and six.
38 & 39 Vict., c. 83	The Local Loans Act, 1875	Sections twenty-one, and twenty-seven.
40 & 41 Vict., c. 59	The Colonial Stock Act, 1877	Section twelve.
43 & 44 Vict., c. 8	The Isle of Man Loans Act, 1880	Section seven, so far as it relates to trustees.
44 & 45 Vict., c. 41	The Conveyancing and Law of Property Act, 1881.	Sections thirty-one to thirty-eight.
45 & 46 Vict., c. 39	The Conveyancing Act, 1882	Section five.
46 & 47 Vict., c. 52	The Bankruptcy Act, 1883	Section one hundred and forty-seven.
51 & 52 Vict., c. 59	The Trustee Act, 1888	The whole Act, except sections one and eight.
52 & 53 Vict., c. 32	The Trust Investment Act, 1889	The whole Act, except sections one and seven.
52 & 53 Vict., c. 47	The Palatine Court of Durham Act, 1889.	Section eight.
53 & 54 Vict., c. 5	The Lunacy Act, 1890	Section one hundred and forty.
53 & 54 Vict., c. 69	The Settled Land Act, 1890	Section seventeen.
55 & 56 Vict., c. 13	The Conveyancing and Law of Property Act, 1892.	Section six.

The Madras and Bombay Armies Act, 1893.

(56 & 57 Vict., c. 62.)

An Act to amend the Law relating to the Madras and Bombay Armies.

[*5th December, 1893.*]

* * * * * * *

1. (1) The offices of Commander-in-Chief of the forces in the Presidencies of Madras and Bombay respectively, and of military secretary to the

Abolition of office of provincial

Commander-in-Chief in India.

government of each of those presidencies, are hereby abolished, and all things which by or under any Act of Parliament are required or authorized to be done by, to, or before any of the officers whose offices are hereby abolished, shall or may be done by, to, or before such officer as the commander-in-chief of the forces in India, with the approval of the Governor General of India in Council, may appoint in that behalf, and the commander-in-chief of the forces in India shall for the purposes of section one hundred and eighty of the Army Act be deemed to be the commander-in-chief in each presidency in India.

(2) The military control and authority exerciseable by the governors in council of the Presidencies of Madras and Bombay shall cease to be exercised by those governors in council, and shall be exerciseable by the Governor General of India in Council and all things which by or under the Army Act are required or authorised to be done by, to, or before the governor in council of the Presidency of Madras or of Bombay, shall or may be done by, to, or before the Governor General of India in Council.[1]

(3) The officers holding at the commencement of this Act the offices of commanders-in-chief of the forces in the Presidencies of Madras and Bombay shall cease to be members of the council of the governors of Madras and Bombay respectively.

Repeal.

2. The Acts specified in the schedule to this Act are hereby repealed to the extent in the third column of that schedule mentioned.

Commencement of Act.

3. This Act shall come into operation at such date as the Governor General of India in Council may by notification in the Gazette of India fix in that behalf.

Short title.

4. This Act may be cited as the Madras and Bombay Armies Act, 1893.

SCHEDULE.

ENACTMENTS REPEALED.

Session and Chapter.	Short Title.	Extent of Repeal.
33 Geo. 3, c. 52	The East India Company Act, 1793.	In section twenty-four, the words "and military," where they occur in relation to the government of the Presidency of Fort St. George or of Bombay.

[1] Expl. by 59 & 60 Vict., c. 2, s. 4, which provides that, "for removing doubts, it is declared that the things which may be done under or in pursuance of section 1 of the Madras and Bombay Armies Act, 1893, may be done either within or without the presidencies of Madras and Bombay respectively."

SCHEDULE—*contd.*

Enactments repealed—*contd.*

Session and Chapter.	Short Title.	Extent of Repeal.
33 Geo. 3, c. 52—*contd.*	The East India Company Act, 1793—*contd.*	In section twenty-five, the words "or of any provincial commander-in-chief of the forces there." Section thirty-two, from "and that when the offices of Governor" to "respective Presidencies."
3 & 4 Will. 4, c. 85 .	The Government of India Act, 1833.	In section sixty-three, the words "Commander-in-Chief or."
43 Vict., c. 3 . .	The Indian Salaries and Allowances Act, 1880.	In the First Schedule, the words "The Commanders-in-Chief of Madras and Bombay."
44 & 45 Vict., c. 58 .	The Army Act . .	In section fifty-four, the words "or if the offender was tried within the limits of any presidency by the Governor General or the Governor of that presidency," and the words "or if the offender has been tried within the limits of any presidency by the Governor General or by the Governor of the Presidency." In section fifty-seven, the words "also as respects persons undergoing sentences in any presidency the Commander in-Chief of the forces in that presidency". In sections sixty, sixty-five, and sixty-seven, the words— "(ii) The Commander-in-Chief of the forces in any presidency in India," and the words— "(iv) The Adjutant General in any presidency in India." In section seventy-three, the words "or the Commander-in-Chief of the forces of any presidency in India." In section one hundred and seventy-two, the words "or in any presidency in India." In section one hundred and seventy-nine, the words "or of any presidency in India." In section one hundred and eighty-three, the words "and also the Commander-in-Chief of the forces in any presidency in India," in each place where they occur.
53 & 54 Vict., c. 4. .	The Army (Annual) Act, 1890.	Section five.

THE EAST INDIA LOAN ACT, 1893.[1]

(56 & 57 Vict., c. 70.)

An Act to enable the Secretary of State in Council of India to raise Money in the United Kingdom for the Service of the Government of India, and for other purposes relating thereto.

[*21st December, 1893.*]

* * * * * * *

Short title. **1.** This Act may be cited as the East India Loan Act, 1893.

Definition. **2.** In this Act the expression "Secretary of State" means the Secretary of State in Council of India, unless the context otherwise requires.

Power to the Secretary of State to raise any sum not exceeding 10,000,000*l.* **3.** It shall be lawful for the Secretary of State, at any time or times, to raise in the United Kingdom for the service of the Government of India, any sum or sums of money not exceeding in the whole ten millions of pounds sterling, such sum or sums to be raised by the creation and issue of bonds, debentures, bills, or capital stock bearing interest, or partly by one of such modes, and partly by another or others.

Issue of bonds. **4.** All bonds issued under the authority of this Act may be issued under the hands of two members of the Council of India, and countersigned by the Secretary of State for India, or one of his under secretaries, or his assistant under secretary, and shall be for such respective amounts, payable after such notice, and at such rate or rates of interest, as the said Secretary of State may think fit.

Signature of debentures and bills. **5.** All debentures and bills to be issued by the Secretary of State under the authority of this or any previous Act of Parliament, instead of being signed by two Members of the Council of India and countersigned, shall bear the name of one of the under secretaries of state for India for the time being, and that name may be impressed or affixed by machinery or otherwise in such manner as the Secretary of State may from time to time direct.

Issue of debentures. **6.** All debentures issued under the authority of this Act may be issued for such respective amounts, and at such rate or rates of interest, as the Secretary of State may think fit, and shall be issued at or for such prices, and on such terms, as may be determined by the Secretary of State.

Payment of principal and interest on debentures. **7.** All debentures issued under the authority of this Act shall be paid off at par at a time or times to be mentioned in such debentures respectively; and the interest on all such debentures shall be paid on such days as shall be mentioned therein; and the principal moneys and interest secured by such debentures shall be payable either at the treasury of the Secretary of State in London or at the Bank of England.

---

[1] For digest, *see* Ilbert's *Government of India*, p. 326.
This Act may be cited, with eighteen others, as the East India Loans Acts, 1859 to 1893—*see* the Short Titles Act, 1896 (59 & 60 Vict., c. 14), printed *post*, p. 1255.

8. The debentures issued under the authority of this Act, and all right to and in respect of the principal and interest moneys secured thereby, shall be transferable by the delivery of such debentures or, at the discretion of the Secretary of State, by deed; provided that the coupons for interest annexed to any debenture issued under the authority of this Act shall pass by delivery. **Transfer of debentures and coupons for interest.**

9. All bills issued under the authority of this Act may be issued for such respective amounts as the Secretary of State may think fit, and shall be issued at or for such prices, and on such terms, as may be determined by the Secretary of State. **Issue of bills.**

10. A bill issued under the authority of this Act shall be a bill for the payment of the principal sum named therein at the date therein mentioned, so that the date be not more than twelve months from the date of the bill; and the principal sum secured by such bill shall be payable either at the treasury of the Secretary of State in London or at the Bank of England. Interest shall be payable in respect of such bill at such rate and in such manner as the Secretary of State may determine. **Description, currency of, and interest on bills.**

11. Any capital stock created under the authority of this Act shall bear such rate of interest as the Secretary of State may think fit; and such capital stock may be issued on such terms as may be determined by the Secretary of State; and any such capital stock may bear interest during such period, and be paid off at par at such time, as the Secretary of State may prescribe previously to the issue of such capital stock. **Creation of capital stock.**

12. In case of the creation and issue of any such capital stock there shall be kept, either at the office of the Secretary of State in London, or at the Bank of England, books wherein entries shall be made of the said capital stock, and wherein all assignments or transfers of the same, or any part thereof, shall be entered and registered, and shall be signed by the parties making such assignments or transfers, or, if such parties be absent, by his, her, or their attorney or attorneys thereunto lawfully authorised by writing under his, her, or their hands and seals, to be attested by two or more credible witnesses; and the person or persons to whom such transfer or transfers shall be made may respectively underwrite his, her, or their acceptance thereof; and no other mode of assigning or transferring the said capital stock or any part thereof, or any interest therein, shall be good and available in law, and no stamp duties whatsoever shall be charged on the said transfers or any of them. **Transfer books of capital stocks.**

13. The whole amount of the principal moneys to be charged on the revenues of India under this Act shall not exceed ten millions of pounds sterling. **Amount charged on revenues of India not to exceed 10,000,000*l*.**

14. Upon or for the repayment of any principal moneys secured under the authority of this Act, the Secretary of State may at any time borrow or **Power to raise money for payment**

of principal money.

raise, by all or any of the modes aforesaid, all or any part of the amount of principal money repaid or to be repaid, and so from time to time as all or any part of any principal moneys under this Act may require to be repaid, but the amount so to be charged on the revenues of India shall not in any case exceed the principal moneys required to be repaid.

Securities to be charged on revenues of India.

15. All bonds, debentures, and bills, issued under this Act, and the principal moneys and interest thereby secured, and all capital stock issued under this Act, and the interest thereon, shall be charged on and payable out of the revenues of India, in like manner as other liabilities incurred on account of the Government of India.

Provisions as to composition for stamp duties on India bonds extended to bonds, debentures, and bills.

16. The provisions contained in section four of the Act fifth and sixth William the Fourth, chapter sixty-four, with respect to the composition and agreement for the payment by the East India Company of an annual sum in lieu of stamp duties on their bonds, and the exemption of their bonds from stamp duties, shall be applicable with respect to the bonds, debentures, and bills to be issued by the Secretary of State under the authority of this or any previous Act, as if such provisions were here and there repeated and re-enacted with reference thereto.

Forgery of debentures, bonds, and bills.

17. All provisions now in force in anywise relating to the offence of forging or altering, or offering, uttering, disposing of, or putting off, knowing the same to be forged or altered, any East India bond, with intent to defraud, shall extend and be applicable to and in respect of any bond, debenture, or bill issued under the authority of this Act.

Saving existing borrowing powers of Secretary of State.

18. This Act shall not prejudice or affect any power of raising or borrowing money vested in the said Secretary of State at the time of passing thereof.

Stock created under this Act to be deemed India stock.

19. Any capital stock created under this Act shall be deemed to be India stock within the Act of the twenty-sixth and twenty-seventh Victoria, chapter seventy-three, anything in the said Act to the contrary notwithstanding.

Amendment of previous East India Loan Acts.

20. Notwithstanding anything to the contrary in the Acts thirty-sixth Victoria, chapter thirty-two, fortieth and forty-first Victoria, chapter fifty-one, and forty-second and forty-third Victoria, chapter sixty, the whole or any part of the moneys which by those Acts respectively the Secretary of State is authorised to borrow, may be raised by the creation of capital stock bearing interest, as well as by any of the other means therein respectively mentioned.

Application of Married Women's Property Act, 1882.

21. The expression public stocks and funds in section seven of the Married Women's Property Act, 1882, shall, as from the commencement of that Act, be deemed to have included and shall include any capital stock issued by the Secretary of State under the authority of Act of Parliament and charged on the revenues of India.

THE TRUSTEE ACT, 1893, AMENDMENT ACT, 1894.

(57 & 58 Vict., c. 10.)

An Act to amend the Trustee Act, 1893.

[*18th June, 1894.*]

* * * * * *

1. In section thirty of the Trustee Act, 1893, the words "as heir, or under the will of a deceased person, for payment of whose debts the judgment was given or order made" shall be repealed. **Amendment of 56 & 57 Vict., c. 53, s. 30.**

2. The powers conferred on the High Court in England by section forty-one of the Trustee Act, 1893, to make vesting orders as to all land and personal estate in Her Majesty's dominions except Scotland, are hereby also given to and may be exercised by the High Court in Ireland. **Extension to Ireland of 56 & 57 Vict., c. 53, s. 41.**

3. In section forty-four of the Trustee Act, 1893, after the word "trustee" in the first two places where it occurs shall be inserted the words "or other person." **Amendment of 56 & 57 Vict., c. 53, s. 44.**

4. A trustee shall not be liable for breach of trust by reason only of his continuing to hold an investment which has ceased to be an investment authorised by the instrument of trust or by the general law. **Liability of trustee in case of change of character of investment.**

5. This Act may be cited as the Trustee Act, 1893, Amendment Act, 1894. **Short title.**

THE INDIAN RAILWAYS ACT, 1894.[1]

(57 & 58 Vict., c. 12.)

An Act to enable Indian Railway Companies to pay Interest out of Capital during construction.

[*3rd July, 1894.*]

* * * * * *

1. This Act may be cited as the Indian Railways Act, 1894. **Short title.**

2. The expression "the Secretary of State" means the Secretary of State in Council of India: **Definitions.**

The expression "Indian Railway Company" means a company registered under the Companies Acts, 1862 to 1890, or any of them, and formed for the

[1] *Cf.* the Indian Railway Companies Act, 1895 (X of 1895). Printed General Acts, Ed. 1898, Vol. VI.

purpose of making and working, or making or working a railway in India, whether alone or in conjunction with other purposes:

The expression "the railway" means the railway in relation to the construction of which interest out of captial is permitted to be paid as herein-after provided.

Payment of interest out of capital.

3. An Indian Railway Company may pay interest on its paid-up share capital out of capital, for the period, and subject to the conditions and restrictions in this section mentioned, and may charge the same to capital as part of the cost of construction of the railway:

(1) Such interest shall be paid only for such period as shall be determined by the Secretary of State; and such period shall in no case extend beyond the close of the half year next after the half year during which the railway shall be actually completed and opened for traffic:

(2) No such payment shall be made unless the same is authorised by the Company's memorandum of association or by special resolution of the Company:

(3) No such payment, whether authorised by the memorandum of association or by special resolution, shall be made without the previous sanction of the Secretary of State:

(4) The amount so paid out of capital by way of interest, in respect of any period, shall in no case exceed a sum which shall, together with the net earnings of the railway during such period, make up the rate of four per cent. per annum:

(5) No such payment of interest shall be made until such Company has satisfied the Secretary of State that two-thirds at least of its share capital, in respect whereof interest is to be so paid, has been actually issued and accepted, and is held by shareholders who, or whose executors, administrators, or assigns, are legally liable for the same:

(6) No such interest shall accrue in favour of any shareholder for any time during which any call on any of his shares is in arrear:

(7) The payment of such interest shall not operate as a reduction of the amount paid up on the shares in respect of which it is paid.

Additional share capital for extensions.

4. If an Indian Railway Company is about to make and work, or to make or work, a railway in addition to, or by way of extension of, a railway owned or worked by such Company, and for that purpose issues further share capital in addition to the capital already issued by it, such Company may pay interest upon such further share capital out of capital, for the period and

subject to the conditions and restrictions in the last preceding section mentioned, the words in that section, "the railway," being read as applying to such addition or extension exclusively.

5. When a Company has power to pay interest under this Act, notice to that effect shall be given in every prospectus, advertisement, or other document inviting subscriptions for shares, and in every certificate of shares. Notice in prospectus and other documents.

6. When any interest has been paid by a Company under this Act, the annual or other accounts of such Company shall show the amount on which, and the rate at which interest has been so paid. Accounts.

7. If by any memorandum of association, articles of association, or other document any power of borrowing money is conferred on an Indian Railway Company, or on its directors, with or without the sanction of any meeting, and if such power of borrowing is limited to an amount bearing any proportion to the capital of such Company, the amount of capital applied or to be applied in payment of interest under this Act shall, for the purpose of ascertaining the extent of such power of borrowing, be deducted from the capital of such Company. Construction of borrowing powers.

8. Where an Indian railway company at any time before the passing of this Act has, with the sanction of the Secretary of State, paid interest out of capital, such payment shall be as valid as if it had been made pursuant to this Act. Sanction of past payments.

9. This Act shall continue in force until the thirty-first day of December one thousand nine hundred and five, and to the end of the then next session of Parliament, and no longer, unless Parliament shall otherwise determine: Provided that all interest, the payment of which shall have been sanctioned by the Secretary of State under this Act, shall continue to be payable to the same extent and for the same period as if this Act had not expired. Duration of Act.

The Finance Act, 1894.[1]

(57 & 58 Vict., c. 30.)

An Act to grant certain Duties of Customs and Inland Revenue to alter other Duties, and to amend the Law relating to Customs and Inland Revenue, and to make other provision for the financial arrangements of the year.

[*31st July, 1894.*]

Most Gracious Sovereign,

We, Your Majesty's most dutiful and loyal subjects, the Commons of the United Kingdom of Great Britain and Ireland in Parliament assembled,

---

[1] See *Chitty's Statutes*, Tit. Revenue, p. 188, and Tit. Death Duties, p. 115.

towards raising the necessary supplies to defray Your Majesty's public expenses and making an addition to the public revenue, have freely and voluntarily resolved to give and grant unto Your Majesty the several duties herein-after mentioned: and do therefore most humbly beseech Your Majesty that it may be enacted, and be it enacted, by the Queen's most Excellent Majesty, by and with the advice and consent of the Lords Spiritual and Temporal, and Commons, in this present Parliament assembled, and by the authority of the same, as follows:—

* * * * * * *

* * * * * * *

British Possessions.

Exception as to property in British possessions.

20.[1] (1) Where the Commissioners are satisfied, that in a British possession to which this section applies, duty is payable by reason of a death in respect of any property situate in such possession and passing on such death, they shall allow a sum equal to the amount of that duty to be deducted from the Estate duty payable in respect of that property on the same death.

(2) Nothing in this Act shall be held to create a charge for Estate duty on any property situate in a British possession, while so situate, or to authorise the Commissioners to take any proceedings in a British possession for the recovery of any Estate duty.

(3) Her Majesty the Queen may, by Order in Council, apply this section to any British possession where Her Majesty is satisfied that, by the law of such possession, either no duty is leviable in respect of property situate in the United Kingdom when passing on death, or that the law of such possession as respects any duty so leviable is to the like effect as the foregoing provisions of this section.

(4) Her Majesty in Council may revoke any such Order, where it appears that the law of the British possession has been so altered, that it would not authorize the making of an Order under this section.

* * * * * * *

* * * * * * *

---

[1] This is the only section of the Act applicable to India.

THE PRIZE COURTS ACT, 1894.

(57 & 58 Vict., c. 39.)

An Act to make further provision for the establishment of Prize Courts, and for other purposes connected therewith.

[*17th August, 1894.*]

* * * * * * * *[1]

1. This Act may be cited as the Prize Courts Act, 1894. Short title.

2. (1) Any commission, warrant, or instructions from Her Majesty the Queen or the Admiralty for the purpose of commissioning or regulating the procedure of a prize court at any place in a British possession may, notwithstanding the existence of peace, be issued at any time, with a direction that the court shall act only upon such proclamation as herein-after mentioned being made in the possession. Constitution of prize courts in British possessions.

(2) Where any such commission, warrant, or instructions have been issued, then, subject to instructions from Her Majesty, the Vice-Admiral of such possession may, when satisfied by information from a Secretary of State or otherwise, that war has broken out between Her Majesty and any foreign State, proclaim that war has so broken out, and thereupon the said commission, warrant, and instructions shall take effect as if the same had been issued after the breaking out of such war and such foreign State were named therein.

(3) The said commission and warrant may authorise either a Vice-Admiralty Court or a Colonial Court of Admiralty, within the meaning of the Colonial Courts of Admiralty Act, 1890, to act as a prize court, and may establish a Vice-Admiralty Court for that purpose. [53 & 54 Vict.,]

(4) Any such commission, warrant, or instructions may be revoked or altered from time to time.

(5) A court duly authorised to act as a prize court during any war shall after the conclusion of the war continue so to act in relation to, and finally dispose of, all matters and things which arose during the war, including all penalties and forfeitures incurred during the war.

3. (1) Her Majesty the Queen in Council may make rules of court for regulating, subject to the provisions of the Naval Prize Act, 1864,[1] and this Act, the procedure and practice of prize courts within the meaning of that Act, and the duties and conduct of the officers thereof, and of the practitioners therein, and for regulating the fees to be taken by the officers of the courts, and the costs, charges, and expenses to be allowed to the practitioners therein. Rules of court for and fees in prize courts. [27 & 28 Vict.,]

[1] Printed Vol. I, p. 379.

(2) Every rule so made shall, whenever made, take effect at the time therein mentioned, and shall be laid before both Houses of Parliament, and shall be kept exhibited in a conspicuous place in each court to which it relates.

(3) This section shall be substituted for section thirteen of the Naval Prize Act, 1864,[1] which section is hereby repealed. 27 & 28 Vict. c. 25.

(4) If any Colonial Court of Admiralty within the meaning of the Colonial Courts of Admiralty Act, 1890,[2] is authorised under this Act or otherwise to act as a prize court, all fees arising in respect of prize business transacted in the court shall be fixed, collected, and applied in like manner as the fees arising in respect of the Admiralty business of the court under the said Act. 53 & 54 Vict. c. 27.

As to Vice-Admiralty Courts.

4. Her Majesty the Queen in Council may make rules of court for regulating the procedure and practice, including fees and costs, in a Vice-Admiralty Court, whether under this Act or otherwise.

Repeal of 39 & 40 Geo. 3. c. 79, s. 25.

5. Section twenty-five of the Government of India Act, 1800, is hereby repealed.

THE UNIFORMS ACT, 1894.[3]

(57 & 58 Vict., c. 45.)

An Act to regulate and restrict the wearing of Naval Military Uniforms.

[*25th August, 1894.*]

BE it enacted by the Queen's most Excellent Majesty, by and with the advice and consent of the Lords Spiritual and Temporal, and Commons, in this present Parliament assembled, and by the authority of the same, as follows:

Short title.

1. This Act may be cited for all purposes as the Uniforms Act, 1894.

Military uniforms not to be worn without authority.

2. (1) It shall not be lawful for any person not serving in Her Majesty's Military Forces to wear without Her Majesty's permission the uniform of any of those forces, or any dress having the appearance or bearing any of the regimental or other distinctive marks of any such uniform: Provided that this enactment shall not prevent—

(*a*) A member of a band from wearing at or for the purpose of a public performance by the band at any time within six years after the passing of this Act any dress which, at the passing of this Act, is the recognised uniform of the band, unless the dress

[1] Printed Vol. I, p. 379.
[2] Printed *ante*, p. 880.
[3] See *Chitty's Statutes*, Tit. Uniforms, p. 1.

is an exact imitation of the uniform of any of Her Majesty's military forces ; or

(*b*) Any persons from wearing any uniform or dress in the course of a stage play performed in a place duly licensed or authorised for the public performance of stage plays, or in the course of a music hall or circus performance, or in the course of any *bonâ fide* military representation.

(2) If any person contravenes this section he shall be liable on summary conviction to a fine not exceeding five pounds.

Penalty for bringing contempt on uniform.

3. If any person not serving in Her Majesty's Naval or Military Forces wears without Her Majesty's permission the uniform of any of those forces, or any dress having the appearance or bearing any of the regimental or other distinctive marks of any such uniform in such a manner or under such circumstances as to be likely to bring contempt upon that uniform, or employs any other person so to wear that uniform or dress, he shall be liable on summary conviction to a fine not exceeding ten pounds, or to imprisonment for a term not exceeding one month.

Interpretation.

4. In this Act—

The expression " Her Majesty's Military Forces " means the regular forces, the reserve forces, and the auxiliary forces within the meaning of the Army Act, other than the naval coast volunteers and naval volunteers :

The expression " Her Majesty's Naval Forces " means the Navy, the naval coast volunteers, and the naval volunteers.

Commencement.

5. This Act shall come into operation on the first day of January one thousand eight hundred and ninety-five.

THE MERCHANT SHIPPING ACT, 1894.[1]

(57 & 58 Vict., c. 60.)

An Act to consolidate Enactments relating to Merchant Shipping.

[*25th August, 1894.*]

* * *

PART I.

REGISTRY.

Qualification for owning British Ships.

Qualification for owning British ship.

1. A ship shall not be deemed to be a British ship unless owned wholly by persons of the following description (in this Act referred to as persons qualified to be owners of British ships), namely,

(*a*) Natural-born British subjects :

---

[1] See *Chitty's Statutes*, Tit Shipping, p. 1 ; also Scrutton, etc.

During the passage of this Volume through the Press, this Act has been further supplemented with respect to the liability of shipowners and others by the Merchant Shipping (Liability of shipowners and others) Act, 1900 (63 & 64, Vict., cap. 32). *See* Gazette of India, 1900, for the month of November, Pt. I.

(*b*) Persons naturalized by or in pursuance of an Act of Parliament of the United Kingdom, or by or in pursuance of an Act or ordinance of the proper legislative authority in a British possession:

(*c*) Persons made denizens by letters of denization; and

(*d*) Bodies corporate established under and subject to the laws of some part of Her Majesty's dominions, and having their principal place of business in those dominions:

Provided that any person who either—

(i) being a natural-born British subject has taken the oath of allegiance to a foreign sovereign or State or has otherwise become a citizen or subject of a foreign state; or

(ii) has been naturalized or made a denizen as aforesaid;

shall not be qualified to be owner of a British ship unless, after taking the said oath, or becoming a citizen or subject of a foreign State, or on or after being naturalized or made denizen as aforesaid, he has taken the oath of allegiance to Her Majesty the Queen, and is during the time he is owner of the ship either resident in Her Majesty's dominions, or partner in a firm actually carrying on business in Her Majesty's dominions.

Obligation to register British ships.

Obligation to register British ships.

2. (1) Every British ship shall, unless exempted from registry, be registered under this Act.

(2) If a ship required by this Act to be registered is not registered under this Act, she shall not be recognised as a British ship.

(3) A ship required by this Act to be registered may be detained until the master of the ship, if so required, produces the certificate of the registry of the ship.

Exemptions from registry.

3. The following ships are exempted from registry under this Act:—

(1) Ships not exceeding fifteen tons burden employed solely in navigation on the rivers or coasts of the United Kingdom, or on the rivers or coasts of some British possession within which the managing owners of the ships are resident:

(2) Ships not exceeding thirty tons burden, and not having a whole or fixed deck, and employed solely in fishing or trading coastwise on the shores of Newfoundland or parts adjacent thereto, or in the Gulf of Saint Lawrence, or on such portions of the coasts of Canada as lie bordering on that gulf.

Procedure for Registration.

Registrars of British ships.

4. (1) The following persons shall be registrars of British ships :—

(a) At any port in the United Kingdom, or Isle of Man, approved by the Commissioners of Customs for the registry of ships, the chief officer of customs :

(b) In Guernsey and Jersey, the chief officers of customs together with the governor :

(c) In Malta and Gibraltar, the governor :

(d) At Calcutta, Madras, and Bombay, the port officer :

(e) At any other port in any British possession approved by the governor of the possession for the registry of ships, the chief officer of customs, or, if there is no such officer there resident, the governor of the possession in which the port is situate, or any officer appointed for the purpose by the governor :

(f) At a port of registry established by Order in Council under this Act, persons of the description in that behalf declared by the Order :

(2) Notwithstanding anything in this section Her Majesty may by Order in Council declare, with respect to any British possession named in the Order, not being the Channel Islands or the Isle of Man, the description of persons who are to be registrars of British ships in that possession.

(3) A registrar shall not be liable to damages or otherwise for any loss accruing to any person by reason of any act done or default made by him in his character of registrar, unless the same has happened through his neglect or wilful act.

Register book.

5. Every registrar of British ships shall keep a book to be called the register book, and entries in that book shall be made in accordance with the following provisions :—

(i) The property in a ship shall be divided into sixty-four shares :

(ii) Subject to the provisions of this Act with respect to joint owners or owners by transmission, not more than sixty-four individuals shall be entitled to be registered at the same time as owners of any one ship ; but this rule shall not affect the beneficial title of any number of persons or of any company represented by or claiming under or through any registered owner or joint owner :

(iii) A person shall not be entitled to be registered as owner of a fractional part of a share in a ship ; but any number of persons not exceeding five may be registered as joint owners of a ship or of any share or shares therein :

(iv) Joint owners shall be considered as constituting one person only as regards the persons entitled to be registered, and shall not be entitled to dispose in severalty of any interest in a ship, or in any share therein in respect of which they are registered:

(v) A corporation may be registered as owner by its corporate name.

Survey and measurement of ship.

6. Every British ship shall before registry be surveyed by a surveyor of ships and her tonnage ascertained in accordance with the tonnage regulations of this Act, and the surveyor shall grant his certificate specifying the ship's tonnage and build, and such other particulars descriptive of the identity of the ship as may for the time being be required by the Board of Trade, and such certificate shall be delivered to the registrar before registry.

Marking of ship.

7. (1) Every British ship shall before registry be marked permanently and conspicuously to the satisfaction of the Board of Trade as follows:—

(*a*) Her name shall be marked on each of her bows, and her name and the name of her port of registry must be marked on her stern, on a dark ground in white or yellow letters, or on a light ground in black letters, such letters to be of a length not less than four inches, and of proportionate breadth;

(*b*) Her official number and the number denoting her registered tonnage shall be cut in on her main beam;

(*c*) A scale of feet denoting her draught of water shall be marked on each side of her stem and of her stern post in Roman capital letters or in figures, not less than six inches in length, the lower line of such letters or figures to coincide with the draught line denoted thereby, and those letters or figures must be marked by being cut in and painted white or yellow on a dark ground, or in such other way as the Board of Trade approve.

(2) The Board of Trade may exempt any class of ships from all or any of the requirements of this section, and a fishing boat entered in the fishing boat register, and lettered and numbered in pursuance of the Fourth Part of this Act, need not have her name and port of registry marked under this section.

(3) If the scale of feet showing the ship's draught of water is in any respect inaccurate, so as to be likely to mislead, the owner of the ship shall be liable to a fine not exceeding one hundred pounds.

(4) The marks required by this section shall be permanently continued, and no alteration shall be made therein, except in the event of any of the particulars thereby denoted being altered in the manner provided by this Act.

(5) If an owner or master of a British ship neglects to cause his ship to be marked as required by this section, or to keep her so marked, or if any person conceals, removes, alters, defaces, or obliterates, or suffers any person under his control to conceal, remove, alter, deface, or obliterate any of the said marks, except in the event aforesaid, or except for the purpose of escaping capture by an enemy, that owner, master, or person shall for each offence be liable to a fine not exceeding one hundred pounds, and on a certificate from a surveyor of ships, or Board of Trade inspector under this Act, that a ship is insufficiently or inaccurately marked, the ship may be detained until the insufficiency or inaccuracy has been remedied.

Application for registry.

8. An application for registry of a ship shall be made in the case of individuals by the person requiring to be registered as owner, or by some one or more of the persons so requiring if more than one, or by his or their agent, and in the case of corporations by their agent, and the authority of the agent shall be testified by writing, if appointed by individuals, under the hands of the appointors, and, if appointed by a corporation, under the common seal of that corporation.

Declaration of ownership on registry.

9. A person shall not be entitled to be registered as owner of a ship or of a share therein until he, or in the case of a corporation the person authorised by this Act to make declarations on behalf of the corporation, has made and signed a declaration of ownership, referring to the ship as described in the certificate of the surveyor, and containing the following particulars:—

(i) A statement of his qualification to own a British ship, or in the case of a corporation, of such circumstances of the constitution and business thereof as prove it to be qualified to own a British ship:

(ii) A statement of the time when and the place where the ship was built, or, if the ship is foreign built, and the time and place of building unknown, a statement that she is foreign built, and that the declarant does not know the time or place of her building; and, in addition thereto, in the case of a foreign ship, a statement of her foreign name, or, in the case of a ship condemned, a statement of the time, place and court at and by which she was condemned:

(iii) A statement of the name of the master:

(iv) A statement of the number of shares in the ship of which he or the corporation, as the case may be, is entitled to be registered as owner:

(v) A declaration that, to the best of his knowledge and belief, no unqualified person or body of persons is entitled as owner to any legal or beneficial interest in the ship or any share therein.

Evidence on first registry.

10. (1) On the first registry of a ship the following evidence shall be produced in addition to the declaration of ownership :—

(*a*) in the case of a British-built ship, a builder's certificate, that is to say, a certificate signed by the builder of the ship, and containing a true account of the proper denomination and of the tonnage of the ship, as estimated by him, and of the time when and the place where she was built, and of the name of the person (if any) on whose account the ship was built, and if there has been any sale, the bill of sale under which the ship, or a share therein, has become vested in the applicant for registry :

(*b*) in the case of a foreign-built ship, the same evidence as in the case of a British-built ship, unless the declarant who makes the declaration of ownership declares that the time and place of her building are unknown to him, or that the builder's certificate cannot be procured, in which case there shall be required only the bill of sale under which the ship, or a share therein, became vested in the applicant for registry :

(*c*) in the case of a ship condemned by any competent court, an official copy of the condemnation.

(2) The builder shall grant the certificate required by this section, and such person as the Commissioners of Customs recognise as carrying on the business of the builder of a ship, shall be included, for the purposes of this section, in the expression "builder of the ship."

(3) If the person granting a builder's certificate under this section wilfully makes a false statement in that certificate, he shall for each offence be liable to a fine not exceeding one hundred pounds.

Entry of particulars in register book.

11. As soon as the requirements of this Act preliminary to registry have been complied with the registrar shall enter in the register book the following particulars respecting the ship :—

(*a*) the name of the ship and the name of the port to which she belongs :
(*b*) the details comprised in the surveyor's certificate :
(*c*) the particulars respecting her origin stated in the declaration of ownership : and
(*d*) the name and description of her registered owner or owners, and if there are more owners than one, the proportions in which they are interested in her.

Documents to be retained by registrar.

12. On the registry of a ship the registrar shall retain in his possession the following documents; namely, the surveyor's certificate, the builder's certificate, any bill of sale of the ship previously made, the copy of the condemnation (if any), and all declarations of ownership.

Port of registry.

13. The port at which a British ship is registered for the time being shall be deemed her port of registry and the port to which she belongs.

Certificate of Registry.

Certificate of registry.

14. On completion of the registry of a ship, the registrar shall grant a certificate of registry comprising the particulars respecting her entered in the register book, with the name of her master.

Custody of certificate.

15. (1) The certificate of registry shall be used only for the lawful navigation of the ship, and shall not be subject to detention by reason of any title, lien, charge, or interest whatever had or claimed by any owner, mortgagee, or other person to, on, or in the ship.

(2) If any person, whether interested in the ship or not, refuses on request to deliver up the certificate of registry when in his possession or under his control to the person entitled to the custody thereof for the purposes of the lawful navigation of the ship, or to any registrar, officer of customs, or other person entitled by law to require such delivery, any justice by warrant under his hand and seal, or any court capable of taking cognizance of the matter, may summon the person so refusing to appear before such justice or court, and to be examined touching such refusal, and unless it is proved to the satisfaction of such justice or court that there was reasonable cause for such refusal, the offender shall be liable to a fine not exceeding one hundred pounds, but if it is shown to such justice or court that the certificate is lost, the person summoned shall be discharged, and the justice or court shall certify that the certificate of registry is lost.

(3) If the person so refusing is proved to have absconded so that the warrant of a justice or process of a court cannot be served on him, or if he persists in not delivering up the certificate, the justice or court shall certify the fact, and the same proceedings may then be taken as in the case of a certificate mislaid, lost, or destroyed, or as near thereto as circumstances permit.

Penalty for use of improper certificate.

16. If the master or owner of a ship uses or attempts to use for her navigation a certificate of registry not legally granted in respect of the ship, he shall, in respect of each offence, be guilty of a misdemeanour, and the ship shall be subject to forfeiture under this Act.

Power to grant new certificate.

17. The registrar of the port of registry of a ship may, with the approval of the Commissioners of Customs, and on the delivery up to him of the certificate of registry of a ship, grant a new certificate in lieu thereof.

Provision for loss of certificate.

18. (1) In the event of the certificate of registry of a ship being mislaid, lost, or destroyed, the registrar of her port of registry shall grant a new certificate of registry in lieu of her original certificate.

(2) If the port (having a British registrar or consular officer) at which the ship is at the time of the event, or first arrives after the event—

(*a*) is not in the United Kingdom, where the ship is registered in the United Kingdom; or,

(*b*) is not in the British possession in which the ship is registered; or,

(*c*) where the ship is registered at a port of registry established by Order in Council under this Act, is not that port;

then the master of the ship, or some other person having knowledge of the facts of the case, shall make a declaration stating the facts of the case, and the names and descriptions of the registered owners of such ship to the best of the declarant's knowledge and belief, and the registrar or consular officer, as the case may be, shall thereupon grant a provisional certificate, containing a statement of the circumstances under which it is granted.

(3) The provisional certificate shall within ten days after the first subsequent arrival of the ship at her port of discharge in the United Kingdom where she is registered in the United Kingdom, or in the British possession in which she is registered, or where she is registered at a port of registry established by Order in Council under this Act at that port, be delivered up to the registrar of her port of registry, and the registrar shall thereupon grant the new certificate of registry; and if the master without reasonable cause fails to deliver up the provisional certificate within the ten days aforesaid, he shall be liable to a fine not exceeding fifty pounds.

Endorsement of change of master on certificate.

19. Where the master of a registered British ship is changed, each of the following persons, that is to say—

(*a*) if the change is made in consequence of the sentence of a naval court, the presiding officer of that court; and

(*b*) if the change is made in consequence of the removal of the master by a court under Part VI of this Act, the proper officer of that court; and

(*c*) if the change occurs from any other cause, the registrar, or if there is none, the British consular officer, at the port where the change occurs,

shall endorse and sign on the certificate of registry a memorandum of the change, and shall forthwith report the change to the Registrar-General of Shipping and Seamen; and any officer of customs at any port in Her Majesty's dominions may refuse to admit any person to do any act there as master of a British ship unless his name is inserted in or endorsed on her certificate of registry as her last appointed master.

20. (1) Whenever a change occurs in the registered ownership of a ship, the change of ownership shall be endorsed on her certificate of registry either by the registrar of the ship's port of registry, or by the registrar of any port at which the ship arrives who has been advised of the change by the registrar of the ship's port of registry. Endorsement of change of ownership on certificate.

(2) The master shall, for the purpose of such endorsement by the registrar of the ship's port of registry, deliver the certificate of registry to the registrar, forthwith after the change if the change occurs when the ship is at her port of registry, and if it occurs during her absence from that port and the endorsement under this section is not made before her return, then upon her first return to that port.

(3) The registrar of any port, not being the ship's port of registry, who is required to make an endorsement under this section may for that purpose require the master of the ship to deliver to him the ship's certificate of registry, so that the ship be not thereby detained, and the master shall deliver the same accordingly.

(4) If the master fails to deliver to the registrar the certificate of registry as required by this section he shall, for each offence, be liable to a fine not exceeding one hundred pounds.

21. (1) In the event of a registered ship being either actually or constructively lost, taken by the enemy, burnt, or broken up, or ceasing by reason of a transfer to persons not qualified to be owners of British ships, or otherwise, to be a British ship, every owner of the ship or any share in the ship shall, immediately on obtaining knowledge of the event, if no notice thereof has already been given to the registrar, give notice thereof to the registrar at her port of registry, and that registrar shall make an entry thereof in the register book. Delivery up of certificate of ship lost or ceasing to be British-owned.

(2) In any such case, except where the ship's certificate of registry is lost or destroyed, the master of the ship shall, if the event occurs in port immediately, but if it occurs elsewhere then within ten days after his arrival in port, deliver the certificate to the registrar, or, if there is none, to the British consular officer there, and the registrar if he is not himself the registrar of her port of registry, or the British consular officer, shall forthwith forward the certificate delivered to him to the registrar of her port of registry.

(3) If any such owner or master fails, without reasonable cause, to comply with this section, he shall for each offence be liable to a fine not exceeding one hundred pounds.

Provisional certificate for ships becoming British owned abroad.

22. (1) If at a port not within Her Majesty's dominions and not being a port of registry established by Order in Council under this Act, a ship becomes the property of persons qualified to own a British ship, the British consular officer there may grant to her master, on his application, a provisional certificate, stating :—

(*a*) the name of the ship ;

(*b*) the time and place of her purchase, and the names of her purchasers ;

(*c*) the name of her master ; and

(*d*) the best particulars respecting her tonnage, build, and description which he is able to obtain ;

and shall forward a copy of the certificate at the first convenient opportunity to the Registrar-General of Shipping and Seamen.

(2) Such a provisional certificate shall have the effect of a certificate of registry until the expiration of six months from its date, or until the ship's arrival at a port where there is a registrar (whichever first happens), and on either of those events happening shall cease to have effect.

Temporary passes in lieu of certificates of registry.

23. Where it appears to the Commissioners of Customs, or to the Governor of a British possession, that by reason of special circumstances it would be desirable that permission should be granted to any British ship to pass, without being previously registered, from any port in Her Majesty's dominions to any other port within Her Majesty's dominions, the Commissioners or the governor may grant a pass accordingly, and that pass shall, for the time and within the limits therein mentioned, have the same effect as a certificate of registry.

Transfers and Transmissions.

Transfer of ships or shares.

24. (1) A registered ship or a share therein (when disposed of to a person qualified to own a British ship) shall be transferred by bill of sale.

(2) The bill of sale shall contain such description of the ship as is contained in the surveyor's certificate, or some other description sufficient to identify the ship to the satisfaction of the registrar, and shall be in the form marked A in the first part of the First Schedule to this Act, or as near thereto as circumstances permit, and shall be executed by the transferor in the presence of, and be attested by, a witness or witnesses.

Declaration of transfer.

25. Where a registered ship or a share therein is transferred, the transferee shall not be entitled to be registered as owner thereof until he, or, in the case of a corporation, the person authorised by this Act to make declarations, on behalf of the corporation, has made and signed a declaration (in this Act called a declaration of transfer) referring to the ship, and containing—

(*a*) a statement of the qualification of the transferee to own a British ship, or if the transferee is a corporation, of such circumstances of the constitution and business thereof as prove it to be qualified to own a British ship; and

(*b*) a declaration that, to the best of his knowledge and belief, no unqualified person or body of persons is entitled as owner to any legal or beneficial interest in the ship or any share therein.

26. (1) Every bill of sale for the transfer of a registered ship or of a share therein, when duly executed, shall be produced to the registrar of her port of registry, with the declaration of transfer, and the registrar shall thereupon enter in the register book the name of the transferee as owner of the ship or share, and shall endorse on the bill of sale the fact of that entry having been made, with the day and hour thereof. Registry of transfer.

(2) Bills of sale of a ship or of a share therein shall be entered in the register book in the order of their production to the registrar.

27. (1) Where the property in a registered ship or share therein is transmitted to a person qualified to own a British ship on the marriage, death, or bankruptcy of any registered owner, or by any lawful means other than by a transfer under this Act:— Transmission of property in ship on death, bankruptcy, marriage, etc.

(*a*) That person shall authenticate the transmission by making and signing a declaration (in this Act called a declaration of transmission) identifying the ship and containing the several statements herein-before required to be contained in a declaration of transfer, or as near thereto as circumstances admit, and also a statement of the manner in which and the person to whom the property has been transmitted.

(*b*) If the transmission takes place by virtue of marriage, the declaration shall be accompanied by a copy of the register of the marriage or other legal evidence of the celebration thereof, and shall declare the identity of the female owner.

(*c*) If the transmission is consequent on bankruptcy, the declaration of transmission shall be accompanied by such evidence as is for the time being receivable in courts of justice as proof of the title of persons claiming under a bankruptcy.

(*d*) If the transmission is consequent on death, the declaration of transmission shall be accompanied by the instrument of representation, or an official extract therefrom.

(2) The registrar, on receipt of the declaration of transmission so accompanied, shall enter in the register book the name of the person entitled under the transmission as owner of the ship or share the property in which has been transmitted, and, where there is more than one such person, shall enter the names of all those persons, but those persons, however numerous, shall for the purpose of the provision of this Act with respect to the number of persons entitled to be registered as owners, be considered as one person.

Order for sale on transmission to unqualified person.

28. (1) Where the property in a registered ship or share therein is transmitted on marriage, death, bankruptcy, or otherwise to a person not qualified to own a British ship, then—

if the ship is registered in England or Ireland, the High Court; or
if the ship is registered in Scotland, the Court of Session; or
if the ship is registered in any British possession, the court having the principal civil jurisdiction in that possession; or
if the ship is registered in a port of registry established by Order in Council under this Act, the British court having the principal civil jurisdiction there;

may on application by or on behalf of the unqualified person, order a sale of the property so transmitted, and direct that the proceeds of the sale, after deducting the expenses thereof, be paid to the person entitled under such transmission or otherwise as the court direct.

(2) The court may require any evidence in support of the application they think requisite, and may make the order on any terms and conditions they think just, or may refuse to make the order, and generally may act in the case as the justice of the case requires.

(3) Every such application for sale must be made within four weeks after the occurrence of the event on which the transmission has taken place, or within such further time (not exceeding in the whole one year from the date of the occurrence) as the court allow.

(4) If such an application is not made within the time aforesaid, or if the Court refuse an order for sale, the ship or share transmitted shall thereupon be subject to forfeiture under this Act.

Transfer of ship or sale by order of court.

29. Where any court, whether under the preceding sections of this Act or otherwise, order the sale of any ship or share therein, the order of the court shall contain a declaration vesting in some person named by the court the right to transfer that ship or share, and that person shall thereupon be entitled to transfer the ship or share in the same manner and to the same extent as if he were the registered owner thereof; and every registrar shall obey the requisition of the person so named in respect of any such transfer to the same extent as if such person were the registered owner.

30. Each of the following courts, namely:— Power of court to prohibit transfer.

(*a*) in England or Ireland the High Court;

(*b*) in Scotland the Court of Session;

(*c*) in any British possession the court having the principal civil jurisdiction in that possession; and

(*d*) in the case of a port of registry established by Order in Council under this Act, the British court having the principal civil jurisdiction there,

may, if the court think fit (without prejudice to the exercise of any other power of the court), on the application of any interested person, make an order prohibiting for a time specified any dealing with a ship or any share therein, and the court may make the order on any terms or conditions they think just, or may refuse to make the order, or may discharge the order when made, with or without costs, and generally may act in the case as the justice of the case requires; and every registrar, without being made a party to the proceeding, shall on being served with the order or an official copy thereof obey the same.

Mortgages.

31. (1) A registered ship or a share therein may be made a security for a loan or other valuable consideration, and the instrument creating the security (in this Act called a mortgage) shall be in the form marked B in the first part of the First Schedule to this Act, or as near thereto as circumstances permit, and on the production of such instrument the registrar of the ship's port of registry shall record it in the register book. Mortgage of ship or share.

(2) Mortgages shall be recorded by the registrar in the order in time in which they are produced to him for that purpose, and the registrar shall by memorandum under his hand notify on each mortgage that it has been recorded by him, stating the day and hour of that record.

32. Where a registered mortgage is discharged, the registrar shall, on the production of the mortgage deed, with a receipt for the mortgage money endorsed thereon, duly signed and attested, make an entry in the register book to the effect that the mortgage has been discharged, and on that entry being made the estate (if any) which passed to the mortgagee shall vest in the person in whom (having regard to intervening acts and circumstances, if any,) it would have vested if the mortgage had not been made. Entry of discharge of mortgage.

33. If there are more mortgages than one registered in respect of the same ship or share, the mortgagees shall, notwithstanding any express, implied, or constructive notice, be entitled in priority, one over the other, Priority of mortgages.

according to the date at which each mortgage is recorded in the register book, and not according to the date of each mortgage itself.

Mortgagee not treated as owner.

34. Except as far as may be necessary for making a mortgaged ship or share available as a security for the mortgage debt, the mortgagee shall not by reason of the mortgage be deemed the owner of the ship or share, nor shall the mortgagor be deemed to have ceased to be owner thereof.

Mortgagee to have power of sale.

35. Every registered mortgagee shall have power absolutely to dispose of the ship or share in respect of which he is registered, and to give effectual receipts for the purchase money; but where there are more persons than one registered as mortgagees of the same ship or share, a subsequent mortgagee shall not, except under the order of a court of competent jurisdiction, sell the ship or share, without the concurrence of every prior mortgagee.

Mortgagee not affected by bankruptcy.

36. A registered mortgage of a ship or share shall not be affected by any act of bankruptcy committed by the mortgagor after the date of the record of the mortgage, notwithstanding that the mortgagor at the commencement of his bankruptcy had the ship or share in his possession, order, or disposition, or was reputed owner thereof, and the mortgage shall be preferred to any right, claim, or interest therein of the other creditors of the bankrupt or any trustee or assignee on their behalf.

Transfer of mortgages.

37. A registered mortgage of a ship or share may be transferred to any person, and the instrument effecting the transfer shall be in the form marked C in the first part of the First Schedule to this Act, or as near thereto as circumstances permit, and on the production of such instrument, the registrar shall record it by entering in the register book the name of the transferee as mortgagee of the ship or share, and shall by memorandum under his hand notify on the instrument of transfer that it has been recorded by him, stating the day and hour of the record.

Transmission of interest in mortgage by death, bankruptcy, marriage, etc.

38. (1) Where the interest of a mortgagee in a ship or share is transmitted on marriage, death, or bankruptcy, or by any lawful means, other than by a transfer under this Act, the transmission shall be authenticated by a declaration of the person to whom the interest is transmitted, containing a statement of the manner in which and the person to whom the property has been transmitted, and shall be accompanied by the like evidence as is by this Act required in case of a corresponding transmission of the ownership of a ship or share.

(2) The registrar on the receipt of the declaration, and the production of the evidence aforesaid, shall enter the name of the person entitled under the transmission in the register book as mortgagee of the ship or share.

Certificates of Mortgage and Sale.

39. A registered owner, if desirous of disposing by way of mortgage or sale of the ship or share in respect of which he is registered at any place out of the country in which the port of registry of the ship is situate, may apply to the registrar, and the registrar shall thereupon enable him to do so by granting a certificate of mortgage or a certificate of sale.

Powers of mortgage and sale may be conferred by certificate.

40. Before a certificate of mortgage or sale is granted, the applicant shall state to the registrar, and the registrar shall enter in the register book, the following particulars; (that is to say,)

Requisites for certificates of mortgage and sale.

(i) the name of the person by whom the power mentioned in the certificate is to be exercised, and in the case of a mortgage the maximum amount of charge to be created, if it is intended to fix any such maximum, and in the case of a sale the minimum price at which a sale is to be made, if it is intended to fix any such minimum:

(ii) the place where the power is to be exercised, or if no place is specified, a declaration that it may be exercised anywhere, subject to the provisions of this Act:

(iii) the limit of time within which the power may be exercised.

41. A certificate of mortgage or sale shall not be granted so as to authorise any mortgage or sale to be made—

Restrictions on certificates of mortgage and sale.

If the port of registry of the ship is situate in the United Kingdom, at any place within the United Kingdom; or

If the port of registry is situate within a British possession, at any place within the same British possession; or

If the port of registry is established by Order in Council under this Act, at that port, or within such adjoining area as is specified in the order; or

By any person not named in the certificate.

42. A certificate of mortgage and a certificate of sale shall contain a statement of the several particulars by this Act directed to be entered in the register book on the application for the certificate, and in addition thereto an enumeration of any registered mortgages or certificates of mortgage or sale affecting the ship or share in respect of which the certificate is given.

Contents of certificates of mortgage and sale.

43. The following rules shall be observed as to certificates of mortgage:—

Rules as to certificates of mortgage.

(1) The power shall be exercised in conformity with the directions contained in the certificate:

(*Sec.* 43.)

(2) Every mortgage made thereunder shall be registered by the endorsement of a record thereof on the certificate by a registrar or British consular officer :

(3) A mortgage made in good faith thereunder shall not be impeached by reason of the person by whom the power was given dying before the making of the mortgage :

(4) Whenever the certificate contains a specification of the place at which, and a limit of time not exceeding twelve months within which, the power is to be exercised, a mortgage made in good faith to a mortgagee without notice shall not be impeached by reason of the bankruptcy of the person by whom the power was given :

(5) Every mortgage which is so registered as aforesaid on the certificate shall have priority over all mortgages of the same ship or share created subsequently to the date of the entry of the certificate in the register book ; and, if there are more mortgages than one so registered, the respective mortgagees claiming thereunder shall, notwithstanding any express, implied, or constructive notice, be entitled one before the other according to the date at which each mortgage is registered on the certificate, and not according to the date of the mortgage :

(6) Subject to the foregoing rules, every mortgagee whose mortgage is registered on the certificate shall have the same rights and powers and be subject to the same liabilities as he would have had and been subject to if his mortgage had been registered in the register book instead of on the certificate.

(7) The discharge of any mortgage so registered on the certificate may be endorsed on the certificate by any registrar or British consular officer, on the production of such evidence as is by this Act required to be produced to the registrar on the entry of the discharge of a mortgage in the register book ; and on that endorsement being made, the interest, if any, which passed to the mortgagee shall vest in the same person or persons in whom it would (having regard to intervening acts and circumstances, if any,) have vested, if the mortgage had not been made:

(8) On the delivery of any certificate of mortgage to the registrar by whom it was granted he shall, after recording in the register book in such manner as to preserve its priority, any unsatisfied mortgage registered thereon, cancel the certificate, and enter the fact

of the cancellation in the register book; and every certificate so cancelled shall be void to all intents.

Rules as to certificates of sale.

44. The following rules shall be observed as to certificates of sale:—

(1) A certificate of sale shall not be granted except for the sale of an entire ship:

(2) The power shall be exercised in conformity with the directions contained in the certificate:

(3) A sale made in good faith thereunder to a purchaser for valuable consideration shall not be impeached by reason of the person by whom the power was given dying before the making of such sale:

(4) Whenever the certificate contains a specification of the place at which, and a limit of time not exceeding twelve months within which, the power is to be exercised, a sale made in good faith to a purchaser for valuable consideration without notice shall not be impeached by reason of the bankruptcy of the person by whom the power was given:

(5) A transfer made to a person qualified to be the owner of a British ship shall be by a bill of sale in accordance with this Act:

(6) If the ship is sold to a person qualified to be the owner of a British ship the ship shall be registered anew; but notice of all mortgages enumerated on the certificate of sale shall be entered in the register book:

(7) Before registry anew there shall be produced to the registrar required to make the same bill of sale by which the ship is transferred, the certificate of sale, and the certificate of registry of such ship:

(8) The last-mentioned registrar shall retain the certificates of sale and registry, and after having endorsed on both of those instruments an entry of the fact of a sale having taken place, shall forward them to the registrar of the port appearing thereon to be the former port of registry of the ship, and the last-mentioned registrar shall thereupon make a memorandum of the sale in his register book, and the registry of the ship in that book shall be considered as closed, except as far as relates to any unsatisfied mortgages or existing certificates of mortgage entered therein:

(9) On such registry anew the description of the ship contained in her original certificate of registry may be transferred to the new register book, without her being re-surveyed, and the declaration

to be made by the purchaser shall be the same as would be required to be made by an ordinary transferee:

(10) If the ship is sold to a person not qualified to be the owner of a British ship, the bill of sale by which the ship is transferred, the certificate of sale, and the certificate of registry shall be produced to a registrar or British consular officer, and that registrar or officer shall retain the certificates of sale and registry and, having endorsed thereon the fact of that ship having been sold to a person not qualified to be the owner of a British ship, shall forward the certificates to the registrar of the port appearing on the certificate of registry to be the port of registry of that ship; and that registrar shall thereupon make a memorandum of the sale in his register book, and the registry of the ship in that book shall be considered as closed, except so far as relates to any unsatisfied mortgages or existing certificates of mortgage entered therein:

(11) If on a sale being made to a person not qualified to be the owner of a British ship, default is made in the production of such certificates as are mentioned in the last rule, that person shall be considered by British law as having acquired no title to or interest in the ship; and further, the person upon whose application the certificate of sale was granted, and the person exercising the power, shall each be liable to a fine not exceeding one hundred pounds:

(12) If no sale is made in conformity with the certificate of sale, that certificate shall be delivered to the registrar by whom the same was granted; and he shall thereupon cancel it and enter the fact of the cancellation in the register book; and every certificate so cancelled shall be void for all intents and purposes.

Power of Commissioners of Customs in case of loss of certificate of mortgage or sale.

45. On proof at any time to the satisfaction of the Commissioners of Customs that a certificate of mortgage or sale is lost or destroyed, or so obliterated as to be useless, and that the powers thereby given have never been exercised, or if they have been exercised, then on proof of the several matters and things that have been done thereunder, the registrar may, with the sanction of the Commissioners, as circumstances require, either issue a new certificate, or direct such entries to be made in the register books, or such other things to be done, as might have been made or done if the loss, destruction, or obliteration had not taken place.

Revocation of certificates

46. (1) The registered owner of any ship or share therein in respect of which a certificate of mortgage or sale has been granted, specifying the places where the power thereby given is to be exercised, may, by an instrument under his hand, authorise the registrar by whom the certificate was granted to give notice to the registrar or British consular officer at every such place that the certificate is revoked. of mortgage and sale.

(2) Notice shall thereupon be given accordingly and shall be recorded by the registrar or British consular officer receiving it, and after it is recorded, the certificate shall be deemed to be revoked and of no effect so far as respects any mortgage or sale to be thereafter made at that place.

(3) The notice after it has been recorded shall be exhibited to every person applying for the purpose of effecting or obtaining a mortgage or transfer under the certificate.

(4) A registrar or British consular officer on recording any such notice shall state to the registrar by whom the certificate was granted whether any previous exercise of the power to which such certificate refers has taken place.

Name of ship.

47. (1) A ship shall not be described by any name other than that by which she is for the time being registered. Rules as to name of ship.

(2) A change shall not be made in the name of a ship without the previous written permission of the Board of Trade.

(3) Application for that permission shall be in writing, and if the Board are of opinion that the application is reasonable, they may entertain it, and thereupon require notice thereof to be published in such form and manner as they think fit.

(4) On permission being granted to change the name, the ship's name shall forthwith be altered in the register book, in the ship's certificate of registry, and on her bows and stern.

(5) If it is shown to the satisfaction of the Board of Trade that the name of any ship has been changed without their permission, they shall direct that her name be altered into that which she bore before the change, and the name shall be altered in the register book, in the ship's certificate of registry, and on her bows and stern accordingly.

(6) Where a ship having once been registered has ceased to be so registered no person unless ignorant of the previous registry (proof whereof shall lie on him) shall apply to register, and no registrar shall knowingly register the ship, except by the name by which she was previously registered, unless with the previous written permission of the Board of Trade.

(7) Where a foreign ship, not having at any previous time been registered as a British ship, becomes a British ship, no person shall apply to register, and no registrar shall knowingly register, the ship, except by the name which

she bore as a foreign ship immediately before becoming a British ship, unless with the previous written permission of the Board of Trade.

(8) If any person acts, or suffers any person under his control to act, in contravention of this section, or omits to do, or suffers any person under his control to omit to do, anything required by this section, he shall for each offence be liable to a fine not exceeding one hundred pounds, and (except in the case of an application being made under the section with respect to a foreign ship which not having at any previous time been registered as a British ship has become a British ship) the ship may be detained until this section is complied with.

Registry of Alterations, Registry anew, and Transfer of Registry.

Registry of alterations.

48. (1) Where a registered ship is so altered as not to correspond with the particulars relating to her tonnage or description contained in the register book, then, if the alteration is made at any port having a registrar, that registrar, or, if it is made elsewhere, the registrar of the first port having a registrar at which the ship arrives after the alteration, shall, on application being made to him, and on receipt of a certificate from the proper surveyor stating the particulars of the alteration, either cause the alteration to be registered, or direct that the ship be registered anew.

(2) On failure to register anew a ship or to register an alteration of a ship so altered as aforesaid, that ship shall be deemed not duly registered, and shall not be recognised as a British ship.

Regulations for registry of alteration.

49. (1) For the purpose of the registry of an alteration in a ship, the ship's certificate of registry shall be produced to the registrar, and the registrar shall, in his discretion, either retain the certificate of registry and grant a new certificate of registry containing a description of the ship as altered, or endorse and sign on the existing certificate a memorandum of the alteration.

(2) The particulars of the alteration so made, and the fact of the new certificate having been granted, or endorsement having been made, shall be entered by the registrar of the ship's port of registry in his register book; and for that purpose the registrar to whom the application for the registry of the alteration has been made (if he is not the registrar of the ship's port of registry), shall forthwith report to the last-mentioned registrar the particulars and facts as aforesaid, accompanied, where a new certificate of registry has been granted, by the old certificate of registry.

Provisional certificate and endorsement where ship is to be registered anew.

50. (1) Where any registrar, not being the registrar of the ship's port of registry, on an application as to an alteration in a ship directs the ship to be registered anew, he shall either grant a provisional certificate, describing the ship as altered, or provisionally endorse the particulars of the alteration on the existing certificate.

(2) Every such provisional certificate, or certificate provisionally endorsed, shall, within ten days after the first subsequent arrival of the ship at her port of discharge in the United Kingdom, if she is registered in the United Kingdom, or, if she is registered in a British possession, at her port of discharge in that British possession, or, if she is registered at a port of registry established by Order in Council under this Act, at that port, be delivered up to the registrar thereof, and that registrar shall cause the ship to be registered anew.

(3) The registrar granting a provisional certificate under this section, or provisionally endorsing a certificate, shall add to the certificate or endorsement a statement that the same is made provisionally, and shall send a report of the particulars of the case to the registrar of the ship's port of registry, containing a similar statement as the certificate or endorsement.

Registry anew on change of ownership.

51. Where the ownership of any ship is changed, the registrar of the port at which the ship is registered may, on the application of the owners of the ship, register the ship anew, although registration anew is not required under this Act.

Procedure for registry anew.

52. (1) Where a ship is to be registered anew, the registrar shall proceed as in the case of first registry, and on the delivery up to him of the existing certificate of registry, and on the other requisites to registry, or in the case of a change of ownership such of them as he thinks material, being duly complied with, shall make such registry anew, and grant a certificate thereof.

(2) When a ship is registered anew, her former register shall be considered as closed, except so far as relates to any unsatisfied mortgage or existing certificates of sale or mortgage entered thereon, but the names of all persons appearing on the former register to be interested in the ship as owners or mortgagees shall be entered on the new register, and the registry anew shall not in any way affect the rights of any of those persons.

Transfer of registry.

53. (1) The registry of any ship may be transferred from one port to another on the application to the registrar of the existing port of registry of the ship made by declaration in writing of all persons appearing on the register to be interested therein as owners or mortgagees, but that transfer shall not in any way affect the rights of those persons or any of them, and those rights shall in all respects continue in the same manner as if no such transfer had been effected.

(2) On any such application the registrar shall transmit notice thereof to the registrar of the intended port of registry with a copy of all particulars relating to the ship, and the names of all persons appearing on the register to be interested therein as owners or mortgagees.

(3) The ship's certificate of registry shall be delivered up to the registrar either of the existing or intended port of registry, and, if delivered up to the former, shall be transmitted to the registrar of the intended port of registry.

(4) On the receipt of the above documents the registrar of the intended port of registry shall enter in his register book all the particulars and names so transmitted as aforesaid, and grant a fresh certificate of registry, and thenceforth such ship shall be considered as registered at the new port of registry, and the name of the ship's new port of registry shall be substituted for the name of her former port of registry on the ship's stern

Restrictions on re-registration of abandoned ships.

54. Where a ship has ceased to be registered as a British ship by reason of having been wrecked or abandoned, or for any reason other than capture by the enemy or transfer to a person not qualified to own a British ship, the ship shall not be re-registered until she has, at the expense of the applicant for registration, been surveyed by a surveyor of ships and certified by him to be seaworthy.

Incapacitated Persons.

Provision for cases of infancy or other incapacity.

55. (1) Where by reason of infancy, lunacy, or any other cause any person interested in any ship, or any share therein, is incapable of making any declaration or doing anything required or permitted by this Act to be made or done in connection with the registry of the ship or share, the guardian or committee, if any, of that person, or, if there is none, any person appointed on application made on behalf of the incapable person, or of any other person interested, by any court or judge having jurisdiction in respect of the property of incapable persons, may make such declaration, or a declaration as nearly corresponding thereto as circumstances permit, and do such act or thing in the name and on behalf of the incapable person; and all acts done by the substitute shall be as effectual as if done by the person for whom he is substituted.

(2) The Trustee Act, 1850, and the Acts amending the same, shall, so far as regards the court exercising jurisdiction in lunacy in Ireland, apply to shares in ships registered under this Act as if they were stock as defined by that Act.

Trusts and Equitable Rights.

Notice of trusts not received.

56. No notice of any trust, express, implied, or constructive, shall be entered in the register book or be receivable by the registrar, and, subject to any rights and powers appearing by the register book to be vested in any other person, the registered owner of a ship or of a share therein shall have power absolutely to dispose in manner in this Act provided of the ship or share, and to give effectual receipts for any money paid or advanced by way of consideration.

57. The expression "beneficial interest", where used in this Part of this Act, includes interests arising under contract and other equitable interests; and the intention of this Act is, that without prejudice to the provisions of this Act for preventing notice of trusts from being entered in the register book or received by the registrar, and without prejudice to the powers of disposition and of giving receipts conferred by this Act on registered owners and mortgagees, and without prejudice to the provisions of this Act relating to the exclusion of unqualified persons from the ownership of British ships, interests arising under contract or other equitable interests may be enforced by or against owners and mortgagees of ships in respect of their interest therein in the same manner as in respect of any other personal property. Equities not excluded by Act.

Liability of Beneficial Owner.

58. Where any person is beneficially interested, otherwise than by way of mortgage, in any ship or share in a ship registered in the name of some other person as owner, the person so interested shall, as well as the registered owner, be subject to all pecuniary penalties imposed by this or any other Act on the owners of ships or shares therein, so nevertheless that proceedings may be taken for the enforcement of any such penalties against both or either of the aforesaid parties, with or without joining the other of them. Liability of owners.

Managing Owner.

59. (1) The name and address of the managing owner for the time being of every ship registered at a port in the United Kingdom shall be registered at the custom house of that port. Ship's managing owner or manager to be registered.

(2) Where there is not a managing owner there shall be so registered the name of the ship's husband or other person to whom the management of the ship is entrusted by or on behalf of the owner; and any person whose name is so registered shall, for the purposes of this Act, be under the same obligations, and subject to the same liabilities, as if he were the managing owner.

(3) If default is made in complying with this section the owner shall be liable, or if there are more owners than one, each owner shall be liable in proportion to his interest in the ship, to a fine not exceeding in the whole one hundred pounds each time the ship leaves any port in the United Kingdom.

Declarations, Inspection of Register, and Fees.

60. When, under this Part of this Act, any person is required to make a declaration on behalf of himself or of any corporation, or any evidence is required to be produced to the registrar, and it is shown to the satisfaction of he registrar that from any reasonable cause that person is unable to make Power of registrar to dispense with declarations and other evidence. the declaration, or that the evidence cannot be produced, the registrar may, with the approval of the Commissioners of Customs, and on the production of such other evidence, and subject to such terms as they may think fit, dispense with the declaration or evidence.

Mode of making declarations. **61.** (1) Declarations required by this Part of this Act shall be made before a registrar of British ships, or a justice of the peace, or a commissioner for oaths, or a British consular officer.

(2) Declarations required by this Part of this Act may be made on behalf of a corporation by the secretary or any other officer of the corporation authorised by them for the purpose.

Application of fees. **62.** All fees authorised to be taken under this Part of this Act, shall, except where otherwise in this Act provided, if taken in any part of the United Kingdom, be applied in payment of the general expenses of carrying into effect this Part of this Act, or otherwise as the Treasury may direct; if taken in a British possession, be disposed of in such way as the Executive Government of the possession direct; and if taken at any port of registry established by Order in Council under this Act, be disposed of as Her Majesty in Council directs.

Returns, Evidence, and Forms.

Returns to be made by Registrars. **63.** (1) Every registrar in the United Kingdom shall at the expiration of every month, and every other registrar at such times as may be fixed by the Registrar-General of Shipping and Seamen, transmit to him a full return, in such form as the said Registrar-General may direct, of all registries, transfers, transmissions, mortgages, and other dealings with ships which have been registered by or communicated to him in his character of registrar and of the names of the persons concerned in the same, and of such other particulars as may be directed by the said Registrar-General.

(2) Every registrar at a port in the United Kingdom shall on or before the first day of February and the first day of August in every year transmit to the Registrar-General of Shipping and Seamen a list of all ships registered at that port, and also of all ships whose registers have been transferred or cancelled at that port since the last preceding return.

Evidence of register book, certificate of registry, and other documents. **64.** (1) A person, on payment of a fee not exceeding one shilling, to be fixed by the Commissioners of Customs, may on application to the registrar at a reasonable time during the hours of his official attendance, inspect any register book.

(2) The following documents shall be admissible in evidence in manner provided by this Act, namely,—

(*a*) Any register book under this Part of this Act on its production from the custody of the registrar or other person having the lawful custody thereof;

(*b*) A certificate of registry under this Act purporting to be signed by the registrar or other proper officer;

(*c*) An endorsement on a certificate of registry purporting to be signed by the registrar or other proper officer;

(*d*) Every declaration made in pursuance of this Part of this Act in respect of a British ship.

(3) A copy or transcript of the register of British ships kept by the Registrar-General of Shipping and Seamen under the direction of the Board of Trade shall be admissible in evidence in manner provided by this Act, and have the same effect to all intents as the original register of which it is a copy or transcript.

Forms of documents, and instructions as to registry.

65. (1) The several instruments and documents specified in the second part of the First Schedule to this Act shall be in the form prescribed by the Commissioners of Customs, with the consent of the Board of Trade, or as near thereto as circumstances permit; and the Commissioners of Customs may, with the consent of the Board of Trade, make such alterations in the forms so prescribed and also in the forms set out in the first part of the said Schedule, as they may deem requisite.

(2) A registrar shall not be required without the special direction of the Commissioners of Customs to receive and enter in the register book any bill of sale, mortgage, or other instrument for the disposal or transfer of any ship or share, or any interest therein, which is made in any form other than that for the time being required under this Part of this Act, or which contains any particulars other than those contained in such form; but the said Commissioners shall, before altering the forms, give such public notice thereof as may be necessary in order to prevent inconvenience.

(3) The Commissioners of Customs shall cause the said forms to be supplied to all registrars under this Act for distribution to persons requiring to use the same, either free of charge, or at such moderate prices as they may direct.

(4) The Commissioners of Customs, with the consent of the Board of Trade, may also, for carrying into effect this Part of this Act, give such instructions to their officers as to the manner of making entries in the register book, as to the execution and attestation of powers of attorney, as to any evidence required for identifying any person, as to the referring to themselves of any question involving doubt or difficulty, and generally as to any act or thing to be done in pursuance of this Part of this Act, as they think fit.

Forgery and false Declarations.

Forgery of documents.

66. If any person forges, or fraudulently alters, or assists in forging or fraudulently altering, or procures to be forged or fraudulently altered, any of the following documents, namely, any register book, builder's certificate, surveyor's certificate, certificate of registry, declaration, bill of sale, instrument of mortgage, or certificate of mortgage or sale under this Part of this Act, or any entry or endorsement required by this Part of this Act to be made in or on any of those documents, that person shall in respect of each offence be guilty of felony.

False declarations.

67. (1) If any person in the case of any declaration made in the presence of or produced to a registrar under this part of this Act, or in any document or other evidence produced to such registrar—

(i) wilfully makes, or assists in making, or procures to be made any false statement concerning the title to or ownership of, or the interest existing in any ship, or any share in a ship; or

(ii) utters, produces, or makes use of any declaration, or document containing any such false statement knowing the same to be false,

he shall in respect of each offence be guilty of a misdemeanour.

(2) If any person wilfully makes a false declaration touching the qualification of himself or of any other person or of any corporation to own a British ship or any share therein, he shall for each offence be guilty of a misdemeanour, and that ship or share shall be subject to forfeiture under this Act, to the extent of the interest therein of the declarant, and also, unless it is proved that the declaration was made without authority, of any person or corporation on behalf of whom the declaration is made.

National Character and Flag.

National character of ship to be declared before clearance.

68. (1) An officer of customs shall not grant a clearance or transire for any ship until the master of such ship has declared to that officer the name of the nation to which he claims that she belongs, and that officer shall thereupon inscribe that name on the clearance or transire.

(2) If a ship attempts to proceed to sea without such clearance or transire, she may be detained until the declaration is made.

Penalty for unduly assuming British character.

69. (1) If a person uses the British flag and assumes the British national character on board a ship owned in whole or in part by any persons not qualified to own a British ship, for the purpose of making the ship appear to be a British ship, the ship shall be subject to forfeiture under this Act, unless the assumption has been made for the purpose of escaping capture by an enemy or by a foreign ship of war in the exercise of some belligerent right.

(2) In any proceeding for enforcing any such forfeiture the burden of proving a title to use the British flag and assume the British national character shall lie upon the person using and assuming the same.

70. If the master or owner of a British ship does anything or permits anything to be done, or carries or permits to be carried any papers or documents, with intent to conceal the British character of the ship from any person entitled by British law to inquire into the same, or with intent to assume a foreign character, or with intent to deceive any person so entitled as aforesaid, the ship shall be subject to forfeiture under this Act; and the master, if he commits or is privy to the commission of the offence, shall in respect of each offence be guilty of a misdemeanour. Penalty for concealment of British or assumption of foreign character.

71. If an unqualified person acquires as owner, otherwise than by such transmission as hereinbefore provided for, any interest, either legal or beneficial, in a ship using a British flag and assuming the British character, that interest shall be subject to forfeiture under this Act. Penalty for acquiring ownership if unqualified.

72. Where it is declared by this Act that a British ship shall not be recognised as a British ship, that ship shall not be entitled to any benefits, privileges, advantages, or protection usually enjoyed by British ships, nor to use the British flag or assume the British national character, but so far as regards the payment of dues, the liability to fines and forfeiture and the punishment of offences committed on board such ship, or by any persons belonging to her, such ship shall be dealt with in the same manner in all respects as if she were a recognised British ship. Liabilities of ships not recognised as British.

73. (1) The red ensign usually worn by merchant ships, without any defacement or modification whatsoever, is hereby declared to be the proper national colours for all ships and boats belonging to any British subject, except in the case of Her Majesty's ships or boats, or in the case of any other ship or boat for the time being allowed to wear any other national colours in pursuance of a warrant from Her Majesty or from the Admiralty. National colours for ships, and penalty on carrying improper colours.

(2) If any distinctive national colours, except such red ensign or except the Union Jack with a white border, or if any colours usually worn by Her Majesty's ships or resembling those of Her Majesty, or if the pendant usually carried by Her Majesty's ships or any pendant resembling that pendant, are or is hoisted on board any ship or boat belonging to any British subject without warrant from Her Majesty or from the Admiralty, the master of the ship or boat, or the owner thereof, if on board the same, and every other person hoisting the colours or pendant, shall for each offence incur a fine not exceeding five hundred pounds.

(3) Any commissioned officer on full pay in the military or naval service of Her Majesty, or any officer of customs in Her Majesty's dominions, or any British consular officer, may board any ship or boat on which any colours or pendant are hoisted contrary to this Act, and seize and take away the colours or pendant, and the colours or pendant shall be forfeited to Her Majesty.

(4) A fine under this section may be recovered with costs in the High Court in England or Ireland, or in the Court of Session in Scotland, or in any Colonial Court of Admiralty or Vice-Admiralty Court within Her Majesty's dominions.

(5) Any offence mentioned in this section may also be prosecuted, and the fine for it recovered, summarily, provided that:—

(*a*) where any such offence is prosecuted summarily, the court imposing the fine shall not impose a higher fine than one hundred pounds; and

(*b*) nothing in this section shall authorise the imposition of more than one fine in respect of the same offence.

Penalty on ship not showing colours.

74. (1) A ship belonging to a British subject shall hoist the proper national colours—

(*a*) on a signal being made to her by one of Her Majesty's ships (including any vessel under the command of an officer of Her Majesty's navy on full pay), and

(*b*) on entering or leaving any foreign port, and

(*c*) if of fifty tons gross tonnage or upwards, on entering or leaving any British port.

(2) If default is made on board any such ship in complying with this section, the master of the ship shall for each offence be liable to a fine not exceeding one hundred pounds.

(3) This section shall not apply to a fishing boat duly entered in the fishing boat register and lettered and numbered as required by the Fourth Part of this Act.

Saving for Admiralty.

75. The provisions of this Act with respect to colours worn by merchant ships shall not affect any other power of the Admiralty in relation thereto.

Forfeiture of Ship.

Proceedings on forfeiture of ship.

76. (1) Where any ship has either wholly or as to any share therein become subject to forfeiture under this Part of this Act,

(*a*) any commissioned officer on full pay in the military or naval service of Her Majesty;

(*b*) any officer of customs in Her Majesty's dominions; or

(*c*) any British consular officer,

may seize and detain the ship, and bring her for adjudication before the High Court in England or Ireland, or before the Court of Session in Scotland, and elsewhere before any Colonial Court of Admiralty or Vice-Amiralty Court n Her Majesty's dominions, and the Court may thereupon adjudge the ship with her tackle, apparel, and furniture to be forfeited to Her Majesty, and make such order in the case as to the court seems just, and may award to the officer bringing in the ship for adjudication such portion of the proceeds of the sale of the ship, or any share therein, as the Court think fit.

(2) Any such officer as in this section mentioned shall not be responsible either civilly or criminally to any person whomsoever in respect of any such seizure or detention as aforesaid, notwithstanding that the ship has not been brought in for adjudication, or if so brought in is declared not liable to forfeiture, if it is shown to the satisfaction of the court before whom any trial relating to such ship or such seizure or detention is held that there were reasonable grounds for such seizure or detention; but if no such grounds are shown the court may award costs and damages to any party aggrieved, and make such other order in the premises as the Court thinks just.

Measurement of ship and Tonnage.

Rules for ascertaining register tonnage.

77. (1) The tonnage of every ship to be registered, with the exceptions herein-after mentioned, shall, previously to her being registered, be ascertained by Rule I in the Second Schedule to this Act, and the tonnage of every ship to which that Rule I can be applied, whether she is about to be registered or not, shall be ascertained by the same rule.

(2) Ships which, requiring to be measured for any purpose other than registry, have cargo on board, and ships which, requiring to be measured for the purpose of registry, cannot be measured by Rule I, shall be measured by Rule II in the said Schedule, and the owner of any ship measured under Rule II may at any subsequent period apply to the Board of Trade to have the ship re-measured under Rule I, and the Board may thereupon, upon payment of such fee not exceeding seven shillings and six-pence for each transverse section as they may authorise, direct the ship to be re-measured accordingly, and the number denoting the register tonnage shall be altered accordingly.

(3) For the purpose of ascertaining the register tonnage of a ship the allowance and deductions herein-after mentioned shall be made from the tonnage of the ship ascertained as aforesaid.

(4) In the measurement of a ship for the purpose of ascertaining her register tonnage, no deduction shall be allowed in respect of any space which has not been first included in the measurement of her tonnage.

(5) In ascertaining the tonnage of open ships Rule IV in the said Schedule shall be observed.

(6) Throughout the rules in the Second Schedule to this Act, the tonnage deck shall be taken to be the upper deck in ships which have less than three

decks, and to be the second deck from below in all other ships, and in carrying those rules into effect all measurements shall be taken in feet, and fractions of feet shall be expressed in decimals.

(7) The Board of Trade may make such modifications and alterations as from time to time become necessary in the rules in the Second Schedule to this Act for the purpose of the more accurate and uniform application thereof, and the effectual carrying out of the principle of measurement therein adopted.

(8) The provisions of this Act relating to tonnage, together with the rules for the time being in force, are in this Act referred to as the tonnage regulations of this Act.

Allowance for engine-room space in steam-ships.

78. (1) In the case of any ship propelled by steam or other power requiring engine room, an allowance shall be made for the space occupied by the propelling power, and the amount so allowed shall be deducted from the gross tonnage of the ship ascertained as in the last preceding section mentioned, and the remainder shall (subject to any deductions hereinafter mentioned) be deemed to be the register tonnage of the ship, and that deduction shall be estimated as follows (that is to say),

(*a*) As regards ships propelled by paddle wheels in which the tonnage of the space solely occupied by and necessary for the proper working of the boilers and machinery is above twenty per cent. and under thirty per cent. of the gross tonnage of the ship, the deduction shall be thirty-seven one-hundredths of the gross tonnage; and in ships propelled by screws, in which the tonnage of such space is above thirteen per cent. and under twenty per cent. of the gross tonnage, the deduction shall be thirty-two one-hundredths of the gross tonnage:

(*b*) As regards all other ships, the deduction shall, if the Board of Trade and the owner both agree thereto, be estimated in the same manner; but either they or he may, in their or his discretion, require the space to be measured and the deduction estimated accordingly; and whenever the measurement is so required, the deduction shall consist of the tonnage of the space actually occupied by or required to be enclosed for the proper working of the boilers and machinery, with the addition in the case of ships propelled by paddle wheels of one-half, and in the case of ships propelled by screws of three-fourths of the tonnage of the space; and in the case of ships propelled by screws, the contents of the shaft trunk shall be added to and deemed to form part of the space; and the measurement of the space shall be governed by Rule III in the Second Schedule to this Act.

(2) Such portion of the space above the crown of the engine-room and above the upper deck as is framed in for the machinery or for the admission of light and air shall not be included in the measurement of the space occupied by the propelling power, except in pursuance of a request in writing to the Board of Trade by the owner of the ship, but shall not be included in pursuance of that request unless—

(*a*) that portion is first included in the measurement of the gross tonnage; and

(*b*) a surveyor of ships certifies that the portion so framed in is reasonable in extent and is so constructed as to be safe and seaworthy, and that it cannot be used for any purpose other than the machinery or for the admission of light and air to the machinery or boilers of the ship.

(3) Goods or stores shall not be stowed or carried in any space measured for propelling power, and if the same are so carried in any ship, the master and owner of the ship shall each be liable to a fine not exceeding one hundred pounds.

Deductions for ascertaining tonnage

79. (1) In measuring or re-measuring a ship for the purpose of ascertaining her register tonnage, the following deductions shall be made from the space included in the measurement of the tonnage, namely:—

(*a*) in the case of any ship,

(i) any space used exclusively for the accommodation of the master, and any space occupied by seamen or apprentices and appropriated to their use, which is certified under the regulations scheduled to this Act with regard thereto;

(ii) any space used exclusively for the working of the helm, the capstan, and the anchor gear, or for keeping the charts, signals, and other instruments of navigation, and boatswain's stores; and

(iii) the space occupied by the donkey engine and boiler, if connected with the main pumps of the ship; and

(*b*) in the case of a ship wholly propelled by sails, any space set apart and used exclusively for the storage of sails.

(2) The deductions allowed under this section, other than a deduction for

a space occupied by seamen or apprentices, and certified as aforesaid, shall be subject to the following provisions, namely:

(a) the space deducted must be certified by a surveyor of ships as reasonable in extent and properly and efficiently constructed for the purpose for which it is intended;

(b) there must be permanently marked in or over every such space a notice stating the purpose to which it is to be applied, and that whilst so applied it is to be deducted from the tonnage of the ship;

(c) the deduction on account of space for storage of sails must not exceed two and a half per cent. of the tonnage of the ship.

Provisions as to deductions in case of certain steamships.

80. In the case of a screw steamship which, on the twenty-sixth day of August, one thousand eight hundred and eighty-nine, had an engine-room allowance of thirty-two per cent. of the gross tonnage of the ship, and in which any crew space on deck has not been included in the gross tonnage, whether its contents have been deducted therefrom or not, the crew space shall, on the application of the owner of the ship, or by direction of the Board of Trade, be measured and its contents ascertained and added to the register tonnage of the ship; and if it appears that with that addition to the tonnage the engine-room does not occupy more than thirteen per cent. of the tonnage of the ship, the existing allowance for engine-room of thirty-two per cent. of the tonnage shall be continued.

Measurement of ships with double bottoms for water ballast.

81. In the case of a ship constructed with a double bottom for water ballast, if the space between the inner and outer plating thereof is certified by a surveyor of ships to be not available for the carriage of cargo, stores, or fuel, then the depth required by the provisions of Rule I relating to the measurement of transverse areas shall be taken to be the upper side of the inner plating of the double bottom, and that upper side shall, for the purposes of measurement, be deemed to represent the floor timber referred to in that Rule.

Tonnage once ascertained to be the tonnage of ship.

82. Whenever the tonnage of any ship has been ascertained and registered in accordance with the tonnage regulations of this Act, the same shall thenceforth be deemed to be the tonnage of the ship, and shall be repeated in every subsequent registry thereof, unless any alteration is made in the form or capacity of the ship, or unless it is discovered that the tonnage of the ship has been erroneously computed; and in either of those cases the ship shall be re-measured, and her tonnage determined and registered according to the tonnage regulations of this Act.

Fees for measurement.

83. Such fees as the Board of Trade determine shall be paid in respect of the measurement of a ship's tonnage not exceeding those specified in the Third Schedule to this Act, and those fees shall be paid into the Mercantile Marine Fund.

Tonnage of ships of foreign countries adopting tonnage regulations.

84. (1) Whenever it appears to Her Majesty the Queen in Council that the tonnage regulations of this Act have been adopted by any foreign country, and are in force there, Her Majesty in Council may order that the ships of that country shall, without being re-measured in Her Majesty's dominions, be deemed to be of the tonnage denoted in their certificates of registry or other national papers, in the same manner, to the same extent, and for the same purposes as the tonnage denoted in the certificate of registry of a British ship is deemed to be the tonnage of that ship.

(2) Her Majesty in Council may limit the time during which the Order is to remain in operation, and make the Order subject to such conditions and qualifications (if any) as Her Majesty may deem expedient, and the operation of the Order shall be limited and modified accordingly.

(3) If it is made to appear to Her Majesty that the tonnage of any foreign ship, as measured by the rules of the country to which she belongs, materially differs from that which would be her tonnage if measured under this Act, Her Majesty in Council may order that, notwithstanding any Order in Council for the time being in force under this section, any of the ships of that country may, for all or any of the purposes of this Act, be re-measured in accordance with this Act.

Space occupied by deck cargo to be liable to dues.

85. (1) If any ship, British or foreign, other than a home-trade ship as defined by this Act carries as deck cargo, that is to say, in any uncovered space upon deck, or in any covered space not included in the cubical contents forming the ship's registered tonnage, timber, stores, or other goods, all dues payable on the ship's tonnage shall be payable as if there were added to the ship's registered tonnage the tonnage of the space occupied by those goods at the time at which the dues become payable.

(2) The space so occupied shall be deemed to be the space limited by the area occupied by the goods and by straight lines inclosing a rectangular space sufficient to include the goods.

(3) The tonnage of the space shall be ascertained by an officer of the Board of Trade or of Customs in manner directed as to the measurement of poops or other closed-in spaces by Rule I in the Second Schedule to this Act, and when so ascertained shall be entered by him in the ship's official log book, and also in a memorandum which he shall deliver to the master, and the master shall, when the said dues are demanded, produce that memorandum in like

manner as if it were the certificate of registry, or, in the case of a foreign ship, the document equivalent to a certificate of registry, and in default shall be liable to the same penalty as if he had failed to produce the said certificate or document.

(4) Nothing in this section shall apply to any ship employed exclusively in trading or going from place to place in any river or inland water of which the whole or part is in any British possession, or to deck cargo carried by a ship while engaged in the coasting trade of any British possession.

Surveyors and regulations for measurement of ships.

86. All duties in relation to the survey and measurement of ships shall be performed by surveyors of ships under this Act in accordance with regulations made by the Board of Trade.

Levy of tonnage rates under local Acts on the registered tonnage.

87. Any persons having power to levy tonnage rates on ships may, if they think fit, with the consent of the Board of Trade, levy those tonnage rates upon the registered tonnage of the ships as determined by the tonnage regulations of this Act, notwithstanding that any local Act under which those rates are levied provides for levying the same upon some different system of tonnage measurement.

Ports of Registry in Place under Foreign Jurisdiction Act.

Foreign ports of registry.

53 & 54 Vict. c. 37.

88. Where, in accordance with the Foreign Jurisdiction Act, 1890, Her Majesty exercises jurisdiction within any port, it shall be lawful for Her Majesty, by Order in Council, to declare that port a port of registry, and by the same or any subsequent Order in Council to declare the description of persons who are to be registrars of British ships at that port of registry, and to make regulations with respect to the registry of British ships thereat.

Registry in Colonies.

Powers of Governors in colonies.

89. In every British possession the governor of the possession shall occupy the place of the Commissioners of Customs with regard to the performance of anything relating to the registry of a ship or of any interest in a ship registered in that possession, and shall have power to approve a port within the possession for the registry of ships.

Terminable certificates of registry for small ships in colonies.

90. (1) The Governor of a British possession may, with the approval of a Secretary of State, make regulations providing that, on an application for the registry under this Act in that possession of any ship which does not exceed sixty tons burden, the registrar may grant, in lieu of a certificate of registry as required by this Act, a certificate of registry to be terminable at the end of six months or any longer period from the granting thereof, and all

certificates of registry granted under any such regulations shall be in such form and have effect subject to such conditions as the regulations provide.

(2) Any ship to which a certificate is granted under any such regulations shall, while that certificate is in force, and in relation to all things done or omitted during that period, be deemed to be a registered British ship.

Application of Part I.

91. This Part of this Act shall apply to the whole of Her Majesty's dominions, and to all places where Her Majesty has jurisdiction. **Application of Part I.**

PART II.

Masters and Seamen.

Certificates of Competency.

92. (1) Every British foreign-going ship and every British home-trade passenger ship, when going to sea from any place in the United Kingdom, and every foreign steamship carrying passengers between places in the United Kingdom, shall be provided with officers duly certificated under this Act according to the following scale:— **Certificates of competency to be held by officers of ships.**

(a) In any case with a duly certificated master:

(b) If the ship is of one hundred tons burden or upwards, with at least one officer besides the master holding a certificate not lower than that of only mate in the case of a foreign-going ship, or of mate in the case of a home-trade passenger ship:

(c) If the ship is a foreign-going ship, and carries more than one mate, with at least the first and second mate duly certificated:

(d) If the ship is a foreign-going steamship of one hundred nominal horse-power or upwards, with at least two engineers, one of whom shall be a first-class and the other a first-class or second-class engineer duly certificated:

(e) If the ship is a foreign-going steamship of less than one hundred nominal horse-power, or a sea-going home-trade passenger steamship with at least one engineer who is a first-class or second-class engineer duly certificated.

(2) If any person—

(a) having been engaged as one of the above-mentioned officers goes to sea as such officer without being duly certificated; or

(b) employs a person as an officer, in contravention of this section without ascertaining that the person so serving is duly certificated,

that person shall be liable for each offence to a fine not exceeding fifty pounds.

(3) An officer shall not be deemed duly certificated, within the meaning of this section, unless he is the holder for the time being of a valid certificate of competency under this Act of a grade appropriate to his station in the ship, or of a higher grade.

Grades of certificates of competency.

93. (1) Certificates of competency shall be granted, in accordance with this Act, for each of the following grades; that is to say,

Master of a foreign-going ship,
First mate of a foreign-going ship:
Second mate of a foreign-going ship;
Only mate of a foreign-going ship;
Master of a home-trade passenger ship;
Mate of a home-trade passenger ship:
First-class engineer,
Second-class engineer.

(2) A certificate of competency for a foreign-going ship shall be deemed to be of a higher grade than the corresponding certificate for a home-trade passenger ship, and shall entitle the lawful holder thereof to go to sea in the corresponding grade in the last-mentioned ship; but a certificate for a home-trade passenger ship shall not entitle the holder to go to sea as master or mate of a foreign-going ship.

Examinations for certificates of competency.

94. (1) For the purpose of granting certificate of competency as masters or mates to persons desirous of obtaining the same, examinations shall be held by Local Marine Boards at their respective ports.

(2) The Board of Trade may make rules which shall be strictly adhered to by the examiners for—

(*a*) the conduct of the examinations; and
(*b*) the qualification of the applicants,

and may depute any of their officers to attend and assist at any examination.

(3) The approval of the Board of Trade shall be necessary so far as regards the number and the remuneration of the examiners, and an examiner shall not be appointed, unless he holds a certificate of qualification to be from time to time granted or renewed by the Board of Trade.

(4) The Board of Trade may, if it appears to them that the examination for two or more ports can be held without inconvenience by the same examiners, provide that the examination be so held, and require the Local Marine Boards of those ports to act as one board for the purpose of the examination.

(5) Subject to the powers of the Board of Trade under this section the Local Marine Board may appoint, remove, and re-appoint examiners, and regulate the conduct of the examinations, and any member of the Local Marine Board may be present at and assist at the examinations held by that Board.

95. Where the business of a mercantile marine office is conducted otherwise than under a Local Marine Board, the Board of Trade may exercise all such powers and make all such provisions for the holding of examinations as may be exercised and made by a Local Marine Board. Examinations by Board of Trade in certain cases.

96. (1) For the purpose of granting certificates of competency as engineers to persons desirous of obtaining the same, examinations shall be held at such places as the Board of Trade direct. Engineers' certificates of competency.

(2) The Board of Trade may appoint times for the examinations, and may appoint, remove, and re-appoint examiners to conduct the same, and determine the remuneration of those examiners, and may regulate the conduct of the examinations and the qualification of the applicants and may do all such acts and things as they think expedient for the purpose of the examinations.

97. An applicant for examination, whether as master, mate, or engineer, shall pay such fees, not exceeding those specified in the Fourth Schedule to this Act, as the Board of Trade direct, and the fees shall be paid to such persons as the Board appoint and carried to the Mercantile Marine Fund. Fees on examination.

98. (1) The Board of Trade shall, subject as herein-after mentioned, deliver to every applicant who is duly reported by the examiners to have passed the examination satisfactorily, and to have given satisfactory evidence of his sobriety, experience, ability, and general good conduct on board ship, such a certificate of competency as the case requires. Grant of certificates on passing examination.

(2) The Board of Trade may, in any case in which a report appears to them to have been unduly made, remit the case either to the examiners who made the report or to any other examiners, and may require a re-examination of the applicant, or a further inquiry into his testimonials and character, before granting him a certificate.

99. (1) A person who has attained the rank of lieutenant, sub-lieutenant, navigating lieutenant, or navigating sub-lieutenant in Her Majesty's Navy, or of lieutenant in Her Majesty's Indian Marine Service, shall be entitled to a certificate of service as master of a foreign-going ship without examination. Certificates of service for naval officers.

(2) A person who has attained the rank of engineer or assistant engineer in Her Majesty's Navy or Indian Marine Service, shall be entitled without

examination, if an engineer, to a certificate of service as first-class engineer, and if an assistant engineer to a certificate of service as second-class engineer.

(3) A certificate of service shall differ in form from a certificate of competency, and shall contain the name and rank of the person to whom it is delivered, and the Board of Trade shall deliver a certificate of service to any person who proves himself to be entitled thereto.

(4) The provisions of this Act (including the penal provisions) shall apply in the case of a certificate of service as they apply in the case of a certificate of competency, except that the provisions allowing a holder of a certificate of competency as master of a foreign-going ship to go to sea as master or mate of a home-trade passenger ship shall not apply.

Form and record of certificate.

100. (1) All certificates of competency shall be made in duplicate, one part to be delivered to the person entitled to the certificate, and one to be preserved.

(2) Such last-mentioned part of the certificate shall be preserved, and a record of certificates of competency and the suspending, cancelling, or altering of the certificates and any other matter affecting them shall be kept in such manner as the Board of Trade direct, by the Registrar-General of Shipping and Seamen, or by such other person as the Board of Trade direct.

(3) Any such certificate and any record under this section shall be admissible in evidence in manner provided by this Act.

Loss of certificate.

101. If a master, mate, or engineer proves to the satisfaction of the Board of Trade that he has, without fault on his part, lost or been deprived of a certificate already granted to him, the Board of Trade shall, and in any other case may, upon payment of such fee (if any), as they direct, cause a copy of the certificate to which, by the record kept in pursuance of this Act, he appears to be entitled, to be certified by the Registrar-General of Shipping and Seamen, or other person directed to keep the record, and to be delivered to him; and a copy purporting to be so certified shall have all the effect of the original.

Colonial certificates of competency.

102. Where the legislature of any British possession provides for the examination of, and grant of certificates of competency to, persons intending to act as masters, mates, or engineers on board ships, and the Board of Trade report to Her Majesty that they are satisfied that the examinations are so conducted as to be equally efficient with the examinations for the same purpose in the United Kingdom under this Act, and that the certificates are granted on such principles as to show the like qualifications and competency as those granted under this Act, and are liable to be forfeited for the like reasons and in the like manner, Her Majesty may by Order in Council,—

(i) declare that the said certificates shall be of the same force if they had been granted under this Act; and

(ii) declare that all or any of the provisions of this Act, which relate to certificates of competency granted under this Act, shall apply to the certificates referred to in the Order; and

(iii) impose such conditions and make such regulations with respect to the certificates, and to the use, issue, delivery, cancellation and suspension thereof, as Her Majesty may think fit, and impose fines not exceeding fifty pounds for the breach of those conditions and regulations.

Production of certificates of competency to superintendent.

103. (1) The master of a foreign-going ship—

(*a*) on signing the agreement with the crew before a superintendent shall produce to him the certificates of competency which the master, mates and engineers of the ship are by this Act required to hold; and

(*b*) in the case of a running agreement shall also, before the second and every subsequent voyage, produce to the superintendent the certificate of competency of any mate or engineer then first engaged by him who is required by this Act to hold a certificate.

(2) The master or owner of every home-trade passenger ship of more than eighty tons burden shall produce to some superintendent within twenty-one days after the thirtieth of June and the thirty-first of December in every year the certificates of competency which the master, mates, and engineers of the ship are by this Act required to hold.

(3) Upon the production of the certificates of competency, the superintendent shall, if the certificates are such as the master, mates, and engineers of the ship ought to hold, give to the master a certificate to the effect that the proper certificates of competency have been so produced.

(4) The master shall, before proceeding to sea, produce the superintendent's certificate to the chief officer of customs, and the ship may be detained until the certificate is produced.

Forgery, etc., of certificate of competency.

104. If any person—

(*a*) forges or fraudulently alters, or assists in forging or fraudulently altering, or procures to be forged or fraudulently altered, any certificate of competency, or an official copy of any such certificate; or (*b*) makes, assists in making, or procures to be made, any false representation for the purpose of procuring either for himself or for any other person a certificate of competency; or

(*c*) fraudulently uses a certificate or copy of a certificate of competency which has been forged, altered, cancelled or suspended, or to which he is not entitled; or

(*d*) fraudulently lends his certificate of competency or allows it to be used by any other person,

that person shall in respect of each offence be guilty of a misdemeanour.

Apprenticeship to the Sea Service.

Assistance given by superintendents as to apprenticeship.

105. All superintendents shall give to persons desirous of apprenticing boys to or requiring apprentices for the sea service, such assistance as may be in their power, and may receive from those persons such fees as the Board of Trade fix, with the concurrence, so far as relates to pauper apprentices in England, of the Local Government Board, and so far as relates to pauper apprentices in Ireland, of the Local Government Board for Ireland.

Apprenticeships of paupers in Great Britain and Ireland.

106. Subject to the special provisions of this Act, apprenticeships to the sea service made by a board of guardians or persons having the authority of a board of guardians shall, if made in Great Britain, be made in the same manner and be subject to the same laws and regulations as other apprenticeships made by such boards or persons; and if made in Ireland, be subject to the following regulations:—

(*a*) The board of guardians or other persons in any poor law union may put out and bind as apprentice to the sea service any boy who, or whose parent, is receiving relief in the union, and who has attained the age of twelve years, and is of sufficient health and strength, and consents to be bound:

(*b*) If the cost of relieving the boy is chargeable to an electoral division of a poor law union, then (except where paid officers act in place of guardians) he shall not be so bound unless the consent in writing of the guardians of that division, or of a majority of them, if more than one, is first obtained, and that consent shall, if possible, be endorsed on the indenture:

(*c*) The expenses incurred in the binding and outfit of any such apprentice shall be charged to the poor law union or electoral division, as the case may be, to which the boy or his parent is chargeable at the time of his being apprenticed:

(*d*) All indentures made in a poor law union may be sued on by the board of guardians of the union, or persons having the authority of such board, by their name of office; and actions so brought shall not abate by reason of any death or change in the persons holding office, but such an action shall not be commenced without the consent of the Local Government Board for Ireland:

(*c*) The amount of the costs incurred in any such action, and not recovered from the defendant, may be charged as the expenses incurred in binding out the apprentice.

Attestation of pauper apprenticeship.

107. Every indenture of apprenticeship to the sea service made in the United Kingdom by a board of guardians, or persons having the authority of a board of guardians, shall be executed by the boy and the person to whom he is bound in the presence of and shall be attested by two justices of the peace, and those justices shall ascertain that the boy has consented to be bound and has attained the age of twelve years and is of sufficient health and strength, and that the person to whom the boy is bound is a proper person for the purpose.

Special provisions as to apprenticeship to the sea service.

108. (1) Every indenture of apprenticeship to the sea service shall be executed in duplicate and shall be exempt from stamp duty.

(2) Every indenture of apprenticeship to the sea service, made in the United Kingdom, and every assignment or cancellation thereof, and, where the apprentice bound dies or deserts, the fact of the death or desertion shall be recorded.

(3) For the purpose of the record—

(*a*) a person to whom an apprentice to the sea service is bound shall within seven days of the execution of the indenture take or transmit to the Registrar-General of Shipping and Seamen, or to a superintendent, the indenture executed in duplicate, and the Registrar-General or superintendent shall keep and record the one indenture and endorse on the other the fact that it has been recorded and re-deliver it to the master of the apprentice;

(*b*) the master shall notify any assignment or cancellation of the indenture, or the death or desertion of the apprentice, to the Registrar-General of Shipping and Seamen, or to a superintendent, within seven days of the occurrence, if it occurs within the United Kingdom; or, as soon as circumstances permit, if it occurs elsewhere.

(4) If any person fails to comply with any requirement of this section, he shall for each offence be liable to a fine not exceeding ten pounds.

Production of indentures to superintendent before voyage in foreign-going ship.

109. (1) The master of a foreign-going ship shall, before carrying an apprentice to sea from a port in the United Kingdom, cause the apprentice to appear before the superintendent before whom the crew are engaged and shall produce to the superintendent the indenture by which the apprentice is bound, and every assignment thereof.

(2) The name of the apprentice, with the date of the indenture and of the assignments thereof, if any, and the names of the ports at which the same have been registered, shall be entered on the agreement with the crew.

(3) If the master fails without reasonable cause to comply with any requirement of this section he shall for each offence be liable to a fine not exceeding five pounds.

Licences to supply Seamen.

Licence for supply of seamen.

110. The Board of Trade may grant to such persons as the Board think fit licences to engage or supply seamen or apprentices for merchant ships in the United Kingdom, and any such licence shall continue for such period, and may be granted and revoked on such terms and conditions as the Board think proper.

Penalty for engaging seamen without licence.

111. (1) A person shall not engage or supply a seaman or apprentice to be entered on board any ship in the United Kingdom, unless that person either holds a licence from the Board of Trade for the purpose, or is the owner or master or mate of the ship, or is *bonâ fide* the servant and in the constant employment of the owner, or is a superintendent.

(2) A person shall not employ for the purpose of engaging or supplying a seaman or apprentice to be entered on board any ship in the United Kingdom any person, unless that person either holds a licence from the Board of Trade for the purpose, or is the owner or master or mate of the ship, or is *bonâ fide* the servant and in the constant employment of the owner, or is a superintendent.

(3) A person shall not receive or accept to be entered on board any ship any seaman or apprentice, if that person knows that the seaman or apprentice has been engaged or supplied in contravention of this section.

(4) If a person acts in contravention of this section, he shall for each seaman or apprentice in respect of whom an offence is committed, be liable to a fine not exceeding twenty pounds, and, if a licensed person, shall forfeit his licence.

Penalty for receiving remuneration from seamen for engagement.

112. (1) A person shall not demand or receive directly or indirectly from a seaman or apprentice to the sea service, or from a person seeking employment as a seaman or apprentice to the sea service, or from a person on his behalf, any remuneration whatever for providing him with employment other than any fees authorised by this Act.

(2) If a person acts in contravention of this section, he shall for each offence be liable to a fine not exceeding five pounds.

Engagement of Seamen.

13. (1) The master of every ship, except ships of less than eighty tons registered tonnage exclusively employed in trading between different ports on the coasts of the United Kingdom, shall enter into an agreement (in this Act called the agreement with the crew) in accordance with this Act with every seaman whom he carries to sea as one of his crew from any port in the United Kingdom. Agreements with crew.

(2) If a master of a ship carries any seaman to sea without entering into an agreement with him in accordance with this Act, the master in the case of a foreign-going ship, and the master or owner in the case of a home-trade ship, shall for each offence be liable to a fine not exceeding five pounds.

114. (1) An agreement with the crew shall be in a form approved by the Board of Trade, and shall be dated at the time of the first signature thereof, and shall be signed by the master before a seaman signs the same. Form periods, and conditions of agreements with crew.

(2) The agreement with the crew shall contain as terms thereof the following particulars:—

(*a*) either the nature, and, as far as practicable, the duration of the intended voyage or engagement, of the maximum period of the voyage or engagement and the places or parts of the world, if any, to which the voyage or engagement is not to extend:

(*b*) the number and description of the crew, specifying how many are engaged as sailors:

(*c*) the time at which each seaman is to be on board or to begin work:

(*d*) the capacity in which each seaman is to serve:

(*e*) the amount of wages which each seaman is to receive:

(*f*) a scale of the provisions which are to be furnished to each seaman:

(*g*) any regulations as to conduct on board, and as to fines, short allowance of provisions, or other lawful punishment for misconduct which have been approved by the Board of Trade as regulations proper to be adopted, and which the parties agree to adopt.

(3) The agreement with the crew shall be so framed as to admit of such stipulations, to be adopted at the will of the master and seaman in each

case, whether respecting the advance and allotment of wages or otherwise, as are not contrary to law.

(4) If the master of a ship registered at a port out of the United Kingdom has an agreement with the crew made in due form according to the law of that port or of the port in which her crew were engaged, and engages single seamen in the United Kingdom, those seamen may sign the agreement so made, and it shall not then be necessary for them to sign an agreement in the form approved by the Board of Trade.

Special provisions as to agreements with crew of foreign-going ships.

115. The following provisions shall have effect with respect to the agreements with the crew made in the United Kingdom in the case of foreign-going ships registered either within or without the United Kingdom:—

(1) The agreement shall (subject to the provisions of this Act as to substitutes) be signed by each seaman in the presence of a superintendent:

(2) The superintendent shall cause the agreement to be read over and explained to each seaman, or otherwise ascertain that each seaman understands the same before he signs it, and shall attest each signature:

(3) When the crew is first engaged the agreement shall be signed in duplicate, and one part shall be retained by the superintendent, and the other shall be delivered to the master, and shall contain a special place or form for the descriptions and signatures of substitutes or persons engaged subsequently to the first departure of the ship:

(4) Where a substitute is engaged in the place of a seaman who duly signed the agreement, and whose services are within twenty-four hours of the ship's putting to sea lost by death, desertion, or other unforeseen cause, the engagement shall, when practicable, be made before a superintendent, and, when not practicable, the master shall, before the ship puts to sea, if practicable, and if not, as soon afterwards as possible, cause the agreement to be read over and explained to the substitute, and the substitute shall thereupon sign the same in the presence of a witness, and the witness shall attest the signature:

(5) The agreements may be made for a voyage, or if the voyages of the ship average less than six months in duration, may be made to extend over two or more voyages, and agreements so made to extend over two or more voyages are in this Act referred to as running agreements:

(6) Running agreements shall not extend beyond the next following thirtieth day of June or thirty-first day of December, or the first arrival of the ship at her port of destination in the United Kingdom after that date, or the discharge of cargo consequent on that arrival:

(7) On every return to a port in the United Kingdom before the final termination of a running agreement, the master shall make on the agreement an endorsement as to the engagement or discharge of seamen, either that no engagements or discharges have been made, or are intended to be made before the ship leaves port, or that all those made have been made as required by law, and if a master wilfully makes a false statement in any such endorsement, he shall for each offence be liable to a fine not exceeding twenty pounds:

(8) The master shall deliver the running agreement so endorsed to the superintendent, and the superintendent shall, if the provisions of this Act relating to agreements have been complied with, sign the endorsement and return the agreement to the master;

(9) The duplicate running agreement retained by the superintendent on the first engagement of the crew shall either be transmitted to the Registrar-General of Shipping and Seamen immediately, or kept by the superintendent until the expiration of the agreement, as the Board of Trade direct.

116. The following provisions shall have effect with respect to the agreements with the crew of home-trade ships for which an agreement with the crew is required under this Act:— Special provisions as to agreements with crew of home-trade ships.

(1) Agreements may be made either for service in a particular ship or for service in two or more ships belonging to the same owner, but in the latter case the names of the ships and the nature of the service shall be specified in the agreement.

(2) Crews or single seamen may, if the master think fit, be engaged before a superintendent in the same manner as they are required to be engaged for foreign-going ships, but if the engagement is not so made, the master shall, before the ship puts to sea, if practicable, and if not, as soon after as possible, cause the agreement to be read and explained to each seaman, and the seaman shall thereupon sign the same in the presence of a witness, and the witness shall attest the signature.

(3) An agreement for service in two or more ships belonging to the same owner may be made by the owner instead of by the master; and the provisions of this Act with respect to the making of the agreement shall apply accordingly.

(4) Agreements shall not, in the case of ships of more than eighty tons burden, extend beyond the next following thirtieth day of June or thirty-first day of December or the first arrival of the ship at her final port of destination in the United Kingdom after that date, or the discharge of cargo consequent on that arrival: Provided that the owner or his agent may enter into time agreements in forms sanctioned by the Board of Trade with individual seamen to serve in any one or more ships belonging to such owner, and those agreements need not expire on the thirtieth day of June or the thirty-first day of December, and a duplicate of every such agreement shall be forwarded to the Registrar-General of Shipping and Seamen within forty-eight hours after it has been entered into.

Changes in crew of foreign-going ship to be reported.

117. (1) The master of every foreign-going ship whose crew has been engaged before a superintendent shall, before finally leaving the United Kingdom, sign, and send to the nearest superintendent, a full and accurate statement, in a form approved by the Board of Trade, of every change which takes place in his crew before finally leaving the United Kingdom, and that statement shall be admissible in evidence in manner provided by this Act.

(2) If a master fails without reasonable cause to comply with this section, he shall for each offence be liable to a fine not exceeding five pounds.

Certificate as to agreements with crew of foreign-going ships.

118. (1) In the case of a foreign-going ship, on the due execution of an agreement with the crew in accordance with this Act, and also, where the agreement is a running agreement, on compliance by the master, before the second and every subsequent voyage made after the first commencement of the agreement, with the provisions of this Act respecting that agreement, the superintendent shall grant the master of the ship a certificate to that effect.

(2) The master of every foreign-going ship shall, before proceeding to sea, produce to the officer of customs that certificate, and any such ship may be detained until the certificate is produced.

(3) The master of every foreign-going ship shall, within forty-eight hours after the ship's arrival at her final port of destination in the United Kingdom or upon the discharge of the crew, whichever first happens, deliver

his agreement with the crew to the superintendent, and the superintendent shall give the master a certificate of that delivery; and an officer of customs shall not clear the ship inwards until the certificate of delivery is produced, and if the master fails without reasonable cause so to deliver the agreement with the crew, he shall for each offence be liable to a fine not exceeding five pounds.

119. (1) The master or owner of a home-trade ship of more than eighty tons burden shall within twenty-one days after the thirtieth day of June and the thirty-first day of December in every year deliver or transmit to a superintendent in the United Kingdom every agreement with the crew made for the ship within six months next preceding those days respectively.

Certificate as to agreements with crew of home-trade ships.

(2) The superintendent on receiving the agreement shall give the master or owner of the ship a certificate to that effect, and the ship shall be detained unless the certificate is produced to the proper officer of customs.

(3) If the master or owner fails without reasonable cause to comply with this section, he shall for each offence be liable to a fine not exceeding five pounds.

120. (1) The master shall at the commencement of every voyage or engagement cause a legible copy of the agreement with the crew (omitting the signatures) to be posted up in some part of the ship which is accessible to the crew.

Copy of agreement to be made accessible to crew.

(2) If the master fails without reasonable cause to comply with this section, he shall for each offence be liable to a fine not exceeding five pounds.

121. If any person fraudulently alters, makes any false entry in, or delivers a false copy of, any agreement with the crew, that person shall in respect of each offence be guilty of a misdemeanour, and if any person assists in committing or procures to be committed any such offence, he shall likewise in respect of each offence be guilty of a misdemeanour.

Forgery, etc., of agreements with crew.

122. Every erasure, interlineation, or alteration in any agreement with the crew (except additions made for the purpose of shipping substitutes or persons engaged after the first departure of the ship) shall be wholly inoperative, unless proved to have been made with the consent of all the persons interested in the erasure, interlineation, or alteration, by the written attestation (if in Her Majesty's dominions) of some superintendent, justice, officer of customs, or other public functionary, or elsewhere, of a British consular officer, or where there is no such officer, of two respectable British merchants.

Alterations in agreements with crew.

123. In any legal or other proceeding a seaman may bring forward evidence to prove the contents of any agreement with the crew or otherwise

Seamen not to be bound to produce agreement.

to support his case, without producing, or giving notice to produce the agreement or any copy thereof.

Engagement of seamen in colonial and foreign ports.

124. (1) With respect to the engagement of seamen abroad, the following provisions shall have effect:—

Where the master of a ship engages a seaman in any British possession other than that in which the ship is registered or at a port in which there is a British consular officer, the provisions of this Act respecting agreements with the crew made in the United Kingdom shall apply subject to the following modifications:—

(*a*) in any such British possession the master shall engage the seaman before some officer being either a superintendent or, if there is no such superintendent, an officer of customs;

(*b*) at any such port having a British consular officer, the master shall, before carrying the seaman to sea, procure the sanction of the consular officer, and shall engage the seaman before that officer;

(*c*) the officer shall endorse upon the agreement an attestation to the effect that the agreement has been signed in his presence and otherwise made as required by this Act, and also, if the officer is a British consular officer, that it has his sanction, and if the attestation is not made the burden of proving that the engagement was made as required by this Act shall lie upon the master.

(2) If a master fails to comply with this section he shall be liable for each offence to a fine not exceeding five pounds.

Agreements with Lascars.

Agreements with lascars.

125. (1) The master or owner of any ship, or his agent, may enter into an agreement with a lascar, or any native of India, binding him to proceed either as a seaman or as a passenger:—

(*a*) to any port in the United Kingdom, and there to enter into a further agreement to serve as a seaman in any ship which may happen to be there, and to be bound to any port in British India; or

(*b*) to any port in the Australian Colonies, and there to enter into a further agreement to serve as a seaman in any ship which may happen to be there, and to be bound to the United Kingdom or to any other part of Her Majesty's dominions.

(2) The original agreement shall be made in such form, and contain such provisions, and be executed in such manner, and contain such conditions for securing the return of the lascar or native to his own country and for other purposes, as the Governor General of India in Council or the Governor in Council of any Indian Presidency in which the agreement is made may direct.

(3) Where any lascar or native bound by the original agreement is, on arriving in the United Kingdom or one of the said colonies, as the case may be, required to enter into such further agreement as aforesaid, some officer appointed for the purpose in the United Kingdom by a Secretary of State in Council of India, or in any such colony by the Governor of the colony, may, on the payment of such fee not exceeding ten shillings, as a Secretary of State in Council of India or the Governor may direct, certify,—

(*a*) that the further agreement is a proper agreement in all respects for the lascar or native to make, and is in accordance with the original agreement; and

(*b*) that the ship to which the further agreement relates is in all respects a proper ship for the lascar or native to serve in and also where the ship is in one of the said Australian colonies that it is properly supplied with provisions; and

(*c*) that there is not, in his opinion, any objection to the full performance of the original agreement;

and thereupon the lascar or native shall be deemed to be engaged under the further agreement and to be for all purposes one of the crew of the ship to which it relates, and the lascar or native shall, notwithstanding a refusal to enter into the further agreement, be liable to the same consequences, and be dealt with in all respects in the same manner, as if he had voluntarily entered into the same.

(4) The master of every ship arriving at a port in the United Kingdom, which has or during any part of her voyage has had on board a lascar or any native of India either as one of her crew or otherwise shall exhibit to the officer of customs, or to such person as the Board of Trade may authorise in that behalf, a statement containing a list and description of all lascars or natives of India who are, or have been, so on board, and an account of what has become of any lascar or native of India who at any time during the voyage has been, but is not then, on board, and the ship shall not be cleared inwards until the statement is exhibited, and if the master fails to exhibit such statement he and the owner of the ship shall be liable jointly and severally

to a fine not exceeding ten pounds for every lascar or native of India in respect of whom the failure takes place.

(5) Nothing in this section shall affect any provisions which are unrepealed of the Act of the fourth year of the reign of King George the Fourth, chapter eighty, intituled "An Act to consolidate and amend the several laws now in force with respect to trade within the limits of the charter of the East India Company, and to make further provision with respect to such trade." 4 Geo. 4, c. 80.

Rating of Seamen.

Rating of seamen.

126. (1) A seaman shall not be entitled to the rating of A.B., that is to say, of an able-bodied seaman, unless he has served at sea for four years before the mast, but the employment of fishermen in decked fishing vessels registered under the first part of this Act shall only count as sea service up to the period of three years of that employment; and the rating of A.B. shall only be granted after at least one year's sea service in a trading vessel in addition to three or more years' sea service on board of decked fishing vessels so registered.

(2) The service may be proved by certificates of discharge, by a certificate of service from the Registrar-General of Shipping and Seamen (granted by the Registrar on payment of a fee not exceeding six pence), specifying in each case whether the service was rendered in whole or in part in steam ship or in sailing ship, or by other satisfactory proof.

Discharge of Seamen.

Discharge before superintendent.

127. (1) When a seaman serving in a British foreign-going ship, whether registered within or without the United Kingdom, is on the termination of his engagement discharged in the United Kingdom, he shall, whether the agreement with the crew be an agreement for the voyage or a running agreement, be discharged in manner provided by this Act in the presence of a superintendent.

(2) If the master or owner of a ship acts in contravention of this section, he shall for each offence be liable to a fine not exceeding ten pounds.

(3) If the master or owner of a home-trade ship so desire, the seamen of that ship may be discharged in the same manner as seamen discharged from a foreign-going ship.

Certificate of discharge and return of certificate to officer on discharge.

128. (1) The master shall sign and give to a seaman discharged from his ship, either on his discharge or on payment of his wages, a certificate of his discharge in a form approved by the Board of Trade, specifying the period of his service and the time and place of his discharge, and if the master

fails so to do, he shall for each offence be liable to a fine not exceeding ten pounds.

(2) The master shall also, upon the discharge of every certificated officer whose certificate of competency has been delivered to and retained by him, return the certificate to the officer, and if without reasonable cause he fails so to do he shall for each offence be liable to a fine not exceeding twenty pounds.

Reports of seaman's character.

129. (1) Where a seaman is discharged before a superintendent, the master shall make and sign, in a form approved by Board of Trade, a report of the conduct, character, and qualifications of the seaman discharged, or may state in the said form that he declines to give any opinion upon such particulars, or upon any of them, and the superintendent before whom the discharge is made shall, if the seaman desires, give to him or endorse on his certificate of discharge a copy of such report (in this Act referred to as the report of character).

(2) The superintendent shall transmit the reports to the Registrar-General of Shipping and Seamen, or to such other person as the Board of Trade may direct, to be recorded.

False or forged certificate of discharge or report of character.

130. If any person—

(*a*) makes a false report of character under this Act, knowing the same to be false; or

(*b*) forges or fraudulently alters any certificate of discharge or report of character or copy of a report of character; or

(*c*) assists in committing, or procures to be committed, any of such offences as aforesaid; or

(*d*) fraudulently uses any certificate of discharge or report of character or copy of a report of character which is forged or altered or does not belong to him,

he shall in respect of each offence be guilty of a misdemeanour.

Payment of Wages.

Payment of wages before superintendent.

131. (1) Where a seaman is discharged before a superintendent in the United Kingdom, he shall receive his wages through or in the presence of the superintendent, unless a competent court otherwise direct, and if in such a case the master or owner of a ship pays his wages within the United Kingdom in any other manner, he shall for each offence be liable to a fine not exceeding ten pounds.

(2) If the master or owner of a home-trade ship so desires, the seamen of that ship may receive their wages in the same manner as seamen discharged from a foreign-going ship.

Master to deliver account of wages.

132. (1) The master of every ship shall before paying off or discharging a seaman deliver at the time and in the manner provided by this Act a full and true account, in a form approved by the Board of Trade, of the seaman's wages, and of all deductions to be made therefrom on any account whatever.

(2) The said account shall be delivered—

(*a*) where the seaman is not to be discharged before a superintendent, to the seaman himself not less than twenty-four hours before his discharge or payment off; and

(*b*) where the seaman is to be discharged before a superintendent, either to the seaman himself at or before the time of his leaving the ship, or to the superintendent not less than twenty-four hours before the discharge or payment off.

(3) If the master of a ship fails without reasonable cause to comply with this section, he shall for each offence be liable to a fine not exceeding five pounds.

Deductions from wages of seamen.

133. (1) A deduction from the wages of a seaman shall not be allowed unless it is included in the account delivered in pursuance of the last preceding section, except in respect of a matter happening after the delivery.

(2) The master shall during the voyage enter the various matters in respect of which the deductions are made, with the amounts of the respective deductions, as they occur, in a book to be kept for that purpose, and shall, if required, produce the book at the time of the payment of wages, and also upon the hearing before any competent authority of any complaint or question relating to that payment.

Time of payment of wages for foreign-going ships.

134. In the case of foreign-going ships (other than ships employed on voyages for which seamen by the terms of their agreement are wholly compensated by a share in the profits of the adventure)—

(*a*) The owner or master of the ship shall pay to each seaman on account, at the time when he lawfully leaves the ship at the end of his engagement, two pounds, or one-fourth of the balance of wages due to him, whichever is least; and shall pay him the remainder of his wages within two clear days (exclusive of any Sunday, fast day in Scotland, or Bank holiday,) after he so leaves the ship:

(*b*) If the seaman consents, the final settlement of his wages may be left to a superintendent under regulations of the Board of Trade, and the receipt of the superintendent shall in that case operate as if it were a release given by the seaman in accordance with this Part of this Act:

(*c*) In the event of the seaman's wages or any part thereof not being paid or settled as in this section mentioned, then, unless the delay is due to the act or default of the seaman, or to any reasonable dispute as to liability, or to any other cause not being the wrongful act or default of the owner or master, the seaman's wages shall continue to run and be payable until the time of the final settlement thereof.

Time of payment of wages for home-trade ships.

135. (1) The master or owner of every home-trade ship shall pay to every seaman his wages within two days after the termination of the agreement with the crew, or at the time when the seaman is discharged, whichever first happens.

(2) If a master or owner fails without reasonable cause to make payment at that time, he shall pay to the seaman a sum not exceeding the amount of two days' pay for each of the days during which payment is delayed beyond that time, but the sum payable shall not exceed ten days' double pay.

(3) Any sum payable under this section may be recovered as wages.

Settlement of wages.

136. (1) Where a seaman is discharged, and the settlement of his wages completed, before a superintentent, he shall sign in the presence of the superintendent a release, in a form approved by the Board of Trade, of all claims in respect of the past voyage or engagement; and the release shall also be signed by the master or owner of the ship, and attested by the superintendent.

(2) The release, so signed and attested, shall operate as a mutual discharge and settlement of all demands between the parties thereto in respect of the past voyage or engagement.

(3) The release shall be retained by the superintendent, and on production from his custody shall be admissible in evidence in manner provided by this Act.

(4) Where the settlement of a seaman's wages is by this Act required to be completed through or in the presence of a superintendent, no payment, receipt, or settlement, made otherwise than in accordance with this Act shall operate as or be admitted as evidence of the release or satisfaction of any claim.

(5) Upon any payment being made by a master before a superintendent, the uperintendent shall, if required, sign and give to the master a statement of the whole amount so paid; and the statement shall as between the master and his employer be admissible as evidence that the master has made the payments therein mentioned.

Decision of questions by superintendents.

137. (1) Where in the case of a foreign-going ship a question as to wages is raised before a superintendent between the master or owner of the ship and a seaman or apprentice, and the amount in question does not exceed five pounds, the superintendent may, on the application of either party, adjudicate, and the decision of the superintendent in the matter shall be final; but if the superintendent is of opinion that the question is one which ought to be decided by a court of law, he may refuse to decide it.

(2) Where any question, of whatever nature and whatever the amount in dispute, between a master or owner and any of his crew is raised before a superintendent, and both parties agree in writing to submit the same to him, the superintendent shall hear and decide the question so submitted; and an award made by him upon the submission shall be conclusive as to the rights of the parties, and the submission or award shall not require a stamp; and a document purporting to be the submission or award shall be admissible as evidence thereof.

Power of superintendent to require production of ship's papers.

138. (1) In any proceeding under this Act before a superintendent relating to the wages, claims, or discharge of a seaman, the superintendent may require the owner, or his agent, or the master, or any mate or other member of the crew, to produce any log books, papers, or other documents in his possession or power relating to a matter in question in the proceeding, and may require the attendance of and examine any of those persons, being then at or near the place, on the matter.

(2) If any person so required fails, without reasonable cause, to comply with the requisition, he shall for each offence be liable to a fine not exceeding five pounds.

Rule as to payment of British seamen in foreign money.

139. Where a seaman has agreed with the master of a British ship for payment of his wages in British sterling or any other money, any payment of or on account of, his wages if made in any other currency than that stated in the agreement, shall, notwithstanding anything in the agreement, be made at the rate of exchange for the money stated in the agreement, for the time being current at the place where the payment is made.

Advance and Allotment of Wages.

Advance notes restricted.

140. (1) (*a*) Where an agreement with the crew is required to be made in a form approved by the Board of Trade, the agreement may contain a stipulation for payment to or on behalf of the seaman, conditionally on his going to sea in pursuance of the agreement, of a sum not exceeding the amount of one month's wages payable to the seaman under the agreement; and

(*b*) Stipulations for the allotment of a seaman's wages may be made in accordance with this Act.

(2) Save as aforesaid an agreement by or on behalf of the employer of a seaman for the payment of money to or on behalf of the seaman conditionally on his going to sea from any port in the United Kingdom shall be void, and any money paid in satisfaction of, in respect of any such agreement shall not be deducted from the seaman's wages, and a person shall not have any right of action, suit, or set-off against the seaman or his assignee in respect of any money so paid or purporting to have been so paid.

Regulations as to allotment notes.

141. (1) Any stipulation made by a seaman at the commencement of a voyage for the allotment of any part of his wages during his absence shall be inserted in the agreement with the crew, and shall state the amounts and times of the payments to be made.

(2) Where the agreement is required to be made in a form approved by the Board of Trade, the seaman may require that a stipulation be inserted in the agreement for the allotment by means of an allotment note, of any part (not exceeding one half) of his wages in favour either of a near relative or of a savings bank.

(3) Allotment notes shall be in a form approved by the Board of Trade.

(4) For the purposes of the provisions of this Act with respect to allotment notes—

(*a*) the expression "near relative" means one of the following persons, namely, the wife, father, mother, grandfather, grandmother, child, grandchild, brother, or sister of the seaman.

(*b*) the expression "savings bank" means a seamen's savings bank under this Act, or a trustee savings bank, or a post office savings bank.

Allotments through savings banks.

142. (1) An allotment in favour of a savings bank shall be made in favour of such persons and carried into effect in such manner as may be prescribed by regulations of the Board of Trade.

(2) The sum received by a savings bank in pursuance of an allotment, shall be paid out only on an application made, through a superintendent or the Board of Trade, by the seaman himself, or, in case of his death, by some person to whom his property, if under one hundred pounds in value, may be paid under this Act.

Right of suing on allotment notes.

143. (1) The person in whose favour an allotment note under this Act is made may, unless the seaman is shown in manner in this Act specified, to have forfeited or ceased to be entitled to the wages out of which the allotment is to be paid, recover the sums allotted, when and as the same are made payable, with costs from the owner of the ship with respect to which the engagement was made, or from any agent of the owner who has authorised the allotment, in the same court and manner in which wages of seamen not exceeding fifty pounds may be recovered under this Act: provided that the wife of a seaman, if she deserts her children, or so misconducts herself as to be undeserving of support from her husband, shall forfeit all right to further payments under any allotment made in her favour.

(2) In any proceeding for such recovery it shall be sufficient for the claimant to prove that he is the person mentioned in the note, and that the note was given by the owner or by the master or some other authorised agent; and the seaman shall be presumed to be duly earning his wages, unless the contrary is shown to the satisfaction of the court, either—

(*a*) by the official statement of the change in the crew caused by his absence, made and signed by the master, as by this Act is required, or

(*b*) by a certified copy of some entry in the official log book to the effect that he has left the ship, or

(*c*) by a credible letter from the master of the ship to the same effect, or

(*d*) by such other evidence as the court in their absolute discretion consider sufficient to show satisfactorily that the seaman has ceased to be entitled to the wages out of which the allotment is to be paid.

Time for payment of allotment note.

144. A payment under an allotment note shall begin at the expiration of one month, or, if the allotment is in favour of a savings bank, of three months, from the date of the agreement with the crew, or at such later date as may be fixed by the agreement, and shall be paid at the expiration of every subsequent month, or of such other periods as may be fixed by the agreement, and shall be paid only in respect of wages earned before the date of payment.

Seamen's Money Orders and Savings Banks.

Remittance of seamen's wages, etc., by seamen's money orders.

145. (1) Facilities shall be given for remitting the wages and other money of seamen and apprentices to the sea service to their relatives or other persons by means of seamen's money orders, issued by superintendents in accordance with this Act.

(2) The Board of Trade may make regulations concerning seamen's money orders, and in particular may specify in those regulations the time and mode of payment, and the persons by or to whom the same are to be paid; and all such regulations, while in force, shall be binding upon all persons interested

or claiming to be interested in the orders as well as upon the officers employed in issuing or paying the same.

146. The Board of Trade may, if they think fit, cause the amount of any seaman's money order to be paid to the person to whom or in whose favour the same has been granted, or to the personal representative, or any legatee, or next-of-kin of such person, notwithstanding that the order may not be in his possession; and, from and after the payment, the Board of Trade, and every superintendent and officer of the Board of Trade shall be freed from all liability in respect of the money order.

Power to pay when order is lost.

147. If any superintendent or officer grants or issues a seaman's money order with a fraudulent intent he shall be guilty of felony, and shall for each offence be liable to penal servitude for a term not exceeding five and not less than three years.

Penalty for issuing money orders with fraudulent intent.

148. (1) The Board of Trade may maintain a central seamen's saving bank in London, and may establish and maintain branch seamen's savings banks at such ports and places in the United Kingdom as they think expedient, and may receive at those banks deposits from or on account of seamen (whether of the Royal Navy, merchant service or other sea service) or the wives, widows, and children of such seamen, so that the aggregate amount of deposits standing at any one time in the name of any one depositor do not exceed two hundred pounds.

Power for Board of Trade to establish savings banks.

(2) The Board of Trade may constitute any mercantile marine office a branch savings bank for seamen, and, if so required, any superintendent of that office shall act as agent of the Board of Trade in executing the provisions of this Act relative to savings banks.

(3) The Board of Trade may make regulations with respect to the persons entitled to become depositors in seamen's savings banks, the making and withdrawal of deposits, the amount of deposits, the rate and payment of interest, the rights, claims, and obligations of depositors, and all other matters incidental to carrying into execution the provisions of this Act with respect to seamen's savings banks, and those regulations while in force shall have effect as if enacted in this Act.

149. (1) The National Debt Commissioners, on the request of the Board of Trade, may receive from and repay to the account of the Board the money paid as deposits in seamen's savings banks.

National Debt Commissioners to receive deposits, etc.

(2) The Commissioners shall invest money so received in the like manner as money received from trustee savings banks, and shall pay to the account of the Board of Trade interest on the money while in their hands, at the same rate as on the money received from trustee savings banks.

Application of deposits of deceased depositor.

150. All sums due from the Board of Trade to the estate of any deceased person on account of any deposit in a seamen's savings bank shall be paid and applied by the Board of Trade as if they were the property of a deceased seaman received by the Board under this Act, and the provisions of this Act respecting that property shall apply accordingly.

Expenses of savings banks.

151. The Board of Trade may, out of the interest received by them from the National Debt Commissioners under this Act, pay any expenses incurred by them in relation to seamen's savings banks.

Accounts and copy of regulations to be laid before Parliament.

152. An annual account of all deposits received and repaid on account of seamen's savings banks by the Board of Trade under this Act, and of the interest thereon, and a copy of all regulations made by the Board of Trade with respect to seamen's savings banks shall be laid before both Houses of Parliament.

Public officers to be exempt from legal proceedings, except in case of wilful default.

153. Legal proceedings shall not be instituted against the Board of Trade, or against any superintendent or officer employed in or about any seamen's savings bank or about any seamen's money order, on account of any regulations made by the Board of Trade with reference to those banks or on account of any act done or left undone in pursuance thereof, or on account of any refusal, neglect, or omission to pay any order or any deposit or interest thereon, unless that refusal, neglect, or omission arises from fraud or wilful misconduct on the part of the person against whom proceedings are instituted.

Forgery of documents, etc., for purposes of obtaining money in seamen's savings bank.

154. If any person, for the purpose of obtaining, either for himself or for any other person, any money deposited in a seamen's savings bank or any interest thereon—

(*a*) forges or fraudulently alters, assists in forging or fraudulently altering, or procures to be forged or fraudulently altered, any document purporting to show or assist in showing any right to any such money or interest ; or

(*b*) makes use of any document which has been so forged or fraudulently altered as aforesaid ; or

(*c*) gives, assists in giving, or procures to be given, any false evidence, knowing the same to be false ; or

(*d*) makes, assists in making, or procures to be made, any false representation, knowing the same to be false ; or

(*e*) assists in procuring any false evidence or representation to be given or made, knowing the same to be false ;

that person shall for each offence be liable to penal servitude for a term not exceeding five years, or to imprisonment for any term not exceeding two years with or without hard labour, or on summary conviction to imprisonment with or without hard labour for any period not exceeding six months.

Rights of Seamen in respect of Wages.

155. A seaman's right to wages and provisions shall be taken to begin either at the time at which he commences work or at the time specified in the agreement for his commencement of work or presence on board, whichever first happens. Right to wages, etc., when to begin.

156. (1) A seaman shall not by any agreement forfeit his lien on the ship, or be deprived of any remedy for the recovery of his wages, to which in the absence of the agreement he would be entitled, and shall not by any agreement abandon his right to wages in case of the loss of the ship, or abandon any right that he may have or obtain in the nature of salvage; and every stipulation in any agreement inconsistent with any provision of this Act shall be void. Right to recover wages, and salvage not to be forfeited.

(2) Nothing in this section shall apply to a stipulation made by the seamen belonging to any ship, which according to the terms of the agreement is to be employed on salvage service, with respect to the remuneration to be paid to them for salvage services to be rendered by that ship to any other ship.

157. (1) The right to wages shall not depend on the earning of freight; and every seaman and apprentice who would be entitled to demand and recover any wages, if the ship in which he has served had earned freight, shall, subject to all other rules of law and conditions applicable to the case, be entitled to demand and recover the same, notwithstanding that freight has not been earned; but in all cases of wreck or loss of the ship, proof that the seaman has not exerted himself to the utmost to save the ship, cargo and stores shall bar his claim to wages. Wages not to depend on freight.

(2) Where a seaman or apprentice who would, but for death, be entitled by virtue of this section to demand and recover any wages, dies before the wages are paid, they shall be paid and applied in manner provided by this Act with respect to the wages of a seaman who dies during a voyage.

158. Where the service of a seaman terminates before the date contemplated in the agreement, by reason of the wreck or loss of the ship, or of his being left on shore at any place abroad under a certificate granted as provided by this Act of his unfitness or inability to proceed on the voyage, he shall be entitled to wages up to the time of such termination, but not for any longer period. Wages on termination of service by wreck or illness.

159. A seaman or apprentice shall not be entitled wages for any time during which he unlawfully refuses or neglects to work when required, Wages not to accrue during refusal to work or imprisonment. whether before or after the time fixed by the agreement for his commencement of such work, nor, unless the court hearing the case otherwise directs, for any period during which he is lawfully imprisoned for any offence committed by him.

Forfeiture of wages, etc., of seaman when illness caused by his own default. **160.** Where a seaman is by reason of illness incapable of performing his duty, and it is proved that the illness has been caused by his own wilful act or default, he shall not be entitled to wages for the time during which he is by reason of the illness incapable of performing his duty.

Costs of procuring punishment may be deducted from wages. **161.** Whenever in any proceeding relating to seamen's wages it is shown that a seaman or apprentice has in the course of the voyage been convicted of an offence by a competent tribunal, and rightfully punished for that offence by imprisonment or otherwise, the court hearing the case may direct any part of the wages due to the seaman, not exceeding three pounds, to be applied in reimbursing any costs properly incurred by the master in procuring the conviction and punishment.

Compensation to seamen improperly discharged. **162.** If a seaman, having signed an agreement, is discharged otherwise than in accordance with the terms thereof before the commencement of the voyage, or before one month's wages are earned, without fault on his part justifying that discharge, and without his consent, he shall be entitled to receive from the master or owner, in addition to any wages he may have earned, due compensation for the damage caused to him by the discharge not exceeding one month's wages, and may recover that compensation as if it were wages duly earned.

Restriction on sale of, and charge upon, wages. **163.** (1) As respects wages due or accruing to a seaman or apprentice to the sea service—

(*a*) they shall not be subject to attachment or arrestment from any court;

(*b*) an assignment or sale thereof made prior to the accruing thereof shall not bind the person making the same;

(*c*) a power of attorney or authority for the receipt thereof shall not be irrevocable; and

(*d*) a payment of wages to the seaman or apprentice shall be valid in law, notwithstanding any previous sale or assignment of those wages, or any attachment, incumbrance, or arrestment thereof.

(2) Nothing in this section shall affect the provisions of this Act with respect to allotment notes.

Mode of recovering Wages.

Summary proceedings for wages. **164.** A seaman or apprentice to the sea service, or a person duly authorised on his behalf, may as soon as any wages due to him, not exceeding fifty pounds, become payable, sue for the same before a court of summary jurisdiction in or near the place at which his service has terminated, or at which he has been discharged, or at which any person on whom the claim is made is or resides, and the order made by the court in the matter shall be final.

Restrictions on suits for wages.

165. A proceeding for the recovery of wages not exceeding fifty pounds shall not be instituted by or on behalf of any seaman or apprentice to the sea service in any superior court of record in Her Majesty's dominions, nor as an admiralty proceeding in any court having admiralty jurisdiction in those dominions, except:—

(i) where the owner of the ship is adjudged bankrupt; or

(ii) where the ship is under arrest or is sold by the authority of any such court as aforesaid; or

(iii) where a court of summary jurisdiction acting under the authority of this Act, refers the claim to any such court; or

(iv) where neither the owner nor the master of the ship is or resides within twenty miles of the place where the seaman or apprentice is discharged or put ashore.

Wages not recoverable abroad in certain cases.

166. (1) Where a seaman is engaged for a voyage or engagement which is to terminate in the United Kingdom, he shall not be entitled to sue in any court abroad for wages, unless he is discharged with such sanction as is required by this Act, and with the written consent of the master, or proves such ill-usage on the part or by authority of the master, as to warrant reasonable apprehension of danger to his life if he were to remain on board.

(2) If a seaman on his return to the United Kingdom proves that the master or owner has been guilty of any conduct or default which but for this section would have entitled the seaman to sue for wages before the termination of the voyage or engagement, he shall be entitled to recover in addition to his wages such compensation not exceeding twenty pounds as the court hearing the case thinks reasonable.

Remedies of master for wages, disbursements, etc.

167. (1) The master of a ship shall, so far as the case permits, have the same rights, liens, and remedies for the recovery of his wages as a seaman has under this Act, or by any law or custom.

(2) The master of a ship, and every person lawfully acting as master of a ship, by reason of the decease or incapacity from illness of the master of the ship, shall, so far as the case permits, have the same rights, liens, and remedies for the recovery of disbursements or liabilities properly made or incurred by him on account of the ship as a master has for the recovery of his wages.

(3) If in any admiralty proceeding in any court having admiralty jurisdiction touching the claim of a master in respect of wages, or of such

disbursements, or liabilities as aforesaid, any right of set-off or counter-claim is set up, the court may enter into and adjudicate upon all questions, and settle all accounts then arising or outstanding and unsettled between the parties to the proceeding, and may direct payment of any balance found to be due.

Power of Courts to rescind Contracts.

Power of court to rescind contract between owner or master and seaman or apprentice.

168. Where a proceeding is instituted in or before any court in relation to any dispute between an owner or master of a ship and a seaman or apprentice to the sea service, arising out of or incidental to their relation as such, or is instituted for the purpose of this section, the court, if having regard to all the circumstances of the case they think it just to do so, may rescind any contract between the owner or master and the seaman or apprentice, or any contract of apprenticeship, upon such terms as the court may think just, and this power shall be in addition to any other jurisdiction which the court can exercise independently of this section.

Property of deceased Seamen.

Property of seamen who die during voyage.

169. (1) If any seaman or apprentice to the sea service belonging to a British ship the voyage of which is to terminate in the United Kingdom, whether a foreign-going or a home-trade ship, dies during that voyage, the master of the ship shall take charge of any money or effects belonging to the seaman or apprentice which are on board the ship.

(2) The master may, if he think fit, cause any of the effects to be sold by auction at the mast or otherwise by public auction.

(3) The master shall enter in the official log book the following particulars:—

(*a*) a statement of the amount of the money and a description of the effects:

(*b*) in case of a sale, a description of each article sold, and the sum received for each:

(*c*) a statement of the sum due to the deceased for wages and of the amount of deductions (if any) to be made from the wages.

(4) The entry shall be signed by the master and attested by a mate and some other member of the crew.

(5) The said money, effects, proceeds of sale of effects, and balance of wages, are in this Act referred to as the property of the seaman or apprentice.

Dealing with and account of property of

170. (1) Where a seaman or apprentice dies as aforesaid and the ship before coming to a port in the United Kingdom touches and remains for forty-eight hours at some port elsewhere, the master shall report the case to the British consular officer at such port, or if the port is in a British possession, to the officer of customs there, and shall give to the officer any information he requires as to the destination of the ship and probable length of the voyage. seamen who die during voyage.

(2) That officer may, if he thinks it expedient, require the property to be delivered and paid to him, and shall thereupon give to the master a receipt thereof, and endorse under his hand upon the agreement with the crew such particulars with respect thereto as the Board of Trade require.

(3) The receipt shall be produced by the master to a superintendent within forty-eight hours after his arrival at his port of destination in the United Kingdom.

(4) Where a seaman or apprentice dies as aforesaid and the ship proceeds at once to a port in the United Kingdom without touching and remaining as aforesaid at a port elsewhere, or the consular officer or officer of customs does not require the delivery and payment of the property as aforesaid, the master shall, within forty-eight hours after his arrival at his port of destination in the United Kingdom, deliver and pay the property to the superintendent at that port.

(5) In all cases where a seaman or apprentice dies during the progress of a voyage or engagement, the master shall give to the Board of Trade, or to the superintendent or officer to whom delivery and payment is made as aforesaid, such account in such form as they respectively require of the property of the deceased.

(6) A deduction claimed by the master in such account shall not be allowed unless verified, if an official log book is required to be kept, by an entry in that book made and attested as required by this Act, and also by such other vouchers (if any) as may reasonably be required by the Board of Trade or by the superintendent or officer to whom the account is given.

(7) A superintendent in the United Kingdom shall grant to a master, upon due compliance with such provisions of this section as relate to acts to be done at the port of destination, a certificate to that effect; and an officer of customs shall not clear inwards a foreign-going ship without the production of that certificate.

Penalty for non-compliance with provision as to property of deceased seamen.

171. (1) If the master of the ship fails to comply with the provisions of this Act with respect to taking charge of the property of a deceased seaman or apprentice, or to making in the official log book the proper entries relating thereto, or to procuring the proper attestation of those entries as required by this Act, or to the payment or delivery of the property, he shall be accountable for the property to the Board of Trade, and shall pay and deliver the same accordingly, and shall in addition for each offence be liable to a fine not exceeding treble the value of the property not accounted for, or if such value is not ascertained, not exceeding fifty pounds.

(2) If any such property is not duly paid, delivered, or accounted for by the master, the owner of the ship shall pay, deliver, and account for the same, and such property shall be recoverable from him accordingly, and if he fails to account for and deliver or pay the same, he shall in addition to his liability for the same be liable to a fine not exceeding treble the value of the property not accounted for, delivered, or paid over, or, if such value be not ascertained, not exceeding fifty pounds.

(3) The property may be recovered in the same court and manner in which the wages of seamen may be recovered under this Act.

Property of deceased seamen left abroad but not on board ship.

172. If any seaman or apprentice to the sea service belonging to a British ship the voyage of which is to terminate in the United Kingdom, or who has within six months preceding his death belonged to any such ship, dies at any place out of the United Kingdom, leaving any money or effects not on board the ship to which he belonged at the time of his death or to which he last belonged before his death, the chief officer of customs in the case of a British possession, and in other cases the British consular officer at or near the place, shall claim and take charge of such money and effects, and such money and effects shall be deemed to be property of a deceased seaman or apprentice within the meaning of this Part of this Act.

Dealing with property of deceased seamen by officers abroad.

173. (1) A chief officer of customs, in a British possession and a British consular officer may, as he thinks fit, sell any of the property of a deceased seaman or apprentice delivered to him or of which he takes charge under this Act, and the proceeds of any such sale shall be deemed to form part of the said property.

(2) Every such officer shall quarterly, or at such times as the Board of Trade require, remit the property in such manner, and shall render such accounts in respect thereof as the Board of Trade require.

Recovery of wages, etc., of seamen lost with their ship.

174. (1) Where a seaman or apprentice is lost with the ship to which he belongs the Board of Trade may recover the wages due to him from the owner of the ship, in the same court and in the same manner in which seamen's wages are recoverable, and shall deal with those wages in the same manner as with the wages of other deceased seamen and apprentices under this Act.

(2) In any proceeding for the recovery of the wages, if it is shown by some official return produced out of the custody of the Registrar General of Shipping and Seamen, or by other evidence, that the ship has twelve months

or upwards before the institution of the proceeding left a port of departure, she shall, unless it is shown that she has been heard of within twelve months after that departure, be deemed to have been lost with all hands on board, either immediately after the time she was last heard of, or at such later time as the court hearing the case may think probable.

(3) Any duplicate agreement or list of the crew made out, or statement of a change of the crew delivered, under this Act, at the time of the last departure of the ship from the United Kingdom, or a certificate purporting to be a certificate from a consular or other public officer at any port out of the United Kingdom, stating that certain seamen and apprentices were shipped in the ship from the said port, shall, if produced out of the custody of the Registrar General of Shipping and Seamen, or of the Board of Trade, be, in the absence of the proof to the contrary, sufficient proof that the seaman and apprentices therein named as belonging to the ship were on board at the time of the loss.

Property of seamen dying at home.

175. If a seaman or apprentice to the sea service dies in the United Kingdom, and is at the time of his death entitled to claim from the master or owner of a ship in which he has served any effects or unpaid wages, the master or owner shall pay and deliver or account for such property to the superintendent at the port where the seaman or apprentice was discharged or was to have been discharged, or to the Board of Trade, or as that Board direct.

Payment over of property of deceased seamen by Board of Trade.

176. (1) Where any property of a deceased seaman or apprentice comes into the hands of the Board of Trade, or any agent of that Board, the Board of Trade, after deducting for expenses incurred in respect of that seaman or apprentice or of his property such sum as they think proper to allow, shall, subject to the provisions of this Act, deal with the residue as follows :—

(*a*) If the property exceeds in value one hundred pounds, they shall pay and deliver the residue to the legal personal representative of the deceased :

(*b*) If the property do not exceed in value one hundred pounds, the Board may as they think fit either pay or deliver the residue to any claimant who is proved to their satisfaction to be the widow or a child of the deceased, or to be entitled to the personalty of the deceased either under his will (if any) or any statute of distribution or otherwise, or to be a person entitled to take out representation, although no such representation has been taken out, and shall be thereby discharged from all further liability in respect of the residue so paid or delivered ; or (*c*) They may, if they think fit, require representation to be taken out and pay and deliver the residue to the legal personal representative of the deceased.

(2) Every person to whom any such residue is so paid or delivered shall apply the same in due course of administration.

Dealing with deceased seaman's property when he leaves a will.

177. (1) Where a deceased seaman or apprentice has left a will the Board of Trade may refuse to pay or deliver the above-mentioned residue;

(*a*) If the will was made on board ship, to any person claiming under the will, unless the will is in writing, and is signed or acknowledged by the testator in the presence of, and is attested by, the master or first or only mate of the ship, and

(*b*) If the will was not made on board ship, to any person claiming under the will, and not being related to the testator by blood or marriage, unless the will is in writing, and is signed or acknowledged by the testator in the presence of, and is attested by, two witnesses, one of whom is a superintendent, or is a minister of religion officiating in the place in which the will is made, or, where there are no such persons, a justice, British consular officer, or an officer of customs.

(2) Whenever the Board of Trade refuse under this section to pay or deliver the residue to a person claiming under a will the residue shall be dealt with as if no will had been made.

Claims by creditors.

178. (1) A creditor shall not be entitled to claim from the Board of Trade the property of a deceased seaman or apprentice, or any part thereof, by virtue of representation obtained as creditor.

(2) A creditor shall not be entitled by any means whatever to obtain payment of his debt out of the property, if the debt accrued more than three years before the death of the deceased, or if the demand is not made within two years after the death.

(3) The demand shall be made by the creditor delivering to the Board of Trade an account in writing in a form approved by the Board, stating the particulars of his demand and the place of his abode, and signed by him and verified by a statutory declaration.

(4) If before the demand is made, any claim to the property of the deceased made by any person has been allowed, that Board shall give notice to the creditor of the allowance of the claim.

(5) If no claim has been allowed, the Board of Trade shall investigate the creditor's account, and may for that purpose require him to prove the same, and to produce all books, accounts, vouchers, and papers relating

thereto; and if by means of them the creditor satisfies the Board of Trade of the justice of the demand, either in the whole or in part, the same shall be allowed and paid accordingly, so far as the property then in the hands of the Board of Trade will extend for that purpose, and the Board of Trade shall thereby be discharged from all further liability in respect of money so paid; but if the Board are not satisfied as to the claim, or if such books, accounts, vouchers, or papers as aforesaid are not produced, and sufficient reason is not given for their non-production, the demand shall be disallowed.

(6) In any case whatever the Board of Trade may delay the investigation of any demand made by a creditor for the payment of his debt for one year from the time of the first delivery of the demand; and if in the course of that time a claim to the property of the deceased is made by any person as widow, next-of-kin, or legatee, and allowed by the Board of Trade under this Act, the Board of Trade may pay and deliver the same to that person.

(7) Where the property has been paid and delivered by the Board of Trade to any person as a widow, next-of-kin, or legatee of the deceased, whether before or after the demand made by the creditor, the creditor shall have the same rights and remedies against that person, as if he had received the property as the legal personal representative of the deceased.

Dealing with unclaimed property of deceased seaman. 45 & 46 Vict., c. 99.

179. Where no claim to the property of a deceased seaman or apprentice received by the Board of Trade is substantiated within six years after the receipt thereof the Board may in their absolute discretion, if any subsequent claim is made, either allow or refuse the claim, and, subject to the allowance of any such claim, shall apply such property in manner provided by Part Twelve of this Act (relating to the Mercantile Marine Fund).

Forgery of documents, etc., for purpose of obtaining property of deceased seamen.

180. If any person, for the purpose of obtaining, either for himself or for any other person, any property of any deceased seaman or apprentice to the sea service,—

(*a*) forges or fraudulently alters, or assists in forging or fraudulently altering, or procures to be forged or fraudulently altered any document purporting to show or assist in showing any right to such property; or

(*b*) makes use of any document which has been so forged or fraudulently altered as aforesaid; or

(*c*) gives or assists in giving, or procures to be given, any false evidence knowing the same to be false; or

(*d*) makes or assists in making, or procures to be made, any false representation, knowing the same to be false; or (*e*) assists in procuring any false evidence or representation to be given or made, knowing the same to be false,

that person shall for each offence be liable to penal servitude for a term not exceeding five years, or to imprisonment for a term not exceeding two years with or without hard labour, or on summary conviction to imprisonment with or without hard labour for any period not exceeding six months.

Property of seamen discharged from Royal Navy.

181. Where a seaman invalided or discharged from any of Her Majesty's ships is sent home in a merchant ship, and dies during the voyage, the provisions of this Act respecting the property of deceased seamen shall apply, with this qualification, that the property shall be delivered, paid over, and disposed of in such manner as the Accountant General of Her Majesty's Navy directs.

Reimbursement of Relief to Seamen's Families.

Relief to seamen's families to be chargeable on a certain proportion of their wages.

182. (1) Whenever, during the absence of any seaman on a voyage, his wife, or any of his children or step-children, becomes chargeable to any union or parish in the United Kingdom, that union or parish shall be entitled to be reimbursed, out of the wages of the seaman earned during the voyage any sums properly expended during his absence in the maintenance of those members of his family or any of them, so that the sums do not exceed the following proportions of his wages; (that is to say,)

(*a*) if only one of those members is chargeable, one-half of the wages:

(*b*) if two or more of those members are chargeable, two-thirds of the wages.

(2) If during the absence of the seaman any sums have been paid by the owner of his ship to or on behalf of any such member as aforesaid, under an allotment note made by the seaman in favour of the member, any claim for reimbursement as aforesaid shall be limited to the excess (if any) of the proportion of the wages hereinbefore mentioned over the sums so paid.

Notice to owner, and enforcement of charge.

183. (1) For the purpose of obtaining such reimbursement as aforesaid, the board of guardians in a poor law union in England or Ireland, and the inspector of the poor in any parish in Scotland, may give to the owner of the ship in which the seaman is serving a notice in writing stating the proportion of the seaman's wages upon which it is intended to make a claim and requiring the owner to retain such proportion in his hands for a period to be therein mentioned, not exceeding twenty-one days from the time of the seaman's return to his port of discharge, and also requiring the owner immediately on the seaman's return to give notice in writing thereof to the board or inspector.

(2) The owner, after receiving any such notice, shall retain the said proportion of wages, and give notice of the seaman's return accordingly, and shall likewise give to the seaman notice of the intended claim.

(3) The board or inspector may, upon the seaman's return, apply to a court of summary jurisdiction having jurisdiction in the union or parish for an order for reimbursement; and that court may make a summary order for the reimbursement to the whole extent claimed, or to such lesser amount as the court, under the circumstances, think fit, and the owner shall pay to the board or inspector out of the seaman's wages the amount so ordered to be paid by way of reimbursement, and shall pay the residue of the wages to the seaman.

(4) If no order for reimbursement is obtained within the period mentioned in the notice given to the owner as aforesaid, the proportion of wages to be retained by him shall immediately on the expiration of that period and without deduction be payable to the seaman.

Destitute Seamen.

Penalty on masters of ships leaving certain (?) seamen in distress in the United Kingdom.

184. (1) If any person being a native of any country in Asia or Africa, or of any island in the South Sea or the Pacific Ocean, or of any other country not having a consular officer in the United Kingdom, is brought to the United Kingdom in a ship, British or foreign, as a seaman, and is left in the United Kingdom, and within six months of his being so left becomes chargeable upon the poor rate, or commits any act by reason whereof he is liable to be convicted as an idle and disorderly person, or any other act of vagrancy, the master or owner of the ship, or in case of a foreign ship the person who is consignee of the ship at the time of the seaman being so left as aforesaid, shall be liable to a fine not exceeding thirty pounds, unless he can show that the person left as aforesaid quitted the ship without the consent of the master, or that the master, owner, or consignee, has afforded him due means of returning to his native country, or to the country in which he was shipped.

(2) The court inflicting the fine may order the whole or any part of the fine to be applied towards the relief or sending home of the person left.

Relief of destitute lascars.

185. (1) It shall be the duty of the Secretary of State in Council of India to make charge of and send home or otherwise provide for all lascars or other natives of India who are found destitute in the United Kingdom.

(2) If any such destitute person is relieved and maintained by a board of guardians in a poor law union in England or Ireland, or by the inspector of the poor in any parish in Scotland, the board or inspector may give notice

thereof in writing to the Secretary of State in Council of India specifying, so far as is practicable, the following particulars; namely,—

(*a*) the name of the person relieved or maintained; and

(*b*) the part of India of which he professes to be a native; and

(*c*) the name of the ship in which he was brought to the United Kingdom; and

(*d*) the port abroad from which the ship sailed, and the port in the United Kingdom at which the ship arrived when he was so brought to the United Kingdom, and the time of the arrival.

4 Geo. 4 c. 80, s. 34, 3 & 4 Will. 4, c. 93.

(3) The Secretary of State in Council of India shall repay to board of guardians or inspector out of the revenues of India all moneys duly expended by them or him in relieving or maintaining the destitute person after the time at which the notice is given, and any money so paid or otherwise paid by the said Secretary of State, on account of the relief or maintenance or passage home of the destitute person, shall be a joint and several debt due to the said Secretary of State from the master and owner of the ship by which the destitute person was brought to the United Kingdom.

(4) This section shall apply only to such lascars or other natives of India as have been brought to the United Kingdom either as seamen, or for employment as seamen, or for employment by the owner of the ship bringing them.

Leaving Seamen Abroad.

Discharge of seamen in foreign countries.

186. (1) In the following cases, namely—

(*a*) where a British ship is transferred or disposed of at any port out of Her Majesty's dominions, and a seaman or apprentice belonging thereto does not in the presence of some British consular officer, or, if there is no such officer there, in the presence of one or more respectable British merchants residing at the port and not interested in the ship, signify his consent in writing to complete the voyage if continued, and

(*b*) where the service of any seaman or apprentice belonging to any British ship terminates at any port out of Her Majesty's dominions,

the master shall give to that seaman or apprentice a certificate of discharge in a form approved by the Board of Trade, and in the case of any certificated officer whose certificate he has retained shall return such certificate to him.

(2) The master shall also besides paying the wages to which the seaman or apprentice is entitled, either—

(*a*) provide him with adequate employment on board some other British ship bound to the port in Her Majesty's dominions at which he was originally shipped, or to a port in the United Kingdom agreed to by the seaman, or

(*b*) furnish the means of sending him back to some such port, or

(*c*) provide him with a passage home, or

(*d*) deposit with the consular officer or merchants as aforesaid such a sum of money as is by the officer or merchants deemed sufficient to defray the expenses of his maintenance and passage home.

(3) The consular officer or merchants shall indorse upon the agreement with the crew of the ship which the seaman or apprentice is leaving the particulars of any payment, provision, or deposit made under this section.

(4) If the master fails, without reasonable cause, to comply with any requirement of this section, the expenses of maintenance or passage home,—

(*a*) if defrayed by the seaman or apprentice shall be recoverable as wages due to him; and

(*b*) if defrayed by the consular officer or by any other person shall (unless the seaman or apprentice has been guilty of barratry) be a charge upon the ship to which the seaman or apprentice belonged and upon the owner for the time being thereof and may be recovered against the owner, with costs, at the suit of the consular officer or other person defraying the expenses, or, in case they have been allowed to him out of public money, as a debt to the Crown, either by ordinary process of law, or in the manner in which wages can be recovered under this Act.

Penalty for forcing seamen on shore or leaving them behind.

187. The master of, or any other person belonging to, a British ship, shall not wrongfully force on shore and leave behind, or otherwise wilfully and wrongfully leave behind, in any place on shore or at sea, in or out of Her Majesty's dominions, a seaman or apprentice to the sea service before the completion of the voyage for which he was engaged or before the return of the ship to the United Kingdom, and if he does so, he shall in respect of each offence be guilty of a misdemeanour.

Seamen not to be discharged or

188. (1) The master of a British ship shall not discharge a seaman or apprentice to the sea service abroad, or leave him behind abroad, ashore, or

left abroad unless sanction or certificate obtained.

at sea, unless he previously obtains, endorsed on the agreement with the crew, the sanction, or in the case of leaving behind the certificate—

(*a*) at any place in a British possession of a superintendent (or in the absence of any such superintendent of the chief officer of customs at or near the place); and

(*b*) at any place elsewhere of the British consular officer for the place, or, in the absence of any such officer, of two merchants resident at or near the place, or, if there is only one merchant so resident, of that merchant,

but nothing in this section shall require such sanction where the discharge is in the British possession where the seaman was shipped.

(2) The certificate shall state in writing the fact and cause of the seaman being left behind whether the cause be unfitness or inability to proceed to sea, desertion, or disappearance.

(3) The person to whom an application is made for a sanction or certificate under this section may, and, if not a merchant, shall, examine into the grounds on which a seaman or apprentice is to be discharged or left abroad, and for that purpose may, if he thinks fit, administer oaths, and may grant or refuse the sanction or certificate as he thinks just.

(4) If a master acts in contravention of this section, he shall be guilty of a misdemeanour, and in any legal proceeding for the offence it shall lie on the master to prove that the sanction or certificate was obtained, or could not be obtained.

Accounts and payment of wages in case of seamen left abroad.

189. (1) Where a master of a British ship leaves a seaman or apprentice on shore abroad, whether within or without Her Majesty's dominions, on the ground of his unfitness or inability to proceed on the voyage, he shall deliver to the person signing the certificate above-mentioned, a full and true account of the wages due to the seaman or apprentice, and if the said person is a consular officer shall deliver the account in duplicate.

(2) If a master fails without reasonable cause to deliver the account he shall for each offence be liable to a fine not exceeding ten pounds, and if he delivers a false account he shall for each offence be liable to a fine not exceeding twenty pounds, in addition in each case to the payment of the wages.

(3) The master shall pay the amount of wages due to a seaman or apprentice so left abroad aforesaid, if he is left in a British possession to the seaman or apprentice himself, and if he is left elsewhere to the British consular officer.

(4) The payment shall be made, whenever it is practicable, in money, and, when not so practicable, by bill drawn on the owner of the ship, but if payment is made by bill—

(*a*) the person signing the certificate shall certify by endorsement on the bill that the same is drawn for seamen's wages, and shall also endorse on the agreement with the crew, the amount for which the bill is drawn, and such further particulars as the Board of Trade requires;

(*b*) if the bill is drawn by the master, the owner of the ship shall be liable to pay the amount to the holder or endorsee thereof; and it shall not be necessary in any proceeding against the owner upon the bill to prove that the master had authority to draw it;

(*c*) a bill purporting to be drawn and endorsed under this section, shall if produced out of the custody of the Board of Trade or of the Registrar General of Shipping and Seamen, or of any superintendent be admissible in evidence; and any endorsement on any such bill purporting to be made in pursuance of this section shall also be admissible as evidence of the facts stated in the endorsement.

(5) If a master fails, without reasonable cause, to make such payment of wages as provided by this section, he shall for each offence be liable in addition to the payment of the wages to a fine not exceeding ten pounds.

(6) Where payment is made to a British consular officer, that officer shall, if satisfied with the account, endorse on one of the duplicates thereof a receipt for the payment, and return it to the master, and the master shall deliver the duplicate within forty-eight hours of his return to his port of destination in the United Kingdom to the superintendent at that port.

(7) The British consular officer shall retain the other duplicate of the account, and shall deal with the sum so paid to him in the following manner, namely,—

(*a*) If the seaman or apprentice subsequently obtains employment at or quits the port at which the payment has been made, he shall deduct out of the sum any expenses incurred by him in respect of the maintenance of the seaman or apprentice under this Act, except such as the owner or master is by this Act required to defray, and shall pay the remainder to the seaman or apprentice, and deliver to him an account of the sums so received and expended on his behalf;

(*b*) if the seaman or apprentice dies before his ship quits the port, he shall deal with the sum as part of the property of a deceased seaman; and

(*c*) if the seaman or apprentice is sent home at the public expense under this Act, he shall account for the sum to the Board of Trade; and the sum, after deducting any expenses duly incurred in respect of the seaman or apprentice, except such expenses as the master or owner of the ship is required by this Act to pay, shall be dealt with as wages of the seaman or apprentice.

Distressed Seamen.

Regulations as to relief and maintenance of distressed seamen.

190. The Board of Trade may make regulations with respect to the relief, maintenance, and sending home of seamen and apprentices found in distress abroad, and may, by those regulations (in this Act referred to as the distressed seamen regulations) make such conditions as they think fit with regard to that relief, maintenance, and sending home, and a seaman shall not have any right to be relieved, maintained, or sent home except in the cases and to the extent and on the conditions provided by those regulations.

Provisions for maintenance and relief of distressed seamen.

191. (1) The following authorities, that is to say, governors of British possessions, British consular officers, and other officers of Her Majesty in foreign countries shall, and, in places where there are no such officers, any two resident British merchants, or if there is only one British merchant so resident that merchant, may in accordance with and on the conditions prescribed by the distressed seamen regulations, provide for the maintenance until a passage home can be procured, of the following seamen and apprentices (who are in this Act included in the term distressed seamen) namely,—

(*a*) seamen and apprentices to the sea service, whether subjects of Her Majesty or not, who by reason of having been discharged or left behind abroad or shipwrecked from any British ship, or any of Her Majesty's ships, are in distress in any place abroad, and

(*b*) seamen and apprentices to the sea service, being subjects of Her Majesty, who have been engaged by any person acting either as principal or agent to serve in a ship belonging to the Government or to a subject or citizen of a foreign country, and are in distress in any place abroad.

(2) For the purpose of providing a distressed seaman with a passage home, the authority shall put him on board a British ship bound either to the United Kingdom or to the British possession to which the seaman belong

(as the case requires), which is in want of men to make up its complement; or if there is no such ship, then the authority shall provide the seaman with a passage home as soon as possible in any ship, British or foreign, bound as aforesaid.

(3) The authority shall endorse on the agreement with the crew of the ship, if a British ship, on board of which a distressed seaman is placed, the name of every person so placed on board with any particulars directed by the distressed seamen regulations to be endorsed.

(4) The authority shall be paid in respect of the expenses of the maintenance and conveyance of distressed seamen such sums as the Board of Trade may allow, and those sums shall, on the production of the bills of disbursements, with the proper vouchers, be paid as hereinafter provided.

192. (1) The master of every British ship so bound as aforesaid shall receive on board his ship, and afford a passage and maintenance to all distressed seamen whom he is required under this Act to take on board his ship, not exceeding one for every fifty tons burden, and shall during the passage provide every such distressed seaman with a proper berth or sleeping place, effectually protected against sea and weather.

Masters of ships compelled to take distressed seamen.

(2) On the production of a certificate, signed by the authority by whose directions any such distressed seaman was received on board, specifying the number and names of the distressed seamen and the time when each of them was received on board, and on a declaration made by the master before a justice of the peace, and verified by the Registrar General of Shipping and Seamen, stating the number of days during which each distressed seaman has received maintenance, and stating the full complement of his crew and the actual number of seamen and apprentices employed on board his ship, and every variation in that number, whilst the distressed seaman received maintenance, the master shall be entitled to be paid, in respect of the maintenance and passage of every seaman or apprentice so conveyed, maintained, and provided for by him, exceeding the number (if any) wanted to make up the complement of his crew, such sum per diem as the Board of Trade allow.

(5) If any master of a British ship fails without reasonable cause to comply with this section in the case of any seaman or apprentice, he shall for each offence be liable to a fine not exceeding one hundred pounds.

193. (1) Where any expenses on account of any such distressed seaman or apprentice as follows, namely:—

Recovery of expenses of relief of distressed seamen.

(*a*) Any seaman or apprentice belonging to a British ship, who has been discharged or left behind abroad, without full compliance on the part of the master with the provisions in that behalf in this Act contained;

(*b*) A subject of Her Majesty, who has been engaged to serve in a ship belonging to the Government or to a subject or citizen of a foreign country,

either for his maintenance, necessary clothing, conveyance home, or, in case of death, for his burial, or otherwise in accordance with this Act are incurred by or on behalf of the Crown, or are incurred by the Government of a foreign country, and repaid to that Government by or on behalf of the Crown, those expenses, together with the wages, if any, due to the seaman or apprentice, shall be a charge upon the ship, whether British or foreign, to which such distressed seaman or apprentice belonged, and shall be a debt to the Crown from the master of the ship, or from the owner of the ship for the time being, and also if the ship be a foreign ship, from the person, whether principal or agent, who engaged the seaman or apprentice for service in the ship.

(2) The debt, in addition to any fines which may have been incurred may be recovered by the Board of Trade on behalf of the Crown either by ordinary process of law, or in the court and manner in which wages may be recovered by seamen.

(3) In any proceeding for such recovery the production of the account (if any) of the expenses furnished in accordance with this Act or the distressed seamen regulations, and proof of payment of the expenses by or on behalf of the Board of Trade, shall be sufficient evidence that the expenses were incurred or repaid under this Act by or on behalf of the Crown.

Payment of expenses out of mercantile marine fund.

194. All expenses paid under this Act by or on behalf of the Crown for the relief of distressed seamen, shall be paid out of the Mercantile Marine Fund, and all sums received or recovered towards those expenses shall be carried to that fund.

Volunteering into the Navy.

Seamen allowed to leave their ships in order to enter the navy.

195. (1) A seaman may leave his ship for the purpose of forthwith entering the naval service of Her Majesty, and in that case shall not by reason of so leaving his ship be deemed to have deserted therefrom, or otherwise be liable to any punishment or forfeiture whatever.

(2) A stipulation introduced into any agreement whereby a seaman is declared to incur a forfeiture or be exposed to a loss in case he enters the naval service of Her Majesty shall be void, and if a master or owner causes any such stipulation to be so introduced he shall for each offence be liable to a fine not exceeding twenty pounds.

196. (1) If a seaman, without having previously committed an act amounting to and treated by the master as desertion, leaves his ship in order to enter the naval service of Her Majesty, and is received into that service, the master shall deliver to him his effects on board the ship, and shall pay, subject to all just deductions, the proportionate amount of his wages down to the time of his entering Her Majesty's service, to the officer authorised to receive the seaman into that service, either in money or by bill drawn upon the owner, and payable at sight to the order of the Accountant General of the Navy; and the receipt of that officer shall be a discharge for the money or bill so given; and the bill shall be exempt from stamp duty.

Money and effects of seamen volunteering into navy.

(2) If the master fails so to deliver the seaman's effects, or to pay his wages, as by this section required, he shall, in addition to his liability to deliver and pay the same, be liable for each offence to a fine not exceeding twenty pounds.

(3) If any such bill be not duly paid when presented, the Accountant General of the Navy or the seaman on whose behalf the bill is given, may sue thereon, or may recover the wages due by all or any of the means by which wages due to seamen are recoverable.

197. (1) Where the wages of a seaman received into Her Majesty's naval service are paid in money, the money shall be credited in the ship's ledger to the account of the seaman.

Wages of seamen received into navy.

(2) Where the wages are paid by bill, the bill shall be noted in the ship's ledger, and sent to the Accountant General of the Navy, who shall cause the same to be presented for payment, and shall credit the produce thereof to the account of the seaman.

(3) An officer who receives any such bill shall not be subject to any liability in respect thereof, except for the safe custody thereof until sent to the Accountant General as aforesaid.

(4) The wages of the seaman shall not be paid to him until the time at which he would have been entitled to receive the same if he had remained in the service of the ship which he has quitted for the purpose of entering Her Majesty's service.

(5) If the owner or master of the ship shows to the satisfaction of the Admiralty, that he has paid or properly rendered himself liable to pay, an advance of wages to or on account of the seaman, and has satisfied that liability, and that the seaman has not at the time of quitting his ship duly earned the advance by service therein, the Admiralty may pay to the owner or master so much of the advance as had not been duly earned, and deduct

the sum so paid from any wages of the seaman earned or to be earned in the naval service of Her Majesty.

(6) Where in consequence of a seaman so leaving his ship and entering Her Majesty's service, it becomes necessary for the safety and proper navigation of the ship to engage any substitute, and the wages or other remuneration paid to the substitute for subsequent service exceed the wages or remuneration which would have been payable to the seaman under his agreement for similar service, the master or owner of the ship may apply to the High Court for a certificate authorising the repayment of the excess, and the application shall be made and the certificate granted in accordance with rules of court.

(7) The certificate shall be sent to the applicant or his solicitor or agent, and a copy thereof shall be sent to the Accountant General of the Navy; and the Accountant General shall, upon delivery to him of the original certificate, together with a receipt in writing purporting to be a receipt from the applicant, pay to the person delivering the certificate, out of the moneys granted by Parliament for Navy services, the amount mentioned in the certificate; and the certificate and receipt shall absolutely discharge the Accountant General and Her Majesty from all liability in respect of the moneys so paid or of the application thereof.

(8) If any person in making or supporting any application under this section—

(*a*) forges or fradulently alters, or assists in forging or fraudulently altering, or procures to be forged or fraudulently altered, any document; or

(*b*) presents or makes use of any document so forged or fraudulently altered; or

(*c*) gives, assists in giving, or procures to be given, any false evidence knowing the same to be false; or

(*d*) makes, assists in making, or procures to be made, any false representation, knowing the same to be false,

that person shall in respect of each offence be guilty of a misdemeanour.

Provisions, Health, and Accommodation.

Complaints as to provisions or water

198. (1) If three or more of the crew of a British ship consider that the provisions or water for the use of the crew are at any time of bad quality, unfit for use, or deficient in quantity, they may complain thereof to any of the following officers, namely, an officer in command of one of Her Majesty's ships, a British consular officer, a superintendent, or a chief officer

of customs, and the officer may either examine the provisions or water complained of or cause them to be examined.

(2) If the officer, or person making the examination, finds that the provisions or water are of bad quality and unfit for use, or deficient in quantity, he shall signify it in writing to the master of the ship, and if the master of the ship does not thereupon provide other proper provisions or water in lieu of any so signified to be of bad quality and unfit for use, or does not procure the requisite quantity of any provisions or water so signified to be deficient in quantity, or uses any provisions or water so signified to be of bad quality and unfit for use, he shall for each offence be liable to a fine not exceeding twenty pounds.

(3) The officer directing, or the person making, the examination shall enter a statement of the result of the examination in the official log book, and send a report thereof to the Board of Trade, and that report shall be admissible in evidence, in manner provided by this Act.

(4) If the said officer certifies in that statement that there was no reasonable ground for the complaint, each of the complainants shall be liable to forfeit to the owner out of his wages a sum not exceeding one week's wages.

199. In either of the following cases; (that is to say,)

Allowance for short or bad provisions.

(i) if during a voyage the allowance of any of the provisions for which a seaman has by his agreement stipulated is reduced (except in accordance with any regulations for reduction by way of punishment contained in the agreement with the crew, and also except for any time during which the seaman wilfully and without sufficient cause refuses or neglects to perform his duty, or is lawfully under confinement for misconduct either on board or on shore); or

(ii) if it is shown that any of those provisions are or have during the voyage been bad in quality and unfit for use;

the seaman shall receive, by way of compensation for that reduction, or bad quality, according to the time of its continuance, the following sums, to be paid to him in addition to, and to be recoverable as, wages; (that is to say,)

(*a*) if his allowance is reduced by not more than one-third of the quantity specified in the agreement, a sum not exceeding fourpence a day:

(*b*) if his allowance is reduced by more than one-third of that quantity, eightpence a day:

(*c*) in respect of bad quality as aforesaid, a sum not exceeding one shilling a day:

But if it is shown to the satisfaction of the court before whom the case is tried that any provisions, the allowance of which has been reduced, could not be procured or supplied in proper quantities, and that proper and equivalent substitutes were supplied in lieu thereof, the court shall take those circumstances into consideration, and shall modify or refuse compensation as the justice of the case requires.

Regulations respecting medicines, anti-scorbutics, etc.

200. (1) The Board of Trade shall issue scales of medicines and medical stores suitable for different classes of ships and voyages, and shall also prepare or sanction books containing instructions for dispensing the same.

(2) The owner of every ship navigating between the United Kingdom and any place out of the same shall provide and cause to be kept on board a supply of medicine and medical stores according to the scale appropriate to the ship, and also the said books or one of them.

(3) The master or owner of every such ship, except in the case of—

(*a*) ships bound to European ports or ports in the Mediterranean Sea; and

(*b*) such ships or classes of ships bound to ports on the eastern coast of America, north of the thirty-fifth degree of north latitude, and to any islands or places in the Atlantic Ocean north of the same limit as the Board of Trade may exempt;

shall provide and cause to be kept on board a sufficient quantity of anti-scorbutics in accordance with the regulations in the Fifth Schedule to this Act, and those regulations shall have effect as part of this section, and the master shall serve out the anti-scorbutics to the crew according to the said regulations, and if a seaman or apprentice refuses or neglects to take the anti-scorbutics when served out, that fact shall be entered in the official log book, and the entry shall be signed by the master and by the mate or some other of the crew, and also by the medical practitioner on board if any.

(4) If any requirement of this section with respect to the provision of medicines, medical stores, book of instruction, or anti-scorbutics is not complied with in the case of any ship, the owner or master of that ship shall, for each offence, be liable to a fine not exceeding twenty pounds, unless he can prove that the non-compliance was not caused through his inattention, neglect or wilful default.

(5) If any requirement of this section with respect to the serving out of anti-scorbutics or making an entry in the official log-book is not complied

with in the case of any ship to which the requirement applies, the master of the ship shall, for each offence, be liable to a fine not exceeding five pounds, unless he can prove that the non-compliance did not arise through any neglect, omission, or wilful default on his part.

(6) If it is proved that some person, other than the master or owner, is in default in any case under this section, that person shall, for each offence, be liable to a fine not exceeding twenty pounds.

(7) If any person manufactures, sells, or keeps, or offers for sale any medicines or medical stores for use on board ship which are of bad quality, he shall, for each offence, be liable to a fine not exceeding twenty pounds.

201. (1) The master of a ship shall keep on board proper weights and measures for determining the quantities of the several provisions and articles served out, and shall allow the same to be used at the time of serving out the provisions and articles in the presence of a witness whenever any dispute arises about the quantities.

Weights and measures on board.

(2) If the master of a ship fails without reasonable cause to comply with this section, he shall for each offence be liable to a fine not exceeding ten pounds.

202. (1) It shall be the duty of the medical inspector of ships for the port appointed under this Part of this Act to inspect the medicines, medical stores, and anti-scorbutics with which a ship is required by this Part of this Act to be provided.

Inspection of medicines, medical stores, and anti-scorbutics.

(2) For the purpose of that inspection a medical inspector of ships shall have all the powers of a Board of Trade inspector under this Act, and shall act, if appointed by a local marine board, under the direction of that board (except in special cases in which the Board of Trade require an inspection to be made), and, if appointed by the Board of Trade, under the direction of the Board of Trade.

(3) The medical inspector of ships shall make his inspection three clear days at least before the ship proceeds to sea, if reasonable notice in writing for the purpose is given to him by the master, owner, or consignee, and, where the result of the inspection is satisfactory, shall not make another inspection before the ship proceeds to sea unless he has reason to suspect that any of the articles inspected have been subsequently removed, injured, or destroyed.

(4) If the medical inspector of ships is of opinion that the articles inspected are deficient in quantity or quality, or are placed in improper vessels, he shall give notice in writing to the chief officer of customs of the port where the ship is lying, and also to the master, owner, or consignee thereof, and the master of the ship before proceeding to sea shall produce to the chief officer of

customs a certificate under the hand of the same or some other medical inspector of ships, that the default found by the inspector has been remedied, and if that certificate is not so produced, the ship shall be detained until the certificate is produced and if the ship proceeds to sea, the owner, master, or consignee of the ship shall, for each offence, be liable to a fine not exceeding twenty pounds.

Medical inspection of seamen.

203. (1) A medical inspector of seamen appointed under this Part of this Act shall, on application by the owner or master of any ship, examine any seaman applying for employment in that ship, and give to the superintendent a report under his hand stating whether the seaman is in a fit state for duty at sea, and a copy of the report shall be given to the master or owner.

(2) The applicant for that medical examination shall pay to the superintendent such fees as the Board of Trade direct, and those fees shall be paid into the mercantile marine fund.

Appointment of medical inspectors.

204. (1) The local marine board at a port may, upon being required by the Board of Trade to do so, appoint and remove a medical inspector of ships for the port, and subject to the control of the Board of Trade may fix his remuneration, and at any port where there is no local marine board, the Board of Trade may appoint and remove a medical inspector of ships and may fix his remuneration.

(2) The local marine board and at a port where there is no such local marine board, the Board of Trade may appoint and remove a medical inspector of seamen, and that inspector shall be paid out of the mercantile marine fund such remuneration as the Board of Trade direct.

Appointment of medical inspector, and regulations as to supply of anti-scorbutics in colonies.

205. The governor of a British possession shall have the power in that possession—

(*a*) of appointing medical inspectors of seamen, of charging fees for medical examinations by those inspectors, and of determining the remuneration to be paid to those inspectors; and,

(*b*) subject to the laws of that possession, to make regulations concerning the supply in that possession of anti-scorbutics for the use of ships, and anti-scorbutics duly supplied in accordance with those regulations shall be deemed to be fit and proper for the use of ships.

Inspection of provisions and water for crew of certain ships.

206. (1) In the case of ships trading or going from any port of the United Kingdom through the Suez Canal, or round the Cape of Good Hope or Cape Horn, the barrels of beef and pork, the preserved meat and vegetables in tins, and the casks of flour or biscuits, intended for the use of the crew of any such ship shall be inspected by such officer and in such manner as rules under this section direct, but before shipment whenever practicable, and, if in the opinion of the inspecting officer they are fit for that use, that officer shall certify the same accordingly in manner directed by such rules.

(2) The inspecting officer may at any time proceed on board any such ship to ascertain whether the stores and water provided have been duly inspected, or, if not, whether they are of a quality fit for the use of the crew of the ship, and if he finds the same not to have been inspected, and to be deficient in quality, the ship shall be detained until the defects are remedied to his satisfaction.

(3) No fee for an inspection under this section shall be levied on the ship.

(4) The Board of Trade may make rules for carrying into effect this section, but all such rules shall be laid before a Parliament within three weeks after they are made, if Parliament be then sitting, and if Parliament be not then sitting, within three weeks after the beginning of the then next meeting of Parliament, and shall not come into operation until they have lain for forty days before both Houses of Parliament during the session of Parliament.

(5) The Board of Trade may appoint officers for the purposes of any inspection under this section, and may, with the concurrence of the Treasury, assign them remuneration to be paid out of moneys provided by Parliament.

Expenses of medical attendance in case of illness.

207. (1) If the master of, or a seaman or apprentice belonging to, a ship receives any hurt or injury in the service of the ship, the expense of providing the necessary surgical and medical advice and attendance and medicine, and also the expenses of the maintenance of the master, seaman, or apprentice until he is cured, or dies, or is brought back, if shipped in the United Kingdom, to a port of the United Kingdom, or if shipped in a British possession to a port of that possession, and of his conveyance to the port, and in case of death the expense (if any) of his burial, shall be defrayed by the owner of the ship, without any deduction on that account from his wages.

(2) If the master or a seaman or apprentice is on account of any illness temporarily removed from his ship for the purpose of preventing infection, or otherwise for the convenience of the ship, and subsequently returns to his duty, the expense of the removal and of providing the necessary advice and attendance and medicine and of his maintenance while away from the ship shall be defrayed in like manner.

(3) The expense of all medicines, surgical and medical advice, and attendance, given to a master, seaman, or apprentice whilst on board his ship shall be defrayed in like manner.

(4) If a seaman or apprentice is ill and has, through the neglect of the master or owner of the ship, not been provided with proper provisions and water according to his agreement, or with such medicines, medical stores, anti-scorbutics, or accommodation, as are required by this Act, then the owner or master, unless it can be proved that the illness has been produced by other causes, shall be liable to pay all expenses (not exceeding on the whole three months' wages) properly and necessarily incurred by reason of the illness either by the seaman himself or by the Crown or any parochial or local authority on his behalf, and those expenses may be recovered as if they were wages duly earned, but this provision shall not affect any further liability of the master or owner for the neglect, or any other remedies possessed by the seaman or apprentice.

(5) In all other cases any reasonable expenses duly incurred by the owner for any seaman in respect of illness, and also any reasonable expenses duly incurred by the owner in respect of the burial of any seaman or apprentice who dies whilst on service, shall, if duly proved, be deducted from the wages of the seaman or apprentice.

Recovery of expenses from owner.

208. (1) If any of the expenses attendant on the illness, hurt, or injury of a seaman or apprentice, which are to be paid under this Act by the master or owner, are paid by any British consular officer or other person on behalf of the Crown, or if any other expenses in respect of the illness, hurt, or injury of any seaman or apprentice whose wages are not accounted for under this Act to that officer, are so paid, those expenses shall be repaid to the officer or other person by the master of the ship.

(2) If the expenses are not so repaid, the amount thereof shall with costs be a charge upon the ship, and be recoverable from the master or from the owner of the ship for the time being, as a debt to the Crown, either by ordinary process of law or in the same court and manner as wages due to seamen.

(3) In any proceeding for such recovery, a certificate of the facts, signed by the said officer or other person, together with such vouchers (if any) as the case requires, shall be sufficient proof that the said expenses were duly paid by that officer or other person.

Certain ships to carry medical practitioners.

209. (1) Every foreign-going ship, having one hundred persons or upwards on board, shall carry on board as part of her complement some duly qualified medical practitioner, and if she does not the owner shall for every voyage of the ship made without a duly qualified medical practitioner be liable to a fine not exceeding one hundred pounds.

(2) Nothing in this section shall apply to an emigrant ship within the meaning of the Third Part of this Act.

210. (1) Every place in any British ship occupied by seamen or apprentices, and appropriated to their use, shall have for each of those seamen or apprentices a space of not less than seventy-two cubic feet, and of not less than twelve superficial feet measured on the deck or floor of that place, and shall be subject to the regulations in the Sixth Schedule to this Act, and those regulations shall have effect as part of this section, and if any of the foregoing requirements of this section is not complied with in the case of any ship, the owner of the ship shall for each offence be liable to a fine not exceeding twenty pounds. Accommodation for seamen.

(2) Every place so occupied and appropriated shall be kept free from goods and stores of any kind not being the personal property of the crew in use during the voyage, and if any such place is not so kept free, the master shall forfeit and pay to each seaman or apprentice lodged in that place the sum of one shilling for each day during which, after complaint has been made to him by any two or more of the seamen so lodged, it is not so kept free.

(3) Such fees as the Board of Trade fix shall be paid in respect of an inspection for the purposes of this section, not exceeding the fees specified in the Sixth Schedule to this Act.

Facilities for making Complaint.

211. (1) If a seaman or apprentice whilst on board ship states to the master of the ship his desire to make a complaint to a justice of the peace, British consular officer, or officer in command of one of Her Majesty's ships, against the master or any of the crew, the master shall, so soon as the service of the ship will permit,— Facilities for making complaint.

(*a*) if the ship is then at a place where there is such a justice or officer as aforesaid, after such statement, and

(*b*) if the ship is not then at such a place, after her first arrival at such a place,

allow the complainant to go ashore or send him ashore in proper custody or, in the case of complaint to a naval officer, to the ship of such officer, so that he may be enabled to take his complaint.

(2) If the master of a ship fails without reasonable cause to comply with this section, he shall for each offence be liable to a fine not exceeding ten pounds.

Protection of Seamen from Imposition.

212. Subject to the provisions of this Act an assignment or sale of salvage payable to a seaman or apprentice to the sea service made prior to the Assignment of sale of salvage invalid.

accruing thereof shall not bind the person making the same; and a power of attorney or authority for the receipt of any such salvage shall not be irrevocable.

No debt exceeding 5s. recoverable till end of voyage.

213. A debt exceeding in amount five shillings incurred by any seaman after he is engaged to serve shall not be recoverable until the service agreed for is concluded.

Seamen's lodging-houses.

214. (1) A local authority hereinafter mentioned whose district includes a seaport may, with the approval of the Board of Trade, make bye-laws relating to seamen's lodging-houses in their district, and those bye-laws shall be binding upon all persons keeping houses in which seamen are lodged and upon the owners thereof and persons employed therein.

(2) The bye-laws shall amongst other things provide for the licensing, inspection, and sanitary conditions of seamen's lodging-houses for the publication of the fact of a house being licensed, for the due execution of the bye-laws for preventing the obstruction of persons engaged in securing that execution, for the preventing of persons not duly licensed holding themselves out as keeping or purporting to keep licensed houses, and for the exclusion from licensed houses of persons of improper character, and shall impose sufficient fines not exceeding fifty pounds for the breach of any bye-law.

(3) The bye-laws shall come into force from a date therein named, and shall be published in the London Gazette and in one newspaper at the least circulating in the district, and designated by the Board of Trade.

(4) If the local authority do not within a time in each case named by the Board of Trade make, revoke, or alter, any bye-laws under this section, the Board of Trade may do so.

(5) Whenever Her Majesty in Council orders that in any district or any part thereof none but persons duly licensed in pursuance of bye-laws under this section shall keep seamen's lodging-houses or let lodgings to seamen from a date therein named, a person acting in contravention of that order shall for each offence be liable to a fine not exceeding one hundred pounds.

(6) A local authority may defray all expenses incurred in the execution of this section out of any funds at their disposal as sanitary authority, and fines recovered for a contravention of this section or of any bye-law under this section shall be paid to such authority and added to those funds.

(7) In this section the expression "local authority" means in the administrative county of London the county council, and elsewhere in England the local authority under the Public Health Acts, and in Scotland the local authority under the Public Health (Scotland) Act, 1867, and the Acts amending the same, and in Ireland the local authority under the Public Health (Ireland) 30 & 31 Vict. c. 101. 41 & 42 Vict. c. 52.

Act, 1878, and the expression "district" means the area under the authority of such local authority.

215. If a person demands or receives from a seaman or apprentice to the sea service payment in respect of his board or lodging in the house of that person for a longer period than the seaman or apprentice has actually resided or boarded therein, that person shall for each offence be liable to a fine not exceeding ten pounds.

Penalty for overcharges by lodging-house keepers.

216. (1) If a person receives or takes into his possession or under his control any money or effects of a seaman or apprentice to the sea service, and does not return the same or pay the value thereof, when required by the seaman or apprentice, subject to such deduction as may be justly due to him from the seaman or apprentice in respect of board or lodging or otherwise, or absconds therewith, he shall for each offence be liable to a fine not exceeding ten pounds.

Penalty for detaining seamen's effects.

(2) A court of summary jurisdiction may, besides inflicting a fine, by summary order direct the amount of the money, or the value of the effects, subject to such deduction as aforesaid (if any) or the effects themselves, to be forthwith paid or delivered to the seaman or apprentice.

217. If within twenty-four hours after the arrival of a ship at a port in the United Kingdom, a person then being on board the ship solicits a seaman to become a lodger at the house of a person letting lodgings for hire, or takes out of the ship any effects of a seaman, except under the personal direction of the seaman, and with the permission of the master, he shall for each offence be liable to a fine not exceeding five pounds.

Penalty for solicitations by lodging-house keepers.

218. Where a ship is about to arrive, is arriving, or has arrived at the end of her voyage, and any person, not being in Her Majesty's service or not being duly authorised by law for the purpose—

Penalty for being on board ship without permission before seamen leave.

(a) goes on board the ship, without the permission of the master, before the seamen lawfully leave the ship at the end of their engagement, or are discharged (whichever last happens); or

(b) being on board the ship, remains there after being warned to leave by the master, or by a police-officer, or by any officer of the Board of Trade or of the Customs,

that person shall for each offence be liable to a fine not exceeding twenty pounds, or, at the discretion of the court, to imprisonment for any term not exceeding six months; and the master of the ship or any officer of the Board of Trade may take him into custody; and deliver him up forthwith to a constable to be taken before a court capable of taking cognizance of the offence.

Application of provisions of previous section to foreign ships.

219. Whenever it is made to appear to Her Majesty that the Government of a foreign country—

(*a*) has provided that unauthorised persons going on board British ships which are about to arrive or have arrived within its territorial jurisdiction shall be subject to provisions similar to those of the last preceding section which are applicable to persons going on board British ships at the end of their voyages; and

(*b*) is desirous that the provisions of the said section shall apply to unauthorised persons going on board ships of that foreign country within British territorial jurisdiction,

Her Majesty in Council may order that those provisions shall apply to the ships of that foreign country, and have effect as if the ships of that country arriving, about to arrive, or having arrived at the end of their voyage, were British ships.

Provisions as to Discipline

Misconduct endangering life or ship.

220. If a master, seaman, or apprentice belonging to a British ship, by wilful breach of duty or by neglect of duty or by reason of drunkenness,—

(*a*) does any act tending to the immediate loss, destruction, or serious damage of the ship, or tending immediately to endanger the life or limb of a person belonging to or on board the ship; or

(*b*) refuses or omits to do any lawful act proper and requisite to be done by him for preserving the ship from immediate loss, destruction, or serious damage, or for preserving any person belonging to or on board the ship from immediate danger to life or limb,

he shall in respect of each offence be guilty of a misdemeanour.

Desertion and absence without leave.

221. If a seaman lawfully engaged, or an apprentice to the sea service commits any of the following offences, he shall be liable to be punished summarily as follows:—

(*a*) If he deserts from his ship he shall be guilty of the offence of desertion, and be liable to forfeit all or any part of the effects he leaves on board, and of the wages which he has then earned, and also, if the desertion takes place abroad, of the wages he may earn in any other ship in which he may be employed until his next return to the United Kingdom, and to satisfy any excess of wages paid by the master or owner of the ship to any substitute engaged in his place at a higher rate of wages than the rate stipulated to be paid to him; and also, except in the United Kingdom, he shall be liable to imprisonment for any period not exceeding twelve weeks with or without hard labour;

(*b*) If he neglects, or refuses without reasonable cause, to join his ship, or to proceed to sea in his ship, or is absent without leave at any time within twenty-four hours of the ship sailing from a port, either at the commencement or during the progress of a voyage, or is absent at any time without leave and without sufficient reason from his ship or from his duty, he shall, if the offence does not amount to desertion, or is not treated as such by the master, be guilty of the offence of absence without leave and be liable to forfeit out of his wages a sum not exceeding two days' pay, and in addition for every twenty-four hours of absence, either a sum not exceeding six days' pay, or any expenses properly incurred in hiring a substitute; and also, except in the United Kingdom, he shall be liable to imprisonment for any period not exceeding ten weeks with or without hard labour.

222. (1) If in the United Kingdom a seaman or apprentice is guilty of the offence of desertion or of absence without leave, or otherwise absents himself from his ship without leave, the master, any mate, the owner, ship's husband, or consignee of the ship, may, with or without the assistance of the local police-officers or constables, convey him on board his ship, and those officers and constables are hereby directed to give assistance if required: Conveyance of deserter on board ship.

(2) Provided that if the seaman or apprentice so requires he shall first be taken before some court capable of taking cognizance of the matter to be dealt with according to law.

(3) If it appears to the court before whom the case is brought that the seaman or apprentice has been conveyed on board or taken before the court on improper or insufficient grounds, that court may inflict on the master, mate, owner, ship's husband, or consignee, as the case may be, a fine not exceeding twenty pounds; but the infliction of that fine shall be a bar to any action, for false imprisonment in respect of the arrest.

223. (1) If out of the United Kingdom, either at the commencement or during the progress of any voyage, a seaman or apprentice is guilty of the offence of desertion or of absence without leave, or otherwise absents himself from his ship without leave, the master, any mate, the owner, ship's husband, or consignee, may in any place in Her Majesty's dominions out of the United Kingdom, with or without the assistance of the local police-officers or constables (and those officers and constables are hereby directed to give assistance if required), and also at any place out of Her Majesty's dominions, if and so far as the laws in force at that place will permit, arrest him without first procuring a warrant. Provisions as to arrest and imprisonment applying out of the United Kingdom.

(2) A person so arresting a seaman or apprentice may in any case, and shall in case the seaman or apprentice so requires and it is practicable, convey him before some court capable of taking cognizance of the matter, to be dealt with according to law, and for that purpose may detain him in custody for a period not exceeding twenty-four hours, or such shorter time as may be necessary; but if the seaman or apprentice does not require to be so taken before a court, or if there is no such court at or near the place, the person arresting him may at once convey him on board his ship.

(3) If it appears to the court before whom the case is brought that an arrest under this section has been made on improper or on insufficient grounds, the master, mate, owner, ship's husband, or consignee who made the arrest, or caused it to be made, shall be liable to a fine not exceeding twenty pounds; but the infliction of that fine shall be a bar to any action for false imprisonment in respect of the arrest.

(4) If out of the United Kingdom, a seaman or apprentice is imprisoned for having been guilty of the offence of desertion or of absence without leave, or for having committed any other breach of discipline, and during his imprisonment and before his engagement is at an end, his services are required on board his ship, a justice of the peace may, on the application of the master or of the owner or his agent, notwithstanding that the period of imprisonment is not at an end, cause the seaman or apprentice to be conveyed on board his ship for the purpose of proceeding on the voyage, or to be delivered to the master or any mate of the ship, or to the owner or his agent, to be by them so conveyed.

Power of Court to order offender to be taken on board ship.

224. (1) Where a seaman or apprentice is brought before a court on the ground of the offence of desertion, or of absence without leave, or of otherwise absenting himself without leave, the court, if the master or the owner or his agent so require, may (and if out of the United Kingdom in lieu of committing him to prison) cause him to be conveyed on board his ship for the purpose of proceeding on the voyage or deliver him to the master, or any mate of the ship, or the owner, or his agent, to be by them so conveyed, and may in such case order any costs and expenses properly incurred by or on behalf of the master or owner by reason of the offence to be paid by the offender, and, if necessary, to be deducted from any wages which he has then earned, or by virtue of his then existing engagement may afterwards earn.

(2) If in the United Kingdom a seaman or apprentice to the sea service intends to absent himself from his ship or his duty, he may give notice of his intention, either to the owner or to the master of the ship, not less than forty-

eight hours before the time at which he ought to be on board his ship; and in the event of that notice being given, the court shall not exercise any of the powers conferred by this section for causing the offender to be conveyed on board his ship.

225. (1) If a seaman lawfully engaged or an apprentice to the sea service commits any of the following offences, in this Act referred to as offences against discipline, he shall be liable to be punished summarily as follows; that is to say,— General offences against discipline.

(*a*) If he quits the ship without leave after her arrival at her port of delivery, and before she is placed in security, he shall be liable to forfeit out of his wages a sum not exceeding one month's pay:

(*b*) If he is guilty of wilful disobedience to any lawful command, he shall be liable to imprisonment for a period not exceeding four weeks, and also, at the discretion of the court, to forfeit out of his wages a sum not exceeding two days' pay:

(*c*) If he is guilty of continued wilful disobedience to lawful commands or continued wilful neglect of duty, he shall be liable to imprisonment for a period not exceeding twelve weeks, and also, at the discretion of the court, to forfeit for every twenty-four hours' continuance of disobedience or neglect, either a sum not exceeding six days' pay, or any expenses properly incurred in hiring a substitute:

(*d*) If he assaults the master or any mate or certificated engineer of the ship, he shall be liable to imprisonment for a period not exceeding twelve weeks:

(*e*) If he combines with any of the crew to disobey lawful commands, or to neglect duty, or to impede the navigation of the ship or the progress of the voyage, he shall be liable to imprisonment for a period not exceeding twelve weeks:

(*f*) If he wilfully damages his ship, or embezzles or wilfully damages any of her stores or cargo, he shall be liable to forfeit out of his wages a sum equal to the loss thereby sustained, and also, at the discretion of the court, to imprisonment for a period not exceeding twelve weeks:

(*g*) If he is convicted of any act of smuggling, whereby loss or damage is occasioned to the master or owner of the ship, he shall be liable to pay to that master or owner a sum sufficient to reimburse the loss or damage; and the whole or a proportionate part of his wages may be retained in satisfaction or on account of that liability, without prejudice to any further remedy.

(2) Any imprisonment under this section may be with or without hard labour.

Summary remedies not to affect other remedies.

226. Nothing in the last preceding section or in the sections relating to the offences of desertion or absence without leave shall take away or limit any remedy by action or by summary procedure before justices which an owner or master would but for those provisions have for any breach of contract in respect of the matters constituting an offence under those sections, but an owner or master shall not be compensated more than once in respect of the same damage.

Penalty for false statement as to last ship or name.

227. (1) If a seaman on or before being engaged wilfully and fraudulently makes a false statement of the name of his last ship or alleged last ship, or wilfully and fraudulently makes a false statement of his own name, he shall for each offence be liable to a fine not exceeding five pounds.

(2) The fine may be deducted from any wages the seaman may earn by virtue of his engagement as aforesaid, and shall, subject to reimbursement of the loss and expenses (if any) occasioned by any desertion previous to the engagement, be paid and applied in the same manner as other fines under this Act.

Entry of offences in official log.

228. If any offence, within the meaning of this Act, of desertion or absence without leave or against discipline is committed, or if any act of misconduct is committed for which the offender's agreement imposes a fine and it is intended to enforce the fine,

(*a*) an entry of the offence or act shall be made in the official log book and signed by the master and also by the mate or one of the crew; and

(*b*) the offender, if still in the ship, shall before the next subsequent arrival of the ship at any port, or if she is at the time in port her departure therefrom, either be furnished with a copy of the entry or have the same read over distinctly and audibly to him, and may thereupon make such reply thereto as he thinks fit; and

(*c*) a statement of a copy of the entry having been so furnished, or of the entry having been so read over, and, in either case, the reply (if any) made by the offender, shall likewise be entered and signed in manner aforesaid; and

(*d*) in any subsequent legal proceeding the entries by this section required shall, if practicable, be produced or proved, and in default of that production or proof the court hearing the case may, in their discretion, refuse to receive evidence of the offence or act of misconduct.

229. (1) In every case of desertion from a ship in any port abroad the master shall produce the entry of the desertion in the official log book to the person by this Act authorised to grant certificates for leaving seamen behind abroad; and that person shall thereupon make and certify a copy of the entry.

Entries and certificates of desertion abroad.

(2) The copy shall be forthwith transmitted to the Registrar-General of Shipping and Seamen in England by the person by whom the copy is made and certified, if he is a public functionary, and if he is not, by the master, and shall be admissible in evidence in manner provided by this Act.

230. A superintendent shall keep at his office a list of the seamen who, to the best of his knowledge and belief, have deserted or failed to join their ships after signing an agreement to proceed to sea in them, and shall on request show the list to a master of a ship, and shall not be liable in respect of any entry made in good faith in the list.

Register of deserters.

231. (1) Whenever a question arises whether the wages of any seaman or apprentice are forfeited for desertion from a ship, it shall be sufficient for the person insisting on the forfeiture to show that the seaman or apprentice was duly engaged in or belonged to the ship, and either that he left the ship before the completion of the voyage or engagement, or, if the voyage was to terminate in the United Kingdom and the ship has not returned, that he is absent from her, and that an entry of his desertion has been duly made in the official log book.

Facilities for proving desertion in proceedings for forfeiture of wages.

(2) The desertion shall thereupon, so far as relates to any forfeiture of wages under this Part of this Act, be deemed to be proved, unless the seaman or apprentice can produce a proper certificate of discharge, or can otherwise show to the satisfaction of the court that he had sufficient reasons for leaving his ship.

232. (1) Where any wages or effects are under this Act forfeited for desertion from a ship, those effects may be converted in to money, and those wages and effects, or the money arising from the conversion of the effects, shall be applied towards reimbursing the expenses caused by the desertion to the master or owner of the ship, and subject to that reimbursement shall be paid into the Exchequer, and carried to the Consolidated Fund.

Application of forfeitures.

(2) For the purpose of such reimbursement, the master or the owner, or his agent may, if the wages are earned subsequently to the desertion, recover them in the same manner as the deserter could have recovered them if not

forfeited; and the court in any legal proceeding relating to such wages may order them to be paid accordingly.

(3) Where wages are forfeited under the foregoing provisions of this Act in any case other than for desertion, the forfeiture shall, in the absence of any specific provision to the contrary, be for the benefit of the master or owner by whom the wages are payable.

Decision of questions of forfeiture and deductions in suits for wages.

233. Any question concerning the forfeiture of or deductions from the wages of a seaman or apprentice may be determined in any proceeding lawfully instituted with respect to those wages, notwithstanding that the offence in respect of which the question arises, though by this Act made punishable by imprisonment as well as forfeiture, has not been made subject of any criminal proceeding.

Ascertainment of amount of forfeiture out of wages.

234. If a seaman contracts for wages by the voyage or by the run or by the share, and not by the month or other stated period of time, the amount of forfeiture to be incurred under this Act shall be an amount bearing the same proportion to the whole wages or share, as a month or any other period hereinbefore mentioned in fixing the amount of such forfeiture (as the case may be) bears to the whole time spent in the voyage or run; and if the whole time spent in the voyage or run does not exceed the period for which the pay is to be forfeited, the forfeiture shall extend to the whole wages or share.

Deduction from wages and payments to superintendents, etc., of fines.

235. (1) Every fine imposed on a seaman for any act of misconduct for which his agreement imposes a fine shall be deducted and paid as follows; that is to say,—

(*a*) if the offender is discharged in the United Kingdom, and the offence, and the entry in the log book required by this Act in respect thereof, are proved to the satisfaction, in the case of a foreign-going ship, of the superintendent before whom the offender is discharged, and in the case of a home-trade ship of the superintendent at or nearest the port at which the crew are discharged, the master or owner shall deduct the fine from the wages of the offender, and pay it to the superintendent;

(*b*) if the offender enters Her Majesty's naval service or is discharged abroad before the final discharge of the crew in the United Kingdom, and the offence and the entry as aforesaid are proved to the satisfaction of the officer in command of the ship he so enters or of the consular officer or other person by whose sanction he is discharged, as the case may be, the fine shall be deducted as aforesaid, and an entry made in the official log book of the ship and signed by the officer or other person to whose satisfaction the offence is proved; and

(*c*) on the return of the ship to the United Kingdom the master or owner shall pay the fine to the superintendent before whom the crew is discharged, or in the case of a home-trade ship to the superintendent at or nearest the port at which the crew are discharged.

(2) If a master or owner fails without reasonable cause so to pay the fine, he shall for each offence be liable to a fine not exceeding six times the amount of the fine not so paid.

(3) An act of misconduct for which any fine has been inflicted and paid by, or deducted from the wages of, the seaman shall not be otherwise punished under this Act.

Penalty for enticing to desert and harbouring deserters.

236. (1) If a person by any means whatever persuades or attempts to persuade a seaman or apprentice to neglect or refuse to join or proceed to sea in or to desert from his ship, or otherwise to absent himself from his duty, he shall for each offence in respect of each seaman or apprentice be liable to a fine not exceeding ten pounds.

(2) If a person wilfully harbours or secretes a seaman or apprentice who has wilfully neglected or refused to join, or has deserted from his ship, knowing or having reason to believe the seaman or apprentice to have so done, he shall for every seaman or apprentice so harboured or secreted be liable to a fine not exceeding twenty pounds.

Penalty on stowaways, and discipline of stowaways and seamen carried under compulsion.

237. (1) If a person secretes himself and goes to sea in a ship without the consent of either the owner, consignee, or master, or of a mate, or of the person in charge of the ship, or of any other person entitled to give that consent, he shall be liable to a fine not exceeding twenty pounds, or, in the discretion of the court, to imprisonment, with or without hard labour, for a period not exceeding four weeks.

(2) Every seafaring person whom the master of a ship is, under the authority of this or any other Act compelled to take on board and convey, and every person who goes to sea in a ship without such consent as aforesaid, shall, so long as he remains in the ship, be deemed to belong to the ship, and be subject to the same laws and regulations for preserving discipline, and to the same fines and punishments for offences constituting or tending to a breach of discipline, as if he were a member of, and had signed the agreement with, the crew.

Deserters from foreign ships.

238. (1) Where it appears to Her Majesty that due facilities are or will be given by the government of any foreign country for recovering and apprehending seamen who desert from British merchant ships in that country, Her Majesty may, by Order in Council, stating that such facilities are or will be given, declare that this section shall apply in the case of such foreign country, subject to any limitations, conditions, and qualifications contained in the Order.

(2) Where this section applies in the case of any foreign country, and a seaman or apprentice, not being a slave, deserts when within any of Her Majesty's dominions from a merchant ship belonging to a subject of that country, any court, justice, or officer that would have had cognisance of the matter if the seaman or apprentice had deserted from a British ship shall, on the application of a consular officer of the foreign country, aid in apprehending the deserter, and for that purpose may, on information given on oath, issue a warrant for his apprehension, and, on proof of the desertion, order him to be conveyed on board his ship or delivered to the master or mate of his ship, or to the owner of the ship or his agent, to be so conveyed; and any such warrant or order may be executed accordingly.

(3) If any person harbours or secretes any deserter liable to be apprehended under this section, knowing or having reason to believe that he has deserted, that person shall for each offence be liable to a fine not exceeding ten pounds.

Official Logs.

Official logs to be kept and to be evidence.

239. (1) An official log shall be kept in every ship (except ships employed exclusively in trading between ports on the coasts of Scotland) in the appropriate form for that ship approved by the Board of Trade.

(2) The Board of Trade shall approve forms of official log books, which may be different for different classes of ships, so that each such form shall contain proper spaces for the entries required by this Act.

(3) The official log may, at the discretion of the master or owner, be kept distinct from, or united with, the ordinary ship's log, so that in all cases the spaces in the official log book be duly filled up.

(4) An entry required by this Act in an official log book shall be made as soon as possible after the occurrence to which it relates, and if not made on the same day as that occurrence shall be made and dated so as to show the date of the occurrence and of the entry respecting it; and if made in respect of an occurrence happening before the arrival of the ship at her final port of discharge shall not be made more than twenty-four hours after that arrival.

(5) Every entry in the official log book shall be signed by the master, and by the mate, or some other of the crew, and also—

(*a*) if it is an entry of illness, injury, or death, shall be signed by the surgeon, or medical practitioner on board (if any); and

(*b*) if it is an entry of wages due to, or of the sale of the effects of, a seaman or apprentice who dies, shall be signed by the mate and by some member of the crew besides the master; and

(*c*) if it is an entry of wages due to a seaman who enters Her Majesty's naval service, shall be signed by the seaman, or by the officer authorised to receive the seaman into that service.

(6) Every entry made in an official log book in manner provided by this Act shall be admissible in evidence.

Entries required in official log book.

240. The master of a ship for which an official log is required shall enter or cause to be entered in the official log book the following matters, (that is to say,)

(1) Every conviction by a legal tribunal of a member of his crew, and the punishment inflicted:

(2) Every offence committed by a member of his crew for which it is intended to prosecute, or to enforce a forfeiture, or to exact a fine, together with such statement concerning the copy or reading over of that entry, and concerning the reply (if any) made to the charge, as is by this Act required:

(3) Every offence for which punishment is inflicted on board and the punishment inflicted:

(4) A statement of the conduct, character, and qualifications of each of his crew, or a statement that he declines to give an opinion on those particulars:

(5) Every case of illness or injury happening to a member of the crew, with the nature thereof, and the medical treatment adopted (if any):

(6) Every marriage taking place on board, with the names and ages of the parties:

(7) The name of every seaman or apprentice who ceases to be a member of the crew, otherwise than by death, with the place, time, manner, and cause thereof:

(8) The wages due to any seaman who enters Her Majesty's naval service during the voyage:

(9) The wages due to any seaman or apprentice who dies during the voyage and the gross amount of all deductions to be made therefrom:

(10) The sale of the effects of any seaman or apprentice who dies during the voyage, including a statement of each article sold, and the sum received for it :

(11) Every collision with any other ship, and the circumstances under which the same occurred: and

(12) Any other matter directed by this Act to be entered.

Offences in respect of official logs.

241. (1) If an official log book is not kept in the manner required by this Act, or if an entry directed by this Act to be made therein is not made at the time and in the manner directed by this Act, the master shall for each offence be liable to the specific fine in this Act mentioned in respect thereof, or where there is no such specific fine, to a fine not exceeding five pounds.

(2) If any person makes or procures to be made, or assists in making, any entry in an official log book in respect of any occurrence happening previously to the arrival of the ship at her final port of discharge more than twenty-four hours after that arrival, he shall for each offence be liable to a fine not exceeding thirty pounds.

(3) If any person wilfully destroys or mutilates or renders illegible any entry in an official log book or wilfully makes or procures to be made or assists in making a false or fraudulent entry in or omission from an official log book, he shall in respect of each offence be guilty of a misdemeanor.

Delivery of official logs to superintendent of mercantile marine office.

242. (1) The master of every foreign-going ship shall within forty-eight hours after the ship's arrival at her final port of destination in the United Kingdom or upon the discharge of the crew, whichever first happens, deliver the official log book of the voyage to the superintendent before whom the crew is discharged.

(2) The master or owner of every home-trade ship for which an official log is required to be kept shall within twenty-one days of the thirtieth day of June and the thirty-first day of December in every year, transmit or deliver the official log book for the preceding half-year to some superintendent in the United Kingdom.

(3) If the master or owner of a ship fails without reasonable cause to comply with this section, he shall be subject to the same consequences and liabilities to which he is subject for the non-delivery of the list of the crew required to be delivered under this Part of this Act.

Official logs to be sent home in case of transfer of ship, and in case of loss.

243. (1) Where by reason of transfer of ownership or change of employment of a ship, the official log ceases to be required in respect of the ship or to be required at the same date, the master or owner of the ship shall, if the ship is then in the United Kingdom, within one month, and if she is elsewhere within six months, after the cessation, deliver or transmit to the superintendent at the port to which the ship belonged the official log book (if any) duly made out to the time of the cessation.

(2) If a ship is lost or abandoned, the master or owner thereof shall, if practicable, and as soon as possible, deliver or transmit to the superintendent at the port to which the ship belonged the official log book (if any) duly made out to the time of the loss or abandonment.

(3) If the master or owner of a ship fails without reasonable cause to comply with this section, he shall for each offence be liable to a fine not exceeding ten pounds.

Local Marine Boards.

Continuance and constitution of local marine board.

244. (1) There shall be local marine boards for carrying into effect this Act under the superintendence of the Board of Trade at those ports of the United Kingdom at which local marine boards are now established and at such other places as the Board of Trade appoint for the purpose.

(2) Every local marine board shall be constituted in manner specified in the Seventh Schedule to this Act, and the regulations in that schedule shall apply to the Board and elections thereof.

(3) A local marine board may regulate the mode in which their meetings are to be held and their business is to be conducted, including the fixing of a quorum, not being less than three.

(4) A local marine board shall keep minutes of their proceedings in the manner (if any) prescribed by the Board of Trade.

(5) Any Act or proceedings of a local marine board shall not be vitiated or prejudiced by reason of any irregularity in the election of any of the members, or of any error in the list of voters entitled to vote at the election, or of any irregularity in making or revising the list, or by reason of any person not duly qualified acting on the board, or of any vacancy in the board.

Control of Board of Trade over local marine boards.

245. (1) Every local marine board shall make and send to the Board of Trade such reports and returns as the Board of Trade require; and all minutes, books, and documents of, or used or kept by, any local marine board or by any superintendent, or by any examiner or other officer or servant under the control of any local marine board, shall be open to the inspection of the Board of Trade and their officers.

(2) If any local marine board, by reason of any election not being held or of the simultaneous resignation or continued non-attendance of all or the greater part of the members, or from any other cause, fail to meet or to discharge their duties, the Board of Trade may, in their discretion, either take

into their own hands the performance of the duties of the local marine board until the next triennial appointment and election thereof, or direct that a new appointment and election of the local marine board shall take place immediately.

(3) If on complaint made to the Board of Trade it appears to them that at any port, any appointments or arrangements made by the local marine board under this Act are not such as to meet the wants of the port, or are in any respect unsatisfactory or improper, the Board of Trade may annul, alter, or rectify the same, as they think expedient, having regard to the intention of this Act and to the wants of the port.

Mercantile Marine Offices.

Establishment and control of mercantile marine offices.

246. (1) A mercantile marine office, with the requisite buildings, property, superintendents, deputies, clerks, and servants shall be maintained at every port of the United Kingdom where there is a local marine board, and may be established and maintained at such other ports as the Board of Trade determine.

(2) In every port where there is a local marine board the board shall procure the said buildings and property, and appoint and remove the superintendents, deputies, clerks, and servants, and regulate the business at, and have the control of, the mercantile marine office, subject as follows:—

(*a*) The sanction of the Board of Trade shall be necessary, so far as regards the number of persons to be so appointed, and the amount of their salaries and wages, and all other expenses:

(*b*) The Board of Trade shall have the immediate control of every such office, as far as regards the receipt and payment of money thereat, and every person appointed to be an officer in any such office shall, before entering upon his duties, give such security (if any) for the due performance thereof as the Board of Trade require:

(*c*) If the Board of Trade have reason to believe that any superintendent, deputy, clerk, or servant appointed by a local marine board does not properly discharge his duties, they may cause the case to be investigated, and if they think fit remove him from his office, and provide for the proper performance of his duties until another person is duly appointed in his place:

(*d*) The Board of Trade may appoint any superintendent of, or other person connected with, any sailors' home in the port of London to be a superintendent with any necessary deputies, clerks and servants, and may appoint an office in any such home to be a mercantile marine office, and all persons and offices so appointed shall be subject to the immediate control of the Board of Trade, and not of the local marine board of the port.

(3) At any port at which the business of a mercantile marine office is conducted otherwise than under a local marine board, the Board of Trade may:—

(*a*) at any time establish a mercantile marine office and for that purpose procure the requisite buildings and property, and appoint and remove all the requisite superintendents, deputies, clerks, and servants, or

(*b*) direct, with the consent of the Commissioners of Customs, that the whole or any part of the business of a mercantile marine office shall be conducted at the custom house, and there upon the custom house shall be a mercantile marine office for the purposes of that business, and any officer of customs there appointed in that behalf by the Board of Trade shall be a superintendent or deputy within the meaning of this Act.

Business of mercantile marine offices.

247. (1) It shall be the general business of superintendents of mercantile marine offices (in this Act referred to as superintendents)—

to afford facilities for engaging seamen by keeping registries of their names and characters:

to superintend and facilitate the engagement and discharge of seamen in manner in this Act provided:

to provide means for securing the presence on board at the proper times of the seamen who are so engaged:

to facilitate the making of apprenticeships to the sea service : and

to perform such other duties relating to seamen, apprentices, and merchant ships as are by or in pursuance of this Act, or any Act relating to merchant shipping, committed to them.

(2) Any act done by, to or before a deputy duly appointed shall have the same effect as if done by, to or before a superintendent.

Embezzlement by officers of local marine boards.

248. (1) A person appointed to any office or service by or under a local marine board shall be deemed to be a clerk or servant within the meaning of section sixty-eight of the Larceny Act, 1861 (relating to embezzlement).

& 25 Vict., 96.

(2) If any person so appointed to an office or service—

(*a*) fraudulently applies or disposes of any chattel, money, or valuable security received by him (whilst employed in such office or service) for or on account of any local marine board, or for or on account of any other public board or department, for his own use, or any use or purpose other than that for which the same was paid, entrusted to, or received by him, or

(*b*) fraudulently withholds, retains, or keeps back the same, or any part thereof, contrary to any lawful directions or instructions which he is required to obey in relation to his office or service aforesaid,

that person shall be guilty of embezzlement within the meaning of the said section sixty-eight of the Larceny Act, 1861. 24 & 25 Vict. c. 96.

(3) In any indictment under this section, it shall be sufficient to charge any such chattel, money, or valuable security as the property either of the local marine board by whom the person was appointed, or of the board or department for or on account of whom the same was received.

(4) Section seventy-one of the Larceny Act, 1861 (relating to the manner of charging embezzlement), shall apply as if an offence under this section were embezzlement under that Act.

Power to dispense with transaction of certain matters at mercantile marine offices.

249. The Board of Trade may dispense with the transaction in a mercantile marine office, or before a superintendent of any matters required by this Act to be so transacted, and thereupon those matters, if otherwise duly transacted, shall be as valid as if they were transacted in such an office or before a superintendent.

Prohibition on taking fees at mercantile marine office.

250. If a superintendent, deputy, clerk, or servant, in a mercantile marine office demands or receives save as provided by any Act, or authorised by the Board of Trade, any remuneration whatever, either directly or indirectly, for hiring or supplying any seaman for a ship or transacting any business which it is his duty to transact, he shall for every such offence be liable to a fine not exceeding twenty pounds, and also to dismissal from his office by the Board of Trade.

Registration of and Returns respecting Seamen.

Establishment of register office.

251. (1) There shall be maintained in the port of London, under the control of the Board of Trade, an office, called the General Register and Record Office of Seamen.

(2) The Board of Trade may appoint and remove a Registrar-General called "The Registrar-General of Shipping and Seamen," and such assistants, clerks, and servants as may be necessary, and, with the consent of the Treasury, regulate their salaries and allowances; and those salaries and allowances,

and all other necessary expenses, shall be paid out of moneys provided by Parliament.

(3) The Board of Trade may direct that the business of the said office at any of the outports be transacted at the mercantile marine office there, or with the consent of the Commissioners of Customs at the Custom House there, and may appoint the superintendent, or with the said consent some officer of customs, as the case may be, to conduct the business, and the business shall thereupon be conducted accordingly, subject to the immediate control of the Board of Trade.

252. The Registrar-General of Shipping and Seamen shall, by means of the documents transmitted to him in pursuance of this Act, and by any other means in his power, keep at his office a register of all persons who serve in ships subject to this Act. **Register of seamen.**

253. (1) The master— **Lists of the crew.**

(*a*) of a foreign-going ship whose crew is discharged in the United Kingdom, in whatever part of Her Majesty's dominions the ship is registered; and

(*b*) of a home-trade ship,

shall make out and sign a list in this Act referred to as the list of the crew, in a form approved by the Board of Trade, and containing the following particulars:—

(i) the number and date of the ship's register, and her registered tonnage:

(ii) the length and general nature of the voyage or employment:

(iii) the names, ages, and places of birth of all the crew including the master and apprentices; their ratings on board, their last ships or other employments, and the dates and places of their joining the ship:

(iv) the names of any of the crew who have ceased to belong to the ship, with the times, places, causes, and circumstances thereof:

(v) the names of any members of the crew who have been maimed or hurt, with the time, place, cause, and circumstances thereof:

(vi) the wages due at the time of death to any of the crew who have died:

(vii) the property belonging to any of the crew who have died, with a statement of the manner in which it has been dealt with, and the money for which any part of it has been sold:

(viii) any marriage which takes place on board with the date thereof, and the names and ages of the parties.

(2) The list of the crew—

(*a*) in the case of a foreign-going ship, shall be delivered by the master within forty-eight hours after the arrival of the ship at her final port of destination in the United Kingdom, or upon the discharge of the crew whichever first happens, to the superintendent before whom the crew is discharged; and

(*b*) in the case of a home-trade ship, shall be delivered or transmitted by the master or owner to some superintendent in the United Kingdom on or within twenty-one days after the thirtieth day of June and the thirty-first day of December in each year;

and the superintendent shall give to such master or owner a certificate of such delivery or transmission, and any such ship may be detained until the certificate is produced, and an officer of customs shall not clear inwards any foreign-going ship until the certificate is produced.

(3) If the master in the case of a foreign-going ship, or the master or owner in the case of a home-trade ship, fails without reasonable cause to deliver or transmit the list of the crew as required by this section, he shall for each offence be liable to a fine not exceeding five pounds.

Return of births and deaths in British ships.

254. (1) The master of every British ship, whether registered or not in the United Kingdom, shall, as soon as may be after the occurrence of the birth of a child or the death of a person happening on board his ship, record in his log book or otherwise the fact of the birth or death, and the particulars required by the Eighth Schedule to this Act to be registered concerning the birth or death, or such of them as may be known to him.

(2) The master of every British ship, upon its arrival at any port in the United Kingdom, or at such other time and place as the Board of Trade may with respect to any ship or class of ships direct, shall deliver or transmit, in such form as the Board of Trade direct a return of the facts recorded by him in respect to the birth of a child or the death of a person on board such ship, to the Registrar-General of Shipping and Seamen.

(3) Where the said return is directed by the Board of Trade to be delivered or transmitted upon the arrival of the ship or the discharge of the crew or otherwise at any port out of the United Kingdom, the Board of Trade may, if they think fit, direct that the return, instead of being delivered or transmitted to the Registrar-General of Shipping and Seamen, shall be delivered, and the same shall accordingly be delivered, if the port is in a British Possession, to the superintendent or chief officer of customs at such port, and if it is elsewhere, to the British consular officer at the port, and such superintendent or

officer shall transmit the same as soon as may be to the Registrar-General of Shipping and Seamen.

(4) The Registrar-General of Shipping and Seamen shall send a certified copy of the returns relating to such births and deaths as follows; that is to say,—

(*a*) if it appears from the return that the father of the child so born, or if the child is a bastard the mother of the child, or that the person deceased was a Scotch or Irish subject of Her Majesty, then to the Registrar-General of Births and Deaths in Scotland or Ireland, as the case may require; and

(*b*) in any other case to the Registrar-General of Births and Deaths in England;

and such Registrar-General of Births and Deaths shall cause the same to be filed and preserved in or copied in a book to be kept by him for the purpose, and to be called the marine register book; and such book shall be a certified copy of the register book within the meaning of the Acts relating to the registration of births and deaths in England, Scotland, and Ireland, respectively.

(5) If the master of any ship fails to comply with any requirement of this section, he shall be liable for each offence to a fine not exceeding five pounds.

255. (1) Where by reason of the transfer of ownership or change of employment of a ship, the list of the crew ceases to be required in respect of the ship, or to be required at the same date, the master or owner of the ship shall, if the ship is then in the United Kingdom, within one month, and, if she is elsewhere, within six months, after that cessation deliver or transmit to the superintendent at the port to which the ship belonged the list of the crew, duly made up to the time of the cessation.

Return in case of transfer or loss of ship.

(2) If a ship is lost or abandoned, the master or owner thereof shall, if practicable, and as soon as possible, deliver or transmit to the superintendent at the port to which the ship belonged the list of the crew, duly made out to the time of the loss or abandonment.

(3) If the master or owner of a ship fails, without reasonable cause, to comply with this section, he shall for each offence be liable to a fine not exceeding ten pounds.

256. (1) All superintendents and all officers of customs shall take charge of all documents which are delivered or transmitted to or retained by them in pursuance of this Act, and shall keep them for such time (if any) as may be necessary for the purpose of settling any business arising at the place where the

Transmission of documents to registrar by superintendents and other officers.] documents come into their hands, or for any other proper purpose, and shall, if required, produce them for any of those purposes, and shall then transmit them to the Registrar-General of Shipping and Seamen, and he shall record and preserve them, and they shall be admissible in evidence in manner provided by this Act, and they shall, on payment of a moderate fee fixed by the Board of Trade, or without payment if the Board so direct, be open to the inspection of any person.

(2) The documents aforesaid shall be public records and documents within the meaning of the Public Record Offices Acts, 1838 and 1877, and those Acts shall, where applicable, apply to those documents in all respects, as if specifically referred to therein. 1 & 2 Vict., c. 94. 40 & 41 Vict., c. 55.

Deposit of documents at foreign ports and in colonies.

257. (1) Whenever a ship, in whatever part of Her Majesty's dominions it is registered (except a ship whose business for the time being is to carry passengers whether cabin or steerage passengers), arrives at a port in a British possession or at a port elsewhere at which there is a British consular officer, and remains thereat for forty-eight hours, the master shall, within forty-eight hours of the ship's arrival, deliver to the chief officer of customs or to the consular officer (as the case may be,) the agreement with the crew, and also all indentures and assignments of apprenticeships, or, if the ship is registered in a British possession, such of those documents as the ship is provided with.

(2) The officer shall keep the documents during the ship's stay in the port, and in cases where any endorsements upon the agreement are required by this Act shall make the same, and shall return the documents to the master within a reasonable time before his departure, with a certificate endorsed on the agreement, stating the time when the documents were respectively delivered and returned

(3) If it appears that the required forms have been neglected, or that the existing laws have been transgressed, the officer shall make an endorsement to that effect on the agreement, and forthwith transmit a copy of the endorsement, with the fullest information he can collect regarding the neglect or transgression, to the Registrar-General of Shipping and Seamen.

(4) If the master of a ship fails without reasonable cause to deliver any document in pursuance of this section, he shall for each offence be liable to a fine not exceeding twenty pounds; and in any prosecution for that fine it shall lie upon the master either to produce the said certificate, or to prove that he duly obtained it, or that it was impracticable for him to obtain it.

Documents to be handed over

258. If during the progress of a voyage the master is removed, or superseded, or for any other reason quits the ship, and is succeeded in the command by some other person, he shall deliver to his successor the various documents relating to the navigation of the ship and to the crew thereof which are in his custody, and if he fails without reasonable cause so to do, he shall be liable to a fine not exceeding one hundred pounds; and his successor shall immediately on assuming the command of the ship enter in the official log book a list of the documents so delivered to him. to successor on charge of master.

Sites for Sailors' Homes.

259. The corporation of a municipal borough, being a port in the United Kingdom, and any body corporate, association, or trustees in any such port, existing or constituted for any public purposes relating to the government or benefit of persons engaged in the British merchant service, or to the management of docks and harbours, or for any other public purposes connected with shipping or navigation, may, with the consent of the Local Government Board, appropriate any land vested in them or in trustees for them as a site for a sailors' home, and may for that purpose either retain and apply the same accordingly, or convey the same to trustees, with such powers for appointing new trustees and continuing the trust as they think fit. Corporations, etc., may grant sites for sailors' homes.

Application of Part II.

260. This Part of this Act shall, unless the context or subject-matter requires a different application, apply to all sea-going ships registered in the United Kingdom, and to the owners, masters, and crews of such ships subject as herein-after provided with respect to— Application of Part II to ships registered in the United Kingdom.

(*a*) ships belonging to any of the three general lighthouse authorities;

(*b*) pleasure yachts; and

(*c*) fishing boats.

261. This Part of this Act shall, unless the context or subject-matter requires a different application, apply to all sea-going British ships registered out of the United Kingdom, and to the owners, masters, and crews thereof as follows; that is to say, Application of Part II to ships registered elsewhere than in the United Kingdom.

(*a*) the provisions relating to the shipping and discharge of seamen in the United Kingdom and to volunteering into the Navy shall apply in every case;

(*b*) the provisions relating to lists of the crew and to the property of deceased seamen and apprentices shall apply where the crew are discharged, or the final port of destination of the ship is, in the United Kingdom; and

(*c*) all the provisions shall apply where the ships are employed in trading or going between any port in the United Kingdom, and any port not situate in the British possession or country in which the ship is registered; and

(*d*) the provisions relating to the rights of seamen in respect of wages to the shipping and discharge of seamen in ports abroad, to leaving seamen abroad and to the relief of seamen in distress in ports abroad, to the provisions, health, and accommodation of seamen, to the power of seamen to make complaints, to the protection of seamen from imposition, and to discipline, shall apply in every case except where the ship is within the jurisdiction of the government of the British possession in which the ship is registered.

Partial application of Part II to ships of lighthouse authorities and pleasure yachts.

262. The following provisions of this Part of this Act shall not apply to ships belonging to the three general lighthouse authorities or to pleasure yachts, or to the owners, masters, and crews thereof, namely, the provisions relating to—

(*a*) the requirement of officers to hold certificates of competency, and the production of those certificates;

(*b*) the exemption from stamp duty and record of indentures of apprenticeship, and matters to be done for the purpose of such record;

(*c*) the entry in the agreement with the crew of the particulars respecting apprentices, and matters to be done for the purpose of such entry;

(*d*) the engagement or supply of seamen or apprentices by or through unlicensed persons;

(*e*) agreements with the crew (except the provisions relating to the engagement of a seaman abroad);

(*f*) the compulsory discharge and payment of seamen's wages before a superintendent and the compulsory delivery of an account of wages;

(*g*) the accommodation for seamen;

(*h*) the deduction and payment of fines imposed under stipulations in the agreement;

(*i*) the delivery of documents at ports abroad to consular or customs officers; or

(*j*) official log books.

Partial application of

263. (1) This Part of this Act (except the provisions thereof relating to the transmission and delivery of lists of crews, volunteering into the Navy and the property of deceased seamen) shall not, subject as herein-after provided with respect to Scotland or by the Fourth Part of this Act, apply to fishing boats exclusively employed in fishing on the coasts of the United Kingdom, or to the owners, skippers, and crews thereof. Part II to fishing boats.

(2) The provisions of this Part of this Act relating to—

(*a*) apprenticeships to the sea service;

(*b*) compulsory agreements with the crew;

(*c*) the alteration, falsification, or posting up of copies of agreements with the crew;

(*d*) compensation to seamen improperly discharged;

(*e*) the delivery of an account of wages;

(*f*) the granting of certificates of discharge and the return of certificates of competency by the master;

(*g*) the decision of questions by the superintendent when referred to him;

(*h*) the production of the ship's papers by the master to the superintendent in proceedings under this Act before him; or

(*i*) the sections constituting the offences of desertion, absence without leave, and offences against discipline;

shall not, subject as in this section mentioned with respect to Scotland, apply to any fishing boats whether or not exclusively employed in fishing on the coasts of the United Kingdom, or to the owners, skippers, and crews thereof.

(3) So far as respects Scotland all of this Part of this Act (except the provisions thereof declared not to apply to ships belonging to the general lighthouse authorities or to pleasure yachts) shall apply to fishing boats, whether or not exclusively employed in fishing on the coasts of the United Kingdom, and to the owners, skippers, and crews thereof in like manner as it applies to other ships, and the owners, skippers, and crews thereof.

264. If the legislature of a British possession, by any law, apply or adapt to any British ships registered at, trading with, or being at, any port in that possession, and to the owners, masters, and crews of those ships, any provisions of this Part of this Act which do not otherwise so apply, such law shall have effect throughout Her Majesty's dominions, and in all places where Her Majesty has jurisdiction in the same manner as if it were enacted in this Act. Application of Part II to Colony by Colonial legislatures.

265. Where in any matter relating to a ship or to a person belonging to a ship there appears to be a conflict of laws, then, if there is in this Part of this Act any provision on the subject which is hereby expressly made to extend to that ship, the case shall be governed by that provision; but if there Conflict of laws.

is no such provision, the case shall be governed by the law of the port at which the ship is registered.

Unregistered ship deemed to be registered in United Kingdom for certain purposes.

266. This Part of this Act shall apply to an unregistered British ship which ought to have been registered under this Act, as if such ship had been registered in the United Kingdom.

PART III.

PASSENGER AND EMIGRANT SHIPS.

1. Definitions.

Definition of Passenger Steamer and Passenger.

Definition of "passenger" and "passenger steamer."

267. For the purposes of this Part of this Act—

The expression "passenger" shall include any person carried in a ship other than the master and crew, and the owner, his family and servants; and

The expression "passenger steamer" shall mean every British steamship carrying passengers to, from, or between any places in the United Kingdom, except steam ferry boats working in chains (commonly called steam bridges) and every foreign steamship carrying passengers between places in the United Kingdom.

Definition of Emigrant Ship, etc.

"Emigrant ship," etc., to which Part applies.

268. For the purposes of this Part of this Act, unless the context otherwise requires—

(1) The expression "emigrant ship" shall mean every sea-going ship, whether British or foreign, and whether or not conveying mails, carrying, upon any voyage to which the provisions of this Part of this Act respecting emigrant ships apply, more than fifty steerage passengers or a greater number of steerage passengers than in the proportion—

(*a*) if the ship is a sailing ship, of one statute adult to thirty-three tons of the ship's registered tonnage; and

(*b*) if the ship is a steam ship of one statute adult to every twenty tons of the ship's registered tonnage; and

includes a ship which, having proceeded from a port outside the British Islands, takes on board at any port in the British Islands such number of steerage passengers whether British subjects or aliens resident in the British Islands, as would, either with or without the steerage passengers which she already has on board, constitute her an emigrant ship;

(2) The expression "statute adult" shall mean a person of the age of twelve years or upwards, and two persons between the ages of one and twelve years shall be treated as one statute adult;

(3) The expression "steerage passenger" shall mean all passengers except cabin passengers, and persons shall not be deemed cabin passengers unless—

(*a*) the space allotted to their exclusive use is in the proportion of at least thirty-six clear superficial feet to each statute adult; and

(*b*) they are messed throughout the voyage at the same table with the master or first officer of the ship; and

(*c*) the fare contracted to be paid by them is in the proportion for every week of the length of the voyage (as determined under this Part of this Act for sailing vessels) of thirty shillings, if the voyage of the ship is from the British Islands to a port south of the equator, and twenty shillings, if the voyage of the ship is from the British Islands to a port north of the equator; and

(*d*) they have been furnished with a duly signed contract ticket in the form prescribed by the Board of Trade for cabin passengers;

(4) The expression "steerage passage" shall include passages of all passengers except cabin passengers;

(5) The expression "upper passenger deck" shall mean and include the deck immediately beneath the upper deck, or the poop, or round house and deck house when the number of passengers, whether cabin or steerage passengers, carried in the poop, round house, or deck house, exceeds one-third of the total number of steerage passengers which the ship can lawfully carry on the deck next below;

(6) The expression "lower passenger deck" shall mean and include the deck next beneath the upper passenger deck not being an orlop deck.

269. For the purpose of this Part of this Act the length of the voyage of an emigrant ship from the British Islands to any port elsewhere shall be determined by such of the scales fixed by the Board of Trade as is applicable thereto, and the Board of Trade may fix the scales by notice published in the London Gazette, and may fix such different lengths of voyage as they think reasonable for different descriptions of ships. **Scale for determining length of voyages.**

270. For the purposes of this Part of this Act a colonial voyage means a voyage from any port in a British possession, other than British India and **Definition of colonial voyage.**

Hong Kong, to any port whatever, where the distance between such ports exceeds four hundred miles, or the duration of the voyage, as determined under this Part of this Act, exceeds three days.

2. Passenger Steamers.

Survey of Passenger Steamers.

Annual survey of passenger steamers.

271. (1) Every passenger steamer which carries more than twelve passengers shall—

(*a*) be surveyed once at least in each year in the manner provided in this Part of this Act; and

(*b*) shall not ply or proceed to sea or on any voyage or excursion with any passengers on board, unless the owner or master has the certificate from the Board of Trade as to survey under this Part of this Act, the same being in force, and applicable to the voyage or excursion on which the steamer is about to proceed.

(2) A passenger steamer attempting to ply or go to sea may be detained until such certificate as aforesaid is produced to the proper officer of Customs.

(3) Provided that, while a steamer is an emigrant ship and the provisions of this Part of this Act as to the survey of the hull, machinery and equipments of emigrant ships have been complied with, she shall not require a survey or certificate under this section.

Mode of survey and declaration of survey.

272. (1) The owner of every passenger steamer shall cause the same to be surveyed by a shipwright surveyor of ships and an engineer surveyor of ships, the shipwright surveyor being, in the case of an iron steamer, a person properly qualified in the opinion of the Board of Trade to survey an iron steamer.

(2) The surveyors, if satisfied on the survey that they can with propriety do so, shall deliver to the owner declarations of survey in a form approved by the Board of Trade.

(3) The declaration of the shipwright surveyor shall contain statements of the following particulars :—

(*a*) that the hull of the steamer is sufficient for the service intended and in good condition:

(*b*) that the boats, life buoys, lights, signals, compasses, and shelter for deck passengers, are such, and in such condition, as are required by this Act:

(*c*) the time (if less than one year) for which the hull and equipments will be sufficient:

(*d*) the limits (if any) beyond which, as regards the hull and equipmentsts the steamer is in the surveyor's judgment not fit to ply:

(*e*) the number of passengers which the steamer is in the judgment of the surveyor fit to carry, distinguishing, if necessary, between the respective numbers to be carried on the deck and in the cabins and in different parts of the deck and cabins; those numbers to be subject to such conditions and variations, according to the time of year, the nature of the voyage, the cargo carried, or other circumstances, as the case requires:

(*f*) that the certificates of the master and mate or mates are such as are required by this Act.

(4) The declaration of the engineer surveyor shall contain statements of the following particulars, namely:—

(*a*) that the machinery of the steamer is sufficient for the service intended, and in good condition:

(*b*) the time (if less than one year) for which the machinery will be sufficient:

(*c*) that the safety-valves and fire hose are such and in such condition as are required by this Act:

(*d*) the limit of the weight to be placed on the safety-valves:

(*e*) the limits (if any) beyond which, as regards the machinery, the steamer is in the surveyor's judgment not fit to ply:

(*f*) that the certificates of the engineer or engineers of the steamer are such as are required by this Act.

Transmission of declaration.

273. (1) The owner of a steamer surveyed shall within fourteen days after the receipt by him of a declaration of survey transmit it to the Board of Trade.

(2) If an owner fails without reasonable cause so to transmit a declaration of survey, he shall forfeit a sum not exceeding ten shillings for every day during which the transmission is delayed, and any sum so forfeited shall be payable on the granting of a certificate in addition to the fee, and shall be applied in the same manner as the fee.

Issue of passenger steamer's certificate.

274. On the receipt of the declarations of survey, the Board of Trade shall, if satisfied that this Part of this Act has been complied with, issue in duplicate a passenger steamer's certificate, that is to say, a certificate stating such compliance and stating, according to the declarations—

(*a*) the limits (if any) beyond which the steamer is not fit to ply; and

(*b*) the number of passengers which the steamer is fit to carry, distinguishing, if necessary, the number to be carried in each part of the steamer, and any conditions and variations to which the number is subject.

Appeal to court of survey.

275. (1) If the owner of a steamer feels aggrieved by the declaration of survey of a shipwright or engineer surveyor, or by the refusal of such a surveyor to give such a declaration, he may appeal to the Court of survey for the port or district where the steamer for the time being is, in manner directed by the rules of that Court.

(2) On any such appeal the judge of the court of survey shall report to the Board of Trade on the question raised by the appeal and the Board, when satisfied that the requirements of the report and of the foregoing provisions of this Part of this Act have been complied with, may grant a passenger steamer's certificate.

(3) Subject to any order made by the judge of the Court of survey the costs of and incidental to the appeal shall follow the event.

(4) A shipwright or engineer surveyor in making a survey of a steamer for the purpose of a declaration of survey shall, if the owner of the steamer so requires, be accompanied on the survey by some person appointed by the owner, and in that case, if the surveyor and the person so appointed agree, there shall be no appeal under this section to the Court of survey.

Transmission of certificate.

276. (1) The Board of Trade shall transmit the passenger steamer's certificate in duplicate to a superintendent or some other public officer at the port mentioned by the owner of the steamer for the purpose, or at the port where the owner or his agent resides, or where the steamer has been surveyed or is for the time lying.

(2) The Board of Trade shall cause notice of the transmission to be given to the master or owner or his agent, and the officer to whom the certificate has been transmitted shall, on the owner, master, or agent applying and paying the proper fee and other sums (if any) mentioned in this Act as payable in that behalf, deliver to him both copies of the certificate.

(3) In proving the issue of a passenger steamer's certificate it shall be sufficient to show that the certificate was duly received by the said officer, and that due notice of the transmission was given to the owner, master, or agent.

Fees for certificate.

277. The grantee of a passenger steamer's certificate shall pay such fees, not exceeding those specified in Part One of the Ninth Schedule to this Act, as the Board of Trade fix.

Duration of certificates.

278. (1) A passenger steamer's certificate shall not be in force for more than one year from the date of its issue, or any shorter time specified in the certificate, nor after notice is given by the Board of Trade to the owner, agent, or master of the steamer, that the Board have cancelled it.

(2) If a passenger steamer is absent from the United Kingdom at the time when her certificate expires, a fine shall not be incurred for want of a certificate

until she first begins to ply with passengers after her next return to the United Kingdom.

Cancellation of certificate.

279. (1) The Board of Trade may cancel a passenger steamer's certificate where they have reason to believe—

(*a*) that any declaration of survey on which the certificate was founded, has been in any particular made fraudulently or erroneously; or,

(*b*) that the certificate has been issued upon false or erroneous information; or,

(*c*) that since the making of the declaration, the hull, equipments, or machinery have sustained any injury, or are otherwise insufficient.

(2) In every such case the Board of Trade may require the owner to have the hull, equipment, or machinery of the steamer again surveyed, and to transmit further declarations of survey, before they re-issue the certificate or grant a fresh one in lieu thereof.

Delivery up of certificate.

280. (1) The Board of Trade may require a passenger steamer's certificate, which has expired or been cancelled, to be delivered up as they direct.

(2) If any owner or master fails without reasonable cause to comply with such requirement, he shall for each offence be liable to a fine not exceeding ten pounds.

Posting up of certificate.

281. (1) The owner or master of every passenger steamer required to have a passenger steamer's certificate shall forthwith, on the receipt of the certificate by him or his agent, cause one of the duplicates to be put up in some conspicuous place on board the steamer, so as to be legible to all persons on board, and to be kept so put up and legible while the certificate remains in force, and the steamer is in use.

(2) If the owner or master fails without reasonable cause to comply with this section, he shall for each offence be liable to a fine not exceeding ten pounds.

(3) If a passenger steamer plies or goes to sea with passengers on board and this section is not complied with, then for each offence the owner thereof shall be liable to a fine not exceeding one hundred pounds, and the master shall also be liable to a further fine not exceeding twenty pounds.

Penalty for forgery of certificate or declaration.

282. If any person—

(*a*) knowingly and wilfully makes, or assists in making, or procures to be made, a false or fraudulent declaration of survey or passenger steamer's certificate; or

(*b*) forges, assists in forging, procures to be forged, fraudulently alters, assists in fraudulently altering, or procures to be fraudulently altered, any such declaration or certificate, or anything contained in, or any signature to any such declaration or certificate;

that person shall in respect of each offence be guilty of a misdemeanor.

Penalty for carrying passengers in excess.

283. The owner or master of any passenger steamer shall not receive on board thereof, or on or in any part thereof, any number of passengers which, having regard to the time, occasion, and circumstances of the case, is greater than the number allowed by the passenger steamer's certificate, and if he does so, he shall for each offence be liable to a fine not exceeding twenty pounds, and also to an additional fine not exceeding five shillings for every passenger above the number so allowed, or if the fare of any passenger on board exceeds five shillings, not exceeding double the amount of the fares of all the passengers above the number so allowed, reckoned at the highest rate of fare payable by any passenger on board.

Colonial certificates for passenger steamers.

284. Where the legislature of any British possession provides for the survey of, and grant of certificates for, passenger steamers, and the Board of Trade report to Her Majesty the Queen that they are satisfied that the certificates are to the like effect, and are granted after a like survey, and in such manner as to be equally efficient with the certificates granted for the same purpose in the United Kingdom under this Act, Her Majesty in Council may—

(1) declare that the certificates granted in the said British possession shall be of the same force as if granted under this Act; and

(2) declare that all or any of the provisions of this Part of this Act, which relate to passenger steamer's certificates shall, either without modification or with such modifications as to Her Majesty may seem necessary, apply to the certificates granted in the said British possession; and

(3) impose such conditions and make such regulations with respect to the certificates, and to the use, delivery, and cancellation thereof, as to Her Majesty may seem fit, and impose fines not exceeding fifty pounds for the breach of those conditions and regulations.

General Equipment of Passenger Steamers.

Equipment of passenger steamers with compasses, hose, deck shelters, and safety appliances.

285. (1) A sea-going passenger steamer shall have her compasses properly adjusted from time to time, to the satisfaction of the shipwright surveyor and according to such regulations as may be issued by the Board of Trade.

(2) A sea-going passenger steamer shall be provided with a hose capable of being connected with the engines of the steamer, and adapted for extinguishing fire in any part of the steamer.

(3) A home-trade passenger steamer shall be provided with such shelter for the protection of deck passengers (if any) as the Board of Trade having

regard to the nature of the passage, the number of deck passengers to be carried, the season of the year, the safety of the ship, and the circumstances of the case, require.

(4) A passenger steamer shall be provided with a safety-valve on each boiler, so constructed as to be out of the control of the engineer when the steam is up, and, if the safety-valve is in addition to the ordinary valve, so constructed as to have an area not less, and a pressure not greater, than the area of and pressure on the ordinary valve.

(5) If a passenger steamer plies or goes to sea from a port in the United Kingdom without being equipped as required by this section, then, for each matter in which default is made, the owner (if in fault) shall be liable to a fine not exceeding one hundred pounds, and the master (if in fault) shall be liable to a fine not exceeding fifty pounds.

286. A person shall not increase the weight on the safety-valve of a passenger steamer beyond the limits fixed by the surveyor, and, if he does so, he shall, in addition to any other liability he may incur by so doing, be liable for each offence to a fine not exceeding one hundred pounds. **Prohibition of increasing weight on safety-valve.**

Keeping Order in Passenger Steamers.

287. (1) If any of the following offences is committed in the case of a passenger steamer for which there is a passenger steamer's certificate in force; that is to say, **Offences in connexion with passenger steamers.**

(*a*) If any person being drunk or disorderly has been on that account refused admission thereto by the owner or any person in his employment, and, after having the amount of his fare, (if he has paid it) returned or tendered to him, nevertheless persists in attempting to enter the steamer:

(*b*) If any person being drunk or disorderly on board the steamer is requested by the owner or any person in his employ to leave the steamer at any place in the United Kingdom, at which he can conveniently do so, and, after having the amount of his fare (if he has paid it) returned or tendered to him, does not comply with the request:

(*c*) If any person on board the steamer, after warning by the master or other officer thereof, molests or continues to molest any passenger:

(*d*) If any person, after having been refused admission to the steamer by the owner or any person in his employ on account of the steamer being full, and having had the amount of his fare (if he has paid it) returned or tendered to him, nevertheless persists in attempting to enter the steamer:

(*e*) If any person having gone on board the steamer at any place, and being requested, on account of the steamer being full, by the owner or any person in his employ to leave the steamer, before it has quitted that place, and having had the amount of his fare (if he has paid it) returned or tendered to him, does not comply with that request:

(*f*) If any person travels or attempts to travel in the steamer without first paying his fare, and with intent to avoid payment thereof:

(*g*) If any person having paid his fare for a certain distance, knowingly and wilfully proceeds in the steamer beyond that distance without first paying the additional fare for the additional distance, and with intent to avoid payment thereof:

(*h*) If any person on arriving in the steamer at a point to which he has paid his fare knowingly and wilfully refuses or neglects to quit the steamer: and

(*i*) If any person on board the steamer fails, when requested by the master or other officer thereof, either to pay his fare or exhibit such ticket or other receipt, if any, showing the payment of his fare, as is usually given to persons travelling by and paying their fare for the steamer:

the person so offending shall for each offence be liable to a fine not exceeding forty shillings, but that liability shall not prejudice the recovery of any fare payable by him.

(2) If any person on board any such steamer wilfully does or causes to be done anything in such a manner as to obstruct or injure any part of the machinery or tackle of the steamer, or to obstruct, impede, or molest the crew, or any of them, in the navigation or management of the steamer, or otherwise in the execution of their duty on or about the steamer, he shall for each offence be liable to a fine not exceeding twenty pounds.

(3) The master or other officer of any such steamer, and all persons called by him to his assistance, may, without any warrant, detain any person who commits any offence against this section and whose name and address are unknown to the master or officer, and convey the offender with all convenient despatch before some justice of the peace to be dealt with according to law, and that justice shall, with all convenient despatch, try the case in a summary manner.

(4) If any person commits an offence against this section and on the application of the master of the steamer, or any other person in the employ of the owner thereof, refuses to give his name and address, or gives a false name or address, that person shall be liable to a fine not exceeding twenty pounds, and the fine shall be paid to the owner of the steamer.

288. The master of any home-trade passenger steamer may refuse to receive on board thereof any person who by reason of drunkenness or otherwise is in such a state, or misconducts himself in such a manner, as to cause annoyance or injury to passengers on board, and if any such person is on board, may put him on shore at any convenient place; and a person so refused admittance or put on shore shall not be entitled to the return of any fare he has paid. **Power to exclude drunken passengers on home-trade passenger steamers.**

3. Emigrant Ships.

Survey of Emigrant Ships.

289. (1) An emigrant ship, in respect of which a passenger steamer's certificate is not in force, shall not clear outwards or proceed to sea on any voyage unless she has been surveyed under the direction of the emigration officer at the port of clearance, but at the expense of the owner or charterer thereof, by two or more competent surveyors to be appointed at any port in the British Islands where there is an emigration officer by the Board of Trade, and at other ports by the Commissioners of Customs, and has been reported by such surveyors to be in their opinion seaworthy and fit for her intended voyage. **Preliminary survey of emigrant ship.**

(2) The survey shall be made before any portion of the cargo is taken on board, except so much as may be necessary for ballasting the ship, and such portion of cargo if laden on board shall be shifted, if required by the emigration officer or the surveyors, so as to expose to view successively every part of the frame of the ship.

(3) If any such surveyors report that the ship is not seaworthy, or not fit for her intended voyage, the owner or charterer may, if he thinks fit, by writing under his hand require the emigration officer to appoint three other competent surveyors (of whom two at least must be shipwrights) to survey the ship at the expense of the owner or charterer, and the said officer shall thereupon appoint such surveyors, and they shall survey the ship, and if by unanimous report under their hands, but not otherwise, they declare the ship to be seaworthy and fit for her intended voyage, the ship shall for the purposes of this Part of the Act be deemed seaworthy and fit for that voyage.

(4) If any requirement of this section is not complied with in the case of any emigrant ship, the owner, charterer or master of the ship or any of them shall for each offence be liable to a fine not exceeding one hundred pounds,

Equipments.

Equipment with compasses, chronometers, fire-engine, anchors, etc.

290. (1) Every emigrant ship shall, in addition to any other requirement under this Act, be provided with the following articles, namely:—

(*a*) with at least three steering compasses, and one azimuth compass; and

(*b*) if proceeding to any place north of the Equator, with at least one chronometer; and

(*c*) if proceeding to any place south of the Equator, with at least two chronometers; and

(*d*) with a fire engine in proper working order and of such description and power, and either with or without such other apparatus for extinguishing fire as the emigration officer may approve; and

(*e*) with three bower anchors of such weight and with cables of such length, size, and material, as in the judgment of the emigration officer are sufficient for the size of the ship; and

(*f*) if a foreign ship, with four properly-fitted lifebuoys kept ready at all times for immediate use; and

(*g*) adequate means, to be approved by the emigration officer at the port of clearance, of making signals by night.

(2) If any requirement of this section is not complied with in the case of any emigrant ship, the master of that ship shall for each offence be liable to a fine not exceeding fifty pounds.

Number of, and Accommodation for, Passengers.

Regulations as to carrying of passengers generally.

291. (1) A ship shall not carry passengers, whether cabin or steerage passengers, on more than two decks, except that cabin passengers not exceeding one for every hundred tons of the ship's registered tonnage, and sick persons placed in hospital as hereinafter provided may be carried in a poop or deck house, although passengers are carried on two other decks.

(2) If steerage passengers are carried under the poop, or in a round house, or deck house, the poop, round house, or deck house shall be properly built and secured to the satisfaction of the emigration officer at the port of clearance.

(3) If any requirement of this section is not complied with in the case of any ship, the master of the ship shall for each offence be liable to a fine not exceeding five hundred pounds.

Limit of number of steerage passengers to be carried on emigrant ships.

292. (1) The number of steerage passengers carried in an emigrant ship shall not exceed the number limited by the regulations in the Tenth Schedule to this Act.

(2) If there is on board any emigrant ship at or after the time of clearance a greater number of steerage passengers than the number so limited (except as increased by births at sea), the master of the ship shall be liable to a fine not exceeding twenty pounds for each steerage passenger constituting such excess.

293. (1) The regulations as to the accommodation for steerage passengers in the Eleventh Schedule to this Act, relating to the construction of passenger decks, to berths, to hospitals, to privies, and to the supply of light and ventilation, shall be observed in the case of all emigrant ships as if they were contained in this section. **Regulations as to accommodation of steerage passengers.**

(2) If any requirement of this section is not complied with in the case of any emigrant ship, the owner, charterer or master of the ship or any of them shall for each offence be liable to a fine not exceeding fifty pounds, except that the master shall alone be liable to the fine where he is in any such regulation expressed to be alone liable.

294. (1) No part of the cargo of the steerage passengers' luggage, or of the provisions, water, or stores, whether for the use of the steerage passengers or of the crew, shall be carried on the upper deck or on the passenger decks, unless, in the opinion of the emigration officer at the port of clearance, the same is so placed as not to impede light or ventilation or to interfere with the comfort of the steerage passengers, nor unless the same is stowed and secured to the satisfaction of the emigration officer; and the space thereby occupied or rendered in the opinion of such officer unavailable for the accommodation of the steerage passengers, shall (unless occupied by the said steerage passengers' luggage) be deducted in calculating the space by which the number of steerage passengers is regulated. **Stowage of goods.**

(2) If any requirement of this section is not complied with in the case of any emigrant ship, the owner, charterer or master or any of them shall for each offence be liable to a fine not exceeding three hundred pounds.

Provisions, Water, and Medical Stores.

295. (1) There shall be placed on board every emigrant ship for the steerage passengers provisions and water of good and wholesome quality and in sweet and good condition, and in quantities sufficient to secure throughout the voyage the issues required by this Part of this Act. **Supply of provisions and water.**

(2) In addition to the allowance of pure water for each steerage passenger, water shall be shipped for cooking purposes sufficient to supply ten gallons for every day of the length of the voyage as determined under this Part of this Act for every one hundred statute adults on board.

(3) There shall also be shipped for the use of the crew and all other persons on board an ample amount of wholesome provisions and pure water, not inferior in quality, to the provisions and water provided for the steerage passengers.

(4) All such water and provisions shall be provided and stowed away by and at the expense of the owner, charterer, or master of the ship.

(5) If any emigrant ship obtains a clearance without being provided with the requisite quantities of water and provisions in accordance with this section, the owner, charterer or master of that ship or any of them shall for each offence be liable to a fine not exceeding three hundred pounds.

(6) Before an emigrant ship is cleared outwards, the emigration officer at the port of clearance shall survey or cause to be surveyed by some competent person the provisions and water by this Act required to be placed on board for the steerage passengers, and shall satisfy himself that the same are of good and wholesome quality and in sweet and good condition, and in the quantities required by this Act.

(7) If the emigration officer considers that any part of the provisions or water is not of a good and wholesome quality, or is not in sweet and good condition, he may reject and mark the same, or the packages or vessels in which it is contained, and direct the same to be forthwith landed or emptied.

(8) If the same are not forthwith landed or emptied, or if after being landed the same or any part thereof are reshipped in the ship, the owner, charterer or master of the ship or any of them, or, if the same are shipped in any other emigrant ship, then the person causing the same to be so shipped, shall for each offence be liable to a fine not exceeding one hundred pounds.

Mode of carrying water.

296. (1) The water to be placed on board emigrant ships as hereinbefore provided shall be carried in tanks or casks approved by the emigration officer at the port of clearance, and the casks shall be sweet and tight, of sufficient strength, and if of wood properly charred inside, and the staves shall not be made of fir, pine, or soft wood, and each cask shall not be capable of containing more than three hundred gallons.

(2) If any requirement of this section is not complied with in the case of any emigrant ship, the owner, charterer or master of the ship, or any of them, shall for each offence be liable to a fine not exceeding fifty pounds.

Provision for touching at intermediate ports to take in water.

297. If an emigrant ship is intended to call at any intermediate port during the voyage for the purpose of taking in water, and if an engagement to that effect is inserted in the master's bond herein-after mentioned, it shall be sufficient to place on board at the port of clearance such supply of water as is required by this Part of this Act for the voyage to the intermediate port, subject to the following conditions; that is to say,

(i) the emigration officer at the port of clearance shall approve in writing the arrangement, and the approval shall be carried among the ship's papers, and shall be exhibited at the intermediate port and delivered on the arrival of the ship at her final port of discharge to the chief officer of customs, or British consular officer, as the case may be:

(ii) if the length of either portion of the voyage, whether to the intermediate port, or from the intermediate port to the final port of discharge, is not determined under this Part of this Act, the emigration officer at the port of clearance shall declare the same in writing as part of his said approval of the arrangement:

(iii) the ship shall have on board at the time of clearance such tanks and water casks of the description by this Part of this Act required, as are sufficient for stowing the quantity of water required for the longest of the aforesaid portions of the voyage.

Issue of water or provisions during voyage.

298. (1) The master of every emigrant ship shall during the voyage, including the time of detention at any place before the termination thereof, issue to each steerage passenger, or where the steerage passengers are divided into messes, to the headman for the time being of each mess, on behalf and for the use of all the members thereof, an allowance of pure water, and sweet and wholesome provisions of good quality, in accordance with the dietary scales in the Twelfth Schedule to this Act, which shall have effect as if they were contained in this section.

(2) The Board of Trade may, by notice published in the London Gazette, add to the dietary scales in the said schedule any dietary scale which in their opinion contains in the whole the same amount of wholesome nutriment as any scale in that schedule, and any dietary scale so added, inclusive of any regulations relating thereto, shall have effect as if they were contained in the said schedule as an alternative of the dietary scales therein contained, and accordingly a master of a ship may issue provisions according to the latter scales or to any scale so added, whichever is mentioned in the contract ticket of the steerage passengers.

(3) If any requirement of this section is not complied with in the case of any emigrant ship, the master of the ship shall for each offence be liable to a fine not exceeding fifty pounds.

Power of Board of Trade to

299. The Board of Trade if satisfied that the food, space, accommodation, or any other particular or thing provided in an emigrant ship for any class of exempt ships. passengers, whether cabin or steerage, is superior to the food, space, accommodation, or other particular or thing required by this Part of this Act, may exempt that ship from any requirement of this Part of this Act with respect to food, space, or accommodation, or other particular or thing, in such manner and upon such conditions as the Board think fit.

Medical stores. **300.** (1) The owner or charterer of every emigrant ship shall provide for the use of the steerage passengers a supply of the following things (in this Part of this Act referred to as medical stores), namely, medicines, medical comforts, instruments, disinfectants, and other things proper and necessary for diseases and accidents incident to sea voyages, and for the medical treatment of the steerage passengers during the voyage, with written directions for the use of such medical stores.

(2) The medical stores shall, in the judgment of the emigration officer a the port of clearance, be good in quality and sufficient in quantity for the probable exigencies of the intended voyage, and shall be properly packed, and placed under the charge of the medical practitioner, when there is one on board, to be used at his discretion.

(3) If any of the above requirements of this section is not complied with in the case of an emigrant ship, the master of the ship shall for each offence be liable to a fine not exceeding fifty pounds.

(4) An emigrant ship shall not clear outwards or proceed to sea unless a medical practitioner appointed by the emigration officer at the port of clearance has inspected the said medical stores, and certified to the emigration officer that they are sufficient in quantity and quality, or unless the emigration officer, in case he cannot on any particular occasion obtain the attendance of a medical practitioner, gives written permission for the purpose.

(5) If an emigrant ship clears outwards or proceeds to sea without such certificate or permission, the master of the ship shall for each offence be liable to a fine not exceeding one hundred pounds.

Dangerous Goods, and Carriage of Cattle.

Regulations as to carriage of dangerous goods, and of horses and cattle. **301.** (1) Subject to the provisions of this Part of this Act as to military stores, an emigrant ship shall not clear outwards or proceed to sea, if there is on board—

(*a*) as cargo, any article which is an explosive within the meaning of the Explosives Act, 1875, or any vitriol, lucifer matches, guano, or green hides, or 38 & 39 c. 17.

(*b*) either as cargo or ballast, any article or number of articles which by reason of the nature, quantity, or mode of stowage thereof are, either singly or collectively, in the opinion of the emigration officer at the port of clearance, likely to endanger the health or lives of the steerage passengers or the safety of the ship, or

(*c*) as cargo, horses or cattle or other animals mentioned in the Thirteenth Schedule to this Act, except they are carried on the conditions stated in that schedule, which shall have effect as if contained in this section.

(2) If any requirement of this section is not complied with in the case of any ship, the owner, charterer or master of the ship or any of them, shall for each offence be liable to a fine not exceeding three hundred pounds.

302. (1) A Secretary of State may, by order under his hand, authorise the carriage as cargo in any emigrant ship (subject to such conditions and directions as may be specified in the order) of naval and military stores for the public service, and those stores may be carried accordingly. Carriage of military stores.

(2) The order shall be addressed to the emigration officer and shall be by him countersigned, and delivered to the master of the ship to which it refers, and shall be delivered up by the master to the chief officer of customs at the port where the stores are discharged.

(3) The master shall comply with all the conditions and directions in the order, and, if he fails to do so, shall for each offence be liable to a fine not exceeding three hundred pounds.

Medical Officer, Staff, and Crew.

303. (1) Subject to any regulations made by Order in Council under this Part of this Act, a duly authorised medical practitioner shall be carried on board an emigrant ship— Medical practitioners.

(*a*) where the number of steerage passengers on board exceeds fifty; and also

(*b*) where the number of persons on board (including cabin passengers, officers and crew) exceeds three hundred.

(2) A medical practitioner shall not be considered to be duly authorised for the purposes of this Act unless—

(*a*) he is authorised by law to practise as a legally qualified medical practitioner in some part of Her Majesty's dominions, or, in the case of a foreign ship, in the country to which that ship belongs: and

(*b*) his name has been notified to the emigration officer at the port of clearance, and has not been objected to by him: and (*c*) he is provided with proper surgical instruments to the satisfaction of that officer.

(3) When the majority of the steerage passengers in any emigrant ship, or as many as three hundred of them, are foreigners, any medical practitioner whether authorised or not may, if approved by the emigration officer, be carried therein.

(4) Where a medical practitioner is carried on board an emigrant ship, he shall be rated on the ship's articles.

(5) If any requirement of this section is not complied with in the case of any emigrant ship, the master of the ship shall for each offence be liable to a fine not exceeding one hundred pounds.

(6) If any person proceeds or attempts to proceed as medical practitioner in any emigrant ship without being duly authorised, or contrary to the requirements of this section, that person and any person aiding and abetting him shall for each offence be liable to a fine not exceeding one hundred pounds.

Steerage passengers, stewards cooks, and interpreters.

304. (1) Every emigrant ship, if carrying as many as one hundred steerage passengers, shall carry a steerage steward, who shall be a seafaring man and rated in the ship's articles as steerage steward, and approved by the emigration officer at the port of clearance: he shall be employed in messing and serving out the provisions to the steerage passengers, and in assisting to maintain cleanliness, order, and good discipline among them, and shall not assist in any way in navigating or working the ship.

(2) Every emigrant ship carrying as many as one hundred steerage passengers shall also carry a steerage cook, and if carrying more than three hundred statute adults two steerage cooks, who shall be seafaring men, and be rated and approved as in the case of steerage stewards, and shall be employed in cooking the food of the steerage passengers.

(3) In every such ship a convenient place for cooking shall be set apart on deck, and a sufficient cooking apparatus, properly covered in and arranged, shall be provided, to the satisfaction of the emigration officer at the port of clearance, together with a proper supply of fuel adequate, in his opinion, for the intended voyage.

(4) Every foreign emigrant ship in which as many as one-half of the steerage passengers are British subjects, shall, unless the master and officers or not less than three of them understand and speak intelligibly the English language, carry, if the number of steerage passengers does not exceed two hundred and fifty, one person, and if it exceeds two hundred and fifty, two persons who understand and speak intelligibly the language spoken by the master and crew and also the English language: those persons shall act as interpreters and be employed exclusively in attendance on the steerage passengers, and not

in working the ship; and any such ship shall not clear outwards or proceed to sea without having such interpreter on board.

(5) If any requirement of this section is not complied with in the case of any emigrant ship, the master of the ship shall for each offence be liable to a fine not exceeding fifty pounds.

305. (1) Every emigrant ship shall be manned with an efficient crew for her intended voyage, to the satisfaction of the emigration officer from whom a certificate for clearance for such ship is demanded: after the crew have been passed by the emigration officer, the strength of the crew shall not be diminished nor any of the men changed without the consent in writing either of that emigration officer or of the superintendent at the port of clearance. Crew of emigrant ship.

(2) Where the consent of a superintendent has been obtained, it shall, within twenty-four hours thereafter, be lodged with the said emigration officer.

(3) If the emigration officer considers the crew inefficient, the owner or charterer of the ship may appeal in writing to the Board of Trade, and the Board shall, at the expense of the appellant, appoint two other emigration officers or two competent persons to examine into the matter, and the unanimous opinion of the persons so appointed expressed under their hands, shall be conclusive on the point.

(4) If any requirement of this section is not complied with in the case of any emigrant ship, the master of that ship shall for each offence be liable to a fine not exceeding fifty pounds.

Medical Inspection.

306. (1) An emigrant ship shall not clear outwards or proceed to sea until— Medical inspection of steerage passengers and crew.

(*a*) either a medical practitioner, appointed by the emigration officer at the port of clearance, has inspected all the steerage passengers and crew about to proceed in the ship, and has certified to the emigration officer, and that officer is satisfied, that none of the steerage passengers or crew appear to be by reason of any bodily or mental disease unfit to proceed, or likely to endanger the health or safety of the other persons about to proceed in the ship; or

(*b*) the emigration officer, if he cannot on any particular occasion obtain the attendance of a medical practitioner, grants written permission for the purpose.

(2) The inspection shall take place either on board the ship, or, in the discretion of the emigration officer, at such convenient place on shore before embarkation as he appoints, and the master, owner or charterer of the ship shall pay to the emigration officer in respect of the inspection, such fee not exceeding twenty shillings for every hundred persons or fraction of a hundred persons inspected, as the Board of Trade determine.

(3) If this section is not complied with in the case of any emigrant ship, the master of the ship shall for each offence be liable to a fine not exceeding one hundred pounds.

Relanding of persons for medical reasons.

307. (1) If the emigration officer is satisfied that any person on board or about to proceed in any emigrant ship is by reason of sickness unfit to proceed, or is for that or any other reason in a condition likely to endanger the health or safety of the other persons on board, the emigration officer shall prohibit the embarkation of that person, or, if he is embarked, shall require him to be relanded; and if the emigration officer is satisfied that it is necessary for the purification of the ship or otherwise that all or any of the persons on board should be relanded, he may require the master of the ship to reland all those persons, and the master shall thereupon reland those persons, with so much of their effects and with such members of their families as cannot, in the judgment of such emigration officer, be properly separated from them.

(2) If any requirement of this section is not complied with in the case of any emigrant ship, the master, owner or charterer of the ship, or any of them, shall for each offence be liable to a fine not exceeding two hundred pounds.

(3) If any person embarks when so prohibited to embark, or fails without reasonable cause to leave the ship when so required to be relanded, that person may be summarily removed, and shall be liable to fine not exceeding forty shillings for each day during which he remains on board after the prohibition or requirement.

(4) Upon such relanding the master of the ship shall pay to each steerage passenger so relanded, or, if he is lodged and maintained in any hulk or establishment under the superintendence of the Board of Trade, then to the emigration officer at the port, subsistence money at the rate of one shilling and six pence a day for each statute adult, until he has been re-embarked or declines or neglects to proceed, or until his passage money, if recoverable under this Part of this Act, has been returned to him.

Return of passage money to persons relanded

308. When a person has been relanded from an emigrant ship on account of the sickness of himself or of any member of his family, and is not re-embarked or does not finally sail in that ship, he, or any emigration officer on his behalf, shall be entitled, on delivery up of his contract ticket, and notwithstanding that the ship has not sailed, to recover summarily, in the case of a steerage passenger the whole, and in the case of a cabin passenger one-half of the money paid by or on account of the passenger and of the members of his family relanded, from the person to whom the same was paid, or from the owner, charterer, or master of the ship, or any of them, at the option of the person recovering the same. for medical reasons.

Master's Bond.

309. (1) Before an emigrant ship clears outwards or proceeds to sea, the master, together with the owner or charterer, or in the event of the owner or charterer being absent or being the master, one other good and sufficient person approved by the chief officer of customs at the port of clearance, shall enter into a joint and several bond, in this Act referred to as the master's bond, in the sum of two thousand pounds, to the Crown. Bond to be given by master of emigrant ship.

(2) The bond shall be executed in duplicate, and shall not be liable to stamp duty.

(3) Where neither the owner nor the charterer of an emigrant ship resides in the British Islands the bond shall be for the sum of five thousand instead of two thousand pounds, and shall contain an additional condition for the payment to the Crown, as a Crown debt, of all expenses incurred under this Act in rescuing, maintaining, and forwarding to their destination, any steerage passengers carried in the ship who by reason of shipwreck or any other cause, except their own neglect or default, are not conveyed by or on behalf of the owner, charterer, or master of the ship to their intended destination.

310. (1) Where an emigrant ship is bound to a British possession the chief officer of customs at the port of clearance shall certify on one part of the master's bond that it has been duly executed by the master of the ship and the other person bound, and shall forward the same to the governor of the said possession, or to such person as the governor may appoint for that purpose. Evidence of bond.

(2) The certificate shall, in any court of a British possession in which the bond may be put in suit, be conclusive evidence of the due execution of the bond by the master and the other person bound, and it shall not be necessary to prove the handwriting of the officer of customs who signed the certificate, nor that he was at the time of signing it chief officer of customs at the port of clearance.

(3) Any such bond shall not be put in suit in a British possession after the expiration of three months next after the arrival of the ship in that possession, nor in the British Islands after the expiration of twelve months next after the return of the ship and of the master to the British Islands.

Passengers' Lists.

Passengers' lists.

311. (1) The master of every ship carrying steerage passengers on a voyage from the British Islands to any port out of Europe and not within the Mediterranean Sea, or on a colonial voyage as herein-before defined, shall, before demanding a clearance for his ship, sign in duplicate a passengers' list, that is to say, a list correctly setting forth the name and other particulars of the ship and of every passenger, whether cabin or steerage on board thereof.

(2) The passengers' list shall be countersigned by the emigration officer if there is one at the port, and then delivered by the master to the officer of customs from whom a clearance is demanded, and that officer shall thereupon countersign and return to the master one duplicate (in this Part of this Act referred to as the "master's list" and shall retain the other duplicate.

(3) If any requirement of this section to be observed by the master is not complied with in the case of any ship or any passengers' list is wilfully false, the master of the ship shall for each offence be liable to a fine not exceeding one hundred pounds.

Lists of passengers embarked after clearance.

312. (1) If at any time after the passengers' list has been signed and delivered as aforesaid any additional passenger, (whether cabin or steerage) is taken on board, the master shall add to the master's list, and also enter on a separate list signed by him the names and other particulars of every such additional passenger.

(2) The separate list shall be countersigned by the emigration officer, where there is one at the port, and shall, together with the master's list to which the addition has been made, be delivered to the chief officer of customs at the port, who shall thereupon countersign the master's list, and return the same to the master, and shall retain the separate list, and so on in like manner whenever any additional passenger is taken on board.

(3) If there is no officer of customs stationed at the port where an additional passenger is taken on board, the said lists shall be delivered to the officer of customs at the next port having such an officer at which the vessel arrives, to be dealt with as herein-before mentioned.

(4) When any additional passenger is taken on board the master shall, before the ship proceeds to sea, obtain a fresh certificate from the emigration officer of the port that all the requirements of this Part of this Act have been complied with.

(5) If any requirement of this section is not complied with in the case of any ship, the master of that ship shall for each offence be liable to a fine not exceeding fifty pounds.

313. (1) If a person is found on board an emigrant ship with intent to obtain a passage therein without the consent of the owner, charterer, or master thereof, he and any person aiding and abetting him, shall be liable to a fine not exceeding twenty pounds, and in default of payment to imprisonment for a period not exceeding three months, with or without hard labour. Attempt to gain passage without payment.

(2) Any person so found on board may, without warrant, be taken before a justice of the peace to be dealt with according to law, and that justice may try the case in a summary manner.

Certificate for Clearance.

314. (1) A ship fitted or intended for the carriage of steerage passengers as an emigrant ship shall not clear outwards or proceed to sea until the master has obtained from the emigration officer at the port of clearance a certificate for clearance, that is to say, a certificate that all the requirements of this Part of this Act, so far as the same can be complied with before the departure of the ship, have been duly complied with, and that the ship is in his opinion seaworthy, in safe trim, and in all respects fit for her intended voyage, and that the steerage passengers and crew are in a fit state to proceed and that the master's bond has been duly executed. Certificate for clearance.

(2) If the emigration officer refuses to grant such certificate, the owner or charterer of the ship may appeal in writing to the Board of Trade, and that Board shall thereupon appoint any two other emigration officers or any two competent persons to examine into the matter at the expense of the appellant, and if the officers or persons so appointed grant the master of the ship under their joint hands a certificate to the same purport as the certificate for clearance, it shall be of the same effect as a certificate for clearance.

315. (1) The master of every ship, whether an emigrant ship or not, which is fitting or intended for the carriage of steerage passengers, or which carries steerage passengers on a voyage from the British Islands to any port out of Europe and not within the Mediterranean Sea, or on a colonial voyage as herein-before defined, shall afford to the emigration officer at any port in Her Majesty's dominions, and, in the case of British ships, to the British consular officer at any port elsewhere at which the ship is or arrives, every facility for inspecting the ship, and for communicating with the steerage passengers and for ascertaining that this Part of this Act, so far as applicable to the ship, has been duly complied with. Facilities to be given for the inspection of ships.

(2) If the master of any ship fails to comply with this section, he shall for each offence be liable to fine not exceeding fifty pounds.

Ships putting back to replenish provisions, etc.

316. (1) If any emigrant ship, after clearance, is detained in port for more than seven days or puts into or touches at any port in the British Islands, she shall not proceed to sea again until—

(*a*) there has been laden on board, at the expense of the owner, charterer, or master of the ship, such further supply of pure water, wholesome provisions of the requisite kinds and qualities, and medical stores, as is necessary to make up the full quantities of those articles required under this Part of this Act to be laden on board for the intended voyage; and

(*b*) any damage which the ship has sustained has been effectually repaired; and

(*c*) the master of the ship has obtained from the emigration officer a certificate for clearance to the same effect as the certificate for clearance at her port of departure.

(2) If any requirement of this section is not complied with in the case of any emigrant ship, the master shall for each offence be liable to a fine not exceeding one hundred pounds.

Emigrant ships putting back to be reported to emigration officer.

317. (1) If any emigrant ship, after clearance, puts into or touches at any port in the British Islands, the master shall, within twelve hours thereafter, report in writing his arrival, and the cause of his putting back, and the condition of his ship and of her provisions, water, and medical stores to the emigration officer at the port, and shall produce to that officer the master's list of passengers.

(2) If the master of an emigrant ship fails to comply with this section, he shall for each offence be liable to a fine not exceeding twenty pounds.

Appeal to Court of Survey.

318. (1) If the owner of an emigrant ship is aggrieved by the refusal by an emigration officer of a certificate for clearance, he may appeal to a court of survey for the port or district where the ship for the time being is in manner directed by the rules of that court.

(2) The judge of the court of survey shall report to the Board of Trade on the question raised by the appeal, and that Board, if satisfied that the requirements of the report and of this Part of this Act have been complied with, may grant or direct the emigration officer to grant a certificate for clearance.

(3) Subject to any order made by the judge of the court of survey, the costs of and incidental to the appeal shall follow the event.

(4) Where a survey of a ship is made for the purpose of a certificate for clearance, the person so appointed to make the survey shall, if so required by the owner, be accompanied on the survey by some person appointed by the

owner, and in such case if the said two persons agree there shall be no appeal to the court of survey in pursuance of this section.

319. (1) If any emigrant ship— Forfeiture of ship proceeding to sea without certificate for clearance.

(*a*) proceeds to sea without the master having obtained the certificate for clearance; or

(*b*) having proceeded to sea, puts into any port in the British Islands in a damaged state, and leaves or attempts to leave that port with steerage passengers on board without the master having obtained the proper certificate for clearance;

that ship shall be forfeited to the Crown, and may be seized by any officer of customs if found within two years from the commission of the offence in any port in Her Majesty's dominions, and shall thereupon be dealt with as if she had been seized as forfeited under the laws relating to the customs.

(2) The Board of Trade may release, if they think fit, any such forfeited ship, on payment, to the use of the Crown, of such sum not exceeding two thousand pounds as the Board specify.

Passengers' Contracts.

320. (1) If any person, except the Board of Trade and persons acting for them and under their direct authority, receives money from any person for or in respect of a passage as a steerage passenger in any ship, or of a passage as a cabin passenger in any emigrant ship, proceeding from the British Islands to any port out of Europe and not within the Mediterranean Sea, he shall give to the person paying the same a contract ticket signed by or on behalf of the owner, charterer, or master of the ship, and printed in plain and legible characters. Contract tickets for passengers.

(2) The contract ticket shall be in a form approved by the Board of Trade and published in the London Gazette, and any directions contained in that form of contract ticket not being inconsistent with this Act shall be obeyed as if set forth in this section.

(3) If any person fails to comply with any requirement of this section, he shall for each offence be liable to a fine not exceeding fifty pounds.

(4) Contract tickets under this section shall not be liable to stamp duty.

321. (1) Any question which arises respecting the breach or non-performance of any stipulation in any such contract ticket may, at the option of any passenger interested, whether a steerage or a cabin passenger, be tried before a court of summary jurisdiction, and the court may award to the complainant such damages and costs as they think just, not exceeding the amount of the passage money specified in the contract ticket and twenty pounds in addition. Summary remedy for breach of contract.

(2) But if a passenger has obtained compensation or redress under any other provision of this Act, he shall not be entitled to recover damages under this section in respect of the same matter.

Penalty for failure to produce contract ticket.

322. If a passenger whether a steerage or a cabin passenger fails, without reasonable cause, on demand of any emigration officer, to produce his contract ticket, and if any owner, charterer, or master of a ship, on like demand, fails without reasonable cause to produce for the inspection of such emigration officer and for the purposes of this Act the counterpart of any contract ticket issued by him or on his behalf, the passenger, owner, charterer, or master, as the case may be, shall for each offence be liable to a fine not exceeding ten pounds.

Penalty for altering, or inducing any one to part with, contract ticket.

323. If any person, after the issue of a contract ticket and during the continuance of the contract of which that ticket is evidence, alters that ticket, or induces any person to part with it, or renders useless, or destroys it, he shall (except it is the contract ticket of a cabin passenger who consents) for each offence be liable to a fine not exceeding twenty pounds.

Regulations as to Steerage Passengers.

Sanitary and other regulations by Order in Council

324. Her Majesty may by Order in Council make regulations—

(i) for preserving order, promoting health, and securing cleanliness and ventilation on board emigrant ships proceeding from the British Islands to any port in a British possession; and

(ii) for prohibiting emigration from any port at any time when choleraic or any epidemic disease is generally prevalent in the British Islands or any part thereof; and

(iii) for reducing the number of steerage passengers allowed to be carried in any emigrant ship, either generally or from any particular ports in the British Islands; and

(iv) for permitting the use on board emigrant ships of apparatus for distilling water and for defining in such case the quantity of fresh water to be carried in tanks and casks for the steerage passengers under the foregoing provisions of this Part of this Act; and

(v) for requiring duly authorised medical practitioners to be carried in emigrant ships where they would not otherwise under this Part of this Act be required to be carried.

Discipline on board.

325. (1) In every emigrant ship the medical practitioner aided by the master or, in the absence of the medical practitioner, the master, shall exact obedience to all regulations made by any such Order in Council as aforesaid.

(2) If any person on board—

(*a*) fails without reasonable cause to obey, or offends against, any such regulation or any provision of this Part of this Act, or

(*b*) obstructs the master or medical practitioner in the execution of any duty imposed upon him by any such regulation, or

(*c*) is guilty of riotous or insubordinate conduct,

that person shall for each offence be liable to a fine not exceeding two pounds, and in addition to imprisonment for any period not exceeding one month.

326. (1) Spirits shall not during the voyage be sold directly or indirectly in any emigrant ship to any steerage passenger.

Sale of spirits prohibited on emigrant ships.

(2) If any person acts in contravention of this section, he shall for each offence be liable to a fine not exceeding twenty pounds.

Maintenance after Arrival.

327. (1) Every steerage passenger in an emigrant ship shall be entitled for at least forty-eight hours next after his arrival at the end of his voyage to sleep in the ship, and to be provided for and maintained on board thereof, in the same manner as during the voyage, unless within that period the ship leaves the port in the further prosecution of her voyage.

Maintenance of steerage passengers after arrival.

(2) If this section is not complied with in the case of any emigrant ship, the master shall for each offence be liable to a fine not exceeding five pounds.

Detention and Wrongful Landing of Passengers.

328. Where a contract has been made by or on behalf of any steerage passenger for a passage in a ship proceeding on a voyage from the British Islands to any port out of Europe and not within the Mediterranean Sea, or proceeding on any colonial voyage as defined by this Part of this Act, and—

Return of passage money and compensation to passengers when passage not provided according to contract.

(i) the steerage passenger is at the place of embarkation before the hour of six o'clock in the afternoon of the day of embarkation appointed in the contract; and

(ii) the stipulated passage money has, if required, been paid;

then if the steerage passenger from any cause whatever [other than his own refusal, neglect, or default, or the prohibition underthis Act of an emigration officer, or the requirement of an Order in Council],

(*a*) is not received on board the ship before the said hour; or,

(*b*) having been received on board, does not either obtain a passage in the ship to the port at which he has contracted to land or, together with all the immediate members of his family who are included in the contract, obtain a passage to the same port in some other equally eligible ship to sail within ten days from the expiration of the said day of embarkation, and is not paid subsistence money from the time and at the rate herein-after provided;

the steerage passenger or any emigration officer on his behalf, may recover summarily all money paid by or on account of the steerage passenger for his passage, together with such further sum not exceeding ten pounds in respect of each such steerage passenger as is in the opinion of the Court a reasonable compensation for the loss or inconvenience occasioned to the steerage passenger by the loss of his passage, and such money and sum may be recovered, either from any person to whom or on whose account any money has been paid under the contract, or if the contract has been made with the owner, charterer, or master of the ship, or with any person acting on behalf or by the authority of any of them, then, at the option of the steerage passenger or emigration officer, from the owner, charterer, or master, or any of them.

Subsistence in case of detention.

329. (1) If any ship, whether an emigrant ship, or otherwise, does not actually put to sea and proceed on her intended voyage before three o'clock in the afternoon of the day next after the day of embarkation appointed in the contract, the owner, charterer, or master of the ship, or his agent, or any of them shall, until the ship finally proceeds on her voyage, pay to every steerage passenger entitled to a passage in the ship, or (if the steerage passenger is lodged and maintained in any hulk or establishment under the superintendence of the Board of Trade) to the emigration officer at the port of embarkation, subsistence money at the following rate; that is to say,

(*a*) for each of the first ten days of detention, one shilling and sixpence, and

(*b*) for every subsequent day, three shillings,

for each statute adult.

(2) Where the steerage passengers are maintained on board in the same manner as if the voyage had commenced—

(*a*) subsistence money shall not be payable for the first two days next after the said day of embarkation, and

(*b*) if the ship is unavoidably detained by wind or weather, or by any cause not attributable in the opinion of the emigration officer to the act or default of the owner, charterer, or master, subsistence money shall not be payable during any part of that period of detention.

Penalty for landing

330. If a steerage passenger is landed from any ship, whether an emigrant ship or not, at any port other than the port at which he has contracted to land, unless with his previous consent, or unless the landing is rendered necessary by perils of the sea or other unavoidable accident, the master of the ship shall for each offence be liable to a fine not exceeding fifty pounds.

steerage passengers at wrong place.

Provisions in case of Wreck.

Provision in case of an emigrant ship being wrecked or damaged in or near British Islands.

331. (1) When any emigrant ship—

(*a*) has, while in any port of the British Islands, or after the commencement of the voyage, been wrecked or otherwise rendered unfit to proceed on her intended voyage and any steerage passengers have been brought back to any port in the British Islands; or

(*b*) has put into any port in the British Islands in a damaged state; the master, charterer, or owner of that ship shall, within forty-eight hours thereafter, give to the nearest emigration officer a written undertaking to the following effect; that is to say,

(i) if the ship has been wrecked or rendered unfit to proceed on her voyage, that the owner, charterer, or master thereof, will embark and convey the steerage passengers in some other eligible ship, to sail within six weeks from the date of the undertaking, to the port for which their passage had been taken:

(ii) if the ship has put into port in a damaged state, that she will be made seaworthy and fit in all respects for her intended voyage, and will within six weeks from the date of the undertaking sail again with the steerage passengers.

(2) In either of the above cases, the owner, charterer, or master shall, until the steerage passengers proceed on their voyage, either lodge and maintain them on board in the same manner as if they were at sea, or pay either to the steerage passengers, or (if they are lodged and maintained in any hulk or establishment under the superintendence of the Board of Trade) to the emigration officer at the port, subsistence money at the rate of one shilling and sixpence a day for each statute adult.

(3) If the substituted ship, or the damaged ship, as the case may be, does not sail within the above-mentioned time, or if default is made in compliance with any requirement of this section, any steerage passenger or any emigration officer on his behalf may recover summarily all money paid by or on account of the passenger for the passage from the person to whom or on whose account the same was paid, or from the owner, charterer, or master of the ship, at the option of the passenger or emigration officer.

(4) The emigration officer may, if he thinks it necessary, direct that the steerage passengers be removed from any damaged emigrant ship at the

expense of the master thereof, and if after that direction any steerage passenger refuses to leave the ship, he shall for each offence be liable to a fine not exceeding forty shillings, or to imprisonment not exceeding one month.

Expenses of rescue and conveyance of wrecked passengers.

332. If any passenger, whether a cabin or a steerage passenger, is either taken off any ship which is carrying any steerage passenger on a voyage from any part of Her Majesty's dominions and is damaged, wrecked, sunk or otherwise destroyed, or if any such passenger is picked up at sea from any boat, raft, or otherwise, it shall be lawful—

(*a*) if the port to which such passenger (in this Act referred to as a "wrecked passenger") is conveyed is in the United Kingdom, for a Secretary of State; and

(*b*) if the port is in a British possession, for the governor of that possession, or any person authorised by him for the purpose; and

(*c*) if the port is elsewhere, for the British consular officer there;

to defray all or any part of the expenses thereby incurred.

Forwarding of passengers by governors or consuls.

333. (1) If any passenger, whether a cabin or a steerage passenger from any ship which is carrying any steerage passenger on a voyage from any port in Her Majesty's dominions, finds himself without any neglect or default of his own at any port outside the British Islands other than the port for which the ship was originally bound, or at which he, or the Board of Trade, or any public officer or other person on his behalf, has contracted that he should land, it shall be lawful—

(*a*) if the place is in a British possession, for the governor of that possession, or any person authorised by the governor for the purpose; and

(*b*) if the place is elsewhere, for the British consular officer there;

to forward the passenger to his intended destination, unless the master of the ship, within forty-eight hours of the arrival of the passenger, gives to the governor or consular officer, as the case may be, a written undertaking to forward or convey within six weeks thereafter the passenger to his original destination, and forwards or conveys him accordingly within that period.

(2) A passenger so forwarded by or by the authority of a governor or a British consular officer shall not be entitled under this Part of this Act to the return of his passage money, or to any compensation for loss of passage.

Recovery of expenses incurred in conveying wrecked passengers and forwarding passengers.

334. (1) All expenses incurred under this Part of this Act by or by the authority of a Secretary of State, governor of a British possession, or consular officer, in respect of a wrecked passenger, or forwarding of a passenger to his destination, including the cost of maintaining the passenger, until forwarded to his destination, and of all necessary bedding, provisions, and stores, shall be a joint and several debt to the Crown from the owner, charterer, and master of the ship on board of which the passenger had embarked.

(2) In any proceeding for the recovery of that debt a certificate purporting to be under the hand of a Secretary of State, governor, or consular officer, and stating the circumstances of the case, and the total amount of the expenses, shall be admissible in evidence in manner provided by this Act, and shall be sufficient evidence of the amount of the expenses, and of the fact that the same were duly incurred, unless the defendant specially pleads and duly proves that the certificate is false and fraudulent, or that the expenses were not duly incurred under this Act.

(3) The sum recovered on account of the expenses shall not exceed twice the total amount of passage money which the owner, charterer, or master of the emigrant ship proves to have been received by him or on his account, or to be due to and recoverable by him or on his account in respect of the whole number of passengers whether cabin or steerage who embarked in the ship.

335. A policy of assurance effected in respect of any steerage passage or of any steerage passage or compensation money by any person by this Part of this Act made liable, in the events aforesaid, to provide such passage or to pay such money, or in respect of any other risk under this Part of this Act, shall not be invalid by reason of the nature of the risk or interest sought to be covered by the policy of assurance. **Validity of insurance of passage money.**

Voyages to the United Kingdom.

336. (1) The master of every ship bringing steerage passengers to the British Islands from any port out of Europe and not within the Mediterranean Sea shall, within twenty-four hours after arrival, deliver to the emigration officer at the port of arrival a correct list, signed by the master, and specifying the name, age, and calling of every steerage passenger embarked, and the port at which he embarked, and showing also any birth which has occurred amongst the steerage passengers, and if any steerage passenger has died, his name and the supposed cause of his death. **List of steerage passengers brought to the British Islands.**

(2) If the master of a ship fails so to deliver the list, or if the list is wilfully false, he shall for each offence be liable to a fine not exceeding fifty pounds.

337. If any ship bringing steerage passengers to the British Islands from any port out of Europe and not within the Mediterranean Sea has on board a greater number of steerage passengers than is allowed by this Act in the case of emigrant ships proceeding from the British Islands, the master of that ship shall, for each statute adult constituting such excess, be liable to a fine not exceeding ten pounds. **Number of steerage passengers on ships bringing passengers to British Islands.**

Provisions and water in ships carrying steerage passengers to British Islands.

338. (1) The master of every ship bringing steerage passengers to the British Islands from any port out of Europe and not within the Mediterranean Sea shall issue to each steerage passenger during the voyage, including the time of detention, if any, at any port before the termination thereof, pure water and good and wholesome provisions in a sweet condition, in quantities not less than the amount required by this Part of this Act in the case of emigrant ships proceeding from the British Islands.

(2) If any requirement of this section is not complied with in the case of any emigrant ship, the master of that ship shall for each offence be liable to a fine not exceeding fifty pounds.

Registration of Births and Deaths.

Application to foreign ships carrying passengers of provisions respecting registration of births and deaths.

339. Where a ship which is not a British ship carries passengers, whether cabin or steerage, to or from any port of the United Kingdom as the port of destination or the port of departure of such ship, the provisions of Part Two of this Act with respect to the registration of births and deaths occurring on board, shall apply as if it were a British ship.

Saving of Right of Action.

Saving of right of action on contract for passage.

340. Nothing in this Part of this Act shall take away or abridge any right of action which may accrue to a steerage passenger in any ship, or to any other person, in respect of the breach or non-performance of any contract made between, or on behalf of, such steerage passenger or other person and the master, charterer, or owner of any such ship, or his agent, or any passage broker.

Passage Brokers.

Passage broker.

341. (1) Any person who sells or lets or agrees to sell or let, or is any wise concerned in the sale or letting of steerage passages in any ship proceeding from the British Islands to any place out of Europe not within the Mediterranean Sea shall for the purposes of this Part of this Act be a passage broker.

(2) The acts and defaults of any person acting under the authority, or as an agent, of a passage broker, shall, for the purposes of this Act, be deemed to be also the acts and defaults of the passage broker.

Passage brokers to enter into bond and obtain licence.

342. (1) A person shall not act directly or indirectly as a passage broker, unless he—

(*a*) has entered, with two good and sufficient sureties approved by the emigration officer nearest to his place of business, into a joint and several bond to the Crown, in the sum of one thousand pounds; and

(*b*) holds a licence for the time being in force to act as passage broker

(2) The bonds shall be renewed on each occasion of obtaining a licence, and shall not be liable to stamp duty; it shall be executed in duplicate, and one part shall be deposited at the office of the Board of Trade, and the other part with the said emigration officer.

(3) The emigration officer may, in lieu of two securities, accept the bond of any guarantee society approved by the Treasury.

(4) There shall be exempted from this section—

(*a*) the Board of Trade, and any person contracting with them or acting under their authority; and

(*b*) any passage broker's agent duly appointed under this Act.

(5) If any person fails to comply with any requirement of this section, he shall for each offence be liable to a fine not exceeding fifty pounds.

343. (1) Application for a licence to act as passage broker shall be made to the licensing authority for the place in which the applicant has his place of business. Granting of licences to passage brokers.

(2) The licensing authority, upon the applicant proving to their satisfaction that he—

(*a*) has entered into and deposited one part of such bond as is required by this Act; and

(*b*) has given to the Board of Trade at least fourteen days' clear notice of his intention to apply for a licence,

may grant the licence, and shall forthwith send to the Board of Trade notice of such grant.

(3) The licensing authority shall be—

(*a*) in the administrative county of London, the justices of the peace at petty sessions;

(*b*) elsewhere in England, the council of a county borough or county district;

(*c*) in Scotland, the sheriff; and

(*d*) in Ireland, the justices in petty sessions.

344. (1) A passage broker's licence shall, unless forfeited, remain in force until the thirty-first day of December in the year in which it is granted and for thirty-one days afterwards. Forfeiture of licence.

(2) Any court, when convicting a passage broker of an offence under this Part of this Act or of any breach or non-performance of the requirements thereof, may order that his licence be forfeited, and the same shall be forfeited accordingly.

(3) The court shall forthwith send to the Board of Trade a notice of any such order.

Passage broker's agents.

345. (1) A passage broker shall not employ as an agent in his business of passage broker any person who does not hold from him an appointment signed by the passage broker, and counter-signed by the emigration officer at the port nearest to the place of business of the passage broker.

(2) Every such agent shall, upon request, produce his appointment to any emigration officer, or to any person treating for a steerage passage under this Part of this Act.

(3) If any person acts in contravention of this section he shall for each offence be liable to a fine not exceeding fifty pounds.

List of agents and runners to be exhibited by brokers, and sent to emigration officers.

346. (1) A passage broker shall keep exhibited in some conspicuous place in his office or place of business a correct list, in legible characters, containing the names and addresses in full of every person for the time being authorised to act as his agent or as an emigrant runner for him, and shall on or before the fifth day, or, if that day be a Sunday on or before the fourth day in every month, transmit a true copy of that list, signed by him, to the emigration officer nearest to his place of business, and shall report to that emigration officer every discharge or fresh engagement of an agent or of an emigrant runner within twenty-four hours of the same taking place.

(2) If a passage broker fails to comply with any requirement of this section, he shall for each offence be liable to a fine not exceeding five pounds.

Emigrant Runners.

Emigrant runner.

347. If any person other than a licensed passage broker or his *bonâ fide* salaried clerk, in or within five miles of the outer boundaries of any port, for hire or reward or the expectation thereof directly or indirectly conducts, solicits, influences, or recommends any intending emigrant to or on behalf of any passage broker, or any owner, charterer or master of a ship, or any keeper of a lodging house, tavern or shop, or any money changer or other dealer or chapman, for any purpose connected with the preparations or arrangements for a passage, or gives or pretends to give to any intending emigrant any information or assistance in any way relating to emigration, that person shall for the purposes of this Part of this Act be an emigrant runner.

Emigrant runner's licence.

348. (1) The licensing authority for passage brokers for the place in which a person wishes to act as an emigrant runner, and to carry on his business, may, upon his application and on the recommendation in writing of an emigration officer, or of the chief constable or other head officer of police in such place (but not otherwise), grant, if they think fit, to the applicant a licence to act as emigrant runner.

(2) The emigrant runner shall, within forty-eight hours after his license is granted, lodge the same with the nearest emigration officer, and that officer shall—

(*a*) register the name and abode of the emigrant runner in a book to be kept for the purpose, and number each name in arithmetical order, and

(*b*) upon receipt of a fee, not exceeding seven shillings, supply to the emigrant runner a badge of such form and description as the Board of Trade approve,

but in case of a renewed licence, the officer need only note the renewal and its date in his registry book against the original entry of the emigrant runner's name.

(3) An emigrant runner's licence shall remain in force until the thirty-first day of December in the year in which it is granted, unless sooner revoked by any justice for any offence against this Act or for any other misconduct committed by the holder of such licence, or unless forfeited under the provisions herein-after contained.

(4) When an emigrant runner changes his abode, the emigration officer shall register the change in his registry book.

Renewal of badge.

349. Where an emigrant runner either satisfies the emigration officer for the port in which he is licensed to act that his badge is lost, or delivers his badge up to such officer in a mutilated or defaced state, and in either case pays such officer five shillings, the officer may, if he thinks fit, supply him with a new badge.

Penalties on persons acting without licence or badge, using badge, not lawfully issued, or employing unlicensed person.

350. (1) A person shall not—

(*a*) act as an emigrant runner without being duly licensed and registered; or

(*b*) retain or use any emigrant runner's badge not issued to him in manner by this Act required; or

(*c*) counterfeit or forge any emigrant runner's badge; or

(*d*) employ as an emigrant runner any person not duly licensed and registered.

(2) If any person acts in contravention of this section, he shall for each offence be liable to a fine not exceeding five pounds.

Penalties on emigrant runners for certain acts of misconduct.

351. (1) An emigrant runner—

(*a*) shall while acting as an emigrant runner wear his badge conspicuously on his breast; and

(*b*) shall lodge his licence with the emigration officer as required by this Act; and (*c*) on changing his abode, shall within forty-eight hours give notice of the change to the emigration officer of the port in which he is licensed to act; and

(*d*) on losing his badge, shall within forty-eight hours give notice to such emigration officer of the loss; and

(*e*) shall produce on demand his badge for inspection, or permit any person to take the number thereof; and

(*f*) hall not mutilate or deface his badge; and

(*g*) shall not wear his badge while unlicensed; and

(*h*) shall not wear any other badge than that delivered to him by the emigration officer; and

(*i*) shall not permit any other person to use his badge.

(2) If an emigrant runner fails to comply with any requirement of this section, he shall for each offence be liable to a fine not exceeding forty shillings, and, if the court thinks fit, to the forfeiture of his licence.

Emigrant runners' commission and fees.

352. (1) An emigrant runner shall not be entitled to recover from a passage broker any fee, commission or reward for or in consideration of any service connected with emigration, unless he is acting under the written authority of that passage broker.

(2) An emigrant runner shall not take or demand from any person about to emigrate any fee or reward for procuring his steerage passage, or in any way relating thereto, and if he does so he shall for each offence be liable to a fine not exceeding five pounds.

Frauds in procuring Emigration.

Frauds in procuring passages.

353. If any person by any false representation, fraud, or false pretence induces any person to engage a steerage passage in any ship, he shall for each offence be liable to a fine not exceeding twenty pounds.

Penalties for fraud in connexion with assisting emigration.

354. If any person—

(*a*) falsely represents himself to be, or falsely assumes to act as, agent of the Board of Trade in assisting persons who desire to emigrate; or

(*b*) sells any form of application, embarkation order, or other document or paper issued by the Board of Trade or by a Secretary of State for the purpose of assisting persons who desire to emigrate; or

(*c*) makes any false representation in any such application for assistance to the Board of Trade, or a Secretary of State, or in any certificate of marriage, birth, or baptism, or other document or statement adduced in support of any such application; or (*d*) forges or fraudulently alters any signature or statement in any such application, certificate, document, or statement, or personates any person named therein; or

(*e*) aids or abets any person in committing any of the foregoing offences;

that person shall, for each offence, be liable to a fine not exceeding fifty pounds.

Emigration Officers.

355. (1) In the British Islands the Board of Trade, and in a British possession the Governor of that possession, may appoint and remove such emigration officers and assistant emigration officers as seem necessary for carrying this Part of this Act into execution, under the direction of the Board or Governor, as the case may be. Emigration officers and assistants.

(2) All powers, functions, and duties to be exercised or performed, and anything to be done in pursuance of this Part of this Act by, to, or before an emigration officer, may be exercised, performed, and done by, to, or before his assistant, or, at any port where there is no emigration officer or assistant, or in their absence, by, to, or before the chief officer of customs for the time being at such port, and in any such case it shall be the duty of the chief officer of customs to do anything which it is the duty of the emigration officer or his assistant to do.

(3) A person lawfully acting as an emigration officer under this Act shall in no case be personally liable for the payment of any money or costs or otherwise in respect of any contract made, or of any legal proceedings for anything done, by him in his official capacity as an emigration officer and on the public service.

Legal Proceedings.

356. All fines and forfeitures under the provisions of this Part of this Act (other than the provisions relating to passenger steamers only) shall be sued for by the following officers; that is to say, Recovery of fines.

(*a*) any emigration officer;

(*b*) any chief officer of customs; and also

(*c*) in the British Islands, any person authorised by the Board of Trade and any officer of customs authorised by the Commissioners of Customs; and

(*d*) in a British possession any person authorised by the Governor of that possession, or any officer of customs authorised by the Government department regulating the customs in that possession.

Recovery of passage and subsistence money, compensation, and damages.

357. All sums of money made recoverable by this Part of this Act in respect of passage money, subsistence money, damages, compensation or costs, may be sued for and recovered before a court of summary jurisdiction by any person entitled thereto or by any of the officers in the last preceding section mentioned on behalf of any one or more of such persons, and in any case either by one or several proceedings.

Protection of persons executing Act.

358. The Public Authorities Protection Act, 1893, shall for the purposes of the provisions of this Part of this Act (other than the provisions relating to passenger steamers only) apply to the whole of Her Majesty's dominions, and to every place where Her Majesty has jurisdiction. 56 & 57 Vict. c. 61.

Supplemental.

Owner responsible for default in absence of agreement.

359. (1) In the absence of any agreement to the contrary, the owner of a ship shall be the person ultimately responsible as between himself and the other persons by this Part of this Act made liable in respect of any default in complying with any requirement thereof.

(2) If any person so made liable pays any money by this Part of this Act made payable to or on behalf of a steerage passenger, he shall be entitled, in the absence of any such agreement as aforesaid, to sue for and recover from the owner the amount so paid, together with costs.

Forms and fees.

360. (1) The forms set out in the Fourteenth Schedule to this Act or forms as near thereto as circumstances admit, shall be used in all cases to which such forms are applicable.

(2) Such fees as the Board of Trade determine shall be paid in respect of the surveys of emigrant ships mentioned in Part II of the Ninth Schedule to this Act not exceeding those specified therein.

(3) If any person employed under this Part of this Act demands or receives, directly or indirectly, otherwise than by the direction of the Board of Trade any fee, remuneration or gratuity whatever in respect of any duty performed by him under this Part of this Act, he shall for each offence be liable to a fine not exceeding fifty pounds.

Posting of abstracts of Part III in emigrant ships.

361. (1) The Board of Trade shall prepare such abstracts as they think proper of all or any of the provisions of this Part of this Act, and of any Order in Council made thereunder, and four copies of the abstracts, together with a copy of this Part of this Act, shall, on demand, be supplied by the chief officer of customs at the port of clearance to the master of every emigrant ship proceeding from the British Islands to any British possession.

(2) The master shall, on request, produce a copy of this Part of this Act to any steerage passenger for his perusal, and shall, before the embarkation of the steerage passengers, post copies of the abstracts in at least two conspicuous

places between the decks on which steerage passengers may be carried, and shall keep them posted so long as any steerage passenger is entitled to remain in the ship.

(3) The master shall be liable to a fine not exceeding forty shillings for every day during any part of which by his act or default such copies of the extracts fail to be so posted.

(4) If any person displaces or defaces any copy of the abstracts posted under this section, he shall for each offence be liable to a fine not exceeding forty shillings.

Bye-laws by harbour authority.

362. (1) The authority having the control of any docks or basins at any port in the British Islands from which emigrant ships are despatched, may, with the approval of a Secretary of State, make bye-laws:—

(*a*) for specifying the docks, basins, or other places at which persons arriving by sea at the port for the purpose of emigration, or actually emigrating therefrom shall be landed and embarked;

(*b*) for regulating the mode of their landing and embarkation;

(*c*) for the storing and safe custody of their luggage;

(*d*) for licensing porters to carry their luggage or otherwise attend upon them; and

(*e*) for admitting persons to and excluding persons from access to the docks and basins.

(2) The authority may attach a fine not exceeding five pounds to a breach of any such bye-law, and instead of an emigration officer the authority shall sue for and recover the fine.

(3) The authority making a bye-law, under this section may, by their officers or servants or by any constable, arrest without warrant any person charged with a breach of the bye-law, and detain him until he can be brought before a justice of the peace, and that justice may try the case in a summary manner.

(4) A bye-law made under this section shall be published in the London Gazette.

Exemption from survey of foreign passenger steamer or emigrant ship in certain cases.

363. Where a foreign ship is a passenger steamer or emigrant ship within the meaning of this Part of this Act, and the Board of Trade are satisfied, by the production of a foreign certificate of survey attested by a British consular officer at a port out of Her Majesty's dominions, that the ship has been officially surveyed at that port, and are satisfied that any requirements of this Act are proved by that survey to have been substantially complied with, the Board may, if they think fit, dispense with any further survey of the ship in respect of any requirement so complied with, and grant or direct one of their officers to grant a certificate, which shall have the same effect as if given upon survey under this Part of this Act:

Provided that Her Majesty in Council may order that this section shall not apply in the case of an official survey at any port at which it appears to Her Majesty that corresponding advantages are not extended to British ships.

Application of Part III as regards Emigrant Ships.

Application to certain voyages.

364. The provisions of this Part of this Act respecting emigrant ships shall apply to all voyages from the British Islands to any port out of Europe and not within the Mediterranean Sea.

Limited application of Part III of Act to colonial voyages.

365. (1) This Part of this Act, so far as the same is applicable, shall apply to every ship carrying steerage passengers on a colonial voyage as defined by this Part of this Act, provided that the enactments thereof relating to—

(*a*) master's bond;

(*b*) steerage passengers' contract tickets;

(*c*) Orders in Council regulating emigration from the British Islands, or prescribing rules for promoting health, cleanliness, order, and ventilation;

(*d*) passage brokers;

(*e*) emigrant runners; and

(*f*) posting of abstracts, and production of a copy, of this Part of this Act,

shall not apply.

(2) Where the duration of a colonial voyage, as determined under this Part of this Act, is less than three weeks, the enactments relating to—

(*a*) the regulations scheduled to this Act as to the accommodation for steerage passengers;

(*b*) medical practitioner, stewards, cooks, cooking apparatus, and manning with an efficient crew; and

(*c*) maintenance of steerage passengers after arrival,

shall also not apply.

(3) Where the duration of a colonial voyage (as determined under this Part of this Act) is less than three weeks, the enactments relating to the issue of provisions shall not, except as to the issue of water, apply to any steerage passenger who has contracted to furnish his own provisions.

366. (1) The Governor of a British possession may by proclamation,—

Modification of provisions of Part III in their application to British possessions.

(*a*) determine what shall be deemed, for the purposes of this Part of this Act, to be the length of the voyage of any ship carrying steerage passengers from any port in that British possession to any other port; and

(*b*) fix dietary scales for steerage passengers during the voyage; and

(*c*) declare what medical stores shall be deemed necessary for the medical treatment of the steerage passengers during the voyage.

(2) Every such proclamation shall take effect from the issue thereof, and shall have effect without as well as within the possession, as if enacted in this Part of this Act.

(3) The Governor of a British possession may authorise such persons as he thinks fit to make a like survey of emigrant ships sailing from that possession as is by this Act required to be made by two or more competent surveyors in the case of emigrant ships sailing from the British Islands.

(4) The Governor of a British possession may authorise any competent person to act as medical practitioner on board an emigrant ship proceeding on a colonial voyage.

367. (1) The Governor of each of the Australasian Colonies, that is to say, New South Wales, Victoria, South Australia, Western Australia, Queensland, Tasmania, New Zealand, and any colony hereafter established in Australia, may by proclamation make such rules as he thinks proper for determining the number of steerage passengers to be carried in any emigrant ship proceeding from one of such colonies to any other of those colonies, and for determining on what deck or decks, and subject to what reservations or conditions, a steerage passenger may be carried in such ship.

Power of Governors of colonies as to numbers of steerage passengers.

(2) The Governor of any British possession may, if he thinks fit, declare by proclamation that ships intended to pass within the tropics from any port in such possession may convey steerage passengers, being natives of Asia or Africa, after the rate of one for every twelve superficial feet of the passenger deck instead of after the rate specified in the Tenth Schedule to this Act.

(3) Every such proclamation shall take effect from the issue thereof, or such other day as may be named therein, and shall have effect without as well as within the possession, as if it were enacted in this Part of this Act in substitution as respects the said ships for the Tenth Schedule to this Act.

(4) The provisions of the Tenth Schedule to this Act, with respect to the number of superficial feet to be allowed to each steerage passenger, shall not apply to any ship proceeding from any port in the island of Ceylon to any port in British India in the Gulf of Manar or Palk's Straits, and the legislature of Ceylon may regulate by law the number of steerage passengers who may be carried on board such ships.

Power for legislature of India to apply Part III.

368. (1) The provisions of this Part of this Act (other than the provisions relating to passenger steamers only) shall not apply to British India except as in this section provided.

(2) The Governor General of India in Council may, by any Act passed for the purpose, declare that all or any provisions of this Part of this Act shall apply to the carriage of steerage passengers upon any voyage from any specified port in British India to any other specified port whatsoever; and may for the purposes of this Part of this Act—

(*a*) fix dietary scales for the voyage, and authorise the substitution of those scales for the scale enacted by this Act;

(*b*) determine what shall be deemed to be the length of any such voyage;

(*c*) determine the persons or officers who in British India shall take the place of emigration officers and officers of customs in the British Islands;

(*d*) declare the space necessary for steerage passengers, and the age at which two children shall be treated as one statute adult, in ships clearing out from any port in British India; and

(*e*) authorise the employment on board any ship of a medical practitioner duly qualified according to Indian law; and

(*f*) provide for the recovery and application in British India of fines and sums of money under this Part of this Act,

and the provisions of any such Act while in force shall have effect without as well as within British India as if enacted by this Act.

(3) Provided that any such Act shall be of no effect under this section, unless it be reserved for the signification of Her Majesty's pleasure thereon, or contain a suspending clause providing that the Act shall not come into operation until Her Majesty's pleasure thereon has been publicly signified in British India.

PART IV.

FISHING BOATS.

* * * * * [1]

PART V.

SAFETY.

Prevention of Collisions.

418. (1) Her Majesty may, on the joint recommendation of the Admiralty and the Board of Trade, by Order in Council, make regulations for the prevention of collisions at sea, and may thereby regulate the lights to be carried and exhibited, the fog signals to be carried and used, and the steering and sailing rules to be observed, by ships, and those regulations (in this Act referred to as the collision regulations), shall have effect as if enacted in this Act. Collision regulations.

(2) The collision regulations, together with the provisions of this Part of this Act relating thereto, or otherwise relating to collisions, shall be observed by all foreign ships within British jurisdiction, and in any case arising in a British court concerning matters arising within British jurisdiction foreign ships shall, so far as respects the collision regulations and the said provisions of this Act, be treated as if they were British ships.

419. (1) All owners and masters of ships shall obey the collision regulations, and shall not carry or exhibit any other lights, or use any other fog signals, than such as are required by those regulations. Observance of collision regulations.

(2) If an infringement of the collision regulations is caused by the wilful default of the master or owner of the ship, that master or owner shall, in respect of each offence, be guilty of a misdemeanor.

(3) If any damage to person or property arises from the non-observance by any ship of any of the collision regulations, the damage shall be deemed to have been occasioned by the wilful default of the person in charge of the deck of the ship at the time, unless it is shown to the satisfaction of the court that the circumstances of the case made a departure from the regulation necessary.

(4) Where in a case of collision it is proved to the court before whom the case is tried, that any of the collision regulations have been infringed,

[1] Section 372 provides that "this Part of this Act shall not, except where otherwise expressly provided, apply to Scotland, or to any British possession." The Part appears to have no application to India, and is, therefore, omitted.

the ship by which the regulation has been infringed shall be deemed to be in fault unless it is shown to the satisfaction of the court that the circumstances of the case made departure from the regulation necessary.

(5) The Board of Trade shall furnish a copy of the collision regulations to any master or owner of a ship who applies for it.

Inspection as to lights and fog signals.

420. (1) A surveyor of ships may inspect any ship, British or foreign, for the purpose of seeing that the ship is properly provided with lights and the means of making fog signals, in conformity with the collision regulations, and if the surveyor finds that the ship is not so provided he shall give to the master or owner notice in writing, pointing out the deficiency, and also what is, in his opinion, requisite in order to remedy the same.

(2) Every notice so given shall be communicated in the manner directed by the Board of Trade to the chief officer of customs at any port at which the ship may seek to obtain a clearance or transire; and the ship shall be detained, until a certificate under the hand of a surveyor of ships is produced to the effect that the ship is properly provided with lights and with the means of making fog signals, in conformity with the collision regulations.

(3) For the purpose of an inspection under this section a surveyor shall have all the powers of a Board of Trade inspector under this Act.

(4) Where the certificate as to lights and fog signals is refused, an owner may appeal to the court of survey for the port or district where the ship for the time being is in manner directed by the rules of that court.

(5) On any such appeal the judge of the court of survey shall report to the Board of Trade on the question raised by the appeal, and the Board of Trade, when satisfied that the requirements of the report and of this Act as to lights and fog signals have been complied with, may grant, or direct a surveyor of ships or other person appointed by them to grant, the certificate.

(6) Subject to any order made by the judge of court of survey the costs of and incidental to the appeal shall follow the event.

(7) A surveyor in making an inspection under this section shall, if the owner of the ship so require, be accompanied on the inspection by some person appointed by the owner, and, if in that case the surveyor and the person so appointed agree, there shall be no appeal under this section to the court of survey.

(8) Such fees as the Board of Trade may determine shall be paid in respect of an inspection of lights and fog signals under this section not exceeding those specified in the Sixteenth Schedule to this Act.

Saving for local rules of navigation

421. (1) Any rules made before or after the passing of this Act under the authority of any local Act, concerning lights and signals to be carried

or the steps for avoiding collision to be taken, by vessels navigating the waters of any harbour, river, or other inland navigation, shall, notwithstanding anything in this Act, have full effect.

in harbours, etc.

(2) Where any such rules are not and cannot be made, Her Majesty in Council on the application of any person having authority over such waters, or if there is no such person, any person interested in the navigation thereof, may make such rules, and those rules shall, as regards vessels navigating the said waters, be of the same force as if they were part of the collision regulations.

Duty of vessel to assist the other in case of collision.

422. (1) In every case of collision between two vessels, it shall be the duty of the master or person in charge of each vessel, if and so far as he can do so without danger to his own vessel, crew and passengers (if any),

(*a*) to render to the other vessel, her master, crew and passengers (if any) such assistance as may be practicable, and may be necessary to save them from any danger caused by the collision, and to stay by the other vessel until he has ascertained that she has no need of further assistance, and also

(*b*) to give to the master or person in charge of the other vessel the name of his own vessel and of the port to which she belongs, and also the names of the ports from which she comes and to which she is bound.

(2) If the master or person in charge of a vessel fails to comply with this section, and no reasonable cause for such failure is shown, the collision shall, in the absence of proof to the contrary, be deemed to have been caused by his wrongful act, neglect or default.

(3) If the master or person in charge fails without reasonable cause to comply with this section, he shall be guilty of a misdemeanor, and, if he is a certificated officer, an inquiry into his conduct may be held, and his certificate cancelled or suspended.

Collisions to be entered in official log.

423. (1) In every case of collision, in which it is practicable so to do, the master of every ship shall immediately after the occurrence cause a statement thereof, and of the circumstances under which the same occurred, to be entered in the official log book (if any), and the entry shall be signed by the master, and also by the mate or one of the crew.

(2) If the master fails to comply with this section, he shall for each offence be liable to a fine not exceeding twenty pounds.

Application of collision regulations to foreign ships.

424. Whenever it is made to appear to Her Majesty in Council that the Government of any foreign country is willing that the collision regulations, or the provisions of this Part of this Act relating thereto or otherwise relating to collisions, or any of those regulations or provisions should apply to the ships of that country when beyond the limits of British jurisdiction, Her Majesty may, by Order in Council, direct that those regulations and provisions shall, subject to any limitation of time, conditions and qualifications contained in the Order, apply to the ships of the said foreign country, whether within British jurisdiction or not, and that such ships shall for the purpose of such regulations and provisions be treated as if they were British ships.

Report of Accidents and Loss of Ship.

Report to Board of Trade of accidents to steamships.

425. When a steamship has sustained or caused any accident occasioning loss of life or any serious injury to any person, or has received any material damage affecting her seaworthiness or her efficiency either in her hull or in any part of her machinery, the owner or master shall, within twenty-four hours after the happening of the accident or damage, or as soon thereafter as possible, transmit to the Board of Trade, by letter signed by the owner or master, a report of the accident or damage, and of the probable occasion thereof, stating the name on the ship, her official number (if any), the port to which she belongs, and the place where she is.

(2) If the owner or master of a steamship fails without reasonable cause to comply with this section, he shall for each offence be liable to a fine not exceeding fifty pounds.

(3) This section shall apply to all British ships, and to all foreign steamships carrying passengers between places in the United Kingdom.

Notice of loss of British ship to be given to the Board of Trade.

426. (1) If the managing owner or, in the event of there being no managing owner, the ship's husband, of any British ship has reason, owing to the non-appearance of the ship or to any other circumstance, to apprehend that the ship has been wholly lost, he shall, as soon as conveniently may be, send to the Board of Trade notice in writing of the loss and of the probable occasion thereof, stating the name of the ship, her official number (if any), and the port to which she belongs.

(2) If a managing owner or ship's husband fails without reasonable cause to comply with this section within a reasonable time, he shall for each offence be liable to a fine not exceeding fifty pounds.

Life-saving Appliances.

Rules as to life-saving appliances.

427. (1) The Board of Trade may make rules (in this Act called rules for life-saving appliances) with respect to all or any of the following matters, namely:—

(*a*) the arranging of British ships into classes, having regard to the services in which they are employed, to the nature and duration of the voyage, and to the number of persons carried;

(*b*) the number and description of the boats, life-boats, life-rafts, life-jackets, and life-buoys to be carried by British ships, according to the class in which they are arranged, and the mode of their construction, also the equipments to be carried by the boats and rafts, and the methods to be provided to get the boats and other life-saving appliances into the water, which methods may include oil for use in stormy weather; and

(*c*) the quantity, quality, and description of buoyant apparatus to be carried on board British ships carrying passengers, either in addition to or in substitution for boats, life-boats, life-rafts, life-jackets, and life-buoys.

(2) All such rules shall be laid before Parliament so soon as may be after they are made, and shall not come into operation until they have lain for forty days before both Houses of Parliament during the session of Parliament; and on coming into operation shall have effect as if enacted in this Act.

(3) Rules under this section shall not apply to any fishing boat for the time being entered in the fishing boat register under Part IV of this Act.

Duties of owners and masters as to carrying live-saving appliances.

428. It shall be the duty of the owner and master of every British ship to see that his ship is provided, in accordance with the rules for life saving appliances, with such of those appliances as, having regard to the nature of the service on which the ship is employed, and the avoidance of undue encumbrance of the ship's deck, are best adapted for securing the safety of her crew and passengers.

Appointment of consultative committee for framing rules.

429. (1) For the purpose of preparing and advising on the rules for life-saving appliances, the Board of Trade may appoint a committee, the members of which shall be nominated by the Board in accordance with the Seventeenth Schedule to this Act.

(2) A member of the committee shall hold office for two years from the date of his appointment, but shall be eligible for re-appointment.

(3) There shall be paid to the members of the committee, out of the Mercantile Marine Fund, such travelling and other allowances as the Board of Trade may fix.

(4) Her Majesty may, by Order in Council, alter the Seventeenth Schedule to this Act.

Penalty for breach of rules.

430. (1) In the case of any ship—

(*a*) If the ship is required by the rules for life-saving appliances to be provided with such appliances and proceeds on any voyage or excursion without being so provided in accordance with the rules applicable to the ship; or (*b*) If any of the appliances with which the ship is so provided are lost or rendered unfit for service in the course of the voyage or excursion through the wilful fault or negligence of the owner or master; or

(*c*) If the master wilfully neglects to replace or repair on the first opportunity any such appliances lost or injured in the course of the voyage or excursion; or

(*d*) If such appliances are not kept so as to be at all times fit and ready for use;

then the owner of the ship (if in fault) shall for each offence be liable to fine not exceeding one hundred pounds, and the master of the ship (if in fault) shall for each offence be liable to a fine not exceeding fifty pounds.

(2) Nothing in the foregoing enactments with respect to life-saving appliances shall prevent any person from being liable under any other provision of this Act, or otherwise, to any other or higher fine or punishment than is provided by those enactments, provided that a person shall not be punished twice for the same offence.

(3) If the court before whom a person is charged with an offence punishable under those enactments thinks that proceedings ought to be taken against him for the offence under any other provision of this Act, or otherwise, the court may adjourn the case to enable such proceedings to be taken.

Survey of ship with respect to life-saving appliances.

431. (1) A surveyor of ships may inspect any ship for the purpose of seeing that she is properly provided with life-saving appliances in conformity with this Act, and for the purpose of that inspection shall have all the powers of a Board of Trade inspector under this Act.

(2) If the said surveyor finds that the ship is not so provided, he shall give to the master or owner notice in writing pointing out the deficiency, and also pointing out what in his opinion is requisite to remedy the same.

(3) Every notice so given shall be communicated in the manner directed by the Board of Trade to the chief officer of customs of any port at which the ship may seek to obtain a clearance or transire, and the ship shall be detained until a certificate under the hand of any such surveyor is produced to the effect that the ship is properly provided with life-saving appliances in conformity with this Act.

General Equipment.

Adjustment of compasses and provision of hose.

432. (1) Every British sea-going steamship if employed to carry passengers, shall have her compasses properly adjusted from time to time and every British sea-going steamship not used wholly as a tug shall be provided with a hose capable of being connected with the engines of the ship and adapted for extinguishing fire in any part of the ship.

(2) If any such British sea-going steamship plies or goes to sea from any port in the United Kingdom and any requirement of this section is not complied with, then for each matter in which default is made, the owner (if in fault) shall be liable to a fine not exceeding one hundred pounds, and the master (if in fault) shall be liable to a fine not exceeding fifty pounds.

Placing undue weight on safety valves.

433. A person shall not place an undue weight on the safety valve of any steamship, and if he does so he shall, in addition to any other liability he may incur by so doing, be liable for each offence to a fine not exceeding one hundred pounds.

Signals of Distress.

Signals of distress.

434. (1) Her Majesty in Council may make rules as to what signals shall be signals of distress, and the signals fixed by those rules shall be deemed to be signals of distress.

(2) If a master of a vessel uses or displays, or causes or permits any person under his authority to use or display, any of those signals of distress except in the case of a vessel being in distress, he shall be liable to pay compensation for any labour undertaken, risk incurred, or loss sustained in consequence of that signal having been supposed to be a signal of distress, and that compensation may, without prejudice to any other remedy, be recovered in the same manner in which salvage is recoverable.

Provision of signals of distress, inextinguishable lights, and life-buoys.

435. (1) Where a ship is a sea-going passenger steamer or emigrant ship within the meaning of the Third Part of this Act, the ship shall be provided to the satisfaction of the Board of Trade—

(*a*) with means for making the said signals of distress at night, including means of making flames on the ship which are inextinguishable in water, or such other means of making signals of distress as the Board of Trade may previously approve; and

(*b*) with a proper supply of lights inextinguishable in water, and fitted for attachment to life-buoys.

(2) If any such ship goes to sea from any port of the United Kingdom without being provided as required by this section, then for each default in any of the above requisites, the owner (if in fault) shall be liable to a fine not exceeding one hundred pounds, and the master (if in fault) shall be liable to a fine not exceeding fifty pounds.

Draught of Water and Load-Line.

Ship's draught of

436. (1) The Board of Trade may, in any case or class of cases in which they think it expedient to do so, direct any person appointed by them

water to be recorded.

for the purpose, to record, in such manner and with such particulars as they direct, the draught of water of any sea-going ship, as shown on the scale of feet on her stem and stern post, and the extent of her clear side in feet and inches, upon her leaving any dock, wharf, port, or harbour for the purpose of proceeding to sea, and the person so appointed shall thereupon keep that record, and shall forward a copy thereof to the Board of Trade.

(2) That record or copy, if produced out of the custody of the Board of Trade, shall be admissible in evidence in manner provided by this Act.

(3) The master of every British sea-going ship shall, upon her leaving any dock, wharf, port, or harbour for the purpose of proceeding to sea, record her draught of water and the extent of her clear side in the official log book (if any), and shall produce the record to any chief officer of customs whenever required by him, and if he fails without reasonable cause to produce the record shall for each offence be liable to a fine not exceeding twenty pounds.

(4) The master of a sea-going ship shall, upon the request of any person appointed to record the ship's draught of water, permit that person to enter the ship and to make such inspections and take such measurements as may be requisite for the purpose of the record; and if any master fails to do so, or impedes, or suffers anyone under his control to impede, any person so appointed in the execution of his duty, he shall for each offence be liable to a fine not exceeding five pounds.

(5) In this section the expression "clear side" means the height from the water to the upper side of the plank of the deck from which the depth of hold as stated in the register is measured, and the measurement of the clear side is to be taken at the lowest part of the side.

Marking of deck-lines.

437. (1) Every British ship (except ships under eighty tons register employed solely in the coasting trade, ships employed solely in fishing, and pleasure yachts, and ships employed exclusively in trading or going from place to place in any river or inland water the whole or part of which is in any British possession), shall be permanently and conspicuously marked with lines (in this Act called deck-lines) of not less than twelve inches in length and one inch in breadth, painted longitudinally on each side amidships, or as near thereto as is practicable, and indicating the position of each deck which is above water.

(2) The upper edge of each of the deck-lines must be level with the upper side of the deck plank next the waterway at the place of marking.

(3) The deck-lines must be white or yellow on a dark ground, or black on a light ground.

(4) In this section the expression "amidships" means the middle of

the length of the load-water-line as measured from the fore side of the stem to the aft side of the stern-post.

438. (1) The owner of every British ship proceeding to sea from a port in the United Kingdom (except ships under eighty tons register employed solely in the coasting trade, ships employed solely in fishing, and pleasure yachts) shall, before the time hereinafter mentioned, mark upon each of her sides, amidships within the meaning of the last preceding section, or as near thereto as is practicable, in white or yellow on a dark ground, or in black on a light ground, a circular disc twelve inches in diameter, with a horizontal line eighteen inches in length drawn through its centre. **Marking of load line.**

(2) The centre of this disc shall be placed at such level as may be approved by the Board of Trade below the deck line marked under this Act and specified in the certificate given thereunder, and shall indicate the maximum load line in salt water to which it shall be lawful to load the ship.

(3) The position of the disc shall be fixed in accordance with the tables used at the time of the passing of this Act by the Board of Trade, subject to such allowance as may be made necessary by any difference between the position of the deck line marked under this Act and the position of the line from which freeboard is measured under the said tables, and subject also to such modifications, if any, of the tables and the application thereof as may be approved by the Board of Trade.

(4) In approving any such modifications the Board of Trade shall have regard to any representations made to them by any corporation or association for the survey or registry of shipping for the time being appointed or approved by the Board of Trade, as hereinafter mentioned, for the purpose of approving and certifying the position of the load line.

439. If a ship is so loaded as to submerge in salt water the centre of the disc indicating the load line, the ship shall be deemed to be an unsafe ship within the meaning of the provisions hereafter contained in this Part of this Act, and such submersion shall be a reasonable and probable cause for the detention of the ship. **Ships with submerged load lines deemed unsafe.**

440. (1) Where a ship proceeds on any voyage from a port in the United Kingdom for which the owner is required to enter the ship outwards, the disc indicating the load line shall be marked, before so entering her, or, if that is not practicable, as soon afterwards as may be. **Time, etc., for marking of load line in case of foreign-going vessels.**

(2) The owner of the ship shall upon entering her outwards insert in the form of entry a statement in writing of the distance in feet and inches between the centre of this disc and the upper edge of each of the deck lines

which is above that centre, and if default is made in inserting that statement, the ship may be detained.

(3) The master of the ship shall enter a copy of that statement in the agreement with the crew before it is signed by any member of the crew, and a superintendent shall not proceed with the engagement of the crew until that entry is made.

(4) The master of the ship shall also enter a copy of that statement in the official log book.

(5) When a ship to which this section applies has been marked with a disc indicating the load line, she shall be kept so marked until her next return to a port of discharge in the United Kingdom.

Time, etc., for marking of load line in case of coasting vessels.

441. (1) Where a ship employed in the coasting trade is required to be marked with the disc indicating the load line, she shall be so marked before the ship proceeds to sea from any port; and the owner shall also once in every twelve months, immediately before the ship proceeds to sea, transmit or deliver to the chief officer of customs of the port of registry of the ship a statement in writing of the distance in feet and inches between the centre of the disc and the upper edge of each of the deck lines which is above that centre.

(2) The owner, before the ship proceeds to sea after any renewal or alteration of the disc, shall transmit or deliver to the chief officer of customs of the port of registry of the ship notice in writing of that renewal or alteration, together with such statement in writing as before mentioned of the distance between the centre of the disc and the upper edge of each of the deck lines.

(3) If default is made in transmitting or delivering any notice or statement under this section, the owner shall, for each offence, be liable to a fine not exceeding one hundred pounds.

(4) When a ship to which this section applies has been marked with a disc indicating the load line, she shall be kept so marked until notice is given of an alteration.

Penalty for offences in relation to marking of load line.

442. (1) If—

(*a*) any owner or master of a British ship fails without reasonable cause to cause his ship to be marked as by this Part of this Act required, or to keep her so marked, or allows the ship to be so loaded as to submerge in salt water the centre of the disc indicating the load line; or

(*b*) any person conceals, removes, alters, defaces, or obliterates, or suffers any person under his control to conceal, remove, alter, deface, or obliterate, any of the said marks, except in the event of the particulars thereby denoted being lawfully altered, or except for the purpose of escaping capture by an enemy,

he shall for each offence be liable to a fine not exceeding one hundred pounds.

(2) If any mark required by this Part of this Act is in any respect inaccurate so as to be likely to mislead, the owner of the ship shall for each offence be liable to a fine not exceeding one hundred pounds.

443. (1) The Board of Trade shall appoint the Committee of Lloyd's Register of British and Foreign Shipping, or, at the option of the owner of the ship, any other corporation or association for the survey or registry of shipping approved by the Board of Trade, or any officer of the Board of Trade specially selected by the Board for that purpose, to approve and certify on their behalf from time to time the position of any disc indicating the load line, and any alteration thereof, and may appoint fees to be taken in respect of any such approval or certificate.

Regulations as to load line.

(2) The Board of Trade may make regulations—

(*a*) determining the lines or marks to be used in connexion with the disc, in order to indicate the maximum load line under different circumstances and at different seasons, and declaring that this Part of this Act is to have effect as if any such line were drawn through the centre of the disc; and

(*b*) as to the mode in which the disc and the lines or marks to be used in connexion therewith are to be marked or affixed on the ship, whether by painting, cutting, or otherwise; and

(*c*) as to the mode of application for, and form of, certificates under this section; and

(*d*) requiring the entry of those certificates, and other particulars as to the draught of water and freeboard of the ship, in the official log-book of the ship, or other publication thereof on board the ship, and requiring the delivery of copies of those entries.

(3) All such regulations shall, while in force, have effect as if enacted in this Act, and if any person fails without reasonable cause to comply with any such regulation made with respect to the entry, publication, or delivery of copies of certificates or other particulars as to the draught of water and freeboard of a ship, he shall for each offence be liable to a fine not exceeding one hundred pounds.

(4) Where in pursuance of the regulations any such certificate is required to be delivered, a statement in writing as to the disc and deck lines of a ship

need not be inserted in the form of entry or transmitted or delivered to a chief officer of customs under the provisions herein-before contained.

Provision as to colonial ships with respect to load lines.

444. Where the legislature of any British possession by any enactment provides for the fixing, marking, and certifying of load lines on ships registered in that possession, and it appears to Her Majesty the Queen that that enactment is based on the same principles as the provisions of this Part of this Act relating to load lines, and is equally effective for ascertaining and determining the maximum load lines to which those ships can be safely loaded in salt water, and for giving notice of the load line to persons interested, Her Majesty in Council may declare that any load line fixed and marked and any certificate given in pursuance of that enactment shall, with respect to ships so registered, have the same effect as if it had been fixed, marked, or given in pursuance of this Part of this Act.

Provision as to foreign ships with respect to load lines.

445. (1) Where the Board of Trade certify that the laws and regulations for the time being in force in any foreign country and relating to overloading and improper loading are equally effective with the provisions of this Act relating thereto, Her Majesty in Council may direct that on proof of a ship of that country having complied with those laws and regulations, she shall not, when in a port of the United Kingdom, be liable to detention for non-compliance with the said provisions of this Act, nor shall there arise any liability to any fine or penalty which would otherwise arise for non-compliance with those provisions.

(2) Provided that this section shall not apply in the case of ships of any foreign country in which it appears to Her Majesty that corresponding provisions are not extended to British ships.

Dangerous Goods.

Restrictions on carriage on dangerous goods.

446. (1) A person shall not send or attempt to send by any vessel, British or foreign, and a person not being the master or owner of the vessel, shall not carry or attempt to carry in any such vessel, any dangerous goods without distinctly marking their nature on the outside of the package containing the same, and giving written notice of the nature of those goods and of the name and address of the sender or carrier thereof to the master or owner of the vessel at or before the time of sending the same to be shipped or taking the same on board the vessel.

(2) If any person fails without reasonable cause to comply with this section, he shall for each offence be liable to a fine not exceeding one hundred pounds; or if he shows that he was merely an agent in the shipment of any such goods as aforesaid, and was not aware and did not suspect and had no

reason to suspect that the goods shipped by him were of a dangerous nature, then not exceeding ten pounds.

(3) For the purpose of this Part of this Act the expression "dangerous goods" means aquafortis, vitriol, naphtha, benzine, gunpowder, lucifer matches, nitro-glycerine, petroleum, any explosives within the meaning of the Explosives Act, 1875, and any other goods which are of a dangerous nature.

38 & 39 Vict., c. 17.

Penalty for misdescription of dangerous goods.

447. A person shall not knowingly send or attempt to send by, or carry or attempt to carry in, any vessel, British or foreign, any dangerous goods under a false description, and shall not falsely describe the sender or carrier hereof, and if he acts in contravention of this section he shall for each offence be liable to a fine not exceeding five hundred pounds.

Power to deal with goods suspected of being dangerous.

448. (1) The master or owner of any vessel, British or foreign, may refuse to take on board any package or parcel which he suspects to contain any dangerous goods, and may require it to be opened to ascertain the fact.

(2) Where any dangerous goods, or any goods, which, in the judgment of the master or owner of the vessel, are dangerous goods, have been sent or brought aboard any vessel, British or foreign, without being marked as aforesaid, or without such notice having been given as aforesaid, the master or owner of the vessel may cause those goods to be thrown overboard, together with any package or receptacle in which they are contained; and neither the master nor the owner of the vessel shall be subject to any liability, civil or criminal, in any court for so throwing the goods overboard.

Forfeiture of dangerous goods improperly sent or carried.

449. (1) Where any dangerous goods have been sent or carried, or attempted to be sent or carried, on board any vessel, British or foreign, without being marked as aforesaid, or without such notice having been given as aforesaid, or under a false description, or with a false description of the sender or carrier thereof, any court having Admiralty jurisdiction may declare those goods, and any package or receptacle in which they are contained, to be, and they shall thereupon be, forfeited, and when forfeited shall be disposed of as the court direct.

(2) The court shall have, and may exercise, the aforesaid powers of forfeiture and disposal notwithstanding that the owner of the goods has not committed any offence under the provisions of this Act relating to dangerous goods, and is not before the court, and has not notice of the proceedings, and notwithstanding that there is no evidence to show to whom the goods belong; nevertheless the court may, in their discretion, require such notice as they may direct to be given to the owner or shipper of the goods before they are forfeited.

Saving for other enactments relating to dangerous goods.

450. The provisions of this Part of this Act relating to the carriage of dangerous goods shall be deemed to be in addition to and not in substitution for, or in restraint of, any other enactment for the like object, so nevertheless that nothing in the said provisions shall be deemed to authorise any person to be sued or prosecuted twice in the same matter.

Loading of Timber.

Loading of timber.

451. (1) If a ship, British or foreign, arrives between the last day of October and the sixteenth day of April in any year at any port in the United Kingdom from any port out of the United Kingdom, carrying as deck cargo, that is to say, in any uncovered space upon deck, or in any covered space not included in the cubical contents forming the ship's registered tonnage, any wood goods as hereinafter defined, the master of that ship, and also the owner, if he is privy to the offence, shall be liable to a fine not exceeding five pounds for every hundred cubic feet of wood goods carried in contravention of this section.

(2) Provided that a master or owner shall not be liable to any fine under this section—

(*a*) in respect of any wood goods which the master has considered it necessary to place or keep on deck during the voyage on account of the springing of any leak, or of any other damage to the ship received or apprehended; or

(*b*) if he proves that the ship sailed from the port at which the wood goods were loaded as deck cargo at such time before the last day of October as allowed a sufficient interval according to the ordinary duration of the voyage for the ship to arrive before that day at the said port in the United Kingdom, but was prevented from so arriving by stress of weather or circumstances beyond his control; or

(*c*) if he proves that the ship sailed from the port at which the wood goods were loaded as deck cargo at such time before the sixteenth day of April as allowed a reasonable interval according to the ordinary duration of the voyage for the ship to arrive after that day at the said port in the United Kingdom, and by reason of an exceptionally favourable voyage arrived before that day.

(3) For the purposes of this section, the expression "wood goods" means—

(*a*) any square, round, waney, or other timber, or any pitch pine, mahogany, oak, teak, or other heavy wood goods whatever; or (*b*) any more than five spare spars or store spars, whether or not made, dressed, and finally prepared for use; or

(*c*) any deals, battens, or other light wood goods of any description to a height exceeding three feet above the deck.

(4) Nothing in this section shall affect any ship not bound to a port in the United Kingdom which comes into any port of the United Kingdom under stress of weather, or for repairs, or for any other purpose than the delivery of her cargo.

Carriage of Grain.

452. (1) Where a grain cargo is laden on board any British ship, all necessary and reasonable precautions (whether mentioned in this Part of this Act or not) shall be taken in order to prevent the grain cargo from shifting.

Obligation to take precautions to prevent grain cargo from shifting.

(2) If those precautions have not been taken in the case of any British ship, the master of the ship and any agent of the owner who was charged with the loading of the ship or the sending of her to sea, shall each be liable to a fine not exceeding three hundred pounds, and the owner of the ship shall also be liable to the same fine, unless he shows that he took all reasonable means to enforce the observance of this section, and was not privy to the breach thereof.

453. (1) Where a British ship laden with a grain cargo at any port in the Mediterranean or Black Sea is bound to ports outside the Straits of Gibraltar or where a British ship is laden with a grain cargo on the coast of North America, the precautions to prevent the grain cargo from shifting, set out in the Eighteenth Schedule to this Act, shall be adopted, unless the ship is loaded in accordance with regulations for the time being approved by the Board of Trade, or is constructed and loaded in accordance with any plan approved by the Board of Trade.

Precautions against shifting of grain cargo laden in port in Mediterranean or Black Sea or on coast of North America.

(2) If this section is not complied with in the case of any ship, reasonable precautions to prevent the grain cargo of that ship from shifting shall be deemed not to have been taken, and the owner and master of the ship and any agent charged with loading her or sending her to sea shall be liable accordingly to a fine under this Part of this Act.

(3) Nothing in this section shall exempt a person from any liability, civil or criminal, to which he would otherwise be subject for failing to adopt any reasonable precautions which, although not mentioned in this section, are reasonably required to prevent grain cargo from shifting.

454. (1) Before a British ship laden with grain cargo at any port in the Mediterranean or Black Sea and bound to ports outside the Straits of Gibraltar, or laden with grain cargo on the coast of North America, leaves her final

Notice by master of kind and quantity of grain cargo

port of loading, or within forty-eight hours after leaving that port, the master shall deliver or cause to be delivered to the British consular officer, or, if the port is in a British possession, to the chief officer of Customs, at that port, a notice stating—

(*a*) the draught of water and clear side, as defined by this Part of this Act, of the said ship after the loading of her cargo has been completed at the said final port of loading; and

(*b*) the following particulars in respect to the grain cargo, namely,

(i) the kind of grain and the quantity thereof, which quantity may be stated in cubic feet, or in quarters, or bushels, or in tons weight; and

(ii) the mode in which the grain cargo is stowed; and

(iii) the precautions taken against shifting.

(2) The master shall also deliver a similar notice to the proper officer of customs in the United Kingdom, together with the report required to be made by the Customs Consolidation Act, 1876, on the arrival of the ship in the United Kingdom. 39 & 40 Vict. c. 36.

(3) Every such notice shall be sent to the Board of Trade, as soon as practicable, by the officer receiving the same.

(4) If the master fails to deliver any notice required by this section, or if in any such notice he wilfully makes a false statement or wilfully omits a material particular, he shall for each offence be liable to a fine not exceeding one hundred pounds.

(5) The Board of Trade may, by notice published in the London Gazette, or in such other way as the Board think expedient, exempt ships laden at any particular port or any class of those ships from this section.

Power of Board of Trade for enforcing provisions as to carriage of grain.

455. For securing the observance of the provisions of this Part of this Act with respect to grain cargo, any officer having authority in that behalf from the Board of Trade, either general or special, shall have power to inspect any grain cargo, and the mode in which the same is stowed, and for that purpose shall have all the powers of a Board of Trade inspector under this Act.

Definition of grain, etc.

456. For the purpose of the provisions of this Part of this Act with respect to grain cargo—

The expression "grain" means any corn, rice, paddy, pulse, seeds, nuts, or nut kernels.

The expression "ship laden with a grain cargo" means a ship carrying a cargo of which the portion consisting of grain is more than one-third of the registered tonnage of the ship, and that third shall be computed, where the grain is reckoned in measures of capacity, at the rate of one hundred cubic feet for each ton of registered tonnage, and where the grain is reckoned in measures of weight, at the rate of two tons weight for each ton of registered tonnage.

Unseaworthy Ships.

457. (1) If any person sends or attempts to send, or is party to sending or attempting to send, a British ship to sea in such an unseaworthy state that the life of any person is likely to be thereby endangered, he shall in respect of each offence be guilty of a misdemeanor, unless he proves either that he used all reasonable means to insure her being sent to sea in a seaworthy state, or that her going to sea in such an unseaworthy state was, under the circumstances, reasonable and justifiable, and for the purpose of giving that proof he may give evidence in the same manner as any other witness.

Sending unseaworthy ship to sea a misdemeanor.

(2) If the master of a British ship knowingly takes the same to sea in such an unseaworthy state that the life of any person is likely to be thereby endangered, he shall in respect of each offence be guilty of a misdemeanor, unless he proves that her going to sea in such an unseaworthy state was, under the circumstances, reasonable and justifiable, and for the purpose of giving such proof he may give evidence in the same manner as any other witness.

(3) A prosecution under this section shall not, except in Scotland, be instituted otherwise than by, or with the consent of, the Board of Trade, or of the governor of the British possession in which the prosecution takes place.

(4) A misdemeanor under this section shall not be punishable upon summary conviction.

(5) This section shall not apply to any ship employed exclusively in trading or going from place to place in any river or inland water of which the whole or part is in any British possession.

458. (1) In every contract of service, express or implied, between the owner of a ship and the master or any seaman thereof, and in every instrument of apprenticeship whereby any person is bound to serve as an apprentice on board any ship, there shall be implied, notwithstanding any agreement to the contrary, an obligation on the owner of the ship, that the owner of the ship, and the master, and every agent charged with the loading of the ship, or the preparing of the ship for sea, or the sending of the ship to sea, shall use all reasonable means to insure the seaworthiness of the ship for the

Obligation of shipowner to crew with respect to use of reasonable efforts to secure seaworthiness.

voyage at the time when the voyage commences, and to keep her in a seaworthy condition for the voyage during the voyage.

(2) Nothing in this section—

(*a*) shall subject the owner of a ship to any liability by reason of the ship being sent to sea in an unseaworthy state where, owing to special circumstances, the sending of the ship to sea in such a state was reasonable and justifiable; or

(*b*) shall apply to any ship employed exclusively in trading or going from place to place in any river or inland water of which the whole or part is in any British possession.

Power to detain unsafe ships, and procedure for detention.

459. (1) Where a British ship, being in any port in the United Kingdom, is an unsafe ship, that is to say, is, by reason of the defective condition of her hull, equipments, or machinery, or by reason of overloading or improper loading, unfit to proceed to sea without serious danger to human life, having regard to the nature of the service for which she is intended, such ship may be provisionally detained for the purpose of being surveyed, and either finally detained or released as follows:—

(*a*) The Board of Trade, if they have reason to believe, on complaint or otherwise, that a British ship is unsafe, may order the ship to be provisionally detained as an unsafe ship for the purpose of being surveyed.

(*b*) When a ship has been provisionally detained there shall be forthwith served on the master of the ship a written statement of the grounds of her detention, and the Board of Trade may, if they think fit, appoint some competent person or persons to survey the ship and report thereon to the Board.

(*c*) The Board of Trade on receiving the report may either order the ship to be released or, if in their opinion the ship is unsafe, may order her to be finally detained, either absolutely, or until the performance of such conditions with respect to the execution of repairs or alterations, or the unloading or reloading of cargo, as the Board think necessary for the protection of human life, and the Board may vary or add to any such order.

(*d*) Before the order for final detention is made a copy of the report shall be served upon the master of the ship, and within seven days after that service the owner or master of the ship may appeal to the court of survey for the port or district where the ship is detained in manner directed by the rules of that court.

(*e*) Where a ship has been provisionally detained, the owner or master of the ship, at any time before the person appointed under this section to survey the ship, makes that survey, may require that he shall be accompanied by such person as the owner or master may select out of the list of assessors for the court of survey, and in that case if the surveyor and assessor agree, the Board of Trade shall cause the ship to be detained or released accordingly, but if they differ, the Board of Trade may act as if the requisition had not been made, and the owner and master shall have the like appeal touching the report of the surveyor as is before provided by this section.

(*f*) Where a ship has been provisionally detained, the Board of Trade may at any time, if they think it expedient, refer the matter to the court of survey for the port or district where the ship is detained.

(*g*) The Board of Trade may at any time, if satisfied that a ship detained under this section is not unsafe, order her to be released either upon or without any conditions.

(2) Any person appointed by the Board of Trade for the purpose (in this Act referred to as a detaining officer), shall have the same power as the Board have under this section of ordering the provisional detention of a ship for the purpose of being surveyed, and of appointing a person or persons to survey her; and if he thinks that a ship so detained by him is not unsafe, may order her to be released.

(3) A detaining officer shall forthwith report to the Board of Trade any order made by him for the detention or release of a ship.

(4) An order for the detention of a ship, provisional or final, and an order varying the same, shall be served as soon as may be on the master of the ship.

(5) A ship detained under this section shall not be released by reason of her British register being subsequently closed.

(6) The Board of Trade may, with the consent of the Treasury, appoint fit persons to act as detaining officers under this section, and may remove any such officer; and a detaining officer shall be paid such salary or remuneration (if any) out of money provided by Parliament as the Treasury direct, and shall for the purpose of his duties have all the powers of a Board of Trade inspector under this Act.

(7) A detaining officer and a person authorised to survey a ship under this section shall for that purpose have the same power as a person appointed by a court of survey to survey a ship, and the provisions of this Act with respect to the person so appointed shall apply accordingly.

Liability for costs and damages.

460. (1) If it appears that there was not reasonable and probable cause, by reason of the condition of the ship or the act or default of the owner, for the provisional detention of a ship under this Part of this Act as an unsafe ship, the Board of Trade shall be liable to pay to the owner of the ship his costs of and incidental to the detention and survey of the ship, and also compensation for any loss or damage sustained by him by reason of the detention or survey.

(2) If a ship is finally detained under this Act, or if it appears that a ship provisionally detained was, at the time of that detention, an unsafe ship within the meaning of this Part of this Act, the owner of the ship shall be liable to pay to the Board of Trade their costs of and incidental to the detention and survey of the ship, and those costs shall, without prejudice to any other remedy, be recoverable as salvage is recoverable.

(3) For the purpose of this section the costs of and incidental to any proceeding before a court of survey, and a reasonable amount in respect of the remuneration of the surveyor or officer of the Board of Trade, shall be part of the costs of the detention and survey of the ship, and any dispute as to the amount of those costs may be referred to one of the officers following, namely, in England or Ireland to one of the masters or registrars of the High Court, and in Scotland to the Auditor of the Court of Session, and the officer shall, on request by the Board of Trade, ascertain and certify the proper amount of those costs.

(4) An action for any costs or compensation payable by the Board of Trade under this section may be brought against the Secretary of that Board by his official title as if he were a corporation sole, and if the cause of action arises in Ireland, and the action is brought in the High Court, that Court may order that the summons or writ may be served on the Crown and Treasury Solicitor for Ireland in such manner and on such terms respecting extension of time and otherwise as the Court thinks fit, and that that service shall be sufficient service of the summons or writ upon the Secretary of the Board of Trade.

Power to require from complainant security for costs.

461. (1) Where a complaint is made to the Board of Trade or a detaining officer that a British ship is unsafe, the Board or officer may, if they or he think fit, require the complainant to give security to the satisfaction of the Board for the costs and compensation which he may become liable to pay as hereinafter mentioned.

(2) Provided that such security shall not be required where the complaint is made by one-fourth, being not less than three, of the seamen belonging to the ship, and is not in the opinion of the Board or officer frivolous or

vexatious, and the Board or officer shall, if the complaint is made in sufficient time before the sailing of the ship, take proper steps for ascertaining whether the ship ought to be detained.

(3) Where a ship is detained in consequence of any complaint, and the circumstances are such that the Board of Trade are liable under this Act to pay to the owner of the ship any costs or compensation, the complainant shall be liable to pay to the Board of Trade all such costs and compensation as the Board incur or are liable to pay in respect of the detention and survey of the ship.

Application to foreign ships of provisions as to detention.

462. Where a foreign ship has taken on board all or any part of her cargo at a port in the United Kingdom, and is whilst at that port unsafe by reason of overloading or improper loading, the provisions of this Part of this Act with respect to the detention of ships shall apply to that foreign ship as if she were a British ship, with the following modifications:—

(i) a copy of the order for the provisional detention of the ship shall be forthwith served on the consular officer for the country to which the ship belongs at or nearest to the said port;

(ii) where a ship has been provisionally detained, the consular officer, on the request of the owner or master of the ship, may require that the person appointed by the Board of Trade to survey the ship shall be accompanied by such person as the consular officer may select, and in that case, if the surveyor and that person agree, the Board of Trade shall cause the ship to be detained or released accordingly, but if they differ, the Board of Trade may act as if the requisition had not been made, and the owner and master shall have the like appeal to a court of survey touching the report of the surveyor as is herein-before provided in the case of a British ship; and

(iii) where the owner or master of the ship appeals to the court of survey, the consular officer, on his request, may appoint a competent person to be assessor in the case in lieu of the assessor who, if the ship were a British ship, would be appointed otherwise than by the Board of Trade.

Survey of ship alleged by seamen to be unseaworthy.

463. (1) Whenever in any proceeding against any seaman or apprentice belonging to any ship for the offence of desertion, or absence without leave or for otherwise being absent from his ship without leave, it is alleged by one-fourth, or if their number exceeds twenty by not less than five, of the seamen belonging to the ship, that the ship is by reason of unseaworthiness, overloading, improper loading, defective equipment, or for any other reason, not in a fit condition to proceed to sea, or that the accommodation in the ship is insufficient, the court having cognizance of the case shall take such means as may be in their power to satisfy themselves concerning the truth or untruth of the allegation, and shall for that purpose receive the evidence of the persons making the same, and may summon any other witnesses whose evidence they may think it desirable to hear, and shall, if satisfied that the allegation is groundless, adjudicate in the case, but if not so satisfied shall before adjudication cause the ship to be surveyed.

(2) A seaman or apprentice charged with desertion, or with quitting his ship without leave, shall not have any right to apply for a survey under this section unless he has before quitting his ship complained to the master of the circumstances so alleged in justification.

(3) For the purposes of this section the court shall require any surveyor of ships appointed under this Act, or any person appointed for the purpose by the Board of Trade, or, if such a surveyor or person cannot be obtained without unreasonable expense or delay, or is not, in the opinion of the court, competent to deal with the special circumstances of the case, then any other impartial surveyor appointed by the court, and having no interest in the ship, her freight, or cargo, to survey the ship, and to answer any question concerning her which the court think fit to put.

(4) Such surveyor or other person shall survey the ship, and make his written report to the court, including an answer to every question put to him by the court, and the court shall cause the report to be communicated to the parties, and, unless the opinions expressed in the report are proved to the satisfaction of the court to be erroneous, shall determine the questions before them in accordance with those opinions.

(5) Any person making a survey under this section shall for the purposes thereof have all the powers of a Board of Trade inspector under this Act.

(6) The costs (if any) of the survey shall be determined by the Board of Trade according to a scale of fees to be fixed by them, and shall be paid in the first instance out of the Mercantile Marine Fund.

(7) If it is proved that the ship is in a fit condition to proceed to sea, or that the accommodation is sufficient, as the case may be, the costs of the survey shall be paid by the person upon whose demand, or in consequence of whose allegation the survey was made and may be deducted by the master or owner out of the wages due or to become due to that person and shall be paid over to the Board of Trade.

(8) If it is proved that the ship is not in a fit condition to proceed to sea, or that the accommodation is insufficient, as the case may be, the master or owner of the ship shall pay the costs of the survey to the Board of Trade,

and shall be liable to pay to the seaman or apprentice, who has been detained in consequence of the said proceeding before the court under this section, such compensation for his detention as the court may award.

PART VI.

Special Shipping Inquiries and Courts.

Inquiries and Investigations as to Shipping Casualties.

464. For the purpose of inquiries and investigations under this Part of this Act a shipping casualty shall be deemed to occur:— Shipping casualties.

(1) when on or near the coasts of the United Kingdom any ship is lost, abandoned, or materially damaged;

(2) when on or near the coasts of the United Kingdom any ship has been stranded or damaged, and any witness is found in the United Kingdom;

(3) when on or near the coasts of the United Kingdom any ship causes loss or material damage to any other ship;

(4) when any loss of life ensues by reason of any casualty happening to or on board any ship on or near the coasts of the United Kingdom;

(5) when in any place any such loss, abandonment, material damage, or casualty as above mentioned occurs, and any witness is found in the United Kingdom;

(6) when in any place any British ship is stranded or damaged, and any witness is found in the United Kingdom;

(7) when any British ship is lost or is supposed to have been lost, and any evidence is obtainable in the United Kingdom as to the circumstances under which she proceeded to sea or was last heard of.

465. (1) Where a shipping casualty has occurred a preliminary inquiry may be held respecting the casualty by the following persons, namely:— Preliminary inquiry into shipping casualties.

(a) where the shipping casualty occurs on or near the coasts of the United Kingdom, by the inspecting officer of the coast-guard or chief officer of customs residing at or near the place at which the casualty occurs; or

(b) where the shipping casualty occurs elsewhere, by the inspecting officer of the coast-guard or chief officer of customs residing at or near any place at which the witnesses with respect to the casualty arrive or are found, or can be conveniently examined; or (*c*) in any case by any person appointed for the purpose by the Board of Trade.

(2) For the purpose of any such inquiry the person holding the same shall have the powers of a Board of Trade inspector under this Act.

Formal investigation of shipping casualties.

466. (1) A person authorized as aforesaid to make a preliminary enquiry shall in any case where it appears to him requisite or expedient (whether upon a preliminary inquiry or without holding such an inquiry) that a formal investigation should be held, and in any case where the Board of Trade so directs, apply to a court of summary jurisdiction to hold a formal investigation, and that court shall thereupon hold the formal investigation.

(2) A wreck commissioner appointed under this Act shall at the request of the Board of Trade hold any formal investigation into a shipping casualty under this section, and any reference to the court holding an investigation under this section includes a wreck commissioner holding such an investigation.

(3) The court holding any such formal investigation shall hold the same with the assistance of one or more assessors of nautical, engineering, or other special skill or knowledge, to be appointed out of a list of persons for the time being approved for the purpose by a Secretary of State in such manner and according to such regulations as may be prescribed by rules made under this Part of this Act with regard thereto.

(4) Where a formal investigation involves or appears likely to involve any question as to the cancelling or suspension of the certificate of a master, mate, or engineer, the court shall hold the investigation with the assistance of not less than two assessors having experience in the merchant service.

(5) It shall be the duty of the person who has applied to a court to hold a formal investigation to superintend the management of the case, and to render such assistance to the court as is in his power.

(6) The court after hearing the case shall make a report to the Board of Trade containing a full statement of the case and of the opinion of the court thereon, accompanied by such report of, or extracts from, the evidence, and such observations as the court think fit.

(7) Each assessor shall either sign the report or state in writing to the Board of Trade his dissent therefrom and the reasons for that dissent.

(8) The court may make such order as the court think fit respecting the costs of the investigation, or any part thereof, and such order shall be enforced by the court as an order for costs under the Summary Jurisdiction Acts.

(9) The Board of Trade may, if in any case they think fit so to do, pay the costs of any such formal investigation.

(10) For the purposes of this section the court holding a formal investigation shall have all the powers of a court of summary jurisdiction when acting as a court in exercise of their ordinary jurisdiction.

(11) Every formal investigation into a shipping casualty shall be conducted in such manner that if a charge is made against any person, that person shall have an opportunity of making a defence.

(12) Formal investigations into shipping casualties under this section shall be held in some town hall, assize or county court or public building, or in some other suitable place to be determined according to rules made under this Part of this Act with regard thereto, and, unless no other suitable place is in the opinion of the Board of Trade available, shall not be held in a court ordinarily used as a police court, and all enactments relating to the court shall for the purposes of the investigation have effect as if the place at which the court is held were a place appointed for the exercise of the ordinary jurisdiction of the court.

(13) Where an investigation is to be held in Scotland, the Board of Trade may remit the same to the Lord Advocate to be prosecuted in such manner as he may direct.

467. (1) The list of persons approved as assessors for the purpose of formal investigations into shipping casualties shall be in force for three years only, but persons whose names are on any such list may be approved for any subsequent list. List of assessors.

(2) The Secretary of State may at any time add or withdraw the name of any person to or from the list.

(3) The list of assessors in force at the passing of this Act shall, subject as aforesaid, continue in force till the end of the year one thousand eight hundred and ninety-five.

468. When any loss of life arises by reason of any casualty happening to or on board any boat belonging to a fishing vessel, the Board of Trade may, if they think fit, cause an inquiry to be made or a formal investigation to be held as in the case of a shipping casualty, and the provisions of this Act relating thereto shall apply accordingly. Inquiry in case of loss of life from fishing vessel's boat.

Power as to Certificates of Officers, etc.

469. The Board of Trade may suspend or cancel the certificate of any master, mate, or engineer if it is shown that he has been convicted of any offence. Power of Board of Trade as to certificate.

Power of court of investigation or inquiry as to certificates.

470. (1) The certificate of a master, mate, or engineer may be cancelled or suspended—

(*a*) by a court holding a formal investigation into a shipping casualty under this Part of this Act, or by a naval court constituted under this Act, if the court find that the loss or abandonment of, or serious damage to, any ship, or loss of life, has been caused by his wrongful act or default, provided that, if the court holding a formal investigation is a court of summary jurisdiction, that court shall not cancel or suspend a certificate unless one at least of the assessors concurs in the finding of the court:

(*b*) by a court holding an inquiry under this Part of this Act into the conduct of a master, mate, or engineer, if they find that he is incompetent, or has been guilty of any gross act of misconduct, drunkenness, or tyranny, or that in a case of collision he has failed to render such assistance or give such information as is required under the Fifth Part of this Act:

(*c*) by any naval or other court where under the powers given by this Part of this Act the holder of the certificate is superseded or removed by that court.

(2) Where any case before any such court as aforesaid involves a question as to the cancelling or suspending of a certificate, that court shall, at the conclusion of the case or as soon afterwards as possible, state in open court the decision to which they have come with respect to the cancelling or suspending thereof.

(3) The court shall in all cases send a full report on the case with the evidence to the Board of Trade, and shall also, if they determine to cancel or suspend any certificate, send the certificate cancelled or suspended to the Board of Trade with their report.

(4) A certificate shall not be cancelled or suspended by a court under this section, unless a copy of the report, or a statement of the case on which the investigation or inquiry has been ordered, has been furnished before the commencement of the investigation or inquiry to the holder of the certificate.

Inquiry into conduct of certificated officer.

471. (1) If the Board of Trade, either on the report of a local marine board or otherwise, have reason to believe that any master, mate or certificated engineer is from incompetency or misconduct unfit to discharge his duties, or that in a case of collision he has failed to render such assistance or give such information as is required under the Fifth Part of this Act, the Board may cause an inquiry to be held.

(2) The Board may either themselves appoint a person to hold the inquiry or direct the local marine board at or nearest the place at which it is convenient for the parties or witnesses to attend to hold the same, or where there is no local marine board before which the parties and witnesses can conveniently attend, or the local marine board is unwilling to hold the inquiry, may direct the inquiry to be held before a court of summary jurisdiction.

(3) Where the inquiry is held by a local marine board, or by a person appointed by the Board of Trade, that board or person—

(*a*) shall hold the inquiry, with the assistance of a local stipendiary magistrate, or, if there is no such magistrate available, of a competent legal assistant appointed by the Board of Trade; and

(*b*) shall have all the powers of a Board of Trade inspector under this Act; and

(*c*) shall give any master, mate, or engineer against whom a charge is made an opportunity of making his defence either in person or otherwise, and may summon him to appear; and

(*d*) may make such order with regard to the costs of the inquiry as they think just; and

(*e*) shall send a report upon the case to the Board of Trade.

(4) Where the inquiry is held by a court of summary jurisdiction, the inquiry shall be conducted and the results reported in the same manner, and the court shall have the like powers, as in the case of a formal investigation into a shipping casualty under this Part of this Act, provided that, if the Board of Trade so direct, it shall be the duty of the person who has brought the charge against the master, mate, or engineer, to the notice of the Board of Trade to conduct the case, and that person shall in that case, for the purpose of this Act, be deemed to be the party having the conduct of the case.

472. (1) Any of the following courts, namely:— Removal of master by Admiralty Court.

In England and Ireland, the High Court,

In Scotland, the Court of Session,

Elsewhere in Her Majesty's dominions any colonial court of Admiralty or Vice-Admiralty court,

may remove the master of any ship within the jurisdiction of that court, if that removal is shown to the satisfaction of the court by evidence on oath to be necessary.

(2) The removal may be made upon the application of any owner of the ship or his agent, or of the consignee of the ship, or of any certificated mate, or of one-third or more of the crew of the ship.

(3) The court may appoint a new master instead of the one removed; but, where the owner, agent, or consignee of the ship is within the jurisdiction of the court, such appointment shall not be made without the consent of that owner, agent, or consignee.

(4) The court may also make such order and require such security in respect of the costs of the matter as the court thinks fit.

Delivery of certificate cancelled or suspended.

473. (1) A master, mate, or engineer whose certificate is cancelled or suspended by any court or by the Board of Trade shall deliver his certificate—

(*a*) if cancelled or suspended by a court, to that court on demand:

(*b*) if not so demanded, or if it is cancelled or suspended by the Board of Trade, to that Board, or as that Board direct.

(2) If a master, mate, or engineer fail to comply with this section, he shall, for each offence, be liable to a fine not exceeding fifty pounds.

Power of Board of Trade to restore certificate.

474. The Board of Trade may, if they think that the justice of the case requires it, re-issue and return the certificate of a master, mate, or engineer which has been cancelled or suspended, whether in the United Kingdom or in a British possession, or shorten the time for which it is suspended, or grant in place thereof a certificate of the same or any lower grade.

Re-hearing of Investigations and Inquiries.

Re-hearing of investigations and inquiries.

475. (1) The Board of Trade may, in any case where under this Part of this Act a formal investigation as aforesaid into a shipping casualty, or an inquiry into the conduct of a master, mate, or engineer has been held, order the case to be re-heard either generally or as to any part thereof, and shall do so—

(*a*) if new and important evidence which could not be produced at the investigation or inquiry has been discovered; or

(*b*) if for any other reason there has in their opinion been ground for suspecting that a miscarriage of justice has occurred.

(2) The Board of Trade may order the case to be re-heard, either by the court or authority by whom the case was heard in the first instance, or by the wreck commissioner, or in England or Ireland by the High Court, or in Scotland by the Senior Lord Ordinary, or any other judge in the Court of Session whom the Lord President of that court may appoint for the purpose, and the case shall be so re-heard accordingly.

(3) Where on any such investigation or inquiry a decision has been given with respect to the cancelling or suspension of the certificate of a master, mate, or engineer, and an application for a re-hearing under this

section has not been made or has been refused, an appeal shall lie from the decision to the following courts, namely :—

(*a*) If the decision is given in England or by a naval court, to the High Court;

(*b*) If the decision is given in Scotland, to either division of the Court of Session;

(*c*) If the decision is given in Ireland, to the High Court in Ireland.

(4) Any re-hearing or appeal under this section shall be subject to and conducted in accordance with such conditions and regulations as may be prescribed by rules made in relation thereto under the powers contained in this Part to this Act.

Supplemental Provisions as to Investigations and Inquiries.

476. (1) Where a stipendiary magistrate is in any place a member of the local marine board, a formal investigation at that place into a shipping casualty shall, whenever he happens to be present, be held before that stipendiary magistrate. Investigations before stipendiary magistrate.

(2) There shall be paid out of the Mercantile Marine Fund to the stipendiary magistrate, if he is not remunerated out of money provided by Parliament under this Act, such remuneration by way of an annual increase of salary, or otherwise, as a Secretary of State, with the consent of the Board of Trade, may direct.

477. The Lord Chancellor may appoint some fit person or persons to be a wreck commissioner or wreck commissioners for the United Kingdom, so that there shall not be more than three of those commissioners at any one time, and may remove any such wreck commissioner; and in case it becomes necessary to appoint a wreck commissioner in Ireland, the Lord Chancellor of Ireland shall have the power to appoint and remove that wreck commissioner. Power to appoint wreck commissioners.

478. (1) The legislature of any British possession may authorise any court or tribunal to make inquiries as to shipwrecks, or other casualties affecting ships, or as to charges of incompetency, or misconduct on the part of masters, mates, or engineers of ships, in the following cases, namely :— Authority for colonial court to make inquiries into shipping casualties and conduct of officers.

(*a*) where a shipwreck or casualty occurs to a British ship on or near the coasts of the British possession or to a British ship in the course of a voyage to a port within the British possession:

(*b*) where a shipwreck or casualty occurs in any part of the world to a British ship registered in the British possession:

(*c*) where some of the crew of a British ship which has been wrecked or to which a casualty has occurred, and who are competent witnesses to the facts, are found in the British possession:

(*d*) where the incompetency or misconduct has occurred on board a British ship on or near the coasts of the British possession, or on board a British ship in the course of a voyage to a port within the British possession:

(*e*) where the incompetency or misconduct has occurred on board a British ship registered in the British possession:

(*f*) when the master, mate, or engineer of a British ship who is charged with incompetency or misconduct on board that British ship is found in the British possession.

(2) A court or tribunal so authorised shall have the same jurisdiction over the matter in question as if it had occurred within their ordinary jurisdiction, but subject to all provisions, restrictions, and conditions which would have been applicable if it had so occurred.

(3) An inquiry shall not be held under this section into any matter which has once been the subject of an investigation or inquiry and has been reported on by a competent court or tribunal in any part of Her Majesty's dominions, or in respect of which the certificate of a master, mate, or engineer has been cancelled or suspended by a naval court.

(4) Where an investigation or inquiry has been commenced in the United Kingdom with reference to any matter, an inquiry with reference to the same matter shall not be held, under this section, in a British possession.

(5) The court or tribunal holding an inquiry under this section shall have the same powers of cancelling and suspending certificates, and shall exercise those powers in the same manner as a court holding a similar investigation or inquiry in the United Kingdom.

(6) The Board of Trade may order the re-hearing of any inquiry under this section in like manner as they may order the re-hearing of a similar investigation or inquiry in the United Kingdom, but if an application for re-hearing either is not made or is refused, an appeal shall lie from any order or finding of the court or tribunal holding the inquiry to the High Court in England: provided that an appeal shall not lie—

(*a*) from any order or finding on an inquiry into a casualty affecting a ship registered in a British possession, or

(*b*) from a decision affecting the certificate of a master, mate, or engineer, if that certificate has not been granted either in the United Kingdom or in a British possession, under the authority of this Act.

(7) The appeal shall be conducted in accordance with such conditions and regulations as may from time to time be prescribed by rules made in relation thereto under the powers contained in this Part of this Act.

479. (1) The Lord Chancellor may (with the consent of the Treasury so far as relates to fees) make general rules for carrying into effect the enactments relating to formal investigations, and to the re-hearing of, or an appeal from, any investigation or inquiry held under this Part of this Act, and in particular with respect to the appointment and summoning of assessors, the procedure, the parties, the persons allowed to appear, the notice to those parties or persons or to persons affected, the amount and application of fees, and the place in which formal investigations are to be held. Rules as to investigations and inquiries.

(2) Any rule made under this section while in force shall have effect as if it were enacted in this Act.

(3) Any rule made under this section with regard to the re-hearing of, or appeals from, any investigation or inquiries, as to the appointment of assessors and as to the place in which formal investigations are to be held, shall be laid before both Houses of Parliament as soon as may be after it is made.

Naval Courts on the High Seas and Abroad.

480. A court (in this Act called a naval court) may be summoned by any officer in command of any of Her Majesty's ships on any foreign station, or, in the absence of such an officer, by any consular officer, in the following cases; (that is to say,) Cases in which naval courts may be summoned.

(i) Whenever a complaint which appears to that officer to require immediate investigation is made to him by the master of any British ship, or by a certificated mate, or by any one or more of the seamen belonging to any such ship;

(ii) Whenever the interest of the owner of any British ship or of the cargo thereof appears to that officer to require it; and

(iii) Whenever any British ship is wrecked, abandoned, or otherwise lost at or near the place where that officer may be, or whenever the crew or part of the crew of any British ship which has been wrecked, abandoned, or lost abroad arrive at that place.

481. (1) A naval court shall consist of not more than five and not less than three members, of whom, if possible, one shall be an officer in the naval service of Her Majesty not below the rank of lieutenant, one a consular officer, and one a master of a British merchant ship, and the rest shall be either officers in the naval service of Her Majesty, masters of British merchant ships, or British merchants, and the court may include the officer summoning the Constitution of naval courts.

same, but shall not include the master or consignee of the ship to which the parties complaining or complained against belong.

(2) The naval or consular officer in the court, if there is only one such officer, or, if there is more than one, the naval or consular officer who, according to any regulations for settling their respective ranks for the time being in force, is of the highest rank, shall be the president of the court.

Functions of naval courts.

482. (1) A naval court shall hear the complaint or other matter brought before them under this Act, or investigate the cause of the wreck, abandonment, or loss, and shall do so in such manner as to give every person against whom any complaint or charge is made an opportunity of making a defence.

(2) A naval court may, for the purpose of the hearing and investigation, administer an oath, summon parties and witnesses, and compel their attendance and the production of documents.

Powers of naval courts.

83. (1) Every naval court may, after hearing and investigating the case, exercise the following powers; (that is to say,)

(*a*) the court may, if unanimous that the safety of the ship or crew or the interest of the owner absolutely requires it, remove the master, and appoint another person to act in his stead; but no such appointment shall be made without the consent of the consignee of the ship if at the place where the case is heard:

(*b*) the court may, in cases in which they are authorised by this Act and subject to the provisions of this Act, cancel or suspend the certificate of any master, mate, or engineer:

(*c*) the court may discharge a seaman from his ship:

(*d*) the court may order the wages of a seaman so discharged or any part of those wages to be forfeited, and may direct the same either to be retained by way of compensation to the owner, or to be paid into the Exchequer, in the same manner as fines under this Act:

(*e*) the court may decide any questions as to wages or fines or forfeitures arising between any of the parties to the proceedings:

(*f*) the court may direct that all or any of the costs incurred by the master or owner of any ship in procuring the imprisonment of any seaman or apprentice in a foreign port, or in his maintenance whilst so imprisoned, shall be paid out of and deducted from the wages of that seaman or apprentice, whether then or subsequently earned:

(*g*) the court may exercise the same powers with regard to persons charged before them with the commission of offences at sea or abroad as British consular officers can under the Thirteenth Part of this Act:

(*h*) the court may punish any master of a ship or any of the crew of a ship respecting whose conduct a complaint is brought before them for any offence against this Act, which, when committed by the said master or member of the crew, is punishable on summary conviction, and shall for that purpose have the same powers as a court of summary jurisdiction would have if the case were tried in the United Kingdom: Provided that—

(i) where an offender is sentenced to imprisonment, the senior naval or consular officer present at the place where the court is held shall in writing confirm the sentence and approve the place of imprisonment, whether on land or on board ship, as a proper place for the purpose; and

(ii) copies of all sentences passed by any naval court summoned to hear any such complaint as aforesaid, shall be sent to the commander-in-chief or senior naval officer of the station:

(*i*) the court may, if it appears expedient, order a survey of any ship which is the subject of investigation to be made, and such survey shall accordingly be made, in the same way, and the surveyor who makes the same shall have the same powers as if such survey had been directed by a competent court in pursuance of the Fifth Part of this Act, in the course of proceedings against a seaman or apprentice for the offence of desertion:

(*j*) the court may order the costs of the proceedings before them or any part of those costs, to be paid by any of the parties thereto, and may order any person making a frivolous or vexatious complaint to pay compensation for any loss or delay caused thereby; and any costs or compensation so ordered to be paid shall be paid by that person accordingly, and may be recovered in the same manner in which the wages of seamen are recoverable, or may, if the case admits, be deducted from the wages due to that person.

(2) All orders duly made by a naval court under the powers hereby given to it shall in any subsequent legal proceedings be conclusive as to the rights of the parties.

(3) All orders made by any naval court shall, whenever practicable, be entered in the official log book of the ship to which the parties to the proceedings before the court belong, and signed by the president of the court.

Report of proceedings of naval courts.

484. (1) Every naval court shall make a report to the Board of Trade containing the following particulars, that is to say:—

(*a*) a statement of the proceedings of the Court, together with the order made by the court, and a report of the evidence;

(*b*) an account of the wages of any seaman or apprentice who is discharged from his ship by the court;

(*c*) if summoned to inquire into a case of wreck or abandonment, a statement of the opinion of the court as to the cause of that wreck or abandonment, with such remarks on the conduct of the master and crew as the circumstances require.

(2) Every such report shall be signed by the president of the court, and shall be admissible in evidence in manner provided by this Act.

Penalty for preventing complaint or obstructing investigation.

485. If any person wilfully and without due cause prevents or obstructs the making of any complaint to an officer empowered to summon a naval court, or the conduct of any hearing or investigation by any naval court, he shall for each offence be liable to a fine not exceeding fifty pounds, or be liable to imprisonment, with or without hard labour, for any period not exceeding twelve weeks.

Application of provisions as to naval courts.

486. (1) The provisions of this Part of this Act with regard to naval courts on the high seas and abroad shall apply to all sea-going ships registered in the United Kingdom (with the exception, in their application elsewhere than in Scotland, of fishing boats exclusively employed in fishing on the coasts of the United Kingdom) and to all ships registered in a British possession, when those ships are out of the jurisdiction of their respective governments, and where they apply to a ship, shall apply to the owners, master, and crew of that ship.

(2) For the purpose of the said provisions an unregistered British ship shall be deemed to have been registered in the United Kingdom.

Courts of Survey.

Constitution of court of survey.

487. (1) A court of survey for a port or district shall consist of a judge sitting with two assessors.

(2) The judge shall be such person as may be summoned for the case in accordance with the rules made under this Act with respect to that court, out of a list approved for the port or district by a Secretary of State, of wreck commissioners appointed under this Act, stipendiary or metropolitan police magistrates, judges of county courts, and other fit persons; but in any special case in which the Board of Trade think it expedient to appoint a wreck commissioner, the judge shall be such wreck commissioner.

(3) The assessors shall be persons of nautical, engineering, or other special skill and experience, subject to the provisions of the Fifth Part of this

Act as regards foreign ships, one of them shall be appointed by the Board of Trade, either generally or in each case, and the other shall be summoned, in accordance with the rules made as aforesaid, by the registrar of the court, out of a list of persons periodically nominated for the purpose by the local marine board of the port, or, if there is no such board, by a body of local shipowners or merchants approved for the purpose by a Secretary of State, or, if there is no such list, shall be appointed by the judge. If a Secretary of State think fit at any time, on the recommendation of the government of any British possession or any foreign country, to add any persons to any such list, those persons shall, until otherwise directed by the Secretary of State, be added to the list, and if there is no such list, shall form the list.

(4) The county court registrar or such other fit person as a Secretary of State may from time to time appoint shall be the registrar of the court, and shall, on receiving notice of an appeal or a reference from the Board of Trade, immediately summon the court to meet forthwith in manner directed by the rules.

(5) The name of the registrar and his office, together with the rules made as aforesaid, relating to the court of survey, shall be published in the manner directed by the rules.

(6) In the application of this section to Scotland the expression "judge of a county court" means a sheriff, and the expression "county court registrar" means sheriff clerk.

(7) In the application of this section to Ireland the expression "stipendiary magistrate" includes any of the justices of the peace in Dublin metropolis and any resident magistrate.

(8) In the application of this section to the Isle of Man the expression "judge of a county court" means the water bailiff, the expression "stipendiary magistrate" means the high bailiff, the expression "registrar of a county court" means a clerk to a deemster or a clerk to justices of the peace.

Power and procedure of court of survey.

488. (1) The court of survey shall hear every case in open court.

(2) The judge and each assessor of the court may survey the ship, and shall have for the purposes of this Act all the powers of a Board of Trade inspector under this Act.

(3) The judge of the court may appoint any competent person or persons to survey the ship and report thereon to the court.

(4) The judge of the court, any assessor of the court, and any person appointed by the judge of the court to survey a ship, may go on board the ship, and inspect the same and every part thereof, and the machinery, equipments, and cargo, and may require the unloading or removal of any cargo, ballast, or

tackle, and any person who wilfully impedes such judge, assessor, or person in the execution of the survey, or fails to comply with any requisition made by him, shall for each offence be liable to a fine not exceeding ten pounds.

(5) The judge of the court shall have the same power as the Board of Trade have to order the ship to be released or finally detained, but, unless one of the assessors concurs in an order for the detention of the ship, the ship shall be released.

(6) The owner and master of the ship and any person appointed by the owner or master, and also any person appointed by the Board of Trade, may attend at any inspection or survey made in pursuance of this section.

(7) The judge of the court shall send to the Board of Trade such report as may be directed by the rules, and each assessor shall either sign the report or report to the Board of Trade the reasons for his dissent.

Rules for procedure of court of survey, etc.

489. The Lord Chancellor may (with the consent of the Treasury so far as relates to fees) make general rules to carry into effect the provisions of this Act with respect to a court of survey, and in particular with respect to the summoning of, and procedure before, the court, the requiring on an appeal security for costs and damages, the amount and application of fees, and the publication of the rules, and those rules shall have effect as if enacted in this Act.

Scientific Referees.

Reference in difficult cases to scientific persons.

490. (1) If the Board of Trade are of opinion that an appeal to a court of survey involves a question of construction or design or of scientific difficulty or important principle, they may refer the matter to such one or more out of a list of scientific referees from time to time approved by a Secretary of State, as may appear to possess the special qualifications necessary for the particular case, and may be selected by agreement between the Board of Trade and the appellant, or in default of any such agreement by a Secretary of State, and thereupon the appeal shall be determined by the referee or referees, instead of by the court of survey.

(2) The Board of Trade, if the appellant in any appeal so requires and gives security to the satisfaction of the Board to pay the costs of and incidental to the reference, shall refer that appeal to a referee or referees so selected as aforesaid.

(3) The referee or referees shall have the same powers as a judge of the court of survey.

Payments to Officers of Courts.

Payments to officers of courts.

491. There may be paid out of money provided by Parliament to any wreck commissioner, judge of a court of survey, assessor in any court of survey or investigation under this Part of this Act, registrar of a court of survey, scientific referee, or any other officer or person appointed for the purpose of any court of survey or investigation under this Part of this Act, such salary or remuneration (if any) as the Treasury may direct.

PART VII.

Delivery of Goods.

Delivery of Goods and Lien for Freight.

Definitions under Part VII.

492. In this Part of this Act unless the context otherwise requires—

The expression "goods" includes every description of wares and merchandise:

The expression "wharf" includes all wharves, quays, docks, and premises in or upon which any goods, when landed from ships, may be lawfully placed:

The expression "warehouse" includes all warehouses, buildings, and premises in which goods, when landed from ships, may be lawfully placed:

The expression "report" means the report required by the customs laws to be made by the master of an importing ship:

The expression "entry" means the entry required by the customs law to be made for the landing or discharge of goods from an importing ship:

The expression "shipowner" includes the master of the ship and every other person authorised to act as agent for the owner or entitled to receive the freight, demurrage, or other charges payable in respect of the ship:

The expression "owner" used in relation to goods means every person who is for the time entitled, either as owner or agent for the owner, to the possession of the goods, subject in the case of a lien (if any), to that lien:

The expression "wharfinger" means the occupier of a wharf as herein-before defined:

The expression "warehouseman" means the occupier of a warehouse as herein-before defined.

Power of shipowner to enter and land goods on default by owner of goods.

493. (1) Where the owner of any goods imported in any ship from foreign parts into the United Kingdom fails to make entry thereof, or, having made entry thereof, to land the same or take delivery thereof, and to proceed therewith with all convenient speed, by the times severally herein-after

(3) At the expiration of those thirty days, unless legal proceedings have in the meantime been instituted by the shipowner against the owner of the goods to recover the said balance or sum, or otherwise for the settlement of any disputes which may have arisen between them concerning the freight or other charges as aforesaid, and notice in writing of those proceedings has been served on the wharfinger or warehouseman, the wharfinger or warehouseman shall pay the balance or sum to the owner of the goods.

(4) A wharfinger or warehouseman shall by any payment under this section be discharged from all liability in respect thereof.

Sale of goods by warehouseman.

497. (1) If the lien is not discharged, and no deposit is made as aforesaid, the wharfinger or warehouseman may, and, if required by the shipowner, shall, at the expiration of ninety days from the time when the goods were placed in his custody, or, if the goods are of a perishable nature, at such earlier period as in his discretion he thinks fit, sell by public auction, either for home use or for exportation, the goods or so much thereof as may be necessary to satisfy the charges herein-after mentioned.

(2) Before making the sale the wharfinger or warehouseman shall give notice thereof by advertisement in two local newspapers circulating in the neighbourhood, or in one daily newspaper published in London, and in one local newspaper, and also, if the address of the owner of the goods has been stated on the manifest of the cargo, or on any of the documents which have come into the possession of the wharfinger or warehouseman, or is otherwise known to him, send notice of the sale to the owner of the goods by post.

(3) The title of a *bonâ fide* purchaser of the goods shall not be invalidated by reason of the omission to send the notice required by this section, nor shall any such purchaser be bound to inquire whether the notice has been sent.

Application of proceeds of sale.

498. The proceeds of sale shall be applied by the wharfinger or warehouseman as follows, and in the following order:

(i) First, if the goods are sold for home use, in payment of any customs or excise duties owing in respect thereof; then

(ii) In payment of the expenses of the sale; then

(iii) In payment of the charges of the wharfinger or warehouseman and the shipowner according to such priority as may be determined by the terms of the agreement (if any) in that behalf between them; or, if there is no such agreement:—

(*a*) in payment of the rent, rates, and other charges due to the wharfinger or warehouseman in respect of the said goods; and then (*b*) in payment of the amount claimed by the shipowner as due for freight or other charges in respect of the said goods;

and the surplus, if any, shall be paid to the owner of the goods.

499. Whenever any goods are placed in the custody of a wharfinger or warehouseman, under the authority of this Part of this Act, the wharfinger or warehouseman shall be entitled to rent in respect of the same, and shall also have power, at the expense of the owner of the goods, to do all such reasonable acts as in the judgment of the wharfinger or warehouseman are necessary for the proper custody and preservation of the goods, and shall have a lien on the goods for the rent and expenses.

Warehouseman's rent and expenses.

500. Nothing in this Part of this Act shall compel any wharfinger or warehouseman to take charge of any goods which he would not have been liable to take charge of if this Act had not been passed; nor shall he be bound to see to the validity of any lien claimed by any shipowner under this Part of this Act.

Warehousemen's protection.

501. Nothing in this Part of this Act shall take away or abridge any powers given by any local Act to any harbour authority, body corporate, or persons, whereby they are enabled to expedite the discharge of ships or the landing or delivery of goods; nor shall anything in this Part of this Act take away or diminish any rights or remedies given to any shipowner or wharfinger or warehouseman by any local Act.

Saving for powers under local Acts.

PART VIII.

Liability of Shipowners.

502. The owner of a British sea-going ship, or any share therein, shall not be liable to make good to any extent whatever any loss or damage happening without his actual fault or privity in the following cases, namely:—

Limitation of shipowner's liability in certain cases of loss of or damage to goods.

(i) where any goods, merchandise, or other things whatsoever taken in or put on board his ship are lost or damaged by reason of fire on board the ship; or

(ii) where any gold, silver, diamonds, watches, jewels, or precious stones taken in or put on board his ship, the true nature and value of which have not at the time of shipment been declared by the owner or shipper thereof to the owner or master of the ship in the bills of lading or otherwise in writing, are lost or damaged by reason of any robbery, embezzlement, making away with, or secreting thereof.

Limitation of owner's liability in certain cases of loss of life, injury, or damage.

503. (1) The owners of ship, British or foreign, shall not, where all or any of the following occurrences take place without their actual fault or privity; (that is to say),

(*a*) Where any loss of life or personal injury is caused to any person being carried in the ship;

(*b*) Where any damage or loss is caused to any goods, merchandise, or other things whatsoever on board the ship;

(*c*) Where any loss of life or personal injury is caused to any person carried in any other vessel by reason of the improper navigation of the ship;

(*d*) Where any loss or damage is caused to any other vessel, or to any goods, merchandise, or other things whatsoever on board any other vessel by reason of the improper navigation of the ship;

be liable to damages beyond the following amounts; (that is to say),

(i) in respect of loss of life or personal injury, either alone or together with loss of or damage to vessels, goods, merchandise, or other things, an aggregate amount not exceeding fifteen pounds for each ton of their ship's tonnage; and

(ii) in respect of loss of, or damage to, vessels, goods, merchandise, or other things, whether there be in addition loss of life or personal injury or not, an aggregate amount not exceeding eight pounds for each ton of their ship's tonnage.

(2) For the purposes of this section—

(*a*) The tonnage of a steam-ship shall be her gross tonnage without deduction on account of engine room; and the tonnage of a sailing ship shall be her registered tonnage:

Provided that there shall not be included in such tonnage any space occupied by seamen or apprentices and appropriated to their use which is certified under the regulations scheduled to this Act with regard thereto.

(*b*) Where a foreign ship has been or can be measured according to British law, her tonnage, as ascertained by that measurement, shall, for the purpose of this section, be deemed to be her tonnage.

(*c*) Where a foreign ship has not been and cannot be measured according to British law, the surveyor general of ships in the United Kingdom, or the chief measuring officer of any British possession abroad, shall, on receiving from or by the direction of the court hearing the case, in which the tonnage of the ship is in question, such evidence concerning the dimensions of the ship as it may be practicable to furnish, give a certificate under his hand stating what would in his opinion have been the tonnage of the ship if she had been duly measured according to British law, and the tonnage so stated in that certificate shall, for the purposes of this section, be deemed to be the tonnage of the ship.

(3) The owner of every sea-going ship or share therein shall be liable in respect of every such loss of life, personal injury, loss of or damage to vessels, goods, merchandise, or things as aforesaid arising on distinct occasions to the same extent as if no other loss, injury, or damage had arisen.

Power of courts to consolidate claims against owners, etc.

504. Where any liability is alleged to have been incurred by the owner of a British or foreign ship in respect of loss of life, personal injury, or loss of or damage to vessels or goods, and several claims are made or apprehended in respect of that liability, then, the owner may apply in England and Ireland to the High Court, or in Scotland to the Court of Session, or in a British possession to any competent court, and that court may determine the amount of the owner's liability and may distribute that amount rateably among the several claimants, and may stay any proceedings pending in any other court in relation to the same matter, and may proceed in such manner and subject to such regulations as to making persons interested parties to the proceedings, and as to the exclusion of any claimants who do not come in within a certain time, and as to requiring security from the owner, and as to payment of any costs as the court thinks just.

Part owners to account in respect of damages.

505. All sums paid for or on account of any loss or damage in respect whereof the liability of owners is limited under the provisions of this Part of the Act, and all costs incurred in relation thereto, may be brought into account among part owners of the same ship in the same manner as money disbursed for the use thereof.

Insurances of certain risks not invalid.

506. An insurance effected against the happening, without the owner's actual fault or privity, of any or all of the events in respect of which the liability of owners is limited under this Part of this Act, shall not be invalid by reason of the nature of the risk.

Proof of passengers on board ship.

507. In any proceeding under this Part of this Act against the owner of a ship or share therein with respect to loss of life, the passenger lists under the Third Part of this Act shall be received as evidence that the person upon whose death proceedings are taken under this Part of this Act was a passenger on board the ship at the time of death.

Liability in certain cases not affected.

508. Nothing in this Part of this Act shall be construed to lessen or take away any liability to which any master or seaman, being also owner or part owner of the ship to which he belongs, is subject in his capacity of master or seaman, or to extend to any British ship which is not recognised as a British ship within the meaning of this Act.

Extent of Part VIII.

509. This Part of this Act shall, unless the context otherwise requires, extend to the whole of Her Majesty's dominions.

PART IX.

Wreck and Salvage.

Vessels in Distress.

Definition of "wreck" and "salvage."

510. In this Part of this Act unless the context otherwise requires—

(1) The expression "wreck" includes jetsam, flotsam, lagan, and derelict found in or on the shores of the sea or any tidal water.

(2) The expression "salvage" includes all expenses properly incurred by the salvor in the performance of the salvage service.

Duty of receiver where vessel in distress.

511. (1) Where a British or foreign vessel is wrecked, stranded, or in distress at any place on or near the coasts of the United Kingdom or any tidal water within the limits of the United Kingdom, the receiver of wreck for the district in which that place is situate shall, upon being made acquainted with the circumstance, forthwith proceed there, and upon his arrival shall take the command of all persons present, and shall assign such duties and give such directions to each person as he thinks fit for the preservation of the vessel and of the lives of the persons belonging to the vessel (in this Part of this Act referred to as shipwrecked persons) and of the cargo and apparel of the vessel.

(2) If any person wilfully disobeys the direction of the receiver, he shall for each offence be liable to a fine not exceeding fifty pounds; but the receiver shall not interfere between the master and the crew of the vessel in reference to the management thereof, unless he is requested to do so by the master.

Powers of the receiver in case of vessels in distress.

512. (1) The receiver may, with a view to such preservation as aforesaid of shipwrecked persons or of the vessel, cargo, or apparel—

(*a*) require such persons as he thinks necessary to assist him:

(*b*) require the master, or other person having the charge, of any vessel near at hand to give such aid with his men, or vessel, as may be in his power:

(*c*) demand the use of any waggon, cart, or horses that may be near at hand.

(2) If any person refuses without reasonable cause to comply with any such requisition or demand, that person shall, for each refusal, be liable to a fine not exceeding one hundred pounds; but a person shall not be liable to pay any duty in respect of any such waggon, cart, or horses, by reason only of the use of the same under this section.

513. (1) Whenever a vessel is wrecked, stranded, or in distress as aforesaid, all persons may, for the purpose of rendering assistance to the vessel, or of saving the lives of the shipwrecked persons, or of saving the cargo or apparel of the vessel, unless there is some public road equally convenient, pass and repass, either with or without carriages or horses, over any adjoining lands without being subject to interruption by the owner or occupier, so that they do as little damage as possible, and may also, on the like condition, deposit on those lands any cargo or other article recovered from the vessel.

Power to pass over adjoining lands.

(2) Any damage sustained by an owner or occupier in consequence of the exercise of the rights given by this section shall be a charge on the vessel, cargo, or articles in respect of or by which the damage is occasioned, and the amount payable in respect of the damage shall, in case of dispute, be determined and shall, in default of payment, be recoverable in the same manner as the amount of salvage is under this Part of this Act determined or recoverable.

(3) If the owner or occupier of any land—

(*a*) impedes or hinders any person in the exercise of the rights given by this section by locking his gates, or refusing, upon request, to open the same, or otherwise; or

(*b*) impedes or hinders the deposit of any cargo or other article recovered from the vessel as aforesaid on the land; or

(*c*) prevents or endeavours to prevent any such cargo or other article from remaining deposited on the land for a reasonable time until it can be removed to a safe place of public deposit;

he shall for each offence be liable to a fine not exceeding one hundred pounds.

514. (1) Whenever a vessel is wrecked, stranded, or in distress as aforesaid, and any person plunders, creates disorder, or obstructs the preservation of the vessel or of the shipwrecked persons or of the cargo or apparel of the vessel, the receiver may cause that person to be apprehended.

Power of receiver to suppress plunder and disorder by force.

(2) The receiver may use force for the suppression of any such plundering, disorder, or obstruction, and may command all Her Majesty's subjects to assist him in so using force.

(3) If any person is killed, maimed, or hurt by reason of his resisting the receiver or any person acting under the orders of the receiver in the

execution of the duties by this Part of this Act committed to the receiver, neither the receiver nor the person acting under his orders shall be liable to any punishment, or to pay any damages by reason of the person being so killed, maimed, or hurt.

Liability for damage in case of a vessel plundered

515. Where a vessel is wrecked, stranded, or in distress as aforesaid, and the vessel or any part of the cargo and apparel thereof, is plundered, damaged, or destroyed by any persons riotously and tumultuously assembled together, whether on shore or afloat, compensation shall be made to the owner of the vessel, cargo, or apparel;

In England in the same manner, by the same authority, and out of the same rate, as if the plundering, damage, injury, or destruction were an injury, stealing, or destruction in respect of which compensation is payable under the provisions of the Riot (Damages) Act, 1886, and in the case of the vessel, cargo, or apparel not being in any police district, as if the plundering, damage, injury, or destruction took place in the nearest police district; 49 & 50 Vict., c. 38.

In Scotland by the inhabitants of the county, city, or borough in or nearest to which such offence is committed, in manner provided by the Riot Act, with respect to prosecutions for repairing the damages of any churches and other buildings, or as near thereto as circumstances permit; and 1 Geo. I, st. 2, c. 5.

In Ireland in manner provided by the Act of the Session held in the sixteenth and seventeenth year of the reign of Her present Majesty, chapter thirty-eight, intituled "An Act to extend the remedies for the compensation of malicious injuries to property in Ireland" with respect to damage to any dwelling-house or other property therein mentioned. 16 & 17 Vict., c. 38.

Exercise of powers of receiver in his absence.

516. (1) Where a receiver is not present, the following officers or persons in succession (each in the absence of the other, in the order in which they are named), namely, any chief officer of customs, principal officer of the coast uard, officer of inland revenue, sheriff, justice of the peace, commissioned officer on full pay in the naval service of Her Majesty, or commissioned officer on full pay in the military service of Her Majesty, may do anything by this Part of this Act authorised to be done by the receiver.

(2) An officer acting under this section for a receiver shall, with respect to any goods or articles belonging to a vessel the delivery of which to the receiver is required by this Act, be considered as the agent of the receiver, and shall place the same in the custody of the receiver; but he shall not be entitled to

any fees payable to receivers, or be deprived by reason of his so acting of an right to salvage to which he would otherwise be entitled.

517. (1) Where any ship, British or foreign, is or has been in distress on the coasts of the United Kingdom, a receiver of wreck, or at the request of the Board of Trade a wreck commissioner or deputy approved by the Board, or, in the absence of the persons aforesaid, a justice of the peace, shall, as soon as conveniently may be, examine on oath (and they are hereby respectively empowered to administer the oath) any person belonging to the ship, or any other person who may be able to give any account thereof or of the cargo or stores thereof, as to the following matters; that is to say,— Examination in respect of ships in distress.

(*a*) the name and description of the ship;

(*b*) the name of the master and of the owners;

(*c*) the names of the owners of the cargo;

(*d*) the ports from and to which the ship was bound;

(*e*) the occasion of the distress of the ship;

(*f*) the services rendered; and

(*g*) such other matters or circumstances relating to the ship, or to the cargo on board the same, as the person holding the examination thinks necessary.

(2) The person holding the examination shall take the same down in writing, and shall send one copy thereof to the Board of Trade, and another to the secretary of Lloyd's in London, and the secretary shall place it in some conspicuous situation for inspection.

(3) The person holding the examination shall, for the purposes thereof, have all the powers of a Board of Trade inspector under this Act.

Dealing with Wreck.

518. (1) Where any person finds or takes possession of any wreck within the limits of the United Kingdom he shall,— Provision as to wreck found in the United Kingdom.

(*a*) If he is the owner thereof, give notice to the receiver of the district stating that he has found or taken possession of the same, and describing the marks by which the same may be recognised;

(*b*) If he is not the owner thereof, as soon as possible deliver the same to the receiver of the district;

and if any person fails, without reasonable cause, to comply with this section, he shall, for each offence, be liable to a fine not exceeding one hundred pounds, and shall in addition, if he is not the owner, forfeit any claim to salvage, and shall be liable to pay to the owner of the wreck if it is claimed, or, if it is unclaimed, to the person entitled to the same, double the value thereof, to be recovered in the same way as a fine of a like amount under this Act.

Penalty for taking wreck at time of casualty.

519. (1) Where a vessel is wrecked, stranded, or in distress at any place on or near the coasts of the United Kingdom or any tidal water within the limits of the United Kingdom, any cargo or other articles belonging to or separated from the vessel, which may be washed on shore or otherwise lost or taken from the vessel shall be delivered to the receiver.

(2) If any person, whether the owner or not, secretes or keeps possession of any such cargo or article, or refuses to deliver the same to the receiver or any person authorised by him to demand the same, that person shall for each offence be liable to a fine not exceeding one hundred pounds.

(3) The receiver or any person authorised as aforesaid may take any such cargo or article by force from the person so refusing to deliver the same.

Notice of wreck to be given by receiver.

520. Where a receiver takes possession of any wreck he shall within forty-eight hours—

(*a*) cause to be posted in the custom house nearest to the place where the wreck was found or was seized by him a description thereof and of any marks by which it is distinguished; and

(*b*) if in his opinion the value of the wreck exceeds twenty pounds, also transmit a similar description to the secretary of Lloyd's in London, and the secretary shall post it in some conspicuous position for inspection.

Claims of owners to wreck.

521. (1) The owner of any wreck in the possession of the receiver, upon establishing his claim to the same to the satisfaction of the receiver within one year from the time at which the wreck came into the possession of the receiver, shall, upon paying the salvage, fees, and expenses due, be entitled to have the wreck or the proceeds thereof delivered up to him.

(2) Where any articles belonging to or forming part of a foreign ship, which has been wrecked on or near the coasts of the United Kingdom, or belonging to and forming part of the cargo, are found on or near those coasts, or are brought into any port in the United Kingdom, the consul general of the country to which the ship or in the case of cargo to which the owners of the cargo may have belonged, or any consular officer of that country authorised in that behalf by any treaty or arrangement with that country, shall, in the absence of the owner, and of the master or other agent of the owner, be deemed to be the agent of the owner, so far as relates to the custody and disposal of the articles.

Immediate sale of wreck by receiver in certain cases.

522. A receiver may at any time sell any wreck in his custody, if in his opinion—

(*a*) it is under the value of five pounds, or

(*b*) it is so much damaged or of so perishable a nature that it cannot with advantage be kept, or

(*c*) it is not of sufficient value to pay for warehousing,

and the proceeds of the sale shall, after defraying the expenses thereof, be held by the receiver for the same purposes and subject to the same claims, rights, and liabilities as if the wreck had remained unsold.

Unclaimed Wreck.

523. Her Majesty and Her Royal successors are entitled to all unclaimed wreck found in any part of Her Majesty's dominions, except in places where Her Majesty or any of Her Royal predecessors has granted to any other person the right to that wreck. **Right of Crown to unclaimed wreck.**

524. (1) Where any admiral, vice-admiral, lord of the manor, heritable proprietor duly infeft, or other person is entitled for his own use to unclaimed wreck found on any place within the district of a receiver, he shall deliver to the receiver a statement containing the particulars of his title, and an address to which notices may be sent. **Notice of unclaimed wreck to be given to persons entitled.**

(2) When a statement has been so delivered and the title proved to the satisfaction of the receiver, the receiver shall, on taking possession of any wreck found at a place to which the statement refers, within forty-eight hours send to the address delivered a description of the wreck and of any marks by which it is distinguished.

525. Where no owner establishes a claim to any wreck, found in the United Kingdom and in the possession of a receiver, within one year after it came into his possession, the wreck shall be dealt with as follows; that is to say, **Disposal of unclaimed wreck.**

(1) if the wreck is claimed by any admiral, vice-admiral, lord of a manor, heritable proprietor, or other person who has delivered such a statement to the receiver as herein-before provided, and has proved to the satisfaction of the receiver his title to receive unclaimed wreck found at the place where that wreck was found, the wreck after payment of all expenses, costs, fees, and salvage due in respect thereof, shall be delivered to him;

(2) if the wreck is not claimed by any admiral, vice-admiral, lord of a manor, heritable proprietor, or other person as aforesaid, the receiver shall sell the same and shall pay the proceeds of the sale (after deducting therefrom the expenses of the sale, and any other expenses incurred by him, and his fees, and paying thereout to the salvors such amount of salvage as the Board of Trade

may in each case, or by any general rule, determine) for the benefit of the Crown, as follows, that is to say:—

(*a*) if the wreck is claimed in right of Her Majesty's duchy of Lancaster, to the receiver-general of that duchy or his deputies as part of the revenues of that duchy;

(*b*) if the wreck is claimed in right of the duchy of Cornwall, to the receiver-general of that duchy or his deputies as part of the revenues of that duchy; and

(*c*) if the wreck is not so claimed, the receiver shall pay the proceeds of sale to the Mercantile Marine Fund during the life of Her present Majesty, and after the decease of Her present Majesty to Her heirs and successors.

Disputed title to unclaimed wreck.

526. (1) Where any dispute arises between any such admiral, vice-admiral, lord of a manor, heritable proprietor, or other person as aforesaid and the receiver respecting title to wreck found at any place, or, where more persons than one claim title to that wreck and a dispute arises between them as to that title, that dispute may be referred and determined in the same manner, as if it were a dispute as to salvage to be determined summarily under this Part of this Act.

(2) If any party to the dispute is unwilling to have the same so referred and determined, or is dissatisfied with the decision on that determination, he may within three months after the expiration of a year from the time when the wreck has come into the receiver's hands, or from the date of the decision, as the case may be, take proceedings in any court having jurisdiction in the matter for establishing his title.

Delivery of unclaimed wreck by receivers not to prejudice title.

527. Upon delivery of wreck or payment of the proceeds of sale of wreck by a receiver, in pursuance of the provisions of this Part of this Act, the receiver shall be discharged from all liability in respect thereof, but the delivery thereof shall not prejudice or affect any question which may be raised by third parties concerning the right or title to the wreck, or concerning the title to the soil of the place on which the wreck was found.

Power to Board of Trade to purchase rights to wreck.

528. (1) The Board of Trade may, with the consent of the Treasury, out of the revenue arising under this Part for this Act, purchase for and on behalf of Her Majesty any rights to wreck possessed by any person other than Her Majesty.

(2) For the purpose of a purchase under this section, the provisions of the Lands Clauses Acts relating to the purchase of lands by agreement shall be incorporated with this Part of this Act, and in the construction of those Acts

for the purposes of this section this Part of this Act shall be deemed to be the special Act, and any such right to wreck as aforesaid shall be deemed to be an interest in land authorised to be taken by the special Act, and Her Majesty shall be deemed to be the promoter of the undertaking.

529. No admiral, vice-admiral, or other person, under whatever denomination, exercising Admiralty jurisdiction, shall, as such, by himself or his agents, receive, take, or interfere with any wreck except as authorised by this Act.

Admiral not to interfere with wreck.

Removal of Wrecks.

530. Where any vessel is sunk, stranded, or abandoned in any harbour or tidal water under the control of a harbour or conservancy authority, or in or near any approach thereto, in such manner as in the opinion of the authority to be, or be likely to become, an obstruction or danger to navigation or to lifeboats engaged in lifeboat service in that harbour or water or in any approach thereto, that authority may—

Removal of wreck by harbour or conservancy authority.

(*a*) take possession of, and raise, remove, or destroy the whole or any part of the vessel; and

(*b*) light or buoy any such vessel or part until the raising, removal, or destruction thereof; and

(*c*) sell, in such manner as they think fit, any vessel or part so raised or removed, and also any other property recovered in the exercise of their powers under this section, and out of the proceeds of the sale reimburse themselves for the expenses incurred by them in relation thereto under this section, and the authority shall hold the surplus, if any, of the proceeds in trust for the persons entitled thereto:

Provided as follows :—

(1) A sale shall not (except in the case of property which is of a perishable nature, or which would deteriorate in value by delay) be made under this section until at least seven clear days' notice of the intended sale has been given by advertisement in some local newspaper circulating in or near the district over which the authority have control; and

(2) At any time before any property is sold under this section, the owner thereof shall be entitled to have the same delivered to him on payment to the authority of the fair market value thereof, to be ascertained by agreement between the authority and the owner, or failing agreement by some person to be named for the

purpose by the Board of Trade, and the sum paid to the authority as the value of any property under this provision shall, for the purposes of this section, be deemed to be the proceeds of sale of that property.

Power of lighthouse authority to remove wreck.

531. (1) Where any vessel is sunk, stranded, or abandoned in any fairway, or on the seashore or on or near any rock, shoal, or bank, in the British Islands, or any of the adjacent seas or islands, and there is not any harbour or conservancy authority having power to raise, remove, or destroy the vessel, the general lighthouse authority for the place in or near which the vessel is situate shall, if in their opinion the vessel is, or is likely to become, an obstruction or danger to navigation or to lifeboats engaged in the lifeboat service, have the same powers in relation thereto as are by this Part of this Act conferred upon a harbour or conservancy authority.

(2) All expenses incurred by the general lighthouse authority under this section, and not reimbursed in manner provided by this Part of this Act, shall be paid out of the Mercantile Marine Fund, but shall be subject to the like estimate, account, and sanction as the expenses of a general lighthouse authority, other than establishment expenses.

Powers of removal to extent to tackle, cargo, etc.

532. The provisions of this Part of this Act relating to removal of wrecks shall apply to every article or thing or collection of things being or forming part of the tackle, equipments, cargo, stores, or ballast of a vessel in the same manner as if it were included in the term "vessel", and for the purposes of these provisions any proceeds of sale arising from a vessel and from the cargo thereof, or any other property recovered therefrom, shall be regarded as a common fund.

Power of Board of Trade to determine certain questions between authorities.

533. If any question arises between a harbour or conservancy authority on the one hand, and a general lighthouse authority on the other hand, as to their respective powers under this Part of this Act for the removal of wrecks, in relation to any place being in or near an approach to a harbour or tidal water, that question shall, on the application of either authority, be referred to the decision of the Board of Trade, and the decision of that Board shall be final.

Powers to be cumulative.

534. The powers conferred by this Part of this Act on a harbour, conservancy or lighthouse authority, for the removal of wrecks shall be in addition to and not in derogation of any other powers for a like object.

Offences in respect of Wreck.

Taking wreck to foreign port.

535. If any person takes into any foreign port any vessel stranded, derelict, or otherwise in distress, found on or near the coasts of the United Kingdom or any tidal water within the limits of the United Kingdom, or any part

of the cargo or apparel thereof, or anything belonging thereto, or any wreck found within those limits, and there sells the same, that person shall be guilty of felony, and on conviction thereof shall be liable to be kept in penal servitude for a term not less than three years and not exceeding five years.

Interfering with wrecked vessel or wreck.

536. (1) A person shall not without the leave of the master board or endeavour to board any vessel which is wrecked, stranded, or in distress, unless that person is, or acts by command of, the receiver or a person lawfully acting as such, and if any person acts in contravention of this enactment, he shall for each offence be liable to a fine not exceeding fifty pounds, and the master of the vessel may repel him by force.

(2) A person shall not—

(*a*) impede or hinder, or endeavour in any way to impede or hinder, the saving of any vessel stranded or in danger of being stranded, or otherwise in distress on or near any coast or tidal water or of any part of the cargo or apparel thereof, or of any wreck;

(*b*) secrete any wreck, or deface or obliterate any marks thereon; or

(*c*) wrongfully carry away or remove any part of a vessel stranded or in danger of being stranded, or otherwise in distress, on or near any coast or tidal water, or any part of the cargo or apparel thereof, or any wreck;

and if any person acts in contravention of this enactment, he shall be liable for each offence to a fine not exceeding fifty pounds, and that fine may be inflicted in addition to any punishment to which he may be liable by law under this Act or otherwise.

Summary procedure for concealment of wreck.

537. (1) Where a receiver suspects or receives information that any wreck is secreted or in the possession of some person who is not the owner thereof, or that any wreck is otherwise improperly dealt with, he may apply to any justice of the peace for a search warrant, and that justice shall have power to grant such a warrant, and the receiver, by virtue thereof may enter any house, or other place, wherever situate, and also any vessel, and search for, seize, and detain any such wreck there found.

(2) If any such seizure of wreck is made in consequence of information given by any person to the receiver, on a warrant being issued under this section, the informer shall be entitled, by way of salvage, to such sum not exceeding in any case five pounds as the receiver may allow.

Marine Store Dealers.

Marine store dealer to have his

538. (1) Every person dealing in, buying, or selling, any of the articles following, that is to say, anchors, cables, sails, old junk, or old iron or other

name and trade painted on his shop.

marine stores of any kind, (in this Part of this Act called a marine store dealer) shall have his name, together with the words, "dealer in marine stores," distinctly painted, in letters of not less than six inches in length on every warehouse and place of deposit belonging to him.

(2) If a marine store dealer fails to comply with the requirements of this section, he shall for each offence be liable to a fine not exceeding twenty pounds.

Marine store dealer to keep proper books.

539. (1) Every marine store dealer shall keep proper books, and enter therein an account of all marine stores of which he becomes possessed, stating in respect of each article the time at which and the person from whom he purchased or received the same, and a description of the business and place of abode of that person.

(2) If a marine store dealer fails to comply with the requirements of this section, he shall be liable to a fine for the first offence not exceeding twenty pounds, and for every subsequent offence not exceeding fifty pounds.

Marine store dealer not to purchase from person under sixteen.

540. (1) A marine store dealer shall not by himself or his agent purchase marine stores of any description from any person apparently under the age of sixteen years.

(2) If a marine store dealer so purchases any marine store, he shall be liable to a fine for the first offence not exceeding five pounds, and for every subsequent offence not exceeding twenty pounds.

Marine store dealer not to cut up cable, etc.

541. (1) A marine store dealer shall not, on any pretence, cut up any cable or other like article exceeding five fathoms in length, or unlay the same into twine or paper stuff without obtaining a written permit as required by this section.

(2) In order to obtain a written permit a marine store dealer shall make a declaration before some justice of the peace having jurisdiction where the dealer resides, stating—

(*a*) the quality and description of the cable or other like article about to be cut up or unlaid;

(*b*) the name and description of the person from whom he purchased or received the same; and

(*c*) that he has purchased or otherwise acquired the same without fraud and without any knowledge or suspicion that it has been come by dishonestly:

and either the justice of the peace before whom the declaration is made, or the receiver of the district, upon the production of the declaration, may grant a permit authorising the marine store dealer to cut up or unlay the cable or other article.

(3) If a marine store dealer cuts up or unlays any cable or other artice without complying with the provisions of this section, he shall be liable to a fine for the first offence not exceeding twenty pounds, and for every subsequent offence not exceeding fifty pounds.

542. (1) A marine store dealer who has obtained a permit as aforesaid shall not proceed by virtue thereof to cut up or unlay any cable or other article until he has for the space of one week, at the least, published in some newspaper circulating in the place where he resides one or more advertisements, notifying the fact of his having so obtained a permit, and specifying the nature of the cable or article mentioned in the permit, and the place where it is deposited, and the time at which it is intended to be so cut up or unlaid. Permit to be advertised before dealer proceeds to act thereon.

(2) If any person suspects or believes that the cable or other article is his property, he may apply to a justice of the peace for a warrant, and that justice may, on the sworn statement of the applicant, grant a warrant entitling the applicant to require the production by the marine store dealer of the cable or article mentioned in the permit, and also of the books required under this Part of this Act to be kept by the marine store dealer, and authorising the applicant to inspect and examine the cable or article or books.

(3) If a marine store dealer fails without reasonable cause to comply with any of the requirements of this section, he shall be liable for the first offence to a fine not exceeding twenty pounds, and for every subsequent offence to a fine not exceeding fifty pounds.

Marking of Anchors.

543. (1) Every manufacturer of anchors shall mark on every anchor manufactured by him in legible characters and both on the crown and also on the shank under the stock his name or initials, and shall in addition mark on the anchor a progressive number and the weight of the anchor. Marking of anchors.

(2) If a manufacturer of anchors fails without reasonable cause to comply with this section, he shall be liable for each offence to a fine not exceeding five pounds.

Salvage.

544. (1) Where services are rendered wholly or in part within British waters in saving life from any British or foreign vessel, or elsewhere in saving life from any British vessel, there shall be payable to the salvor by the owner of the vessel, cargo, or apparel saved, a reasonable amount of salvage, to be determined in case of dispute in manner herein-after mentioned. Salvage payable for saving life.

(2) Salvage in respect of the preservation of life when payable by the wners of the vessel shall be payable in priority to all other claims for salvage.

(3) Where the vessel, cargo, and apparel are destroyed, or the value thereof is insufficient, after payment of the actual expenses incurred, to pay the amount of salvage payable in respect of the preservation of life, the Board of Trade may, in their discretion, award to the salvor, out of the Mercantile Marine Fund, such sum as they think fit in whole or part satisfaction of any amount of salvage so left unpaid.

Salvage of life from foreign vessels.

545. When it is made to appear to Her Majesty that the government of any foreign country is willing that salvage should be awarded by British courts for services rendered in saving life from ships belonging to that country, when the ship is beyond the limits of British jurisdiction, Her Majesty may, by Order in Council, direct that the provisions of this Part of this Act with reference to salvage of life shall, subject to any conditions and qualifications contained in the Order, apply, and those provisions shall accordingly apply to those services as if they were rendered in saving life from ships within British jurisdiction.

Salvage of cargo or wreck.

546. Where any vessel is wrecked, stranded, or in distress at any place on or near the coasts of the United Kingdom or any tidal water within the limits of the United Kingdom, and services are rendered by any person in assisting that vessel or saving the cargo or apparel of that vessel or any part thereof, and where services are rendered by any person other than a receiver in saving any wreck, there shall be payable to the salvor by the owner of the vessel, cargo, apparel, or wreck, a reasonable amount of salvage to be determined in case of dispute in manner herein-after mentioned.

Procedure in Salvage.

Determination of salvage disputes.

547. (1) Disputes as to the amount of salvage whether of life or property, and whether rendered within or without the United Kingdom arising between the salvor and the owners of any vessel, cargo, apparel or wreck, shall, if not settled by agreement, arbitration, or otherwise, be determined summarily in manner provided by this Act, in the following cases, namely:—

(*a*) In any case where the parties to the dispute consent:

(*b*) In any case where the value of the property saved does not exceed one thousand pounds:

(*c*) In any case where the amount claimed does not exceed in Great Britain three hundred pounds, and in Ireland two hundred pounds.

(2) Subject as aforesaid, disputes as to salvage shall be determined by the High Court in England or Ireland, or in Scotland the Court of Session, but if the claimant does not recover in any such court in Great Britain more

than three hundred pounds, and in any such court in Ireland more than two hundred pounds, he shall not be entitled to recover any costs, charges, or expenses incurred by him in the prosecution of his claim, unless the court before which the case is tried certify that the case is a fit one to be tried otherwise than summarily in manner provided by this Act.

(3) Disputes relating to salvage may be determined on the application either of the salvor or of the owner of the property saved, or of their respective agents.

(4) Where a dispute as to salvage is to be determined summarily under this section it shall be referred and determined as follows:—

(*a*) In England it shall be referred to and determined by a county court having Admiralty jurisdiction by virtue of the County Courts Admiralty Jurisdiction Act, 1868, or any Act amending the same: [& 32 Vict., 71.]

(*b*) In Scotland it shall be referred to and determined by the sheriff's court:

(*c*) In Ireland it shall be referred to the arbitration of and determined by two justices of the peace, or a stipendiary magistrate, or the recorder of any borough having a recorder, or the chairman of quarter sessions in any county, and any such justices, stipendiary magistrate, recorder, or chairman are herein-after included in the expression "arbitrators."

(5) Nothing in this Act relating to the procedure in salvage cases shall affect the jurisdiction or procedure in salvage cases of a county court having Admiralty jurisdiction by virtue of the County Courts Admiralty Jurisdiction Act, 1868, or the Court of Admiralty (Ireland) Act, 1867, or any Act amending either of those Acts. [& 31 Vict., 14.]

548. (1) Disputes as to salvage which are to be determined summarily in manner provided by this Act shall— [Determination of disputes as to salvage summarily.]

(*a*) where the dispute relates to the salvage of wreck be referred to a court or arbitrators having jurisdiction at or near the place where the wreck is found:

(*b*) where the dispute relates to salvage in the case of services rendered to any vessel or to the cargo or apparel thereof or in saving life therefrom be referred to a court or arbitrators having jurisdiction at or near the place where the vessel is lying, or at or near the port in the United Kingdom into which the vessel is first brought after the occurrence by reason whereof the claim of salvage arises.

(2) Any court or arbitrators to whom a dispute as to salvage is referred for summary determination may, for the purpose of determining any such dispute, call in to their assistance any person conversant with maritime affairs as assessor, and there shall be paid as part of the costs of the proceedings to every such assessor in respect of his services such sum not exceeding five pounds as the Board of Trade may direct.

Appeal in case of salvage disputes.

549. (1) Where a dispute relating to salvage has been determined summarily in manner provided by this Act, any party aggrieved by the decision may appeal therefrom—

(*a*) in Great Britain, in like manner as in the case of any other judgment in an Admiralty or maritime cause of the county court or sheriff's court, as the case may be; and

(*b*) in Ireland, to the High Court, but only if the sum in dispute exceeds fifty pounds, and the appellant within ten days after the date of the award gives notice to the arbitrators of his intention to appeal and, within twenty days after the date of the award takes such proceedings as, according to the practice of the High Court, are necessary for the institution of an appeal.

(2) In the case of an appeal from arbitrators in Ireland the arbitrators shall transmit to the proper officer of the court of appeal a copy on unstamped paper certified under their hands to be a true copy of the proceedings had before them or their umpire (if any) and of the award so made by them or him, accompanied with their or his certificate in writing of the gross value of the article respecting which salvage is claimed; and such copy and certificate shall be admitted in the court of appeal as evidence in the case.

As to arbitrators in Ireland.

550. (1) The Lord Lieutenant in Ireland may appoint, out of the justices for any borough or county, a rota of justices, by whom jurisdiction in salvage cases under this Part of this Act shall be exercised.

(2) Where no such rota is appointed the salvors may, by writing addressed to the justices' clerk, name one justice and the owner of the property saved may in like manner name another justice to be arbitrators; and if either party fails to name a justice within a reasonable time the case may be tried by two or more justices at petty sessions.

(3) Where a dispute as to salvage is referred to justices under this Act, they may, if a difference of opinion arises between them, or without such difference, if they think fit, appoint some person conversant with maritime affairs as umpire to decide the point in dispute.

(4) The arbitrators, within forty-eight hours after any such dispute has been referred to them, and the umpire (if any) within forty-eight hours after

his appointment, shall make an award as to the amount of salvage payable, with power nevertheless for such arbitrators or umpire, by writing, duly signed, to extend the time for so making the award.

(5) There shall be paid to every umpire appointed as aforesaid, in respect of his services, such sum not exceeding five pounds as the Board of Trade may direct.

(6) All the costs of such arbitration, including any such payment to an umpire as aforesaid, shall be paid by the parties to the dispute, in such manner, and in such shares and proportions, as the arbitrators or umpire may direct by the award.

(7) The arbitrators or umpire may call for the production of any documents in the possession or power of either party which they or he may think necessary for determining the question in dispute, and may examine the parties and their witnesses on oath, and administer the oaths necessary for that purpose.

(8) A Secretary of State may determine the scale of costs to be awarded in salvage cases determined by arbitrators under this Part of this Act.

Valuation of property by receiver.

551. (1) Where any dispute as to salvage arises, the receiver of the district where the property is in respect of which the salvage claim is made, may, on the application of either party, appoint a valuer to value that property, and shall give copies of the valuation to both parties.

(2) Any copy of the valuation purporting to be signed by the valuer and to be certified as a true copy by the receiver, shall be admissible as evidence in any subsequent proceeding.

(3) There shall be paid in respect of the valuation by the person applying for the same such fee as the Board of Trade may direct.

Detention of property liable for salvage by a receiver.

552. (1) Where salvage is due to any person under this Act, the receiver shall—

(*a*) if the salvage is due in respect of services rendered in assisting any vessel, or in saving life therefrom, or in saving the cargo or apparel thereof, detain the vessel and cargo or apparel; and

(*b*) if the salvage is due in respect of the saving of any wreck, and the wreck is not sold as unclaimed under the Act, detain the wreck.

(2) Subject as herein-after mentioned, the receiver shall detain the vessel and the cargo and apparel, or the wreck (herein-after referred to as detained property) until payment is made for salvage, or process is issued for the arrest or detention thereof by some competent court.

(3) A receiver may release any detained property if security is given to

his satisfaction or, if the claim for salvage exceeds two hundred pounds and any question is raised as to the sufficiency of the security, to the satisfaction in England or Ireland of the High Court, and in Scotland of the Court of Session, including any division of that court, or the lord ordinary officiating on the bills during vacation.

(4) Any security given for salvage in pursuance of this section to an amount exceeding two hundred pounds may be enforced by such court as aforesaid in the same manner as if bail had been given in that court.

Sale of detained property by receiver.

553. (1) The receiver may sell any detained property if the persons liable to pay the salvage in respect of which the property is detained are aware of the detention, in the following cases, namely—

(*a*) where the amount is not disputed, and payment of the amount due is not made within twenty days after the amount is due, or

(*b*) where the amount is disputed, but no appeal lies from the first court to which the dispute is referred, and payment is not made within twenty days after the decision of the first court, or

(*c*) where the amount is disputed and an appeal lies from the decision of the first court to some other court, and within twenty days of the decision of the first court neither payment of the sum due is made nor proceedings are commenced for the purpose of appeal.

(2) The proceeds of sale of detained property shall, after payment of the expenses of the sale, be applied by the receiver in payment of the expenses, fees, and salvage, and, so far as not required for that purpose, shall be paid to the owners of the property, or any other persons entitled to receive the same.

Agreement as to salvage.

554. (1) Where services for which salvage is claimed are rendered either by the commander or crew or part of the crew of any of Her Majesty's ships or of any other ship, and the salvor voluntarily agrees to abandon his lien upon the ship, cargo, and property alleged to be salved, then, upon the master entering into a written agreement attested by two witnesses to abide the decision of the High Court in England, or of a Vice-Admiralty Court or Colonial Court of Admiralty, and thereby giving security in that behalf to an amount agreed on by the parties to the agreement, that agreement shall bind the ship, and the cargo, and freight, respectively, and the respective owners of the ship, cargo, and freight, and their respective heirs, executors, and administrators, for the salvage which may be adjudged to be payable in respect of the ship, cargo, and freight respectively to the extent of the security given.

(2) Any agreement made under this section may be adjudicated on and enforced in the same manner as a bond executed under the provisions of thi

Part of this Act relating to salvage by Her Majesty's ships, and on any such agreement being made the salvor and the master shall respectively make the statements required by this Part of this Act to be made in the case of the bond, but their statements need not be made on oath.

(3) The salvor shall transmit the statements made, as soon as practicable, to the court in which the agreement is to be adjudicated upon.

Apportionment of salvage under 200*l.* by receiver.

555. (1) Where the aggregate amount of salvage payable in respect of salvage services rendered in the United Kingdom has been finally determined, either summarily in manner provided by this Act or by agreement, and does not exceed two hundred pounds, but a dispute arises as to the apportionment thereof among several claimants, the person liable to pay the amount may apply to the receiver for liberty to pay the same to him; and the receiver shall, if he thinks fit, receive the same accordingly, and shall grant to the person paying the amount a certificate of the amount paid and of the services in respect of which it is paid, and that certificate shall be a full discharge and indemnity to the person by whom the money is paid, and to his vessel, cargo, apparel, and effects against the claims of all persons whomsoever in respect of the services mentioned in the certificate.

(2) The receiver shall with all convenient speed distribute any amount received by him under this section among the persons entitled to the same on such evidence, and in such shares and proportions, as he thinks fit, and may retain any money which appears to him to be payable to any person who is absent.

(3) A distribution made by a receiver in pursuance of this section shall be final and conclusive as against all persons claiming to be entitled to any portion of the amount distributed.

Apportionment of salvage by Admiralty courts.

556. Whenever the aggregate amount of salvage payable in respect of salvage service rendered in the United Kingdom has been finally ascertained, and exceeds two hundred pounds, and whenever the aggregate amount of salvage payable in respect of salvage services rendered elsewhere has been finally ascertained, whatever that amount may be, then, if any delay or dispute arises as to the apportionment thereof, any court having Admiralty jurisdiction may cause the same to be apportioned amongst the persons entitled thereto in such manner as it thinks just, and may for that purpose, if it thinks fit, appoint any person to carry that apportionment into effect, and may compel any person in whose hands or under whose control the amount may be to distribute the same, or to bring the same into court to be there dealt with as the court may direct, and may for the purposes aforesaid issue such processes as it thinks fit.

Salvage by Her Majesty's Ships.

Salvage by Her Majesty's ships.

557. (1) Where salvage services are rendered by any ship belonging to Her Majesty or by the commander or crew thereof, no claim shall be allowed for any loss, damage, or risk caused to the ship, or her stores, tackle, or furniture, or for the use of any stores or other articles belonging to Her Majesty, supplied in order to effect those services, or for any other expense or loss sustained by Her Majesty by reason of that service, and no claim for salvage services by the commander or crew, or part of the crew of any of Her Majesty's ships, shall be finally adjudicated upon, unless the consent of the Admiralty to the prosecution of that claim is proved.

(2) Any document purporting to give the consent of the Admiralty for the purpose of this section, and to be signed by the Secretary to the Admiralty or on his behalf, shall be evidence of that consent.

(3) If a claim is prosecuted and the consent is not proved, the claim shall stand dismissed with costs.

Salvage by Her Majesty's ships abroad.

558. (1) Where services are rendered at any place out of the limits of the United Kingdom or the four seas adjoining thereto by the commander or any of the crew of any of Her Majesty's ships in saving any vessel or cargo or property belonging to a vessel, the vessel, cargo, or property, alleged to be saved shall, if the salvor is justified by the circumstances of the case in detaining it, be taken to some port where there is a consular officer or a colonial court of admiralty, or a vice-admiralty court.

(2) The salvor and the master, or other person in charge of the vessel, cargo, or property, saved shall within twenty-four hours after arriving at the port each deliver to the consular officer or judge of the colonial court of admiralty or vice-admiralty court, as the case may be, a statement on oath, specifying so far as possible, and so far as those particulars are applicable, the particulars set out in the first part of the Nineteenth Schedule to this Act, and also in the case of the master or other person his willingness to execute a bond in the form, so far as circumstances will permit, set out in the second part of that Schedule.

Provisions as to bond to be executed.

559. (1) The bond shall be in such sum as the consular officer or judge thinks sufficient to answer the demand for salvage service, but the sum fixed shall not exceed one-half of the amount which, in the opinion of the consular officer or judge, is the value of the property in respect of which salvage has been rendered.

(2) Where the vessel, cargo, or property in respect of which salvage services are rendered is not owned by persons domiciled in Her Majesty's dominions, the master shall procure such security for the due performance of the bond

as the consular officer or judge thinks sufficient to be lodged with that officer or judge, or with that officer or judge and such other persons jointly as the salvor may appoint.

(3) The consular officer or judge shall fix the amount of the bond within four days after the receipt of the statements required by this Part of this Act, but if either of those statements is not delivered within the time required by this Part of this Act, he may proceed *ex parte*.

(4) A consular officer may for the purposes of this section take affidavits.

(5) Nothing in this section shall authorise the consular officer or judge to require the cargo of any ship to be unladen.

560. (1) The consular officer or judge on fixing the sum to be inserted in the bond shall send notice thereof to the salvor and master, and on the execution of the bond by the master in the sum fixed in the presence of the consular officer or judge (who shall attest the same) and upon delivery thereof to the salvor, and in cases where security is to be lodged, on that security being duly lodged, the right of the salvor to detain the vessel, cargo, or property shall cease. **Execution of bond.**

(2) The bond shall bind the respective owners of the vessel, cargo, and freight, and their heirs, executors, and administrators for the salvage adjudged to be payable in respect of the vessel, cargo, and freight respectively.

561. (1) The bond shall be adjudicated on and enforced in the High Court in England, unless the salvor and master agree at the time of the execution of the bond that the bond may be adjudicated on and enforced in any specified colonial court of admiralty or vice-admiralty court, but that court shall in that case have the same power and authorities for the purpose as the High Court in England. **Enforcement of bond.**

(2) The High Court in England shall have power to enforce any bond given in pursuance of this Part of this Act in any colonial court of admiralty or vice-admiralty court in any part of Her Majesty's dominions, and any court exercising admiralty jurisdiction in Scotland, Ireland, the Isle of Man, or the Channel Islands shall assist that court in enforcing those bonds.

(3) Where security has been given for the performance of a bond, the persons with whom the security is lodged shall deal with the same as the court adjudicating upon the bond direct.

(4) The consular officer or judge shall at the earliest opportunity transmit the statements and documents delivered to him and the notice of the sum fixed in the bond to the High Court in England or the colonial court of admiralty or vice-admiralty court in which the bond is to be enforced, as the case may be.

Saving for other salvage rights.

562. (1) Nothing contained in this Part of this Act shall prejudice the right of the salvor where salvage services have been rendered by one of Her Majesty's ships, or by the commander or any of the crew thereof, to proceed for the enforcement of the salvage claim otherwise than in manner provided by this Act, but the salvor shall have no right to detain the vessel, cargo, or property saved, unless he elects to proceed under this Part of this Act.

(2) Nothing contained in this Part of this Act shall affect the right of the salvor, where salvage services have been rendered by one of Her Majesty's ships or by the commander or any of the crew thereof, in any case which is not provided for therein.

Exemption from stamp duty.

563. Any bond, statement, agreement, or other document made or executed in pursuance of the provisions of this Part of this Act relating to salvage by Her Majesty's ships shall, if made or executed out of the United Kingdom, be exempt from stamp duty.

Punishment for forgery and false representations.

564. If any person in any proceeding under the provisions of this Part of this Act relating to salvage by Her Majesty's ships—

(*a*) forges, assists in forging, or procures to be forged, fraudulently alters, assists in fraudulently altering, or procures to be fraudulently altered, any document; or

(*b*) puts off or makes use of any forged or altered document, knowing the same to be so forged or altered; or

(*c*) gives or makes, or assists in giving or making, or procures to be given or made, any false evidence or representation, knowing the same to be false,

that person shall for each offence be liable to imprisonment, with or without hard labour, for any period not exceeding two years, or, on summary conviction, to imprisonment, with or without hard labour, for any period not exceeding six months.

Jurisdiction of High Court in Salvage.

Jurisdiction of High Court in salvage.

565. Subject to the provisions of this Act, the High Court, and in Scotland, the Court of Session, shall have jurisdiction to decide upon all claims whatsoever relating to salvage, whether the services in respect of which salvage is claimed were performed on the high seas or within the body of any county, or partly on the high seas and partly within the body of any county, and whether the wreck in respect of which salvage is claimed is found on the sea or on the land, or partly on the sea and partly on the land.

Appointment of Receivers of Wreck.

566. The Board of Trade shall have the general superintendence throughout the United Kingdom of all matters relating to wreck, and may, with the consent of the Treasury, appoint any officer of customs, or of the coastguard, or any officer of inland revenue, or, where it appears to such Board to be more convenient, any other person, to be a receiver of wreck (in this Part of this Act referred to as a receiver), in any district, and to perform the duties of receiver under this Part of this Act, and shall give due notice of the appointment.

Appointment of receivers of wreck.

Fees of Receivers of Wreck.

567. (1) There shall be paid to every receiver the expenses properly incurred by him in the performance of his duties, and also, in respect of the several matters specified in the Twentieth Schedule to this Act, such fees not exceeding the amounts therein mentioned as may be directed by the Board of Trade, but a receiver shall not be entitled to any remuneration other than those payments.

Receivers' fees.

(2) The receiver shall, in addition to all other rights and remedies for the recovery of those expenses or fees, have the same rights and remedies in respect thereof as a salvor has in respect of salvage due to him.

(3) Whenever any dispute arises in any part of the United Kingdom as to the amount payable to any receiver in respect of expenses or fees, that dispute shall be determined by the Board of Trade, and the decision of that Board shall be final.

(4) All fees received by a receiver in respect of any services performed by him as receiver shall be carried to and form part of the Mercantile Marine Fund, but a separate account shall be kept of those fees, and the money arising from them shall be applied in defraying any expenses duly incurred in carrying into effect this Act in such manner as the Board of Trade direct.

568. (1) Where services are rendered by any officers or men of the coastguard service in watching or protecting shipwrecked property, then, unless it can be shown that those services have been declined by the owner of the property or his agent at the time they were tendered, or that salvage has been claimed and awarded for those services, the owner of the property shall pay in respect of those services remuneration according to a scale to be fixed by the Board of Trade; and that remuneration shall be recoverable by the same means, and shall be paid to the same persons, and accounted for and applied in the same manner as fees received by receivers under the provisions of this Part of this Act.

Remuneration for services by coastguard.

(2) The scale fixed by the Board of Trade shall not exceed the scale by which remuneration to officers and men of the coastguard for extra duties in the ordinary service of the Commissioners of Customs is for the time being regulated.

Duties on Wreck.

Provisions as to duties, etc., on wrecked goods.

569. (1) All wreck, being foreign goods brought or coming into the United Kingdom or Isle of Man, shall be subject to the same duties as if the same was imported into the United Kingdom or Isle of Man respectively, and if any question arises as to the origin of the goods, they shall be deemed to be the produce of such country as the Commissioners of Customs may on investigation determine.

(2) The Commissioners of Customs and Inland Revenue shall permit all goods, wares, and merchandise saved from any ship stranded or wrecked on her homeward voyage to be forwarded to the port of her original destination, and all goods, wares, and merchandise saved from any ship stranded or wrecked on her outward voyage to be returned to the port at which the same were shipped; but those Commissioners shall take security for the due protection of the revenue in respect of those goods.

Supplemental.

Powers of Sheriff in Scotland.

570. Any matter or thing which may be done under this Part of this Act by or to a justice of the peace or a court of summary jurisdiction, may in Scotland be done by or to the sheriff of the county.

Saving for Cinque ports.

571. Nothing in this Part of this Act shall prejudice or affect any jurisdiction or powers of the Lord Warden or any officers of the Cinque ports or of any court of those ports or of any court having concurrent jurisdiction within the boundaries of these ports, and disputes as to salvage arising within those boundaries shall be determined in the manner in which they have been hitherto determined.

PART X.

Pilotage.[1]

* * * * * * *

* * * * * * *

PART XI.

Lighthouses.

* * * * * * *

* * * * * * *

1 S. 572 provides that "this Part of this Act extends to the United Kingdom and the Isle of Man only, but applies to all ships British and Foreign." The Part is, therefore, omitted.

Lighthouses, etc., in Colonies.

[1]670. (1) Where any lighthouse, buoy, or beacon has, either before or after the passing of this Act, been erected or placed on or near the coasts of any British possession by or with the consent of the legislature of that possession, Her Majesty may by Order in Council fix such dues (in this Act referred to as colonial light dues) to be paid in respect of that lighthouse, buoy, or beacon by the owner or master of every ship which passes the same and derives benefit therefrom, as Her Majesty may deem reasonable, and may by like order increase, diminish, or repeal such dues, and those dues shall from the time mentioned in the Order be leviable throughout Her Majesty's dominions. Dues for colonial lighthouses, etc.

(2) Colonial light dues shall not be levied in any British possession unless the legislature of that possession has by address to the Crown, or by Act or Ordinance duly passed, signified its opinion that the dues ought to be levied.

671. (1) Colonial light dues shall in the United Kingdom be collected and recovered so far as possible as light dues are collected and recovered under this Part of this Act. Collection and recovery of colonial light dues.

(2) Colonial light dues shall in each British possession be collected by such persons as the Governor of that possession may appoint for the purpose, and shall be collected by the same means, in the same manner, and subject to the same conditions so far as circumstances permit, as light dues under this Part of this Act, or by such other means, in such other manner, and subject to such other conditions as the legislature of the possession direct.

672. Colonial light dues levied under this Act shall be paid over to Her Majesty's Paymaster-General at such times and in such manner as the Board of Trade direct, and shall be applied, paid, and dealt with by him for the purposes authorised by this Act, in such manner as that Board direct. Payment of colonial light dues to Paymaster-General.

673. Colonial light dues shall, after deducting the expenses of collection, be applied in payment of the expenses incurred in erecting and maintaining the lighthouse, buoy, or beacon in respect of which they are levied, and for no other purpose. Application of colonial light dues.

674. (1) The Board of Trade may raise such sums as they think fit for the purpose of constructing or repairing any lighthouse, buoy, or beacon in respect of which colonial light dues are levied or are to be levied on the security of those dues so levied or to be levied. Advances for construction and repair of colonial lighthouses, etc.

(2) Any sums so to be raised may be advanced by the Treasury out of moneys provided by Parliament, or by the Public Works Loan Commissioners or by any other persons, but any such advances shall be made and secured

---

[1] Ss. 670-675 are the only sections in this Part applicable to India.

in the same manner and subject to the same provisions as similar advances for the purpose of lighthouses in the United Kingdom under this Part of this Act.

Accounts of colonial light dues.

675. (1) Accounts shall be kept of all colonial light dues received under this Act and of all sums expended in the construction, repair, or maintenance of the lighthouse, buoy, or beacon in respect of which those dues are received.

(2) These accounts shall be kept in such manner as the Board of Trade direct, and shall be laid annually before Parliament and audited in such manner as may be directed by Order in Council.

PART XII.

Mercantile Marine Fund.

Sums payable to the Mercantile Marine Fund.

676. (1) The common fund called the Mercantile Marine Fund shall continue to exist under that name, and subject to the provisions of this Act there shall be accounted for and paid to that fund—

(*a*) all fees, charges, and expenses payable in respect of the survey or measurement of ships under this Act:

(*b*) all fees and other sums (other than fines and forfeitures) received by the Board of Trade under the Second and Fifth Parts of this Act, including all fees payable in respect of the medical inspection of seamen under the Second Part of this Act:

(*c*) the moneys arising from the unclaimed property of deceased seamen, except where the same are required to be paid as directed by the Accountant General of Her Majesty's Navy:

(*d*) any sums recovered by the Board of Trade in respect of expenses incurred in relation to distressed seamen and apprentices under the Second Part of this Act:

(*e*) all fees and other sums payable in respect of any services performed by any person employed under the authority of the Third Part of this Act:

(*f*) all fees paid upon the engagement or discharge of members of the crews of fishing boats when effected before a superintendent:

(*g*) such proceeds of the sale of unclaimed wreck as are directed to be paid thereto during the lifetime of Her present Majesty under the Ninth Part of this Act:

(*h*) any fees received by receivers of wreck under the Ninth Part of this Act:

(*i*) all light dues or other sums received by or accruing to any of the General Lighthouse Authorities under the Eleventh Part of this Act:

& 46 Vict., 22. & 54 Vict., 15.

(*k*) all costs and expenses ordered by the court to be paid to the Board of Trade in pursuance of the Boiler Explosions Acts, 1882 and 1890:

(*l*) any sums which under this or any other Act are directed to be paid to the Mercantile Marine Fund.

(2) All fees mentioned in this section shall be paid at such time and in such manner as the Board of Trade direct.

Application of Mercantile Marine Fund.

677. Subject to the provisions of this Act and to any prior charges that may be subsisting on the Mercantile Marine Fund under any Act of Parliament or otherwise, there shall be charged on and payable out of that fund the following expenses so far as they are not paid by any private person:

(*a*) the salaries and other expenses connected with Local Marine Boards and Mercantile Marine Offices and with the examinations conducted under the Second and Fourth Parts of this Act:

(*b*) the salaries of all surveyors of ships and officers appointed under this Act and all expenses incurred in connection with the survey and measurement of ships under this Act, and the remuneration of medical inspectors of seamen under the Second Part of this Act:

(*c*) the salaries and expenses of persons employed under the Third Part of this Act:

(*d*) the superannuation allowances, gratuities, pensions and other allowances granted either before or after the passing of this Act to any of the said surveyors, officers or persons:

(*e*) the allowances and expenses paid for the relief of distressed British seamen and apprentices, including the expenses declared under this Act to be payable as such expenses, and any contributions to seamen's refuges and hospitals:

(*f*) any sums which the Board of Trade, in their discretion, think fit to pay in respect of claims to moneys carried to the Mercantile Marine Fund on account of the property of deceased seamen, or on account of the proceeds of wreck:

(*g*) all expenses of obtaining depositions, reports and returns, respecting wrecks and casualties:

(*h*) all expenses incurred in carrying into effect the provisions of this Act with regard to receivers of wrecks and the performance of their duties under this Act:

(*i*) all expenses incurred by the General Lighthouse Authorities in the works and services of lighthouses, buoys, and beacons, or in the execution of any works necessary or expedient for the purpose of permanently reducing the expense of those works and services :

(*k*) any pensions or other sums payable in relation to the duties formerly performed by the Trinity House in respect of lastage and ballastage in the River Thames:

(*l*) such expenses for establishing and maintaining on the coasts of the United Kingdom proper lifeboats with the necessary crews and equipments, and for affording assistance towards the preservation of life and property in cases of shipwreck and distress at sea, and for rewarding the preservation of life in such cases, as the Board of Trade direct:

(*m*) such reasonable costs, as the Board of Trade may allow, of advertising or otherwise making known the establishment of, or alterations in, foreign lighthouses, buoys, and beacons to owners, and masters of, and other persons interested in, British ships:

(*n*) all costs and expenses incurred by the Board of Trade under the Boiler Explosions Acts, 1882 and 1890, so far as not otherwise provided for, including any remuneration paid in pursuance of section seven of the Boiler Explosions Act, 1882, and any costs and expenses ordered by the court in pursuance of those Acts to be paid by the Board of Trade :

45 & 46 Vict., c. 22. 53 & 54 Vict., c. 35.

(*o*) any expenses which are charged on or payable out of the Mercantile Marine Fund under this or any other Act of Parliament.

Subsidy from Parliament to Mercantile Marine Fund.

678. There shall be paid to the Mercantile Marine Fund out of moneys provided by Parliament such sum in each year as may be determined by the Treasury, with the concurrence of the Board of Trade, having regard to the receipts and expenditure of the Mercantile Marine Fund under this Act.

Accounts and audit

679. (1) The accounts of the Mercantile Marine Fund shall be deemed to be public accounts within the meaning of section thirty-three of the Exchequer and Audit Departments Act, 1866, and shall be examined and audited accordingly.

29 & 30 Vict., c. 39.

(2) The Board of Trade shall as soon as may be after the meeting of Parliament in every year cause the accounts of the Mercantile Marine Fund for the preceding year to be laid before both Houses of Parliament.

PART XIII.

Legal Proceedings.

Prosecution of Offences.

680. (1) Subject to any special provisions of this Act and to the provisions herein-after contained with respect to Scotland,— Prosecution of offences.

(*a*) an offence under this Act declared to be a misdemeanor, shall be punishable by fine or by imprisonment not exceeding two years, with or without hard labour, but may, instead of being prosecuted as a misdemeanor, be prosecuted summarily in manner provided by the Summary Jurisdiction Acts, and if so prosecuted shall be punishable only with imprisonment for a term not exceeding six months, with or without hard labour, or with a fine not exceeding one hundred pounds.

(*b*) an offence under this Act made punishable with imprisonment for any term not exceeding six months, with or without hard labour, or by a fine not exceeding one hundred pounds, shall be prosecuted summarily in manner provided by the Summary Jurisdiction Acts.

(2) Any offence committed or fine recoverable under a bye-law made in pursuance of this Act may be prosecuted or recovered in the same manner as an offence or fine under this Act.

681. (1) The Summary Jurisdiction Acts shall, so far as applicable, apply— Application of Summary Jurisdiction Acts in certain cases.

(*a*) to any proceeding under this Act before a court of summary jurisdiction, whether connected with an offence punishable on summary conviction or not; and

(*b*) to the trial of any case before one justice of the peace, where, under this Act, such a justice may try the case.

(2) Where under this Act any sum may be recovered as a fine under this Act, that sum, if recoverable before a court of summary jurisdiction, shall, in England, be recovered as a civil debt in manner provided by the Summary Jurisdiction Acts.

682. Where a person is convicted summarily in England of an offence under this Act, and the fine inflicted or the sum ordered to be paid exceeds five pounds in amount, that person may appeal to quarter sessions against the conviction in manner provided by the Summary Jurisdiction Acts. Appeal on summary conviction.

683. (1) Subject to any special provisions of this Act neither a conviction for an offence nor an order for payment of money shall be made under Limitation of time for

summary proceeding.

this Act in any summary proceeding instituted in the United Kingdom, unless that proceeding is commenced within six months after the commission of the offence or after the cause of complaint arises as the case may be; or, if both or either of the parties to the proceeding happen during that time to be out of the United Kingdom, unless the same is commenced, in the case of a summary conviction within two months, and in the case of a summary order within six months, after they both first happen to arrive, or to be at one time, within the United Kingdom.

(2) Subject to any special provisions of this Act neither a conviction for an offence nor an order for payment of money shall be made under this Act in any summary proceeding instituted in any British possession, unless that proceeding is commenced within six months after the commission of the offence or after the cause of complaint arises as the case may be; or, if both or either of the parties to the proceeding happen during that time not to be within the jurisdiction of any court capable of dealing with the case, unless the same is commenced, in the case of a summary conviction within two months, and in the case of a summary order within six months, after they both first happen to arrive, or to be at one time, within that jurisdiction.

(3) No law for the time being in force under any Act, Ordinance or otherwise, which limits the time within which summary proceedings may be instituted, shall affect any summary proceeding under this Act.

(4) Nothing in this section shall affect any proceeding to which the Public Authorities Protection Act, 1893, applies. 56 & 57 Vict., c. 61.

Jurisdiction.

Provision as to jurisdiction in case of offences.

684. For the purpose of giving jurisdiction under this Act, every offence shall be deemed to have been committed and every cause of complaint to have arisen either in the place in which the same actually was committed or arose, or in any place in which the offender or person complained against may be.

Jurisdiction over ships lying off the coasts.

685. (1) Where any district within which any court, justice of the peace, or other magistrate, has jurisdiction either under this Act or under any other Act or at common law for any purpose whatever is situate on the coast of any sea, or abutting on or projecting into any bay, channel, lake, river, or other navigable water, every such court, justice, or magistrate, shall have jurisdiction over any vessel being on, or lying or passing off, that coast, or being in or near that bay, channel, lake, river, or navigable water, and over all persons on board that vessel or for the time being belonging thereto, in the same manner as if the vessel or persons were within the limits of the original jurisdiction of the court, justice, or magistrate.

(2) The jurisdiction under this section shall be in addition to and not in derogation of any jurisdiction or power of a court under the Summary Jurisdiction Acts.

686. (1) Where any person, being a British subject, is charged with having committed any offence on board any British ship on the high seas or in any foreign port or harbour or on board any foreign ship to which he does not belong, or, not being a British subject, is charged with having committed any offence on board any British ship on the high seas, and that person is found within the jurisdiction of any court in Her Majesty's dominions, which would have had cognizance of the offence if it had been committed on board a British ship within the limits of its ordinary jurisdiction, that court shall have jurisdiction to try the offence as if it had been so committed.

Jurisdiction in case of offences on board ship.

(2) Nothing in this section shall affect the Admiralty Offences (Colonial) Act, 1849.

[& 13 Vict., c. 96]

687. All offences against property or person committed in or at any place either ashore or afloat out of Her Majesty's dominions by any master, seaman, or apprentice who at the time when the offence is committed is, or within three months previously has been, employed in any British ship shall be deemed to be offences of the same nature respectively, and be liable to the same punishments respectively, and be inquired of, heard, tried, determined, and adjudged in the same manner and by the same courts and in the same places as if those offences had been committed within the jurisdiction of the Admiralty of England; and the costs and expenses of the prosecution of any such offence may be directed to be paid as in the case of costs and expenses of prosecutions for offences committed within the jurisdiction of the Admiralty of England.

Offences committed by British seamen at foreign ports, to be within Admiralty jurisdiction.

Damage occasioned by Foreign Ship.

688. (1) Whenever any injury has in any part of the world been caused to any property belonging to Her Majesty or to any of Her Majesty's subjects by any foreign ship, and at any time there-after that ship is found in any port or river of the United Kingdom or within three miles of the coast thereof, a judge of any court of record in the United Kingdom (and in Scotland the Court of Session and also the sheriff of the county within whose jurisdiction the ship may be) may, upon its being shown to him by any person applying summarily that the injury was probably caused by the misconduct or want of skill of the master or mariners of the ship, issue an order directed to any officer of Customs or other officer named by the judge, court, or sheriff, requiring him to detain the ship until such time as the owner, master, or consignee thereof has made satisfaction in respect of the injury, or has given security to

Power to arrest foreign ship that has occasioned damage.

be approved by the judge, court, or sheriff, to abide the event of any action, suit, or other legal proceeding that may be instituted in respect of the injury, and to pay all costs and damages that may be awarded thereon; and any officer of Customs or other officer to whom the order is directed shall detain the ship accordingly.

(2) Where it appears that, before an application can be made under this section, the ship in respect of which the application is to be made will have departed from the limits of the United Kingdom or three miles from the coast thereof, the ship may be detained for such time as will allow the application to be made, and the result thereof to be communicated to the officer detaining the ship, and that officer shall not be liable for any costs or damages in respect of the detention unless the same is proved to have been made without reasonable grounds.

(3) In any legal proceeding in relation to any such injury aforesaid, the person giving security shall be made defendant or defender, and shall be stated to be the owner of the ship that has occasioned the damage; and the production of the order of the judge, court, or sheriff made in relation to the security shall be conclusive evidence of the liability of the defendant or defender to the proceeding.

Provisions in case of Offences Abroad.

Conveyance of offenders and witnesses to United Kingdom or British possession.

689. (1) Whenever any complaint is made to any British consular officer—

(*a*) that any offence against property or person has been committed at any place, either ashore or afloat, out of Her Majesty's dominions by any master, seaman, or apprentice, who at the time when the offence was committed, or within three months before that time, was employed in any British ship: or

(*b*) that any offence on the high seas has been committed by any master, seaman, or apprentice belonging to any British ship,

that consular officer may inquire into the case upon oath, and may, if the case so requires, take any steps in his power for the purpose of placing the offender under the necessary restraint and of sending him as soon as practicable in safe custody to the United Kingdom, or to any British possession in which there is a court capable of taking cognizance of the offence, in any ship belonging to Her Majesty or to any of Her subjects, to be there proceeded against according to law.

(2) The consular officer may order the master of any ship belonging to any subject of Her Majesty bound to the United Kingdom or to such British

possession as aforesaid to receive and afford a passage and subsistence during the voyage to any such offender as aforesaid, and to the witnesses, so that the master be not required to receive more than one offender for every one hundred tons of his ship's registered tonnage, or more than one witness for every fifty tons of that tonnage; and the consular officer shall endorse upon the agreement of the ship such particulars with respect to any offenders or witnesses sent in her as the Board of Trade require.

(3) Any master of a ship to whose charge an offender has been so committed shall, on his ship's arrival in the United Kingdom or in such British possession as aforesaid, give the offender into the custody of some police officer or constable, and that officer or constable shall take the offender before a justice of the peace or other magistrate by law empowered to deal with the matter, and the justice or magistrate shall deal with the matter as in cases of offences committed upon the high seas.

(4) If any master of a ship, when required by any British consular officer to receive and afford a passage and subsistence to any offender or witness, does not receive him and afford a passage and subsistence to him, or does not deliver any offender committed to his charge into the custody of some police officer or constable as herein-before directed, he shall for each offence be liable to a fine not exceeding fifty pounds.

(5) The expense of imprisoning any such offender and of conveying him and the witnesses to the United Kingdom or to such British possession as aforesaid in any manner other than in the ship to which they respectively belong, shall, where not paid as part of the costs of the prosecution, be paid out of moneys provided by Parliament.

Inquiry into cause of death on board ship.

690. (1) Where a case of death happens on board any foreign-going British ship, the superintendent at the port where the crew of the ship is discharged, shall, on the arrival of the ship at that port, inquire into the cause of the death, and shall make in the official log an endorsement to the effect, either that the statement of the cause of death in the log is in his opinion true, or the contrary, according to the result of the inquiry.

(2) A superintendent shall for the purpose of an inquiry under this section have the powers of a Board of Trade inspector under this Act; and if in the course of any such inquiry it appears to a superintendent that any such death has been caused on board the ship by violence or other improper means, he shall either report the matter to the Board of Trade, or, if the emergency of the case so requires, shall take immediate steps for bringing the offender or offenders to justice.

(3) This section shall not apply—

(*a*) except in Scotland, to fishing boats, nor

(*b*) to ships registered in a British possession when those ships are within the jurisdiction of the government of that possession; nor

(*c*) to pleasure yachts, or ships belonging to any of the three General Lighthouse Authorities.

Depositions to be received in evidence when witness cannot be produced.

691. (1) Whenever in the course of any legal proceeding instituted in any part of Her Majesty's dominions before any judge or magistrate, or before any person authorised by law or by consent of parties to receive evidence, the testimony of any witness is required in relation to the subject matter of that proceeding, then upon due proof, if the proceeding is instituted in the United Kingdom that the witness cannot be found in that kingdom, or if in any British possession that he cannot be found in that possession, any deposition that the witness may have previously made on oath in relation to the same subject matter before any justice or magistrate in Her Majesty's dominions, or any British consular officer elsewhere, shall be admissible in evidence, provided that—

(*a*) if the deposition was made in the United Kingdom, it shall not be admissible in any proceeding instituted in the United Kingdom; and

(*b*) if the deposition was made in any British possession, it shall not be admissible in any proceeding instituted in that British possession; and

(*c*) if the proceeding is criminal, it shall not be admissible, unless it was made in the presence of the person accused.

(2) A deposition so made shall be authenticated by the signature of the judge, magistrate, or consular officer before whom it is made; and the judge, magistrate, or consular officer shall certify, if the fact is so, that the accused was present at the taking thereof.

(3) It shall not be necessary in any case to prove the signature or official character of the person appearing to have signed any such deposition, and in any criminal proceeding a certificate under this section shall, unless the contrary is proved, be sufficient evidence of the accused having been present in manner thereby certified.

(4) Nothing herein contained shall affect any case in which depositions taken in any proceeding are rendered admissible in evidence by any Act of Parliament, or by any Act or ordinance of the legislature of any colony, so far as regards that colony, or interfere with the power of any colonial legislature

to make those depositions admissible in evidence, or to interfere with the practice of any court in which depositions not authenticated as herein-before mentioned are admissible.

Detention of Ship and Distress on Ship.

692. (1) Where under this Act a ship is to be or may be detained, any commissioned officer on full pay in the naval or military service of Her Majesty, or any officer of the Board of Trade, or any officer of Customs, or any British consular officer may detain the ship, and if the ship after detention or after service on the master of any notice of or order for detention proceeds to sea before it is released by competent authority, the master of the ship, and also the owner, and any person who sends the ship to sea, if that owner or person is party or privy to the offence, shall be liable for each offence to a fine not exceeding one hundred pounds. Enforcing detention of ship.

(2) Where a ship so proceeding to sea takes to sea when on board thereof in the execution of his duty any officer authorised to detain the ship, or any surveyor or officer of the Board of Trade or any officer of Customs, the owner and master of the ship shall each be liable to pay all expenses of and incidental to the officer or surveyor being so taken to sea, and also to a fine not exceeding one hundred pounds, or, if the offence is not prosecuted in a summary manner, not exceeding ten pounds for every day until the officer or surveyor returns, or until such time as would enable him after leaving the ship to return to the port from which he is taken, and the expenses ordered to be paid may be recovered in like manner as the fine.

(3) Where under this Act a ship is to be detained an officer of Customs shall, and where under this Act a ship may be detained an officer of Customs may, refuse to clear that ship outwards or to grant a transire to that ship.

(4) Where any provisions of this Act provides that a ship may be detained until any document is produced to the proper officer of Customs, the proper officer shall mean, unless the context otherwise requires, the officer able to grant a clearance or transire to such ship.

693. Where any court, justice of the peace, or other magistrate, has power to make an order directing payment to be made of any seaman's wages, fines, or other sums of money, then, if the party so directed to pay the same is the master or owner of a ship, and the same is not paid at the time and in manner prescribed in the order, the court, justice of the peace, or magistrate who made the order may, in addition to any other powers they may have for the purpose of compelling payment, direct the amount remaining unpaid to be levied by distress or poinding and sale of the ship, or her tackle, furniture, and apparel. Sums ordered to be paid leviable by distress on ship.

Evidence, Service of Documents, and Declarations.

Proof of attestation not required.

694. Where any document is required by this Act to be executed in the presence of or to be attested by any witness or witnesses, that document may be proved by the evidence of any person who is able to bear witness to the requisite facts without calling the attesting witness or the attesting witnesses or any of them.

Admissibility of documents in evidence.

695. (1) Where a document is by this Act declared to be admissible in evidence, such document shall, on its production from the proper custody, be admissible in evidence in any court before any person having by law or consent of parties authority to receive evidence, and, subject to all just exceptions, shall be evidence of the matters stated therein in pursuance of this Act or by any officer in pursuance of his duties as such officer.

(2) A copy of any such document or extract therefrom shall also be so admissible in evidence if proved to be an examined copy or extract, or if it purports to be signed and certified as a true copy or extract by the officer to whose custody the original document was entrusted, and that officer shall furnish such certified copy or extract to any person applying at a reasonable time for the same, upon payment of a reasonable sum for the same, not exceeding four pence for every folio of ninety words, but a person shall be entitled to have—

(*a*) a certified copy of the particulars entered by the registrar in the register book on the registry of the ship, together with a certified statement showing the ownership of the ship at the time being; and

(*b*) a certified copy of any declaration, or document, a copy of which is made evidence by this Act,

on payment of one shilling for each copy.

(3) If any such officer wilfully certifies any document as being a true copy or extract knowing the same not to be a true copy or extract, he shall for each offence be guilty of a misdemeanor, and be liable on conviction to imprisonment for any term not exceeding eighteen months.

(4) If any person forges the seal, stamp, or signature of any document, to which this section applies, or tenders in evidence any such document with a false or counterfeit seal, stamp, or signature thereto, knowing the same to be false or counterfeit, he shall for each offence be guilty of felony, and be liable to penal servitude for a term not exceeding seven years, or to imprisonment for a term not exceeding two years, with or without hard labour, and whenever any such document has been admitted in evidence, the court or the person who admitted the same may on request direct that the same shall be impounded, and

be kept in the custody of some officer of the court or other proper person for such period or subject to such conditions as the court or person thinks fit.

696. (1) Where for the purposes of this Act any document is to be served on any person, that document may be served— Service of documents.

(*a*) in any case by delivering a copy thereof personally to the person to be served or by leaving the same at his last place of abode; and,

(*b*) if the document is to be served on the master of a ship, where there is one, or on a person belonging to a ship, by leaving the same for him on board that ship, with the person being or appearing to be in command or charge of the ship; and,

(*c*) if the document is to be served on the master of a ship, where there is no master, and the ship is in the United Kingdom, on the managing owner of the ship, or, if there is no managing owner, on some agent of the owner residing in the United Kingdom, or where no such agent is known or can be found, by affixing a copy thereof to the mast of the ship.

(2) If any person obstructs the service on the master of a ship of any document under the provisions of this Act relating to the detention of ships as unseaworthy, that person shall for each offence be liable to a fine not exceeding ten pounds, and, if the owner or master of the ship is party or privy to the obstruction, he shall in respect of each offence be guilty of a misdemeanor.

697. Any exception, exemption, proviso, excuse, or qualification, in relation to any offence under this Act, whether it does or does not accompany in the same section the description of the offence, may be proved by the defendant, but need not be specified or negatived in any information or complaint, and, if so specified or negatived, no proof in relation to the matter so specified or negatived shall be required on the part of the informant or complainant. Proof, etc., of exemption.

698. Any declaration required by this Act to be taken before a justice of the peace or any particular officer may be taken before a commissioner for oaths. Declarations.

Application of Penalties and Costs of Prosecutions.

699. (1) Where any court, justice of the peace, or other magistrate, imposes a fine under this Act for which no specific application is herein provided, that court, justice of the peace, or magistrate, may if they think fit direct the whole or any part of the fine to be applied in compensating any person for any wrong or damage which he may have sustained by the act or default in respect of which the fine is imposed, or to be applied in or towards payment of the expenses of the proceedings. Application of penalties.

(2) Subject to any directions under this section or to any specific application provided under this Act, all fines under this Act shall, notwithstanding anything in any other Act—

(*a*) if recovered in the United Kingdom, be paid into the Exchequer in such manner as the Treasury may direct, and be carried to and form part of the Consolidated Fund; and

(*b*) if recovered in any British possession, be paid over into the public treasury of that possession, and form part of the public revenue thereof.

Expenses of prosecution of misdemeanor.

700. Where an offence under this Act is prosecuted as a misdemeanor the court before whom the offence is prosecuted may in England make the same allowances and order payment of the same costs and expenses as if the offence were a felony, and in any other part of Her Majesty's dominions may make such allowances and order payment of such costs and expenses as are payable or allowable upon the trial of any misdemeanor or under any law for the time being in force therein.

Payment of costs of prosecution of offences committed in Admiralty jurisdiction.

701. Such costs and expenses of and incidental to any prosecution for a felony or misdemeanor as are by law payable out of any county or other local rate shall, where the felony or misdemeanor has been committed within the jurisdiction of the Admiralty of England, be paid in the same manner and subject to the same regulations as if the felony or misdemeanor had been committed in the county in which the same is heard and determined, or where the same is heard and determined at the Central Criminal Court, as if the same had been committed in the county of London, and all sums properly paid out of any county or other local rate in respect of those costs and expenses shall be repaid out of money provided by Parliament.

Procedure in Scotland.[1]

* * * *

Prosecution of Offences in Colonies.

Prosecution of offences in British possession.

711. Any offence under this Act shall, in any British possession, be punishable by any court or magistrate by whom an offence of a like character is ordinarily punishable, or in such other manner as may be determined by any Act or ordinance having the force of law in that possession.

Application of Part XIII.

Application of Part XIII.

712. This Part of this Act shall, except where otherwise provided, apply to the whole of Her Majesty's dominions.

---

[1] Ss. 702-710 are omitted as being inapplicable to India.

PART XIV.

SUPPLEMENTAL.

General Control of Board of Trade.

713. The Board of Trade shall be the department to undertake the general superintendence of all matters relating to merchant shipping and seamen, and are authorised to carry into execution the provisions of this Act and of all Acts relating to merchant shipping and seamen for the time being in force, except where otherwise provided by those Acts, or except so far as those Acts relate to the revenue. Superintendence of merchant shipping by Board of Trade.

714. All consular officers and officers of customs abroad, and all local marine boards and superintendents, shall make and send to the Board of Trade such returns or reports on any matter relating to British merchant shipping or seamen as the Board may require. Returns as to merchant shipping to Board of Trade.

715. All superintendents shall, when required by the Board of Trade, produce to that Board or to its officers all official log-books and other documents which are delivered to them under this Act. Production of log-books, etc., by superintendents.

716. (1) All fees and other sums (other than fines) received by the Board of Trade under the Second, Fourth, and Fifth Parts of this Act shall be carried to the account of the Mercantile Marine Fund. Application of fees, fines, etc.

(2) All fines coming into the hands of the Board of Trade under this Act shall be paid into the Exchequer as the Treasury may direct, and shall be carried to and form part of the Consolidated Fund.

717. The Board of Trade may take any legal proceedings under this Act in the name of any of their officers. Legal proceedings.

Expenses of Commissioners of Customs.

718. All expenses incurred by the Commissioners of Customs in the conduct of suits or prosecutions, or otherwise in carrying into effect the provisions of this Act, shall be considered as expenses having reference to the Revenues of Customs, and shall be paid accordingly; but the Board of Trade may, with the consent of the Treasury, repay out of the Mercantile Marine Fund all or any part of such of the expenses so paid as are under this Act chargeable on that fund. Expenses incurred by Commissioners of Customs.

Documents and Forms.

719. All documents purporting to be made, issued, or written by or under the direction of the Board of Trade, and to be sealed with the seal of the Board, or to be signed by their secretary or one of their assistant secretaries, or, if a certificate, by one of the officers of the Marine Department, shall be admissible in evidence in manner provided by this Act. Proof of documents.

Power of Board of Trade to prescribe forms.

720. (1) Subject to any special provisions of this Act the Board of Trade may prepare and sanction forms for any book, instrument, or paper required under this Act, other than those required under the First Part of this Act, and may make such alterations in these forms as they think fit.

(2) The Board shall cause every such form to be sealed with their seal or marked with some other distinguishing mark, and before finally issuing any form or making any alteration in a form shall cause public notice thereof to be given in such manner as the Board think requisite in order to prevent inconvenience.

(3) The Board of Trade shall cause all such forms to be supplied at all custom houses and mercantile marine offices in the United Kingdom, free of charge, or at such moderate prices as the Board may fix, or the Board may license any persons to print and sell the forms.

(4) Every such book, instrument, or paper, required under this Act shall be made in the form (if any) approved by the Board of Trade, or as near thereto as circumstances permit, and unless so made shall not be admissible in evidence in any civil proceeding on the part of the owner or master of any ship.

(5) Every such book, instrument, or paper, if made in a form purporting to be the proper form, and to be sealed or marked in accordance with this section, shall be deemed to be in the form required by this Act unless the contrary is proved.

Exemption from stamp duty.

721. The following instruments shall be exempt from stamp duty:—

(*a*) any instruments used for carrying into effect the First Part of this Act; and

(*b*) any instruments used by or under the direction of the Board of Trade in carrying into effect the Second, Fifth, Eleventh, and Twelfth Parts of this Act; and

(*c*) any instruments which are by those parts of this Act required to be in a form approved by the Board of Trade, if made in that form.

Offences as to use of forms.

722. (1) If any person—

(*a*) forges, assists in forging, or procures to be forged, the seal or any other distinguishing mark of the Board of Trade on any form issued by the Board of Trade under this Act; or

(*b*) fraudulently alters, or assists in fraudulently altering, or procures to be fraudulently altered, any such form,

that person shall in respect of each offence be guilty of a misdemeanor.

(2) If any person—

(*a*) when a form approved by the Board is, under the Second Part of this Act, required to be used, uses without reasonable cause a form not purporting to be a form so approved; or

(*b*) prints, sells, or uses any document purporting to be a form approved by the Board of Trade, knowing the same not to be the form approved for the time being, or not to have been prepared or issued by the Board of Trade,

that person shall, for each offence, be liable to a fine not exceeding ten pounds.

Powers for enforcing Compliance with Act.

Powers for seeing that Act is complied with.

723. (1) Where any of the following officers, namely:—

any officer of the Board of Trade,

any commissioned officer of any of Her Majesty's ships on full pay,

any British consular officer,

the Registrar-General of Shipping and Seamen or his assistant,

any chief officer of Customs in any place in Her Majesty's dominions, or

any superintendent,

has reason to suspect that the provisions of this Act, or any law for the time being in force relating to merchant seamen or navigation is not complied with, that officer may—

(*a*) require the owner, master, or any of the crew of any British ship to produce any official log-books or other documents relating to the crew or any member thereof in their respective possession or control;

(*b*) require any such master to produce a list of all persons on board his ship, and take copies of the official log-books, or documents, or of any part thereof;

(*c*) muster the crew of any such ship; and

(*d*) summon the master to appear and give any explanation concerning the ship or her crew or the official log-books or documents produced or required to be produced.

(2) If any person, on being duly required by an officer authorised under this section, fails without reasonable cause to produce to that officer any such official log-book or document as he is required to produce under this section, or refuses to allow the same to be inspected or copied, or impedes any muster of the crew required under this section, or refuses or neglects to give any explanation which he is required under this section to give, or knowingly

misleads or deceives any officer authorised under this section to demand any such explanation, that person shall for each offence be liable to a fine not exceeding twenty pounds.

Surveyors of Ships.

Appointment of surveyors.

724. (1) The Board of Trade may, at such ports as they think fit, appoint either generally or for special purposes, and on special occasion, any person they think fit to be a surveyor of ships for the purposes of this Act, and a person so appointed (in this Act referred to as a surveyor of ships) may be appointed either as a shipwright surveyor or as an engineer surveyor or as both.

(2) The Board of Trade may also appoint a surveyor general of ships for the United Kingdom.

(3) The Board of Trade may remove any surveyors of ships and fix and alter their remuneration, and may make regulations as to the performance of their duties, and in particular as to the manner in which surveys of passenger steamers are to be made, as to the notice to be given by them when surveys are required, and as to the amount and payment of any travelling or other expenses incurred by them in the execution of their duties, and may by such regulations determine the persons by whom and the conditions under which the payment of those expenses is to be made.

(4) If a surveyor of ships demands or receives directly or indirectly any fee, remuneration, or gratuity whatever in respect of any duties performed by him under this Act otherwise than by the direction of the Board of Trade, he shall for each offence be liable to a fine not exceeding fifty pounds.

(5) The duties of a surveyor of ships shall be performed under the direction of the Board of Trade, and in accordance with the regulations made by that Board.

Power of surveyor for purpose of survey of ships.

725. (1) A surveyor of ships in the execution of his duties may go on board any steamship at all reasonable times, and inspect the same or any part thereof, or any of the machinery, boats, equipments, or articles on board thereof, or any certificates of the master, mate, or engineer to which the provisions of this Act or any of the regulations made under this Act apply, not unnecessarily detaining or delaying the ship from proceeding on any voyage, and if in consequence of any accident to the ship or for any other reason they consider it necessary so to do, may require the ship to be taken into dock for the purpose of surveying the hull thereof.

(2) If any person hinders any surveyor of ships from going on board any steamship or otherwise impedes him in the execution of his duties under this Act, that person shall for each offence be liable to a fine not exceeding five pounds.

726. (1) Surveyors of ships shall make such returns to the Board of Trade as that Board may require with respect to the build, dimensions, draught, burden, rate of sailing, room for fuel, and the nature and particulars of machinery and equipments of ships surveyed by them.

Returns by surveyors to Board of Trade.

(2) The owner, master, and engineer of any ship so surveyed shall, on demand, give to the surveyors all such information and assistance within his power as they require for the purpose of those returns.

(3) If any owner, master, or engineer, on being applied to for that purpose, fails without reasonable cause to give any such information or assistance, he shall for each offence be liable to a fine not exceeding five pounds.

727. The Governor of a British possession may appoint and remove surveyors of ships within the limits of the possession for any purposes of this Act to be carried into effect in that possession.

Appointment of surveyors in colonies.

Board of Trade Inspectors.

728. The Board of Trade may as and when they think fit appoint any person as an inspector to report to them—

Appointment of inspectors to report on accidents, etc.

(*a*) upon the nature and causes of any accident or damage which any ship has sustained or caused, or is alleged to have sustained or caused; or

(*b*) whether the provisions of this Act, or any regulations made under or by virtue of this Act, have been complied with; or

(*c*) whether the hull and machinery of any steamship are sufficient and in good condition.

729. (1) An inspector so appointed (in this Act referred to as a Board of Trade inspector) and any person having the powers of a Board of Trade inspector—

Powers of inspectors.

(*a*) may go on board any ship and inspect the same or any part thereof, or any of the machinery, boats, equipments, or articles on board thereof to which the provisions of this Act apply, not unnecessarily detaining or delaying her from proceeding on any voyage; and

(*b*) may enter and inspect any premises the entry or inspection of which appears to him to be requisite for the purpose of the report which he is directed to make; and

(*c*) may, by summons under his hand, require the attendance of all such persons as he thinks fit to call before him and examine for the purpose of his report, and may require answers or returns to any inquiries he thinks fit to make; and (*d*) may require and enforce the production of all books, papers, or documents which he considers important for the purpose of his report; and

(*e*) may administer oaths, or may, in lieu of requiring or administering an oath, require every person examined by him to make and subscribe a declaration of the truth of the statements made by him in his examination.

(2) Every witness summoned under this section shall be allowed such expenses as would be allowed to a witness attending on subpœna to give evidence before any court of record, or if in Scotland to a witness attending on citation the Court of Justiciary; and in case of any dispute as to the amount of those expenses, the same shall be referred in England or Ireland to one of the masters or registrars of the High Court, and in Scotland to the Queen's and Lord Treasurer's Remembrancer, and the officer shall, on request made to him for that purpose under the hand of the inspector or person having the powers of an inspector, ascertain and certify the proper amount of those expenses.

(3) If any person refuses to attend as a witness before a Board of Trade inspector or before any person having the powers of a Board of Trade inspector, after having been required to do so in manner provided by this section and after having had a tender made to him of the expenses (if any) to which he is entitled under this section, or refuses or neglects to make any answer, or to give any return, or to produce any document in his possession, or to make or subscribe any declarations which an inspector or person having the powers of an inspector is hereby empowered to require, that person shall for each offence be liable to a fine not exceeding ten pounds.

Penalty for obstructing inspectors in the execution of their duty.

730. If any person wilfully impedes a Board of Trade inspector or any person having the powers of a Board of Trade inspector in the execution of his duty, whether on board a ship or elsewhere, that person shall for each offence be liable to a fine not exceeding ten pounds, and may be seized and detained by the inspector or person having the powers of an inspector, or by any person or persons whom that inspector or person may call to his assistance, until he can be conveniently taken before some justice of the peace or other officer having proper jurisdiction.

Exemption from Rates and Harbour Dues.

Exemption from rates.

731. All lighthouses, buoys, beacons, and all light dues, and other rates, fees, or payments accruing to or forming part of the Mercantile Marine Fund, and all premises or property belonging to or occupied by any of the General Lighthouse Authorities or by the Board of Trade, which are used or applied

for the purposes of any of the services for which those dues, rates, fees, and payments are received, and all instruments or writings used by or under the direction of any of the General Lighthouse Authorities or of the Board of Trade in carrying on those services, shall be exempted from all public parochial, and local taxes, duties, and rates of every kind.

732. All vessels belonging to or used by any of the General Lighthouse Authorities or the Board of Trade shall be entitled to enter, resort to, and use any harbours, ports, docks, or piers in the United Kingdom without payment of any tolls, dues, or rates of any kind. Exemption from harbour dues.

Private Signals.

733. (1) If a shipowner desires to use for the purpose of a private code any rockets, lights, or other similar signals, he may register those signals with the Board of Trade, and that Board shall give public notice of the signals so registered in such manner as they think requisite for preventing those signals from being mistaken for signals of distress or signals for pilots. Registration of private code of signals.

(2) The Board may refuse to register any signals which in their opinion cannot easily be distinguished from signals of distress or signals for pilots.

(3) Where a signal has been registered under this section, the use or display thereof by any person acting under the authority of the shipowner in whose name it is registered shall not subject any person to any fine or liability under this Act for using or displaying signals improperly.

Application of Act to Foreign Ships by Order in Council.

734. Where it has been made to appear to Her Majesty that the Government of any foreign country is desirous that any of the provisions of this Act, or of any Act hereafter to be passed amending the same, which do not apply to the ships of that country, should so apply and there are no special provisions in this Act for that application, Her Majesty in Council may order that such of those provisions as are in the Order specified shall (subject to the limitations, if any, contained therein) apply to the ships of that country, and to the owners, masters, seamen, and apprentices of those ships, when not locally within the jurisdiction of the government of that country, in the same manner in all respects as if those ships were British ships. Application by Order in Council of provisions of Merchant Shipping Acts to foreign ships.

Powers of Colonial Legislature.

735. (1) The legislature of any British possession may by any Act or Ordinance, confirmed by Her Majesty in Council, repeal, wholly or in part, any provisions of this Act (other than those of the Third Part thereof Power of Colonial Legislature to alter pro-

visions of Act.

which relate to emigrant ships), relating to ships registered in that possession; but any such Act or Ordinance shall not take effect until the approval of Her Majesty has been proclaimed in the possession, or until such time thereafter as may be fixed by the Act or Ordinance for the purpose.

(2) Where any Act or Ordinance of the legislature of a British possession has repealed in whole or in part as respects that possession any provision of the Acts repealed by this Act, that Act or Ordinance shall have the same effect in relation to the corresponding provisions of this Act as it had in relation to the provision repealed by this Act.

Regulation of coasting trade by colonial legislature.

736. The legislature of a British possession may, by any Act or Ordinance, regulate the coasting trade of that British possession, subject in every case to the following conditions:—

(*a*) the Act or Ordinance shall contain a suspending clause providing that the Act or Ordinance shall not come into operation until Her Majesty's pleasure thereon has been publicly signified in the British possession in which it has been passed:

(*b*) the Act or Ordinance shall treat all British ships (including the ships of any other British possession) in exactly the same manner as ships of the British possession in which it is made:

(*c*) where by treaty made before the passing of the Merchant Shipping (Colonial) Act, 1869 (that is to say, before the thirteenth day of May eighteen hundred and sixty-nine), Her Majesty has agreed to grant to any ships of any foreign State any rights or privileges in respect of the coasting trade of any British possession, those rights and privileges shall be enjoyed by those ships for so long as Her Majesty has already agreed or may hereafter agree to grant the same, anything in the Act or Ordinance to the contrary notwithstanding.

32 & 33 Vict. c. 11.

Provision for Foreign Places where Her Majesty has Jurisdiction.

Provision for foreign places where Her Majesty has jurisdiction.

737. Where under this Act anything is authorised to be done by, to or before a British consular officer, and in any place outside Her Majesty's dominions in which Her Majesty has jurisdiction there is no such officer, such thing may be done in that place by, to or before such officer as Her Majesty in Council may direct.

Orders in Council.

Provision as to Orders in Council.

738. (1) Where Her Majesty has power under this Act, or any Act hereafter to be passed amending the same, to make an Order in Council, Her Majesty may from time to time make that Order in Council, and by Order in Council revoke, alter or add to any Order so made.

(2) Every such Order in Council shall be published in the London Gazette, and shall be laid before both Houses of Parliament within one month after it is made, if Parliament be then sitting, or, if not, within one month after the then next meeting of Parliament.

(3) Subject to any special provisions of this Act, upon the publication of any such Order, the Order shall, as from the date of the publication or any later date mentioned in the Order, take effect as if it were enacted by Parliament.

Transmission and Publication of Documents.

Notices, etc., to be in writing and provision as to sending by post.

739. (1) Where by this Act any notice, authority, order, direction, or other communication is required or authorised to be given or made by the Board of Trade, or the Commissioners of Customs, or the Governor of a British possession, to any person not being an officer of such Board, or Commissioners, or Governor, the same shall be given or made in writing.

(2) Where any notice or document is by this Act required or authorised to be transmitted or sent, the same may be transmitted or sent by post.

Publication in London Gazette.

740. Where a document is required by this Act to be published in the London Gazette, it shall be sufficient if notice thereof is published in accordance with the Rules Publication Act, 1893.

57 Vict.,

Exemption of Her Majesty's Ships.

Exemption of Her Majesty's ships.

741. This Act shall not, except where specially provided, apply to ships belonging to Her Majesty.

Definitions and Provisions as to Application of Act.

Definitions

742. In this Act, unless the context otherwise requires, the following expressions have the meanings hereby assigned to them, that is to say—

"Vessel" includes any ship or boat, or any other description of vessel used in navigation;

"Ship" includes every description of vessel used in navigation not propelled by oars;

"Foreign-going ship" includes every ship employed in trading or going between some place or places in the United Kingdom, and some place or places situate beyond the following limits, that is to say, the coasts of the United Kingdom, the Channel Islands, and Isle of Man, and the continent of Europe between the River Elbe and Brest inclusive;

"Home-trade ship" includes every ship employed in trading or going within the following limits, that is to say, the United Kingdom, the Channel Islands, and Isle of Man, and the continent of Europe between the River Elbe and Brest inclusive;

"Home-trade passenger ship" means every home-trade ship employed in carrying passengers;

"Master" includes every person (except a pilot) having command or charge of any ship;

"Seaman" includes every person (except masters, pilots, and apprentices duly indentured and registered), employed or engaged in any capacity on board any ship;

"Wages" includes emoluments;

"Effects" includes clothes and documents;

"Salvor" means, in the case of salvage services rendered by the officer or crew or part of the crew of any ship belonging to Her Majesty, the person in command of that ship;

"Pilot" means any person not belonging to a ship who has the conduct thereof;

"Court" in relation to any proceeding includes any magistrate or justice having jurisdiction in the matter to which the proceeding relates;

"Colonial Court of Admiralty" has the same meaning as in the Colonial Courts of Admiralty Act, 1890; 3 & 54 Vict. . 27.

"A Commissioner for Oaths" means a commissioner for oaths within the meaning of the Commissioners for Oaths Act, 1889; 52 & 53 Vict. c. 10.

"Chief Officer of Customs" includes the collector, superintendent, principal coast officer, or other chief officer of customs at each port;

"Superintendent" shall, so far as respects a British possession, include any shipping master or other officer discharging in that possession the duties of a superintendent;

"Consular Officer" when used in relation to a foreign country, means the officer recognised by Her Majesty as a consular officer of that foreign country;

"Bankruptcy" includes insolvency;

"Representation" means probate, administration, confirmation, or other instrument constituting a person the executor, administrator, or other representative of a deceased person;

"Legal Personal Representative" means the person so constituted executor, administrator, or other representative, of a deceased person;

"Name" includes a surname;

(Sec. 742.)

"Port" includes place;

"Harbour" includes harbours properly so called, whether natural or artificial, estuaries, navigable rivers, piers, jetties, and other works in or at which ships can obtain shelter, or ship and unship goods or passengers;

"Tidal Water" means any part of the sea and any part of a river within the ebb and flow of the tide at ordinary spring tides and not being a harbour;

"Harbour Authority" includes all persons or bodies of persons corporate or unincorporate, being proprietors of, or intrusted with, the duty or invested with the power of constructing, improving, managing, regulating, maintaining, or lighting a harbour;

"Conservancy Authority" includes all persons or bodies of persons, corporate or unincorporate, intrusted with the duty or invested with the power of conserving, maintaining, or improving the navigation of a tidal water;

"Lighthouse" shall, in addition to the ordinary meaning of the word, include any floating and other light exhibited for the guidance of ships, and also any sirens and any other description of fog signals, and also any addition to a lighthouse of any improved light, or any siren, or any description of fog signal;

"Buoys and Beacons" includes all other marks and signs of the sea;

"The Trinity House" shall mean the master wardens and assistants of the guild, fraternity, or brotherhood of the most glorious and undivided Trinity and of St. Clement in the parish of Deptford Strond in the county of Kent, commonly called the corporation of the Trinity House of Deptford Strond;

"The Commissioners of Irish Lights" means the body incorporated by that name under the local Act of the session held in the thirtieth and thirty-first years of the reign of Her present Majesty, chapter eighty-one, intituled "An Act to alter the constitution of the Corporation for preserving and improving the Port of Dublin and for other purposes connected with that body and with the Port of Dublin Corporation" and any Act amending the same;

"Lifeboat Service" means the saving, or attempted saving of vessels, or of life, or property on board vessels, wrecked or aground or sunk or in danger of being wrecked or getting aground or sinking.

Any reference to failure to do any act or thing shall include a reference to refusal to do that act or thing.

Application of Act to ships propelled by electricity, etc.

743. Any provisions of this Act applying to steamers or steamships shall apply to ships propelled by electricity or other mechanical power with such modifications as the Board of Trade may prescribe for the purpose of adaptation.

Application of Act to certain fishing vessels.

744. Ships engaged in the whale, seal, walrus, or Newfoundland cod fisheries shall be deemed to be foreign-going ships for the purpose of this Act and not fishing boats, with the exception of ships engaged in the Newfoundland cod fisheries, which belong to ports in Canada or Newfoundland.

Repeal and Savings.

Repeal.

745. (1) The Acts mentioned in the Twenty-second Schedule to this Act are hereby repealed to the extent specified in the third column of that Schedule.

Provided that—

(*a*) Any Order in Council, licence, certificate, bye-law, rule, or regulation made or granted under any enactment hereby repealed shall continue in force as if it had been made or granted under this Act.

(*b*) Any officer appointed, any body elected or constituted, and any savings bank or office established, under any enactment hereby repealed shall continue and be deemed to have been appointed, elected, constituted, or established, as the case may be, under this Act.

(*c*) Any document referring to any Act or enactment hereby repealed shall be construed to refer to this Act, or to the corresponding enactment of this Act.

(*d*) Any penalty may be recovered, and any offence may be prosecuted, under any provision of the Merchant Shipping Acts, 1854 to 1892, which is not repealed by this Act, in the same manner as fines may be recovered and offences prosecuted under this Act.

(*e*) Ships registered under the Merchant Shipping Act, 1854, and the Acts amending the same, or duly registered before the passing of the Merchant Shipping Act, 1854, shall be deemed to have been registered under this Act. 17 & 18 Vict. c. 120.

(*f*) Nothing in this Act shall affect the Behring Sea Award Act, 1894, and that Act shall have effect as if this Act had not passed. 57 & 58 [Vict.] c. 2.

(2) The mention of particular matters in this section shall not be held to prejudice or affect the general application of section thirty-eight of the Interpretation Act, 1889, with regard to the effect of repeals. 52 & 53 [Vict.] c. 63.

(3) The tonnage of every ship not measured or remeasured in accordance with the Merchant Shipping (Tonnage) Act, 1889, shall be estimated for all purposes as if any deduction prohibited by the Merchant Ship- 52 & 53 [Vict.] c. 43.

ping (Tonnage) Act, 1889, had not been made, and the particulars relating to the ship's tonnage in the registry book and in her certificate of registry shall be corrected accordingly.

& 19 Vict., 104. **746.** (1) Nothing in this Act shall affect the Chinese Passengers Act, 1855. Savings.

(2) Any local Act which repeals or affects any provisions of the Acts repealed by this Act shall have the same effect on the corresponding provisions of this Act as it had on the said provisions repealed by this Act.

(3) Nothing in this Act shall affect the rating of any seaman who was rated and served as A.B. before the second day of August one thousand eight hundred and eighty.

Short title and Commencement.

747. This Act may be cited as the Merchant Shipping Act, 1894. Short title.

748. This Act shall come into operation on the first day of January one thousand eight hundred and ninety-five. Commencement.

SCHEDULES.

FIRST SCHEDULE.

Part I.

[*The forms in this Part of the Schedule are subject to alteration from time to time by the Commissioners of Customs, with the consent of the Board of Trade.*]

Form A.—Bill of Sale.

Official No.	Name of ship.	No., Date, and Port of Registry.

No., Date, and Port of previous Registry (if any).

Whether British or Foreign built.	Whether a sailing or Steamship, and if a Steamship, how propelled.	Where built.	When built.	Name and address of builders.

			Feet.	Tenths.
No. of Decks . No. of Masts . Rigged . Stern . . . Build . . . Galleries . .	Head . . . Framework and description of vessel . . No. of Bulkheads No. of water ballast tanks and their capacity in tons.	Length from fore part of Stem, under the bowsprit, to the aft side of the Head of the Stern-post. . . . . . Length at quarter of depth from top of weather deck at side amidships to bottom of keel . . . . . Main breadth to outside of Plank . Depth in Hold from Tonnage Deck to Ceiling at Midships . . . . Depth in Hold from Upper Deck to Ceiling at Midships in the case of three Decks and upwards . . . . . Depth from top of Beam amidships to top of Keel . . . . . Depth from top of Deck at side amidships to bottom of Keel . . . . . Round of Beam . . . . . Length of Engine Room, if any . . .		

PARTICULARS OF DISPLACEMENT.

Total to quarter the depth from weather deck at side amidships to bottom of keel ... tons.	Ditto per inch immersion at same depth ... tons.

PARTICULARS OF ENGINES (if any).

No. of Engines.	Description.	Whether British or Foreign made.	When made.	Name and Address of makers.	No. of and Diameter of Cylinders.	Length of Stroke.	N. H. P., I. H. P., Speed of Ship.
	Engines.		Engines.	Engines.			
	Boilers. Number . . Iron or Steel . Pressure when loaded . .		Boilers.	Boilers.			

PARTICULARS OF TONNAGE.

GROSS TONNAGE.	No. of Tons.	DEDUCTIONS ALLOWED.	No. of Tons.
Under tonnage Deck . . . . . Closed-in Spaces above the tonnage Deck, if any . . . . Space or Spaces between Deck . Poop . . . . Forecastle . . . . . . Roundhouse . . . . . Other closed-in Spaces, Spaces for Machinery, Light and Air, if any .		On account of Space required for Propelling Power . . . . . . On account of Spaces occupied by Seamen or Apprentices, and appropriated to their use, and certified under the regulations scheduled to this Act. These Spaces are the following, viz. On account of space used exclusively for accommodation of master, for the working of the helm, the capstan and the anchor gear, or for keeping the charts, signals, and other instruments of navigation, and boatswain's stores, and for space occupied by donkey engine and boiler, and in case of sailing ships for space used for storage of sails. Cubic Metres.	
Gross Tonnage . . Deductions as per Contra .			
Registered Tonnage .		Total deductions .	

a "I or we." b "Me" or "us." c "I" or "we." d "Myself and my" or "ourselves and our." e "His," "her," or "their."

I[a]

in consideration of the Sum of ________ paid to[b] ____ by ________ the receipt whereof is hereby acknowledged, transfer ____________ shares in the ship above particularly described, and in her boats, guns, ammunition, small arms, and appurtenances, to the said ________________.

Further [c] ____________ the said ____________ for [d] ____________ heirs covenant with the said ________________ and [e] ____________ assigns, that [a] ______ have power to transfer in manner aforesaid the premises hereinbefore expressed to be transferred, and that the same are free from incumbrances [b] ______.

In witness whereof ______ ha___ hereunto subscribed ______ name ____ and affixed ______ seal this ______ day of ____________ One thousand eight hundred and ______________.

Executed by the above-named ______________
in the presence of ______________

[a] "I" or "we."
[b] If there be any subsisting Mortgage, or outstanding certificate of Mortgage, add "save as appears by the Registry of the said Ship.";

NOTE.—A Purchaser of a Registered British Vessel does not obtain a complete title until the Bill of Sale has been recorded at the Port of Registry of the Ship; and neglect of this precaution may entail serious consequences.

FORM B.—MORTGAGE.

[*Insert description of ship and particulars as in Bill of Sale.*]

i. TO SECURE PRINCIPAL SUM AND INTEREST.

[a] ________ the undersigned ______________________ in consideration of ______________ this day lent to [b] ______ by ______ do hereby for [c] _____ and [d] ______ heirs, covenant with the said ________ firstly. That [a] ______ or [d] ________ heirs, executors, or administrators, will pay to the said __________ the said sum of ______________ together with interest thereon at the rate of ____ per cent. per annum on the _____ day of ________ next; and secondly, that if the said principal sum is not paid on the said day [a] ______ or [d] ________ heirs, executors, or administrators, will, during such time as the same or any part thereof remains unpaid, pay to the said ________________ interest on the whole or such part thereof as may for the time being remain unpaid, at the rate of _______ per cent. per annum, by equal half-yearly payments on the ________ [f] day of ____________ and _____ [f] day of ________ in every year; and for better securing to the said ______________ the repayment in manner aforesaid of the said principal sum and interest [a] ______ hereby mortgage to the said ______________ shares, of which [a] ________ the Owner ____ in the Ship above particularly described, and in her boats, guns, ammunition, small arms, and appurtenances. Lastly, [a] ________ for [b] ______ and [d] _____ heirs, covenant with the said __________ and __________ assigns that [a] ____________ power to mortgage in manner aforesaid the abovementioned shares, and that the same are free from incumbrances [e] ______________.

In witness whereof [a] ________ ha ____ hereto subscribed [d] ___________ name ______ and affixed [d] ______ seal ______ this _____ day of ________ One thousand eight hundred and ____________.

[a] "I" or "we."
[b] "Me" or "us."
[c] "Myself" or "ourselves."
[d] "My" or "our."
[f] Insert the day fixed for payment of principal as above.

[a] "I am" or "we are."

[a] "I" or "we."
[b] "Myself" or "ourselves."
[d] "My" or "our."
[e] If any prior incumbrance, add, "save as appears by the Registry of the said Ship."

Executed by the above-named ______________ }
in the presence of ______________ }

NOTE—The prompt registration of a Mortgage Deed at the Port of Registry of the Ship is essential to the security of the mortgagee, as a mortgage takes its priority from the date of production for registry, *not from the date of the instruments.*

ii. TO SECURE ACCOUNT CURRENT, ETC.

Here state by way of recital that there is an account current between the Mortgagor (describing him) and the Mortgagee (describing him); and describe the nature of the transaction so as to show how the amount of principal and interest due at any given time is to be ascertained and the manner and time of payment.

g "His" or "their."

h "I am" or "we are."

i If any prior incumbrance, add, "save as appears by the Registry of the said Ship."

Whereas f ______________

Now a ______ the undersigned ______________ in consideration of the premises for b ______ and d ______ heirs covenant with the said ______ and g ______ assigns, to pay to him or them the sums for the time being due on this security, whether by way of principal or interest, at the times and manner aforesaid. And for the purpose of better securing to the said ______________ the payment of such sums as last aforesaid, a ______ do hereby mortgage to the said ______________ shares, of which h ______ the Owner ____ in the Ship above particularly described, and in her boats, guns, ammunitions, small arms, and appurtenances.

Lastly, a ______ for b ______ and d ______ heirs, covenant with the said ______________ and g ______ assigns that a ______________ ha ______ power to mortgage in manner aforesaid the above-mentioned shares, and that the same are free from incumbrances i ______________.

In witness whereof a ______ ha ______ hereto subscribed b ______ name ______ and affixed b ______ seal ______ this ______ day of ______ One thousand eight hundred and ______________.

Executed by the above-named ______________ }
in the presence of ______________ }

NOTE.—The prompt registration of a Mortgage Deed at the Port of Registry of the Ship is essential to the security of the Mortgagee, as a mortgage takes its priority from the date of production for registry, *not from the date of the instrument.*

FORM C.—TRANSFER OF MORTGAGE.

[*To be indorsed on the original mortgage.*]

a "I" or "we."

b "My" or "our."

c "Me" or "us."

d "To him" "them."

a ______ the within-mentioned ______________ in consideration of ______ this day paid to c ______ by ______________ hereby transfer to d ______ the benefit of the within written security. In witness whereof a ______ ha ______ hereunto subscribed b ______ name ______ and affixed b ______ seal ______, this ______ day of ______________ One thousand eight hundred and ______________

Executed by the above-named ______________ }
in the presence of ______________ }

PART II.

Documents of which the forms are to be prescribed by the Commissioners of Customs and sanctioned by the Board of Trade.

Certificate of surveyor.
Declaration of ownership by individual owner.
Declaration of ownership on behalf of a corporation as owner.
Certificate of registry.
Provisional certificate.
Declaration of ownership by individual transferee.
Declaration of ownership on behalf of a corporation as transferee.
Declaration of owner taking by transmission.
Declaration by mortgagee taking by transmission.
Certificate of mortgage.
Certificate of sale.
Revocation of certificate of sale or mortgage.

SECOND SCHEDULE.

Rules for Measurement of Tonnage.

Sections 77, 78, 81, 85.

MEASUREMENT OF TONNAGE.

Rule 1.

RULE I.

Measurement of ships to be registered and other ships of which the hold is clear.

Lengths.

(1) Measure the length of the ship in a straight line along the upper side of the tonnage deck from the inside of the inner plank (average thickness) at the side of the stem to the inside of the midship stern timber or plank there, as the case may be (average thickness), deducting from this length what is due to the rake of the bow in the thickness of the deck, and what is due to the rake of the stern timber in the thickness of the deck, and also what is due to the rake of the stern timber in one-third of the round of the beam; divide the length so taken into the number of equal parts required by the following table, according to the class in such table to which the ship belongs:

TABLE.

Class 1. Ships of which the tonnage deck is according to the above measurement 50 feet long or under, into 4 equal parts:

Class 2. Ships of which the tonnage deck is according to the above measurement above 50 feet long and not exceeding 120, into 6 equal parts:

Class 3. Ships of which the tonnage deck is according to the above measurement above 120 feet long and not exceeding 180, into 8 equal parts:

Class 4. Ships of which the tonnage deck is according to the above measurement above 180 feet long and not exceeding 225, into 10 equal parts:

Class 5. Ships of which the tonnage deck is according to the above measurement above 225 feet long, into 12 equal parts:

Transverse areas.

(2) Then the hold being first sufficiently cleared to admit of the required depths and breadths being properly taken, find the transverse area of the ship at each point of division of the length as follows:—Measure the depth at each point of division, from a point at a distance of one-third of the round of the beam below the tonnage deck, or, in case of a break, below a line stretched in continuation thereof, to the upper side of the floor timber at the inside of the limber strake, after deducting the average thickness of the ceiling which is between the bilge planks and limber strake (subject, however, to the provisions of this Act in the case of a ship constructed with a double bottom for water ballast); then if the depth at the midship division of the length do not exceed sixteen feet, divide each depth into four equal parts; then measure the inside horizontal breadth at each of the three points of division, and also at the upper and lower points of the depth, extending each measurement to the average thickness of that part of the ceiling which is between the points of measurement; number these breadths from above (*i.e.*, numbering the upper breadth one, and so on down to the lowest breadth); multiply the second and fourth by four, and the third by two; add these products together, and to the sum add the first breadth and the fifth; multiply the quantity thus obtained by one-third of the common interval between the breadths, and the product shall be deemed the transverse area; but if the midship depth exceed sixteen feet, divide each depth into six equal parts instead of four, and measure as before directed the horizontal breadths at the five points of division, and also at the upper and lower points of the depth; number them from above as before; multiply the second, fourth, and sixth by four, and the third and fifth by two; add these products together, and to the sum add the first breadth and the seventh; multiply the quantity thus obtained by one-third of the common interval between the breadths, and the product shall be deemed the transverse area.

Computation from areas.

(3) Having thus ascertained the transverse area at each point of division of the length of the ship as required by the above table, proceed to ascertain the register tonnage under the tonnage deck in the following manner:—Number the areas respectively 1, 2, 3, etc., No. 1 being at the extreme limit of the length at the bow, and the last No. at the extreme limit at the length at the stern; then, whether the length be divided according to the table

into four or twelve parts as in classes 1 and 5, or any intermediate number as in classes 2, 3, and 4, multiply the second and every even numbered area by four, and the third and every odd numbered area (except the first and last) by two; add these products together, and to the sum add the first and last if they yield any thing; multiply the quantity thus obtained by one-third of the common interval between the areas, and the product will be the cubical contents of the space under the tonnage deck; divide this product by one hundred, and the quotient, being the tonnage under the tonnage deck, shall be deemed to be the register tonnage of the ship subject to any additions and deductions under this Act.

In case of decks above the tonnage deck.

(4) If the ship had a third deck, commonly called a spar deck, the tonnage of the space between it and the tonnage deck shall be ascertained as follows:—

Measure in feet the inside length of the space at the middle of its height from the plank at the side of the stem to the lining on the timbers at the stern, and divide the length into the same number of equal parts into which the length of the tonnage deck is divided as above directed; measure (also at the middle of its height) the inside breadth of the space at each of the points of division, also the breadth at the stem and the breadth at the stern; number them successively 1, 2, 3, etc., commencing at the stem; multiply the second and all the other even numbered breadths by four, and the third and all the other odd numbered breadths (except the first and last) by two; to the sum of these products add the first and last breadths; multiply the whole sum by one-third of the common interval between the breadths, and the result will give in superficial feet the mean horizontal area of the space; measure the mean height of the space, and multiply by it the mean horizontal area, and the product will be the cubical contents of the space; divide this product by one hundred, and the quotient shall be deemed to be the tonnage of the space and shall be added to the tonnage of the ship ascertained as aforesaid. If the ship has more than three decks the tonnage of each space between decks above the tonnage deck shall be severally ascertained in manner above described, and shall be added to the tonnage of the ship ascertained as aforesaid.

Poop, deck-house, forecastle, and any other closed-in space.

(5) If there be a break, a poop, or any other permanent closed-in space on the upper deck, available for cargo or stores, or for the berthing or accommodation of passengers or crew, the tonnage of that space shall be ascertained as follows:—Measure the internal mean length of the space in feet, and divide it into two equal parts; measure at the middle of its height three inside breadths, namely, one at each end and the other at the middle of the length; then to the sum of the end breadths add four times the middle breadth and multiply the whole sum by one-third of the common interval between

the breadths, the product will give the mean horizontal area of the space; then measure the mean height, and multiply by it the mean horizontal area; divide the product by one hundred, and the quotient shall be deemed to be the tonnage of the space, and shall be added to the tonnage under the tonnage deck ascertained as aforesaid. Provided that no addition shall be made in respect of any building erected for the shelter of deck passengers, and approved by the Board of Trade.

RULE II.

Measurement of ships not requiring registry with cargo on board and ships which cannot be measured under Rule I.

Rule II.

(1) Measure the length on the uppermost deck from the outside of the outer plank at the stem to the aft side of the stern post, deducting therefrom the distance between the aft side of the stern post and the rabbet of the stern post at the point where the counter plank crosses it; measure also the greatest breadth of the ship to the outside of the outer planking or wales, and then, having first marked on the outside of the ship on both sides thereof the height of the upper deck at the ship's sides, girth the ship at the greatest breadth in a direction perpendicular to the keel from the height so marked on the outside of the ship on the one side to the height so marked on the other side by passing a chain under the keel; to half the girth thus taken add half the main breadth; square the sum; multiply the result by the length of ship taken as aforesaid; then multiply this product by the factor ·0018 (eighteen ten-thousandths) in the case of ships built of wood, and ·0021 (twenty-one ten-thousandths) in the case of ships built of iron, and the product shall be deemed the register tonnage of the ship, subject to any additions and deductions under this Act.

Length. Breadth.

Girthing of the ship.

Poop, deck-house, forecastle, and other closed-in spaces on upper deck.

(2) If there be a break, a poop, or other closed-in space on the upper deck, the tonnage of that space shall be ascertained by multiplying together the mean length, breadth, and depth of the space, and dividing the product by 100, and the quotient so obtained shall be deemed to be the tonnage of the space, and shall be added to the tonnage of the ship ascertained as aforesaid.

RULE III.

Measurement of allowance for engine room space in steam ships.

Rule III.

(1) Measure the mean depth of the space from its crown to the ceiling at the limber strake, measure also three, or, if necessary, more than three breadths of the space at the middle of its depth, taking one of those measurements at each end, and another at the middle of the length; take the mean of those breadths; measure also the mean length of the space between the foremost and aftermost bulkheads or limits of its length, excluding such parts, if any, as are not actually occupied by or required for the proper working of th

machinery ; multiply together these three dimensions of length, breadth, and depth, divide the product by 100, and the result shall be deemed the tonnage of the space below the crown; then find the cubical contents of the space or spaces, if any, above the crown aforesaid, which are framed in for the machinery or for the admission of light and air, by multiplying together the length, depth, and breadth thereof; add such contents to the cubical contents of the space below the crown; divide the sum by 100; and the result shall (subject to the provisions herein-after contained) be deemed to be the tonnage of the space.

(2) If in any ship in which the space for propelling power is to be measured the engines and boilers are fitted in separate compartments, the contents of each shall be measured severally in like manner, according to the above rules, and the sum of their several results shall be deemed to be the tonnage of the said space.

(3) In the case of screw steamers in which the space for propelling power is to be measured, the contents of the shaft trunk shall be ascertained by multiplying together the mean length, breadth, and depth of the trunk, and dividing the product by 100.

(4) If in any ship in which the space aforesaid is to be measured any alteration be made in the length or capacity of the spaces or if any cabins be fitted in the space, the ship shall be deemed to be a ship not registered until remeasurement.

Rule IV.

RULE IV

Measurement of open ships.

(4) In ascertaining the tonnage of open ships the upper edge of the upper strake is to form the boundary line of measurement, and the depths shall be taken from an athwartship line, extended from upper edge to upper edge of the said strake at each division of the length.

THIRD SCHEDULE.

Section 83.

TABLE OF MAXIMUM FEES TO BE PAID FOR THE MEASUREMENT OF MERCHANT SHIPS.

	£	s.	d.
For a ship under 50 tons register tonnage	1	0	0
" from 50 to 100 tons "	1	10	0
" " 100 to 200 " "	2	0	0
" " 200 to 500 " "	3	0	0
" " 500 to 800 " "	4	0	0
" " 800 to 1,200 " "	5	0	0
" " 1,200 to 2,000 " "	6	0	0
" " 2,000 to 3,000 " "	7	0	0
" " 3,000 to 4,000 " "	8	0	0
" " 4,000 to 5,000 " "	9	0	0
" " 5,000 and upwards "	10	0	0

FOURTH SCHEDULE.

Section 97. TABLE OF MAXIMUM FEES TO BE PAID BY APPLICANTS FOR EXAMINATION.

For Certificates as Masters and Mates.

	£	s.	d.
Certificate as Master	2	0	0
Certificate as Mate	1	0	0

For Certificates as Engineers.

	£	s.	d.
Certificate as first-class Engineer	2	0	0
Certificate as second-class Engineer	1	0	0

FIFTH SCHEDULE.

REGULATIONS TO BE OBSERVED WITH RESPECT TO ANTI-SCORBUTICS.

Furnishing of Anti-Scorbutics.

(1) The anti-scorbutics to be furnished shall be lime or lemon juice, or such other anti-scorbutics (if any) of such quality, and composed of such materials, and packed and kept in such manner, as Her Majesty by Order in Council may direct.

Section 200. (2) No lime or lemon juice shall be deemed fit and proper to be taken on board ship, for the use of crew or passengers thereof, unless it has been obtained from a bonded warehouse for and to be shipped as stores.

(3) Lime or lemon juice shall not be so obtained or delivered from a warehouse as aforesaid, unless—

(*a*) it is shown, by a certificate under the hand of an inspector appointed by the Board of Trade, to be proper for use on board ship, the certificate to be given upon inspection of a sample, after deposit of the lime or lemon juice in the warehouse; and

(*b*) it contains fifteen per cent. of proper and palatable proof spirit, to be approved by the inspector or by the proper officer of customs, and to be added before or immediately after the inspection thereof; and

(*c*) it is packed in such bottles at such time and in such manner and is labelled in such manner as the Commissioners of Customs may direct.

(4) If the lime or lemon juice is deposited in a bonded warehouse, and has been approved as aforesaid by the inspector, the spirit, or the amount of

spirit necessary to make up fifteen per cent., may be added in the warehouse, without payment of any duty thereon; and when any spirit has been added to any lime or lemon juice, and the lime or lemon juice has been labelled as aforesaid, it shall be deposited in the warehouse for delivery as ship's stores only upon such terms and subject to such regulations of the Commissioners of Customs as are applicable to the delivery of ship's stores from the warehouse.

(5) The lime or lemon juice with which a ship is required by this Act to be provided shall be taken from the warehouse duly labelled as aforesaid, and the labels shall remain intact until twenty-four hours at least after the ship has left her port of departure on her foreign voyage.

Serving out of Anti-Scorbutics.

(6) The lime or lemon juice shall be served out with sugar (the sugar to be in addition to any sugar required by the agreement with the crew).

(7) The anti-scorbutics shall be served out to the crew so soon as they have been at sea ten days; and during the remainder of the voyage, except during such time as they are in harbour, and are there supplied with fresh provisions.

(8) The lime or lemon juice and sugar shall be served out daily at the rate of an ounce each per day to each member of the crew, and shall be mixed with a due proportion of water before being served out.

(9) The other anti-scorbutics, if any, provided in pursuance of an Order in Council, shall be served out at such time and in such quantities as the Order in Council directs.

SIXTH SCHEDULE.

Regulations to be observed with respect to Accommodation on board Ships.

(1) Every place in a ship occupied by seamen or apprentices, and appropriated to their use, shall be such as to make the space which it is required by the Second Part of this Act to contain available for the proper accommodation of the men who are to occupy it, and shall be securely constructed, properly lighted and ventilated, properly protected from weather and sea, and, as far as practicable, properly shut off and protected from effluvium which may be caused by cargo or bilge water.

Accommodation.
Sections 79, 210.

(2) A place so occupied and appropriated as aforesaid shall not authorise a deduction from registered tonnage under the tonnage regulations of this Act unless there be in the ship properly constructed privies for the use of the crew, of such number and of such construction as may be approved by the surveyor of ships.

(3) Every place so occupied and appropriated as aforesaid shall, whenever the ship is registered or re-registered, be inspected by one of the surveyors of ships under this Act, who shall, if satisfied that the same is in all respects such as is required by this Act, give to the collector of customs a certificate to that effect, and if the certificate is obtained, but not otherwise, the space shall be deducted from the register tonnage.

(4) No deduction from tonnage as aforesaid shall be authorised unless there is permanently cut in a beam, and cut in or painted on or over the doorway or hatchway of every place so occupied and appropriated, the number of men which it is constructed to accommodate, with the words "Certified to accommodate seamen."

(5) Upon any complaint concerning any place so occupied and appropriated as aforesaid, a surveyor of ships may inspect the place, and if he finds that any of the provisions of this Act with respect to the same are not complied with, he shall report the same to the chief officer of customs at the port where the ship is registered, and thereupon the register tonnage shall be altered, and the deduction aforesaid in respect of space disallowed, unless and until it be certified by the surveyor, or by some other surveyor of ships, that the provisions of this Act in respect of the place are fully complied with.

Maximum Fees for Inspection.

(6) The fee for each visit to the ship shall not exceed ten shillings.

(7) The aggregate amount of the fees for any such inspection shall not exceed one pound, whatever be the number of separate visits.

(8) When the accommodation is inspected at the same time with the measurement of the tonnage, no separate fee shall be charged for the inspection.

SEVENTH SCHEDULE.

Constitution of Local Marine Boards.

Elections.

Constitution of local marine board. Section 244.

1. A local marine board shall consist of the following members, viz.,—

(*a*) The mayor or provost and the stipendiary magistrate, or such of the mayors or provosts and stipendiary magistrates of the place (if more than one) as the Board of Trade appoint:

(*b*) Four members appointed by the Board of Trade from among persons residing or having places of business at the port or within seven miles thereof:

(*c*) Six members elected by the owners of such foreign-going ships and home-trade passenger ships as are registered at the port.

2. The elections shall be held on the twenty-fifth day of January one thousand eight hundred and ninety-six, and on the twenty-fifth day of January in every third succeeding year, and the appointments shall be made within one month after the elections.

3. Upon the conclusion of that month and the constitution of a new board, the functions of the then existing board shall cease, and the board, consisting of the members then newly elected and appointed, shall take its place.

4. A casual vacancy happening in the intervals between the general elections and appointments, by death, resignation, disqualification, or otherwise, shall be filled up within one month after it happens; and every person elected or appointed to fill a casual vacancy shall continue a member until the next constitution of the new board.

5. The mayor or provost shall fix the place and mode of conducting elections, and also, in the case of casual vacancies, the day of election, and shall give at least ten days' notice thereof.

6. The Board of Trade may decide any question raised concerning any election.

Registry and Votes of Electors.

7. Owners of foreign-going ships and of home trade passenger ships registered at the port shall have votes at the election as follows, namely,

Every registered owner of not less than 250 tons in the whole of such shipping shall at every election have one vote for each member for every 250 tons owned by him, so that his votes for any one member do not exceed ten.

8. The qualification of electors shall be ascertained as follows:—

(*a*) In the case of a ship registered in the name of one person, that person shall be deemed the owner:

(*b*) In the case of a ship registered in distinct and several shares in the names of more persons than one the tonnage shall be apportioned among them as nearly as may be in proportion to their respective shares, and each of them shall be deemed the owner of the tonnage so apportioned to him:

(*c*) In the case of a ship or shares of a ship registered jointly without severance of interest in the names of more persons than one the tonnage shall, if sufficient either alone or together with other tonnage, if any, owned by the joint owners, to give a qualification to each of them, be apportioned equally between or among the joint owners, and each of them shall be deemed the owner of the equal share so apportioned to him; but if it is not so sufficient the whole of the tonnage shall be deemed to be owned by such one of the joint owners resident or having a place of business at the port or within seven miles thereof as is first named on the register:

(*d*) In making any such apportionment any portion of the tonnage may be struck off so as to produce a divisible amount:

(*e*) The whole amount of tonnage so owned by each person, whether in ships or shares of or interest in ships, shall be added together and if sufficient, shall constitute his qualification.

9. The chief officer of customs in the port shall, with the assistance of the Registrar-General of Shipping and Seamen, on or before the twenty-fifth day of December in the year one thousand eight hundred and ninety-five, and in every third succeeding year, make out an alphabetical list of the persons entitled by this Act to vote at the election, containing the name and residence of each such person, and the number of votes to which he is entitled, and shall sign the list, and shall cause a sufficient number of copies thereof to be printed, and shall cause copies thereof to be fixed on or near the doors of the custom house of the port for two entire weeks next after the list has been made, and shall keep two copies of the list and permit the same to be perused by any person, without payment, at all reasonable hours during those two weeks.

10. The mayor or provost of the port, or such of them, if more than one, as is or are for the time being so appointed as aforesaid, shall, at least twenty days before the twenty-fifth day of January one thousand eight hundred and ninety-six, and in each succeeding third year nominate two justices of the peace (in this schedule referred to as the revisors) to revise the list.

11. The revisors shall, between the eighth and fifteenth days of January, both inclusive, in the year in which they are nominated, revise the list at the custom house of the port, or in some convenient place near thereto, to be hired. if necessary, by the said chief officer.

12. The revisors shall give three clear days' notice of the revision by advertising the same in some local newspaper, and by affixing a notice thereof on or near to the doors of the custom house.

13. The revisors shall make the revision by inserting in the list the name of every person who claims to have his name inserted therein and gives proof, satisfactory to the revisors, of his right to have his name so inserted, and by striking out therefrom the name of every person to the insertion of whose name an objection is made by any other person named in the list who gives

proof, satisfactory to the revisors, that the name objected to ought not to have been inserted therein.

14. The decision of the revisors with respect to every such claim or objection shall be conclusive.

15. The revisors shall, immediately after the revision, sign their names at the foot of the list so revised.

16. The list so revised shall be the register of votes at elections for three years from the twenty-fifth day of January then next ensuing inclusive to the twenty-fourth day of January inclusive in the third succeeding year.

17. The revised list, when so signed, shall be delivered to the mayor or provost as aforesaid, who shall, if necessary, cause a sufficient number of copies thereof to be printed, and shall cause a copy thereof to be delivered to every voter applying for the same.

18. The chief officer shall, if required, for the assistance of the revisors in revising the list, produce to them the books containing the register of ships registered at the port; and the Registrar-General of Shipping and Seamen, if required, shall also produce or transmit to them such certified extracts or returns from the books in his custody as may be necessary for the same purpose.

19. The revisors shall certify the expenses properly incurred by the chief officer in making and printing the list and in the revision thereof, and the Board of Trade shall pay the same, and also all expenses properly incurred by the mayor or provost in printing the same, or in any election; and the Board of Trade may disallow any items of any of those expenses in their opinion improperly incurred.

20. Every person whose name appears on the revised list and no other person, shall be qualified to vote at the election on the twenty-fifth day of January next after the revision, and at any election for a casual vacancy held at any time between that day and the next ordinary triennial election.

Qualification of Members.

21. Every male person who is, according to the revised list, entitled to a vote, shall be qualified to be elected a member, and no other person shall be so qualified; and if any person elected ceases after election to be an owner of such quantity of tonnage as would entitle him to a vote he shall no longer continue to act or be considered a member, and thereupon another member shall be elected in his place.

Application to Corporations.

22. A corporation owning a ship shall be entitled to be registered in like manner as any individual, with the substitution of the office of the corporation

for the residence of the individual. The vote of such corporation shall be given by some person whom the corporation may appoint in that behalf, and that person shall be qualified to be elected a member, and if the corporation ceases after his election to be an owner of such quantity of tonnage as entitles the corporation to be registered as a voter, that person shall cease to be a member and another member shall be elected in his place.

EIGHTH SCHEDULE.

Section 254

PARTICULARS TO BE REGISTERED BY MASTER OF A SHIP CONCERNING A BIRTH AT SEA.

Date of birth.
Name (if any) and sex of the child.
Name and surname, rank, profession, or occupation of the father.
Name and surname, and maiden surname of the mother.
Nationality and last place of abode of the father and mother.

Particulars to be registered by Master of a Ship concerning a Death at Sea.

Date of Death.
Name and surname.
Sex.
Age.
Rank, profession, or occupation.
Nationality, and last place of abode.
Cause of death.

NINTH SCHEDULE.

Sections 277, 360.

PART I.

Maximum Fees to be paid for Passenger Steamer's Certificate.

	£	s.	d.
For passenger steamers not exceeding 100 tons.	4	0	0
Exceeding 100 tons and not exceeding 300 tons	6	0	0
Exceeding 300 tons and not exceeding 600 tons	8	0	0
And for every additional 300 tons above 600 an additional	2	0	0

PART II.

Maximum Fees for Survey of Emigrant Ships.

	£	s.	d.
For an ordinary survey of the ship, and of her equipments, accommodation, stores, light, ventilation, sanitary arrangements, and medical stores	10	0	0
For a special survey	15	0	0

TENTH SCHEDULE.

REGULATIONS AS TO NUMBER OF PERSONS CARRIED ON EMIGRANT SHIPS. Sections 292, 367.

(1) An emigrant ship shall not carry under the poop or in the round house or deck house or on the upper passenger deck, a greater number of steerage passengers than in the proportion of one statute adult to every fifteen clear superficial feet of deck allotted to their use.

(2) An emigrant ship shall not carry on the lower passenger deck a greater number of steerage passengers than in the proportion of one statute adult to every eighteen clear superficial feet of deck allotted to their use.

(3) Provided, that if the height between the lower passenger deck and the deck immediately above it is less than seven feet, or if the apertures (exclusive of side scuttles) through which light and air are admitted together to the lower passenger deck are less in size than in the proportion of three square feet to every one hundred superficial feet of that deck, the ship shall not carry a greater number of steerage passengers on that deck than in the proportion of one statute adult to every twenty-five clear superficial feet thereof.

(4) An emigrant ship, whatever be her superficial space of decks, shall not carry a greater number of steerage passengers on the whole than in the proportion of one statute adult to every five superficial feet, clear for exercise, on the upper deck or poop, or on any round house or deck house which is secured and fitted on the top with a railing or guard to the satisfaction of the emigration officer at the port of clearance.

(5) In the measurement of the passenger decks, poop, round house or deck house, the space for the hospital, and the space occupied by that part of the personal luggage of the steerage passengers which the emigration officer permits to be carried there, shall be included.

ELEVENTH SCHEDULE.

REGULATIONS AS TO THE ACCOMMODATION FOR STEERAGE PASSENGERS.

Construction of Passenger Decks. Section 293.

(1) The beams supporting the passenger decks shall form part of the permanent structure of the ship. They shall be of adequate strength in the judgment of the emigration officer at the port of clearance, and shall be firmly secured to the ship to his satisfaction.

(2) The passenger decks shall be at least one inch and a half thick, and shall be laid and firmly fastened on the beams continuously from side to side of the compartment in which the steerage passengers are berthed.

(3) The height between that part of any deck on which steerage passengers are carried and the deck immediately above it shall not be less than six feet.

Berths.

(4) There shall not be more than two tiers of berths on any one deck. The interval between the floor of berths and the deck immediately beneath it shall not be less than six inches. The interval between each tier of berths and between the uppermost tier and the deck above it shall not be less than two feet six inches.

(5) The berths shall be securely constructed and of dimensions not less than six feet in length and eighteen inches in breadth for each statute adult and shall be sufficient in number for the proper accommodation of all the steerage passengers contained in the lists of passengers by this Act required to be delivered by the master of the ship.

(6) No part of any berth shall be placed within nine inches of any water closet erected in the between-decks.

(7) All male steerage passengers of the age of fourteen years and upwards (except those who occupy berths with their wives) shall, to the satisfaction of the emigration officer at the port of clearance, be berthed in the fore part of the ship in a compartment divided off from the space appropriated to the other steerage passengers by a substantial and well-secured bulkhead without opening into or communicating with any adjoining steerage passenger's berth, or, if the ship is fitted with enclosed berths, in separate rooms.

(8) Not more than one steerage passenger, except in the case of husband and wife, or females, or children under the age of twelve years, shall be placed in or occupy the same berth.

(9) Berths occupied by steerage passengers during the voyage shall not be taken down until forty-eight hours after the arrival of the ship at the port of final discharge, unless all the steerage passengers have voluntarily quitted the ship before the expiration of that time. The master of the ship shall alone be liable to a fine for breach of this regulation.

Hospitals.

(10) Sufficient space shall be set apart in every emigrant ship for use exclusively as a hospital for the steerage passengers, properly divided off, to the satisfaction of the emigration officer at the port of clearance.

(11) The space set apart for a hospital shall be under the poop or in the round house, or in any deck house which shall be properly built and secured to the satisfaction of the emigration officer at the port of clearance, or on the upper passenger deck, and not elsewhere.

(12) The space so set apart shall contain not less than eighteen clear superficial feet for every fifty steerage passengers whom the ship carries; and shall be fitted with bed-places, and supplied with proper beds, bedding, and utensils to the satisfaction of the emigration officer at the port of clearance, and shall throughout the voyage be kept so fitted and supplied.

Privies.

(13) Every emigrant ship shall be provided to the satisfaction of the emigration officer at the port of clearance with at least two privies, and with two additional privies on deck for every one hundred steerage passengers on board, and in ships carrying as many as fifty females steerage passengers with at least two water-closets under the poop or elsewhere on the upper deck to the satisfaction of the emigration officer for the exclusive use of women and young children. The privies shall be placed in equal numbers on each side of the ship, and need not in any case exceed twelve in number.

(14) All such privies and water-closets shall be firmly constructed and maintained in a serviceable and cleanly condition throughout the voyage, and shall not be taken down until the expiration of forty-eight hours after the arrival of the ship at the final port of discharge, unless all the steerage passengers quit the ship before the expiration of that time.

(15) The master of the ship shall alone be liable to a fine for breach of the regulations as to privies.

Light and Ventilation.

(16) Every emigrant ship shall be supplied with such provision for affording light and air to the passenger decks as the circumstances of the case may, in the judgment of the emigration officer at the port of clearance, require, and if there are as many as one hundred steerage passengers on board, shall be supplied with an adequate and proper ventilating apparatus, to be approved by such emigration officer and fitted to his satisfaction.

(17) The steerage passengers shall have the free and unimpeded use of the whole of each hatchway situated over the space appropriated to them, and over each such hatchway there shall be erected such a boobyhatch or other substantial covering as will, in the opinion of the emigration officer, afford the greatest amount of light and air, and of protection from wet, which the case will admit.

TWELFTH SCHEDULE.

Water and Provisions.

Water and provisions shall be issued to the steerage passengers according to the following dietary scales, that is to say,—

Water.

Three quarts daily to each statute adult, exclusive of the quantity necessary for cooking any article issued under this schedule in a cooked state.

Provisions.

Weekly, per statute adult:—

——	Scale A. For Voyages *not exceeding* 84 Days for Sailing Ships or 50 days for Steamships or ships having steam power in aid of sails.		Scale B. For Voyages *exceeding* 84 Days for Sailing Vessels or 50 Days for Steamships or ships having steam power in aid of sails.	
	lbs.	ozs	lbs.	ozs.
Bread or biscuit, not inferior to navy biscuit	3	8	3	8
Wheaten flour	1	0	2	0
Oatmeal	1	8	1	0
Rice	1	8	0	8
Peas	1	8	1	8
Beef	1	4	1	4
Pork	1	0	1	0
Butter	—		0	4
Potatoes	2	0	2	0
Sugar	1	0	1	0
Tea	0	2	0	2
Salt	0	2	0	2
Mustard	0	½	0	½
Pepper (white or black), ground	0	¼	0	¼
Vinegar	One gill.		One gill.	

(*Twelfth Schedule.*)

Provisions—continued.

Weekly, per statute adult—*continued.*

—	SCALE A. For Voyages *not exceeding* 84 Days for Sailing Ships or 50 Days for Steamships or ships having steam power in aid of sails.		SCALE B. For Voyages *exceeding* 84 Days for Sailing Vessels or 50 Days for Steamships or ships having steam power in aid of sails.	
	lbs.	ozs.	lbs.	ozs.
Preserved meat			1	0
Suet			–	–
Raisins				
Lime juice			0	6
			(*See below*).	

Substitutions.

Substitutions at the following rates may, at the option of the master of any emigrant ship, be made in the above dietary scales, as follows; that is to say,

1¼ lb. of soft bread baked on board	for	1 lb. of flour, or 1 lb. of biscuit, or 1¼ lb. of oatmeal, or 1 lb. of rice, or 1 lb. of peas.
1 lb. of preserved meat	for	1 lb. of salt pork or beef.
1 lb. of flour or of bread or biscuit, or ½ lb. of beef or of pork	for	1¼ lb. of oatmeal, or 1 lb. of rice, or 1 lb. of peas.
1 lb. of rice	for	1¼ lb. of oatmeal, or *vice versâ.*
½ lb. of preserved potatoes	for	1 lb. of potatoes.
10 oz. of currants	for	8 oz. of raisins.
3½ oz. of cocoa or of coffee, roasted and ground	for	2 oz. of tea.
¾ lb. of treacle	for	½ lb. of sugar.
1 gill of mixed pickles	for	1 gill of vinegar.

Provided that the substituted articles are set forth in the contract tickets of the steerage passengers.

Regulations as to Lime Juice.

Lime juice. When the ship is not in the tropics, it shall not be obligatory to issue lime juice, but lime juice may be issued at the discretion of the medical practitioner on board, or if there is no such medical practitioner, at the discretion of the master.

Regulations as to Messes and Issue of Provisions.

(1) Steerage passengers may be divided into messes, but a mess shall not consist of more than ten statute adults.

(2) Members of the same family, whereof one at least is a male adult, shall be allowed to form a separate mess.

(3) Water and provisions according to the above scales shall be issued daily before two o'clock in the afternoon to the head person for the time being of each mess, on behalf and for the use of the members thereof.

(4) The first of the issues shall be made before two o'clock in the afternoon of the day of embarkation to such of the steerage passengers as are then on board.

(5) Such provisions as require to be cooked shall be issued in a properly cooked state.

THIRTEENTH SCHEDULE.

Conditions for Carriage of Horses and Cattle in Emigrant Ships.

Section 301. (1) The animals shall not be carried below any deck on which steerage passengers are berthed, nor in any compartment in which steerage passengers are berthed, nor in any adjoining compartment, except in a ship built of iron, and of which the compartments are divided off by water-tight bulkheads extending to the upper deck.

(2) Clear space on the spar or weather deck shall be left for the use and exercise of the steerage passengers, at the rate of at least ten superficial feet for each statute adult.

(3) No greater number of steerage passengers shall be carried than in the proportion of fifteen to every one hundred tons of the ship's registered tonnage.

(4) In emigrant ships of less than five hundred tons registered tonnage not more than two head of large cattle shall be carried, nor in emigrant ships of larger tonnage more than one additional head of large cattle for every additional two hundred tons of the ship's registered tonnage, nor more in all in any emigrant ship than ten head of large cattle. The expression "large cattle" includes both sexes of horned cattle, deer, horses, and asses; and four sheep

of either sex, or four female goats, shall be equivalent to, and may, subject to the same conditions, be carried in lieu of one head of large cattle.

(5) Proper arrangements shall be made, to the satisfaction of the emigration officer at the port of clearance, for the housing, maintenance, and cleanliness of the animals, and for the stowage of their fodder.

(6) Not more than six dogs, and no pigs or male goats, shall be conveyed as cargo in any emigrant ship.

FOURTEENTH SCHEDULE.

Section 360.

Forms under Part III (Passenger and Emigrant Ships).

Form I.

Form of Master's Bond.

Know all men by these presents, that we, [a]
are held and firmly bound unto our Sovereign , by the Grace of God, of the United Kingdom of Great Britain and Ireland defender of the faith, in the sum of [b] *two thousand* pounds of good and lawful money of Great Britain, to be paid to our said Sovereign Her [His] heirs and successors; to which payment well and truly to be made we bind ourselves and every of us, jointly and severally, and our heirs, executors, and administrators, and every of them, firmly by these presents. Sealed with our seals. Dated this day of one thousand eight hundred and .

Whereas by Part III of the Merchant Shipping Act, 1894, it is amongst other things enacted, that, before any emigrant ship clears outwards or proceeds to sea, the master, together with the owner or charterer, or in the event of the owner or charterer being absent, or being the master, one other good and sufficient person, approved by the chief officer of customs at the port of clearance, shall enter into a joint and several bond to the Crown, in the sum of two thousand pounds:

Now the condition of this obligation is such, that if the ship whereof the above bounden is master, bound to is in all respects seaworthy, [c] [and if the said ship shall call at the port of and there shall be shipped on board at such port pure water for the use of the steerage passengers, sufficient in quantity to afford an allowance of three quarts daily to each statute adult for the period of days on the voyage from such port to the final port or place of discharge of such ship,] and if (notwithstanding any

(*Fourteenth Schedule.*)

fine by the said Act imposed, and whether the same may have been sued for and recovered or not) all and every the requirements of the said Merchant Shipping Act, 1894, (except such of them as relate exclusively to passage brokers and emigrant runners) and of the Board of Trade acting under the said Act, and of any Order of Her Majesty in Council relating to "emigrant ships" and now in force, shall in all respects be well and truly performed, *[and if the master for the time being of the said ship shall submit himself, in like manner as a British subject being the master of a British emigrant ship, to the jurisdiction of the tribunals in Majesty's possessions abroad, empowered by the said Act to adjudicate on offences committed against the said Act,] and if moreover all fines and forfeitures which the master of such ship may be adjudged to pay for or in respect of the breach or nonfulfilment of any of such requirements as aforesaid shall be well and truly paid, and if all expenses incurred by a Secretary of State or governor of a British possession or British consular officer under the said Act shall also be well and truly paid, then this obligation to be void, otherwise to remain in full force and virtue.

interna[l] port to [t]… in water[s] provid[ed] Part III… the Mer[chant] Shipping 1894.

* This clause to [be] inserted [in] the ca[se of] a foreign emigrant proceedi[ng to] any Bri[tish] possessio[n].

Signed, sealed, and delivered by the above bounden and in the presence of [b]

[b] Insert names, address[es] full of [the] witness[es].

*[I hereby certify, that the above bond was duly signed, sealed, and delivered according to the law of the United Kingdom by the said master of the said ship and by the said (*other obligor*).]

(Signature) ________________ Chief Officer of Customs for the port of

(Date) ________________ 18

* Certi[ficate] to be si[gned] by the Officer [of] Custom[s], forward[ed] with th[e] to the … accordi[ng to] s. 319 … Act.

Form II.

Form of Passenger's List.

Ship's name.	Master's name.	Tons per Register.	Aggregate Number of Superficial Feet in several Compartments set apart for Steerage Passengers.	Total Number of Statute Adults, exclusive of Master, Crew, and Cabin Passengers, which the Ship can legally carry.	Where bound.

I hereby certify, that the provisions actually laden on board this ship are sufficient, according to the requirements of Part III of the Merchant Shipping Act, 1894, for statute adults for a voyage of days.

(Signature)____________________ Master.

Date__________________18 .

Names and Descriptions of Passengers.

Ports of Embarkation.	Number of Contract Ticket.	Names of Passengers.	Profession, Occupation, or Calling of Passenger.	ENGLISH.								SCOTCH.								IRISH.								FOREIGNERS.								Port at which Passengers have contracted to land.
				AGE OF EACH ADULT OF 12 YEARS AND UPWARDS.				Ages of children between 1 and 12 years		Infants.		AGE OF EACH ADULT OF 12 YEARS AND UPWARDS.				Ages of children between 1 and 12 years.		Infants.		AGE OF EACH ADULT OF 12 YEARS AND UPWARDS.				Ages of children between 1 and 12 years.		Infants.		AGE OF EACH ADULT OF 12 YEARS AND UPWARDS.				Ages of children between 1 and 12 years.		Infants.		
				Married.		Single.						Married.		Single.						Married		Single.						Married		Single.						
				Males.	Females.	Males.	Females.	Males.	Females.	Males.	Females.	Males.	Females.	Males.	Females.	Males.	Females.	Males.	Females.	Males.	Females.	Males.	Females.	Males.	Females.	Males.	Females.	Males.	Females.	Males.	Females.	Males.	Females.	Males.	Females.	

Summary of Steerage and Cabin Passengers.

Nationalities.	NUMBER OF SOULS.							
	ADULTS OF 12 YEARS OF AGE AND UPWARDS				Children between 1 and 12 years.		Infants.	
	Married.		Single.					
	M.	F.	M.	F.	M.	F.	M.	F.
English								
Scotch								
Irish								
Foreigners								
TOTAL								

	No.
Total Number of Adults	
Children between 1 and 12; equal to Statute Adults	
Total Number of Statute Adults	

We hereby certify, that the above is a correct list of the names and descriptions of all the passengers who embarked at the port of __________

(Signed) __________ Master.

__________ Emigration Officer.

(Countersigned) __________ Officer of Customs at __________

Date __________ 18 .

N.B.—Lines should be ruled in the same form for any additions to the list after the ship first clears out; and similar certificates be subjoined to such additions according to the requirements of the Act.

FORM III.

Form of Governor's or Consular Officer's Certificate of Expenditure in the case of Passengers Wrecked or Forwarded.

I hereby certify that, acting under and in conformity with the provisions of the Merchant Shipping Act, 1894, I have defrayed the expenses incurred in rescuing, maintaining, supplying with necessary bedding, provisions, and stores,[a] and in forwarding to their destination steerage passengers [b][and cabin passengers], who were proceeding from to in the ship , which was wrecked at sea, etc.[c]

And I further certify, for the purposes of Part III of the said Act, that the total amount of such expenses is pounds, and that such expenses were duly incurred by me under the said Act.

Given under my hand, this day of 18

{ *Governor of, etc.*, (or as the case may be) *British Consular Officer at*

[a] If more passengers were re[...] than forwarded, o[...] bedding, [...] was not s[...] plied, al[...] the certifi[...] to suit th[...] facts of t[...] case.

[b] Omit w[...] in brack[...] when n[...] sary.

[c] State g[...] ally the n[...] ture of the disaster a[...] where it o[...] curred. If the p[...] sengers w[...] only left b[...] hind, w[...] any defa[...] their own, state the [...] according[...]

Form IV.

Section 350.

Form of Passage Broker's Bond.

Know all men by these presents, that we, *A.B.*[d] of C. *D.* of *etc.* and *E.F.* of *etc.* are held and firmly bound unto our Sovereign by the Grace of God of the United Kingdom of Great Britain and Ireland defender of the faith, in the sum of one thousand pounds of good and lawful money of Great Britain, to be paid to our said Sovereign, Her [His] heirs and successors; to which payment well and truly to be made we bind ourselves and every of us, jointly and severally, and our heirs, executors, and administrators, and every of them, firmly by these presents. Sealed with our seals. Dated this day of one thousand eight hundred and .

[d] Insert n[...] and surn[...] in full, w[...] occupation and addre[...] each of the parties.

Whereas by Part III of the Merchant Shipping Act, 1894, it is amongst other things enacted, that a person shall not, save as therein excepted, directly or indirectly act as a passage broker in respect of steerage passages from the British Islands to any port out of Europe, and not within the Mediterranean Sea, unless such person has entered, with two good and sufficient sureties, to be approved by the emigration officer nearest to his place of business, into a joint and several bond to the Crown, in the sum of one thousand pounds: And whereas the said *C.D.* and *E.F.* have been duly approved by the proper emigration officer as sureties for the said *A.B.*:

Now the condition of this obligation is such, that if the above-bounden *A.B.*, and every agent whom he may employ in his business of a passage broker, shall well and truly observe and comply with all the requirements of the said Act, so far as the same relate to passage brokers, and further shall well and truly pay all fines and forfeitures, and also all sums of money, by way of subsistence money, or of return of passage money or compensation, to any steerage passenger, or on his account, together with all costs which the above bounden *A.B.*, or any of his agents as aforesaid, may at any time be adjudged to pay under or by virtue of the said Act, then and in such case this obligation to be void, otherwise to remain in full force.

Signed, sealed, and delivered by the above-bounden *A.B.*, *C.D.*, and *E.F.*, in the presence of[a]

[a] [In]sert the [name]s and [addr]esses in [full] of the [witn]esses.

N.B.—This bond is to be executed in duplicate, in the presence of and to be attested by an emigration officer or his assistant, or an officer of Customs, or a magistrate, or a notary public. One part is to be deposited with the Board of Trade and the other part with the emigration officer at the port nearest to the place of business of the broker.

Each member of a firm or partnership who acts as a passage broker must give a separate bond with two sureties.

The bond is exempt from stamp duty, but must be renewed annually with the licence.

Form V.

Form of Passage Broker's Licence.

A.B.[b] of in the having shown to the satisfaction of the council of [*or* (me) *or* (us) the undersigned], that he hath given bond to the Crown, as required by the Merchant Shipping Act, 1894, and also given fourteen days' previous notice to the Board of Trade of his intention to apply for a licence to carry on the business of a passage broker in respect of steerage passages from the British Islands to any port out of Europe, and not within the Mediterranean Sea, the said council [*or* I (*or* we), the undersigned], having had no sufficient cause shown and seeing no valid reason why the said *A.B.* should not receive such licence, do hereby license and authorise the said *A.B.* to carry on

[b] The names and surnames in full, with the address and trade or occupation of the party applying for the Licence, must be correctly inserted. If a member of a firm, the names and surnames of

all the members must be given.

the business of a passage broker as aforesaid until the end of the present year, and thirty-one days afterwards, unless this licence shall be sooner determined by forfeiture for misconduct on the part of the said *A.B.* as provided in the Merchant Shipping Act, 1894.

Given under the common seal of the said council [*or* my hand and seal (*or* our respective hands and seals)], this day of 18 at

(L.S.) [Signature authenticating seal]-

[*or* Signature] ______________ (L.S.) { Sheriff, *or* sheriff substitute, *or* justices of the peace *as the case may be.*

NOTE.—Each member of a firm or partnership who acts as a passage broker must have a separate licence.

FORM VI.

Form of Notice to be given to the Board of Trade by Licensing Authority granting a Licence.

Gentlemen,

This is to give you notice, that the council of [*or* we (*or* I), the undersigned], did on the day of 18 license *A.B.* of * to carry on the business of a passage broker under the provisions of the Merchant Shipping Act, 1894.

* Insert the names and surnames in full, with the address and occupation of the party.

Signatures____________________
____________________ { Clerk of the said Council *or* sheriff *or* justices of the peace, *or as the case may be.*

Place______________

Date____________________

To the Board of Trade, London

FORM VII.

Form of Notice to be given to the Board of Trade by an Applicant for a Passage Broker's Licence.

Gentlemen,

I *A.B.*[a] of in do hereby give you notice that it is my intention to apply, after the expiration of fourteen clear days from the date of putting this notice into the post to the council for the city *or* borough *or* district of *or if in Scotland* to the sheriff *or* sheriff substitute of *or if in Ireland* to the justices assembled in petty sessions to be held[b], *as the case may be*, for a licence to carry on the business of a passage broker under the Merchant Shipping Act, 1894.

Signature____________________

Date____________________

To the Board of Trade, London.

[a] The names and surnames in full, with the address and trade or occupation of the party applying for a licence, must be here correctly inserted.

[b] The place or district in which the party giving the notice has his place of business.

FORM VIII.

Form of Notice of forfeiture of a Passage Broker's Licence to be given by the Court by which it is forfeited to the Board of Trade.

Gentlemen,

This is to give you notice, that the licence granted on the day of 18 to *A.B.*[a] of in to act as a passage broker, was on the day of now last past duly declared by me (*or* us) the undersigned to be forfeited.[c]

Signatures____________________

____

Place and date________________18

To the Board of Trade, London.

[c] Here state generally the reason of forfeiture.

FORM IX.

Form of Appointment of Passage Broker's Agent.

Insert in the proper places the names and surnames in full, with the correct addresses and designations of the constituent and agent respectively.

I, *A. B.* of, *etc.* (*or as the case may be*) one of the partners and on behalf of the firm of, *etc.*, (*name all the partners and the style of the firm*) carrying on the business of at , do hereby nominate and appoint you *C. D.* of, *etc.*, to act as my agent and on my behalf in the sale or letting of steerage passages and otherwise in the business of a passage broker, according to the Merchant Shipping Act, 1894.

Signature in full. __________

Place and date __________

Countersignature __________ { Emigration officer at the port of __________

FORM X.

Form of Emigrant Runner's Annual Licence.

[a] The names and surnames in full, with the address of the party applying for the licence, must be here correctly inserted.

[b] District, town, or place in which the emigrant runner is to carry on his business.

A. B.[a] of in the having made application in writing to the council of [*or* me, the sheriff, *or* us, the undersigned justices of the peace assembled in petty sessions, for the of] to grant to him a licence to enable him to be registered as an emigrant runner in and for[b] , and the said [*A.B.*] having also been recommended as a proper person to receive such licence by an emigration officer, *or* by the chief constable [*or other head officer of police, as the case may be*] of [*the district, town, or place in which the said A B. is to carry on his business*] : the said council [*or* I, the sheriff, *or* we, the undermentioned justices] having no sufficient cause shown and seeing no valid reason why the said *A.B.* should not receive such licence, do hereby grant to him this licence for the purposes aforesaid, subject nevertheless to be revoked for misconduct on the part of the said *A.B.* as provided in the Merchant Shipping Act, 1894.

(Signatures, and authenticating seal.)

Section 375.

FIFTEENTH SCHEDULE.

Number and Dimensions of Boats for Fishing Boats entered in the Fishing Boat Register.

Registered Tonnage.		Column 1. — To be carried by Sailing Boats and Steam Boats.								Column 2. — To be carried by Sailing Boats and by Steam Boats when they do not carry the Boats in Column 3.				Column 3. — To be carried by Steam Boats which do not carry the Boats in Column 2.				Column 4. — Total Number of Boats.	
Sailing Boats.	Steam Boats.	Boats.				Boats.				Launches.				Boats.				Sailing Boats.	Steam Boats.
		Number.	Length.	Breadth.	Depth.	Number.	Length.	Breadth.	Depth.	Number.	Length.	Breadth.	Depth.	Number.	Length.	Breadth.	Depth.		
Tons.	Tons.		Ft.	Ft. In.	Ft. In.		Ft.	Ft. In.	Ft. In.		Ft.	Ft. In.	Ft. In.		Ft.	Ft. In.	Ft. In.		
400 and upwards.	240 and upwards.	1	16	5 6	2 3	1	22	5 6	2 5	1	22	6 6	3 3	2	22	5 6	2 6	3	3 or 4 (as the case may be.)
200 to 400	120 to 240.	1	14	5 0	2 2	...	...	...	...	1	20	6 0	3 0	2	22	5 6	2 6	2	2 or 3 (as the case may be.)
100 to 200	60 to 120.	1	14	5 0	2 2	...	...	...	...	1	16	5 6	2 9	2	18	5 6	2 4	2	2 or 3 (as the case may be.)
Under 100	Under 60.	1	14	5 0	2 2	...	...	...	...	...	...	...	...	...	...	...	...	1	1

Note.—In sailing boats carrying the number of boats above specified, and steam boats carrying the larger of the two numbers above specified, the boats are to be considered sufficient, if their aggregate cubic contents are equal to the aggregate cubic contents of the boats specified.

In steam boats carrying the smaller of the two numbers, specified in column 4, one of the boats must be a launch of the capacity specified in column 2.

In sailing boats of 200 tons burden and under, not carrying passengers, a dingy may be substituted for the boat in column 1.

In sailing boats of 150 tons burden and under, not carrying passengers, a substantial boat of capacity sufficient to carry the crew may be substituted for those above specified.

In all steam boats, two paddlebox boats may be substituted for the boats in column 3.

SIXTEENTH SCHEDULE.

Maximum Fees for Inspection of Lights and Fog Signals.

Section 420.		£	s.	d.
	For each visit made to a ship on the application of the owner and for each visit made where the lights or fittings are found defective		0	10

Provided that the aggregate amount of fees for any such inspection shall not exceed one pound, whatever may be the number of separate visits.

SEVENTEENTH SCHEDULE.

Life Saving Appliances.

Constitution of the Committee.

Section 429. (1) Three shipowners selected by the Council of the Chamber of Shipping of the United Kingdom.

(2) One shipowner selected by the Shipowners Association of Glasgow and one shipowner selected by the Liverpool Steamship Owners Association and the Liverpool Shipowners Association conjointly.

(3) Two shipbuilders selected by the Council of the Institution of Naval Architects.

(4) Three persons practically acquainted with the navigation of vessels selected by the shipmasters societies recognised by the Board of Trade for this purpose.

(5) Three persons being or having been able-bodied seamen selected by seamen's societies recognised by the Board of Trade for this purpose.

(6) Two persons selected conjointly by the Committee of Lloyd's, the Committee of Lloyd's Register Society, and the Committee of the Institute of London Underwriters.

EIGHTEENTH SCHEDULE.

Precautions as to Grain Cargo.

Section 453. (1) There shall not be carried between the decks, or if the ship has more than two decks, between the main and upper decks, any grain in bulk, except such as may be necessary for feeding the cargo in the hold, and is carried in properly constructed feeders.

(2) Where grain (except such as may be carried in properly constructed feeders) is carried in bulk in any hold or compartment, and proper provision for filling up the same by feeders is not made, not less than one-fourth of the grain carried in the hold or compartment (as the case may be) shall be in

bags supported on suitable platforms laid upon the grain in bulk: Provided that this regulation with respect to bags shall not apply—

(*a*) To oats, or cotton seed; nor

(*b*) To a ship which is a sailing ship of less than four hundred tons registered tonnage, and is not engaged in the Atlantic trade; nor

(*c*) To a ship laden at a port in the Mediterranean or Black Sea, if the ship is divided into compartments which are formed by substantial transverse partitions, and are fitted with longitudinal bulkheads or such shifting boards as herein-after mentioned, and if the ship does not carry more than one-fourth of the grain cargo, and not more than one thousand five hundred quarters in any one compartment, bin, or division, and provided that each division of the lower hold is fitted with properly constructed feeders from the between decks; nor

(*d*) To a ship in which the grain cargo does not exceed one-half of the whole cargo of the ship, and the rest of the cargo consists of cotton, wool, flax, barrels, or sacks of flour, or other suitable cargo so stowed as to prevent the grain in any compartment, bin, or division from shifting.

(3) Where grain is carried in the hold or between the decks, whether in bags or bulk, the hold or the space between the decks shall be divided by a longitudinal bulkhead or by sufficient shifting boards which extend from deck to deck or from the deck to the keelson and are properly secured, and if the grain is in bulk are fitted grain-tight with proper fillings between the beams.

(4) In loading the grain shall be properly stowed, trimmed, and secured.

NINETEENTH SCHEDULE.

Part I.

Statements in the Case of Salvage by Her Majesty's Ships.

(1) Particulars to be stated both by the salvor and by the master or other person in charge of the vessel, cargo, or property saved:— Section 568.

(*a*) the place, condition, and circumstances in which the vessel, cargo, or property was at the time when the services were rendered for which salvage is claimed:

(*b*) the nature and duration of the services rendered.

(2) Additional particulars to be stated by the salvor:—

(*a*) the proportion of the value of the vessel, cargo, and property, and of the freight which he claims for salvage, or the values at which he estimates the vessel, freight, cargo, and property respectively, and the several amounts that he claims for salvage in respect of the same:

(*b*) any other circumstances which he thinks relevant to the said claim.

(3) Additional particulars to be stated by the said master or other person in charge of the said vessel, cargo, or property:—

(*a*) a copy of the certificate of registry of the said vessel, and of the indorsements thereon, stating any change which (to his knowledge or belief) has occurred in the particulars contained in the certificate; and stating also to the best of his knowledge and belief, the state of the title to the vessel for the time being, and of the incumbrances and certificates of mortgage or sale, if any, affecting the same, and the names and places of business of the owners and incumbrancers:

(*b*) the name and place of business or residence of the freighter (if any) of the said vessel, and the freight to be paid for the voyage on which she then is:

(*c*) a general account of the quantity and nature of the cargo at the time the salvage services were rendered:

(*d*) the name and place of business or residence of the owner of the cargo and of the consignee thereof:

(*e*) the values at which the master or person making the statement estimates the vessel, cargo, and property, and the freight respectively, or, if he thinks fit, in lieu of the estimated value of the cargo, a copy of the vessel's manifest:

(*f*) the amounts which the master thinks should be paid as salvage for the services rendered:

(*g*) an accurate list of the property saved in cases where the vessel is not saved:

(*h*) an account of the proceeds of the sale of the vessel, cargo, or property, in cases where the same or any of them are sold at the port where the statement is made:

(*i*) the number, capacities, and condition of the crew of the vessel at the time when the services were rendered; and

(*k*) any other circumstances he thinks relevant to the matters in question.

PART II.

Salvage Bond.

[*N.B.—Any of the Particulars not known, or not required, by reason of the Claim being only against the Cargo, etc., may be omitted.*]

Whereas certain salvage services are alleged to have been rendered by the vessel [*insert names of vessel and of commander*], commander, to the merchant vessel [*insert names of vessel and master*], master, belonging to [*name and place of business or residence of owner of vessel*], freighted by [*the name of the freighter*] and to the cargo therein, consisting of [*state very shortly the descriptions and quantities of the goods, and the names and addresses of their owners and consignees*]:

And whereas the said vessel and cargo have been brought into the port of [*insert name and situation of port*], and a statement of the salvage claim has been sent to [*insert the name of the consular officer or judge of the colonial court of admiralty or vice-admiralty court and of the office he fills*], and he has fixed the amount to be inserted in this bond at the sum of [*state the sum*].

Now I, the said [*master's name*], do hereby, in pursuance of the Merchant Shipping Act, 1894, bind the several owners for the time being of the said vessel and of the cargo therein and of the freight payable in respect of that cargo and their respective heirs, executors, and administrators, to pay among them such sum not exceeding the said sum of [*state the sum fixed*], in such proportions and to such persons as [*if the parties agree on any other court, substitute the name of it here*], the High Court in England shall adjudge to be payable as salvage for the services so alleged to have been rendered as aforesaid.

In witness whereof I have hereunto set my hand and seal, this [*insert the date*] day of

Signed, sealed, and delivered by the said [*master's name.*]

(L. S.)

In the presence of [*name of consular officer or judge of the colonial court of admiralty or vice-admiralty court, and of the office he fills.*]

TWENTIETH SCHEDULE.

MAXIMUM FEES AND REMUNERATION OF RECEIVERS.

Section 567.

	£	s.	d.
For every examination on oath instituted by a receiver with respect to any vessel which may be or may have been in distress, a fee not exceeding	1	0	0

	£ s. d.
But so that in no case shall a larger fee than two pounds be charged for examinations taken in respect of the same vessel and the same occurrence, whatever may be the number of the deponents.	
For every report required to be sent by the receiver to the secretary of Lloyd's in London, the sum of	0 10 0
For wreck taken by the receiver into his custody, a percentage of five per cent. upon the value thereof.	
But so that in no case shall the whole amount of percentage so payable exceed twenty pounds.	
In cases where any services are rendered by a receiver, in respect of any vessel in distress, not being wreck, or in respect of the cargo or other articles belonging thereto, the following fees instead of a percentage; that to is say,	
If that vessel with her cargo equals or exceeds in value six hundred pounds, the sum of two pounds for the first, and the sum of one pound for every subsequent day, during which the receiver is employed on that service, but if that vessel with her cargo is less in value than six hundred pounds, one moiety of the above-mentioned sum.	

TWENTY-FIRST SCHEDULE.

(*Omitted as being inapplicable to India.*)

TWENTY-SECOND SCHEDULE.

Section 745.

REPEAL.

Session and Chapter.	Short Title.	Extent of Repeal.
17 Edw. 2. Stat. 2. c. 11. (Prerog. Reg. Stat. temp. incert. c. 13 in Rev. Edition.)	Prerogative Regis . . .	The words "wreck of the sea."
4 Geo. 4, c. 80 . .	An Act to consolidate and amend the several laws now in force with respect to trade within the limits of the charter of the East India Company, and to make further provision with respect to such trade.	Section twenty-seven, section twenty-eight, from "and for every omission" to "herein is required" and the word "omission" after "non-observance," and section thirty-four.

(Twenty-second Schedule.)

REPEAL—*contd.*

Session and Chapter.	Short Title.	Extent of Repeal.
15 & 16 Vict., c. 26 .	The Foreign Deserters Act, 1852 .	The whole Act.
16 & 17 Vict., c. 84 .	An Act to amend the Passengers Act, 1852, so far as relates to the passages of natives of Asia or Africa, and also passages between the Island of Ceylon and certain parts of the East Indies.	The whole Act.
17 & 18 Vict., c. 104 .	The Merchant Shipping Act, 1854.	The whole Act.
17 & 18 Vict., c. 120 .	The Merchant Shipping Repeal Act, 1854.	Section sixteen.
18 & 19 Vict., c. 91 .	The Merchant Shipping Act (Amendment) Act, 1855.	The whole Act.
18 & 19 Vict., c. 119 .	The Passengers Act, 1855 . . .	The whole Act.
19 & 20 Vict., c. 41 .	The Seamen's Savings Bank Act, 1856.	The whole Act.
24 & 25 Vict., c. 10 .	The Admiralty Court Act, 1861 .	Sections nine, twelve, and twenty-four.
24 & 25 Vict., c. 52 .	The Australian Passengers Act, 1861.	The whole Act.
25 & 26 Vict., c. 63 .	The Merchant Shipping Amendment Act, 1862.	The whole Act.
26 & 27 Vict., c. 51 .	The Passengers Act Amendment Act, 1863.	The whole Act.
30 & 31 Vict., c. 114 .	The Court of Admiralty (Ireland) Act, 1867.	Sections thirty-five and forty-five.
30 & 31 Vict., c. 124 .	The Merchant Shipping Act, 1867	The whole Act, except section one as far as "Act, 1867," and section twelve.
31 & 32 Vict., c. 45 .	The Sea Fisheries Act, 1868 . .	Sections twenty-two to twenty-four.
31 & 32 Vict., c. 129 .	The Colonial Shipping Act, 1868 .	The whole Act.
32 & 33 Vict., c. 11 .	The Merchant Shipping (Colonial) Act, 1869.	The whole Act.
33 & 34 Vict., c. 95 .	The Passengers Act (Amendment) Act, 1870.	The whole Act.
34 & 35 Vict., c. 110 .	The Merchant Shipping Act, 1871	The whole Act.

(*Twenty-second Schedule.*)

REPEAL—*contd.*

Session and Chapter.	Short Title.	Extent of Repeal.
35 & 36 Vict., c. 73 .	The Merchant Shipping Act, 1872.	The whole Act, except sections one, ten, and seventeen.
36 & 37 Vict., c. 85 .	The Merchant Shipping Act, 1873.	The whole Act.
37 & 38 Vict., c. 88 .	The Births and Deaths Registration Act, 1874.	Section thirty-seven, except sub-section (6), and except so far as the section relates to Her Majesty's ships.
38 & 39 Vict., c. 17 .	The Explosives Act, 1875 . .	Section forty-two.
39 & 40 Vict., c. 27 .	The Local Light Dues Reduction Act, 1876.	The whole Act.
39 & 40 Vict., c. 80 .	The Merchant Shipping Act, 1876.	The whole Act.
40 & 41 Vict., c. 16 .	The Removal of Wreck Act, 1877 .	The whole Act.
42 & 43 Vict., c. 72 .	The Shipping Casualties Investigation Act, 1879.	The whole Act.
43 & 44 Vict., c. 16 .	The Merchant Seamen Payment of Wages and Rating Act, 1880.	The whole Act, except the first paragraph of section one and section eleven.
43 & 44 Vict., c. 18 .	The Merchant Shipping Act (1854) Amendment Act, 1880.	The whole Act.
43 & 44 Vict., c. 22 .	The Merchant Shipping (Fees and Expenses) Act, 1880.	Sections two, five, six and seven.
43 & 44 Vict., c. 43 .	The Merchant Shipping (Carriage of Grain) Act, 1880.	The whole Act.
45 & 46 Vict., c. 55 .	The Merchant Shipping (Expenses) Act, 1882.	The whole Act, except the first paragraph of section one and section eight.
45 & 46 Vict., c. 76 .	The Merchant Shipping (Colonial Inquiries) Act, 1882.	The whole Act.
46 & 47 Vict., c. 22 .	The Sea Fisheries Act, 1883 .	Section eight.
46 & 47 Vict., c. 41 .	The Merchant Shipping (Fishing Boats) Act, 1883.	The whole Act.
49 & 50 Vict., c. 38 .	The Riot (Damages) Act, 1886 .	In section six, Paragraph (*a*), and the words "plundering, damage," before "injury"; and from "and as if" to the end of the section.

REPEAL—*concld.*

Session and Chapter.	Short Title.	Extent of Repeal.
50 & 51 Vict., c. 4 .	The Merchant Shipping (Fishing Boats) Act, 1887.	The whole Act.
50 & 51 Vict., c. 62 .	The Merchant Shipping (Miscellaneous) Act, 1887.	The whole Act.
51 & 52 Vict., c. 24 .	The Merchant Shipping (Life Saving Appliances) Act, 1888.	The whole Act
52 & 53 Vict., c. 5 .	The Removal of Wrecks Act, 1877, Amendment Act, 1889.	The whole Act.
52 & 53 Vict., c. 29 .	The Passenger Acts Amendment Act, 1889.	The whole Act.
52 & 53 Vict., c. 43 .	The Merchant Shipping (Tonnage) Act, 1889.	The whole Act.
52 & 53 Vict., c. 46 .	The Merchant Shipping Act, 1889.	The whole Act.
52 & 53 Vict., c. 68 .	The Merchant Shipping (Pilotage) Act, 1889.	The whole Act.
52 & 53 Vict., c. 73 .	The Merchant Shipping (Colours) Act, 1889.	The whole Act.
53 & 54 Vict., c. 9 .	The Merchant Shipping Act, 1890.	The whole Act.
55 & 56 Vict., c. 37 .	The Merchant Shipping Act, 1892.	The whole Act.

THE NATURALIZATION ACT, 1895.

(58 & 59 Vict., c. 43.)

An Act to amend the Naturalization Act, 1870, so far as respects Children of Naturalized British Subjects in the service of the Crown resident out of the United Kingdom.

[*6th July, 1895.*]

* * * * * * *

Amendment of 33 & 34 Vict., c. 14, s. 10, as respects children of naturalized British subjects resident abroad.

1. (1) The residence of a child of a naturalized British subject with his father while in the service of the Crown out of the United Kingdom, shall have, and be deemed always to have had, the same effect, for the purpose of sub-section five of section ten of the Naturalization Act, 1870, as residence with such father in the United Kingdom.

(2) Sub-section five of section ten of the Naturalization Act, 1870, shall have effect as if the words "or with such father while in the service of the

Crown out of the United Kingdom" had been inserted therein after the words "part of the United Kingdom," and every copy of the Naturalization Act, 1870, hereafter printed may be printed accordingly.

Short title. 2. This Act may be cited as the Naturalization Act, 1895.

The Judicial Committee Amendment Act, 1895.

(58 & 59 Vict., c. 44.)

An Act to amend the Law relating to the Judicial Committee of Her Majesty's Privy Council.

[*6th July, 1895.*]

* * * * * * *

Provision as to persons being or having been Colonial Chief Justices or Judges. 1. (1) If any person being or having been Chief Justice or a Judge of the Supreme Court of the Dominion of Canada, or of a Superior Court in any province of Canada, of any of the Australasian colonies mentioned in the schedule to this Act, or of either of the South African colonies mentioned in the said schedule, or of any other Superior Court in Her Majesty's Dominions named in that behalf by Her Majesty in Council, is a member of Her Majesty's Privy Council, he shall be a member of the Judicial Committee of the Privy Council.

(2) The number of persons being members of the Judicial Committee by reason of this Act shall not exceed five at any one time.

(3) The provisions of this Act shall be in addition to, and shall not affect, any other enactment for the appointment of or relating to members of the Judicial Committee.

Short title. 2. This Act may be cited as the Judicial Committee Amendment Act, 1895.

SCHEDULE.

Australasian Colonies.

New South Wales.
New Zealand.
Queensland.
South Australia.
Tasmania.
Victoria.
Western Australia.

South African Colonies.

Cape of Good Hope.
Natal.

The Derelict Vessels (Report) Act, 1896.

(59 & 60 Vict., c. 12.)

An Act for the better reporting of Floating Derelicts.

[*2nd July, 1896.*]

* * * * * * *

1. This Act may be cited as the Derelict Vessels (Report) Act, 1896. Short title.

2. Every master or other person for the time being in command of any British ship, after the passing of this Act, who shall become aware of the existence on the high seas of any floating derelict vessel, shall notify the same to the Lloyd's agent at his next place of call or arrival, and shall, together with such notification, furnish to the Lloyd's agent all such information as he may possess as to the supposed locality or identity of such derelict vessel, and the date when and place where the same may have been observed by or reported to him, and the Lloyd's agent shall forthwith on receipt of such notification and information transmit the same to the secretary of Lloyd's in London. Notice of derelict vessels to be given by masters to Lloyd's agents.

And if any such master fails to make such a report he shall be liable, on summary conviction, to a penalty not exceeding five pounds.

3. If there shall be no Lloyd's agent at the next place of call or arrival, then and in such case the notification shall be made and the information furnished by such master or other person as aforesaid, to the secretary of Lloyd's, London. Letters to be sent to Lloyd's in default of agents.

4. Any information received by the society of Lloyd's as aforesaid, in pursuance of this Act, shall be published by the society forthwith in the same manner and to the same extent as its reports of shipping casualties, and the society shall also forthwith communicate such information to the Board of Trade. Information to be published by Lloyd's.

The Short Titles Act, 1896.[1]

(59 & 60 Vict., c. 14.)

An Act to facilitate the Citation of Sundry Acts of Parliament.

[*20th July, 1896.*]

* * * * * * *

1. Each of the Acts mentioned in the First Schedule[2] to this Act may without prejudice to any other mode of citation, be cited by the short title therein mentioned in this behalf. Citation of Acts in first Schedule.

[1] See Lely's *Annual Statutes*, 1896, p. 1.

[2] As the short titles conferred by this Act on the Statutes printed in this Collection have been given *in loco*, this Schedule has not been reproduced.

Collective titles.

2. (1) Each of the groups of Acts mentioned in the Second Schedule[1] to this Act may, without prejudice to any other mode of citation, be cited by the collective title therein mentioned in that behalf.

(2) If it is provided that any Act passed after this Act may, as to the whole or any part thereof, be cited with any of the groups of Acts mentioned in the Second Schedule to this Act, or with any groups of Acts to which a collective title has been given by any Act passed before this Act, that group shall be construed as including that Act or part, and, if a collective title of the group states the first and last years of the group, the year in which that Act is passed shall be substituted for the last year of the group, and so on as often as a subsequent Act or part is added to the group.

Effect of repeal of enactments giving short titles.

3. Notwithstanding the repeal of an enactment giving a short title to an Act, the Act may, without prejudice to any other mode of citation, continue to be cited by that short title.

Repeal of 55 & 56 Vict., c. 10.

4. The Short Titles Act, 1892, is hereby repealed.

Short title.

5. This Act may be cited as the Short Titles Act, 1896.

(*Schedules omitted—see footnotes to sections 1 and 2 above.*)

THE EAST INDIA LOAN ACT, 1898.

(61 & 62 Vict., c. 13.)

An Act to enable the Secretary of State in Council of India to raise Money in the United Kingdom for the Service of the Government of India.

[*1st July, 1898.*]

* * * * * * *

Short title.

1. This Act may be cited as the East India Loan Act, 1898.

Definition.

2. In this Act the expression "Secretary of State" means the Secretary of State in Council of India, unless the context otherwise requires.

Power to Secretary of State to raise sum not exceeding 10,000,000*l*.

3. It shall be lawful for the Secretary of State, at any time or times, to raise in the United Kingdom, for the service of the Government of India, any sum or sums of money not exceeding in the whole ten millions of pounds sterling, such sum or sums to be raised by the creation and issue of bonds, debentures, bills, or capital stock bearing interest, or partly by one of such modes, and partly by another or others.

---

[1] It has been thought needless to reproduce this schedule, the necessary notes having been added to the Statutes concerned.

4. The whole amount of the principal moneys to be charged on the revenues of India under this Act shall not exceed ten millions of pounds sterling. Limit of amount charged on revenues of India.

5. Upon or for the repayment of any principal moneys secured under the authority of this Act, the Secretary of State may at any time borrow or raise, by all or any of the modes aforesaid, all or any part of the amount of principal money repaid or to be repaid, and so from time to time as all or any part of any principal moneys under this Act may require to be repaid, but the amount so to be charged on the revenues of India shall not in any case exceed the principal moneys required to be repaid. Power to raise money for payment of principal money.

6. All bonds, debentures, and bills issued, under this Act, and the principal moneys and interest thereby secured, and all capital stock issued under this Act, and the interest thereon, shall be charged on and payable out of the revenues of India, in like manner as other liabilities incurred on account of the Government of India. Securities to be charged on revenues of India.

7. This Act shall not prejudice or affect any power of raising or borrowing money vested in the said Secretary of State at the time of passing thereof. Saving.

8. The provisions of the East India Loan Act, 1893, as to the issue, signature, verification, terms, and conditions of bonds, debentures, and bills, and the payment of principal and interest on debentures, and the creation, registration, and transfer, of capital stock, and the composition for stamp duties, and as to criminal offences, and as to the application of the India Stock Certificate Act, 1863, shall apply in the case of bonds, debentures, and bills issued, and capital stock created, under this Act, as the case may be. Provisions of 56 & 57 Vict., c. 70, 1893, to apply.

The Army (Annual) Act, 1899.

(62 & 63 Vict., c. 3.)

An Act to provide, during Twelve Months, for the Discipline and Regulation of the Army.

[*27th April, 1899.*]

Whereas the raising or keeping of a standing army within the United Kingdom of Great Britain and Ireland in time of peace, unless it be with the consent of Parliament, is against law:

And whereas it is adjudged necessary by Her Majesty and this present Parliament, that a body of forces should be continued for the safety of the United Kingdom and the defence of the possessions of Her Majesty's Crown, and that the whole number of such forces should consist of one hundred and eighty-four thousand eight hundred and fifty-three including those to be employed at the depôts in the United Kingdom of Great Britain and Ireland for the training of recruits for service at home and abroad, but exclusive of the numbers actually serving within Her Majesty's Indian possessions:

And whereas it is also judged necessary for the safety of the United Kingdom, and the defence of the possessions of this realm, that a body of Royal Marine forces should be employed in Her Majesty's fleet and naval service, under the direction of the Lord High Admiral of the United Kingdom, or the Commissioners for executing the office of Lord High Admiral aforesaid:

And whereas the said marine forces may frequently be quartered or be on shore, or sent to do duty or be on board transport ships or vessels, merchant ships or vessels, or other ships or vessels, or they may be under other circumstances in which they will not be subject to the laws relating to the government of Her Majesty's forces by sea:

And whereas no man can be forejudged of life or limb, or subjected in time of peace to any kind of punishment within this realm by martial law, or in any other manner than by the judgment of his peers and according to the known and established laws of this realm; yet nevertheless it being requisite, for the retaining all the before-mentioned forces, and other persons subject to military law, in their duty, that an exact discipline be observed, and that persons belonging to the said forces who mutiny or stir up sedition, or desert Her Majesty's service, or are guilty of crimes and offences to the prejudice of good order and military discipline, be brought to a more exemplary and speedy punishment than the usual forms of the law will allow:

And whereas the Army Act will expire in the year one thousand eight hundred and ninety-nine on the following days: 44 & 45 Vict. c. 58.

(*a*) In the United Kingdom, the Channel Islands, and the Isle of Man, on the thirtieth day of April, and

(*b*) Elsewhere in Europe, inclusive of Malta, also in the West Indies and America, on the thirty-first day of July; and

(*c*) Elsewhere whether within or without Her Majesty's dominions, on the thirty-first day of December :

* * * * * * *

Short title, Army Act (44 & 45

1. This Act may be cited as the Army (Annual) Act, 1899.

2. (1) The Army Act shall be and remain in force during the periods

hereinafter mentioned, and no longer, unless otherwise provided by Parliament; that is to say, Vict., c. 58) to be in force for specified times.

(a) Within the United Kingdom, the Channel Islands and the Isle of Man, from the thirtieth day of April one thousand eight hundred and ninety-nine to the thirtieth day of April one thousand nine hundred, both inclusive; and

(b) Elsewhere in Europe, inclusive of Malta, also in the West Indies and America, from the thirty-first day of July one thousand eight hundred and ninety-nine to the thirty-first day of July one thousand nine hundred, both inclusive; and

(c) Elsewhere, whether within or without Her Majesty's dominions, from the thirty-first day of December one thousand eight hundred and ninety-nine to the thirty-first day of December one thousand nine hundred, both inclusive;

and the day from which the Army Act is continued in any place by this Act is in relation to that place referred to in this Act as the commencement of this Act.

(2) The Army Act, while in force, shall apply to persons subject to military law, whether within or without Her Majesty's dominions.

(3) A person subject to military law shall not be exempted from the provisions of the Army Act by reason only that the number of the forces for the time being in the service of Her Majesty, exclusive of the marine forces, is either greater or less than the number hereinbefore mentioned.

3. There shall be paid to the keeper of a victualling house for the accommodation provided by him in pursuance of the Army Act the prices specified in the schedule to this Act. Prices in respect of billeting

Amendment of Army Act.

4. (1) In section ninety-one and in sub-section (3) of section one hundred and thirty-eight, and in sub-section (2) of section one hundred and forty-five, of the Army Act, after the words "a Secretary of State" in each place where they occur shall be inserted the words "or any officer deputed by him for the purpose," and after the words "the Secretary of State" in each place where they occur shall be inserted the words "or officer." Amendment of 44 & 45 Vict., c. 58, ss. 91, 138, 145.

(2) In sub-section (2) of section ninety one of the Army Act, the words "or under the hand of an under secretary," and in proviso (a) of section one hundred and thirty-eight the words by a "court martial," commanding officer, or Secretary of State," are hereby repealed.

5. After the words "of the forces in India" where they occur in sub-section (2) of section fifty-seven, sub-section (3) of section seventy-three, and sub- Amendment of 44 & 45 Vict., c. 58,

ss. 57, 73, 183, as amended by 56 & 57 Vict., c. 62, as to powers of Commander-in-Chief in India.

section (2) and proviso (5) of section one hundred and eighty-three, of the Army Act, shall be inserted the words "or such officer as the Commander-in-Chief of the forces in India, with the approval of the Governor-General of India in Council, may appoint."

Amendment of 44 & 45 Vict., c. 58, ss. 83, 190, as amended by 58 Vict., c. 7, as to certain corps.

6. (1) In sub-section (6) of section eighty-three of the Army Act, the words "or in the corps of armourer sergeants, or in the medical staff corps, or in the army service corps" and the words "or in the corps of mounted military police" shall be repealed.

(2) In section one hundred and ninety of the Army Act, sub-section (15) (A) (iii), the words "the Army Service Corps, the Medical Staff Corps, and" and the word "other" shall be repealed.

SCHEDULE.

Accommodation to be provided.	Maximum Price.
Lodging and attendance for soldier where hot meal furnished.	Four pence per night.
Hot meal as specified in Part I of the Second Schedule to the Army Act.	One shilling and three pence halfpenny each.
Breakfast as so specified	One penny halfpenny each.
Where no hot meal furnished, lodging and attendance; and candles, vinegar, salt, and the use of fire, and the necessary utensils for dressing and eating his meat.	Four pence per day.
Ten pounds of oats, twelve pounds of hay, and eight pounds of straw per day for each horse.	One shilling and nine pence per day.
Lodging and attendance for officer	Two shillings per night.

NOTE.—An officer shall pay for his food.

THE RESERVE FORCES ACT, 1899.

(62 & 63 Vict., c. 40.)

An Act to amend the Law relating to the Reserve Forces.

[*9th August, 1899.*]

* * * * * * *

Permission to Army Reserve men

1. Where a soldier of the regular forces, when entitled to be transferred to the reserve, is serving out of the United Kingdom, he may, at his own

request, be transferred to the reserve without being required to return to the United Kingdom, but subject to such conditions, as to residence, as to liability to be called out for annual training or on permanent service or in aid of the civil power, or as to any other matters, as may be prescribed by regulations under section twenty of the Reserve Forces Act, 1882, and thereupon the provisions of that Act, and of the Acts amending that Act, shall apply in the case of the soldiers so transferred with such adaptations as may be made by those regulations.

to reside out of United Kingdom.

5 & 46 Vict., 48

Short title.

2. This Act may be cited as the Reserve Forces Act, 1899.

APPENDIX.

THE COINAGE ACT, 1870.

(33 & 34 Vict., c. 10.)

An Act to consolidate and amend the law relating to the Coinage and Her Majesty's Mint.

[*4th April 1870.*]

[PREAMBLE.]

1. This Act may be cited as "The Coinage Act, 1870." Short title.

2. In this Act— Definitions of terms.

the term "Treasury" means the Lord High Treasurer for the time being, or the Commissioners of Her Majesty's Treasury for the time being, or any two of them;

the term "the Mint" means, except as expressly provided, Her Majesty's Royal Mint in England;

the term "British possession" means any colony, plantation, island, territory, or settlement within Her Majesty's dominions and not within the United Kingdom; and

the term "person" includes a body corporate.

3. All coins made at the Mint of the denominations mentioned in the first schedule to this Act shall be of the weight and fineness specified in that schedule, and the standard trial plates shall be made accordingly. Standard of coins.

If any coin of gold, silver, or bronze, but of any other denomination than that of the coins mentioned in the first schedule to this Act, is hereafter coined at the Mint, such coin shall be of a weight and fineness bearing the same proportion to the weight and fineness specified in that schedule as the denomination of such coin bears to the denominations mentioned in that schedule.

Provided that in the making of coins a remedy (or variation from the standard weight and fineness specified in the said first schedule)[1] shall be allowed of an amount not exceeding the amount specified in that schedule.

4. A tender of payment of money, if made in coins which have been issued by the Mint in accordance with the provisions of this Act, and have not been called in by any proclamation made in pursuance of this Act, and have not become diminished in weight, by wear or otherwise, so as to be of less weight than the current weight, that is to say, than the weight (if any) Legal tender.

[1] For amendment of schedule, *see* 54 & 55 Vict., c. 72, s. 2, *ante*, p. 908.

specified as the least current weight in the first schedule to this Act, or less than such weight as may be declared by any proclamation made in pursuance of this Act, shall be a legal tender,—

in the case of gold coins for a payment of any amount:

in the case of silver coins for a payment of an amount not exceeding forty shillings, but for no greater amount:

in the case of bronze coins for a payment of an amount not exceeding one shilling, but for no greater amount.

Nothing in this Act shall prevent any paper currency which under any Act or otherwise is a legal tender from being a legal tender.

Prohibition of other coins and tokens.

5. No piece of gold, silver, copper, or bronze, or of any metal or mixed metal, of any value whatever, shall be made or issued, except by the Mint, as a coin or a token for money, or as purporting that the holder thereof is entitled to demand any value denoted thereon. Every person who acts in contravention of this section shall be liable on summary conviction to a penalty not exceeding twenty pounds.

Contracts, etc., to be made in currency.

6. Every contract, sale, payment, bill, note, instrument, and security for money, and every transaction, dealing, matter, and thing whatever relating to money, or involving the payment of or the liability to pay any money, which is made, executed, or entered into, done or had, shall be made, executed, entered into, done and had according to the coins which are current and legal tender in pursuance of this Act, and not otherwise, unless the same be made, executed, entered into, done or had according to the currency of some British possession or some foreign state.

Defacing light gold coin.

7. Where any gold coin of the realm is below the current weight as provided by this Act, or where any coin is called in by any proclamation, every person shall, by himself or others, cut, break, or deface any such coin tendered to him in payment, and the person tendering the same shall bear the loss.

If any coin cut, broken, or defaced in pursuance of this section is not below the current weight, or has not been called in by any proclamation, the person cutting, breaking, or defacing the same shall receive the same in payment according to its denomination. Any dispute which may arise under this section may be determined by a summary proceeding.

Coining of bullion taken to the Mint.

8. Where any person brings to the Mint any gold bullion, such bullion shall be assayed and coined, and delivered out to such person, without any charge for such assay or coining, or for waste in coinage:

(*Secs. 9-11.*)

Provided that—

(1) if the fineness of the whole of the bullion so brought to the Mint is such that it cannot be brought to the standard fineness under this Act of the coin to be coined thereout, without refining some portion of it, the master of the Mint may refuse to receive, assay, or coin such bullion:

(2) where the bullion so brought to the Mint is finer than the standard fineness under this Act of the coin to be coined thereout, there shall be delivered to the person bringing the same such additional amount of coin as is proportionate to such superior fineness.

No undue preference shall be shown to any person under this section, and every person shall have priority according to the time at which he brought such bullion to the Mint.

9. The Treasury may from time to time issue to the master of the Mint, out of the growing produce of the Consolidated Fund, such sums as may be necessary to enable him to purchase bullion in order to provide supplies of coin for the public service. Purchase of bullion.

10. All sums received by the master of the Mint, or any deputy master or officer of the Mint, in payment for coin produced from bullion purchased by him, and all fees and payments received by the master or any deputy master or officer of the Mint as such, shall (save as otherwise provided in the case of any branch mint in a British possession by a proclamation respecting such branch mint) be paid into the receipt of the Exchequer, and carried to the Consolidated Fund. Payment of profits, etc., to Exchequer.

11. It shall be lawful for Her Majesty, with the advice of Her Privy Council, from time to time by proclamation to do all or any of the following things; namely, Regulations by proclamation.

(1) to determine the dimension of and design for any coin:

(2) to determine the denominations of coins to be coined at the Mint:

(3) to diminish the amount of remedy allowed by the first schedule to this Act in the case of any coin:

(4) to determine the weight (not being less than the weight (if any) specified in the first schedule to this Act) below which a coin, whether diminished in weight by wear or otherwise, is not to be a current or a legal tender:

(5) to call in coins of any date or denomination, or any coins coined before the date in the proclamation mentioned:

(6) to direct that any coins, other than gold, silver, or bronze, shall be current and be a legal tender for the payment of any amount not exceeding the amount specified in the proclamation, and not exceeding five shillings:

(7) to direct that coins coined in any foreign country shall be current and be a legal tender, at such rates, up to such amounts, and in such portion of Her Majesty's dominions as may be specified in the proclamation; due regard being had in fixing those rates to the weight and fineness of such coins, as compared with the current coins of this realm.

(8) to direct the establishment of any branch of the Mint in any British possession, and impose a charge for the coinage of gold thereat; determine the application of such charge; and determine the extent to which such branch is to be deemed part of the Mint, and to which coins issued therefrom are to be current and be a legal tender, and to be deemed to be issued from the Mint:

(9) to direct that the whole or any part of this Act shall apply to and be in force in any British possession, with or without any modifications contained in the proclamation:

(10) to regulate any matters relative to the coinage and the Mint within the present prerogative of the Crown which are not provided for by this Act:

(11) to revoke or alter any proclamation previously made.

Every such proclamation shall come into operation on the date therein in that behalf mentioned, and shall have effect as if it were enacted in this Act.

Trial of the pyx.

12. For the purpose of ascertaining that coins issued from the Mint have been coined in accordance with this Act, a trial of the pyx shall be held at least once in every year in which coins have been issued from the Mint.

It shall be lawful for Her Majesty, with the advice of Her Privy Council, from time to time, by order, to make regulations respecting the trial of the pyx and all matters incidental thereto, and in particular respecting the following matters; *viz.*,

(1) the time and place of the trial:

(2) the setting apart out of the coins issued by the Mint certain coins for the trial:

(3) the summoning of a jury of not less than six out of competent freemen of the mystery of goldsmiths of the city of London or other competent persons:

(4) the attendance at the trial of the jury so summoned, and of the proper officers of the Treasury, the Board of Trade, and the Mint, and the production of the coins so set apart, and of the standard trial plates and standard weights:

(5) the proceedings at and conduct of the trial, including the nomination of some person to preside thereat, and the swearing of the jury, and the mode of examining the coins:

(6) the recording and the publication of the verdict, and the custody of the record thereof, and the proceedings (if any) to be taken in consequence of such verdict.

Every such order shall come into operation on the date therein in that behalf mentioned, and shall have effect as if it were enacted in this Act, but may be revoked or altered by any subsequent order under this section.

13. The Treasury may from time to time do all or any of the following things: Regulations by Treasury.

(1) fix the number and duties of the officers of and persons employed in the Mint:

(2) make regulations and give directions (subject to the provisions of this Act and any proclamation made thereunder) respecting the general management of the Mint, and revoke and alter such regulations and directions.

Master and Officers of Mint.

14. The Chancellor of the Exchequer for the time being shall be the master, worker, and warden of Her Majesty's Royal Mint in England, and governor of the Mint in Scotland. Master of Mint.

Provided that nothing in this section shall render the Chancellor of the Exchequer incapable of being elected to or of sitting or voting in the House of Commons, or vacate the seat of the person who at the passing of this Act holds the office of Chancellor of the Exchequer.

All duties, powers, and authorities imposed on or vested in or to be transacted before the master of the Mint may be performed and exercised by or transacted before him or his sufficient deputy.

15. The Treasury may from time to time appoint deputy masters and other officers and persons for the purpose of carrying on the business of the Mint Deputy masters, officers.

in the United Kingdom or elsewhere, and assign them their duties, and award them their salaries.

The master of the Mint may from time to time promote, suspend, and remove any such deputy masters, officers, and persons.

Standard Trial Plates and Weights.

Custody, etc., of standard trial plates.

16. The standard trial plates of gold and silver used for determining the justness of the gold and silver coins of the realm issued from the Mint, which now exist or may hereafter be made, and all books, documents, and things used in connexion therewith, or in relation thereto, shall be in the custody of the Board of Trade, and shall be kept in such places and in such manner as the Board of Trade may from time to time direct; and the performance of all duties in relation to such trial plates shall be part of the business of the Standard Weights and Measures Department of the Board of Trade.

The Board of Trade shall from time to time, when necessary, cause new standard trial plates to be made and duly verified, of such standard fineness as may be in conformity with the provisions of this Act.

Standard weights for coins.

17. * * * * * * *[1]

The master of the Mint shall from time to time cause copies to be made of such standard weights, and once at least in every year the Board of Trade and the master of the Mint shall cause such copies to be compared and duly verified with the standard weights in the custody of the Board of Trade.

* * * * * * *[1]

Legal Proceedings.

Summary procedure.

18. Any summary proceeding under this Act may be taken, and any penalty under this Act may be recovered,—

in England, before two justices of the peace in manner directed by the Act of the session of the eleventh and twelfth years of the reign of Her present Majesty, chapter forty-three, intituled "An Act to facilitate the performance of the duties of justices of the peace out of sessions within England and Wales with respect to summary convictions and orders," and any Act amending the same;

in Scotland, in manner directed by The Summary Procedure Act, 1864;

in Ireland, so far as respects Dublin, in manner directed by the Acts regulating the powers of justices of the peace or the police of Dublin metropolis, and elsewhere in manner directed by The Petty Sessions (Ireland) Act, 1851, and any Act amending the same.

---

[1] Words repealed by 41 & 42 Vict., c. 49, s. 86, are omitted.

In any British possession, in the courts, and before such justices or magistrates, and in the manner in which the like proceedings and penalties may be taken and recovered by the law of such possession, or as near thereto as circumstances admit, or in such other courts, or before such other justices or magistrates, or in such other manner as any Act or Ordinance having the force of law in such possession may from time to time provide.

Miscellaneous.

19. This Act, save as expressly provided by this Act, or by any proclamation made thereunder, shall not extend to any British possession. **Extent of Act.**

20. The Acts mentioned in the first part of the second schedule to this Act are hereby repealed to the extent in the third column of such schedule mentioned, and those mentioned in the second part of the same schedule are hereby repealed entirely. **Repeal of Acts and parts of Acts in second schedule.**

Provided that,—

(1) this repeal shall not affect anything already done or suffered, or any right already acquired or accrued:

(2) all weights for weighing coin which have before the passing of this Act been marked at the Mint or by any proper officer shall be deemed to have been marked under this Act:

(3) every branch of the Mint which at the passing of this Act issues coins in any British possession shall, until the date fixed by any proclamation made in pursuance of this Act with respect to such branch Mint, continue in all respects to have the same power of issuing coins and be in the same position as if this Act had not passed, and coins so issued shall be deemed for the purpose of this Act to have been issued from the Mint:

(4) the said Acts (unless relating to a branch Mint and unless in the said schedule expressly otherwise mentioned) are not repealed so far as they apply to any British possession to which this Act does not extend until a proclamation directing that this Act or any part thereof, with or without any modification contained in the proclamation, shall be in force in such British possession, comes into operation.

SCHEDULES.

FIRST SCHEDULE.[1]

Denomination of coin.	Standard Weight.		Least Current Weight.		Standard Fineness.	Remedy Allowance.		
						Weight per Piece.		
	Imperial Weight.	Metric Weight.	Imperial Weight.	Metric Weight.		Imperial.	Metric.	Millesimal [illegible]
	Grains.	Grams.	Grains.	Grams.		Grains.	Grams.	
Gold:								
Five Pound	616·37239	39·94028	612·50000	39·69935	Eleven-twelfths fine gold, one-twelfth alloy; or millesimal fineness 916·6	1·00000	0·06479	[illegible]
Two Pound	246·54895	15·97611	245·00000	15·87574		0·40000	0·02592	
Sovereign	123·27447	7·98805	122·50000	7·93787		0·20000	0·01296	
Half Sovereign	61·63723	3·99402	61·12500	3·96083		0·10000	0·00648	
Silver:								
Crown	436·36363	28·27590	...	...	Thirty-seven-fortieths fine silver, three-fortieths alloy; or millesimal fineness 925.	1·81818	0·11781	[illegible]
Half Crown	218·18181	14·13795	...	...		0·90909	0·05890	
Florin	174·54545	11·31036	...	...		0·72727	0·04712	
Shilling	87·27272	5·65518	...	...		0·36363	0·02356	
Sixpence	43·63636	2·82759	...	...		0·18181	0·01178	
Groat or Fourpence	29·09090	1·88506	...	...		0·12121	0·00785	
Threepence	21·81818	1·41379	...	...		0·09090	0·00589	
Twopence	14·54545	0·94253	...	...		0·06060	0·00392	
Penny	7·27272	0·47126	...	...		0·03030	0·00196	
Bronze:								
Penny	145·83333	9·44984	...	...	Mixed metal, copper tin, and zinc.	2·91666	0·18899	None.
Halfpenny	87·50000	5·66990	...	...		1·75000	0·11339	
Farthing	43·75000	2·83495	...	...		0·87500	0·05666	

The weight and fineness of the coins specified in this Schedule are according to what is provided by the Act fifty-six George the Third, chapter sixty-eight, that the gold coin of the United Kingdom of Great Britain and Ireland should hold such weight and fineness as were prescribed in the then existing Mint indenture (that is to say), that there should be nine hundred and thirty-four sovereigns and one ten shilling piece contained in twenty pounds weight troy of standard gold, of the fineness at the trial of the same of twenty-two carats fine gold and two carats of alloy in the pound weight troy; and further, as regards silver coin, that there should be sixty-six shillings in every pound troy of standard silver of the fineness of eleven ounces two pennyweights of fine silver and eighteen pennyweights of alloy in every pound weight troy.

[1] For amendment of schedule, *see* 54 & 55 Vict., c. 72, s. 2, *ante*, p. 906.

SCHEDULES—*contd.*

SECOND SCHEDULE.

FIRST PART.

Acts partly repealed.

Year and Chapter.	Title.	Extent of Repeal.
2 Hen. 6. c. 17.* .	For regulating and ascertaining the fineness of silver work.	So much as relates to the master of the Mint.
29 & 30 Vict. c. 82 .	An Act to amend the Acts relating to the standard weights and measures, and to the standard trial pieces of the coin of the realm.	Section thirteen.

* c. 14. in Ruffhead.

SECOND PART.

Acts wholly repealed.

Year and Chapter.	Title.
18 & 19 Cha. 2. c. 5.* .	An Act for encouraging of coinage.
6 Anne, c. 57.†‡ . .	An Act for ascertaining the rates of foreign coins in Her Majesty's plantations in America.
‡13 Geo. 3. c. 57. . .	An Act to explain and amend an Act made in the fourth year of His present Majesty, intituled "An Act to prevent paper bills of credit "hereafter to be issued in any of His Majesty's "colonies or plantations in America from being "declared to be a legal tender in payments of "money, and to prevent the legal tender of such "bills as are now subsisting from being pro-"longed beyond the periods limited for calling "in and sinking the same."

* 18 Cha. 2. in Ruffhead. † c. 30 in Ruffhead.

‡ Repealed as to the whole of Her Majesty's dominions upon the passing of this Act.

SCHEDULES—*contd.*

SECOND SCHEDULE—*contd.*

SECOND PART—*contd.*

Acts wholly repealed—contd.

Year and Chapter.	Title.
14 Geo. 3. c. 70. . .	An Act for applying a certain sum of money for calling in and recoining the deficient gold coin of this realm; and for regulating the manner of receiving the same at the Bank of England, and of taking there an account of the deficiency of the said coin and making satisfaction for the same; and for authorizing all persons to cut and deface all gold coin that shall not be allowed to be current by His Majesty's proclamation.
14 Geo. 3. c. 92. . .	An Act for regulating and ascertaining the weights to be made use of in weighing the gold and silver coin of this kingdom.
15 Geo. 3. c. 30. . .	An Act for allowing the officer appointed to mark or stamp the weights to be made use of in weighing the gold and silver coin of this kingdom, in pursuance of an Act made in the last session of Parliament, to take certain fees in the execution of his office.
39 Geo. 3. c. 94. . .	An Act to ascertain the salary of the master and worker of His Majesty's Mint.
52 Geo. 3. c. 138. . .	An Act for the further prevention of the counterfeiting of silver tokens issued by the Governor and Company of the Bank of England called dollars, and of silver pieces issued and circulated by the said Governor and Company called tokens, and for the further prevention of frauds practised by the imitation of the notes or bills of the said Governor and Company.
52 Geo. 3. c. 157. . .	An Act to prevent the issuing and circulating of pieces of gold and silver or other metal, usually called tokens, except such as are issued by the Banks of England and Ireland respectively.

SCHEDULES—*contd.*

SECOND SCHEDULE—*contd.*

SECOND PART—*contd.*

Acts wholly repealed—contd.

Year and Chapter.	Title.
54 Geo. 3. c. 4.	An Act to continue until six weeks after the commencement of the next session of Parliament an Act passed in the last session of Parliament, intituled "An Act to continue and amend an "Act of the present session, to prevent the issuing "and circulating of pieces of gold and silver or "other metal, usually called tokens, except such "as are issued by the Banks of England and "Ireland respectively."
56 Geo. 3. c. 68	An Act to provide for a new silver coinage, and to regulate the currency of the gold and silver coin of this realm.
57 Geo. 3. c. 46	An Act to prevent the issuing and circulating of pieces of copper or other metal usually called tokens.
57 Geo. 3. c. 67	An Act to regulate certain offices, and abolish others, in His Majesty's Mints in England and Scotland respectively.
57 Geo. 3. c. 113	An Act to prevent the further circulation of dollars and tokens issued by the Governor and Company of the Bank of England for the convenience of the public.
6 Geo. 4. c. 79	An Act to provide for the assimilation of the currency and monies of account throughout the United Kingdom of Great Britain and Ireland.
6 Geo. 4. c. 98	An Act to prevent the further circulation of tokens issued by the Governor and Company of the Bank of Ireland for the convenience of the public, and for defraying the expense of exchanging such tokens.
1 & 2 Will. 4. c. 10	An Act to reduce the salary of the master and worker of His Majesty's Mint.

SCHEDULES—*concld.*

SECOND SCHEDULE—*concld.*

SECOND PART—*concld.*

Acts wholly repealed—concld.

Year and Chapter.	Title.
7 Will. 4. & 1 Vict. c. 9	An Act to amend several Acts relating to the Royal Mint.
12 & 13 Vict. c. 41.	An Act to extend an Act of the fifty-sixth year of King George the Third, for providing for a new silver coinage, and for regulating the currency of the gold and silver coin of this realm.
22 & 23 Vict. c 30.	An Act to extend the enactments relating to the copper coin to coin of mixed metal.
26 & 27 Vict. c. 74	An Act to enable Her Majesty to declare gold coins to be issued from Her Majesty's Branch Mint at Sydney, New South Wales, a legal tender for payments; and for other purposes relating thereto.
29 & 30 Vict c. 65.	An Act to enable Her Majesty to declare gold coins to be issued from Her Majesty's Colonial Branch Mints a legal tender for payments; and for other purposes relating thereto.

INDEX TO VOLUMES I AND II.

(The references are to pages.)

INDEX TO VOL. II.

* Volume I ends with page 530.

* Volume I ends with page 520.

* Volume I ends with page 520.

* Volume I ends with page 530.

* Volume I ends with page 530.

* Volume I ends with page 320.

* Volume I ends with page 530.

* Volume I ends with page 530.

Pages*

* Volume I ends with page 530.

* Volume I ends with page 530.

* Volume I ends with page 530.

* Volume I ends with page 530.

Pages*

* Volume I ends with page 830.

* Volume I ends with page 630.

* Volume I ends with page 520.

* Volume I ends with page 520.

*Volume I ends with page 530.

* Volume I ends with page 530.

* Volume I ends with page 530.

* Volume I ends with page 530.

G. I. C. P. O.—No. 55 L. D.—29-1-1901.—7,000.—H. R. and G. R.

CPSIA information can be obtained
at www.ICGtesting.com
Printed in the USA
BVHW081053231118
533754BV00023B/1379/P